Midwest Studies in Philosophy
Volume XXIII

MIDWEST STUDIES IN PHILOSOPHY

EDITED BY PETER A. FRENCH
HOWARD K. WETTSTEIN

Many papers in MIDWEST STUDIES IN PHILOSOPHY are invited and all are previously unpublished. The editors will consider unsolicited manuscripts that are received by January of the year preceding the appearance of a volume. All manuscripts must be pertinent to the topic area of the volume for which they are submitted. Address manuscripts to MIDWEST STUDIES IN PHILOSOPHY, Department of Philosophy, University of California, Riverside, CA 92521.

The articles in MIDWEST STUDIES IN PHILOSOPHY are indexed in THE PHILOSOPHER'S INDEX.

Forthcoming

Volume XXV 2000 Life and Death: Ethics and Metaphysics

Announcement

Beginning with Volume 23 onwards, we are pleased to announce that *Midwest Studies in Philosophy* will be published by Blackwell Publishers, Inc. *Midwest Studies in Philosophy* was originally published by the University of Minnesota Press and most recently by the University of Notre Dame Press.

Midwest Studies in Philosophy Volume XXIII

New Directions in Philosophy

Editors

Peter A. French
University of South Florida

Howard K. Wettstein
University of California, Riverside

BLACKWELL PUBLISHERS • BOSTON, MA & OXFORD, UK

Blackwell Publishers,Inc.
350 Main Street
Malden, MA 02148 USA

Blackwell Publishers, Ltd.
108 Cowley Road
Oxford OX4 1JF
United Kingdom

ISBN 0-63121-593-X
ISBN 0-63121691-X (P)
ISSN 0363-6550

Midwest Studies in Philosophy
Volume XXIII
New Directions in Philosophy

Locke and the Crisis of Postmodern Epistemology . . . . Richard Foley 1

A Priori Philosophy after an A Posteriori Turn . . . . Richard Fumerton 21

The Ontological Turn . . . . C. B. Martin and John Heil 34

Things and Their Parts . . . . Kit Fine 61

The Mystery of the Physical and the Matter of Qualities:
A Paper for Professor Shaffer . . . . Peter Unger 75

How Ontology Might Be Possible:
Explanation and Inference in Metaphysics . . . . Chris Swoyer 100

Existential Relativity . . . . Ernest Sosa 132

Unity without Identity:
A New Look at Material Constitution . . . . Lynne Rudder Baker 144

Identity in the Talmud . . . . Eli Hirsch 166

Distrusting Reason . . . . Hilary Kornblith 181

Reasons and the Deductive Ideal . . . . Larry Wright 197

Criteria and Truth . . . . Bernard Harrison 207

Born Yesterday:
Personal Autonomy for Agents without a Past . . . . David Zimmerman 236

The Ethics of Belief: Off the Wrong Track . . . . Jonathan E. Adler 267

Empirically and Institutionally Rich Legal
and Moral Philosophy . . . . Carl F. Cranor 286

Late in the Quest:
The Study of Malory's *Morte Darthur*
as a New Direction in Philosophy . . . . Felicia Ackerman 312

Contributors 343

Midwest Studies in Philosophy
Volume XXIII

Midwest Studies in Philosophy, XXIII (1999)

Locke and the Crisis of Postmodern Epistemology

RICHARD FOLEY

Locke is arguably the first great modern epistemologist. This may seem a surprising claim given that Descartes is usually accorded this honor. Nevertheless, there is a constellation of positions, closely associated with modern epistemology, that appeared for the first time with Locke.

Drawing upon work by Nicholas Wolterstorff,[1] I will describe a set of key themes in Locke's epistemology, and argue that underlying these themes are presuppositions that Locke takes almost entirely for granted and that mark him off as a distinctly modern epistemologist. Identifying these presuppositions will set the stage for a discussion of epistemology's future, the link being that Locke's presuppositions have come under fierce attack in our postmodern age. The attacks have produced a set of specific challenges for postmodern epistemology but also a general lack of confidence in its importance. Locke had no doubts about why it was important to do epistemology, and this confidence is a direct result of the presuppositions that define his modernism. We, by contrast, are filled with doubts about these same presuppositions.

1

One of the keys to understanding Locke's epistemology is to appreciate that his main concern is not with how we acquire knowledge but rather with how we regulate opinion. For Locke, knowledge requires certainty and, thus, is extremely scanty. We have knowledge only of the mind and its modifications. About all other subjects and issues, we have only opinions, not knowledge. Accordingly, Locke is principally concerned with the regulation of opinion.

It is in the relatively neglected Book IV of *An Essay Concerning Human Understanding* where these concerns are most extensively treated. Of the four books of the *Essay*, this is the one that should be of most concern to us today, for both positive and negative reasons. Negatively, Books I–III depend heavily on a psychology that is largely discredited. Positively, the issues that motivate Locke in Book IV—the fractured moral and religious situation of seventeenth-century Europe and the need for an epistemology capable of dealing with the resulting social upheaval—are still with us. Indeed, they are more pressing than ever.

In Book IV Locke makes a constellation of claims concerning the regulation of opinion. Among the most important of these claims are the following: all of us have an obligation to try to make our opinions as accurate as possible; the way to meet this obligation is to gather evidence and then to proportion our degree of confidence in the proposition or hypothesis in question to the strength of the evidence; and, appeals to the intellectual authority of others have only a very limited role to play in the proper regulation of opinion.

Underlying these claims is a set of presuppositions that Locke does not explicitly address but that shape his epistemology at every turn: his intellectual optimism, his individualism, and his egalitarianism. At the deepest level, it is these presuppositions that make Locke a paradigmatic modern epistemologist. However, contemporary thinkers have enormous difficulty sharing these presuppositions, and this creates a problem, indeed a crisis, for contemporary epistemology. More on this crisis later.

2

Locke says we have an obligation to do our best to have accurate opinions. This obligation is the result of God's commanding us to have accurate beliefs.[2] Locke recognized that believings can have other desirable or undesirable features, but he had little tolerance for the idea that we have an obligation to pursue these other desiderata. Our obligations, as they apply to our believings, center on truth and falsity, and derivatively on probability. In governing beliefs, we are to practice "indifference" to all other merits and demerits of believings. We have an obligation to try to get things right and the way to do this is to follow what Wolterstorff calls Locke's "principles of evidence and proportionality":[3]

1. *Principle of evidence*: Base opinion on evidence, where evidence consists of what one knows.
2. *Principle of appraisal*: Examine the evidence one has collected to determine its force, that is, appraise the probability of the proposition in question on that evidence.
3. *Principle of proportionality*: Adopt a level of confidence in the proposition that is proportioned to its probability on one's evidence.

3

According to Locke, we have an obligation to try our best to have accurate beliefs and the way to do this is to follow the principles of evidence and proportionality. However, he issues various qualifications and restrictions on this basic claim.

The most important of these qualifications is that the obligation to try our best to have accurate beliefs applies only to propositions of maximal "concernment." The paradigmatic examples of such propositions are ones concerning the fundamental issues of morality and religion. In addition. Locke thinks that everyone has an obligation to seek the truth "concerning various practical matters which pertain specifically to him or her,"[4] for example, gathering information about an illness that is threatening the life of one's child. But having noted such practical matters, Locke then pretty much ignores them and focuses instead on the obligation to discover the truth on matters of morality and religion. It is the latter that occupies most of his attention because, first, no one really has to be convinced about the importance of acquiring information on matters of pressing personal concern and because, second, it is matters of morality and religion that were tearing at the social fabric of seventeenth-century Europe.

For propositions of maximal concernment, the obligation to seek the truth is not just a prima facie obligation. Rather, it is an obligation that is never overridden by other considerations or other obligations. By contrast, for other propositions, that is, propositions not of maximal concernment, we are not obligated to do our intellectual best.

> If it be objected that this will require every man to be a scholar, and quit all his other business, and betake himself wholly to study, I answer, I propose no more to anyone than he has time for. Some men's state and conditions requires no great extent of knowledge: the necessary provision for life swallows the greater part of it. (*Conduct of the Understanding*, §37)[5]

Indeed, the point is even stronger. It is not just that we are under no obligation to do our best with respect to propositions not of maximal concernment; we are often obligated not to do our best, since doing so would take us away from matters of more pressing concern.[6] If one's children are seriously ill, one has an obligation not to spend one's time trying to discover the truth about, say, Goldbach's conjecture (the still unproven conjecture that there is no even number greater than two that is not the sum of two primes).

4

Locke thinks that we have an absolute obligation to try to have accurate opinions about the fundamental claims of morality and religion, because these propositions are crucially important for our happiness, indeed our everlasting happiness. They affect our prospects for salvation. It is this which explains why the obligation to try to get at the truth with respect to these matters is never overridden by other considerations. Too much is at stake.

One obvious objection to this position is that it is too demanding on ordinary people. Fishmongers, carpenters, and laborers have neither the time nor training to think through the issues of religion and morality in accordance with Locke's principles of evidence and proportionality. Perhaps wealthy people and intellectuals can do so, but others cannot.

Locke disagrees, however. With respect to issues other than morality and religion, he concedes that the needs and demands of everyday life are often such as to outweigh any intellectual duty to discover the truth about these issues, but he holds firm with respect to propositions of morality and religion:

> No man is so wholly taken up with the attendance on the means of living, as to have no spare time at all to think of his soul, and inform himself in matter of religion. (*Essay Concerning Human Understanding*, IV, xx, 3)

In other words, because matters of religion and morality are so centrally important (nothing less than the salvation of our souls is at stake), everyone has an intellectual duty to do one's best to seek out the truth on these matters.

Underlying this position is Locke's intellectual optimism, which will not admit any thought that it might be futile to engage in such intellectual pursuits. Locke assumes that individual human beings, even ordinary humans, *can* have reliable beliefs about matters of morality and religion. They need only to make proper use of their intellectual faculties, and this means following the principles of evidence and proportionality. Locke does not claim that in following his principles, one is altogether assured of having only true beliefs. On the contrary, his view is that religion and morality are not areas about which we can have knowledge with its attendant certainty. But we can be assured, it seems, that our beliefs will at least not be wildly mistaken if we follow his principles. I say "it seems" because Locke never explicitly addresses this possibility. However, there is no hint in Locke that one who follows his rules might possibly fall into massive error. A basic, general intellectual optimism is simply taken for granted.

5

What is the source of Locke's optimism? The quick answer is God, but there are two aspects to this answer, one that is concerned with the intellectual equipment God has bestowed upon us, and one that is concerned with how God chooses to reveal himself and his commands to us.

Locke assumes that the cognitive equipment provided us by God is well-designed to generate accurate opinions.[7] The following is a characteristic remark:

> Every man carries about him a touchstone if he will make use of it, to distinguish substantial gold from superficial glittering, truth from appearances . . . [T]his touchstone . . . is natural reason. (*Conduct of the Understanding*, §3)

Moreover, Locke assumes that God would not reveal Himself in an evidential vacuum. The assumption, in other words, is that God will play by the rules of evidence.[8] Accordingly, if we follow the rules of evidence and proportionality, we will not be terribly misled.

> Since our faculties are not fitted to penetrate into the internal fabric and real essence of bodies; but yet plainly discover to us the being of a God, and the

> knowledge of ourselves, enough to lead us into a full and clear discovery of our duty, and great concernment, it will become us, as rational creatures, to employ those faculties we have about what they are most adapted to, and follow the direction of nature, where it seems to point us out the way. For 'tis rational to conclude, that our proper employment lies in those enquiries, and in that sort of knowledge, which is most suited to our natural capacities, and carries in it our greatest interest, i.e., the condition of our eternal state. Hence I think I may conclude, that morality is the proper science, and business of mankind in general; (who are both concerned, and fitted to search out their *Summum Bonum*). (*Essay Concerning Human Understanding*, IV, xii, 11)

Thus, Locke thinks we have a duty to seek out the truth in matters of religion and morality because knowing the truth about such matters is so centrally important for us; they concern "the condition of our eternal state" and our "*Summum Bonum*." In addition, he thinks that God has properly equipped us for this task. All we need do is use our faculties for "what they are most adapted to, and follow the direction of nature, where it seems to point us out the way."

In the above passages, it is easy to discern another of Locke's basic presuppositions, what I am calling his "individualism." Locke's idea is that within normal adult human beings there is a faculty of reason, and this faculty is the individual's personal authority on intellectual issues. Wolterstorff puts the point in this way:

> Locke's picture of the community of responsible believers is the picture of a democracy in which each listens to his or her own inner voice of reason and no one treats any voice outside himself or herself as authoritative—unless his or her own reason tells him to do so.[9]

Moreover, Locke's individualism is closely tied to the third presupposition that I listed earlier, his egalitarianism. Unlike Descartes, whose recommended method of inquiry was intended only for philosopher/scientists, Locke intends his recommendations for everyone. Even ordinary men and women can have credible opinions about religion and morality.

Locke fully recognizes that there are significant differences in intellectual capacity among humans:

> Those who want skill to use those evidence they have of probabilities; who cannot carry a train of consequences in their heads, nor weigh exactly the preponderancy of contrary proofs and testimonies, making every circumstance its due allowance, may be easily misled to assent to positions that are not probable. There are some men of one, some but of two syllogisms, and no more; and others that can but advance one step further. These cannot always discern that side on which the strongest proofs lie; cannot constantly follow that which in itself is the more probable opinion. (*Essay Concerning Human Understanding*, IV, xx, 5)

However, Locke thinks that even "these men of one or two syllogisms" can sufficiently well regulate their opinions on matters of religion and morality if only they will apply themselves to such questions. Moreover, he also thinks that they have sufficient time to do so. Even laborers have sufficient leisure to devote thought to matters of maximal concernment and even the dullest of them can discover the important basic truths of religion and morality.

Thus, Locke is an egalitarian, and his being so is grounded in his intellectual optimism and his individualism, which together imply that every normal person's faculty of reason is well-suited to seek out and discern the truth about matters of morality and religion, not with the absolute certainty of knowledge, but nonetheless with a reliability that is suitable for our needs.

6

Locke's optimism is far from naive. He goes to considerable lengths to point out that there are various "distempers of the mind," or what he sometimes calls "wrong measures of probability." These are weaknesses or defects or dispositions that distort the workings of our intellectual faculties. Locke lists four principal wrong measures of probability:

1. False propositions are inculcated in us from youth as self-evident.
2. We become attached to familiar explanations and do not even consider alternatives.
3. Our opinions are motivated or influenced by our emotions rather than being the products of a disinterested concern for truth.
4. We give allegiance to authority.

This last flaw, Locke adds, is especially destructive:

> The fourth and last wrong measure of probability I shall take notice of, and which keeps in ignorance, or errour, more people than all the others together, is that which I have mentioned in the fore-going chapter, I mean, the giving up our assent to the common received opinions, either of our friends, or party; neighborhood, or country. How many men have no other ground of their tenets, than the supposed honesty, or learning, or number of those of the same profession? As if honest, or bookish men could not err; or truth were to be established by the vote of the multitude: yet this with most men serves the turn. The tenet has had the attestation of revered antiquity, it comes to me with the passport of former ages, and therefore I am secure in the reception I give it: other men have been, and are of the same opinion, for that is all is said, and therefore it is reasonable for me to embrace it. A man may more justifiably throw up cross and pile for his opinions, than take them up by such measure. (*Essay Concerning Human Understanding*, IV, xx, 17)

The above list is from the *Essay*. A similar list appears in *The Conduct of the Understanding*. There he lists the principal intellectual "miscarriages" people are guilty of as shortsightedness (seeing but one side of the matter), passion, and tradition.[10]

In both lists, tradition and allegiance to authority is stressed as especially likely to mislead. For the medievals, tradition was generally seen as a repository of wisdom. By contrast, Locke saw it as a source of error and took individual reason to be the corrective. Some of the most impassioned passages in Locke's work are on this point:

> For, I think, we may as rationally hope to see with other men's eyes, as to know by other men's understandings. So much as we ourselves consider and comprehend of truth and reason, so much we possess of real and true knowledge. The floating of other men's opinions in our brains makes us not one jot the more knowing though they happen to be true. What in them was science, is in us but opiniatrety, whilst we give up our assent only to reverend names, and do not, as they did, employ our own reason to understand those truths, which gave them reputation. (*Essay Concerning Human Understanding*, I, iv, 23)

How does one avoid these wrong measures of probability? Locke's answer is that one does so by using reason in accordance with the principles of evidence and proportionality. These principles require that we be indifferent, that we collect evidence, that we weigh this evidence, and that we then be no more confident in our opinions than the evidence warrants.

So although Locke is an intellectual optimist, his optimism is restricted to individuals relying on their own reason. He is utterly suspicious of reliance on tradition and authority, which he views as an excuse for not bringing one's own intelligence to bear on the issues at hand. It is a recipe for error and for what we in the twentieth century would call "groupthink."

7

I have been arguing that underlying Locke's epistemology is a tightly knotted package of three presuppositions. First, there is his optimism: if individuals use their intellectual equipment well, following the principles of evidence and proportionality, they can expect to have relatively accurate opinions. Second, there is his individualism: in regulating their opinions, individuals are to follow the principles of evidence and proportionality, which require them to exercise their own judgment about how strongly the evidence supports the hypothesis in question. Finally, there is his egalitarianism: his principles are intended for everyone, not just the intellectually elite.

This combination of optimism, individualism, and egalitarianism makes Locke a paradigmatic modern epistemologist, and indeed perhaps the first unqualifiedly modern epistemologist.

8

Locke's presuppositions, and the various positions they encourage, have been hugely influential on Western epistemology and Western thought generally. However, there is plenty of evidence that this combination of presuppositions has just about run its course.

Locke's epistemology has always had its detractors. Hume and Reid, among others, were powerful critics of Locke. They successfully attacked a number of the key elements of Locke's epistemology. They argued, for example, that Locke's foundationalism is far too restrictive. It restricts the acceptable processes of immediate belief formation to episodes of direct awareness, whereas in fact there are a variety of cognitive faculties and processes for immediate belief formation. Similarly, there are modes of mediate belief formation other than the few that Locke proposes, namely, deductive proof and his principles of evidence and proportionality.[11]

As damaging as these attacks were for Locke's epistemological system, they did not constitute a frontal attack upon the basic presuppositions of his views: his optimism, individualism, and egalitarianism. The frontal attack, as I am calling it, did not come until the twentieth century, but it then came with full force.

I am going to describe, albeit briefly, a few of the major themes in these attacks, and then go on to suggest that despite the attacks, there is something in each of Locke's presuppositions worth preserving. The trick is to find an appropriate balance between the undeniable force of the attacks and the undeniable insight that informs Locke's presuppositions. The search for this balance is the most serious epistemological challenge of the postmodern period. Locke's optimism, individualism, and egalitarianism characterize modernism in epistemology, but these presuppositions are no longer tenable in the strong form that Locke held them. Yet the postmodernist period has brought with it temptations to err in the opposite direction, that is, in the direction of pessimism, anti-individualism, and elitism.

9

Of the three presuppositions, it is Locke's egalitarianism that has survived best in the twentieth century. We still tend to side with Locke against Descartes and the medievals in thinking that all of us, and not just the intellectually elite, have a responsibility to think carefully about matters of importance and to come to our own opinions about them.

Nevertheless, there are contemporary threats to egalitarianism, and nowhere are these threats more overt than in the deference given to the opinions of experts in technical fields. Such deference is not unmotivated. Knowledge has become increasingly specialized. As our societies have become more complex, so inevitably have our ways of organizing our intellectual pursuits. Moreover, we have witnessed what a powerful tool the division of intellectual labor can be. Enormous progress on important intellectual questions has been made by breaking up complex problems into smaller, more manageable ones.

The increasing division of intellectual labor, and the specialization it brings with it, has made deference to expert opinion a common occurrence. Of course, the elitism implicit in such deference is different from the elitism that was Locke's concern. His principal enemy was a system in which intellectual elites were set up as the authorities on issues of morality and religion, and his critique of this system presupposed that ordinary people, not just intellectuals, have the capacity to form their own opinions about these matters. They only need make proper use of the faculty of reason that God has given them for this purpose. Moreover, according to Locke, ordinary people, even those engaged in demanding labor, have enough free time to have credible opinions about these issues.

Whatever one thinks of this as a strategy for responding to seventeenth-century religious elitism, it is decidedly not an adequate strategy for responding to the challenges of twentieth-century scientific elitism. Contemporary elitists plausibly claim that many truths in technical fields are simply beyond the capacities of nonexperts. The nonexperts lack the training to understand these truths, and moreover in many cases it is too late for them to obtain the training. It is not as if one can devote one's spare weekends to string theory and expect to have informed opinions about the field. Moreover, nonexperts are frequently not in a good position even to judge the qualifications of the purported experts who make claims in the field.

Challenges of this sort to egalitarianism are already serious, and they are going to become even more serious in the coming years. We need a theoretically adequate way of understanding and treating these challenges. An adequate treatment will acknowledge that there is something fundamentally right in Locke's reaction to religious and moral elitism that is also applicable to scientifically based elitism. To be sure, Locke underestimated the difficulties of being able to make up one's own mind on complex issues. Nonetheless, he was right in thinking that it is profoundly disturbing for nonexperts to be told that they must simply defer to the experts. This is, or at least should be, as disturbing to us today as it was to Locke in the seventeenth century. It is as objectionable to defer mindlessly to immunologists and quantum theorists as it is to defer mindlessly to religious authorities and the tradition of the church.

On the other hand, it is also objectionable, indeed every bit as objectionable, to ignore or reject the conclusions and achievements of modern science. So, there is a balancing act to be performed. One of the most pressing intellectual demands of our age is how to achieve this balance. We need to find a way of reserving a place for egalitarian instincts in an age of experts and to do so without becoming Luddites. We do not have an adequate solution to this problem yet, but it is possible to discern at least the general direction of the solution.

The first step is to recognize that what is most dangerous about deference to the authority of scientific experts is identical with what Locke found most dangerous about deference to the authority and the traditions of the church. Namely, both can too easily become an excuse for not bringing one's intelligence to bear on important issues. A central question for us in the late twentieth and early twenty-first centuries is how to bring our intelligence to bear on issues connected to technical and scientific expertise, especially given that it is not a realistic option for us to acquire the expertise ourselves.

The answer, in roughest form, has two parts. The first is to demarcate as carefully as possible those issues and claims on which expertise directly bears from those on which expertise does not directly bear. It is especially important to distinguish genuinely scientific issues from nonscientific ones, for example, related public policy issues, and to be on guard that whatever deference is awarded to experts on the former does not get automatically transferred, via a halo effect, to the latter. Of course, it is often difficult to determine precisely where scientific issues end and nonscientific ones begin, but sorting the two to the extent possible is an important first step in thinking clearly about scientific expertise.

However, something beyond this sorting is also possible. Even when it is not feasible for educated persons to become experts themselves in a field, it is possible for them to form credible opinions about the overall workings of the system that produces specialized knowledge claims in the field. Of course, even this is immensely difficult and often enough immensely controversial, as the recent "science/humanities wars" attest. However, it is at least a practicable project, whereas achieving the firsthand expertise usually is not.

Moreover, the single most important thing for nonexperts to know about the practice of science is that it is designed, ideally, to be a self-correcting system. It requires that theories and hypotheses be testable; it requires that the tests be publicly observable and repeatable, thus allowing one inquirer to verify the conclusions reached by other inquirers; it requires the unfettered flow of information among inquirers; and so on. Of course, even when the system is working well, there is no absolute guarantee that errors will in fact be corrected. The claim on behalf of science is only that it is reasonable for us to think that the system will move us in the direction of greater accuracy when it is operating properly.

This is a statement about how the system is ideally supposed to work. The real world is a different matter, however, and it is about the real world of science that individuals, even nonscientists, can and should have opinions. In particular, the question about which individuals can be entitled to have opinions is whether science as it is actually practiced is sufficiently close to the ideal to make its results trustworthy. It bears repeating that it is immensely difficult to have credible opinions even about this issue, but there are some general markers to look for. Anything that interferes with the free flow of information, for example, is especially worrisome, since it potentially disrupts the above-described self-correcting mechanisms of science.

The Lockean point here is that as difficult as it may be to have credible opinions about the workings of science as actually practiced, this is at least potentially achievable if nonexperts bring their intelligence to bear on the issue. The further Lockean point is that, given the increasing impact of science in our lives, it is important for us to have credible opinions on this issue. Our efforts need not be aimed at a mastery of the fields and subfields themselves. Rather, the efforts can be aimed at the workings of the overall system, with the goal of coming to an opinion of its overall credibility.

10

Of Locke's three presuppositions, it is his individualism that has come under the most fierce attack in the twentieth century.

Locke worried about the threat of overly easy intellectual conformity and correspondingly stressed the need for intellectual autonomy. He was right to be worried. Few things are more difficult than resisting domination by one's intellectual environment. Locke assumed that reason is resistant to such domination and hence is able to protect us against it. It is no longer possible to be so sanguine. We recognize that even the way we reason and deliberate is shaped by our intellectual heritage and surroundings. The recognition of this point has made it easy to slide into positions that so emphasize the "social construction" of our opinions and ways of reasoning that little or no room is left for intellectual autonomy.

Twentieth-century intellectual life is marked by an increased emphasis on communities and groups, as opposed to individuals, as the most appropriate and interesting objects of study. This trend can be found across the social sciences and humanities. It has helped create, and in turn been reinforced by, a public political discourse that increasingly focuses on the rights, privileges, and histories of groups as opposed to individuals. Epistemology is no exception to this trend. If in Locke's epistemology we see an apotheosis of the individual and his or her reason, in much of contemporary epistemology we see an apotheosis of the social.

An emphasis on communities of inquirers is especially common in work on the epistemology of science. This should not be surprising. Science is largely cumulative, with one generation building on the work of the previous; its methods emphasize the use of publicly observable and repeatable experiments, thus allowing inquirers to test each other's hypotheses; and the nature of its problems often requires a division of intellectual labor, which brings with it a need to rely on the work of others. Observations such as these convinced C. S. Peirce that scientific justification is essentially social; hypotheses are justified only because they are products of a set of methods employed by a community of inquirers over an extended period of time. More recently, philosophers of science as otherwise diverse as Thomas Kuhn, Bruno Latour, Philip Kitcher, Helen Longino, and Miriam Solomon have defended similar views.[12]

Feminist epistemologists have also argued for such views and added a political warning. Our intellectual and scientific standards cannot be disentangled from our social arrangements, and because of this, these standards can be wielded as political tools to empower some groups and disempower others.

Some philosophers go further, claiming that the justification of our opinions is entirely social. For example, both Ludwig Wittgenstein and Richard Rorty flirt with the view that one's opinion on an issue is rational only if the manner in which one has arrived at the opinion is intellectually acceptable in one's community.

Locke and the generations of philosophers influenced by him overestimated the ability of individuals to escape the influence of their intellectual inheritance and surroundings. The above movements and positions are effective antidotes to this excessive individualism, but there is a danger of overreaction, that is, of epistemology's becoming excessively social. It may be difficult to determine the exact point at which the reaction to individualism threatens to becomes excessive, but there are at least some markers to indicate when things have gone too far. For example, an epistemology should not a priori preclude the possibility of individuals' being rational when their standards, practices, methods, and opinions differ greatly from those of their communities or traditions. Similarly, an epistemology has become excessively social if it a priori precludes the possibility of individuals' engaging in radical but rational critiques of the prevailing standards, practices, methods, and opinions of their communities or traditions. No matter how entrenched or widely accepted the standards, practices, methods, and opinions of a given community may be, an epistemology ought not to make it utterly impossible for an individual within that community to depart from them, or to explicitly reject them, and to do so rationally.

The notion of rationality and the associated notions of reason, reasonability, and justification come down to us historically with a variety of senses. With some oversimplification, the senses can divided into two broad categories. One sense tends to be externally focused, objective, and closely connected with knowledge, that is, with what is required for us to stand in a relation of knowledge to our environment. The other tends to be internally focused, more subjective, and closely connected with responsible believing, that is, with what is required for us to put our own intellectual house in order and with having personal intellectual integrity.

Both senses are important for thinking about our intellectual lives, and both are important for understanding the history of epistemology. Indeed, a number of the great modern epistemologists assumed that a single unified notion of rationality could capture both senses. For example, Descartes thought that if we were responsible believers, believing only that which is "clear and distinct," we could also be completely assured of not falling into error.

Epistemologists no longer think that there are intellectual guarantees of this sort, in large part because the ambitious, foundationalist projects of modern epistemology have failed. However, the lesson is not that the one or the other aspects of these projects has to be entirely abandoned and that we have to choose between the sense of rationality that tends to be externally focused, objective, and closely connected with knowledge and the sense that tends to be internally focused, subjective, and closely connected with responsible believing. The lesson, rather, is that there are different projects for epistemologists to pursue, and although it is natural to conceive of both projects as being concerned with issues of rationality, reason, and justification, and hence also natural to report the conclusions of these investigations using the language of rationality, these projects must not be confused with one another.

It is the latter sense of rationality, the one that is closely connected with responsible believing, that I am principally concerned with here, and my claim is that accounts of even this sense of rationality must leave room for the possibility of individuals' radically but rationally rejecting the prevailing standards, practices, and opinions of their communities. However widely accepted or cherished these standards, practices, and opinions may be, it still ought not to be impossible for an individual rationally to reject them. There may be limits as to how much can be rationally challenged at any given moment, but even if this is so, the limits are distant ones, not ones that preclude the possibility of radical critiques. Moreover, no particular standard, practice, or opinion is sacrosanct from rational challenge.

The sense of rationality being appealed to here is thus Lockean in spirit, in that it presupposes the possibility of individuals' being rational while also being deeply at odds with their traditions and communities. Of course, it is one thing for an epistemology to leave room for the possibility of this sort of intellectual independence, and it is another for individuals actually to be independent. One of the challenges for contemporary epistemology is to explain how meaningful, intellectual autonomy is possible, given what is known about the power of one's intellectual inheritance and surroundings to shape one's concepts, one's opinions, and even the way one reasons.

Intellectual autonomy cannot be plausibly conceived as being based on the ability to cast off wholesale one's intellectual tradition, but if this is not the its basis, what is?

As with the challenge to Locke's egalitarianism, this challenge can be met only by finding a proper balance. We cannot ignore the extent to which our concepts, opinions, and ways of reasoning are shaped by our surroundings, but we must also find a way of understanding how intellectual autonomy is possible.

The solution, at least in rough form, is to conceive autonomy as being grounded in the ability to use our existing methods and opinions to examine these very same methods and opinions—the very ability, not coincidentally, that makes epistemology possible. We have the ability to engage in intellectual metacritiques, that is, to make our intellectual selves into an object of study, to evaluate and monitor ourselves, and moreover to do so in terms of our own standards, while fully recognizing that these standards have themselves been shaped by our surroundings and inheritance.[13]

We rightfully worry that our communities and traditions mold us intellectually to such an extent that there is no room for intellectual autonomy, but according to the conception I am suggesting, it is also true that we would not have developed the abilities required for autonomy had we not been nurtured by and trained within a rich and enveloping social community and tradition. The training we receive from others, the intellectual heritage we inherit, and the complex social arrangements we are raised in spur the development of the very intellectual abilities that make sophisticated, critical self-monitoring possible.

There are further ironies. Worries about intellectual autonomy have increased with our increasing awareness of the rich variety of intellectual traditions and environments. Familiarity with cultural diversity heightens our awareness of how extensively a culture shapes the intellectual standards and opinions of individuals within it, and this in turn raises worries about intellectual autonomy. As I have been saying, these are legitimate worries, but it is worth reminding ourselves that familiarity with diversity, especially firsthand familiarity, also makes it simpler for individuals to achieve a measure of independence from their traditions. It does so by relieving them of the need to imagine or invent standards, practices, and opinions that are alternatives to the ones prevailing in their community. Instead, they are confronted with such alternatives simply by looking around them. The point, obvious enough as soon as it is stated, is that it is easier for individuals to avoid being the captive of any one tradition in a pluralistic society than in a nonpluralistic one.

So to return to the main thesis, the ability to use our methods and opinions to examine these very same methods and opinions creates a space for intellectual autonomy. It bears repeating, however, that it is only a space. Self-monitoring in terms of one's own standards does not eliminate the threat of complete intellectual domination. Foucault and Marx have both pointed out that the most effective and therefore most chilling kind of control is that which is internalized. We accept as our own the very norms by which we are controlled without realizing we are being controlled.

Be this as it may, our only alternative is to monitor ourselves for this as well. In this respect, the possibility of complete domination is not much different from the complete deception envisioned by the skeptical hypotheses that so preoccupied Descartes. Just as a powerful enough demon might use our own sense experiences to deceive us thoroughly without our being aware of it, so too a powerful enough dominating force, whether impersonal or personal, might use our own standards to control us thoroughly without our being aware of it. However, neither of these threats is a reason for thinking that our intellectual projects are pointless.

No amount of self-monitoring will provide us with absolute certainty that a powerful demon is not using our own experiences to deceive us, but in itself this does not imply that perceptual knowledge is altogether impossible for us. What it does show is that a significant measure of intellectual self-trust is unavoidable if we are to engage in intellectual projects at all. We must trust that our faculties and procedures are reasonably well-suited to yield accurate opinions, and we are entitled to this trust even if we cannot prove with utter certainty that it is well-placed.

Precisely analogous points hold with respect to intellectual autonomy. No amount of self-monitoring will provide us with absolute guarantees that powerful intellectual forces are not completely controlling us by means of our very own intellectual standards, but in itself this does not imply that autonomy is utterly impossible for us. What it does show is that we must presume ourselves to have at least some capacity for intellectual independence if our thinking critically about prevailing opinions, procedures, and practices is to have any point at all. We must make this presumption, and are entitled to make it, even if we cannot prove with utter certainty that it is correct.

11

Intellectual optimism runs through Locke's work in epistemology. Our cognitive faculties, he assumed, can be trusted to yield accurate opinions provided that we employ them properly. He recognized that we are susceptible to various "distempers of the mind," but he was convinced that if we are responsible believers, we can avoid the errors such distempers would otherwise produce.

Three hundred years later optimism does not come so easily. An outpouring of studies in cognitive psychology has shown that what Locke called the "distempers of mind" are not always easy to avoid. Moreover, even when specific "distempers" are avoided, we are dubious of our ability to discover truths in the areas in which Locke thought it was most important to discover them, religion and morality. Both points constitute serious challenges to Locke's optimism, but I will consider here only the latter.

According to Locke, we have an absolute obligation to do our best to have accurate opinions about matters of religion and morality. His conclusion is based on several assumptions.

First, it is important for us to have accurate opinions about these matters, since the salvation of our souls is at stake. Locke also thought that there were major social benefits to be won by the proper regulation of opinion. Moral and religious disputes were creating a social crisis in seventeenth-century Europe, and he thought that an adequate epistemology was needed to address this crisis. His assumption, stated most baldly, is that if people would only proportion their opinions on moral and religious issues to the evidence, social and political chaos could be avoided.

Second, Locke assumes that even ordinary human beings are intellectually well equipped to have accurate opinions about religion and morality. God chooses not to hide these truths from us and has provided us with the requisite faculties. We need only to make proper use of these faculties.

Third, not only do ordinary people have the raw intellectual capacities to discover these truths, it is also feasible for them to do so. It does not demand an enormous investment of time or special training. All that is required is that one devote some "spare time . . . to think of his soul, and inform himself in matters of religion."

The optimism characteristic of the Enlightenment and of modernism in general undergirds these assumptions. By contrast, our postmodern age has doubts about each of these assumptions.

We are less confident than Locke that the tangled issues of morality and religion can be sorted out in our spare time. More seriously, we are less confident that we have the capacities to sort them out. The fundamental truths of religion and morality may be beyond us, no matter how much time and energy we devote to them. More seriously still, we are less confident that there are any fundamental truths of religion and morality to be discovered. Religion and morality are perhaps best understood not as sets of purported truths about which it is possible to have more or less accurate beliefs, but rather as systems of commands, metaphors, or myths, which are concerned with something other than literal truths. Finally, we are less confident than Locke that conflicts among traditions and cultures can be avoided or significantly reduced if people would only employ reason appropriately about matters of religion and morality.

These doubts are familiar to anyone with a knowledge of twentieth-century thought about religion, morality, and politics, but what it less frequently noted are the implications of such doubts for epistemology. Locke's epistemology, like many of the great epistemologies of modern philosophy, has a moral basis. According to Locke, it is important to use our cognitive faculties well, because it is important to discover moral truths. Big issues, both personal and social, were at stake for Locke in regulating opinion appropriately, and hence big issues were also at stake in doing epistemology well.

Locke's answer to the question, Why is it important to have accurate opinions? is no longer regarded as credible by most philosophers, but if so, the challenge, indeed arguably the single most important challenge for postmodern epistemology, is to provide an alternative answer. Why do we think it is important to have accurate opinions? If Locke's answer, to save our souls and to minimize social conflict, is no longer acceptable, what is an acceptable answer?

This question is underdiscussed in contemporary epistemology, but when it is raised, the usual, quick answer is self-interest, and more specifically self-preservation. It is important for us to have accurate beliefs if we are to successfully make our way about the world and, more fundamentally, if we as a species are to survive. Not surprisingly, this answer is often placed in an evolutionary framework rather than the moral and theological framework in which Locke placed his answer. Locke's view was that God has provided us with the cognitive faculties we need for that inquiry "which is most suited to our natural capacities, and carries in it our greatest interest, i.e., the condition of our eternal state." The contemporary view, by contrast, is that the processes of natural selection have provided us with cognitive systems that are well-designed for survival, and these systems would not be well-designed for survival unless they were generally reliable.[14]

In other words, the contemporary view has evolution playing a role analogous to the role played by God in Locke's epistemology. Why is it important for us to have accurate beliefs? The answer is not salvation but survival. Similarly, if we wonder whether it might not be futile to devote time and energy to having accurate opinions, the reassurances given us are evolutionary not theological. Whereas Locke says that God has provided us with faculties suitable to our intellectual inquiries, the contemporary view is that natural selection has provided us with faculties suitable for our intellectual inquiries. It is the workings of natural selection, rather than the works of God, that provide grounds for optimism.

Unfortunately, neither aspect of this view will do. Quick appeals to our survival as a species are incapable of providing a satisfactory explanation of why it is important for us to have accurate beliefs, and quick arguments based on natural selection are incapable of providing assurances that our cognitive equipment is reliable. Consider first the arguments based on natural selection. The theory of natural selection simply does not have the implications it needs to have for the arguments to succeed.[15]

First, nothing in the theory implies that evolution is only caused by natural selection; other factors (e.g., random genetic drift) can also lead to changes in gene frequency, and these other factors need not exert pressure in the direction of well-designed systems.

Second, nothing in the theory implies that the set of genetic options that are available for natural selection to choose among will be large and varied enough to include ones that will produce "well-designed" cognitive systems. The fact that we have survived up until this point is not in itself an adequate argument.

Third, nothing in the theory implies that all, or even the majority, of our most characteristic intellectual procedures, methods, and dispositions are the products of biological evolution at all. They may instead be social and cultural products.

Fourth, and perhaps most importantly, even if it is granted that our most characteristic intellectual procedures, methods, and dispositions are the products of evolution, nothing in the theory implies that these procedures are well designed to generate accurate opinions in our current environment. At best the theory implies that we have been well designed for survival in the Pleistocene, when humans are thought to have evolved. But what constitutes a good design for survival need not also be a good design for having accurate opinions.[16] A fortiori what constitutes a good design in the Pleistocene for survival need not be a good design for having accurate opinions in our current environment.

So no quick appeal to natural selection will provide guarantees that our cognitive equipment can be trusted to generate accurate opinions, and hence no such appeal will provide guarantees that our self-interest, or even our prospects for survival, are enhanced by devoting significant time and effort to having accurate opinions.

Similarly, casual appeals to self-interest or self-preservation do not provide a satisfactory explanation of why it is important for us to have accurate beliefs. The assumption that our interests, as individuals or as a species, are well-served by having accurate opinions is comforting but also increasingly in need of a defense. Consider the expansion of scientific knowledge, with its attendant development of technologies, as a case in point. Given what we now know about the consequences of such development (the threats posed by nuclear weapons, the harms inflicted on the environment, and so forth), it is no longer credible simply to assume that the overall, long-term effects of such knowledge and technology are benign. Nor is it credible simply to assume that increasing technological sophistication will provide remedies for the harms and risks associated with past technological development. The most that can be assumed is something far more cautious, namely, that expanding scientific knowledge and technological skills are capable of being used to further our interests. Any assumption about the inevitability of their doing so is no longer tenable.

Analogous points hold with respect to the self-interest of individuals. It cannot be simply assumed that accuracy of opinions inevitably serves one well. Whether or not this is so depends on the content of what one comes to know (becoming aware of truths is sometimes destructive), on the uses one makes of the knowledge (witness the familiar example of one who gathers all the relevant information about a problem and still makes an unwise decision), and on what the circumstances are (even when one makes wise use of knowledge, conditions may conspire to produce a harmful, even a disastrous, result).

Whatever its other shortcomings, Locke's epistemology had the virtue of trying to provide a serious defense of the importance of our having accurate opinions and, thus, a defense also of the importance of intellectual inquiry. Contemporary epistemology ought to have comparably ambitious aims. In particular, part of its agenda should be the development of a serious, sustained defense of the intellectual part of our lives. Superficial appeals to self-interest and self-preservation are not a substitute for such a defense.

I share enough of Locke's optimism to think that this search can and will be successful. Epistemology is a field in transition. Indeed, the most salient feature of current epistemology is its diversity. Throughout much of the twentieth century, epistemology was dominated by foundationalism. There is no longer a dominant "-ism" in epistemology. Foundationalism's demise has brought with it a bewildering but also intoxicating array of new views, approaches, and questions. There have been bold new attempts to refute skepticism; reliabilism, coherentism, and probabilism have all staked their claims to be the successors of foundationalism; naturalized epistemologies and socialized epistemologies have proposed novel approaches to epistemological questions; and it is no longer taken for granted that the task of epistemologists is simply to provide conceptual analyses of key epistemological concepts.

The immediate aim of all this activity is to provide accounts of knowledge and rational belief that avoid the weaknesses of traditional foundationalism, but as was the case with Locke's epistemology, there are large issues and assumptions lurking in the background of these accounts. One of the most basic of these assumptions, I have been pointing out, is that it is valuable for us to have accurate beliefs, and hence also valuable for us to engage in intellectual inquiry. Epistemologists need to bring this assumption to the foreground and provide a defense of it.

Some features of the eventual defense are already discernible. For example, as I argued above, the defense will need to acknowledge that our pragmatic interests are not necessarily well-served by having accurate opinions. However, the upshot of this observation is not that pragmatic considerations are out of place in an explanation of the importance of intellectual inquiry. The point, rather, is that the explanation cannot be a simplistic one, which posits a direct and inevitable link between the accuracy of beliefs and self-interest. The corollary, and this is perhaps the most important point to keep in mind in searching for the needed explanation, is that there is no single, overriding goal that we are seeking in our intellectual pursuits. Correspondingly, there is no single, overriding reason for us to engage in such pursuits. Rather, there are varied and overlapping goals and reasons.

This observation sounds banal when stated in isolation, but fully acknowledging it potentially has profound implications for epistemology. Much of contemporary epistemology is written as if the sole end of intellectual inquiry were to have true beliefs and avoid false beliefs. Correspondingly, the primary focus of most contemporary epistemology is on the reasons or justifications one has for believing particular propositions or hypotheses rather than on the reasons or justifications for engaging in intellectual inquiry generally. Given this narrow focus, issues about the rationale for, the practices governing, and the constraints upon intellectual inquiry do not naturally arise. Unfortunately, an epistemology that does not address such issues is destined to seem barren to everyone except specialists.

What would an epistemology that adequately addressed such concerns look like? This is the main question that needs answering, and I do not pretend to have an answer for it. However, I do have some speculations.

First, and most importantly, it would identify, and distinguish among, the intellectual as well as the nonintellectual goals of inquiry. Some tangential discussion of this issue has already found its way into the literature, but it usually occurs within a discussion of epistemic reasons as opposed to the pragmatic reasons for belief, and concerns itself with the accompanying question of whether the former can ever override the latter. This is an important theoretical issue if only because adequately dealing with it requires that one to try to distinguish clearly between epistemic goals and nonepistemic goals.[17] On the other hand, in our everyday intellectual lives, such issues almost never arise. Why they do not is itself an interesting issue,[18] but for my present purposes the point to notice is that the narrowness of these discussions is a consequence of contemporary epistemology's focus on the reasons one has for believing particular propositions or hypotheses as opposed to the reasons or justifications for engaging in intellectual inquiry generally.[19]

Second, an adequate defense of intellectual inquiry will acknowledge that except for perhaps a few rare occasions, pragmatic considerations influence our intellectual inquiries indirectly rather than by virtue of being the direct goal of such inquiries. They primarily shape inquiry by placing constraints on the amount of time, energy, and resources it is reasonable for us to devote to trying to have accurate opinions. We have numerous ends and needs, most of which are not intellectual, and these nonintellectual ends and needs sharply constrain the effort it is reasonable to devote to our intellectual ends and needs. Pragmatic considerations also enormously influence which subjects it is reasonable to investigate. Not every truth is worth knowing, and in large measure we distinguish those that are worth knowing from those that are not on pragmatic grounds.

So pragmatic considerations do help determine not only which subjects are worthy of investigation but also how much time and effort it makes sense to devote to these subjects. However, and this is the important point, once pragmatic considerations have helped determine the direction and extent of the inquiry, they ordinarily drop out as unimportant. The point then becomes to discover the truth about the subject in question within the established constraints. In other words, the considerations that guide the actual investigation are largely intellectual, not pragmatic. The aim is to have as accurate opinions as possible within the constraints.

Third, an adequate defense of intellectual inquiry will acknowledge that although pragmatic considerations are important in determining which subjects are worthy of inquiry and important also in determining how much effort to devote to these inquiries, they do not do so exclusively. One rationale for inquiry is simple curiosity. To be sure, we engage in many intellectual projects because we are convinced that we need additional information to adequately pursue our various practical ends, but it is equally the case that in many instances, especially in the basic sciences, mathematics, philosophy, and other such disciplines, we engage in inquiry not just because we think it will serve us well, but also because we want to understand our world and ourselves. We may believe or at least hope that such understanding will also serve us well at least in the long run, but the value of these projects for us is not entirely dependent on their having "cash value." We are needy beings but also curious beings, and no adequate answer to the question, Why is it important to accurate beliefs? can ignore this aspect of our constitution and of our intellectual lives.

An epistemology that managed in a coherent and compelling way to address these concerns and other like concerns about the rationale for, the practices governing, and the constraints upon intellectual inquiry would be an epistemology that matters. It would be an epistemology that was more than an exercise in puzzle solving. It would be an epistemology that provided a vindication of our intellectual pursuits and, more generally, of the intellectual parts of our lives.

12

Like other great works, Locke's essays on epistemology, which have been so hugely influential on Western thought, have different values for different ages. One of the principal values of Locke's epistemology for our age is that it helps define our intellectual predicament.

Many of the substantive claims of Locke's epistemology are no longer credible. We can provide an account of these differences between us and him without any feeling of discomfort that it is we, and not Locke, who are mistaken or who are overlooking something significant. However, when we turn our attention to Locke's conviction that intellectual inquiry is important, comfort does not come so easily. The problem is not that we cannot understand why there is this difference between Locke and us. The value of intellectual pursuits for Locke was a natural consequence of a battery of presuppositions that seemed obvious to him and that define his modernism, while by contrast we are filled with postmodern doubts about these same presuppositions and assumptions. The problem, rather, is that with respect to these differences between Locke and us, it is hard to avoid the feeling that it is we who are missing out on something important. Like Locke, we are convinced of the value of intellectual inquiry, but unlike Locke, we have no account of its value that is clear and compelling for us.

As I have suggested, I believe there are signs that we are working our way through this crisis, but for the moment I am content with preparing the ground for a serious discussion of why, if at all, intellectual inquiry is important. What I have been arguing is that there is no better way to prepare this ground than by getting clear on the differences between Locke and us on this issue.

NOTES

1. Nicholas Wolterstorff, *John Locke and the Ethics of Belief* (Cambridge: Cambridge University Press, 1996).
2. Wolterstorff, 63–64.
3. Wolterstorff, 67–73.
4. Wolterstorff, 72.
5. See also *An Essay Concerning Human Understanding*, IV, xvi, 3 and IV, xx, 2.
6. Wolterstorff, 70.
7. "Locke never so much as considers the possibility that God, in designing us, might have had in mind more desiderata than truth for the beliefs produced in us by our belief-forming faculties." Wolterstorff, 11.
8. Wolterstorff, 120.
9. Wolterstorff, 87.
10. *Conduct of the Understanding*, §3.
11. Wolterstorff, 78.
12. Thomas Kuhn, *The Structure of Scientific Revolution*, 2nd ed. (Chicago: University of Chicago Press, 1970); Bruno Latour, *Science in Action* (Cambridge: Harvard University Press, 1987); Philip Kitcher, *The Advancement of Science* (Oxford: Oxford University Press, 1993); Helen Longino, *Science as Social Knowledge* (Princeton: Princeton University Press, 1990); and Miriam Solomon, "Social Empiricism," *Nous* 28 (1994).
13. For a similar view, see Keith Lehrer, *Self-Trust* (Oxford: Oxford University Press, 1997).
14. "Creatures inveterately wrong in their inductions have a pathetic but praiseworthy tendency to die before reproducing their kind." W. V. O. Quine, "Natural Kinds," in *Ontological Relativity and Other Essays* (New York: Columbia University Press, 1969), 114–38.
15. For a good discussion of these issues, see Stephen Stich, *The Fragmentation of Reason* (Cambridge: MIT Press, 1990), 55–74.
16. "[T]he selection pressures felt by organisms are dependent on the costs and benefits of various consequences. We think of hominids on the savannah requiring an accurate way to discriminate leopards and conclude that parts of the ancestral schemes of representation, having evolved under strong selection, must accurately depict the environment. Yet, where selection is intense the way it is here, the penalties are only severe for failures to recognize present predators. The hominid representation can be quite at odds with natural regularities, lumping all kinds of harmless things with potential dangers, provided that the false positives are evolutionarily inconsequential and provided that the representation always cues the danger." Kitcher, *The Advancement of Science*, 300.
17. For a treatment of these distinctions, see Richard Foley, *Working without a Net* (Oxford: Oxford University Press, 1993), especially 15–21 and 94–96.
18. See Foley, *Working without a Net*, 15–19.
19. For a notable exception, see Stich, *The Fragmentation of Reason*, especially chap. 6.

Midwest Studies in Philosophy, XXIII (1999)

A Priori Philosophy after an A Posteriori Turn

RICHARD FUMERTON

INTRODUCTION

It certainly seems on the face of it that philosophy has taken a pronounced and dramatic turn away from the a priori "armchair" philosophy on which many of us in the analytic tradition were raised.[1] One might, of course, argue that the twentieth-century emphasis on philosophy as an a priori discipline was itself the aberration, a detour in the historical evolution of our field. Certainly Aristotle, Descartes, Locke, Hume, Hobbes, and countless others didn't always sharply distinguish their philosophical inquiries from studies of physics, biology, sociology, and psychology. It might, however, be possible to represent more perspicuously the history of philosophy by arguing that the intellectual giants of the past were simply interested in more than one field. They weren't attempting to answer philosophical questions through scientific investigation. Rather, they were simply interested in a great many questions other than philosophical questions.

However we fit our century of philosophizing into the history of philosophy, it does seem that in the last thirty years philosophy has taken an a posteriori turn. In philosophy of language causal theories of reference for terms referring to natural kinds cast serious doubt on the very enterprise of a priori conceptual analysis. Cognitive science is all the rage in both philosophy of mind and epistemology. The Churchlands are as likely to be reading papers to neurophysiologists (albeit neurophysiologists who fancy themselves as having a kind of philosophical bent) as they are to philosophers. Dretske attempts to understand intentionality and knowledge by studying information processing.[2] Quine's injunction to naturalize epistemology,[3] to study knowledge employing the methods of science, has found an ally and a conceptual justification in popular reliabilist or tracking accounts of justification and knowledge. In ethics, Brandt attempts to give us insights into an important examination of theoretical ethics by enlightening us with respect to cognitive psychotherapy,[4] and the positivists' injunction to eschew normative ethics for metaethics has long fallen by the wayside. In courses and conferences we now address normative ethical issues that even the most fanatical anticonsequentialists must concede require extensive empirical knowledge to resolve.

I'm sure a great many philosophers are excited by these mergers of philosophy and science. Those distressed by a singular lack of philosophical progress (if progress is defined in terms of consensus) might optimistically suppose that if we can incorporate science into our philosophy we can share in some of the dazzling success that science has unquestionably enjoyed. It is, however, difficult to teach an old dog new tricks, and this old dog can't quite muster the enthusiasm or energy necessary to acquire the knowledge that would seem to be necessary to navigate successfully a dramatic a posteriori turn. I've often claimed that it is a defining characteristic of a fundamental philosophical question that no empirical evidence beyond that which everyone already possesses is relevant to answering it. I still think that's true, although in the end it may be that I am simply prescribing a definition of "fundamental philosophy." In this paper, I want to try to reassure myself that the field of philosophy isn't leaving me behind completely. More specifically, I want to examine some of the trends in areas of philosophy mentioned above and argue first that a good part of what goes on in those fields—indeed the most fundamental part—is traditional armchair philosophy. Secondly, I want to argue that when we appear to be dealing with questions that involve empirical matters, we can sometimes turn those questions into hypothetical questions to which we can offer armchair conditional answers.

A PRIORI OR ARMCHAIR PHILOSOPHY

Before attempting to discover what is left for a priori philosophy, it might be helpful to say a few words about what this alleged divide is between a priori and a posteriori philosophy. I chose the title of the paper for its rhetorical ring, but it is probably better to contrast "armchair" with "scientific" philosophy. Strictly speaking, I don't think it is plausible to construe the traditional philosophy I'm concerned with defending as a priori, if that implies that the traditional philosopher is concerned only with discovering necessary truths.[5] Even the most extreme positivists who claimed to be interested only in analytic truths were almost always also relying on phenomenological evidence. They were paying close "introspective" attention to the character of their experience and what was "given" to them through that experience. In dealing with the traditional problems of perception, the modern philosophers and their empiricist successors in the twentieth century felt free to rely on "familiar" facts about perceptual relativity, facts that, however familiar they may be, are not discoverable a priori. To be sure, apparent reliance on contingent facts can sometimes be eliminated. Dream arguments for skepticism don't need to rely on the contingent truth that people dream, only on the necessary truth that it is possible that people dream. The same holds true of appeal to the existence of illusion as a way of attacking direct realism: the possibility of illusion, a possibility one could in principle discover a priori, would have done just as well. But facts about the qualitative or fleeting character of sensory states are empirical facts, and it probably isn't going to be possible to eliminate reference to these in reconstructing a philosophical investigation of perception that is truly a priori.

The expression "armchair philosophy," then, is probably better to capture the philosophical methodology I'm concerned with defending. The armchair philosopher seeks an answer to philosophical questions employing a priori methods of investigation and relying only on the kind of empirical data one can't help getting by simply living one's life. The armchair philosopher claims that one doesn't need to engage in highly specialized investigations into the structure of the brain, the causal origin of language, the fundamental laws governing the physical universe, or complex sociological/psychological facts about people in order to get an answer to the questions that preoccupy them. Is this view plausible? Let's look more carefully at some of these empirical revolutions within philosophy, and let's begin with views in philosophy of language that might seem to challenge the possibility of conceptual analysis as traditionally conceived.[6]

ARMCHAIR PHILOSOPHY AND CAUSAL AND DIRECT THEORIES OF REFERENCE

The causal theory of reference was first introduced as a way of understanding how proper names refer.[7] A token of the word "Aristotle" on a given occasion of its use refers to some individual whose "baptismal" ceremony has the "right" sort of causal connection to the token's use. The theory was offered as an alternative to the Russellean view that most ordinary names are disguised definite descriptions, as such, having both meaning and denotation.[8] On most popular versions of direct reference theories, using a name with the appropriate causal history is only one way of successfully using it to refer. One can also "fix the reference" of a name using a definite description. But the anti-Russellean emphasizes one must not suppose that the name whose reference is so fixed acquires the meaning of the definite description—the meaning of the name is its referent. Direct reference theories of proper names were quickly expanded to propose a way of understanding how we succeed in talking about kinds of things. Thus I can talk about water by "fixing the reference" of water using some description, for example, the kind of stuff that presents a certain appearance, or by inheriting my use of the term from someone else who has successfully fixed its reference.

Crude statements of "direct" theories of reference require enormous work before they become even prima facie plausible. Apparently meaningful expressions that fail to denote and deviant causal chains that must be distinguished from the "right" causal ancestry that determines reference are just two of the problems that must be overcome. I've argued elsewhere that the critical concept of "fixing reference" is problematic and that Kripke's arguments against Russell fail.[9] But my concern is not to revisit these issues here. What would be the implications of a successful causal or direct reference theory of natural kinds for the traditional conception of philosophical analysis as conceptual analysis? On the face of it the implications are enormous. Given the direct reference theory of names for natural kinds of things, we typically discover what kinds of things we succeed in referring to only as a result of empirical investigation. We discovered through empirical investigation that we should analyze water as stuff with a certain molecular structure. Having isolated the referent of our term, we might continue our investigation in an attempt to discover its essential properties. But some proponents of direct reference theories will identify essential properties of a thing or kind of thing with those that occupy an important place in lawful explanation of a thing's behavior.[10] On such a view, the discovery of essential properties is itself a complex empirical matter. If (and this is a big if) one extends the theory to cover the meaning of such terms as "mind," "knowledge," "property," "law of nature," "causation," or even "good," then one might suppose that we have reassigned classical philosophical investigations into the nature of mind, knowledge, properties, laws of nature, causation, and goodness to the purview of empirical investigation. Empirically investigate the causal origins of our use of these terms, or find some plausible reference fixing definite descriptions and empirically investigate their denotation. Having discovered the kinds of things referred to, do some more empirical investigation and report the properties that appear to be essential (from the perspective of the best-worked-out science). If the theory could be made this broad and were correct, what would be left for the armchair philosopher?

The answer is, of course, at one level, simple. The theory of reference itself is one whose plausibility we can and do evaluate from the armchair. Interestingly enough, critics of Russell and proponents of direct reference theories do not appear to be investigating the nature of reference empirically. They test various proposed accounts of reference employing the thought experiments that are the stock and trade of armchair philosophers. We are asked to think of exotic hypothetical situations involving swamp men, twin earthers, ants leaving trails that resemble caricatures of Winston Churchill, and brains in a vat. We are asked hypothetical questions about how we would characterize the referent of a symbol, or putative symbol, in these situations. We take our armchair answers to these questions and formulate a theory of reference around them. What is the modal status of the theory so formulated? I don't think proponents of direct reference theories give this question nearly enough attention. Nothing in the way they approach the issue, however, suggests that they take themselves to be investigating an empirical question. Indeed, for all the world, the analysis of reference looks very much like conceptual analysis. They are investigating the semantic rules we implicitly follow in communicating, where these semantic rules a given philosopher thinks he or she is following are investigated from the comfort of the armchair.

Now it is true that the results of the direct reference theorists' analyses, if correct, may imply that other attempts at conceptual analysis of natural kinds are futile. I suspect that may be why so many philosophers who are primarily interested in defending this theory tend not to be interested in many of the other classical philosophical questions that have preoccupied analytic philosophers. But at least we can rest comfortably knowing that the fundamental question with which they are concerned is approached precisely the way we have always approached analysis of fundamental philosophical concepts.

Furthermore, everything just now said about the analysis of reference applies to the analysis of the concept of an essential property. Again, direct reference theorists, who are prone to speculate about what is or is not an essential property of some kind of thing, are often shy about offering a detailed analysis of what makes something an essential property. But when the question is addressed, it seems relatively clear that it is addressed from the armchair. Although given a certain analysis of what being essential involves, it may turn out that the discovery of essential properties involves empirical investigation, it seems absurd on the face of it to suppose that one could conduct an empirical investigation that would tell us what it is for a property to be essential.

Can we broaden the scope of conceptual analysis still further while accepting some of the tenets of the direct reference theorist? Well, we have already alluded to the critical concept of reference-fixing definite descriptions that some direct reference theorists allow are indispensable to the introduction of terms referring both to individuals and natural kinds. These definite descriptions, the direct theorist claims, are not equivalent in meaning to the terms introduced using them, but they do nevertheless employ predicate expressions that must be understood in order for them to serve their reference-fixing function. These predicate expressions themselves might be given their referential "life" through still other reference-fixing definite descriptions, but if we are to avoid a vicious regress there must be some predicate expressions whose meaningful use by us is not parasitic upon understanding some definite description. Those predicate expressions will no doubt include "causes" and its synonyms. Most of the examples of reference-fixing definite descriptions for terms referring to kinds of things effect reference through descriptions that pick out these kinds through reference to their causal properties. But of course, that leaves us with the question of how to understand the critical concept of causation we use in fixing reference.

One can retreat at this point to a "pure" causal theory for meaningful terms whose ability to refer is not parasitic upon their being "attached" to reference-fixing definite descriptions. If such an analysis of reference were correct, then it may be that the task of conceptual analysis should really begin and end with the analysis of reference. But as we have already said, at least that part of philosophy of language would be armchair philosophy, and as I noted earlier, its not clear to me that philosophers who have reached that conclusion have much interest in doing anything other than arguing about the correctness of their understanding of the semantic rules governing reference.

ARMCHAIR PHILOSOPHY, COGNITIVE SCIENCE, PHILOSOPHY OF MIND, AND EPISTEMOLOGY

The way in which one can secure a role for armchair philosophy should by now be obvious. The very views that seem to turn much of traditional philosophy over to empirical science are themselves views that proponents and opponents alike evaluate using the familiar method of thought experiments. In philosophy of mind, one might get interested in exploring the way in which our brains instantiate mental states understood as functional properties, but one better first defend the view that mental states should receive a functional analysis. That philosophical task is not one that could even in principle be decided by empirical investigation. Qualia, the Achilles' heel of all physicalist reductions of the mental, must be dealt with, and I can't even imagine an empirical discovery that bears on the question of whether the "given" character of a pain state could be identified with some physical property. Again, once one decides that some version of physicalism is true, one could, I suppose, join those philosophers of mind who engage in quasi-scientific investigation into the detailed workings of the brain. Although I might be able to do the usual philosophical kibitzing concerning problematic inferences, ambiguity, or failure to consider alternatives, I'd be the first to concede that my armchair contributions to this enterprise will not be terribly illuminating. But then as a philosopher I was never much interested in how the brain worked anyway. I am content to issue the challenge at the fundamental level. Show me an empirical discovery—indeed describe for me a possible empirical discovery—that would settle the question of whether we should be token or type mind-brain identity theorists, functionalists, substance dualists, or property dualists.[11]

Let me illustrate the pattern of argument I am employing by examining a field I have written much more about, epistemology. Epistemologists seem to be more and more interested in cognitive science because of the increasing popularity of externalist analyses of epistemic concepts. If some form of reliabilism is true, for example, then to discover the "legitimate" rules of reasoning we follow in reaching conclusions about the world around us, we would have no choice but to investigate the workings of the brain. To understand how we reason (something the externalist emphasizes we do not need to do in order to reason correctly), we should investigate the "software" of the brain and the way in which it responds to stimuli by producing cognitive states.[12]

Given the plausibility of externalist analyses of epistemic concepts, has epistemology any alternative but to merge with cognitive science? Again, we must recognize that the most fundamental epistemological questions have nothing whatsoever to do with cognitive science. In epistemology, as in ethics, we must distinguish metaquestions from first-level questions. Metaepistemological questions are questions that concern the nature of knowledge, justification, and evidence. It is only after we answer these questions that we will have any excuse for an excursion into cognitive science. But metaepistemological questions are not answered through empirical investigation. No one even pretends to be confirming the externalist analyses of epistemic concepts by employing the methods of science. Goldman has a good reason, I suppose, to be interested in cognitive science given his metaepistemological views, but you'll notice that when he writes a large book with a portion heavily devoted to cognitive science,[13] the vast majority of philosophers don't pay the slightest attention to that material. They focus immediately on the critical analysis of justified belief in terms of beliefs that are reliably produced in "normal" worlds, and normal worlds reliabilism is evaluated by Goldman and his critics in precisely the way philosophers have been evaluating proposed analyses of fundamental concepts for millennia. We are clearly looking for necessary and sufficient conditions for a belief's being justified and the analysis of justification stands or falls on its ability to withstand the kind of counterexample that can be constructed from the armchair.[14]

But even if we grant that the most fundamental questions in epistemology, metaepistemological questions, are not to be answered through empirical investigation, might metaepistemology not lead us to the conclusion that first-level epistemological questions concerning what we know or are justified in believing must be answered employing the methods of science? Might not an externalist metaepistemology convince us that Quine was right after all in suggesting that we turn to science if we want to investigate how we know the world? That may, indeed, be true, and I do not want to understate the dramatic implications of what may be a genuine externalist revolution in epistemology. A good part of the history of epistemology was concerned with an attempt to refute skepticism, and the skeptic is most naturally construed as raising questions about what we are in fact justified in believing (often simply presupposing some account of knowledge or justified belief). I do think that if the externalist has the right account of knowledge or justified belief we must either stop doing first-level epistemology or start learning something about how the brain works. Faced with that choice, I'd stop doing first-level epistemology, but I certainly have no objections to a philosopher's deciding to learn a new field.

Empirical evidence might seem to be an indispensable part of first-level epistemology even if one rejects contemporary externalist accounts of knowledge and justification. Almost all epistemologists agree that whether or not a belief is justified depends in part on whether the belief is based on appropriate evidence or justification. I may have perfectly good evidence available that would entitle me to infer that Jones is guilty of a particular crime, but if the reason I believe that Jones is guilty is that a fortune-teller told me he is guilty, my belief is not a justified belief. Although there is some disagreement over how to understand the critical concept of basing, it is at least tempting to suppose that what one bases one's beliefs on is in part a function of what causally sustains the beliefs. My belief is not based on evidence if my possession of the evidence plays no causal role in my believing what I do. But if that is so, it looks as if we must engage in psychological (empirical) investigation in order to discover whether any beliefs are justified. It's hard to see how an investigation into the causal origins of belief can be an appropriate subject for armchair philosophy.

I think the above argument is sound, but I also think that the appropriate moral to draw is that we misconceive the philosophical task of the epistemologist if we think of it as preoccupied with the question of what we know or justifiably believe. If what causally sustains our beliefs is relevant to questions about what we know or justifiably believe, then we should limit our epistemological inquiry to questions about whether there is available justification to support beliefs and whether it *would* yield knowledge *were* the believer to be influenced in the appropriate way by that justification. As a philosopher I'm hardly in a position to speculate intelligently about the causes of beliefs and if I need to know something about the causes of belief to know what we justifiably believe, then I'm not in a position as a philosopher to speculate intelligently about what we justifiably believe. Our first-level epistemological conclusions should concern only the existence of justification and conditional claims about what we would be justified in believing were the available justification playing the appropriate causal role.

The above conclusion should, however, be liberating. In philosophy of science, it has long been useful to distinguish psychological/sociological questions about the context of discovery from philosophical/epistemological questions about the context of justification. To discover that there is available evidence that would support a given conclusion is not to discover anything about what does or does not produce or causally sustain belief, and vice versa. But it's good that these discoveries are independent of one another. It is precisely for that reason that we can afford to ignore most of what goes on in the sociology or psychology of belief under the guise of feminist or social epistemology. Feminist epistemologists often speculate about the ways in which biases of one sort or another might have causally influenced the conclusions historians, biologists, psychologists, sociologists, and philosophers have reached on this, that, or the other subject. For all I know they are right. But if the critical questions in epistemology have nothing to do with the causal origins of beliefs, why should we be concerned with such possible biases except, if possible, to guard against them when we do our legitimate epistemologizing?

The above is perhaps an overstatement. It is natural for epistemologists to turn to causal hypotheses about the origins of beliefs both to raise skeptical doubts and to make it easier for us to swallow skeptical conclusions. Thus Descartes begins the *Discourse* by pointing out the extraordinary diversity of incompatible belief systems, hinting strongly that what one believes is heavily influenced not by rational consideration of evidence, but by the environment in which one is raised. When we reflect on this apparent fact, he suggests, we should be much more wary about assuming that what we believe is rationally defensible. Similar observations should, I suspect, give philosophers a certain sense of humility with respect to their philosophical views when they realize that it is highly likely that they hold many of their cherished theories primarily because of the influence of the philosophical school in which they were taught. It should go without saying, however, that none of these observations entail that we can find no justification for our believing what we do, and they should play no role whatsoever in our attempt to find such justification.

Just as one can reflect on psychological/sociological causes of belief in order to generate psychological doubt that might soften one up for the oncoming skeptical attack, so the skeptic will sometimes offer a causal explanation for our believing what we do when the skeptic wants to ease the counterintuitive consequences of the claim that we are massively mistaken with respect to some subject matter. If, for example, after suffering innumerable attacks by the skeptic, the theist wants to know how it could be that so many people are so badly mistaken with respect to their religious beliefs, it probably doesn't hurt to offer some Freudian causal explanations for the existence of these beliefs. But these are philosophical "afterthoughts," so to speak. The heart of the debate between the theist and the atheist arguing over the epistemological status of religious beliefs has nothing whatsoever to do with the truth of causal hypotheses about the origin of belief.

In distinguishing questions about the discovery of conclusions from questions about the justification of conclusions, I also do not want to minimize the causal role that science has often played in generating philosophical ideas. It seems pretty obvious that the modern philosophers' preoccupation with skeptical questions involving an appearance/reality distinction was partly fueled by a developing physics that led them to think of the structure of physical objects (collections of spatially scattered constitutents) as quite different from the structure of their appearance. But although the new physics might have focused their attention on the appearance/reality distinction, that distinction and its skeptical implications, if any, were available to armchair philosophers for millenia. Similarly, it's no coincidence that externalist theories of intentionality and epistemology came into such prominence in the age of the computer. Even the terminology used in advocating reliabilism is full of "input/output" jargon. But again, even if there are causal connections between developments in the world of science and ideas philosophers get, one must carefully separate the philosophical justification of those ideas from any speculation about what causally influenced them.

ARMCHAIR PHILOSOPHY AND ETHICS

Let me conclude this (somewhat defensive) defense of a role for armchair philosophy by turning finally to the field of ethics. The first step in resisting a complete a posteriori turn in ethics should by now be obvious. Philosophers must carefully distinguish metaethical questions from normative ethical questions. Metaethical questions are questions that concern the analysis of fundamental ethical concepts such as good, bad, right, wrong, should, shouldn't, and a host of concepts (e.g., murder, theft, sadism) that are probably definable in part by reference to our paradigm ethical concepts. I suppose I've already admitted earlier the abstract possibility that a direct reference theorist might insist that ethical terms have their reference fixed by reference-fixing definite descriptions. If reference fixing were intelligible, we might determine that it's possible that we succeed in referring to intrinsic goodness, for example, by fixing the reference of "good" using some description such as "the property the presence of which gives rise to this feeling of approbation." It then might become an empirical question as to whether there is some unique property that always gives rise to this sentiment and if there is, what it is. But certainly both historical and contemporary metaethical debate seems to suggest that we are doing something that looks much more like traditional meaning analysis.

In today's enthusiasm for "scientific" philosophy, of course, even metaethical views are occasionally defended by appeal to empirical facts. Harman's defense of ethical relativism as the "best explanation" for data consisting of our ethical judgments[15] made it sound as if we are engaged in some sort of scientific explanation of the occurrence of moral judgments or moral experience. But the term "explanation" has many different connotations. We do want our analyses to account for (explain, if you prefer) our intuitions concerning various thought experiments. In that sense trying to find the best explanation for the available phenomenological evidence, where that includes intuitions about hypothetical situations, is surely part of what one does when one offers a philosophical analysis of any concept. Explaining, in the sense of accommodating, intuitions is hardly the kind of scientific explanation that we associate with empirical investigation. On the other hand, until we have an analysis of the content of moral beliefs, we don't even know what we are trying to explain causally, if causal explanations are really the object of our search. Without conceptual analysis we don't know what it is that we believe when we accept a moral conclusion.

I'm not suggesting that philosophers never try to bring in genuinely scientific data in support of a metaethical view. The rise in popularity of so-called evolutionary ethics seems to be an attempt to bring information about a scientific theory to bear on the plausibility of a metaethical theory. But when the smoke clears, it's always clear that the evolutionary causal explanations of the attitudes, sentiments, or even moral judgments we make is quite irrelevant to any account of their content. Ruse appears to argue that once we have a causal explanation for why people make the normative ethical judgments they do, that account "makes inappropriate the inquiry into the justification of what we believe."[16] The reason is that he thinks he can provide a causal explanation of why we treat moral judgments as objective (act as if they were objective) even though they are not. The position he is probably trying to advocate is similar to Mackie's suggestion that if we are concerned with meaning in ethics, we should probably embrace metaethical objectivism, even though the correct ontological view of the world should recognize that there are no objective values to make our moral judgments true.[17] Mackie's position might in the end be defensible—it is certainly worth considering. But as Mackie realizes, and Ruse should realize, no empirical evidence is relevant to the plausibility of conceptual analysis. Once one concludes, as Mackie essentially does, that given a certain conceptual analysis all of our positive normative ethical judgments are false, we may be interested in hearing some explanation (and here we are talking about a causal explanation) of why people could be so misguided as to accept error on such a massive scale. And just as the religious skeptic sometimes offers an explanation for widespread irrationality with respect to theistic beliefs, so also the evolutionist might offer a causal explanation worth considering. If we have independent reason to suppose that we are guilty of massive confusion in ethics, it might be interesting to speculate about possible causal explanations of such confusion. I emphasize again, however, that the interest of these causal explanations is parasitic upon the independent plausibility of armchair analyses of ethical concepts.

If metaethics, understood as conceptual analysis, is still an appropriate subject for the armchair philosopher, what of normative ethics? To what extent can we do normative ethics without engaging in empirical research? It's almost always useful in ethics to distinguish normative questions about intrinsic goodness from normative questions about how we ought to act. That we make a distinction between things that are intrinsically good and things that are only instrumentally good is a datum that any successful analysis of good must accommodate.[18] Depending on how one analyzes intrinsic goodness, we may or may not need to leave the armchair to discover what is intrinsically good. To take a wildly implausible view, if being intrinsically good is identified with being valued intrinsically by the majority of people, that would relegate the discovery of what is intrinsically good to sociological/psychological investigation. Even if we are relativists, questions about what is intrinsically good may require extensive empirical investigation. Crudely inspired by Brandt, we may identify the fact that something has intrinsic value for S with the fact that S values X intrinsically where that attitude would not be extinguished through certain kinds of therapy. Short of engaging in the relevant therapy, or, minimally, studying the kinds of values that tend to be influenced by therapy, it's hard to see how I would be in a particularly good position as an armchair philosopher to know what would have genuine intrinsic value for me. On the other hand, if Moore were right about intrinsic goodness,[19] then I could discover a priori synthetic necessary truths about the natural properties upon which intrinsic goodness supervenes, and confidently accept at least conditional propositions that assert that if something exemplifies certain natural properties, then that thing is intrinsically good. Even on Moore's view, however, discovering whether something is intrinsically good may involve empirical investigation in that without such inquiry we may have no basis on which to conclude that the thing exemplifies the relevant natural properties.

On a great many views, then, one may be forced to the conclusion that armchair philosophizing about intrinsic goodness ends with the metaethical question of how to understand or analyze intrinsic goodness and various conditional propositions describing what would be intrinsically good were certain other conditions met. If this is true about intrinsic goodness, it is even more obviously true of ethical questions concerning right and wrong, ethical questions concerning how we ought to behave. Even the most extreme deontologists will surely concede that one must know the consequences of an action or the consequences of action kinds in order to reach rational conclusions about how we ought to behave. The most straightforward consequentialism, act consequentialism, takes the rightness of an action to be a function of the sum of the value (perhaps adjusted for probabilities) of actual, probable, or possible consequences of that action compared to alternatives. Rule consequentialists require us to know the actual, probable, or possible consequences of people in general following alternative possible rules in order to know what the right thing to do is. As I said, even deontologists will almost always include among prima facie duties the duty of beneficence, and to discover in any actual situation that the duty kicks in and overrides some other prima facie obligation would require extensive knowledge of the consequences that would result from this action. There is simply no getting around the conclusion that figuring out how one ought to live one's life requires extensive empirical knowledge of the consequences of actions. Any ethical view that denies this conclusion will be subject to relatively straightforward reductio.[20]

The armchair philosopher can, once again, contribute to the metaethical questions concerning the analysis of right and wrong. There simply can be no scientific discovery that bears on the questions of whether act or rule consequentialism is correct, or whether consequentialism, deontological views, or Divine Command theories are correct. It is the task of the philosopher qua philosopher to answer these questions. But although we live in an age of philosophical toleration, I urge us to take seriously the positivists' disparaging remarks about normative ethics as a field of philosophy. After we settle the metaethical questions, what's left to do but "plug in" the relevant empirical evidence to "churn out" the relevant normative conclusions? Who's got the relevant empirical evidence? I wouldn't trust a philosopher, not even a philosopher who works a great deal in applied ethics. Philosophers tend to lead lives that are far too sheltered from the realities of life. The people with the best empirical evidence to settle ethical disputes that arise in medicine, business, agriculture, warfare, and so on are doctors, economists, psychologists, sociologists, soldiers, and generally people who exhibit good common sense. I'm not saying no philosophers have good common sense, but you've sat in on as many department meetings as I have. Of course the people with the best empirical evidence don't necessarily have the kind of theoretical knowledge that would enable them to put their empirical knowledge to the best use.

I do think it would be a good idea for doctors, lawyers, businesspeople, biologists, and just about everyone else to have had a really good theoretical course in ethics. They would then be in a better position to make a rational choice of ethical theory that they could then employ in their decision making. But the idea that one might be a philosophical specialist in medical ethics, for example, whose job is to help resolve ethical crises as they arise in hospitals strikes me as prima facie absurd. God help the hospital that hires the philosopher with the wrong metaethical view. That philosopher will be consistently churning out ethical conclusions with the wrong theoretical machinery. The philosopher qua philosopher can come up with complex *conditional* normative claims describing what we ought to do under various conditions. But when we examine such conditionals closely, we will see that they are never any more plausible than the underlying presupposed metaethical theories which assert conceptual or synthetic necessary connections between the states of affairs referred to in the antecedents and the states of affairs referred to in the consequents of the conditionals. In short the philosophical contribution of the philosopher who offers us conditional "normative" claims is exhausted by the underlying metaethical theory that is the ethical philosopher's legitimate field of expertise.

CONCLUSION

The a posteriori turn in philosophy is not so dramatic after all. It may be that if correct, certain "revolutions" in philosophy of language, philosophy of mind, and epistemology will severely narrow the scope of armchair philosophy. But the methods of traditional philosophy will be the only available methods to settle the most fundamental questions in these areas. In ethics, the contributions of armchair philosophy may well begin and end with metaethics, but the importance of that contribution to sensible discussion of normative issues is so enormous that one shouldn't be the slightest bit apologetic if one doesn't care to get one's philosophical hands dirty toiling in the messy world of empirical facts that are crucial to reaching conclusions in applied ethics.[21]

NOTES

1. Alright, so there is a generational gap. I'm talking about those of us creaking through middle age.

2. Fred Dretske, *Knowledge and the Flow of Information* (Cambridge: MIT Press, 1981) and elsewhere.

3. W. V. Quine, "Epistemology Naturalized," chap. 3 of *Ontological Relativity and Other Essays* (New York: Columbia University Press, 1969).

4. Richard Brandt, *A Theory of the Good and the Right* (Oxford: Clarendon Press, 1979).

5. I'm ignoring for the moment the movements in philosophy of language that have challenged the view that we should view as coextensive the class of a priori truths and the class of necessary truths.

6. Of course, it is wildly misleading to write as if there was some one conception of conceptual analysis. Philosophers comfortable with the label "analytic philosopher" agree that much of what they do when they philosophize is analyze, but they don't agree on what they are analyzing, or on the modal status of the products of their analysis. I defend my own conception of philosophical analysis most fully in "The Paradox of Analysis," *Philosophy and Phenomenological Research* 43 (1983), 477–97.

7. The most influential and important work was, of course, Saul Kripke's *Naming and Necessity* (Cambridge: Harvard University Press, 1972). That seminal piece was followed by an explosion of important papers supporting, expanding, and criticizing the ideas put forth by Kripke.

8. Russell defends the central idea behind construing names as having meaning and denotation in *The Problems of Philosophy* (Oxford: Oxford University Press, 1959), chap. 5, and elsewhere.

9. In "Russelling Causal Theories of Reference," in C. Wade Savage and C. Anthony Anderson, eds., *Rereading Russell* (Minneapolis: Univesity of Minnesota Press, 1989).

10. See, for example, Evan Fales, "Relative Essentialism," *British Journal for Philosophy of Science* 30 (1979), 349–70.

11. It is perhaps tempting to suppose that empirical evidence could at least discredit type mind-brain identity theories, but even that would be a mistake. The type identity theorist need only be forced by empirical evidence to construe the relevant property types as disjunctive. One might have good philosophical reasons to reject the existence of genuine disjunctive properties but one certainly won't have any good empirical reasons to reject the existence of such properties.

12. One might hold that such an investigation will inevitably be circular in so far as it will employ the very rules of reasoning for which we are searching. I have argued in *Metaepistemology and Skepticism* (Lanham, MD: Rowman and Littlefield, 1995) that this concern really reflects an implicit rejection of externalist analyses of epistemic concepts—at least when we move to metalevels. A thoroughgoing externalist should have no compunctions about using a method of reasoning to investigate, and even discover the legitimacy, of that very method of reasoning.

13. Alvin Goldman, *Epistemology and Cognition* (Cambridge: Harvard University Press, 1986).

14. The necessary and sufficient conditions need not be analytically necessary and sufficient conditions. Goldman, for one, prefers to think of his task as the discovery of nonepistemic conditions on which epistemic properties supervene. It is clear, however, that the relevant species of supervenience is something rather strong—claims about this kind of supervenience are appropriately tested using the thought experiments of the armchair philosopher.

15. Gilbert Harmon, *The Nature of Morality* (New York: Oxford University Press, 1977).

16. See Michael Ruse, "Evolution and Ethics: The Sociobiological Approach," in Louis Pojman, ed., *Ethical Theory* (Belmont, CA: Wadsworth, 1998).

17. See J. L. Mackie, *Ethics: Inventing Right and Wrong* (New York: Penguin, 1977).

18. And radically different metaethical accounts of goodness can accommodate the datum. Moore will identify intrinsic goodness with a simple, unanalyzable, nonnatural property, whereas the radical relativist will insist that being intrinsically good is elliptical for being intrinsically good for some person, a property that can ultimately be understood in terms of an attitude that person has toward that thing considered in and of itself.

19. G. E. Moore, *Principia Ethica* (Cambridge: Cambridge University Press, 1903).

20. The extent to which armchair philosophy can reach normative questions about right and wrong does still depend on whether or not one is a consequentialist or a deontologist. The deontologist may have a view that entails that one can discover a priori what action kinds are prima facie right or wrong. Just as Moore thought that goodness supervenes on natural properties, so the deontologist might argue that prima facie rightness supervenes on natural properties, and one can discover a priori what those properties are. Certain versions of contractualism, when the contractors are idealized persons (persons we can approximate through thought experiments) may also leave room for armchair discovery of certain general normative principles. I take this as perfectly consistent with my claim that deciding what to do in any particular situation would require extensive empirical knowledge.

21. I would like to thank my colleague Diane Jeske for her helpful comments on a draft of this paper.

Midwest Studies in Philosophy, XXIII (1999)

The Ontological Turn

C. B. MARTIN AND JOHN HEIL

Contemporary philosophy of mind, like much contemporary philosophy, has become mired in sterile disputes over technical issues apparently of interest only to professional philosophers. One symptom of the current malaise is the difficulty philosophers have in motivating central themes to outsiders. Attention lavished on possible worlds, the causal relevance of mental content, and supervenience, for instance, is difficult to justify to anyone who has not been conditioned by an appropriately comme il faut Ph.D. program.

We exempt from this assessment those philosophers who consider themselves scientists: cognitive scientists. The latter regard the pursuit of traditional philosophical aims as laughably naive. The role of the philosopher in the investigation of the mind, they tell us, is that of lending a hand to those who do the real work: the neuroscientists, cognitive psychologists, computer scientists, and linguists. Philosophers can usefully summarize empirical results, provide inspiration, and serve as conceptual police. The idea that philosophy has anything substantive to offer, however, is considered an embarrassing remnant of an earlier tradition that we have now—thankfully—mostly outgrown.

This self-effacing attitude has a long history, predating Hume, but it is treated with every revival as original: a sign that philosophy has come of age. It persists until philosophers regain the intellectual curiosity and courage to ask of some mathematized theory, for instance, how the world must be if that theory is correct; or of some thesis peopled with nonspatial, nontemporal entities, "What does this really come to?" These are questions that many of the best scientists, mathematicians, and logicians themselves ask and cannot be stopped from asking even when a philosopher tells them with a superior smile that they are not real, or more modestly, not fruitful questions.

Although we regard the dismissal of traditional philosophical pursuits as misguided, our focus here will be on the side effects of technical and formalistic approaches to ontology and the philosophy of mind. Our thesis is that excessive reliance on technical and formal methods can have a corrupting effect on our thinking. We do not oppose such methods per se. Our point is that they too often divert attention from ontologically deeper matters. We believe that the philosophy of mind—and probably philosophy generally—needs an infusion of ontological seriousness.

We defend this belief by briefly examining popular approaches to currently salient topics of discussion. Next, by way of contrast, we sketch what we regard as a promising ontology of properties. We apply this ontology to a few representative problems that have resisted technical solutions, and show that puzzles associated with the philosophy of mind are, in some cases, self-inflicted. These become manageable given a suitable ontology. Our conclusion: philosophers of mind must spend less time working out epicycles for going theories and more time scrutinizing potential truth-makers for these theories. This requires replacing an excessive dependence on technical exercises with the more chancy pursuit of fundamental ontology.

1. A PRELIMINARY: ANTIREALISM AND ONTOLOGY

Philosophers who defend versions of antirealism are often keen to leave the impression that they owe no ontological debts. This is a mistake. Antirealism about a particular domain implies realism about some other domain: truly "global" antirealism is incoherent. Berkeley is an antirealist about the physical world, but a realist about minds and ideas. Antirealists about minds are realists about physical objects. In general, anyone who takes one category of entities to be a construct must accept the reality of the constructing entities; anyone denying the existence of a domain eliminates that domain in favor of some other.

We propose the following precept:

(*P*) In evaluating a strain of antirealism, scrutinize the resulting ontology.[1]

In many cases, we believe, the charm of the antirealist position wears thin once its ontology is made explicit.

By way of illustration, imagine that someone denies the existence of natural divisions in the world: all depends on language. Language "carves up" reality; and to the extent that language is arbitrary or conventional, so are the elements of reality. Before you rush to embrace a view of this sort, however, you should ask yourself what it implies about the ontology of language. The nonlinguistic world is made dependent on language. But what is language, and what are the repercussions of privileging it in this way? Are we supposed to regard tables, mountains, and electrons with suspicion, while accepting syllables and morphemes as immune to doubt? If the world is a linguistic construct, then it is hard to see how language could itself be a part of the world. But then what is it? In this case it would not do to regard language as an abstract entity. That would imply, absurdly, that concrete entities—tables, mountains, and electrons—depend for their being on an abstract entity. But if language is concrete, why should it be exempt from the kinds of dependence thought to pertain to other concrete entities?

We do not claim that every form of antirealism is defective. We are merely pointing out that it is a mistake to imagine that devotees of antirealism are off the hook ontologically. Our suggestion is that much can be learned by pressing antirealists to make their ontology explicit. The strategy forces discussion back down to earth.

2. LINGUISTICISM

In an effort to avoid messy ontological considerations, philosophers in the twentieth century have engaged in what, in polite circles, is called "semantic ascent." Substantive ontological issues are transmogrified into issues concerning language and its application. In this way, talk of states of mind, for instance, is replaced by talk of mental attributions; talk of properties is replaced by talk of predicates; talk of causation is replaced by talk of theories; and talk of objects or states of affairs is replaced by talk of statements, propositions, or sentences.

Linguisticism—our preferred label for this approach—regards ontology with suspicion. Ontology is unwholesome, dubious, something to be avoided or, if that is inconvenient or impossible, to be minimized. Linguisticism finds expression in the quasi-technical shift from the "material mode" to the "formal mode," and is linked to the old idea that reduction requires entailment or translation.[2] This has allowed philosophers to argue that, because physical object statements do not entail statements about (actual and possible) sense experiences, physical objects are not reducible to (actual and possible) sense experiences, although the "information content" of physical object statements is exhausted by statements about actual and possible sense experiences (see Martin 1997, 214–15).

There is a natural bond between linguisticism and species of antirealism, and indeed these can shade off imperceptibly into one another. The flight from ontology, however, is scarcely more than an institutionalized form of repression. If we replace talk of properties with talk of predicates, for instance, we are left with the question of the ontological status of predicates. If properties strike you as odd or ungainly, surely predicates are worse. Are predicates concrete particulars? Classes of particulars? Abstracta? In comparison, being square and having mass $9.11(10)^{-28}$ g (the mass of an electron) seem utterly transparent.

Linguisticism does not succeed in replacing or eliminating ontology, but only diverting attention and postponing the hard questions. The mistake is to imagine that it is philosophically innocent.

3. SUPERVENIENCE

D. M. Armstrong's use of "supervenience" is clear and ontologically candid (see Armstrong 1997, 11–12). According to Armstrong, if αs supervene on βs, αs are nothing "over and above" βs. We are not sure about anyone else's uses. They are many, mixed, and confusing. By couching claims in terms of supervenience, philosophers keep ontology at arm's length. If αs supervene on βs, are αs anything "over and above" βs or not? The question is neither obscure nor unfair.

Consider being equilateral and being equiangular applied to triangles. These characteristics, though distinct, necessarily covary. In consequence, each, it would seem, supervenes on the other. The strength of a supervenience claim, then, is no indication whether items in the supervenience relation are distinct ("over and above" one another) or not. Weaker causal forms of supervenience (as in Searle 1992), appear inconsistent with the Humean contention that what is necessarily connected cannot be distinct, and what is causal cannot be necessarily connected.

Some philosophers reject these Humean theses, holding that what is distinct may be necessarily covariant, and what is distinct and causal may be necessarily connected. After all of the different breeds of supervenience (other than Armstrong's) are offered, we remain in the dark as to whether the items in a supervenience relation are necessarily connected (even necessarily covariant) and distinct, or whether Searle-style causally supervenient items are necessarily connected. (For more on Searle, see section 5.) The appeal to supervenience is a game for the ontologically uncurious and uncandid.

The most basic domain over which supervenience floats is that of the supposed supervenience of wholes on their parts. The world, considered as a whole, owes its character to the nature and arrangement of elementary items that make it up. This is sometimes put in terms of supervenience: all the facts supervene on the elementary physical facts. We are happy to grant the supervenience claim, but we would like to be clear on its ontological significance. As we have noted, supervenience is consistent both with the idea that supervening items are "nothing over and above" subvening items, and with the very different idea that what is supervenient, although ontologically distinct from its subvenient basis, covaries with that basis.

Appeals to supervenience have, in the main, allowed philosophers to avoid the messy details of ontology (see Heil 1998b). We follow Armstrong, however, in understanding the thought that the macroscopic character of the world supervenes on its microscopic particulars as amounting to the idea that the macroscopic is nothing over and above the microscopic. This places us at odds with philosophers who appeal to supervenience en route to a defense of the existence of levels of being. Levels talk is appropriate for descriptions and explanations, perhaps, but not for reality. In support of this preference we propose a single-level—or better, no-level—ontology that we believe reconciles the scientific image with important pretheoretical commitments (see section 5).

4. POSSIBLE WORLDS

Some readers will have noticed that we have thus far managed to refrain from mentioning possible worlds. It has not been easy. Discussions of supervenience are riddled with possible world talk. One reason to introduce such talk in the first place is to provide truth-makers for certain philosophically puzzling categories of locution. Counterfactual and subjunctive conditionals, for instance, appear to be straightforwardly true or false. Even if they are thought of as Rylean "inference tickets" (Ryle 1949) or INUS conditions (Mackie 1980), or some other abstract of connivance, we evidently need something in the world to make counterfactuals true, inference tickets "valid," or INUS conditions satisfied. When you are told that you would not have caught cold if you had not stood in a draft, you may agree. But to what exactly are you agreeing? What makes it the case, what makes it true that had you not stood in a draft, you would not have caught cold? The notion of a counter-to-the-facts fact-of-the-matter seems only to label the problem, not to resolve it.

Believers in real alternative worlds—"modal realists"—have an answer to the puzzle as to what might ground counterfactual truths (and other truths as well; in the interests of brevity, we shall focus exclusively on counterfactuals). The idea is that a counterfactual conditional assertion is true just in case no world in which the antecedent of the conditional (you do not stand in a draft) is true and the consequent (you do not catch cold) is false is "closer"—that is, more similar in its details—to the actual world than some world in which both the antecedent and the consequent are true. This arrangement of alternative worlds serves as truth-maker for the counterfactual assertion: if the assertion is true, it is true in virtue of this arrangement.[3]

We do not believe in philosophers' alternative worlds. Truths such worlds are called upon to ground can be anchored in perfectly ordinary features of our own world. According to the truth-maker principle, if a statement about the world is true, there is something about the world in virtue of which it is true. Realism about alternative worlds is based in part on acceptance of this principle. A true counterfactual conditional assertion, like any empirical assertion, requires a truth-maker. If nothing in the actual world is available to do the job, we are left with features of possible worlds or collections of possible worlds.[4]

Realism about possible worlds strikes many philosophers as implausible. What too often goes unrecognized is that those who are skeptical of the existence of nonactual possible worlds, yet persist in appealing to possible worlds in analyses or explanations of particular concepts or locutions, owe the rest us an account of the truth-makers of their claims. Suppose you contend that a counterfactual conditional assertion is true when, in the "nearest" worlds in which its consequent is false, its antecedent is false as well. What grounds your contention if there are no alternative worlds? And if you reject the need for truth-makers, what can be the point of appealing to these other worlds?

You might respond by noting that you are relying on talk of alternative worlds only as an illuminative device, a metaphor. It is convenient to translate talk of counterfactual conditionals (and much else, as well) into talk of possible worlds. Such talk enables us to organize and keep track of what would be more difficult to sort out otherwise.

We grant that this might be so if we had reason to accept that there really are alternative worlds—and enough of them. The ontology is on the scene and ready to be extended metaphorically. But if you do not believe in alternative worlds, then what exactly do your claims about alternative worlds and relations they allegedly bear to one another amount to? What—or where—are the truth-makers for those claims? If your talk of alternative worlds is purely metaphorical, how do we determine whether that talk is apt? To what features of the world do we direct our attention in assessing it?

Suppose we reject alternative worlds. We then accept that claims about the world are true, if they are true, in virtue of features intrinsic to our world. If we couch those claims in terms of alternative worlds, or appeal to alternative worlds when we set out to explain or defend them, we merely postpone consideration of whatever it is in virtue of which they hold. The impression that we have said all that needs saying, or even that we have made philosophical progress, is illusory. The appearance of content here when there is none stems from the fact that many of us have become comfortable with talk of alternative worlds. By and large we can count on our audience's going along with the ruse. But to revel in the trappings of alternative worlds while rejecting the ontology is to court mystery.

Note that we are not explicitly arguing against an ontology of alternative worlds. We think there are good arguments against an indefinite number of real worlds other than our own. Our brief is against those who advert to alternative worlds but reject the ontology. Even so, it is worth noting that those who accept an ontology of alternative worlds are not thereby excused from responsibility for providing an account of the ontology of this world. The "closeness" or "remoteness" of worlds to our world turns on intrinsic features of our world. If a counterfactual conditional assertion is true because in the "closest" worlds in which its antecedent is true, its consequent is true, then there must be something about our world in virtue of which those worlds are "closer" to it than some other worlds. In this regard, "distance" between worlds differs from distance between cities or planets. The latter is an external relation, the former is internal—it is fixed by intrinsic properties and spatiotemporal relations of the objects in question.

The upshot of all this is that we had better start thinking seriously about the ontology of our own world. It might turn out that, when we do so, the motivation for introducing alternative worlds will diminish. In any case, what we cannot do is to persist in the pretense that talk of alternative worlds relieves us of the need to get down to the messy details of the ontology of the actual world.

5. PARTS, WHOLES, AND LEVELS OF BEING

Proponents of hierarchical conceptions of reality have not done much to clarify the ontology. This may be due in part to an overreliance on modal concepts like supervenience and the jargon of possible worlds. Consider a recent author's remarks on levels of reality:

> It should be understood that the primacy of physics in ontological matters does not mean that everything is an element of a strictly physical ontology . . . physicalism . . . allows for non-physical objects, properties, and relations. The primacy of the physical ontology is that it grounds a structure that contains everything, not that it includes everything. . . . [W]ith regard to ontological matters, physicalism should not be equated with the identity theory in any of its forms. . . . I prefer the idea of a hierarchically structured system of objects grounded in a physical basis by a relation of *realization* to the idea that all objects are token identical to physical objects. (Poland 1994, 18)

For our part, we have difficulty understanding the nature of "grounding relations" when these are described in such a way that grounded properties remain wholly dependent on, but nevertheless distinct from, properties that serve as grounds. Perhaps some of our readers share our puzzlement.

One apparent consequence of a commitment to levels of being is a subsidiary commitment to forms of "vertical"—"upward" or "downward"—causation. This latter commitment stems from the idea that objects or properties occupy distinct levels of reality, coupled with the idea that genuine objects and properties cannot be causally inert. If some property, *P*, of an object, *o*, is grounded in, or realized by a distinct property, *G*, then *P* must (it would seem) make a contribution to the causal powers of *o* distinct from the contribution made by *G*. Were that not so, it is hard to see how anyone could think that both *P* and *G* could be simultaneously possessed by *o*. Indeed, if the causal contribution of *P* is exhausted by *G*, it looks as though anyone ascribing both properties to *o* would be guilty of a kind of double counting.

One need not, in any case, look far to find authors willing to embrace both "downward" and "upward" causation. Here is John Searle on "bottom-up" neuronal-to-mental causation:

> There is nothing mysterious about such bottom-up causation; it is quite common in the physical world. Furthermore, the fact that the mental features are supervenient on the neuronal features in no way diminishes their causal efficacy. The solidity of the piston is causally supervenient on its molecular structure, but this does not make solidity epiphenomenal; and similarly, the causal supervenience of my present back pain on micro events in my brain does not make the pain epiphenomenal. (Searle 1992, 125–26)

If micro-to-macro "bottom-up" causation is "common in the physical world," then what of "top-down," macro-to-micro causation? According to R. W. Sperry, "the concept of emergent downward causation" affords "a direct contradiction to prior atomistic, exclusively bottom-up" conceptions (Sperry 1991, 236). Sperry recommends that we embrace a recent "well-documented paradigm shift" that

> requires a shift to a new form of causality, a shift specifically from conventional microdeterminism to a new macromental determinism involving "top-down" emergent control (and referred to variously as emergent interaction, emergent or downward causation, and also as macro, emergent, or holistic determinism . . .). (Sperry 1991, 222)

We are not confident that we grasp the details of Searle's and Sperry's views. We propose only to point out a simple, and seemingly obvious, problem for any proponent of "vertical causation." Think, first, of "bottom-up" causation. How, exactly, are the constituents of a whole to be thought of as having effects upon a whole that includes themselves? When we turn to putative cases of "downward" causation, it is natural to wonder how a whole, something made up of particular constituents, could be thought of as affecting those very constituents? The affected constituents must apparently be parts of their own cause.[5] Searle's remarks to the contrary, there is indeed something "mysterious about bottom-up causation" and its "top-down" counterpart.

We can avoid mystery by thinking more clearly about a sensible compositional model according to which wholes and their properties do not "emerge" from, are nothing "over and above" parts and their properties. The key to understanding the model is to consider wholes not merely as simple aggregates, collections that cease to exist with the addition or subtraction of a single element. Instead, think of a particular kind of whole as comprising its constituents in all their interrelations and interactivities (actual and potential) for one another and for whatever might be external to them (with varying degrees of stability of all of these), while at the same time allowing for degrees of addition, subtraction, alteration, configuration, and even qualitative transformation, within whatever rough limits pertain to wholes of that kind.

Suppose a whole is considered as something distinct from all of its constituents with all of their interrelations, interactions, and dispositions for these. Then the "over and aboveness" of the whole is regarded as a causal factor quite apart from causal operativenesses of its individual constituents, even all of its individual constituents. As we have pointed out, effects of this "emergent" whole include effects upon its constituents ("top-down" causation) as well as effects on other things not traceable to the causal operativenesses of any, or even all, of its parts. Searle's "bottom-up" causation incorporates effects of a whole that outrun the effects of its parts and whatever is external to them (where these effects include the acquisition of further dispositions).

The threat of causes and effects duplicated at every level has not deterred philosophers from embracing multilevel ontologies. Perhaps one reason for the popularity of such ontologies is the inadequacy of traditional ways of thinking about compositionality. Once a plausible account of the constituents of a whole is in play, however, an account that includes the complex roles of constituents, the notion that wholes and their properties are "over and above" their constituents appears incredible. The ordinary conception of a collection (or a whole, or an object) is one that allows for the addition, subtraction, or substitution of constituents, and for changes in properties of those constituents (as when constituents are heated or cooled). Wholes survive changes like these, not because they are "over and above" their constituents, but because such changes are allowable for the kinds of whole in question.

Reflect for a moment on the familiar example of a statue and the bronze of which it is composed. One apparent problem for a compositional accounting of the statue is its status as an artifact created with a certain purpose in mind. But consider: the statue is just the bronze in a particular shape and size within rough limits of deformation, and loss, addition, or substitution of parts, as well as changes in properties of those parts, with the additional condition that the statue's character is the intentional product of an agent or agents for whom a compositional account can be given.

Imagine God setting out to create a world containing statues. God can do so by creating simple elements and insuring that these bear the right relations to one another. The creation of a single statue could well require the creation of a dynamic arrangement of simple elements extending over time and taking in a sizable spatial region. If statues require the existence of intelligent creatures with particular thoughts, then other collections of simple elements with similarly extended spatial and temporal relations would need to be included as well.

To determine what kind of compositional account might work for a given kind of object or whole, you must first determine the spatial and temporal boundaries of such wholes, their properties and relations, their capacities for affecting (and being affected by) other actual and possible things, and what degrees of addition, subtraction, and substitution of parts are allowable. Only after this is done is it possible to begin (1) plotting the spatial and temporal bounds formed by the constituents; (2) specifying an allowable range of interrelations and interactions (and the capacities or dispositions of these) with one another (and with whatever might be external to them); (3) determining allowable degrees of gain, loss, and substitution of constituents; and (4) determining allowable degrees of alteration in the properties of constituents. All this is required to render an object or whole, without remainder, in terms of its constituents.

A view of this sort is ontologically, but neither conceptually nor explanatorily, reductionist. There is no prospect of providing a useful definition, or even a finite set of necessary and sufficient conditions for something's being a statue appealing only a vocabulary limited to particles and relations among these. To regard this as a difficulty for the compositional view, however, is to miss the point. Our contention is not that talk of statues is translatable into, or finitely analyzable in terms of, talk of particles and their relations. The idea, rather, is that this is all statues are; statues are nothing other than, distinct from, or "over and above" collections of particles, where "collection" is taken in the relaxed sense spelled out above.

The composition model stems from the thought that, although there are undoubtedly levels of description and explanation, there are no levels of being. There is only a single level of ultimate constituents. Further, an object's constituents—in all their interrelatednesses and interreactivenesses, remember, their dispositions for these with one another and with whatever may be external, in all their varying degrees of stability—fully constitute and together are the whole (again, allowing additions, subtractions, and alterations of properties and configuration consistent with being a whole of that kind). Insofar as the properties and relations of the sorts of entity we have been considering are complex, these entities must have simpler constituents, and the properties and relations of these constituents must be simpler. What, then, are the ultimate constituents? This question is best left to the physicists.

As will become clear, we are not recommending the replacement of metaphysics by physics. It may be, as some theorists believe, that a true and complete physics will forever elude the human intellect. Even so, we are in a position to say something about the properties of the ultimate constituents of nature. Such properties, for instance, cannot be purely qualitative (in "pure act") any more than macroscopic or structural properties could be purely qualitative. The properties of whatever we count as elementary and noncomposite must include a capability for more than they manifest at any given time.

Perhaps this is uncontroversial—or relatively so. But consider one implication. Any account of properties that proved inapplicable to a domain of elementary constituents would thereby be inadequate.[6] Accounts of dispositionality that envisage the grounding of dispositions in structural features of complex objects appear incapable of explaining how ultimate constituents, items lacking structure, could be capable of more than they manifest.[7]

It might be useful to pause and reflect on grounds for the belief in a realm of "elementary" constituents. This belief, we contend, is prior to the pursuit of science. It is founded on a number of simple considerations.

First, we come to a grasp of a notion of composition according to which objects of particular kinds are wholly constituted by (and so no more than) parts of different kinds appropriately related. The parts of a hut are not huts, the parts of a sheep are not sheep, the parts of a stew are not stew.

Second, we find that objects grow larger by the addition of parts and smaller by a loss of parts.

Third, we come to see that a plant grows larger, and stone steps gradually wear down. In each case, changes occur indiscernibly. Observe the plant or the stone as closely as you like, and you will not detect an increase by addition of parts or a decrease by a loss of parts. Rejecting the notion that increases and decreases in size might be due to objects' expanding and contracting like balloons, we fasten on the idea that an object grows or shrinks by the addition or loss of insensible particles constitutive of the object.

This much comes to us without the benefit of science. Gradually we learn that appearance is not always a reliable indicator of reality. When we add science to the mix, we move further in this direction. We find it convenient, for instance, to distinguish primary and secondary properties of objects, and we are told that what is apparently solid and stable is, in reality, made up of tiny particles, widely separated in space, and in constant motion.

Our basic, pretheoretical, prescientific repertoire of concepts will undoubtedly require bending and twisting before these concepts can be deployed in attempts to understand some of current physics's more startling theses. Even here, however, even among the most unintuitive theories vying for serious attention today, one can recognize some conception of edges of boundednesses. There might be, for instance, relative degrees of density of aggregations of particles or aspects of fields, and relative degrees of stability of that density. This is at least analogous, in the realm of the elementary, to sizes, shapes, edges, continuity, and movement of macroscopic objects, and it further reinforces our realist compositional model of the relationship of the macroscopic and microscopic.

We are by no means suggesting that philosophers must toil in the shadows of science.[8] The pursuit of ontology is an attempt to devise a model of how the world might be, a model more abstract even than the model provided by physics. An ontological model incorporates placeholders for scientific results, and thereby constrains possible theories, excluding tempting confusions. Theoretical science and ontology can, with luck, advance one another's interests. (We shall return to this point in section 8.) Compositionalism is not scientism. Compositionalism leaves open the real possibility that science has thus far produced an incomplete and partial picture of the finer interstices of nature.

6. AN ONTOLOGY OF PROPERTIES

In this section, we outline a position that, taken together with the compositional model, provides a respectable ontological starting point for discussions in metaphysics and the philosophy of mind. In one regard our discussion will violate what we consider an essential metaprinciple of ontology. According to that principle, it is a mistake to pursue ontology piecemeal. Ontology resembles meteorology: small differences in one spot, tiny miscalculations, can have monumental repercussions elsewhere. Philosophers, long suspicious of ontology, may find themselves pushed to endorse a view of laws, or properties, or causation, for instance, in the course of discussing something else. This is to pick and choose a position on these basic topics that, although appearing no worse than alternatives that come to mind, promises a simple solution to some pressing difficulty. If the upshot yields embarrassments elsewhere, it saves effort to bite the bullet, and move on.

Every ontological theory (indeed every scientific theory) must posit a level of brute fact. It would be a mistake, however, to confuse the necessity of positing certain brute facts with a frank willingness to accept implausible consequences of a favored view. In engaging in ontology, our aim should be the advancement of a plausible overall scheme, one that minimizes brute facts and meshes with empirical theorizing and common understanding. Ontology does not lend itself to one-off answers to particular difficulties.

Still, one must begin somewhere. In section 5 we defended a compositional model of being. Here, we extend the view to properties. Our goal is not to advance a completed theory, but only to say enough to reveal the shape such a theory might have. (For detailed arguments see Martin 1980, 1992, 1993, 1994, 1997; Martin and Heil 1998; Heil 1998a, chap. 6.) Perhaps we can say enough to make clear the power inherent in the position we endorse.

In section 2, we distinguished predicates and properties. Whatever properties are, they cannot be simply whatever answers to predicates. Some predicates designate properties, no doubt, and, in general, predicates hold true of objects in virtue of properties possessed by those objects. But it would be a mistake to imagine that every predicate, even every predicate that figures in a going empirical theory, designates a property.

Why should anyone believe in properties in the first place, whether viewed as particulars (tropes), Platonic universals, or Armstrong's "all" in each of the many? One philosophical tradition shuns properties, preferring, instead, resemblance classes or sets of similar objects. The predicate "is spherical," for instance, might be taken to designate a class of objects, those, namely, belonging to the class of spherical things. A friend of properties will regard this as placing the cart before the horse. If objects belong to classes in virtue of similarities or resemblances they bear to one another, they resemble one another in virtue of their properties. Objects do not resemble one another *tout court*, but in some way or respect. You can think of these ways or respects as properties.

Consider two balls, one red and the other blue. Do these objects resemble one another? Yes, both are spherical. Do they differ? Again, yes, they are differently colored. It is natural to suppose that being spherical, being red, and being blue are properties possessed by the balls. Differently put: there is something about one ball in virtue of which it is true to say of it "the ball is spherical," and something about the ball—something else about the very same ball—in virtue of which it is true to say of it "the ball is red." These somethings about the ball are its properties; each endows the ball with a distinctive qualitative character and a distinctive range of powers or dispositionalities.

Objects resemble or fail to resemble one another in particular ways or respects. These ways or respects, we have suggested, are properties. Properties themselves can resemble or fail to resemble one another, but they do not do so or fail to do so in particular ways or respects. Two balls can be similar with respect to their shapes. The balls' shapes are similar, not with respect to anything, but similar *tout court*. Properties are the bases of similarities; they account for similarities among objects.

The balls, we say, while differing in color, have *the same* shape; they *share* a property. What is the significance of the italicized expressions in the previous sentence? Philosophers who regard properties as universals are inclined to read "the same" in such sentences as "the selfsame" or "one and the same." There is some one thing that the balls literally have in common or share: their shape. But, if the balls occupy distinct, nonoverlapping regions of space, then their sharing a property cannot be like two spectators at a golf match sharing an umbrella, or teenagers sharing a pizza. Rather, the sharing must be sui generis. Each ball is or encompasses a distinct instance of the universal sphericity. Universals differ from particulars precisely in this capacity to be "fully in" each particular.

We shall not pause here to discuss different accounts of universals.[9] We follow Locke in taking properties to be particulars. Two distinct, spatially nonoverlapping spherical objects possess distinct, though similar, properties, both of which answer to the general term "sphericity." What sense, then, can we make of talk of distinct objects sharing a property or possessing the same property? Two people can share a dislike for bagpipes or okra, and two stockbrokers can arrive at work wearing the same tie. In neither case do we have anything like identity or selfsameness, nor anything that would tempt us to imagine that aversions and ties are not, like everything else, entirely particular. Sameness in such cases need not be anything more than resemblance. For that matter, identical twins are twins, and objects with identical shapes need not be objects that stand in a unique relation of instantiation to a single universal entity.

On our view, then, one ball's sphericity is entirely distinct from the sphericity of another ball. To be sure, the sphericity of the first ball might be exactly similar to the sphericity of the second. But the sphericity of the first ball is a (particular) way the first ball is and the sphericity of the second ball is a (particular) way the second ball is.

Properties, then, can be real without being universals. A common name for properties thus considered is "tropes."[10] We have resisted the term, however, because we differ from other friends of tropes in rejecting the idea that objects are nothing more than bundles of tropes. We shall not go into details here, but for our money, the bundle theory treats properties inappositely as parts of objects.[11] Objects can have parts, but an object's properties are not its parts, they are particular ways the object is. A baseball's sphericity is not a part of the baseball in the way the baseball's cover is a part of it. A traditional label for properties considered as particularized ways is "modes." Rather than introduce a new term into the discussion, however, we shall stick with "property."

Our first claim, then, is that properties are particulars, not universals. Second, we hold that every property has a dual nature: in virtue of possessing a property, an object possesses both a particular dispositionality and a particular qualitative character. The overall dispositionality and qualitative character of an object depend on the properties it possesses and relations these bear to one another. A ball's sphericity, for instance, gives it (in concert with the ball's other properties) a distinctive appearance and disposes it in particular ways. (It will roll, for instance, and reflect light in a certain pattern.)

Philosophers commonly distinguish dispositional and categorical properties. Dispositional properties endow their possessors with particular dispositions or powers; categorical properties endow objects with nondispositional qualities. Some philosophers have denied the existence of categorical properties, arguing that every property is purely dispositional (see, for instance, Mellor 1974; Shoemaker 1980). Others deny dispositional properties (Armstrong 1968, 85–88). Still others have regarded dispositional properties with suspicion, treating them as grounded in or realized by categorical properties (see Prior, Pargetter, and Jackson 1982; and Jackson 1996). On such a view, the fundamental properties are qualitative; dispositional properties are "second-order" properties, properties possessed by objects in virtue of their possession of first-order qualitative properties.[12]

The debate has had the form of one side's finding its opponents' position implausible and declaring victory by default. Those who regard properties as dispositional, for instance, point out that nondispositional properties could make no causal difference to their possessors. A nondispositional property would be, like God or the number two, "in pure act," incapable of anything further. For its part, science seems to care nothing for qualities. The magnitudes figuring in physical theories identify powers possessed by objects. Properties, then, must be dispositional, not categorical.[13]

On the other side, those who regard dispositionality as ontologically derivative point out that purely dispositional properties would resemble promissory notes backed by promissory notes, themselves backed by promissory notes, backed by. . . . Every disposition is a disposition for some manifestation. But if every manifestation is itself purely dispositional, then it will be for some further disposition for some manifestation, and this manifestation, in turn, nothing more than a disposition for some manifestation, . . . and so on. A world consisting of pure dispositions would seem to be a world whose inhabitants, although poised to act, never get around to doing anything.[14]

We believe that both sides of the dispute are right, and both wrong. Properties are not purely qualitative (the proponents of dispositionality are right about that). But neither are properties purely dispositional (in this we agree with those suspicious of pure dispositionality). Instead, every property is at once dispositional and categorical—or, as we prefer, dispositional and qualitative. Dispositionality and qualitativity are built into each property; indeed, they *are* the property. The inseparability of a property's dispositionality and qualitativity is analogous to the inseparability of the old lady and the young woman in Leeper's famous ambiguous figure (see Heil 1998a, p. 189).

A property—and unless we signal otherwise, we shall focus exclusively on intrinsic properties—is a two-faced dispositional-qualitative coin. Properties are not compounds, however. A property's dispositionality or qualitativity cannot be abstracted as entirely distinct or separable ingredients. A property's dispositionality and qualitativity must be thought of as unrealizable limits for different ways of being that property. Because dispositionality and qualitativity are equally basic and irreducible, there is no asymmetry here. A property's qualitativity, for instance, does not "ground" or serve as a supervenience base for its dispositionality. A property just *is* a certain dispositionality that just *is* a certain qualitativity.

We are not entirely happy characterizing a property's dispositionality and qualitativity as "different ways of being" the property. This mode of description remains too suggestive of a mixture. Talk of covariance—as in equiangular and equilateral—is also potentially misleading.

What we propose boils down to a surprising identity: the dispositional and the qualitative are identical with one another and with the unitary intrinsic property itself. The suggested identity is surprising only because we have grown used to distinguishing the dispositional and the qualitative. Once it is recognized that these are simply different ways of representing the selfsame property, the identity can be seen to resemble countless others.

For any intrinsic, irreducible property, then, what is dispositional and what is qualitative are one and the same property differently considered: considered as what the property exhibits of its nature, and considered as what the property is directive and selective for as its manifestations. These cannot be prized apart into the purely qualitative and the exclusively dispositional. The qualitative informs and determines the "forness" of the dispositional, and the "forness" of the dispositional informs and determines the qualitative. There is neither a direction of priority or dependence, nor a reduction of one to the other.

One impediment to recognizing that the dispositional and qualitative are one and the same is an unfortunate tendency to regard the qualitative as nonrelational and the dispositional as relational. Dispositions are not relations between dispositional states and their manifestations or whatever elicits their manifestations. A disposition can be fully present and "ready to go," yet never manifest itself. Indeed a disposition can exist despite the nonexistence of reciprocal disposition partners needed for its manifestation. Their absence or nonexistence does not affect the readiness of the dispositional state; that state need not change in any way in order to be manifested. A salt crystal remains soluble in water even if it never dissolves, even if no water exists within its light cone, even if it exists in a world entirely devoid of water.

To summarize: Our suggestion is that dispositionality and qualitativity are to be identified: a property's dispositionality and qualitativity are, at bottom, the property looked at in two complementary ways. This identity thesis must be distinguished from a view according to which dispositionality and qualitativity are taken to covary, even when the covariance is strictly necessary—as in the case of a triangle's equilaterality and equiangularity.

The necessity of a connection between nonspecific size and shape of an object is of little interest. In defending the identity of a property's qualitativity and dispositionality, we mean to be speaking only of specific, maximally definite or determinate qualities and dispositions. Reality traffics in specifics. This is the locus of necessities (and nonnecessities), identities (and nonidentities). Imagine a triangle with a particular size and shape. If the quality of the triangle's size or shape changes, so must its dispositionality—and vice versa. The covariance here is not that of one's being caused by the other, nor is it merely accidental.

A particular triangle comprises three straight lines or edges, their three points of connection forming a three-sided plane figure with three angles. If the sides of the figure are equal in length, then, necessarily, the angles formed by the intersection of these sides are equal. Disproportional increases or decreases of the lengths of sides are matched by increases or decreases of the angles. However, proportional increases or decreases of the lengths of the sides are not matched by increases or decreases of the angles. There is no necessary covariance between sides and angles, then, insofar as these are understood (as they must be if we are concerned with particular objects) as possessing definite magnitudes. The length of the side of an equilateral triangle can vary independently of the size of the angles, provided only that the lengths vary together.

Equiangularity is supervenient (in Armstrong's "nothing over and above" sense) on the sides of a triangle having some particular length when this length happens to be equal. The same is true, *mutatis mutandis*, of equilaterality. The particular length of the sides of an equilateral triangle, then, do not covary with such triangles' angles in the way the dispositionality and qualitativity of a property necessarily covary.

Let us recapitulate. First, properties are particularized ways objects are. When distinct objects "share properties," each object possesses a distinct, but exactly similar property.

Second, the notion that an intrinsic property is either purely qualitative or purely dispositional is a nonstarter. Leaving aside God (and perhaps the number two), no property is in "pure act"; no property is at any time utterly lacking in unfulfilled potency. Nor is any property purely a capacity for the production of further capacities for the production of. . . . On the contrary, properties must be qualitative as well as dispositional (and dispositional as well as qualitative). The dispositionality and qualitativity of a property are correlative, complementary, inseparable, and covariant when these appear in their intrinsic and irreducible form in "the finer interstices" of nature.[15]

An ontology of properties constrains the empirical question of what properties in particular there are (or might be, or could be) in the material domain (which includes the "theoretical" entities) and in the mental domain.

Finally, what of universals? If properties are identified with universals, then the instantiation relation—the relation between a universal and its particular instances —must be explained. On some views, universals are wholly present in each of their numerically and spatially distinct instances (see Armstrong 1978, 1997). On other views, universals can exist apart from, yet somehow be present spatiotemporally in, their instances (Tooley 1987). We believe that there is no need for universals, however conceived. When a general term—"sphericity," for instance—designates a property, it can apply to every exactly similar property. If you like, the general term can be said to designate a class of exactly similar properties. Other general terms—most, perhaps—designate looser classes, classes of resembling, but not exactly resembling, qualities.

7. APPLICATIONS

We have outlined a theory of parts and wholes and a theory of properties. How are such theories to be evaluated? Our answer is that it would be a mistake to imagine that an ontological thesis could be assessed a priori: by eyeballing, so to speak, its components. The test of an ontological picture is its power: how much it enables us to explain and tie together. A defense of an ontology of possible worlds, for instance, does not turn on the a priori plausibility of the thesis that our world is merely one of an infinitude of alternative worlds. An ontology of possible worlds deserves to be taken seriously to the extent that it provides unified and satisfying answers to persisting questions.

We believe that the ontology sketched here (and elsewhere; see references) is at least as powerful as any competitor. Our defense of this claim will consist in applications of the view to issues of contemporary concern. Along the way, we shall indicate how a sensible account of properties can displace reliance on possible worlds, and provide the kind of ontological grounding philosophers have sought in appeals to supervenience and the phenomenon of multiple realizability.

Modal Realism without Possible Worlds

Imagine for a moment that we are right: every property is dispositional. The dispositionality of a property is intrinsic to it, a facet of its nature. The dispositionalities of objects are the result of the dispositionalities of the object's properties, and relations these bear to one another.[16] Manifestations of dispositions are typically mutual manifestations of reciprocal disposition partners.[17] Consider a grain of salt's disposition to dissolve in water and the reciprocal disposition of water to dissolve salt. The grain of salt's dissolving is a mutual manifestation of these reciprocal partners. A given disposition can manifest itself differently with different reciprocal partners. That property of the salt in virtue of which it dissolves in water may be very differently manifested when subjected to heat, for instance, or pressure.

One way to put this point is to note that dispositions are projective for an indefinite range of alternative manifestations with alternative reciprocal disposition partners. At any given time, every disposition is capable of endless (perhaps literally endless) manifestations (Martin and Heil 1998). These possibilities are built into the disposition itself. They are present even if unmanifested, even if the reciprocal partners for their manifestation are absent or nonexistent.

This gives us everything we need to ground counterfactual assertions. It is true of this grain of salt that, had it been immersed in water, it would have dissolved, not because in some nearby world the salt (or its counterpart) is immersed and dissolves, but because, even undissolved, the salt retains its power to dissolve in water. It is true of you that, had you not stood in a draft, you would not have caught cold, because your catching cold is a mutual manifestation of your being overheated and your having stood in a cool draft.

The intrinsic dispositionalities of objects provide, as well, a grounding for claims about what is or is not possible, what is or is not necessary. In this way, intrinsic dispositionalities underlie laws of nature and their modal status. We prefer to think of laws governing occurrences in the actual world as truths that hold in virtue of existing objects and their properties. The modal force of the statement of a law stems from the dispositional character of the law's truth-makers. Because a property's dispositionality is included in its nature, there can be no question of worlds containing the same properties with different dispositionalities. And, by extension, there can be no question of there being worlds with the same properties, yet different laws of nature. The laws of nature are contingent to the extent that it is contingent that the properties that exist do in fact exist.

We can also begin to make sense of the much discussed distinction between so-called strict laws and hedged ceteris paribus laws. The manifestation of a disposition can be blocked or inhibited by the presence or absence of particular reciprocal disposition partners. A grain of salt, although water soluble, will not dissolve in water if the water is already saturated or if the salt is coated in a chemical that prevents its dissolving. In these cases, the salt retains its disposition, but fails to manifest it in the presence of an appropriate reciprocal partner owing to the presence of some further disposition. To the extent that such possibilities are built into the properties that ground statements of laws of nature, those statements will admit of exceptions. It may be possible to write these exceptions into laws applying to the very simplest constituents of our world. But it is hopeless to try to do so when it comes to laws ranging over complex objects with complex dispositionalities. We shall have more to say on this topic presently.

The dispositionalities built into properties gives us genuine in re possibilities and necessities without the introduction of nonactual possible worlds. They provide a way of locating possibilities and necessities in the world—in our world—where they might be thought, pretheoretically, to belong. This conclusion is reached, not via an ad hoc theory of possibility and necessity, but as a natural outgrowth of what we regard as an independently plausible ontology of properties.

Multiple Realizability

Philosophers of mind, particularly those of a functionalist bent, are fond of the idea that mental properties are "multiply realizable." We know of no clear account of multiple realizability, but the idea is roughly this:

> (MR) A property, Ψ, is multiply realizable, when an object, x's, possessing Ψ depends on and is determined by x's possessing some property, σ, from a (nonempty, and possibly open-ended) set of properties, Σ. When a member of Σ is present, it realizes Ψ.[18]

We do not claim much for this characterization of multiple realizability. What we have to say, however, depends only on the idea that when a property, Ψ, is multiply realized, objects possessing Ψ are taken to possess both Ψ and some realizing property, σ.

One much-discussed problem facing those who regard mental properties as multiply realizable is the problem of mental causation. If a mental property is realized by a physical property, then the physical realizer threatens to preempt any causal contribution on the part of the realized mental property. The difficulty, however, is perfectly general. It applies to any multiply realized property, mental or not.

Attempts to reconcile multiple realizability and causal efficacy have included appeals to purely counterfactual accounts of causation, to the idea that any property that figures in a causal law (even a "hedged" ceteris paribus law) possesses causal efficacy, and to assorted varieties of reductionism: mental properties are identical with their realizers or with disjunctions of their realizers. We are suspicious of all these strategies. Rather than arguing the point here, however, we shall sketch an alternative picture of multiple realizability. This alternative picture takes seriously the ontology of properties (and causality!), and applies our earlier observations about predicates and properties.

Suppose, if you will, that some mental predicates, those featured in appeals to multiple realizability, do not designate properties. Such predicates are satisfied by objects, and they are satisfied by those objects in virtue of their properties. But the properties in virtue of which objects satisfy predicates of this kind, although similar, are not precisely similar. An octopus, a rabbit, and an infant human being can all experience pain. Is this a matter of their sharing a property—the property of being in pain—designated by the predicate "is in pain"? We doubt it.[19] The octopus, the rabbit, and the infant possess properties that are pertinently similar and, in virtue of this, each satisfies the predicate "is in pain."

We hope we have said enough to make it clear that this need not be a form of eliminativism about the mental. Nor, plainly, is it a form of reductionism. Reductionism requires something to reduce, and the suggestion is that, in the cases at issue, there are no properties to be reduced. No, the idea is that mental predicates standardly thought to designate multiply realizable properties—"is in pain," for instance—apply to objects that are similar in certain respects: similar enough to merit application of the predicate. These similarities stem from the objects' possession of certain properties. But the properties need not be the same in every case: objects are not exactly similar in those respects in virtue of which it is true of them that they satisfy the predicate "is in pain."

A view of this sort has a number of virtues: it allows us to be realists about pains; it does not lead to worries about pains being epiphenomenal; and it accommodates the notion that what it is in virtue of which a creature is in pain could vary widely across individuals or species. Imagine, for instance, that pain is at least in part a functional notion. That is, a creature satisfies the predicate "is in pain" partly in virtue of being in a state that plays a certain complex causal role in the creature's psychological economy.[20] As functionalists never tire of pointing out, many different kinds of state could assume this role. (This is especially clear because any specification of the role will, of necessity, incorporate a measure of vagueness.) Very different kinds of creature, then, could be in pain. They are all in pain, however, not because they share a "second-order" property, the property of being in pain, but because they possess similar first-order properties. This similarity, which is not to be confused with exact similarity or with identity, is enough to allow objects possessing distinct and less than perfectly similar properties to satisfy the predicate "is in pain."

If something like this is right, then multiple realizability is not, as it is usually thought to be, a relation among properties. It is simply an instance of the familiar phenomenon of predicates applying to objects in virtue of properties possessed by those objects, but not in virtue of designating some property shared by those objects. And it would seem that this is something that holds of most of the predicates we deploy in everyday life and in the practice of science.

Multiple realizability—regarded as a relation among properties—has been accorded a central place in contemporary philosophy of mind. Our suggestion is that multiple realizability remains attractive only so long as we fail sharply to distinguish predicates and properties. It is but a short step from this to the idea that every predicate satisfied by an object names a property. Thus, if distinct objects satisfy the same predicate, they must have a property in common. Failure to locate any obvious candidates leads to the idea that the predicates must name properties distinct from, but somehow rooted in, properties on the scene.

If pain is multiply realizable, however, this means only that the predicate "is in pain" applies to different kinds of object in virtue of their possessing different, pertinently similar (though not exactly similar) properties. We are now in a position to see how something like this is precisely what we ought to expect, and why statements of laws in which multiply realizable predicates figure are bound to be hedged.

Return for a moment to pain. Suppose that your being in pain—your having a sore throat, for instance—is a matter of your possessing a particular property, P_1. It is true of you that you are in pain in virtue of your possessing P_1. Now, imagine that an octopus is in pain. We shall imagine that the octopus is very differently constituted, so that it is true of the octopus that it is in pain in virtue of the octopus's possessing P_2. On the view we recommended, P_1 and P_2 are similar, but not exactly similar properties. (P_1 and P_2 are similar enough so that the presence of either satisfies the predicate "is in pain.") To the extent that they are similar, we can expect their dispositionalities to be similar.[21] The lawlike generalizations we construct in which the predicate "is in pain" figure will hold of objects that can be counted on to behave similarly, though not necessarily identically, in similar circumstances. In our terms: similar dispositions will have similar manifestations with similar reciprocal partners.

To the extent that other psychological predicates resemble "is in pain," they will be "projectable" (owing to their being satisfied by a range of similar dispositions), but loose (owing to their being satisfied by similar, but not exactly similar, dispositions). Generalizations in which such predicates figure, then, will be unavoidably hedged. Further, such generalizations will not be translatable into generalizations couched in some "more basic" vocabulary—the vocabulary of neuroscience, for instance. This is a consequence of the apparent fact that predicates figuring in those generalizations are satisfied by properties distinct from those satisfying predicates in the "more basic" vocabulary.

This is just another way of expressing our view of multiple realizability. The view honors the antireductionist idea that there is no prospect of deducing psychological truths from descriptions of physical objects and properties (in the vocabulary of neuroscience, for instance) without requiring a commitment to the idea that psychological truths hold in virtue of agents' possession of assorted "higher-level" properties. There are levels, to be sure, but the levels are linguistic and explanatory, not ontological.

Functionalism

Although we have noted that the ordinary concept of pain may include functional components, we wish to distinguish our view sharply from functionalism. We have been assuming realism concerning dispositionality (see Martin 1992, 1994, 1997; and Martin and Heil 1998). Dispositions are real, intrinsic features of the world; functions, in contrast, are abstractions. Dispositions ground functional attributions. But in speaking of a disposition as a function, we consider it only as for a very small set of manifestations. Functional ascriptions are manifestation bound. This puts blinkers on viewing the world that can be distortive for science itself.

Talking realistically about real objects, any particular disposition state is ready with an infinite number of alternative reciprocal disposition partners—nonactual as well as actual—for an infinite number of mutual manifestations. The dispositional states of any real object or real machine or real person are not bound to any small set of manifestations.

The concept of reciprocal disposition partnerhood for mutual manifestation loosens the simplistic linguistic bondage of a specific and unique dispositionality for a specific and unique manifestation. Instead, it allows that one and the same dispositional state with different reciprocal disposition partners can have different mutual manifestations. The differences can be striking. Water thrown on burning wood and water (identically the same water) thrown on burning oil has strikingly different mutual manifestations.[22] The importance of this point for neuroscience and the philosophy of mind will become clear presently.

Supervenience

Our earlier reflections on multiple realizability lead naturally to an alternative understanding of supervenience relations. First, as we have seen (section 3), it is a mistake to imagine that supervenience is a kind of relation holding between properties or property domains. The concept of supervenience as it is standardly characterized is a modal concept, one satisfied by a variety of distinct kinds of relation among a variety of distinct sorts of entity.

Second, once we recognize this, and once we take the trouble to distinguish predicates and properties, we can see that, in many cases, supervenience will hold when a given predicate ("is in pain," for instance) is satisfied by objects possessing distinct, though similar properties. Indeed, this seems to have been one motivation for introducing talk of supervenience into ethical theory in the first place. "Is good" holds of objects in virtue of properties possessed by those objects, but it does not follow that "is good" designates a property shared by every good object (in our terms, precisely similar properties). Nevertheless, if two objects, a and b, are identical with respect to their properties, and the predicate "is good" holds of a, then it must hold of b as well.

It is easy to see now that supervenience will hold trivially of any predicate that designates a property (or designates a class of exactly similar properties). It will hold as well of any multiply realizable predicate. "Is in pain" holds of you in virtue of your possession of P_1, and of an octopus in virtue of its possession of a similar, but not exactly similar property, P_2. "Is in pain" will hold, as well, of any other creature that possesses P_1, or P_2, or any other property sufficiently similar to P_1 or P_2.

Once we move to accept supervenience as a constraint on the application of predicates rather than a relation between properties or property families, there is no need to posit levels of properties and thus to fall prey to a host of philosophical difficulties raised by such a conception.[23]

8. PLACEHOLDERS AND PLACE FILLERS

Ontology should not just limply follow (à la Quine) the latest efforts of scientific research with timorous attempts at their conceptual clarification. If science can be thought of as providing abstract theoretical models of facets of the world, then ontology should be regarded as providing an even more abstract model. Ontology's abstractness provides what amount to constraints or placeholders for certain kinds of less abstract model in science. We illustrate the idea by mentioning examples of placeholders indicated by our ontology and place fillers obligingly provided by recent work in the empirical domain.

Placeholder

Although it is common to identify dispositions by reference to a single kind of manifestation, this is, as we have shown, potentially misleading. No disposition has a single kind of manifestation. Actual disposition states have alternative reciprocal disposition partners for alternative mutual manifestations. It can appear otherwise because nature may provide us much of the time with the comfort of mostly similar reciprocal disposition partners for mostly similar mutual manifestations.

Nature is not always reliable in this regard, however. If you have a simplistic view of dispositions and manifestations, you will miss the underlying complexity of what are different reciprocal partners and different mutual manifestations.

Place Filler

For many years, the information flow (through the medium of neurotransmitters) or vector-directional path circuitry model held dominance in neuroscience. The model fits the American Sunday driver who treats every destination point as just another point of departure. The vast complexity of what is at any destination point is unnoticed. In the brain, this array of complexity is not found in the comparatively simple transmitters, but at the postsynaptic receptors side, which has been relatively ignored. It is here that the very same transmitters, in the very same dispositional states, with very different disposition state partners at the receptor level, have different mutual manifestations at the extremes of excitation or inhibition. The point is made forcefully by Morrison and Hof (1992).

> [Our] discussion is greatly oversimplified because it implies that a given neurotransmitter will have only one cellular effect. In reality not only can a neurotransmitter's effect be modified by other postsynaptic or intracellular events, but also a high degree of receptor diversity exists such that there may be

> several different receptor subtypes for a given neurotransmitter. This receptor subtype diversity not only gives the neurotransmitter greater latitude in its effect but also complicates the spatial domain of a given neurotransmitter. Since the different receptor subtypes have different functional properties, the complete characterization of a synapse will require precise knowledge of the molecular identity of the postsynaptic receptor as well as the neurotransmitter employed. (28–29)

> Presently we assume that all of these projections will use glutamate and/or aspartate as their neurotransmitter and in that sense we make the assumption that the neurotransmitter neurobiology of these projections is relatively simplistic. However, this is likely to be a conceptual error in that the neurotransmitter nature of these connections may be relatively simplistic on the presynaptic side but it is likely to be extremely complicated on the postsynaptic side. (34)

> Therefore, while we know that the major excitatory afferents to cortex come from the thalamus and other cortical sites, we will have very little appreciation of the precise nature of these circuits until we have characterized the postsynaptic side and the degree to which postsynaptic specificity of glutamate receptor proteins is the defining characteristic of a glutamatergic circuit. (35)

Placeholder

Integral to the account of properties outlined in section 6 is the idea that the "projectivity" of dispositions provides a promising backdrop to a naturalistic account of intentionality. A disposition incorporates projectivity for particular kinds of response with particular kinds of reciprocal disposition partner. Projectivity—a kind of primitive of-ness or for-ness—is found throughout nature. To the extent that dispositionality goes "all the way down," so does this projectivity. We believe that this holds the key to understanding the intentionality of thought and language.[24]

We envisage an account of intentionality that begins with the nonintentional, then introduces intentional conscious thought at a primitive, prelinguistic stage, then ties this to the acquisition and use of language. Martin 1987 includes a worked-out theoretical model for explaining semantic, rule-governed, idiolectal procedural activities (in the head or in behavior) that are prelinguistic in the history of the race and the individual. These are basic to nonlinguistic conscious thinking and basic to the life and continuance of language itself. Prelinguistic intentionality is more than a precondition for language, however, its deployment is thoroughly intertwined with the use of language.

Place Filler

Developmental psychologists and neuropsychologists are uncovering sophisticated mental capacities of prelinguistic infants and children. (See, for instance, Spelke et al. 1992.) Too often psychological testing has relied on linguistic or gross behavioral data. A pair of developments in testing have led to the discovery of surprising cognitive abilities at very early ages. One is founded on the sucking response, which is correlated with attention and interest. The other is enabled by sophisticated, noninvasive brain scanners such as magnetic resonance imaging (MRI). It is noteworthy that some investigators have seen the need for, and central function of, nonstatic imagery in procedural activity that can be richly semantic (Weiskrantz 1988). Our chief reservation concerning this research is its emphasis on the visual at the expense of the other senses.

Placeholder

Given the many and varied roles of thought without language described philosophically (Martin 1987) and substantiated in research by neuropsychologists (Weiskrantz 1988), it seems evident that such precursors and supports of language cannot be based in utterly disparate areas of the brain. That would be taking modularity too far. Broca's area, for example, should not be speech specific and anatomically distinct from areas devoted to spatial processing. No one wants action at a distance.

Place Filler

Broca's area appears to have a visual-spatial processing function (Kosslyn et al. 1993) that can partly explain the etiology of prelinguistic imagistic task uses, and motor-perceptual task uses and the emergence of the capacity for speech in the development of the individual and the race. Intimations of this surfaced as early as 1972 in the work of Roger Shepard (Shepard and Feng 1972) but were overlooked by most researchers until recently.

Placeholder

Any disposition has actual readinesses for an infinite number of alternative actual and nonactual reciprocal disposition partners for an infinity of alternative mutual manifestations.

Place Filler

Instead of Richard Feynman's infinity of world lines or an infinity of real alternative worlds, the infinities and the mathematics needed in theoretical physics can rest in the infinities of the actual disposition states of whatever are the ultimate posits of a more complete physics than we have now (see Martin and Heil 1998).

9. CONCLUDING REMARKS

Contemporary analytical philosophy, we contend, has been ill-served by a tendency to rely too heavily on technical devices. Technical accoutrements have hindered, and in some cases displaced, serious thinking about ontological matters. The result is an arid climate of discussion. Theorists rest content with adding epicycles to theories expressed in a medium guaranteed to keep ontology at arm's length and so dodge the deeper questions.

The solution, we have argued, is the inculcation of an attitude of ontological seriousness. Ontology is with us, whether we like it or not. Attempts to repress ontological themes or to transform them via semantic ascent merely muddy the water and postpone the inevitable. We have sought to illustrate this idea by addressing topics central to contemporary philosophy of mind and showing how discussion of these topics might benefit from an infusion of ontological seriousness. We do not claim to have provided anything like a complete account of the issues we take up. We believe we have said enough to get our point across to open-minded readers, however. Philosophy is hard enough. We only make matters worse by forcing ourselves to view the territory through the lens of a technical apparatus with the power to conceal as much as it reveals.

NOTES

1. For a detailed defense of this precept, see Martin 1993.

2. Rather than purging philosophy of ontology, the practice of semantic ascent has rather served as an evasion or obfuscation of ontological views. Proponents have pretended that entailments were possible when they are not. When entailments have had to be abandoned for nonentailment ontological reductions, they have refused to see these reductions as ontological and have labeled only the entailment form as phenomenalism, etc. See, for example, Ayer 1956 and Wisdom 1938.

3. We do not present this as an analysis of the counterfactual conditional under discussion. We intend only to illustrate the rudiments of appeals to possible worlds in attempts to ground such conditionals. The most influential advocate of possible worlds is David Lewis. See Lewis 1986; see also Stalnaker 1976.

4. What we are dealing with is an effulgence, an indefinite number of real worlds that includes our own world. These alternative worlds are distinct from one another, although they can parallel (that is, be closest neighbors) to one another and to our world in virtue of their intrinsic properties.

5. There is an additional problem here: the problem of causal overdetermination that seems to occur at all levels. A clear, though unremarked, depiction of such overdetermination can be found in Searle 1983, 269.

6. We are content to leave it entirely open as to whether these ultimate constituents are corpuscular, or whether they are fields or regions of space-time. We leave it open, as well, whether items we are calling "elementary" or "ultimate" might not themselves be complex. Our objection to accounts of dispositionality that "ground" dispositions in structures is that this rules out a priori the possibility of ultimately simple objects.

7. We take it as obvious that structural properties themselves involve dispositionality and thus cannot be used to explain or "ground" dispositionality.

8. Nor should philosophers regard science with the kind of cynicism born of the thought that the history of science is a history of theories embraced, regarded as obvious, then later rejected. The history of science should stand as a reminder that there are many different ways the world might be.

9. For a clear, fair-minded summary, see Armstrong 1989.

10. See Williams 1966, chap. 7. See also Armstrong 1989, chap. 6; Campbell 1990; Simons 1994; and Bacon 1995.

11. It is important to distinguish bundle theories, according to which objects are made up of properties, from a view according to which objects are regarded as regions of space-time that possess properties. We regard this latter view as an open possibility, providing only that the properties in question are nontransferable, nonexchangeable between entities or space-time regions. See Martin 1980.

12. For an extended discussion of the relation between dispositionality and qualitativity, see Armstrong, Martin, and Place 1996, especially §§ 1, 5, 6, 8, 9, and 11.

13. See Blackburn 1990. Might something exist in a purely qualitative state utterly lacking in dispositionality? It seems possible to imagine something altogether inert and unchanging. This is importantly different from something's altogether lacking dispositionality, however. An entity or property intrinsically incapable of affecting or being affected by anything else, actual or possible, is not merely inert; it amounts to no-thing.

14. For possible worlds enthusiasts, Blackburn (1990, p. 64) puts the point as follows: "To conceive of *all* the truths about a world as dispositional is to suppose that a world is entirely described by what is true at *neighboring* worlds. And since our argument was a priori, these truths in turn vanish into truths about yet other neighboring worlds, and the result is that there is no truth anywhere." See also Foster 1982, p. 68.

15. It is easy to be put off the scent in such cases by focusing on secondary qualities: colors, sounds, or feels. If you begin with a consideration of colored objects, for instance, you may be baffled (as Locke was) by the connection between colors as qualities and colors as dispositions. Difficulties are compounded when philosophers attempt to distinguish between "phenomenal color" and "physical color." If colors might fail to exist in nature, how can they exist in nature? Is phenomenal color a color experience (versus a colored experience)? Then how does an inanimate object like a stone have such an experiential property (and why not an experiential ache as well)?

16. An object's dispositionalities can depend, as well, on dispositionalities of objects external to it. Think of an object the sphericity of which depends on its being suspended in a particular gravitational field. The dispositionalities possessed by the object in virtue of its sphericity themselves depend on the dispositionalities of distinct, spatially discontinuous objects (whose dispositionalities may in turn depend on the dispositionalities of . . .). In such cases, as Locke (1690/1978, bk. IV, chap. VI, § 11) puts it, everything "owes the being it has . . . to its neighbours." To simplify the discussion, we shall ignore complications of this sort in what follows.

17. Typically, but not invariably. An atom's disposition to decay may be "self-manifesting." Again, to simplify the discussion, we ignore this complication here.

18. In most discussions of multiple realizability, the presumption is that properties are universals. On our view, properties are particulars. The points that follow, however, go through in either case. If you accept universals, then you will interpret talk of objects sharing properties or possessing the same property as talk of objects instantiating a single universal. If you take properties to be particulars, then you will (like us) interpret such talk as holding true of objects in virtue of their possessing exactly similar properties.

19. We doubt it for roughly the reasons proponents of multiple realizability like to harp on. Compare the predicate "is a game." Is anyone tempted to regard being a game as a "second-order" property realized by particular games?

20. To the extent that functional concepts can be assimilated to dispositional concepts, we have no objection to this idea. We do object, however, and on entirely general ontological grounds, to the further claim (essential to functionalism) that all there is to pain is this dispositionality. See below.

21. And if the functionalists were right, this would be all that mattered in their satisfying the predicate "is in pain."

22. Let us look more closely at this example (for which we thank Kevin Sauvé). What happens when water is thrown on flaming wood? Water extinguishes the flame, first, by absorbing thermal energy (some of the water turning into steam) thereby decreasing the temperature of both flame and wood and decreasing the chances that the fire will spread to portions of wood not already burning; and second, because it penetrates wood slowly, water that does not turn to steam coats the surface of the wood separating the wood from ambient oxygen required for combustion.

Matters are quite different when water is sprayed on a pool of burning oil. Although water can reduce the temperature of the oil by absorbing thermal energy from the flames, water molecules not converted to steam as they pass through the flames work their way beneath the oil. This water, when heated to its boiling point, produces bubbles of steam that rise upward through the burning oil, increasing the fuel-to-air surface area, thereby intensifying the fire.

Water can quickly penetrate burning oil, but water penetrates wood much more slowly. In virtue of the very same intrinsic properties, water yields utterly different manifestations when its disposition partners are as different as flaming oil and flaming wood. For more details, see Hawthorne 1987, 27–30.

23. The problem of mental causation being perhaps chief among these; see Heil and Mele 1993. For an account of mental causation that falls within the spirit of our discussion, see Robb 1997.

24. The connection between dispositionality and intentionality is discussed in Martin and Pfeifer 1986 and, in more detail, in Martin and Heil 1998.

REFERENCES

Armstrong, D. M. 1968. *A Materialist Theory of the Mind*. London: Routledge and Kegan Paul.

Armstrong, D. M. 1978. *A Theory of Universals*. Vol. 2 of *Universals and Scientific Realism*. Cambridge: Cambridge University Press.

Armstrong, D. M. 1989. *Universals: An Opinionated Introduction*. Boulder, CO: Westview Press.

Armstrong, D. M. 1997. *A World of States of Affairs*. Cambridge: Cambridge University Press.

Armstrong, D. M., Martin, C. B., and Place, U. T. 1996. *Dispositions: A Debate*, ed. Tim Crane. London: Routledge.

Ayer, A. J. 1956. *The Problem of Knowledge*. Harmondsworth, UK: Penguin Books.

Bacon, J. 1995. *Universals and Property Instances: The Alphabet of Being*. Oxford: Basil Blackwell.

Bacon, J., Campbell, K., and Reinhardt, L., eds. 1992. *Ontology, Causality, and Mind*. Cambridge: Cambridge University Press.

Blackburn, S. 1990. "Filling in Space," *Analysis* 50: 62–65.

Campbell, K. 1990. *Abstract Particulars*. Oxford: Basil Blackwell.

Foster, J. 1982. *The Case for Idealism*. London: Routledge and Kegan Paul.

Hawthorne, E. 1987. *Petroleum Liquids: Fire and Emergency Control*. Englewood Cliffs, NJ: Prentice-Hall.

Heil, J. 1998a. *Philosophy of Mind: A Contemporary Introduction*. London: Routledge.

Heil, J. 1998b. "Supervenience Deconstructed." *European Journal of Philosophy* 6: 146–55.

Heil, J., and Mele, A., eds. 1993. *Mental Causation*. Oxford: Clarendon Press.

Jackson, F. 1996. "Mental Causation." *Mind* 105: 377–413.

Kosslyn, S. M., Alpert, N. M., Thompson, W. L., Maljkovic, V., Weise, S. B., Chabris, C. F., Hamilton, S. E., Rauch, S. L., and Buonanno, F. S. 1993. "Visual Mental Imagery Activates Topographically Organized Visual Cortex: PET Investigations." *Journal of Cognitive Neuroscience* 5: 263–87.

Lewis, D. 1986. *On the Plurality of Worlds*. Oxford: Basil Blackwell.

Locke, J. 1978. *An Essay Concerning Human Understanding*, ed. P. H. Nidditch. Oxford: Clarendon Press. Original work published in 1690.

Mackie, J. L. 1980. *The Cement of the Universe: A Study of Causation*. Oxford: Clarendon Press.

Martin, C. B. 1980. "Substance Substantiated," *Australasian Journal of Philosophy* 58: 3–10.

Martin, C. B. 1987. "Proto-Language." *Australasian Journal of Philosophy* 65: 277–289.

Martin, C. B. 1992. "Power for Realists," in Bacon et al., 1992, 175–86.

Martin, C. B. 1993. "The Need for Ontology: Some Choices," *Philosophy* 68: 505–522.

Martin, C. B. 1994. "Dispositions and Conditionals." *Philosophical Quarterly* 44: 1–8.

Martin, C. B. 1997. "On the Need for Properties: The Road to Pythagoreanism and Back." *Synthese* 112: 193–231.

Martin, C. B., and Heil, J. 1998. "Rules and Powers." *Philosophical Perspectives* 12: 283–312.

Martin, C. B., and Pfeifer, K. 1986. "Intentionality and the Non-Psychological." *Philosophy and Phenomenological Research* 46: 531–554.

Mellor, Hugh. 1974. "In Defense of Dispositions." *Philosophical Review* 83: 157–81.

Morrison, J. H., and Hof, P. R. 1992. "The Organization of the Cerebral Cortex: From Molecules to Circuits." *Discussion in Neuroscience* 9: 10–80.

Poland, J. 1994. *Physicalism: The Philosophical Foundations*. Oxford: Clarendon Press.

Prior, E. W., Pargetter, R., and Jackson, F. 1982. "Three Theses about Dispositions." *American Philosophical Quarterly* 19: 251–57.
Robb, D. 1997. "The Properties of Mental Causation." *Philosophical Quarterly* 47: 178–94.
Ryle, G. 1949. *The Concept of Mind*. London: Hutchinson.
Searle, J. 1983. *Intentionality: An Essay in the Philosophy of Mind*. Cambridge: Cambridge University Press.
Searle, J. 1992. *The Rediscovery of the Mind*. Cambridge: MIT Press.
Shepard, R., and C. Feng. 1972. "A Chronometric Study of Mental Paper Folding." *Cognitive Psychology* 3: 228–43.
Shoemaker, Sydney. 1980. "Causality and Properties," in van Inwagen, 1980, 109–35.
Simons, P. 1994. "Particulars in Particular Clothing: Three Trope Theories of Substance." *Philosophy and Phenomenological Research* 54: 553–75.
Spelke, E. S., Breinlinger, K., Macomber, J., and Jacobson, K. 1992. "Origins of Knowledge." *Psychological Review* 99: 605–32.
Sperry, R. W. 1991. "In Defense of Mentalism and Emergent Interaction." *Journal of Mind and Behavior* 12: 221–46.
Stalnaker, R. 1976. "Possible Worlds." *Noûs* 10: 65–75.
Tooley, M. 1987. *Causality: A Realist Approach*. Oxford: Clarendon Press.
van Inwagen, P., ed. 1980. *Time and Cause*. Dordrecht, the Netherlands: Reidel Publishing Co.
Weiskrantz, L., ed. 1988. *Thought without Language*. Oxford: Clarendon Press.
Williams, D. C. 1966. *Principles of Empirical Realism*. Springfield, IL: Charles Thomas.
Wisdom, J. 1938. "Metaphysics and Verification (I)." *Mind* 47: 452–98.

Midwest Studies in Philosophy, XXIII (1999)

Things and Their Parts

KIT FINE

I wish to sketch a theory of the general nature of material things. It is a theory on which I have been working for some time; and what I present here is the merest sketch. Details are slid over, significant questions not raised, and controversial assumptions left undefended. But I hope, all the same, that enough is said to indicate the relevance of the theory to questions concerning the nature of material things and the plausibility of its answers.

One way into the theory is through consideration of part-whole. Things have parts; and so we are led to consider how they are capable of having the parts that they do. What in their nature accounts for their division into parts? It has often been supposed that we may give an adequate answer to this question by conceiving of a material thing as the material content of a space-time region or as a successive stream of matter. But I believe that there are enormous difficulties with these positions and that, once they are taken into account, we are led to adopt a very different conception of a material thing and of its relationship to its parts.

Central to the paper is a distinction between two different ways in which one thing can be part of another. It can, in the first place, be a part in a way that is relative to a time. It is in this way, for example, that a newly installed carburetor is now a part of my car, whereas earlier it was not, or that certain molecules are now parts of my body though later, through the exercise of natural bodily functions, they no longer will be.

In the second place, one object can be a part of another in a way that is not relative to a time. For something that is a part in this way, it is not appropriate to ask *when*, or *for how long*, it is a part; it just is a part. It is in such a way that the pants and the jacket, for example, are parts of a suit or various atoms are parts of a water molecule, or two particular pints of milk are parts of a quart of milk, or various time-slices, if there are such things, are parts of a persisting individual.

It is by attempting to understand the relations of temporary and timeless part that we hope to come to a better understanding of material things. I begin by criticizing the standard mereological conceptions and argue that they are incapable of providing an adequate account either of timeless part (section 1) or of temporary part (section 2). I then propose an alternative account that I believe is immune from the difficulties in the standard conceptions. This account takes seriously the idea that there is both a formal and material aspect to most material things. Thus it falls squarely within the hylomorphic tradition of Aristotle.

The particular version of hylomorphism developed here I call the *theory of embodiment*. It is in two main parts: the first, the theory of *rigid* embodiment, provides an account of the timeless relation of part (section 3); and the second, the theory of *variable* embodiment, provides an account of the temporary relation (section 4). This theory requires us to accept two new kinds of whole and, in addition to its mereological consequences, has significant consequences for the nature of material things, their existence, their classification into sorts, and their interconnection with abstract objects (section 5).[1]

1. TIMELESS PART

I have a ham sandwich before me. It is (timelessly) composed of two slices of bread and a piece of ham.[2] Clearly, these ingredients are parts of the sandwich. But what is it for them to be parts?

It might be thought that standard mereology provides us with an answer to this question. For given certain material things $a, b, c, \ldots$, it posits an object $a + b + c + \ldots$ that is the *sum* or *fusion* of those parts. Now let us denote the two slices of bread by s_1 and s_2 and the ham by h. Then can we not take the ham sandwich to be the sum $s_1 + s_2 + h$ and can we not suppose that the ham sandwich contains the ingredients s_1, s_2, and h as parts in exactly the same way that any sum contains its components as parts?

Not, it must be said, on the standard "aggregative" understanding of what the sum is. For on this understanding, a sum of material things is regarded as being spread out through time in much the same way as a material thing is ordinarily regarded as being spread out in space. Thus the sum $a + b + c + \ldots$ will exist *whenever* any of its components $a, b, c, \ldots$ exists (just as it is located, at any time, *wherever* any of its components are located). It follows that, under the proposed analysis of the ham sandwich, it will exist as soon as the piece of ham or either slice of bread exists. Yet surely this is not so. Surely the ham sandwich will not exist until the ham is actually placed between the two slices of bread. After all, one *makes* a ham sandwich; and to make something is to bring into existence something that formerly did not exist.

Nor does it help to add further components to the sum. For they can only serve to augment, not diminish, the time during which the sum exists.

A somewhat different stategy for dealing with the difficulty is to suppose that the sandwich is not the sum $s_1 + s_2 + h$ itself but the temporal restriction of the sum $s_1 + s_2 + h$ to those times at which the sandwich exists. This immediately delivers the correct existence conditions, but it is not clear that it delivers the correct judgments of part. For why should we now say that the slices of bread or the ham are *parts* of the sandwich?

It might be suggested that it is in an extended sense of *part* that the ingredients are to be regarded as parts. Given any two objects, we may say that the first is, in this extended sense, a part of the second if the restriction of the first to the times at which the second exists is (in the unextended sense) a part of the second. Thus for the purpose of making such judgments of part, we ignore what there is to the first object outside of the time at which the second exists. Since the restriction of each ingredient to the time at which the restricted sum exists is, in the unextended sense, a part of the restricted sum, we may conclude that each ingredient is, in the extended sense, a part of the restricted sum.

In response to this proposal, it should be noted that it is not at all clear why the proposed sense of part should even be taken to *be* a sense of part. After all, the sandwich is not an aggregative sum of its ingredients. Nor does there appear any other reasonable operation of summation by which the sandwich can be taken to be formed from its parts. But if the sandwich is not the *sum* of its ingredients, then how can they be regarded as its *parts*?

In any case, the proposed sense of part will not deliver the correct results. Consider the sum of the ham and Cleopatra or, more dramatically, the sum of the ham and all objects that existed only before or after the sandwich existed. Then the restriction of this sum to the time the sandwich exists is the same as the restriction of just the ham and hence must also be a part of the sandwich. But it is ludicrous to suppose that this monstrous object—of which Cleopatra and all merely past and future galaxies are parts—is itself a part of the ham sandwich.

Thus there seems to be no reasonable way, under the present conception of mereological sum, in which one might regard the slices of bread and the ham as parts of the ham sandwich.

But there is a another, somewhat different way of understanding the notion of mereological sum. We may suppose that a mereological sum is spread out only in space, not also in time. Thus for a "compound" sum $a + b + c + \ldots$ to exist at a time, its identity as a sum must be preserved and hence *all* of its components $a, b, c, \ldots$ must exist at the time.[3]

If we now take the sandwich to be the compound sum $s_1 + s_2 + h$, we do not have the difficulty that the sandwich begins to exist as soon as any of the ingredients exist. But we do have a related difficulty. For the sandwich will exist as long as all of the ingredients exist. And again, surely this need not be so. If the sandwich is to exist, it is not sufficient for the ingredients merely to be around. They must be appropriately assembled.

In this case, however, we may attempt to remedy the difficulty by adding further components; for these *may* serve to diminish the time during which the sum exists. And there is an obvious choice of component to add. For we may suppose that, in addition to the slices of bread and piece of ham, the sandwich should contain a trope or particularized relation of betweenness (or assembly). Thus it will be supposed that there is a relation r of betweenness holding between the ham and the slices of bread that is peculiar to the sandwich in question and that must also be taken to be one of the components of the sandwich. The sandwich will therefore be of the form

$s_1 + s_2 + h + r$ and, as long as the trope r is taken to exist only when the ham is between the slices of bread, we will obtain the required existence conditions for the sandwich.

However, even if we grant that the trope is a part of the sandwich, it is hard to believe that it is a part in the same way as the standard ingredients. Thus we should not regard the sandwich as a straightforward mereological sum of s_1, s_2, h, and r, but in some other way that has yet to be made clear. Indeed, one of the differences between the standard ingredients and the trope is that it is only the former that are properly determinative of when the object exists or where it is located. Suppose one held the extraordinary view that the trope did not exist in time or that it did but filled the whole of space at any time at which it existed. Then that should not lead one to change one's view of when the sandwich existed or where it was located. One would not want to say that the sandwich always failed to exist or that it filled the whole of space whenever it did exist.

We conclude that neither conception of mereological sum, as aggregate or compound, yields a satisfactory account of the ham sandwich or its parts and that, in the absence of any alternatives, it is unclear how standard mereology can shed any light on the nature of the part-whole relationship in these cases.

2. TEMPORARY PART

We turn now to the parallel questions concerning temporary part. How is one to provide a satisfactory account of what it is for one object to be a temporary part of another—of what it is, for example, for this carburetor to be currently a part of my car?

It has commonly been supposed that standard mereology can provide such an account. Given that my car and its carburetor currently exist, there will be a time-slice, or temporal restriction, of each of them to the current time. Armed with this notion of time-slice, we may say that the carburetor is currently a part of my car if the current time-slice of the carburetor is a timeless part of the current time-slice of the car. More generally, given any two objects x and y that exist at a given time t, we may say that x is a part of y at t if the time-slice of x at t is a timeless part of the time-slice of y at t (or, in symbols, $x \leq_t y =_{df} x_t \leq y_t$).

Part of what makes this account so natural is the thought that a judgment of temporary part simply depends upon the identities of the part and whole at the time in question—upon what, in some vague and intuitive sense, they then are. Combine this thought with the view that the identity of an object at a given time is its time-slice at that time, and the present account appears irresistible.

But natural as the account may be, it is subject to grave difficulties. Perhaps the most significant of these is the analogue of the "monster objection." Consider the aggregate of the current time-slice of the carburetor with Cleopatra or, if you like, with all things whatever that do not currently exist. The current time-slice of this monster aggregate is the same as the current time-slice of the carburetor. Given that the carburetor is currently part of the car, it follows, on the present account, then the monster is as well. But surely this is absurd. How can an object that contains

Cleopatra as a part—not to mention all past and future galaxies—currently be a part of my car?

It might be thought that it is the strangeness of the monster object that is somehow responsible for leading our intuitions astray in these cases. But consider the analogous case in which the *car* is replaced by the aggregate of the car with Cleopatra. This is an object that begins its life as a queen and, after a considerable lapse of time, is "reincarnated" as a means of transport. In this case, we seem to be in no doubt that the carburetor is currently a part of the monster whole. For surely the ancestry of the whole, how it once was, is irrelevant to its current constitution. But then why should our intuitions be led astray in the one case and yet not in the other?

We detect here a fundamental asymmetry between temporary part and whole. A temporary part belongs, as a whole, to a given whole. Its whole identity is relevant to whether it is a part. On the other hand, a given temporary part belongs to a whole in its capacity as a part. It is only the identity of the whole at the given time that is relevant to whether the temporary part is a part. To put it in Heideggerese, "the part, as a whole, belongs to the whole, as a part." What the examples concerning monsters reveal is the failure of the standard account in terms of time-slices to respect this fundamental asymmetry in the status of part and whole.

3. RIGID EMBODIMENT

I should like to provide a positive account of how the problem cases of part-whole are to be resolved. We begin with the theory of rigid embodiment, which is intended to deal with the cases of timeless part, and then turn our attention to the theory of variable embodiment.

We wish to give an account of the ham sandwich that makes it clear how it has the (timeless) parts that it does. As we have seen, we cannot take it to be a *mere* mereological sum, whether the sum be conceived as a compound or an aggregate. Nor can we take it to be the temporal restriction of a mereological sum. What then can we take it to be?

I should like to suggest that we take the bold step of recognizing a new kind of whole. Given objects *a*, *b*, *c*, . . . and given a relation *R* that may hold or fail to hold of those objects at any given time, we suppose that there is a new object—what one may call "the objects *a*, *b*, *c*, . . . in the relation *R*." So, for example, given some flowers and given the relation of *being bunched*, there will be a new object—the flowers in the relation of being bunched (what might ordinarily be called a "bunch of flowers").

Intuitively, this new object is an amalgam or composite of the component objects *a*, *b*, *c*, . . . and the relation *R*. But it is a composite of a very special sort. For the components and the relation do not come together as coequals, as in a regular mereological sum. Rather, the relation *R* preserves its predicative role and somehow serves to modify or qualify the components. However, the result of the modification is not a fact or state. It is a whole, whose components are linked by the relation, rather than the fact or state of the components being so linked.

An object of this special sort will be called a *rigid embodiment*, since the "form" *R* is embodied in the fixed "matter" *a*, *b*, *c*, ... Let us agree to designate such an object by the term "*a*, *b*, *c*, . . . /*R*." The relation *R* will then be called the *principle of rigid embodiment*, and the operation by which a rigid embodiment is formed from the objects *a*, *b*, *c*, . . . and a relation *R*, the *operation of rigid embodiment*.

Our view is that the operation of rigid embodiment is sui generis; it is not to be understood in terms of any other way of forming wholes from parts, whether from standard mereology or elsewhere. But still, we may obtain an implicit understanding of the operation in terms of the postulates by which it is governed. There are five main types of postulates in all, of which I merely give a sketch.

The *existence postulate* states when a rigid embodiment exists. It takes the form:

(R1) The rigid embodiment *a*, *b*, *c*, . . . /*R* exists at a time *t* iff *R* holds of *a*, *b*, *c*, . . . at *t*.

The *location postulate* states where a rigid object is. It assumes the form:

(R2) If the rigid embodiment *e* = *a*, *b*, *c*, . . . /*R* exists at time *t*, then *e* is located at the point *p* at *t* iff at least one of *a*, *b*, *c*, . . . is located at *p*.

The *identity postulate* states when rigid embodiments are the same. The simplest criterion of this sort is as follows:

(R3) The rigid embodiments *e* = *a*, *b*, *c*, . . . /*R* and *a*′, *b*′, *c*′, . . . /*R*′ are the same iff *a* = *a*′, *b* = *b*′, *c* = *c*′, . . . and *R* = *R*′.

However, such a postulate results in an embarrassing diversity of rigid embodiments. If, for example, *a* and *b* were two blocks, *R* the relation of *being on top of*, and *R*′ the relation of *being beneath*, then we would have to distinguish between the tower *a*, *b*/*R* and the tower *b*, *a*/*R*.

A somewhat more satisfactory criterion is as follows:

(R3′) The rigid embodiments *a*, *b*, *c*, . . . /*R* and *a*′, *b*′, *c*′, . . . /*R*′ are the same iff the state of *a*, *b*, *c*, . . . standing in the relation *R* is the same as the state of *a*′, *b*′, *c*′, . . . standing in the relation *R*′.

Since the state of *a*’s being on top of *b* is plausibly taken to be the same as the state of *b*’s being beneath *a*, we can now maintain that the two previous towers are the same. However, under this criterion, the same rigid embodiment may involve two distinct principles of forms. A criterion without an embarrassing diversity of either forms or embodiments may be obtained by reworking the underlying theory of relations.[4]

The *postulates of part-whole* state what parts a rigid embodiment has. We certainly want:

(R4) The objects *a*, *b*, *c*, . . . are (timeless) parts of *a*, *b*, c, . . . /*R*.

If we adopt a criterion of identity in terms of states, then we might also want to adopt a corresponding criterion of parthood:

(R4′) The rigid embodiment *e* = *a*, *b*, *c*, . . . /*R* is a part of the rigid embodiment *a*′, *b*′, *c*′, . . . /*R*′ if the state of *a*, *b*, *c*, . . . standing in the relation *R* is a part of the state of *a*′, *b*′, *c*′, . . . standing in the relation *R*′.

Regardless of whether we adopt (R4) or (R4′), we may also wish to adopt:

(R5) The relation R is a (timeless) part of $a, b, c, \ldots /R$. In this case, the relation R itself is taken to be a (constitutive) aspect of the corresponding rigid embodiment.

There are also postulates that set limits on what timeless parts there are. If one does not believe in temporal restrictions, then one will want to claim that the parts under (R4) (or under both [R4] and [R5]) are essentially the only parts of a rigid embodiment that there are:

(R6) Any timeless part of $a, b, c, \ldots /R$ is a (timeless) part of one of $a, b, c, \ldots$ (or of R).

(And similarly if one adopts [R4′] in place of [R4].) If one allows temporal restrictions, then they must also be included among the parts that may serve as intermediaries.

The *character postulates* state what descriptive properties a rigid embodiment will have—whether, for example, it is red or heavy or much admired. What these postulates are will depend upon the properties and the sort of rigid embodiment in question. So, for example, whether a rigid embodiment $a, b, c, \ldots /R$ is *scattered* will depend upon whether its location (as given by principle [R2]) is scattered. On the other hand, whether a *bunch* $a, b, c, \ldots /R$ is tight will depend upon whether the component objects $a, b, c, \ldots$ are tightly bunched.

Once a theory of this sort is in place, we can give a satisfactory account of the ham sandwich, one that accounts for its parts and yet is compatible with, and even predicts, all the other things we wish to say about it. For we may take the ham sandwich (under certain simplifying assumptions) to be the rigid embodiment $s_1, h, s_2/B$, where s_1 and s_2 are the two slices of bread, h is the piece of ham, and B is the relation of betweenness, that is, the relation that holds between three objects x, y, and z just in case y is between x and z.

It then follows from postulate (R4) that the two slices of bread and the piece of ham are (timeless) parts of the sandwich, just as we want. By postulate (R1), the sandwich will exist *when* it should, namely, when the ham is between the slices of bread; and by postulate (R2), it will exist *where* it should, namely, where the slices of bread and the ham exist. Thus we secure the desired result, in a straightforward manner, without doing violence either to the notion of part or to when or where the sandwich should be.

I believe that there are many other cases of objects that may plausibly be treated in this way (and without the aid of any simplifying assumptions). We have already mentioned the cases of molecules and suits. Any molecule—or, at least, any suitably small molecule—may be taken to be the rigid embodiment that is the various atoms in the relation of being suitably bonded; and any suit may be taken to be the rigid embodiment that is the pants and jacket under the relation of being made for one another. Similarly, to give an organic example, a nut may be regarded as a kernel and shell under the relation of being suitably connected.

An especially important class of cases are those in which the principle of embodiment is a property P rather than a polyadic relation R. The rigid embodiment is then of the form "a/P" and may be read as "a qua P" or as "a under the description P." An airline passenger, for example, is not the same as the person who is the passenger since, in counting the passengers who pass through an airport on a given weekend, we may legitimately count the same person several times. This therefore suggests that we should take an airline passenger to be someone under the description of being flown on such and such a flight. And similarly for mayors and judges and other "personages" of this sort.

Here are some other examples. Most, if not all, actions are also cases of qua objects. Oswald's act of killing Kennedy, for example, is his act of shooting the gun under the description of causing Kennedy's death. A musical work will be a certain characteristic pattern of sounds under the description of being rendered realizable in a suitable way and in such and such circumstances. A token of a given word will be the corresponding expression token under the description of being an instance of that word (thus the token must be understood in terms of the type, not the type in terms of the token). A trope will be a universal under the description of being possessed by such and such an object. If this latter suggestion is correct, we see that our earlier attempt to explain rigid embodiments as a sum of the components with a trope was flatly circular, since the trope itself must be understood as a special case of rigid embodiment.

4. VARIABLE EMBODIMENT

I wish now to provide a more satisfactory account of the car, one that will accommodate what we take to be its temporary parts and yet will avoid monsters and other such counterintuitive results.

Let us begin with a somewhat simple example. We may talk of "the water in a river." But this phrase may be understood in two rather different ways. On the one hand, it may be taken to signify that given quantity of water that is, at a given time, the water in the river. In this sense of the phrase, the water in the river at one time is rarely, if ever, the same as the water at another time. On the other hand, the phrase may signify a variable quantity of water—that water, whatever it is, that is in the river. It is in this sense of the phrase that we may say that the water in the river is rising, since it is the very same thing that was once relatively low and now is relatively high.

I take it that the water in the river in the second sense—what we may call the *variable* water—is now constituted by one quantity of water and now by another. But what is the variable water? Clearly, it is not any one of the quantities of water that is in the river at any one time. Nor is it the aggregate of all such quantities, since the water would then overflow its natural spatiotemporal boundaries. Nor is it the restriction of the aggregate to those boundaries, since then there would be no clear sense in which the variable water was constituted by water rather than by aggregative monsters. What then can we take the variable water to be?

Again, I would like to take the bold step of supposing that there is here a hitherto unrecognized method by which wholes may be formed from parts. In the case of the variable water, there is a function, or "principle," that determines which quantity of water constitutes the variable water at any given time. This is the principle that we might express by the phrase "the quantity of water in the river"; it picks out, at any time t at which the river exists, the quantity of water in the river at that time (and fails to pick out anything at any other time). What I would like to suggest is that there is a new kind of whole corresponding to this principle, a whole that exists when and only when the principle picks out some water and that is constituted at any such time *t* by the quantity of water picked out by the principle at *t*. And it is this object that I take to be the variable water of the river.

In general, we will suppose, given any suitable function or principle *F* (taking times to things), that there is a corresponding object standing in the same relationship to *F* as the variable water of the river stands to *its* principle. We call this object the *variable embodiment of F* and designate it by /*F*/. The principle *F* in /*F*/ will be called a *principle of variable embodiment*, the various objects picked out by the principle *F* the *manifestations* of the variable embodiment /*F*/, and the operation "/ /" by which /*F*/ is formed from the principle *F* the *operation* of variable embodiment. In contrast to the case of a rigid embodiment *a*, *b*, *c*, . . . /*R*, the matter of a variable embodiment is not given independently of the form or principle, but is itself specified by means of that principle.

Here is one way of getting an intuitive grip on the notion of a variable embodiment. Imagine a container into and out of which water flows. We may then distinguish between three things: (a) the container itself, (b) the water that is in it at any given time, and (c) the container with the water in it. We may think of (c) as a single object that has different water as a part at different times. Let us now make two modifications to our conception of the container. First, we suppose that it not merely a passive recipient of the water but somehow determines which water is to be in it at any one time. It plays an active role, as it were, in determining what its content is to be over time. Second, we suppose that the container is not another physical object but something of a more abstract or conceptual nature. Thus the varying contents of the container will be determined by conceptual rather than by physical means. With these two modifications in place, we may then obtain a pretty good model for our notion of variable embodiment, with the container being the principle of embodiment *F* and the container-cum-content being the variable embodiment /*F*/.

I suggest that we take the variable water of the river to be the variable embodiment /*F*/, where *F* is the principle that picks out the water in the river at each time at which the river exists. But what of the car? Since it has a varying constitution, we also wish to take it to be a variable embodiment /*F*/. But what objects, in this case, does the principle *F* pick out? What are the manifestations of the car? They cannot just be the matter of the car at different times. For the engine or the chassis are not parts of this matter and so it is not clear, on this view, how we are to secure the result that they are parts of the car.

It will be helpful, at this point, to combine the two theories of embodiment. I would like to suggest that at each time at which a particular car exists, it is constituted by a certain rigid embodiment. This embodiment will be the various major parts of the car (the engine, the chassis, etc.) arranged in the general manner characteristic of a car. As these parts change or as the general arrangement changes then so will the rigid embodiment. Thus the car will be a variable embodiment /*F*/ whose principle *F* picks out various rigid embodiments. And since these rigid embodiments will include the engine and the like as timeless parts, there will be no difficulty in supposing that they are temporary parts of the car.

Thus we see that two different kinds of embodiment are involved in saying what the car is—a variable embodiment, which accounts for its variation over time, and a rigid embodiment, which accounts for its mereological structure at a time. I believe that it was the failure of Aristotle to distinguish between these two different roles for form that principally accounts for the inadequacy of his hylomorphic conception of material things, which, in other broad respects, is so close to our own.[5]

Let us now sketch the theory on the basis of which these and various other considerations can be made precise. Where $f = /F/$ is a variable embodiment, we shall use f_t for the object selected by F at t, that is, for the manifestation of f at t. The postulates of existence, location and identity are then as follows:

(V1) The variable embodiment $f = /F/$ exists at time t iff it has a manifestation at t.

(V2) If the variable embodiment $f = /F/$ exists at t, then its location is that of its manifestation f_t (assuming that f_t has a location).

(V3) The variable embodiments $/F/$ and $/G/$ are the same iff their principles F and G are the same.

The postulates for temporary part and for character are less straightforward. The fundamental postulate governing temporary part is:

(V4) Any manifestation of a variable embodiment at a given time is a temporary part of the variable embodiment at that time (in symbols: $f_t \leq_t f$).

This postulate helps distinguish the variable embodiment $f = /F/$ from its underlying principle F. For the principle F stands in a purely external relationship to the manifestation f_t, whereas the manifestation is actually part of the embodiment. (Analogously, the container merely encloses its content, whereas the contain-cum-content has the content as a part.)

Two further postulates extend the range of the relationships of temporary part:

(V5a) If a is a timeless part of b that exists at t and if b is a part of c at t, then a is a part of c at t.

(V5b) If a is a part of b at t and if b is a timeless part of an object c that exists at t, then a is a part of c at t.

In other words, the result of chaining a temporary part with a timeless part is itself a temporary part.

We see from the last three postulates how we may get temporary parts at successively deeper levels. Consider, for example, the car $f = /F/$. By (V4), the current manifestation f_t of the car is a temporary part of the car (at t). But the manifestation f_t is itself a rigid embodiment $a, b, c, \ldots /R$, namely, the engine, chassis, and body in a certain automative relation. By (R4), the engine, chassis, and body are timeless parts of the rigid embodiment f_t and hence, by (V5a), are temporary parts of the car f. But the engine itself is a variable embodiment and so, in a similar manner, it will have temporary parts, which will then be temporary parts of the car.

A final postulate states that if one object is a temporary part of another it must be possible to show that it is a temporary part by means of the previous postulates. Let us be more exact. Say that a link between two objects is a *fundamental link* at t if it holds between the manifestation f_t of a variable embodiment and the variable embodiment f itself; and say that a link is an *auxiliary link* at t if it holds between two objects a and b, where a and b both exist at t and a is a timeless part of b. Call a sequence $(a_1, a_2), (a_2, a_3), \ldots, (a_{n-1}, a_n)$ of connected links a *mereological chain* at t if (1) each link in the sequence is either a fundamental or auxiliary link at t and (2) at least one link in the sequence is fundamental. We then have the following restriction on relationships of temporary part:

> (V6) If a is a temporary part of b at t, then there is a mereological chain at t connecting a to b.

Thus, according to this postulate, all relationships of temporary part must be mediated through the fundamental link of a manifestation to its variable embodiment, all other relationships of temporary part being the result of chaining these fundamental links with the auxiliary links of timeless part. Thus variable embodiments, on this view, become the ultimate source of temporary parthood. It is only because there are variable embodiments, manifesting themselves differently at different times, that there are any relationships of temporary part at all.

When we compare the present account of temporary part with the previous account in terms of time-slices, we see two main differences. First, our account is asymmetric in its treatment of temporary part and whole. For whether the object e is a part of f at t depends upon what f is at the time (i.e., upon f_t) but depends upon e in its entirety (i.e., upon e itself rather than e_t or some other part of e). Second, the present account is informed by a very different conception of the "temporary identity" of an object, of what it is at a time. On the earlier account, the temporary identity of an object was its time-slice at the time in question. But for us, it is characteristically a rigid embodiment, something with a "life" and structure of its own.

The final principle of our theory concerns character. In contrast to the case for rigid embodiments, it is possible to state a general principle of character for variable embodiments. Call a property of objects *pro tem* if its holding at a given time depends only upon how the object is at that time. We then have the following transfer principle:

> (V7) The pro tem properties of a variable embodiment f at a given time t are the same as those of its manifestation f_t.

For example, whether something is red at a given time depends only upon how it is at that time. So by this principle, a variable embodiment will be red at a given time just in case its manifestation is red at that time.

Given these postulates, we are able to secure the desired results concerning the properties and parts of the car. We take the car to be a variable embodiment /*F*/, where *F* picks out, at each time at which the car exists, a suitable rigid embodiment of its principal parts. By (V1) and (V2), the car will then exist when and where it should. From (V4) and (V5), as we have seen, the car will have the engine and *its* various parts as temporary parts. On the other hand, it follows from (V6) that the "monsters" will not be temporary parts, since there is no mereological chain connecting them to the car. Finally, by (V7), the car will share in the pro tem properties of the rigid embodiment; it will be red, for example, shiny, and largely metallic.

In a similar way, we may give an account of any other object that is capable of having a variable constitution. This includes most of the material things that we ordinarily talk about. However, there is no need for a variable embodiment or its manifestations to be material things. A process—such as the erosion of a cliff, for example—may be taken to be a variable embodiment whose manifestations are the different states of erosion of the cliff. There is not even any need for the manifestations to be something in time. The "law of the land," for example, is constituted at different times by different bodies of law. But a body of law is something abstract, existing in neither space nor time. The theory is therefore capable of accounting for the identity of a wide range of different entities.

5. CONSEQUENCES

Apart from its particular applications, the present account has consequences of more general relevance to the nature of material things. Let me here merely say what they are without attempting a detailed defense. But it should be noted that these consequences, if accepted, will call for a radical revision in the way we conceive the material world.

The first is that the majority of material objects, on our account, will submit to a hierarchical division into parts. Just as a car will have an engine, a chassis, and a body as immediate parts (these being the components of the rigid embodiment that is the current manifestation of the car), these immediate parts will themselves have further immediate parts, and so on all the way down until we reach the most basic forms of matter. Thus a material object will be like a set, with its hierarchical division into members, members of members, and so on.

Moreover, this division into parts will be largely unique; very few of the spatial divisions of the object will actually correspond to a mereological division via the operations of variable and rigid embodiment. Of course, everyone can grant that some spatial divisions of an object are more natural than others. The division of a car down the middle, for example, is far less natural than the division into an engine, a chassis, and a body. But on the present view, the natural division is intrinsic to the identity of the object in a way that the other divisions are not.

Consider, by analogy, the set {Plato, Aristotle, Mozart, Beethoven}. There is a natural division of this set into the subsets {Plato and Aristotle} and {Mozart and Beethoven}. But this division is not intrinsic to the identity of the set; it is *we* who privilege the subsets, not the set itself. On the other hand, the set {{Plato, Aristotle}, {Mozart, Beethoven}} has what is both a natural and an intrinsic division into the member sets {Plato, Aristotle}, {Mozart, Beethoven}; in this case, it is the set itself that sanctions this division, rather than us.

The division of a material object into its natural parts is, I suggest, more analogous to the latter case, division by member, than to the former, division by subset. Traditional mereology would have us believe otherwise. Indeed, its very notion of part was conceived by analogy with the notion of subset. But, if I am right, it is the hierarchical conception of sets and their members, rather than the linear conception of set and subset or of aggregate and component, that provides us with the better model for the structure of part-whole in its application to material things.

A second consequence of our account is that there will be an intensional or conceptual element to the identity of many material objects. For a rigid embodiment *a*, *b*, *c*, . . . /*R* is to be understood partly in terms of its material components, but also partly in terms of its relational principle *R*; and a variable embodiment /*F*/ is to be understood wholly in terms of its functional principle *F*. Thus these principles, which are intensional or conceptual in nature, are directly implicated in the identity of the embodiments and hence also in the identity of the material things that are explained by their means. Indeed, I believe that it may plausibly be argued that these principles are *parts* of their embodiments and hence parts of the corresponding material things.

The material world is standardly conceived in extensional terms. It is allowed, under this conception, that material things may have properties or enter into relations, but these properties or relations are not themselves taken to be constitutive of material things in the same kind of way that they are constitutive of the propositions concerning those things. But on the view I wish to advocate, properties and relations will be as much involved in the identity of the one as of the other. Thus, if I am right, we see yet another respect in which the divide between the concrete and abstract realms is not as great as it is commonly taken to be.

A third consequence of our theory—at least under its most plausible development—is that there will be many more material objects than is commonly supposed. We are familiar with the prodigious ontology of the mereologists, according to which any occupied region of space-time, no matter how scattered or gerrymandered, will determine a material object. But this is nothing compared to the ontology of the present view. For to each such object of the mereologist, there will correspond a multitude of rigid embodiments, differing in their choice of components or relational principle, and a multitude of variable embodiments, differing in their actual or possible manifestations. Also bear in mind that the components and manifestations may themselves be rigid or variable embodiments, and we see that the flat unstructured objects of the mereologist represent a mere fraction of what there is.

Of course, this is not to say that there need be any *ultimate* commitment to these objects. But I would wish to maintain that the objects we ordinarily recognize —chairs and tables and the like—are not ontologically privileged. Whatever kind of ontological commitment we have to them we should also have to the more bizarre forms of rigid and variable embodiment.

Given this superabundance of objects, the possibilies for coincidence on the present view will be much greater than on the standard mereological view. Consider a tree, for example. Then just as we may distinguish the variable water of the river, so we may distinguish the wood (and protoplasm) of the tree. But the wood of the tree, in this sense, will necessarily coincide with the tree; they will necessarily coexist and they will be necessarily colocated whenever they do exist. But although they necessarily coincide, there is a clear explanation of their difference; for the tree will have a trunk, the branches, and the leaves, etc., as temporary parts, whereas the wood will not. The wood is, as it were, a relatively unstructured version of the tree just as the set {a, b, c, d} is an unstructured counterpart of the set {{a, b}, {c, d}}; and it should be considered no more surprising, on the present view, that so many material objects should coincide than that so many sets should be constructible from the same underlying individuals.

The possibility of necessary coincidence has, in its turn, important implications for the notion of sort. It is often supposed that a sort is determined by the associated persistence conditions, that is, by the conditions for the identification of an object of that sort at a given time and by the conditions for its reidentification at different times and in different possible circumstances. But objects that necessarily coincide will satisfy the same persistence conditions and so cannot, under this view, be of different sorts. Since the tree and its wood *are* of different sorts, the view must therefore be mistaken. In determining a sort, attention must be given not only to the persistence conditions of the objects but also to their mereological complexity.

We are led, by these considerations, to a picture of the material world that has much more in common with the abstract realms of sets or of propositions than with the realms of concreta envisaged by the mereologist or even by his "three-dimensional" opponent. Material things enjoy a hierarchical structure; they can embody a significant intensional element; and they will belong to a vast superstructure, of which the objects we usually recognize are but a small part. Thus, if I am right, it is only by abandoning our usual conception of material things as relatively unstructured, completely unconceptual, and ontologically limited in their nature that we can attain a proper understanding of what they are.

NOTES

1. An early version of the theory is to be found in Fine 1982. The theory of rigid embodiment is there restricted to qua objects, and the theory of variable embodiment omitted altogether. A much fuller version of the present theory is to be developed in a forthcoming book.

I should like to thank the many people who have helped me clarify my ideas in various talks and seminars; and I am especially grateful to David Barnett, Ruth Chang, and Peter Kung for their detailed comments on a previous draft.

2. The assumption that they are *timeless* parts is a little dubious. Those who do not like it can substitute a water molecule for the sandwich, hydrogen atoms for the slices of bread, and an oxygen atom for the piece of ham.

3. The distinction between aggregative and compound sums is further discussed in Fine 1994b.

4. Something I discuss in a forthcoming paper, "Neutral Relations."

5. See Fine 1994a.

REFERENCES

Fine, K. 1982. "Acts, Events and Things," in *Language and Ontology* (Vienna: Holder-Pichler-Tempsky), 97–105, as part of the proceedings of the Sixth International Wittgenstein Symposium, August 23–30, 1981, Kirchberg/Wechsel (Austria).

Fine, K. 1994a. "A Puzzle Concerning Matter and Form," in *Unity, Identity, and Explanation in Aristotle's Metaphysics* (ed. Scaltsas, Charles, Gill), 13–40, Clarendon Press: Oxford.

Fine, K. 1994b. "Compounds and Aggregates," *Nous* 28(2), 137–58.

Midwest Studies in Philosophy, XXIII (1999)

The Mystery of the Physical and the Matter of Qualities: A Paper for Professor Shaffer*

PETER UNGER

1. INTRODUCTION: A RUSSELLIAN RESPECT FOR THE MYSTERY OF THE PHYSICAL

For some fifty years now, nearly all work in mainstream analytic philosophy has made no serious attempt to understand the *nature of physical reality*, even though most analytic philosophers take this to be all of reality, or nearly all. Whereas we've worried much about the nature of our own experiences and thoughts and languages, we've worried little about the nature of the vast physical world that, as we ourselves believe, has them all as only a small part.

In this central respect, we've been very different from the man emerging as the century's preeminent analytic philosopher, Bertrand Russell. Although Russell thought hard about the things that have preoccupied us, *he also thought hard about the nature of physical reality*. Why has there been such a great disparity?

By contrast with Russell, most contemporary workers in core analytic areas just assume that, largely as a legacy from the physical sciences, we have been granted a happily adequate conception of physical reality: Thanks to physics, we have a pretty good understanding of physical reality, even if there may be some serious deficiencies in our understanding.

When in this frame of mind, we philosophers aren't moved to think hard about the nature of physical reality, even if we believe it to be all of reality. Rather, we're much more moved by thoughts like this: "Let's leave such terribly large matters to so many successful scientists, and to the few philosophers so concerned to interpret the work of the many."

Just so, when we trouble ourselves about what's what with things grossly physical, or with physical reality that's extralinguistic, and extramental, and so on, our concerns are with quite superficial matters. For example, we may reflect on the apparent fact that, if an ordinary rock should be split down the middle, with the two resulting "halves" never even coming close to being rejoined, the rock that was split ceases to exist, while two substantially smaller rocks then begin to exist. And, then, we may reflect on the apparent fact that, when a rock that's as famous as Plymouth Rock is similarly bisected, there's still that rock that's then in two salient pieces, whether or not there are also two smaller rocks then coming into existence. Based on these two reflections, we may aspire to a complex theory that "capturing intuitions" about both cases will serve to illuminate the "persistence conditions" for rocks in general, both the famous and also the obscure. But won't such a theory reflect our own interests more than it will tell us about the nature of physical reality? At all events, it won't deliver anything very deep, or very illuminating, about physical reality.

Even while knowing all that very well, we still don't trouble ourselves to be more searching. Rather, we're still affected by thoughts like, "Let's leave such terribly large matters to so many successful scientists, and our few colleagues who know their science." Especially in this fearfully complacent philosophical day and age, we do well to remember what Russell counseled: About the rest of concrete reality, we don't know anything nearly so intimately, nor nearly so fully, as we know our experience or, maybe better, as we know the phenomena apprehended in experience. (This remains true, of course, even if what we know most fully, and intimately, might be known less fully, and less intimately, than it can often appear.) And, we do well to recall that Russell did not exaggerate much, if at all, when, in a generally robust epistemological spirit, he said, "as regards the world in general, both physical and mental, everything that we know of its intrinsic character is derived from the mental side."[1] Nor did he exaggerate very much when, in a specifically materialistic spirit, he said, "we know nothing about the intrinsic quality of physical events except when these are mental events that we directly experience."[2]

If there's to be appropriately ambitious analytic philosophy done any time soon, then we'd best pay heed to such Russellian reminders. And though our philosophical efforts might diverge from his in many respects, they should be guided by the same realization that so greatly moved Russell: Except for what little of the physical world we might apprehend in conscious experience, which is available if materialism should be true, *the physical is mysterious to us*.

So we should wonder: To what extent, if any at all, do we have a philosophically adequate conception of physical reality? Do we have a conception well enough related to the human mind for it to ground a metaphysic in terms of which physical reality can be understood, at all well, by us very limited human thinkers?

Inspired by Russell and others, I'll try to give decent answers to such daunting questions. In the course of the effort, I may do more toward raising further questions than toward giving decent answers. But if they are fresh questions, that might be all to the good.

2. A BRIEF EXPOSITION OF THE SCIENTIFICAL METAPHYSIC

As a first step in this effort, I'll sketch, very briefly, what I take to be the metaphysical worldview that, for several centuries and with no letup anywhere in sight, has been the dominant metaphysic of the highly educated in cultures much affected by the development of the natural sciences. It will be useful to have a memorable name for this dominant worldview, but not a name loaded with positive connotations, like "the scientific metaphysic," or with negative ones, like "the scientistic metaphysic." For a name that's reasonably memorable and neutral, I'll introduce a word that's meant to parallel "philosophical" and, with it, I'll coin the naming phrase "the *scientifical* metaphysic."

Though various modifications of it appear required by certain twentieth-century scientific developments, notably, by quantum mechanics and relativity theory, the heart of our scientifical metaphysic is, apparently, essentially the same as before the advent of the twentieth century. So, even if folks versed in contemporary physics would rightly prefer esoteric analogues of the ordinary terms I feel most comfortable using for the job, for my main philosophical purposes the following few paragraphs may serve to express our dominant worldview.

First, differently distributed in space at different times, there is physical stuff or *matter*. Placing aside the thought that this matter may have been, very long ago, created by some Extraordinarily Powerful Mind (or Minds), and placing aside thoughts of how such a SuperMind might, even nowadays, occasionally affect matter, this matter is *independent of minds*: To exist, the matter needn't be sensed by, or be thought about by, sentient beings.

Second (again placing to the side all such "theological" ideas, which from now on will generally be done only implicitly), insofar as it's determined by anything at all and isn't merely random, the distribution of this matter at any given time is determined by the distribution of the matter at earlier times, with the determination proceeding in line with our world's basic natural laws, which are physical laws.

Third, owing to the variety in these material distributions, at certain times some of the world's matter, or possibly much of the matter, is configured so as to compose various complex material structures and systems, ranging from the slightly complex through the fairly complex to the highly complex. Among the more complex of even these highly complex material structures and systems are living entities, or those serving to constitute living entities.

Fourth, among the more complex of even these living material entities, and possibly even among some (very distant) nonliving material complexes, there are those that are thinking, feeling, experiencing physical entities. Or, more cautiously, complexly composed of some matter, there are the living physical bodies of such thinking physical entities.

Fifth, there are certain properties that are the *naturally important* properties of matter, both matter that's involved in composing a highly complex material system and, equally, matter that's never so interestingly involved. To date, it's mainly been the work of physics to discover what actually are these properties.

Sixth, beyond what physics aims to discover, there are other naturally important properties. The most salient of these properties are to be found in a most intimate connection with the minds of the sentient beings of the world: These salient properties will qualify the conscious immediate experiences of these beings; or, if not quite that, they'll qualify whatever it is that such beings most immediately experience, perhaps manifolds of qualia. So, these properties will include (absolutely specific) phenomenal color properties and, just as well, (absolutely specific) phenomenal pain properties. None of these properties are, of course, even remotely like mere powers of material bodies to promote, in finite minds, any sort of experience. Because they figure prominently in my inquiry, I'll refer to the phenomenal properties as the *Qualities*, which capitalized term I'll reserve for them and only such other properties as are strongly and deeply analogous to phenomenal properties.

Seventh, the six preceding paragraphs are to be understood as implying that our scientifical metaphysics conflicts with many traditional metaphysical systems, even though it's not in conflict with many others. Thus, whereas Berkeley's subjective idealism conflicts with our scientifical metaphysic, other metaphysical views comport with it well. For example, Descartes's dualism, or at least a view much like the Cartesian metaphysic, provides a consistent line for further specification of our scientifical metaphysic. And it appears a materialistic worldview provides a quite different consistent line.

Although I've sketched the main thrust of our scientifical metaphysic in the seven paragraphs just preceding, I've ignored some very large matters. For example, I've offered nothing about what this metaphysic might say, or might not say, regarding questions of genuine choice, or free will. Still, even with only as much of the scientifical metaphysic as what's been presented, there may be raised questions of philosophical importance. In this paper, we'll explore some of them.

3. THIS METAPHYSIC, THREE KINDS OF PROPERTY, AND THE RESTRICTION OF QUALITIES TO MINDS

For a discussion that we may hope to be as profitable as it's protracted, I'll move deliberately toward displaying a doctrine that's assumed true by most who embrace the scientifical metaphysic, even if it might not be so much as actually implied by the dominant worldview. Toward succinctly presenting this popular proposition, which I'll call the *Restriction of Qualities to Minds*, it will be useful to notice *three categories of basic natural property* (of whatever entities, or entity, might serve to constitute physical reality.)

First, I'll take note of what might be called the purely *spatiotemporal* properties or, for short, the *Spatiotemporals*. Central to this group are, with one exception, what Descartes regarded as "the primary or real properties of matter . . . shape, size, position, duration, movability, divisibility and number. This list we can immediately diminish by one, because it is clear that *number* is an interloper here."[3] As concrete reality might have very many dimensions, this group may include, in addition to geometric properties, topological properties and, perhaps, other such "mathematically recognized" properties. Of course, even such determinables as Descartes's are just a starting point here; more to the concrete point are such absolutely specific determinate properties as, say, *being perfectly spherical*.

As I'm understanding the Spatiotemporals, even absolutely empty regions will, at least when limited in some dimensions or respects, have Spatiotemporal properties whether at an instant or over time, even if they might be devoid of all other basic properties. And, at least in many possible worlds, there's nothing more to the having of Spatiotemporal properties than what a perfectly empty region has, at an instant or over time.

As I'm painfully aware, the scientifical metaphysic *might not* help provide us with any understanding of concrete reality that's even modestly adequate. But, if it does profit us in that large regard, then we must think of very much of this reality, even if not absolutely all of it, as having spatiotemporal properties. Indeed, though I'm far less confident of it, I suggest that we should accept even this much more ambitious proposition: For the scientifical metaphysic to do much *for our understanding* of concrete reality, there must be *some* truth in the thought that much of this reality has the three-dimensional nondirectional spatial structure, and the correlative one-dimensional directional temporal structure that, in our conscious perception of reality, are spatiotemporal properties that physical reality appears to have. For although such perception might provide us with only a *very partial perspective* on reality, and with a *quite superficial* perspective, still and all, unless there's *something about physical reality* in virtue of which it has these familiar spatiotemporal properties, the scientifical metaphysic will, I think, do far more toward providing intellectual illusion than toward giving us even a very modestly adequate understanding of reality. But in the present essay, I will rely only on less ambitious propositions. At all events, so much for my first category of basic natural properties, the Spatiotemporals.

Second, I'll notice what, for want of a better expression, I'll call the *propensity properties* or, more briefly, the *Propensities*. Often, these properties, or some of them, have been called "powers"; but inappropriately for us, that term connotes positive force. Others have called the properties "dispositions"; but despite the valiant efforts of C. B. Martin and others, that term has been so badly abused that it will arouse, in the minds of too many, undue confusion.[4]

Now, at least for the meanwhile, we'll understand the Propensities as being distinct from, even if they might be importantly related to, the Spatiotemporals. On this understanding, regions of absolutely empty space, or perfect vacuums, can have spatiotemporal properties; but as it at least appears, no such physically empty regions will themselves have any powers or, as I'll say, any Propensities. By contrast with such vacuums, we may envision a finite spatial region that's precisely occupied by an electron, where our supposed electron is well suited to making true an early theory of such supposedly simple physical things. Then what's in that small finite region will be something that has, in addition to its spatiotemporal properties, *unit negative electric charge*. Its having *that* property is, we may suppose, the electron's having a certain complex Propensity or, perhaps the same, its having a cluster of simpler Propensities. The complex Propensity of our electron will include, for salient examples, its Propensity to repel any other electron with such-and-such a force in so-and-so a direction, and its Propensity to attract any proton with such-and-such a force in so-and-so a direction. As with any entity's having any Propensity, the electron's having this one is not dependent, not even in the minutest degree, on there ever actually being any protons, or there being any other electrons. In contradistinction to there being any *chance for* the Propensity of our electron to be *manifested*, which does require there to be things external to it, the electron's *just having* the indicated Propensity doesn't depend on there ever being *any* such external entity.

Third, and last, I'll notice what I call the *Qualities*, a group of properties whose most accessible members are the phenomenal properties available in our conscious experience. But the Qualities may also include other properties: Beyond the properties experientially available to us, and even beyond those available to any of the world's finite minds, there may be properties that are *deeply analogous to* at least some of the phenomenal properties. Through *extrapolative analogical thinking*, perhaps we might get some grasp as to the nature of some of these farther-fetched properties, even if, perhaps, never a grasp that's very rich, firm, or clear.

So on the one hand, consider those phenomenal properties best suited to filling space, or to being spread through space. Here, we may consider a perfectly specific sort of translucent red, and an equally specific "colorless transparency," as with what's apprehended in experience of, say, a typical windowpane, and an equally specific "silveriness," as with what's experienced in, say, seeing some shiny silver. Since they're so well suited to filling space, we'll call these *Extensible Qualities*. Now, and on the other hand, consider some phenomenal properties that seem *unsuited* to filling space. Here we may consider a perfectly specific sort of taste of sweet chocolate, and a perfectly specific sort of pleasant sound, as with what's apprehended in one's experience of, say, a certain rendition of a favorite song, and a perfectly specific sort of elation, as with what's experienced upon, say, hearing some wonderful news. Since they're so unsuited to filling space, suppose, we'll call them *Nonextensible Qualities*. Now, we can have a conception, it appears, of properties that, though they're *not* available in experience to the world's finite minds, are very much *more like each* of our indicated Extensible Qualities than they're like *any* of our indicated Nonextensible Qualities.

The qualities we're analogically contemplating are very much more like our indicated Extensibles than our indicated Nonextensibles both overall and, as well, in those respects, whatever precisely they may be, that have our Extensibles be so very much more suited to filling space than are our Nonextensibles. By way of such extrapolative analogical thinking, I'm suggesting, we may have a contentful conception of (even if not yet any reason to believe in) a world featuring many instantiations of Extensible Qualities that can't, at least as a matter of natural fact, be experienced by any of the world's finite minds. In parallel, we can also conceive of properties that, though they're likewise unavailable to experience, are much more like each of our indicated *Nonextensible* Qualities than they're like any of our indicated Extensible Qualities. Here, too, there may be properties that, though they're not properly phenomenal properties, are among a world's farther-fetched Qualities.

In marked contrast with how things were fifty years ago, nowadays it appears almost universally believed by analytic philosophers that the phenomenal properties are properties of, and only of, conscious experiences; and, rather than being any mere contingent truth, this belief runs, it's conceptually and necessarily true that the phenomenal properties are all properties of, and only of, the mental, and even just the experiential. Let's suppose this belief is correct. Then it might be that, though the phenomenal color properties *seem well suited* to filling space, that's an illusory appearance. For as far as any of us can tell, it might be that conscious experiences can't literally occupy spatial regions.

Let's further suppose that, whether or not for that reason, none of the phenomenal properties are actually Extensible, are Qualities well suited to filling space. Well, even in such an event, it's still true to say this: The phenomenal properties may be peculiarly helpful leads for our only quite partially grasping, through extrapolative analogical thinking, Qualities whose instances *are* so prevalent in our mind-independent spatiotemporal reality.

Having said that, I'll also say this: Apparently against almost all other contemporary analytic philosophers, I *don't* believe that the phenomenal properties are features only of conscious experiences. Rather, I'm quite agnostic. Toward explaining this unfashionable agnosticism, in the next section I'll offer two sorts of consideration. Here it suffices to note that the present project doesn't depend on what's the best approach to this interesting issue. To indicate what's much more relevant, I display this from Russell:

> To assert that the material *must* be very different from percepts is to assume that we know a great deal more than we do in fact know of the intrinsic character of physical events. If there is any advantage in supposing that the light-wave, the process in the eye, and the process in the optic nerve, contain events qualitatively continuous with the final visual percept, nothing that we know of the physical world can be used to disprove the supposition.
>
> The gulf between percepts and physics is not a gulf as regards intrinsic quality, for we know nothing of the intrinsic quality of the physical world, and therefore do not know whether it is, or is not, very different from that of percepts. The gulf is as to what we know about the two realms. We know the quality of percepts, but we do not know their laws so well as we could wish. We know the laws of the physical world, in so far as these are mathematical, pretty well, but we know nothing else about it. If there is any intellectual difficulty in supposing that the physical world is intrinsically quite unlike that of percepts, this is a reason for supposing that there is not this complete unlikeness. And there is a certain ground for such a view, in the fact that percepts are part of the physical world, and are the only part that we can know without the help of rather elaborate and difficult inferences.[5]

At all events, at least for the meanwhile we may understand the Qualities as being distinct from, though perhaps importantly related to, both the Spatiotemporals and the Propensities. On this understanding, whereas the spatiotemporal properties can be possessed by regions of absolutely empty space, it is at least somewhat doubtful that any of the Qualities, including even any of the Extensible Qualities, can be possessed by an *absolutely* perfect vacuum. For now, that's all for this last sort of basic natural property.

With this threefold classification providing the context for it, I can briefly display the doctrine that, at this section's start, I said was assumed by most who hold with the scientifical metaphysic, even if it's not actually implied by the dominant worldview:

> *The Restriction of Qualities to Minds.* Unlike the Spatiotemporal properties and the Propensities, which are so widely instantiated in what's physical, there are not (any instantiations of) any of the Qualities in physical reality, with the possible exception, at any given time, of such a small part as may subserve the minds of sentient beings.

According to the *Restriction*, to use this doctrine's short name, all the world's matter, or almost all, has no Qualities, whatever might be its Spatiotemporal properties and its Propensities.

Though they need fleshing out if they're ever to be of much philosophical interest, here are a couple of questions that, I'll suggest, may already be of some interest: If we *add* the Restriction to our scientifical metaphysic and, thus, obtain a *deeply segregated* worldview, what will be, for us, the advantages of, and the disadvantages of, such a view of the world? On the opposite hand, if we add the *Denial* of the Restriction to our scientifical metaphysic, obtaining a *deeply integrated* worldview, what will be the advantages and disadvantages?

4. MIGHT PHENOMENAL QUALITIES OUTRUN EXPERIENCE?

Before inquiring into the implications of the Restriction, which will soon be my main order of business, I'll offer two groups of ideas, each complementing the other, that serve to motivate this pretty unusual philosophical stance of mine: Apparently against almost all my analytically philosophical contemporaries, I *don't* believe that the phenomenal properties are possessed only by experiences. Rather, I'm agnostic about the matter. Though providing motivation for this unfashionable stance isn't crucial for my project, my doing that will help contemporary readers appreciate, rather well, what I mean to say about the implications of the Restriction.

For the first group of motivating ideas, I'll quote at length from Michael Lockwood's wonderfully stimulating book, *Mind, Brain and the Quantum*:

> I find it plausible to suppose that the phenomenal qualities themselves are less fickle than one's attention, and may persist even when one's awareness of them lapses. On this view, phenomenal qualities are neither realized by/being sensed nor sensed by being realized. . . . The realization of a phenomenal quality is one thing, I contend; its being an object of awareness is something else, ...
>
> At first hearing, the present proposal may seem wildly eccentric. . . .
>
> . . . But now consider the following example. Suppose we have three colour patches projected close together on to a screen; call them *L* (left), *M* (middle) and *R* (right). Suppose, further, that in the absence of *R*, *L* is indistinguishable from *M*, and that in the absence of *L*, *M* is indistinguishable from *R*. *L*, however (in the presence or absence of *M*), *is* distinguishable from *R*. . . . So what are we to suppose happens if we start with a screen containing only *L* and *M*, which are *ex hypothesi* indistinguishable, then add *R*, so that all three patches are

present, and finally remove *L*, leaving *M* and *R*, which are likewise indistinguishable?

There are only two possibilities, surely. By far the more plausible, to my mind, is that the phenomenal colours corresponding to *L* and *M* are distinct, even in the absence of *R*: there *is* a phenomenal difference here, but one too small to register in consciousness, no matter how closely the subject attends. Adding together two phenomenal differences of this magnitude does, however, produce a difference that registers in consciousness; hence the subject's ability to distinguish *L* from *R*. The only alternative is to suppose that the effect, either of adding *R* or of removing *L*, is to induce a qualitative change in the phenomenal colour corresponding to one or the other of the remaining patches. But it surely won't *seem* to the subject that this is what happens. So on this supposition too, there would be phenomenal differences—or at least, phenomenal *transitions*—that defied conscious detection.

Not only, in such perceptual cases, does the phenomenal character of what one is immediately aware of outrun one's awareness of it; it actually seems to do so. . . . What I am suggesting, in effect, is that we should allow phenomenal qualities quite generally to outrun awareness. Those who think they understand what it is for phenomenal qualities to inhere in portions of their visual field of which . . . they are not currently conscious, now have a model for what, . . . the unsensed portion of the physical world is like in itself, quite generally—even in regions beyond the confines of the brains of sentient beings, where awareness, as far as we know, never intrudes.[6]

These passages provide extremely suggestive argumentation, even if no decisive argumentation, to the effect that there are instances of phenomenal color qualities that outrun experience (and also *fairly* suggestive reasoning that these Qualities outrun even nonconscious mentality).

Much as the quotation from Lockwood indicates, insofar as philosophers now think they have difficulty understanding the suggestion that phenomenal qualities may outrun mentality, it's generally because they think they have difficulties with the suggestion that phenomenal qualities might ever outrun *conscious* mentality. But what's just been quoted serves to confute the latter thought. So most of these philosophers should reject the former as well.

While many may still find it hard to *believe* phenomenal properties outrun all of mentality, myself included, by now few should have trouble with the thought that the suggestion is a *coherent* proposition. With that said, there's enough from the first group of motivating ideas.

For the second group of ideas, I'll relate the results of some bouts of phenomenological thinking, and some analysis pertaining thereto: When lying still in silence and darkness, sometimes I vividly experience my body as filling space. Then, it appears, I apprehend *Qualities felt as suffusing space*. Naturally enough, I'll call these Extensible Qualities the *Felt Bodily Qualities*. Now, with the Felt Bodily Qualities I can conceive *only* of there being such instances as are *experienced*; indeed, with *these* Qualities, I conceive only of such instances as are *experienced as extending through space occupied by (some of) a being that experiences them.*

By contrast with the Felt Bodily Qualities, it seems clear, I can conceive of there being instances of *color* Qualities that *aren't* ever experienced; indeed, I can do that about as well, it appears, as I can conceive instances that *are* experienced. (To me, this has been intuitive for as long as I can remember, long before any encounter with *arguments* in support of such an idea, like what's just been displayed from Lockwood.)

In marked contrast to the phenomenal colors, it appears, the Felt Bodily Qualities are *essentially mental* Qualities, which can be instanced only when they figure in experience. By that same contrast, the phenomenal colors, and the Extensibles strongly analogous with them, *aren't essentially mental* Qualities, and can be instanced *even when they don't* figure in experience. So as it appears, we have tolerably clear conceptions of two quite different sorts of Extensible Quality. Considerations like these serve to motivate my agnosticism as to whether the phenomenal qualities may outrun experience, or even mentality.

Having had both groups of motivating ideas presented, perhaps readers will be sympathetic to the idea that the phenomenal qualities can outrun experience. And with that reasonably open-minded stance, perhaps they'll appreciate, rather well, what I'll now say about the implications of the Restriction. At all events, it's high time for that main order of business.

5. THE RESTRICTION, PARTICLES IN SPACE AND SPACES IN A PLENUM

For the scientifical metaphysic to provide us with a reasonably adequate view of our world, do its bare bones need such Qualitative flesh as can be had only with the Denial of the Restriction? My conjecture is that the question receives an affirmative answer.

Toward motivating this conjecture, I'll *suppose that the Restriction holds* and, in terms of the scientifical metaphysic as thus limited, I'll begin two *extremely simple attempts to characterize* our world. (Toward the Restriction's being fully in force, I'll stipulate that both are mainly aimed at characterizing the world well before there were any [finite] minds.)

First, and familiarly, I'll begin an attempt to characterize physical reality in generally Newtonian terms: Moving about in what's otherwise uniformly empty space, there are many particles of matter, grandiosely labeled Particles, whose motion is governed by physical laws. In that we're supposing the Restriction to hold, we must suppose that, in this *Particulate World*, the laws concern only Nonqualitative properties that the Particles might have, not Qualities.

Second, and unusually, I begin this attempt to characterize physical reality: In what's otherwise a continuous material plenum, or a continuous field of matter, there are little perfectly empty spaces, or absolute vacua, or *Bubbles*: As regards both shape and size, each Bubble is precisely similar to a certain Particle, its *counterpart* Particle, in the Particulate World. And, wherever there's a Particle in our Particulate World, there's a counterpart place with a counterpart Bubble in this *Plenumate World*. So, if there are eight spherical Particles arrayed in a quite cubical pattern in a certain region of our Particulate World, then in the counterpart region of our Plenumate World there'll be eight such Bubbles arrayed in just such a pattern.

Even as various Particles may instance certain physical properties that will have them be suited for governance by certain physical laws, so various regions of a physical Plenum may have certain correlative physical properties that will have them be correlatively suited for governance by apt parallels of, or nice inversions of, the Particle-governing laws. So, in a nice parallel with the law-governed behavior of the Particles in our Particulate World, this Plenumate World features laws governing the distribution of its Plenum throughout all its time. And, since its Bubbles always *are* at just the places in the World where there *isn't* any Plenum, this World's laws also serve to determine the distribution of all its *Bubbles* over time. So, our Plenumate World's Bubbles will move through its material field along trajectories that, over time, perfectly parallel the trajectories of the Particulate World's Particles through its empty space.

Always supposing the Restriction holds, I'd make two extremely simple attempts, it appears, at starting to characterize our world. Before concluding the section, it may be useful to comment on what may be the two most salient respects in which my attempts were so simple.

First, there's the point that my attempts were conducted in the general framework of classical physics, with its quite intuitive conceptions of space and of time, rather than the framework of more recent physics, with its quite *unintuitive* conceptions, like the notion of *spacetime*. One reason for this, I blush to confess, is that I know precious little about contemporary physical science. A more important reason is that I'm engaged in an endeavor that's meant to transcend the differences between classical physics and more recent scientific developments. And it's perfectly possible, it appears, for there to be an endeavor that succeeds in being that comprehensive: Since recent scientific developments make no Completely Revolutionary Break with earlier science, what's new in the recent scientific conceptions doesn't affect the question of how we might, with the Restriction fully in force, ever have an intelligible worldview that, far from being any sort of idealism, is an adequate specification of the scientifical metaphysic.

Apparently with complete sincerity, that's what I've been told by philosophers knowledgeable about contemporary physics. So apparently, my employing the framework of classical physics means no loss of generality for these philosophical exercises.

Second, there's the point that, in trying to characterize a Particulate World, and also a Plenumate World, I forswore saying anything about complex material structures or systems, much less anything about any minds that any material complexes might subserve. That was done for several reasons, the most important being that such a simplification would be helpful toward having the Restriction be fully in force. Even if it might be unnecessary, I'll again implore my readers: When trying to think of a Particulate World, *don't do anything even remotely like*, say, thinking of *light grey* spheres moving through a *dark grey* space or field; and, when attempting thoughts of a Plenumate World, don't do anything even remotely like thinking of dark grey spheres moving through a light grey space or field!

For holding to this supposition, it will be useful to discuss some relations regarding the scientifical metaphysic, the instantiation of Qualities, and "the place of mind in the world order," or, as it might turn out, what just appear to be some such relations: Even while they try to have the Restriction be in force, some may have these following thoughts regarding the scientifical metaphysic. As our dominant metaphysic seems fully to allow, where and when a World features creatures with conscious minds, there and then there'll be someplace in the World for Qualities to be instantiated. So, if we should endeavor to characterize, say, a Particulate World, at greater length, then, as we may make specifications for complex living material creatures, and so consciously experiencing creatures, we may thus characterize a part of the world in which Qualities will be instanced, even while supposing the Restriction to hold. So, if we just go further in our attempts to characterized Worlds, even while supposing the Restriction, won't we do quite a lot toward characterizing a Particulate World, and also a Plenumate World?

No, we won't, for the situation is this: Whenever there's something that seems to characterize an experiencing creature as constituted of many Particles, there's also something, in correlative Plenumate terms, that seems to characterize that creature, with just as much propriety, as not being so constituted. Let me explain.

In an attempt to characterize an experiencing creature that features a body as well as a mind with *Particulate* terms, we may say this: Ever so many material Particles, perhaps billions and billions, serve to *constitute* the material creature with a mind. Or at the very least, they all serve to constitute the body of the creature; and because so many of this body's Particles are going through an appropriately complex sequence of arrangements, this body, it may then be said, subserves the creature's mind. When the duly constituted creature has experiences, Qualities are, through or in the creature's mind, instanced in the Particulate World.

But using *Plenumate* terms, we can say *this* about any materially realized experiencing creature: Ever so many Bubbles in the Plenum, perhaps billions and billions, serve to *institute* the physical creature with a mind, to coin a euphonious Plenumate term. Or at least they serve to institute the body of the creature, which body subserves the creature with a mind. When the duly instituted creature has experiences, Qualities are, through or in the creature's mind, instanced in the Plenumate World.

In this section, serious questions were raised about any attempt to contemplate physical reality within the confines of the Restriction. Initially, it may have appeared that each of my attempts to characterize physical reality, one with Particulate wording and one with the Plenumate terms, clearly contrasted with the other. But mightn't it be that I actually made just one extremely insubstantial start twice over, first using one mutually connected group of terms, the "Particulate terms," and then using another, the "Plenumate terms"? Mightn't it be that, as long as any attempt to conceive of our world is limited by the Restriction, it will be doomed to futility?

6. WHEN LIMITED BY THE RESTRICTION, HOW TO CONCEIVE A PARTICLE'S PROPENSITIES?

In my two attempts at characterizing Worlds, I tried to attribute Spatiotemporal properties to the objects of the Worlds. For example, I said that, in one sort of World, there are spherical Particles and, in the other, there are spherical Bubbles. By contrast, I did little, or nothing, as regards the other basic natural properties of the intended objects, the Propensities and the Qualities. Of course, as the Restriction was fully in force, it was forbidden to attribute any Quality to a Particle or to a Plenum. But what about Propensities?

On this we can hardly do better, I should think, than to consider what, historically, appears the propensity most saliently proposed for philosophical consideration, the supposed *solidity* of things material. And, on that, we can hardly do better than to begin with book 2, chapter 4 of the *Essay Concerning Human Understanding*, which is "Of Solidity," in which Locke aims to present an "Idea" that serves to distinguish material Bodies from the mere Space they may occupy:

> That which thus hinders the approach of two Bodies, when they are moving one towards another, I call *Solidity*. . . . but if any one think it better to call it *Impenetrability*, he has my Consent. . . . This of all other, seems the *Idea* most intimately connected with, and essential to Body, so as no where else to be found or imagin'd, but only in matter: . . . the Mind, . . . considers it, as well as Figure, in the minutest Particle of Matter, that can exist; and finds it inseparably inherent in Body, where-ever, or however modified.
>
> This is the *Idea*, belongs to Body, whereby we conceive it *to fill space*.[7]

As with other passages, we should understand Locke here as assuming, if not affirming, that the Restriction holds. Even as Newton's physics ignores Qualities, Locke excludes them from the world's vast material realm, restricting them to our Minds (*Essay*, 136–37).

For Locke, solidity is impenetrability. But, with the Restriction in force, what can such solidity do for our conception of a Particle? An excellent discussion of the question can be found in John Foster's terribly difficult but at least occasionally brilliant book, *The Case for Idealism*. According to Foster:

> Locke . . . thought that the nature of solidity is revealed in tactual experience. . . . But in this Locke was clearly mistaken. . . . The tactual experience of solidity is no more nor less than the experience of voluminous resistance, and, in so far as our concept of solidity is acquired through tactual experience, the specification of matter as solid is opaque. All it adds to the specification of matter as a voluminous substance is that there is *something* in its intrinsic nature (it does not say *what*) which makes material objects mutually obstructive.[8]

Now, I do not know that Foster is right in his suggestion that Locke thought that solidity was not a Power of material objects. More likely, it seems to me, in "Of Solidity" Locke was involved in muddles: How could *Impenetrability*, which Locke says is the very same as Solidity, *not* be a Power of resistance on the part of Impenetrable Bodies. But philosophically, there's no more to be gained from Locke here than what Foster contends, nothing much at all. Indeed, insofar as Foster's reading of Locke may be mistaken, his error will be, apparently, *undue charity* toward the old philosopher.

At all events, where Foster is most helpful is in his own discussion of the quite general question of the "Powers of Material Bodies." This occurs in an appendix to chapter 4 of the book. As Foster's thinking there is so very helpful, I'll quote this appendix at length:

> The only properties of fundamental particles which can be transparently specified in physical terms are (1) spatiotemporal properties, such as shape, size and velocity and (2) causal and dispositional properties, such as mutual obstructiveness, gravitational power and electric charge. From this, I have concluded that . . . the intrinsic nature of the particles can, in physical terms, only be specified opaquely, as that on which their behavioural dispositions and causal powers are grounded. But, is this conclusion justified? An alternative would be to say that . . . each particle is, in itself, no more than a mobile cluster of causal powers, there being no "substantial" space-occupant which possesses the powers and on whose categorical nature the powers are grounded. Such a thesis has been endorsed, in different forms, by a number of distinguished scientists and philosophers. [Here, Foster has a note naming such intellectual heavyweights as Leibniz, Boscovich, Kant, Priestley and Faraday.] If it is coherent, this thesis certainly has some appeal. . . .
>
> But is the powers-thesis (PT) coherent? The main problem is that if all the fundamental particles are construed in this way, there seem to be no physical items in terms of whose behaviour the content of the powers could be specified, and consequently, it seems that, in the last analysis, there is nothing which the powers are powers to do. Let us begin with a concrete example. We will assume that the atoms are the only fundamental particles and that all atoms are of exactly the same type. Now each atom has a number of causal powers. It has a power of resistance, whereby any two atoms are mutually obstructive. It has a power of gravitational attraction, whereby, between any two atoms, there is a force of attraction inversely proportional to the square of their distance. . . . And it has a number of other powers which we need not list. For PT to be true, it is necessary some subset of these powers constitutes the essential nature of an atom. Let us suppose, for simplicity, we select the power of resistance as the only (putatively) essential atomic power and leave the other powers to depend on the contingent laws of nature governing the behavior of atoms. Thus each atom is construed as a mobile sphere of impenetrability, the behavior and causal interaction of these spheres, apart from their mutual obstructiveness, being governed by additional laws. The problem arises when we ask: "To what is a sphere of impenetrability impenetrable?" The answer is: "To other atoms, i.e., to other spheres of impenetrability." But this means that the specification of the content of the atom-constituting power is viciously regressive: each atom is a sphere of impenetrability to any other sphere of impenetrability to any other sphere of impenetrability . . . and so on *ad infinitum*. From which it follows that the notion of such a power is incoherent, since there is nothing which the power is a power to do. . . .
>
> The problem is not avoided if we include further powers in the essential nature of the atom. Thus we might take the atomic nature to combine a power

> of resistance with a power of attraction, so that each atom is constituted by a mobile sphere of impenetrability surrounded by a more extensive (perhaps infinitely extended) field of gravitational potential (the field being structured, in accordance with the inverse-square-law, around the centre of the sphere). We could then try to specify the content of the power of resistance in terms of the behavior of gravitational fields or specify the content of the power of attraction in terms of the behavior of spheres of impenetrability. But neither specification blocks the regress, since it merely specifies the content of one power in terms of another. The only way of avoiding the regress, it seems, is to construe at least one of the powers as a power to affect the behavior of some . . . space occupant . . . with an intrinsic nature independent of its causal powers and dispositions. But such occupants are just what PT excludes. (67–69)

> My conclusion, therefore, is that the powers-thesis is incoherent. And consequently, I stand by my previous conclusion that, apart from their shape and size, the intrinsic nature of the fundamental space-occupants (assuming there are occupants at all) cannot be empirically discovered or transparently specified in physical terms. (72)

Now, I'm not sure that the considerations Foster marshals show that the powers-thesis is so much as *incoherent*. But, it does seem clear that they show there to be grave difficulties, perhaps even insuperable ones, with the thought we can understand certain regions of space, or certain entities occupying the regions, to have just so many Spatiotemporal properties and Propensity properties without their having any Qualities at all.

To take full advantage of them, I'll conjoin Foster's ideas with some complementary considerations. Toward setting out these considerations, I'll quote from "Of the Modern Philosophy," a marvelous section of Hume's *Treatise*:

> The idea of solidity is that of two objects, which being impell'd by the utmost force, cannot penetrate each other; but still maintain a separate and distinct existence. Solidity, therefore, is perfectly incomprehensible alone, and without the conception of some bodies, which are solid, and maintain this separate and distinct existence. Now what idea have we of these bodies? The ideas of colours, sounds, and other secondary qualities are excluded. The idea of motion depends on that of extension, and the idea of extension on that of solidity. 'Tis impossible, therefore, that the idea of solidity can depend on either of them. For that wou'd be to run in a circle, and make one idea depend on another, while at the same time the latter depends on the former. Our modern philosophy, therefore, leaves us no just nor satisfactory idea of solidity; nor consequently of matter.
>
> Add to this, that, properly speaking, solidity or impenetrability is nothing, but an impossibility of annihilation, ... An impossibility of being annihilated cannot exist, and can never be conceived to exist, by itself; but necessarily requires some object or real existence, to which it may belong. Now the

> difficulty still remains, how to form an idea of this object or existence, without having recourse to the secondary and sensible qualities.[9]

We should now understand Hume, like Locke before him, as assuming the Restriction to hold. And as these passages then serve to show, in fixing on solidity, or on *what's left of that notion when the Restriction has been supposed*, Locke found nothing to distinguish adequately between Particles of Matter and Bubbles in a material Plenum.

Now, right before the quote just displayed, there are these sentences:

> The idea of extension is a compound idea; but as it is not compounded of an infinite number of parts or inferior ideas, it must at last resolve itself into such as are perfectly simple and indivisible. Those simple and indivisible parts, not being ideas of extension, must be non-entities, unless conceiv'd as colour'd or solid. Color is excluded from any real existence. The reality, therefore, of our idea of extension depends upon the reality of that of solidity, nor can the former be just while the latter is chimerical. Let us, then, lend our attention to the examination of the idea of solidity. (228)

As Hume's here suggesting, without phenomenal colors available, or any similarly helpful Qualities, we'll lack the resources for an adequate conception of something's being physically solid or impenetrable. As Hume also seems rightly to suggest, the same pertains to any other alleged physical Propensity. (Except that Locke fixed on solidity as his favorite, there's nothing very special about that candidate, as the passages from Foster can be seen to show.)

In light of what's been presented in this section, we may be able to make useful comments concerning the questions that, at the just previous section's end, arose for my attempts to characterize a Particulate World, and also a Plenumate World: Though it may have appeared that each of my attempts to characterize physical reality, one with Particulate wording and one with the Plenumate terms, clearly contrasted with the other, mightn't it be that I actually made just one extremely insubstantial start twice over, first using one mutually connected group of terms and then using another? Indeed, it may now be so plain that those questions have affirmative answers that the whole matter's no longer interesting.

What may still be interesting, I think, is to notice these further points: With those attempts, even my *very talk of particles* may have been badly misleading, as was my *talk of a plenum*. As I'm suggesting, it may be that something's *being a particle* isn't ever a completely Nonqualitative matter, and the question of whether there's *a plenum* might not be wholly Nonqualitative. With the *Restriction in place*, it may be that we're unable to think of a World as containing any *particles*; when supposing the Restriction to hold while trying to think of a "Particulate World," perhaps the most we can do is think, very abstractly indeed, about a physical World where "Quality-purged correlates of true particles" are to play a certain role in the history of the World. And, with the Restriction in place while trying to think of a "Plenumate World," perhaps the most we can do is think, just as abstractly, about a World where "Quality-purged correlates of a true plenum" play a perfectly parallel role, or maybe even the very same role, in the history of the World. With thoughts so abstract, perhaps there's no significant difference between what we're thinking at the one time and at the other.

7. EXTENSIBLE QUALITIES AND INTELLIGIBLE PROPENSITIES

With the Restriction in force and no Qualities available, we'll have no adequate conception of physical reality. By contrast, with Qualities having "real existence" in the physical realm, we may have a systematically rich variety of physical conceptions, perhaps far beyond anything imagined by Locke or Hume. Directly, I'll explain.

Whether or not we scientifically educated philosophers now can *believe* that any matter is a certain Qualitative color, say, that it's a certain Absolutely Specific shade of phenomenal red, it certainly seems that we can *conceive* of there being matter, even perfectly insensate matter, that's entirely just such a red, and that has no other Absolutely Specific Quality. As I'll say, we're to contemplate matter that is *Red*.

It may also be helpful to have our considered stuff be, through and through, *pretty highly phenomenally transparent* (and *somewhat phenomenally translucent*). As with any Quality our matter may have, it's (degree of) transparency must be Absolutely Specific. So, it's Red Transp-Taso matter that we're to conceive. For easy exposition, we'll call our matter just by its first name, Red.

Though it might not be believable for you and me, it's perfectly conceivable, even to us, that all of a World's matter be Red. In particular, it's conceivable that all of a World's matter be distributed so as to comprise eight Red congruent material spheres, each separated from the others by Qualityless empty space, and with nothing else in such a region having any Qualities, while what's where any sphere is has just the color Quality we're contemplating.

Consonant with such a conception, there may be clear content in *each of several different ideas of impenetrability*. For just one salient way of cutting the conceptual pie, we may have clear content both in (1) the idea of a sphere that's impenetrable to, or by, *all* the matter that's external to it and in (2) the idea of a sphere that's impenetrable to *some*, but *not all*, the matter external to it. In turn, I'll illustrate both ideas.

1. We may think of an infinity of Red spheres each of which is absolutely impenetrable to every other, with the matter of these spheres comprising all the matter of the World in which there are the spheres. When two such spheres collide, then each directly recedes from the other, without either making any intrusion into the bounds of the other.
2. In addition to all our Red spheres, we may contemplate an infinity of spheres that are each an Absolutely Specific shade of phenomenal blue and a certain Absolutely Specific phenomenal transparency, an infinity of *Blue* spheres. Now, just as each Red sphere is completely impenetrable to all other Red spheres, each Blue sphere is impenetrable to all other Blue spheres. More interestingly, each *Red* sphere will be *perfectly penetrable* by any *Blue* sphere, and *vice versa*; so without even the least resistance or temporal delay in trajectory, Red spheres and Blue spheres will pass through each other, as will parts of such

Qualitatively different spheres. To conceive such a "perfect passing" most vividly, we may think of a region where a Blue and a Red sphere overlap as suffused with a certain Absolutely Specific transparent purple, as being *Purple* regions.

As this discussion of impenetrability suggests, any intelligible conception of physical Propensities, and any adequate conception of physical entities, has a central place for Extensible Qualities. At the same time, there's an abundance of such good conceptions that do that.

It's not surprising, then, to observe that, just as thought of Extensible Qualities allows us to have intelligible ideas of physical objects, variously distributed through spacetime and disposed toward various possible interactions, so it allows us to make intelligible specifications of Particulate Worlds, and clearly contrasting characterizations of Plenumate Worlds.

With attempts at Worldly characterization, we'll now have there be instanced some Extensible Quality *wherever there is matter*, from the minutest particle to a material expanse infinitely extensive in all directions. And, it's *only where* there's matter, or only where there's physical reality, that there'll be Extensible Quality instantiated.

In a Particulate World, there'll be Extensible Quality where, and only where, there are Particles, these being relatively small bounded regions of materially filled space, or spacetime. Each suffused with Extensible Quality, each particle is surrounded by a region that, as it's completely devoid of Quality, will also lack any real physical Propensity.

In a Perfectly Plenumate Physical World, Extensible Quality is instanced everywhere, and always, in the whole space (or spacetime) of the World. And, this Qualified space will be equally pervaded with physical Propensities; so, then, the World is filled with matter.

In a Plenumate World with Bubbles, finally, such well-Qualified materially filled space won't exhaust the space of the World. Rather, with each separated from the others by well-Qualified matter, there'll be many regions without Quality, and without anything of physical reality.

8. INTELLIGIBLE PHYSICAL REALITY AND A PRINCIPLE OF CONTINGENCY

In terms of our three kinds of basic property, what's required for there to be a humanly intelligible mind-independent *physical* reality, whether or not it's the World's only realm of reality? Without much detail, I'll try to give the question a serviceable answer.

First, some words about some necessary relations: For a World to feature *physical* reality, it *must* include at least one entity such that (1) it has *some* Spatiotemporal Properties—even if it may be, in a quite extreme case, only the property of being, in all directions, infinitely extensive, and (2) it has *some* Extensible Qualities—even if it may be, in a quite extreme case, only the property of being, everywhere and always, the very same Quality, and also (3) it has *some* Propensities—even if it may be, in a quite extreme case, only the Propensity to exemplify, in each place at each time, exactly the same Quality it exemplifies right there at the just previous time. The necessity just stressed is the same as with this more familiar proposition: As does any Euclidean geometrical closed solid, a physical entity precisely bounded by such a figure *must* be such that (1) it has *some* shape and also (2) it has *some* size.

As far as its being required of a physical entity that it instantiate some Extensible Quality, we need only recall the discussion of the previous section. As far as its being required that it instantiate some Spatiotemporal Property, we need only note that, for any thing to exemplify any Extensible Quality, there must be some space (or spacetime) that's occupied by that thing and suffused with that Quality. And as far as its being required that our physical entity instantiate some Propensity, we've already observed the point to hold even in the extreme case of a physically homogeneous reality.

Second, some complementary words about some contingent relations: Even with regard to something that's a *physical* entity, there is *no necessary connection* between (1) *which* Spatiotemporal Properties the thing has, and (2) *which* Qualities the thing has, and (3) *which* Propensities are those of that physical thing. The *lack* of necessity just stressed, and the *contingency* just indicated, is the same as with this proposition: As is true of the Euclidean closed solid figures that precisely bound them, physical entities precisely bounded by such figures *may* be a certain given *shape* even while being *any* one of *numerous distinct sizes* and, equally, they *may* be a certain given *size* even while being *any* one of *numerous distinct shapes*. As seems fitting, I'll call the proposition this paragraph aims to express the *Principle of Contingency (of Relations among the Basic Properties.)*

For an easy appreciation of this Principle, recall the most recent remarks on characterizing Particulate and Plenumate Worlds. Perfectly in line with them all, for each of numerous Particulate Worlds, for example, there may be specified distinct exemplifications of Extensible Qualities. Even with a World specified as being "fully monochromatic" in Extensible Quality, there are numerous Particulate Worlds to countenance: Some are some Worlds where all the Particles are Red; others have all Blue Particles, and so on. Equally, just as there are Plenumate Worlds where the Plenum is Red, there are others with a Blue Plenum, and so on.

For ease of exposition, we'll focus on Particulate Worlds, and we'll narrow the focus to Worlds whose Particles are like the Newtonian entities familiar from the quote from Foster. In these Worlds, each of enormously many Particles has the same "mass" and the same "amount of matter," and each will attract the others with a force that varies inversely with the square of the distance between the centers of the interacting Particles. In some of these monochromatic Newtonian Worlds, all the Particles are Red; in others, all are Blue Particles, and so on. Whereas that's old hat, we newly notice this: In *Tutti-Frutti* Particulate Worlds, many Particles are Red and many others Blue, with yet many others being Yellow, and also Green, and Brown, and Grey, and Silvery, and Goldenish, and so on. (Along with such Qualitative variety, in many Tutti-Frutti Worlds there's also much Qualitative stability; there, any Particle that's Red will always be Red, and it will never have any other Quality, not Blue, not Yellow, and so on.)

Our supposition of Tutti-Frutti Worlds is as perfectly intelligible as it's vividly imaginable. So, as I'll suggest, our Principle of Contingency may be both perfectly intelligible and entirely unobjectionable.

9. QUALITIES AS A FACTOR IN THE DEVELOPMENT OF PHYSICAL REALITY: A PROBLEM

As it often appears, the Qualities of physical things won't be much of a factor in determining the development of any physical reality. The problematic appearance is most acute with physically well-behaved Worlds that, while otherwise heterogeneous, lack Qualitative variation, as with many monochromatic Worlds. What are we to make of this appearance? This question poses the *Problem of the Roles for Qualities (in Physical Reality).*

Without thinking long and hard about the possible relations between physical entities and Qualities, there's little likelihood of encountering this Problem. So, as I expect, most contemporary philosophers will find this to be their first encounter with it. But many may quickly come to appreciate the puzzle quite well.

To that purpose, we'll focus on the comparison between a monochromatic Newtonian World and, on the other hand, a Tutti-Frutti Newtonian World. Except that the first has no Qualitative variety and the second has a great deal, the two Worlds may be exceedingly similar. So the behavior of the Tutti-Frutti World's Particles may precisely parallel the behavior of the Particles in the monochromatic World. And then all its Qualitative variety will make no difference to the physical development of the Tutti-Frutti World. But, then, are there *any* Worlds where Qualitative variety means much more than that for the development of the World's physical reality? All too often, it seems there are none. So, our Problem often appears acute.

To appreciate this Problem properly, however, it's also important that we not overestimate the apparent predicament: Our Problem is *not* to show how it might be true that, in *every* World with physical reality, all the Qualities of physical things are very significant factors in the physical development of the World. Nor is it to show even how it might be that, in every such World, *at least some* such Qualities are such significant factors. Indeed, it follows from the Principle of Contingency (of Relations among the Basic Properties) that there's no more chance of doing such a thing than of drawing a perfectly round square. Rather than any of that, our Problem asks us to show how it might be that, in *some* Worlds with physical reality, some Qualities of physical things are quite significant factors in the development of that reality.

10. THE PROBLEM OF THE ROLES FOR QUALITIES IN PHYSICAL REALITY: A SOLUTION

At least since Galileo, physics has made great progress by ignoring, it appears, thoughts as to Qualities. Because we're so impressed by that, when we contemplate physical Propensities such thoughts are excluded from our consideration. For progress with the Problem of the Roles for Qualities, we must rectify this intellectually restrictive situation.

To that end, I'll first characterize a World whose salient Propensities we find it easy to take seriously. Using this *Size-Propensity* World as a model for further characterization, I'll then characterize various *Quality-Propensity* Worlds, whose quite different Propensities we can also take seriously. When we fully acknowledge these Quality-directed Propensities, perhaps we'll have found a solution to our Problem.

First, we'll contemplate a monochromatic Particulate World: Whereas all the World's Particles have the very same Extensible Quality, perhaps *Grey*, these spherical Particles come in ten different Sizes, with many Particles of each Size. As regards both its volume and its "amount of matter," each of the smallest Particles is one-tenth as great as each of the largest Particles; each of the next smallest is two-tenths as great as a largest Particle, and so on. Now, each Particle has the Propensity to attract each of the others, and to be attracted by each of the others, with a force that varies directly with its Size (and, say, inversely with the square of the distance between its center and the centers of the each of the other Particles). It's easy enough to take seriously the thought that a World might work in that way.

Next, we'll contemplate a *multichromatic* Particulate World: Whereas all this World's Particles have the very same Size, perhaps the Size of the smallest Particles in the foregoing monochromatic World, these spherical Particles come in ten different "Achromatic Colors," with many Particles of each such Color. The lightest Particles, each of them Snow White, each have one-tenth "the amount of matter" of the darkest, each of which is Jet Black; each of the next lightest Particles, each of them Very Light Grey, is two-tenths as "massive" as the darkest, and so on. Here, each Particle has the Propensity to attract each of the others, and to be attracted by each of the others, with a force that varies directly with its *Qualitative Darkness* (and, say, inversely with the square of the distance). Though there might be *no good reason for it*, as I'll suggest, it may be quite hard to take seriously the thought that a World might work in *this* way.

To make progress on our Problem, we must overcome this difficulty. We must take seriously not only the thought that physical entities have Qualities, but also the thought that, at least in some Worlds, such entities have Propensities *with respect to Qualities*. In other words, we must adopt a *more inclusive mode of thinking* than the one that, apparently, proved so successful for Galileo and so many successors. For adopting such more inclusive thinking, what's most helpful, I imagine, is more experience with such thinking.

Accordingly, we may do well to contemplate a different contrasting pair of Particulate Worlds, again one a Size-Propensity World and the other a Quality-Propensity World. In both of these Worlds, there are four sorts of spherical Particles: Each exactly the same as the other in Quality, there are Large Red Particles and Small Red Particles, with the former being ten times the Size of the latter. And, each of them having a Quality very different from that of any Red Particle, there are Large Blue Particles and Small Blue Particles, the former being exactly the same size as the Large Red Particles and the latter the same as the Small Red Particles.

Now, in the first of our two Worlds, each Particle will have a Propensity to attract any Particle that's different from it in Size, and a Propensity to repel any Particle that's the same Size. In this World, the Large Red Particles and the Large Blue Particles will repel each other, as will the Small Red and the Small Blue Particles.

And the Large Particles, both Red and Blue, will attract, and will be attracted by, the Small Particles, Red and Blue. As I'm envisioning this World, when Particles attract, or repel, other Particles, it's *because* the former have Propensities *with respect to the very Size* the latter possess.

In the second World, no Particle will have any of those Propensities. Rather, each will have a Propensity to attract any Particle that's different from it in *Quality*, and a Propensity to repel any Particle that's the same Quality. In this World, the Red Particles, Large and Small, will attract, and will be attracted by, the Blue Particles, Large and Small. Far from repelling each other, here the Large Red Particles and the Large Blue Particles will *attract* each other. As I'm envisioning this other World, when Particles attract, or repel, other Particles, it's *because* the former have Propensities *with respect to the very Quality* the latter possess.

Toward gaining comfort with the good thought that, in addition to their having Qualities, many physical entities have Propensities *with respect to Qualities*, I've considered a couple of relevantly contrasting pairs of Particulate Worlds. Although the job is a tad more complex, we can do as well with, say, apt pairs of Plenumate Worlds. But even without actually encountering such a variety of illustrative examples, we see how the Qualities of physical entities can be a very significant factor in the development of physical reality.

11. CONCLUDING AND CONTINUING QUESTIONS

In comparison with most recent papers in philosophy, this one has been quite ambitious. But it is not nearly so ambitious as might appear. So it might sometimes seem that I have attempted an argument, very largely a priori, to the effect that, in this actual world, certain sorts of properties are basic properties, to wit, Spatiotemporals, Propensities, and Qualities. But of course, it's futile for anyone to argue, in such an a priori fashion, to any such substantial effect. And of course, I haven't really attempted anything like that much.

Much more modestly, I've argued only for conditional propositions. Conspicuous among them is this: If the scientifical metaphysic provides us with a tolerably accurate understanding of this world, then, as basic properties instanced in the actual world, there are Spatiotemporal Properties, and Propensities, and also Qualities. As we should bear in mind, it *might* be that this dominant worldview provides us with no such thing.

When the limits of the present essay are appreciated, we see large questions for future inquiry. Salient among them is this: If the scientifical metaphysic should be inadequate, then what might we best suppose are the basic properties of concrete reality? As a first pass at this fearful question, I hazard the conjecture that we should still countenance Qualities and Propensities, and perhaps Temporal Properties but no Spatial Properties.

In the present climate, I may be a greater friend of qualities than any other admittedly ambitious metaphysician. Yet I have doubts about that. Now, especially as this essay is dedicated to Jerome Shaffer, for a most salient example of work that fuels these doubts it's especially fitting to consider work from a most salient student of Professor Shaffer's. So, I ask: What does David Lewis denote with "qualities" in this schematic metaphysical passage?

> Many of the papers, here and in Volume I, seem to me in hindsight to fall into place within a prolonged campaign on behalf of the thesis I call "Humean supervenience."...
>
> Humean supervenience is named in honor of the greater denier of necessary connections. It is the doctrine that all there is to the world is a vast mosaic of local matters of particular fact, just one little thing and then another. (But it is no part of the thesis that these local matters are mental.) We have geometry: a system of external relations of spatio-temporal distance between points. Maybe points in spacetime itself, maybe point-sized bits of matter or aether or fields, maybe both. And at those points we have local qualities: perfectly natural intrinsic properties which need nothing bigger than a point at which to be instantiated. For short: we have an arrangement of qualities. And that is all. There is no difference without difference in the arrangement of qualities. All else supervenes on that.[10]

Though Lewis clearly uses "qualities" for *some* metaphysically basic properties, it's not clear what these properties are. Are his qualities much like our Qualities?

Following Russell, who followed Hume, in characterizing the Qualities I wanted there to be *some* connection, however indirect and tenuous, between the properties targeted and what we might experience, if only with the experience enjoyed in imaginative understanding. Without *any* connection to *any* such aid to intelligibility, what are we humans to understand by *anyone's* metaphysical reference to qualities? So it is that, in trying to say *something intelligible about what are* Qualities, I referred us to phenomenal qualities. Anyway, as Lewis's qualities are absolutely basic in his metaphysics, it should be asked: In humanly intelligible terms, what's there to say as to *what are* these items on whose arrangement, perhaps, all else supervenes?

This paper serves also to raise questions about the work of other students of Shaffer's, including the work in this very paper itself: When I said that, if the Extensible Qualities don't include phenomenal colors, then they should be strongly and deeply analogous to such colors, what sort of analogy could I sensibly have had in mind? More specifically, *in what respects* are such Extensible Qualities to be so analogous to phenomenal colors?

The previous section's discussion promotes the appearance that, for an intelligible conception of the actual world as comprising a heterogeneous physical reality, we need only a very few Qualities, and these may bear very much the same relations to each other as obtain among a *very few achromatic* phenomenal colors, perhaps much as obtain between just a certain Light Grey, say, and a certain Dark Grey. So, perhaps we can do a fair amount to sharpen our questions, and even to place limits on the range of sensible answers: What is it about the relations among, or even between, a few colors that, at least to a quite significant degree, must find a parallel in relations among Extensible Qualities, if thinking in terms of these Qualities will do much toward our having an adequate conception of physical reality?

As I've just observed, there's been the appearance that an adequate conception of what seems most of our world requires us to conceive only a very few Qualities as basic properties, perhaps just two Extensible Qualities. But that appearance might be illusory. To do justice to even just the Qualities apparently available in, or through, our immediate experience, perhaps we must regard as basic all the known phenomenal qualities, both such as seem Extensible and such as seem Nonextensible. Now, insofar as it may come to seem that the truth lies in such a more expansive vein, then, however restricted the academically respectable options of the time, serious philosophers will have to confront such extensive considerations as this final question: Might it possibly be that, rather than with the scientifical metaphysic, only with a more mentalistic worldview, maybe one where neither the physical nor the mental is most basic, will we have anything like an adequate conception of what's actually concrete reality?

NOTES

*In 1995, David Lewis dedicated a paper to Professor Jerome Shaffer, his undergraduate philosophy teacher, for the occasion of Jerry Shaffer's retirement from teaching philosophy: "Should a Materialist Believe in Qualia?" *Australasian Journal of Philosophy*, Vol. 73, 1995, 140–44, and *Faith and Philosophy*, 1995, 467–71. Now, I much more belatedly dedicate this paper to Shaffer, who was also my undergraduate philosophy teacher. Not only for his understanding and encouragement, but especially for that, I'll always be grateful to Jerry Shaffer.

For many years, Shaffer's thought hard about the relation between the mental and the physical. Now, I try to write usefully about part of what may be sustaining his thinking.

With this effort, help came from many others: In the fall of 1997, it was discussed by those regularly attending the graduate seminar I gave at New York University with John Gibbons. In addition to Gibbons, I gratefully thank Mark Bajakian, David Barnett, Geoff Helmreich, Peter Kung, Brian Leftow, Barbara Montero, and Sebastien Pennes. Grateful thanks also go to Robert Adams, David Armstrong, Gordon Belot, Michael Della Rocca, Hartry Field, Kit Fine, Brian Loar, Michael Lockwood, Barry Loewer, Graham Priest, Michael Rea, and Galen Strawson. For almost incredible efforts, very special great thanks go to John Carroll, John Heil, and C. B. (Charlie) Martin.

1. Bertrand Russell, *The Analysis of Matter* (London: Kegan Paul, 1927), 407. My own copy of the work is a reprinting by Dover Publications, New York, 1954. In that, see p. 402. Anyway, the quoted words are from the book's penultimate sentence.

2. Bertrand Russell, "Mind and Matter," in *Portraits from Memory* (Nottingham, England: Spokesman, 1956), 153. Until recently, truths like those just quoted were, for centuries, influential with serious philosophers. For a seminal example, "the father of modern philosophy" advances some in Descartes' *Principles of Philosophy*, part 1, paragraph 11: "How our mind is better known than our body," as in *The Philosophical Writings of Descartes*, trans. J. Cottingham, R. Stoothoff, and D. Murdoch, Vol. 1 (Cambridge: Cambridge University Press, 1985).

3. The quote is from David Armstrong, *Perception and the Physical World* (London: Routledge and Kegan Paul, New York: Humanities Press, 1961), 184. For Descartes's list, Armstrong refers us to "the second paragraph in the Fifth Meditation, and elsewhere."

4. Though some of Martin's writings on this subject are very hard to understand, others are helpfully clear. For work that helps clarify the fact that *dispositions are as categorical as anything*, see C. B. Martin, "Dispositions and Conditionals," *Philosophical Quarterly*, Vol. 44, 1994, and Martin's contribution to D. M. Armstrong, C. B. Martin, and U. T. Place, *Dispositions: A Debate*, ed. Tim Crane (London and New York: Routledge, 1996).

5. Bertrand Russell, *The Analysis of Matter* (London: Kegan Paul), 1927. My copy is a reprinting by Dover Publications, New York, 1954. In this reprinting, see pp. 263–64.

6. Michael Lockwood, *Mind, Brain and the Quantum* (Oxford: Basil Blackwell, 1989), pp. 164–65.

7. In P. H. Nidditch's edition of John Locke's *An Essay Concerning Human Understanding* (Oxford: Oxford University Press, 1975), the quoted words can be found on p. 123.

8. John Foster, *The Case for Idealism* (London: Routledge & Kegan Paul, 1982), 63. By contrast with the passages from it that I'll cite, much of the book is written in a very difficult technical style. From the parts I've managed to understand, I'm convinced that the work deserves serious study. A few of its last words convey the thrust of the courageous book: "I hope one day to . . . make the case for mentalism irresistible. But until then, I must be content with a Defence of idealism in its anti-realist and phenomenalist forms."

With his paper, "The Succinct Case for Idealism," in H. Robinson (ed.), *Objections to Physicalism* (Oxford: Oxford University Press, 1993), Foster gives an overview of the difficult work.

9. David Hume, *A Treatise of Human Nature*, book 1, part 4, section IV. My copy of the *Treatise* is the P. H. Nidditch edition, based on L. A. Selby-Bigge's earlier edition, from the Oxford University Press (Oxford, 1978). In this edition, the quoted words are on pp. 228–29.

10. David Lewis, "Introduction," *Philosophical Papers*, Vol. 2 (New York: Oxford University Press, 1986), *ix*.

Midwest Studies in Philosophy, XXIII (1999)

How Ontology Might Be Possible: Explanation and Inference in Metaphysics

CHRIS SWOYER

Even people who like philosophy often don't like metaphysics. Ontology in particular, with its arcane discussions of universals and particulars, is frequently cited as a paradigm of desiccated Scholasticism. I don't foresee the day when works on universals top the best-seller list, but I do think that updated versions of many traditional views in ontology can be more responsive to the real world and more interesting than is often supposed. To keep the discussion manageable, I will focus on properties or universals.

My proposal is that we need a reorientation in ontology, one in which we construe arguments for the existence of properties or universals as inferences to the best explanation. I think that many traditional and current arguments for the existence of properties are quite plausibly construed in this way, so the proposed reorientation wouldn't send us back to square one. But the proposal is not simply to attach a fashionable new label to venerable practices; it has three practical consequences.

First, we should acknowledge that there will virtually never be knockdown, demonstrative arguments for (or against) any theory of properties. But this doesn't mean that such theories are empty. They can, if successful, receive *cumulative confirmation* by helping to explain a variety of phenomena. On this picture, the goal is to make one's ontological case by piling up pieces of evidence in its favor. This means that the *unit of evaluation* in ontology should be a research program (rather than a paper or book or even someone's collected works) involving a number of explanations, independent tests, and refinements. Such programs are more likely to prosper if they are pursued by a number of philosophers working toward a common end, rather than by a solitary thinker.

Second, instead of beginning with a detailed picture of the nature of properties, we would gradually come to learn what properties are like by examining the *roles* they are postulated to fill. With luck, various explanations will allow us to triangulate in on the nature of properties. Of course it may turn out that no single kind of entity can perform all of the tasks properties have been invoked to perform. But if this is so, the approach suggested here would help us see that too.

Third, if properties can explain things of interest to philosophers who don't specialize in metaphysics, things like mathematical truth or the logical form of English sentences or the nature of natural laws, then they will appear more interesting. Unlike the substantial forms so derided by early modern philosophers as dormitive virtues, properties will pay their way by doing interesting and important work.

In section 1 I develop these themes in more detail, and in section 2 I quickly sketch a number of traditional arguments in metaphysics and urge that they are very naturally construed as inference to the best explanation. In section 3 I note how several traditional arguments for properties are naturally viewed as inferences to the best explanation, and in section 4 I make several preliminary points about explanation in philosophy. Sections 5–7 are the heart of the paper. Here I present three case studies, mathematical knowledge and truth, semantics of natural languages, and the nature of natural laws, in some detail and show how properties have recently been invoked in efforts to explain them. In the final section I draw several conclusions about inferences to the best explanation in ontology. Along the way I try to respond to the most serious arguments that such inferences are illegitimate, but my conclusions are more aporetic than I would wish. Still, if I am right there is no other metaphysical game in town. So if inference to the best explanation isn't possible in ontology, ontology isn't possible either.[1]

1. SUPERANNUATED IDEALS

There are two reasons for regarding most of the familiar arguments for the existence of properties as inferences to the best explanation. First, on the more traditional construals of such arguments, they are utter failures. Second, many of the arguments look like inferences to the best explanation, and they often make good sense if we interpret them that way. I will consider these points in turn.

1.1. Ontology as Demonstration

The *demonstrative ideal* of ontology as fundamental, first philosophy still enjoys considerable currency. On this picture, ontology is a demonstrative, a priori enterprise that proceeds from secure premises, step by deductively valid step, to secure conclusions. The traditional standards for security were very high, requiring necessary, a priori, self-evident premises. After centuries of failure, philosophers have lowered their standards, and nowadays most would gladly settle for deductions from premises that were uncontroversially true. It's a noble ideal, but it doesn't work. If we judge arguments in metaphysics by these standards they not only fail—*they fail miserably*. Even a philosophical novice, for example, can often spot seven different reasons why the teleological and the cosmological arguments are unsound.

Furthermore, there are always competing answers to the Big Questions in philosophy, and to demonstrate that our favorite answer to one of them is right, we would have to demonstrate that all the competing answers, indeed *all possible competing answers*, are wrong. But when we look at the ways philosophers actually argue against rival positions we find knockdown arguments only in those rare instances where a view can be shown inconsistent (and even here a well-chosen epicycle or two can usually save the day). Instead we typically find arguments that turn on delicate judgments about simplicity, appropriateness of primitive notions, and the like.

1.2. Ontology as Conceptual Analysis

In this century philosophers have sometimes seen philosophy as conceptual analysis, and this might yield secure conclusions without requiring incontrovertible first principles. But quite apart from doubts about whether there is such a thing as conceptual analysis, what concepts could the proponent of properties be analyzing? We don't seem to have any univocal and precise everyday conception of properties, much less of universals. Moreover, none of the familiar arguments for the existence of properties look anything like Socrates's probings about the nature of piety or recent epistemologists' attempts to plumb our intuitions about the conditions under which "*x* knows that *p*."

1.3. Ontology as Reduction

Earlier in this century some philosophers saw the task of ontology as reduction, as showing that some things are really nothing over and above certain other things. The idea here is that there is an ontological bedrock; certain kinds of things are ontologically basic, and everything else somehow derives from them. On this conception the arguments for the existence of certain entities are not deductions from first principles. Rather, a philosopher argues that we can't really reduce certain sorts of things away, but that we can reduce many other things to them. Perhaps, for example, we can reduce physical objects to bundles of properties or numbers to properties.

At one time the typical reductionist's aim was epistemological security. But hopes for a foundationalist epistemology have faded, and nowadays the most common motivation for ontological reduction is ontological economy. The goal is to effect a *purge*, liquidating as many would-be items in our ontology as possible. But although no one wants metaphysical Rube Goldberg machines, reductionist projects typically award parsimony a disproportionate role, making it the most important thing when it is just one good thing among many. Quite apart from this, however, the fact is that reductionist programs don't work. There are no good reasons to think that such projects *can* succeed and countless failures to suggest they can't. Finally, even if one reduction comes close to succeeding, there will be many others that work equally well, and there will typically be no principled way to choose among them (we will return to this issue in section 5.4).

1.4. Applications of Theories Confirmed Elsewhere

Nowadays philosophers sometimes propose an account of some phenomenon, say mental causation or measurement, that relies on properties. Frequently they help themselves to properties with the causal remark that there are good independent reasons to believe that properties exist, so they will be using them without defending them. They can't be faulted for this; life is short, and a philosopher can't be expected to rehearse a detailed defense of properties each time she wants to make use of them. Still, support for the claim that properties exist must originate *somewhere*. On the view I am urging, it comes, a bit at a time, from *each* project that uses properties in a plausible explanation.

Often philosophers agree, since after their claim that there are good independent reasons to think that properties exist, they slip in the remark that if their current project is successful it adds one more reason to the list. My recommendation is that we take this addendum seriously. Projects that employ properties to explain something are, *in the very process of doing this*, arguments that properties exist. This much shouldn't be controversial. But I will also be defending the stronger thesis that this is the *only* plausible kind of argument for the existence of properties.

In short, many of the traditional conceptions of ontology just don't wash. At best they fit uneasily with philosophical practice, and often they make nonsense of it. But to dislodge such ideals, even when our practices rarely match them, we need an alternative. The claim that the most plausible arguments for properties are inferences to the best explanation, that the existence of properties is the best explanation of the success of the projects that employ them, is meant to provide just that.

2. A NEW IDEAL: ONTOLOGY AS INFERENCE TO THE BEST EXPLANATION

The style of argument that Peirce calls *abduction* and that more recent writers call *inference to the best explanation* is far more modest and fallibilistic than traditional pictures of metaphysical argument. As with explanation in general, there is no generally accepted account of inference to the best explanation. As we proceed I hope to shed some light on it, but to get things started we can think of it like this: Some phenomenon is noted. A hypothesis is proposed that, if true, would explain it. Then, to the extent that the hypothesis offers a better explanation than its competitors, we have some reason to suppose that it is true and that any entities it postulates really *do* exist. In this section I will say a bit more about the consequences of taking this seriously.

2.1. Cumulative Support

In many types of inquiry, from the courtroom to the laboratory, we marshal support for a hypothesis by painstakingly piling up pieces of evidence of its behalf. No single bit of evidence establishes our case, but the cumulative weight of the evidence often makes a hypothesis quite plausible. If this is true of arguments for the existence of properties, we shouldn't evaluate them in an all-or-none way, as though they must prove their case if they are to be worth considering. Instead we should consider the contribution each argument makes to the sum total of evidence supporting a given hypothesis about properties.

2.2. Explanatory Roles: Properties Are as Properties Do

Viewing arguments for the existence of properties as inferences to the best explanation also provides a principled way to learn what properties are *like*. If they are invoked to play definite explanatory roles, we can ask what they would *have* to be like in order to play the roles they are called on to fill. What, for example, would their existence or identity conditions have to be for them to explain causation? The answers to such questions won't come easily, for there are bound to be disagreements about the merits of various explanations. Still, if properties can explain a number of different things, this would enable us to triangulate in on their nature using a metaphysical counterpart of Whewell's method of the *consilience of inductions*.

Just over a century ago Bradley characterized metaphysics as the finding of bad reasons for things we believe on instinct (adding that to find such reasons is no less an instinct). Nowadays it would be closer to the truth to characterize it as the formalization of things we believe on instinct (with formalization perhaps on its way to becoming an instinct itself). But if we learn about properties bit by bit, then the plodding work of a detective is a better model for the development of an account of properties than the axiomatic projects of set theorists or topologists. Formalization is often useful, but it should be judged by its fruits rather than the intuitive plausibility of its axioms.

It may turn out that no single kind of entity could play all the roles properties have been invoked to fill. It may be, for example, that the identity or existence conditions of entities well suited to one task are ill suited for entities with a different job to do. If so, what we thought of as properties may fragment into several different kinds of entities. If this is how things turn out, it's how they turn out. But as fragmentation increases, cumulative support and consilience will begin to slip away.

2.3. Making Properties More Interesting

Discussions or properties sometimes seem boring or barren because they are so isolated from other topics. But if we can use properties to help solve problems about the nature of mathematical truth or the semantics of natural languages or the nature of natural laws, they become more interesting because they bear on issues that are interesting.

2.4. Theories of Properties

Properties alone can't explain much. What does the explaining is a *theory* of properties, an *account* of what they are like and how they do the things they are called on to do. In some cases the account might be rather minimal, but in others (e.g., in accounts that use properties to explain mathematical truth or logical form) it will have to be much more detailed, and it will also require the aid of auxiliary hypotheses.

2.5. Nobody Does It Better

A theory doesn't get top billing for explaining something if a competing theory explains it better. Hence, a champion of a theory of properties will have to buttress her explanations with arguments that rival accounts, both competing realist theories as well as the going versions of nominalism and conceptualism, cannot explain some phenomenon or that they cannot explain it as well as her account can. If the demonstrative ideal for ontology were sound such arguments should aim to be knockdown, but in fact almost none of them come close. Once the weakest theories have been eliminated, disputes among the survivors often turn on subtle trade-offs between things, like ontological parsimony or simplicity of primitive notions, that everyone agrees are desirable. Indeed, it is hard to see how they could proceed in any other way.

2.6. The Fundamental Ontological Trade-Off

We will see several such trade-offs below, but one occurs so frequently that it is worth noting now. I will call it *the fundamental ontological trade-off*. It is the perennial trade-off between a rich, abundant ontology with what looks like great explanatory power, on the one hand, and a more modest ontology that promises more epistemological security, on the other. The tension is reflected in the frequent charge that with so much machinery, all those properties or propositions or possible worlds, it's not surprising that an abundant theory can explain a great deal. But, the worry continues, it is difficult to believe in the existence of all that machinery. We will see that this skepticism can be backed by arguments that rich ontologies often require entities we couldn't know about or talk about and, ironically, that this undermines their ability to account for the very things they were introduced to explain. Of course the choice needn't be all or none—feast on an abundant realm of properties of famine with few or none—and a principled middle ground is always worth striving for. But a trade-off here can seldom be avoided.

3. HISTORICAL PRECEDENTS

In this section I will gesture, quite superficially, toward several traditional arguments in metaphysics and note how they are plausibly construed as inferences to the best explanation. I won't go into detail, much less urge that all of these explanations are compelling. The point is simply to indicate how a wide range of arguments that look weak when judged by the demonstrative ideal look much stronger when construed as inferences to the best explanation.

3.1. Substance, God, and Senses

Various philosophical entities have been defended on the grounds that they explain one thing or another. For example, some of the traditional arguments for the existence of God aim to show that His existence would explain what would otherwise be puzzling features of the world, including its intricacy, its order, and even its existence. The concept of substance has also been introduced to explain such things as the persistence of things through change or the individuation of persons and physical objects.

In more recent times facts have been introduced to explain truth (construed as correspondence to the facts), and Fregean Senses, propositions, and possible worlds have be postulated to explain a host of phenomena involving meaning and modality. For example, it has been argued that if words have senses we could explain why some identity statements are informative and account for certain puzzling features of sentences ascribing propositional attitudes.

None of the arguments for (or against) the existence of such entities look like the last word on any of these matters (the arguments against senses come the closest, though even here there is room to maneuver). And once we abandon the demonstrative ideal, it is difficult to see how to view these arguments except as attempts at inference to the best explanation.

This is not to say that the champions of these (putative) entities actually viewed themselves as proposing inferences to the best explanation. Often they construed their argument as an inference to the *only remotely plausible explanation* or an inference to the *only explanation anyone in their right mind would accept* or, even, as an inference to the *only possible* explanation.

In a famous passage Paley describes a watch washed up on the shore. He urges that its intricate workings would naturally lead us to infer that it had been designed by a being with intelligence and skill. It now seems plausible to view this as a proposed inference to the best explanation. The best explanation for the watch is an intelligent designer; analogously, the argument continues, the best explanation for the endlessly intricate world around us is a designer with incomparably more intelligence and skill than the watchmaker. Such an argument faces formidable difficulties, many of which had been noted by Hume (unbeknownst to Paley) before Paley set pen to paper. Still, even those of us who reject Paley's conclusion can, I think, view his discussion as a serious abductive argument that might form part of a cumulative case for the existence of God. This isn't how Paley sees it, though, for he goes on to urge that the existence of God is the *only possible explanation* for the intricacy and order of the world. He tells us that we think this inference to be "inevitable, that the watch must have had a maker" who designed it to tell time (Paley 1802, chap. 1).

In short, my proposal is not that the historical figures who gave the sorts of arguments alluded to here saw themselves as proposing inferences to the best explanation. It is instead a claim about how *we* should judge and evaluate these arguments *today*, in trying to decide whether they point in the direction of accounts that could be plausible for us, here and now. The reason for this is that none of these arguments look very good when judged by the demonstrative ideal. But some look much better when viewed as inferences to the best explanation, and they look better still if they are part of a cumulative case for the conclusion that God or senses or facts exist.

3.2. Universals: The Thirteen Ways

In this subsection I will note thirteen arguments for the existence of properties that are quite plausibly construed as inferences to the best explanation. The arguments vary greatly in plausibility, and they are not intended to indicate a golden, thirteen-way path to platonism. But a mixed bag like this usefully illustrates the range of things that properties have been invoked to explain. In sections 5–7 I will consider several of these cases in more detail.

1. *Resemblance and Qualitative Recurrence.* Some things are alike in certain ways—they have the same color or shape or rest mass—and other things differ. Possession of a common property, for example, a given shade of red, or a mass of 3 kilograms, has often been thought to explain such resemblance, whereas possession of different color properties or mass properties explains their

differences. This has been a traditional motivation for realism with respect to universals, and it continues to motivate many realists today (e.g., Armstrong 1984, 250; cf. Butchvarov 1966).

2. *Recognition*. Many philosophers have argued that an organism's ability to recognize and classify new and novel things as red, circular, or the like is best explained by the hypothesis that the things have a common property, for example, *redness* or *circularity*, and that the organism has somehow learned to recognize it.
3. *A Priori Knowledge*. Some philosophers have argued that the possibility of a priori knowledge is not easily explained unless it is viewed as knowledge of relations among universals (e.g., Russell 1912, chap. 10).
4. *Knowledge versus Belief*. Plato attempted to explain the difference between knowledge and belief by arguing that universals (the Forms) are the objects of the former but not the latter (e.g., *Timaeus*, 51d3ff).
5. *Change*. From Parmenides on, the problem of flux vexed Greek thinkers. Plato argued that change is only possible against a background of things that do not change, and he urged that the Forms provided this (*Theaetetus*, 181c–183b; *Cratylus*, 439d3ff). Nowadays we are likely to reject the demand for some permanent backdrop for change, but properties may still be cited in a quite different account of change. If an individual *a* is red all over at one time and green all over later, then *a* alone can't explain the change. After all, the object *a* persists throughout. But we can explain the alteration by noting that *a* exemplifies the property *redness* at an earlier time and the property *greenness* later.
6. *Causal powers*. Objects have various powers or dispositions, and their properties are often cited to explain these. The liquid in the glass caused the litmus paper to turn blue because the liquid is an alkaline (not because the liquid also happens to be blue); the Earth exerts a gravitational force on the moon because of their respective gravitational masses; smoking tends to cause cancer. Explanations frequently advert to properties, often because they cite causes: the liquid's being an alkaline explains why it turned the litmus paper blue.
7. *Mathematics*. Many philosophers have believed that numbers could be "reduced" to sets, but in the last couple of decades several philosophers have argued that a reduction of mathematics to property theory has various advantages over this more traditional approach. On such accounts we explain things like the truth conditions of the sentences of number theory by construing their subjects and predicates as referring to properties and relations of a certain kind (e.g., Bealer 1982, chaps. 5–6; Jubien 1989; Pollard and Martin 1986). We will return to this example in section 5.
8. *Semantics of General Terms*. General terms like "red" apply to some things but not to others. Many thinkers, ancient and modern, have argued that the possession of a common property (together with certain linguistic conventions) would explain why general terms apply to the things that they do. Thus, Plato noted that "we are in the habit of postulating one unique Form for each plurality of objects to which we apply a common name" (*Republic*, 596A; see also *Phaedo*, 78e; *Timaeus*, 52a; *Parmenides*, 133d; Russell 1912, 93).

9. *Logical Form.* Certain sentences appear to quantify over properties ("There are no acquired characteristics") or to contain singular term in subject position that seem to be anaphorically linked to predicates earlier in the sentence ("John is tall, and that is a good property for a basketball player"). Some philosophers and linguists have tried to explain the semantic behavior of such sentences, including the logical relations (like entailment) among them, by ascribing truth conditions to them in which linguistic expressions (predicates, abstract singular terms, some pronouns) denote or express properties. We will return to this example in section 6.
10. *Laws of Nature.* Some philosophers have argued that viewing natural laws as relations among properties provides the best explanation of various features of laws, including their ability to be confirmed by their instances, support counterfactuals, explain empirical phenomena, and be discovered rather than invented (Armstrong 1978; Dretske 1977; Tooley 1977; Swoyer 1982). We will return to this example in section 7.
11. *Measurement.* The view that what we directly measure are the properties of things has been held to explain why alternative procedures can be used for measuring the same magnitude, the possibility of measurement errors, the use of properties (e.g., a given wavelength of light) to provide basic units of measurement, and to show how to integrate facts about measurement into a realist account of laws and causation (Swoyer 1987, §1; cf. Mundy 1987).
12. *Intensional Logic.* It is often argued that a semantic account of linguistic contexts containing intensional idioms like *believes*, *imagines*, and *desires* requires properties (e.g., Bealer 1982; Menzel 1993; Zalta 1983, 1988).
13. *Cognitive Phenomena and Content.* It has also been urged that philosophical explanations of such mental states as beliefs, imaginings, and desires require properties (e.g., Zalta 1988).

In some cases, for instance, 4, the arguments may seem weak or even pointless. Some seem weak because they are, but the appearance of pointlessness is more interesting. Perhaps one reason for it is that judgments about the relative importance of the things needing explanation alter over time. During the Middle Ages, for example, theological phenomena were very important, and the Trinity and the Eucharist were high on the list of things a philosopher needed to explain. Nowadays far more philosophers yearn for naturalistically respectable explanations of things like causation or the nature of natural laws. But my point here is concerns the form of these arguments (construed as charitably as possible) rather than their plausibility. In sections 5–7 we will consider three of these cases in more detail, but it will be useful to note two points first.

4. CURRENT EXPLANATIONS

4.1. Synonyms of "Explain"

The word "explain" often figures explicitly in arguments for the existence of properties. One reason, we are told, to think that there are properties is that their existence would *explain* qualitative recurrence or some tricky feature of logical form. But even when the word "explain" is absent, we often find claims that some phenomenon holds *in virtue of*, or *because of*, this or that property, that a property is the *ground* or *foundation* of the some phenomenon, or that a property is (in part) the *truth maker* for a sentence describing the phenomenon. The role of such expressions is to give reasons, to answer why-questions, and this is a central point of explanation.

4.2. Preliminary Doubts

Various doubts can be raised about inference to the best explanation in philosophy. We will be in a better position to evaluate them once we have inspected the case studies in subsequent sections, but I want to acknowledge several of them here.

4.2.1. *First challenge: There is nothing to explain.* The first challenge is that the things the realist wants to explain are illusory. For example, very able philosophers have denied that the sentences of mathematics have truth values, that words have determinate semantic values, and that there are any natural laws. Some of these challenges may be more plausible than others, but all three represent minority views, and to keep things manageable I will simply assume that various features of arithmetic, the semantics of English, and natural laws are genuine things that might be capable of philosophical explanation.

4.2.2. *Second challenge: No explanation is required.* Some philosophers agree that such phenomena are genuine but deny that they require any special, philosophical sort of explanation. Deflationary accounts of reference and truth often have this consequence; for example, on such views sentences or arithmetic do have truth values, but there are no deep philosophical explanation of their truth conditions. This line may be more plausible in some cases than in others, but these issues will be easier to evaluate once we have examined some concrete cases.

4.2.3. *Third challenge: Philosophical explanation is impossible.* Finally, there can be doubts about the nature of ontological explanation itself. Is it like scientific explanation, or is it somehow unique? Whether it is much like scientific explanation depends on what scientific explanation is like, and there is nothing like a consensus about this. I think that many discussions of scientific explanation involve false dilemmas and that there are a number of distinct explanatory virtues. (See Salmon 1989, 180ff, for one way of defending this claim.) Often these virtues accompany each other, but like most good things they are sometimes in tension. Some of the explanatory virtues in science, for example, pinpointing causal mechanisms or citing statistically relevant information, are not likely to be found in ontology, but others, like unification, might be. The only way to get clearer on the matter, though, is to consider examples.

Some of the realist's traditional *explananda*, for example, resemblance and qualitative recurrence, are still with us. But taken alone, the explanations properties provide for such things are rather thin, and they bear on few topics outside of ontology itself. In the next three sections I will examine three topics—arithmetic, semantics, and natural laws—that seem to require more elaborate explanations that do bear on topics of wider philosophical interest.

5. MATHEMATICS

5.1. Mathematics: What Is to Be Explained

Number theory (arithmetic) is only a small portion of mathematics. It is the part that has received the most philosophical attention, however, and many of the philosophical issues in other parts are similar to the problems that arise here, so I will focus on it. There are disagreements over which features of number theory require explanation, but many philosophers would accept something like the following list.

1. At least many of the statements of arithmetic are either true or false.
2. Statements in number theory have the truth values they do quite independently of human language and thought. Fermat's last theorem was true before Andrew Wiles proved it, and it would still have been true even if no one had ever discovered a proof.
3. The surface syntax of many sentences in arithmetic strongly suggests that they contain singular terms that refer to things and predicates that express properties and relations. For example, the surface form of "6 > 2" looks a lot like that of "Sam is taller than Ted," which at least suggests that "6" and "2" refer to objects and that ">" expresses a binary relation.
4. Claims about mathematics must be capable of justification by proofs. (In its more recondite regions this is the only method of justification.) Proofs employ inference rules that are in turn justified by the fact that they are necessarily truth-preserving. So a philosophical account of number theory should explain how standard modes of inference (from *modus ponens* to mathematical induction) can legitimately be applied to arithmetical claims.
5. The statements of number theory necessarily have the truth values that they do.
6. It is possible to have reliable and justified beliefs and, indeed, knowledge in mathematics.
7. It is possible to have a priori knowledge of many mathematical truths.

Some of these items (like the claim that sentences of number theory can be true or false) are more central than others (like the claim about apparent logical form). But other things being equal, most philosophers would agree, the more of them a theory can explain, the better.

5.2. Mathematics: How Properties Explain

My aim now is to indicate how recent theories of properties have been mobilized in attempts to explain the items on this list. I will consider questions about the plausibility of these explanations later in the paper.

The dominant program in the foundations of mathematics for over a century has been what might be called *identificationism*. The idea is to *identify* the natural numbers with some other sort of things (or, better, with things that we hadn't realized were really the numbers). Frege and Russell in effect identified numbers with sets (though neither thought of their enterprise literally in terms of sets), and Zermelo, von Neumann, and many others since identified numbers with sets quite explicitly.

But there is nothing about identificationism that requires that numbers be identified with sets, and in recent years several philosophers (e.g., Bealer 1982, chaps. 5–6; Pollard and Martin 1986; Jubien 1989) have argued that we should instead identify numbers with properties.

As we will see in section 5.4, there can be various motivations for a property-based identificationism. But whatever the rationale, the goal is to define property-theoretic proxies of arithmetical creatures (like zero and successor), and then to prove that these induce translations that carry truths of arithmetic to truths of the reducing property theory and carry falsehoods to falsehoods. The basic recipe goes as follows.

First, find a realm of properties to be the natural numbers. Since there is a countable infinity of natural numbers, we need a realm with at least a countable infinity of properties.

Second, the sequence of natural numbers is structured in a very special way (it's called an ω-sequence). Sequences with this structure have a unique first member and no repetitions, and each member has a unique member coming right after it. So we must postulate some structure in our realm of properties so that they form (or contain) an ω-sequence.

Third, identify some particular property in our realm of properties (the first in the sequence) with zero and some relation with the successor relation, and then identify the natural numbers with all of the objects in the realm that bear the ancestral of this relation to the object we paired up with zero (much as von Neumann identified 0 with the empty set and the successor of x with $x \cup \{x\}$).

Fourth, the relevant features of the natural numbers are distilled in Peano's Postulates. So we must prove that we can derive our property-theoretic translations of Peano's Postulates (or their equivalents, or at least a first-order approximation) from (definitional extensions) of the first principles of our theory of properties.

There are two very general ways to proceed. The first employs a very powerful property theory that includes axioms analogous to those of familiar set theories (minus the axiom of extensionality, and perhaps with other minor emendations). On this approach the above steps are straightforward, since they retrace much of the same ground as set-theoretic versions of identificationism.

The second approach identifies numbers with properties, at least some of which are exemplified in the actual world (e.g., Armstrong 1989, chap. 9; Bigelow and Pargetter 1990). Champions of this approach must work harder to find all the properties they need to serve as the natural numbers (to say nothing of the real numbers or transfinite cardinals), since they cannot simply postulate them with a set of axioms at the outset. The two approaches have different strengths and weaknesses (I have discussed the second approach in Swoyer 1996, §5), but their explanations of most of the items on our list proceed in similar ways.

5.3. Mathematics: The Explanations

In addition to the claim that there is a realm of properties of the appropriate size with the appropriate structure, property-based identificationism requires several auxiliary hypotheses in order to explain anything. The central auxiliaries are (i) the *metaphysical* hypothesis that the natural numbers really are just the properties our identificatory scheme says they are, and (ii) the *semantic* hypothesis that the numerals and arithmetic predicates of natural languages refer to or express the appropriate properties ("0" refers to the property we identify as zero, etc.).

Once this machinery is in place it is straightforward to explain the first four items on our list. The syntax of the simple sentences of arithmetic seems to involve singular terms that refer to numbers (item 3) because that is precisely what they do. Moreover, since the terms are correlated with mind-independent properties standing in the appropriate mind-independent relations, we can explain the mind-independent truth values of sentences of number theory (items 1 and 2). And since we can give a standard account of the truth conditions of the sentences of arithmetic in first-order (or, if you prefer, second-order) logic, we explain the applicability of standard rules of inference (item 4) by noting that the rules necessarily preserve truth so defined.

Many philosophers hold that the sentences of number theory *necessarily* have the truth values that they do (item 5). In the present context this requires an infinite collection of properties that *exist necessarily*. So accounts like Armstrong's that treat properties as contingent beings will either have severe problems explaining this putative datum or else they will have to explain it away.

The last two (putative) *explananda* are epistemological. We can have reliable, justified beliefs about arithmetic, for example, that 1 + 1 = 2 (item 6). Furthermore, according to many philosophers we can have a priori knowledge of mathematical truths (item 7). Accounts like Armstrong's that identify numbers with properties exemplified in the natural world have an edge with item 6, since it is a bit easier to see how we might come to know something about them, but this gives them a harder time with item 7. But any account of these two *explananda* will require substantive empirical auxiliary hypotheses about human cognition, and there are no well-confirmed hypotheses of this sort available today.

5.3.1. *Best explanations versus indispensability arguments.* It is worth pausing briefly to contrast such accounts with Quine's influential indispensability argument. Quine develops his argument in the context of a holistic account of theory confirmation. Our beliefs—our total body of theory—confront the tribunal of evidence as a whole, and since our scientific theory incorporates claims that seem to quantify over numbers (or sets, to which Quine thinks numbers can be reduced), the claim that numbers exist is confirmed every time we confirm any part of our overall theory about the world.

Quine's account *can* be reconstrued as a inference to the best overall explanation, but one needn't endorse his sprawling holism to conclude that numbers or sets or properties exist because their existence explains various things. In science and in daily life we certainly do bring different bits of evidence to bear on different subsets of our beliefs or different parts of our general theories. (See Glymour 1980 for an account of one way this might work.) It is not clear why things should be different in philosophy. At all events, the seven *explananda* on the list above are quite specifically about mathematics, and one can try to explain them without any commitment to holism whatsoever.

5.4. Mathematics: Why Explanations Using Properties Are Best

Thus far we have examined the property theorist's claims that properties, together with several auxiliary hypotheses, can explain the various items on our list of *explananda*. Her next step in constructing an inference to the best explanation is to argue that her account provides a *better* explanation than the available alternatives.

5.4.1. *The competition.* The word *available* is important. There is no general way to show that a property theorist's account of arithmetic provides better explanations than all possible rivals. Indeed, arguments that one theory provides a better explanation of mathematical phenomena than another does often turn on quite detailed and specific features of the two accounts.

Later we will consider cases where properties have features, for example, intensional identity conditions, that might enable them to explain phenomena that extensional creatures like sets cannot. But mathematical phenomena are extensional, and there are two serious realist alternatives to property identificationism. The first is the view that the natural numbers are unique abstract objects that aren't identical with sets or properties or anything else. The second is a family of views whose members identify numbers with sets in one way or another.

Like property identificationism, both of these views seem well suited to explaining the early items on our list involving truth and objectivity, whereas all three rivals fare less well in explaining the later items involving epistemology. Moreover, both of property identificationism's rivals have advantages over it. The view that there are natural numbers, period, doesn't require any formal account of properties (or, for that matter, sets), it's extensional, and it takes many of our naive intuitions about numbers at face value. And the view that the natural numbers are sets, though less intuitive, has its natural home in an extensional theory of sets that has been developed and explored over many decades, and that now provides a powerful and unified framework in which most of mathematics can be developed. So a property theorist must argue that the apparent strengths of these views are illusory or else that properties offer enough advantages to compensate for these disadvantages. The first response is difficult for a realist to defend, but the second is more promising.

5.4.2. *We need them anyway.* It is difficult to argue that properties are better than numbers or sets as long as we focus solely on mathematics. The best arguments for property identificationism are those that claim that we need properties for tasks outside of the philosophy of mathematics; since we need them anyway, we should use them in our philosophy of mathematics. They can do all of the work of sets (or numbers) and more besides. At this point the property theorist might argue sets and numbers don't exist (on grounds of ontological parsimony), or he might argue that sets are derivative, constructible from certain sorts of properties (cf. Bealer 1982, chaps. 5–6).

In short, the argument goes, the view that sets (or just plain numbers) afford better philosophical accounts of arithmetic results from a metaphysical myopia. If we step back from mathematics and consider the bigger picture, we find that we need only one sort of entity, properties, to explain things in a variety of domains. So properties provide the best global, overall explanation. This does mean that champions of properties have little hope of making their case by focusing exclusively on mathematics. The arguments in this realm will need buttressing by arguments from other areas, which of course fits nicely with the claim that the case for the existence of properties will be cumulative. Still, arithmetic is a good place to begin, since it provides especially clear *explananda* and explanations.

5.4.3. *Other fronts: Family quarrels.* To streamline exposition I have treated property identificationism as a generic view, but different philosophers develop this approach in different ways, and there are family quarrels among them. The important point here is that the arguments each side gives for thinking its explanations better than its rival's are far from demonstrative. Indeed, there will typically be limiting cases in which it will be difficult to give *any* argument that one account is better than certain of its rivals. For if there is one way to pair numbers with the properties postulated by a given theory of properties, there will be many ways, and it will often be difficult to make any case that one out of the many possible pairings delivers the Metaphysical Truth. (This point was stressed by Benacerraf [1965] about attempts to identify numbers with sets, but it arises equally for attempts to identify numbers with properties, cf. Swoyer 1996, §5.)

5.4.4. *Other fronts: Antirealists.* The property identificationist also has to fight on a broader front against various antirealist views of mathematics. Here the disputes are more about what the phenomena are. For example, many people agree that the sentences of arithmetic certainly *seem* to have truth values. The realist will insist that we take this appearance at face value, whereas the antirealist will try to explain it away. But here again, it is difficult to see how either side could give a demonstrative argument that the other side is wrong. As always, there are pluses and minuses.

To begin with, there is the fundamental ontological trade-off, the recurring tension between an opulent ontology (that aims to account for a host of things) and a more modest ontology with greater epistemological security. The more we postulate, the harder it is to believe in all of it, and very rich theories of properties court the danger of paradox (a nice word for inconsistency). If numbers are abstract objects it may seem that we can explain how claims about them can be timelessly and necessarily true. But it becomes harder to see how we can get into epistemic touch with them, and this raises questions about whether we could even have beliefs *about them*, much less justified beliefs. This in turn raises questions about how we could link our words to them; if we can't, this would subvert a number of the explanations (e.g., of logical form) that properties were introduced to provide.

This dialectic is especially dramatic in disputes between realists and antirealists, but it can arise in family quarrels between identificationists. For example, someone like Armstrong can argue that since he identifies numbers with properties that are instantiated in the actual world, we have epistemic access to them in a way that we couldn't have to properties existing outside space and time.

There are other trade-offs as well. Is a simple account of the logical form of the sentences of arithmetic that is homogeneous with a semantics for the rest of English (to the extent that we have one) sufficiently valuable to justify a rich ontology? (A nominalistic program like Hellman's [1989], which requires a lot of reparsing, looks more plausible if the answer is "no.") Is it better to have a richly detailed explanation of a narrower range of phenomena or a less detailed explanation of a wider range? Should we accept more entities in order to have fewer primitive notions? Are the primitives of one account more perspicuous than those of another, and how much should it matter if they aren't? Such considerations are unavoidable—what else *could* we go on? But once we eliminate the most obviously unpromising theories, the issues among those that remain are often nebulous or delicate, and arguments about them rarely look demonstrative.

There are various accounts in the foundations of mathematics that I haven't considered, but I have tried to say enough to make three claims plausible. First, there are good arguments for property identificationism, and most of them turn on the ability of properties to *explain* various mathematical phenomena. Second, most of these arguments proceed in tandem with arguments that property identificationism (or some particular version of it) provides *better* explanations than its rivals. Third, although the arguments in both of these stages may be strong, they are *not demonstrative*, and there is little prospect of strengthening them so that they are. If this is right, it is difficult to resist the conclusion that such arguments are attempts to provide inferences to the best explanation.

6. SEMANTICS AND LOGICAL FORM

Language and logic have always been a fruitful source of data for ontologists. In the paper in which he announced his theory of definite descriptions, Russell said that a logical theory should be tested by its capacity for dealing with puzzles, and he urged that his theory solved three problems about substitutivity, truth, and negative existentials. Russell's motivations were partly metaphysical and epistemological, but it is quite possible to view his theory of descriptions as a piece of semantic theory about the meanings of English definite descriptions. And he is surely right that if a theory explains things that its rivals cannot, things like the informativeness of certain identity statements or the nonsubstitutivity of coreferential expressions in belief contexts, that is a mark in its favor.

In recent years several philosophers and linguists have devised theories of properties with the express purpose of providing semantic theories of natural language (e.g., Chierchia and Turner 1988), and several other writers have invoked properties to account for various semantic features of natural language (e.g., Bealer 1982; Zalta 1983, 1988; Menzel 1993).

6.1. Semantics: What Is to Be Explained

The surface structure of an English sentence is often an unreliable indicator of its logical capacities, telling us little about which sentences it entails or which sentences entail it. Sentences that appear quite similar may behave quite differently in these respects, and sentences that appear quite different may behave similarly. This has led many thinkers to embrace a theoretical notion of *logical form.* The aim is to provide *theoretical redescriptions* of sentences in terms of their logical forms in way that allows us to *explain* semantic properties like logical truth, consistency, and entailment.

In the context of such accounts properties have been invoked in an effort to explain the following:

1. General terms like "red" and "round" can apply to different individuals. Furthermore, many predicates that in fact have the same extension might have had different extensions; even if exactly the same things are red and round, for example, this is an empirical accident, not a deep or necessary feature of either language or the world.
2. Some words and phrases, for example, nominalizations like "honesty," seem to be referring singular terms, and many of the sentences containing these terms are not easily paraphrased in ways that dispel this appearance. Cases in point include "Honesty is a virtue" and "Red resembles orange more than it resembles blue."
3. We use pronouns and other singular terms in subject position that are anaphorically linked back to predicates: "Washington was honest, and *that* is a good feature for a President to have."
4. Many English sentences appear to quantify over the semantic values of predicates, and often these quantifications are not easily paraphrased away or otherwise dismissed as mere figures of speech. Examples include "Napoleon had all the properties of a great general, but Custer did not," "There are several different properties that account for the forces that particles exert on each other," and "There are some properties that will never be named." (If the last sentence is true, it precludes a semantic account of these sentences that treats their quantifiers substitutionally.)
5. These apparent quantifications seem to be entailed by their substitution instances. For example, "Clinton and Gingrich are both tenacious" seems to entail "There is some property (feature, quality) that Clinton and Gingrich both have."
6. We can count the things that predicates seem to stand for; for example, "Clinton and Gingrich have two important things (features, qualities, properties) in common."
7. Some sentences seem to involve identity claims about properties: "According to some versions of the doctrine of the unity of virtue, courage and temperance are the same thing."
8. Various English constructions, including relative clauses and conjoined and disjoined verb phrases, are naturally construed as *complex predicates*. For example, "Rover is an Alsatian that bit someone Tom hit" is naturally parsed as predicating "is an Alsatian that bit someone Tom hit" of "Rover." Such expressions are also employed as parts of generalized quantifiers like "some high and mighty politicians" and "most six-year-olds who don't believe in Santa."
9. Complex predicates can involve subtle scope distinctions. For example, "The color of my true love's hair is necessarily black" can mean that she necessarily has black hair *or* that the actual color of her hair, namely black, is necessarily black.
10. English brims with intentional idioms like *believes*, *imagines*, and *desires*, and these present difficult problems for any theory of meaning for English.

6.2. Semantics: How Properties Explain

The basic idea is to explain these phenomena by postulating properties to serve as the semantic values of predicates and their nominalizations. We need a very rich theory of properties to supply enough semantic values, and we will also need some substantive auxiliary hypotheses.

6.2.1. *Auxiliary hypotheses.* First, we need a hypothesis about the underlying logic (as determined by the recursion clauses in a truth definition) that will be used in an account of logical form. In programs like Davidson's this is basically first-order logic, but in most accounts that invoke properties it is much richer. For example Zalta's (1983, 1988) theory incorporates a full theory of types along with modal and tense operators, predicates that denote properties and relations, devices for forming complex predicates, and a powerful logic that delivers every instance of a comprehension schema (according to which every well-formed condition on objects expressible by any formula meeting certain restrictions determines a property).

Second, we need a linguistic hypothesis that the sentences of English have certain logical forms; for example, we might claim that the logical form our sentence about Rover really does contain a complex predicate.

Third, we need hypotheses—bridge principles—pairing linguistic expressions with the properties that are to serve as their semantic values. Among other things we need a hypothesis that predicates (at least often) express properties, and that their nominalizations denote the property that the predicate expresses. For example, "honest" expresses the property *honesty* and "honesty" denotes it.

Fourth, we eventually need an account of the way in which actual expressions in a natural language come to have the semantics values they do (although no one now is close to having a detailed and general account about this).

6.3. Semantics: The Explanations

We can explain the behavior of simple general terms (item 1) with a fairly rudimentary account of properties. An English sentence of the form $\ulcorner a \text{ is } F \urcorner$ is true just in case a denotes some object α, F denotes (or expresses) some property ϕ, and α exemplifies ϕ. With the right auxiliary hypotheses a rich theory of properties can also explain items 2–7, and it can do so without requiring a wholesale regimentation of English. Thus, in many recent accounts nominalizations seem to function like referring singular terms (item 2) because they *are* singular terms that refer to properties. This also enables us to adapt any standard account of anaphora (item 3) to handle properties, since an anaphoric pronoun can now refer back to the property that is the semantic value of an earlier predicate or nominalization.

When a Lamarkian says "There is some acquired characteristic that Lassie has," the sentence behaves like an existential quantification because it *is* an existential quantification and, indeed, an objectual one. Hence, the sentence is true just in case there is at least one property that is an acquired characteristic of Lassie's, and this is so whether that property is the semantic value of any English expression or not (item 4). This also allows us to use completely standard and familiar logical principles to explain why existential quantifications are entailed by their substitution instances; if an object exemplifies the property expressed by a predicate "F," then there is some property that it exemplifies (item 5). And since properties are genuine things, we can count them (item 6) and use different expressions to stand for the same property (item 7).

These rough and ready explanations can be made precise if we develop a formal logic (of the sort described briefly below) and represent English sentences by interpreted sentences of the formalism. One might view the sentences in the formal language as providing deep structures of English sentences and develop transformation rules mapping them to surface structures of English sentences. But current accounts are less precise about the match between the formal sentences and sentences of English, relying primarily on heuristics and rules of thumb, so-called "translation lore."

The next step is to introduce a semantic account for the logic that places a domain of properties alongside the domain of individuals in each model (e.g., Zalta 1988); alternatively, we can employ an untyped formal language, and simply dump all of the properties and relations into a single domain alongside the individual objects (e.g., Bealer 1982; Menzel 1993). Either way, we then add an extension function to each model that assigns the appropriate sort of extension to each property; it assigns a (possibly empty) set of things to each one-place property, a (possibly empty) set of ordered pairs of things to each two-place relation, and so on. If we like, we can extend this machinery by adding sets of times, worlds, or other indices to our model structures and assigning extensions to properties at times, worlds, or other indices.

We then define satisfaction for monadic atomic formulas in terms of our primitive notion of extension: a value assignment satisfies the open sentence $\ulcorner x \text{ is } \phi \urcorner$ just in case the individual it assigns to x is in the extension of the property denoted (or expressed) by ϕ (this extends routinely to predicates with any number of argument places). We can then define satisfaction for complex sentences, including existential quantifications, with the usual sorts of recursion clauses (except that we now allow quantification over the semantic values of properties). There are various ways to implement the details, but most of them are variations on this approach (see Zalta 1983; Menzel 1993; Swoyer 1998; Bealer's [1982]) approach is somewhat different but secures essentially the same results). We can then make our intuitive explanations of the first seven items on our list quite precise. For example, existential quantifications are entailed by their substitution instances (item 5) because the recursion clause for existential quantifications in our truth definition guarantees that existential generalization is necessarily truth-preserving.

What about the last three items on our list? If we view phrases like "is high and mighty" and "does not believe in Santa" as complex predicates that express "compound" properties, we can explain why they seem to apply to a variety of objects (item 8). We can also draw various useful scope distinctions (item 9; cf. Swoyer 1997; Linsky 1984). But what *is* a compound property?

Many complex predicates have what looks like a logical structure; for example, the first predicate in the previous paragraph looks like a conjunction and the second looks like a negation. The idea is to take these appearances at face value by postulating a set of logical operations that carry properties into more "complex" properties. For example, a conjunctive operation would carry the properties *being red* and *being square* into the conjunctive property *being red and square*. We then place constraints on extension assignments so that something exemplifies this conjunctive property just in case it exemplifies both *redness* and *squareness*. We needn't think of this property as literally being structured or compound; to say that it is conjunctive is just to say that something exemplifies just in case it exemplifies *redness* and *squareness*.

Similar operations guarantee the existence of properties like *loving Sam* and *loving someone*. We then classify predicates into kinds (e.g., conjunctions, existential quantifications) and provide a recursive definition of the denotation (or expression) of these predicates. This can be done in such a way that conjunctive predicates denote conjunctive properties, negative predicates denote negative properties, and so on (Zalta 1983 contains a particularly elegant way of doing this), and this machinery enables us to explain many features of the behavior of complex predicates.

Explanations of the semantic behavior of intentional idioms (item 10) like "believes that" typically require properties that are very finely individuated, probably as finely individuated as the linguistic expressions that denote them. For example if the properties *redness and squareness* and *squareness and redness* are distinct, we can account for the fact that Sam believes that the cube on the table is red and square while doubting that it is square and red. Few people would be guilty of a blatant lapse like Sam's, but we can all fail to realize that two properties necessarily have the same extensions when they are described in complicated ways.

We can obtain very fine-grained identity conditions for compound properties by placing tight constraints on the operations that generate them. We may wonder whether this gives us distinctions without differences (as when it distinguishes a relation like *loving* from the converse of the converse of itself). And it is not clear that we can dissolve all of the paradoxes of intensionality with even the most fine-grained properties. But if we think that really finely individuated properties will help solve some of the puzzles of intensionality, this approach provides a principled way to get them.

6.4. Semantics: Why Explanations Using Properties Are Best

There are two general alternatives to property-based semantic theories.

6.4.1. *The competition: Sets.* The first alternative takes the semantic values of predicates to be sets of individuals. Various general semanticists have adopted this approach, but the best-known example of it is Davidson's (1984) program, which aims to provide a theory of meaning for a fragment of English by providing a first-order theory of truth for it.

Although a great deal in ingenuity has gone into Davidsonian accounts, they face several serious problems, and some of them would persist even if we employed a logic with more resources (e.g., devices for dealing with predicate modifiers or complex predicates). The program requires a great deal of regimentation, some of which seems rather unnatural, but the main problem is that some kinds of sentences seem almost certain to resist treatment in this framework. The chief difficulty is that sets are much too coarse-grained to provide semantics for the predicates of a natural language. If the set of red things and the set of round things happened to have the same extensions (including an empty extension), then they would have the same semantic values. There are many problematic constructions for this approach, several of which are illustrated by the sentence "Red resembles orange more than it resembles blue, and Sally thinks that Tom believes that there are only two colors that she prefers to it."

6.4.2. *The competition: Intensions.* Other theorists have identified properties with functions, sometimes called *intensions*, that assign an extension to each predicate at each time in each possible world (or in terms of other set theoretical constructions that encode the same information). These approaches typically use more powerful formal languages than first-order logic, and in the hands of Montague (e.g., 1974) and philosophers and linguists he inspired (e.g., Lewis 1970), they have led to work of great depth and elegance. But their treatment of predicates still leads to problems.

First, we learn the meanings of many predicates by ostension, and we seem to group objects together when they share a property (rather than thinking they share a property because they are all members of some set). Property theorists explain this by saying that we learn to recognize a property, and we can then determine whether other objects fall into its extension. But these simple facts become mysterious on the possible-worlds approach, since it treats the meaning of a predicate as an incredibly complicated set-theoretic entity that involves infinitely many times in infinitely many possible worlds. We might overlook this difficulty by viewing intensions simply as parts of a formal model that reflects various features of English. But the account of the semantics of predicates would still be too coarse-grained, since it treats predicates that are necessarily coextensive, like "lasted a fortnight" and "lasted two weeks," as expressing the same property. This will make it very difficult to explain how "Wilbur believed the jail term lasted two weeks" could be true while "Wilbur believed the jail term lasted a fortnight" was false.

The possible worlds account requires a rich ontology, but property-based theorists are ill advised to throw stones here, since the most obvious way to deal with puzzling intensional constructions is to employ a semantics that assigns an extension to each property at every time in every world. It may be that worlds and times can be constructed from properties (cf. Zalta 1988) or that possible worlds can be avoided entirely (Bealer 1982, esp. §46). But property-theoretic approaches to semantics still require a great many properties, and it isn't clear that they offer a substantially leaner ontology than possible-worlds accounts do.

6.4.3. *Family quarrels.* Of course there are alternative ways to use properties in the semantics for natural languages. One key difference is between accounts that employ a typed language (e.g., Zalta 1988; Swoyer 1993) and those that do not (e.g., Bealer 1982; Menzel 1993). The former may reduce the risk of paradoxes stemming from self-predication, but judiciously designed versions of the latter may do so as well, and they are much more flexible. With enough ingenuity, though, both approaches can handle a wide range of phenomena, and there are no utterly decisive arguments for (or against) either approach.

6.4.4. *Evaluating the alternatives.* There are two types of arguments that a semanticist can give against a competitor's account. The first cites specific kinds of constructions that her own account can handle but the competing account cannot. For example, a sentence that takes the semantic values of predicates to be sets will have a very difficult time explaining the semantical behavior of sentences attributing propositional attitudes. Indeed, some sentences, like "The temperature is ninety and rising," have almost become test cases for various approaches.

Since the arguments here depend on the details of the specific case, there is nothing very general to say about all of them. But it is worth noting that they often end in a grudging admission that perhaps a rival account *can* handle certain constructions, but it does so in a way that is unnatural or ugly. For example, "The King of France is bald" looks like a subject-predicate sentence, but on Russell's account of definite descriptions, it dissolves into an existential quantification containing a cloud of logical constants. Again, Davidson's paratactic account of belief sentences seems unnatural to many. But although such arguments often carry a good deal of weight, they are far from being demonstrative.

The second kind of arguments involves trade-offs between one desideratum and another. Is it better for a theory to assign logical forms that stick closely to the syntactic structures of sentences (at the price of a powerful logic and rich ontology), or is it better to employ a lot of regimentation in order to scrimp by on a simpler logic and sparser ontology? Is it worth trading a compositional semantics—one in which the semantic values of complex syntactic expressions are functions of the semantic values of their constituents—to avoid problems with belief sentences? Again, arguments for alternative answers to these questions are often important, but they are rarely decisive.

6.4.5. *There are no crucial experiments.* It is also difficult to make tests bear directly on the *ontologies* of competing semantics accounts. A semantic theory for a natural language will include several complex auxiliary hypotheses, and when something goes wrong it is always possible, and often plausible, to pin the blame on one of them.

For example, semantic theories pass judgments about the validity or invalidity of many of the arguments in their jurisdiction, and we can check our intuitions to see whether their verdicts are right. But our intuitions about validity are often cloudy and unsystematic. It may seem extremely odd for someone to endorse the premises of a particular argument while rejecting its conclusion. It doesn't follow that the argument is valid, though, since there may well be alternative explanations for the oddity. For example, it may seem odd because of a conversational implicature; it may violate some norm of conversation (like being relevant) to endorse the premises without endorsing the conclusion. Or the argument from the premises to the conclusion may be valid, but not formally so; for example, if "Today is Sunday" is true, then "Tomorrow is Monday" must be true as well. Again, there may be some lawlike regularity that leads speakers to think that if the premises are true the conclusion must be true as well: "Sue had a baby, so Sue is female."

The point is that if a semantic theory fails to count an intuitively good argument as valid, its proponents can often explain this away by urging that any intuitions that it seems valid actually stem from some other source (e.g., we mistake a conventional or a conversational implicature for a logical entailment). After a certain point such maneuvers may be ad hoc, but there is no definite point at which they are forbidden, and so once again such considerations are not decisive.

My aim in this section has been (1) to shed light on the ways in which properties might help explain a range of semantic phenomena, (2) to note that their proponents also try to show that their explanations are better than alternatives, and (3) to indicate several reasons why their arguments are not demonstrative. In short, the uses of properties in semantics represent an attempt to draw an inference to the best explanation.

7. LAWS OF NATURE

7.1. Natural Laws: What Is to Be Explained

In recent years several writers (e.g., Armstrong 1978, 1984; Dretske 1977; Tooley 1977, 1987; Swoyer 1983) have argued that properties or universals, along with an auxiliary hypothesis about the nature of laws, explain the central features of natural laws and explain them better than rival accounts can. I will call these theories *universalist accounts of laws*. I will focus on deterministic laws. (Probabilistic laws are at least as important, but if the current accounts can't get deterministic laws right they aren't likely to work for anything else.) There are a number of features of laws that we might want to explain (Armstrong 1983, 99ff, lists thirteen), but the following five are among the most central:

1. Laws are objective. We don't invent laws, we discover them.
2. Laws, unlike accidental generalizations, are confirmed by their instances and they underwrite predictions.
3. Laws have genuine explanatory power. They play a central role in scientific explanation that mere universal generalizations do not.
4. Laws have some sort of modal force. This shows up when we describe laws (or their implications) using words like "must," "cannot," and "impossible."
5. Laws entail, but are not entailed by, their corresponding universal generalizations.

None of the *explananda* on this list are completely uncontroversial. But they are standardly cited symptoms of nomologicality and most philosophers would agree that, other things being equal, the more of them an account of laws can explain, the better.

7.2. Natural Laws: How Properties Explain

Universalists have developed their accounts in somewhat different ways, but here I will focus on the simple, common core of their accounts. The universalist's thesis is that laws are relations among properties. Universal generalizations (sentences of the form ⌜All *F*s are *G*s⌝) are often used to gesture toward laws, but they are not laws themselves. The real law involves a relation among the properties *F* and *G*, which will typically be determinate physical magnitudes like a mass of 0.56 kg or a kinetic energy of 3×10^{-2} joules. The law does *not* hold because all of the individuals that are *F*s are also *G*s. It holds because there is something about being an *F* that makes a thing (or a thing related to it in the appropriate way) be a *G*.

For example, in a Newtonian world any body that has the (conjunctive) property of having a certain net force *f* (a vector, and hence a relational property) acting on it and a mass *m* (a scalar, and hence a monadic property) would also have a determinate acceleration property *f/m*. Some writers call this higher-order relation among physical magnitudes *nomic necessitation* ("*N*," for short). So on this account statements of at least the simpler deterministic laws have the logical form ⌜*N*(*F*,*G*)⌝.

One advantage of construing the universalists' arguments as inferences to the best explanation is that it enables them to respond to two recent criticisms of universalism. The first criticism is that we have no idea what the relation *N* is like (the second is the identification problem that is mentioned below). But if we view the arguments for universalism as inferences to the best explanation, we should approach this question by asking what *N* would *have* to be like in order to explain the things it is postulated to explain. So the answer (to the extent that there is one) will emerge only as we look at the explanations the account offers.

In the preceding sections I discussed the explanations offered by property theorists in one subsection and their arguments that their explanations are better than their rivals' in another. But the development of universalism is so thoroughly intertwined with criticisms of its chief rivals, regularity theories of laws, that it will be clearer to consider the two stages together.

7.2.1. *Regularity theories.* There are many versions of the regularity theory, but they share the core idea that laws are simply contingent regularities (or the sentences expressing them), differing from accidental generalizations only in having some special epistemic, pragmatic, or logical trappings (e.g., containing projectible predicates like "rest mass" rather than "grue," or being part of a powerful yet simple deductive theory of nature). The most prominent variant nowadays is the Ramsey-Lewis account, according to which laws are those universal generalizations that would be part of the overall systematization of our theories about the world that best combines simplicity and strength.

Earlier in this century regularity theories typically talked about predicates and sentences rather than properties. This is not surprising, because such theories were favored by empiricists who often found properties epistemically suspect, but a regularity theorist could talk about regularities among properties. Even if the regularity theorist and the universalists both invoke properties, however, we will see that there are still large differences between their accounts.

There are various problems with regularity theories (see Carroll 1994, chap. 2, for a good discussion), but the major issue between universalists and regularity theorists involves—yet again—the fundamental ontological trade-off. Regularity theories have a relatively low epistemological cost. We observe instances of regularities here in the actual world, and the additional features used to upgrade universal generalizations to laws don't seem epistemically problematic in any deep or ineluctable way. The problem, according to the universalist, is that this epistemic security is only achieved by making the account so weak that it can't explain the fundamental, distinctive features of laws.

7.3. Natural Laws: The Explanations

To bring these points down to earth, it will be useful to consider a few universalist attempts to explain the items on our list above.

7.3.1. *Objectivity*. The universalist argues that laws are objective because the *N*-relation relates those properties it does quite independently of our language and thought (in the case of properties that don't specifically involve us or our language or thought). By contrast, regularity theories depend on features that are too subjective or anthropomorphic to account for the objectivity of laws. Which predicates are entrenched in our language, what explanations we actually give, and perhaps even what theories are simplest depend too much on contingent facts about us and our practices.

7.3.2. *Confirmation and prediction*. According to the universalist, it is unclear what could justify accepting a mere generalization short of checking all of its instances. If laws merely record regularities, why should the fact that observed *F*s are *G*s lead us to conclude that *F*s we haven't encountered will be *G*s too? If the *F*s I have observed are to be relevant to my belief that unobserved *F*s will be *G*s, then there needs to be something about an object's being *F* that requires (or, in the case of probabilistic laws, makes it probable) that it will be a *G*. And if the properties stand in a nomic relation, there is something about an object's being an *F* that will make it be a *G*, and the examined cases will be related to the unexamined cases in the relevant way.

7.3.3. *Explanation*. The accidental regularity that all of the cars I saw today were red doesn't explain why any particular one of them is red. But, universalists sometimes argue, if one property nomically necessitates a second, that does explain why anything having the first property has the second.

This isn't the universalist's best argument. If there are many different explanatory virtues, this may well afford a glimmer of understanding; it tells us that the correlation holds as a matter of law and that we shouldn't look around for particular facts in the world to explain it (as we might for the fact that all the cars I've seen today have been red). Of course this won't be a very deep or informative explanation; it doesn't provide causal mechanisms, for example, or a more fundamental and far-reaching story about the relevant properties. But with the most basic laws something like this may well be all we can offer by way of explanation. At some point we may hit the end of the explanatory road; perhaps it simply is a law that bodies that have certain forces acting on them accelerate in certain ways. And, says the universalist, better there should be genuine laws at this point then mere, brute regularities (however the regularity theorist might propose to deck them out).

7.3.4. *Modal force*. Perhaps the most distinctive features of laws is their modal force, the way they seem to require some things and preclude others. Pauli's exclusion principle *requires* that two fermions occupy different quantum states; the special theory of relativity *doesn't allow* a signal to be propagated at a velocity exceeding that of light; the laws of thermodynamics show the *impossibility* of perpetual motion machines. Conservation laws assure us that such quantities as angular momentum, mass-energy, and charge *cannot* be created or destroyed. The modal force of laws may seem to show up in the way that laws commonly support counterfactuals; if there had been a tenth planet, it too would have obeyed Kepler's laws.

Regularity theorists maintain that laws are contingent universal generalizations with some special, but nonmodal, additional features, so it isn't surprising that it is difficult for them to account for the modal force of laws. It is also difficult to explain this modal force if it is a *purely contingent* fact that two properties stand in the ***N***-relation. How, for example, does such an account support claims about the impossibility of a perpetual-motion machine? Indeed, if it is purely contingent whether two properties stand in the ***N***-relation, then this relation doesn't unite them because of what they are like; it just happens to link some properties in the actual world while linking completely different properties in others. On this account light could have had the phenomenal properties of molasses, photons the mass of the solar system, and elementary particles could retain their identity while swapping all their quantum numbers.

The moral is that you can't derive a *must* from an *is*. Not a *genuine* nomological *must*, anyway (though perhaps you can pull some sort of ersatz *must* out of a hat full of nonmodal facts). If we want genuine modal force to fall out at the end, we have to build it in at the beginning, and on the universalist account there is no place to put it except in the relation ***N*** itself. If this is correct, there is reason to think that ***N*** involves a fundamental *de re* connection among properties (as it would if such connections among properties were metaphysically necessary). But if we move in this direction, the fundamental ontological trade-off becomes more pressing, and the epistemic cost of universalism begins to rise.

7.3.5. *Laws necessitate their corresponding generalizations.* If it is a law that all *F*s are *G*s, it follows that each particular *F* is a *G*. It is easy for regularity theorists to explain this. According to them a law is, in effect, a conjunction of a universal generalization and something else, so the law certainly entails the universal generalization. But it is more difficult for a universalist to explain why the inference from ⌜*N*(*F*,*G*)⌝ to ⌜All *F*s are *G*s⌝ is legitimate (van Fraassen 1989, 96, calls this the *inference problem*).

Universalists have produced some very subtle solutions to the inference problem (e.g., Tooley 1987, 128ff), but I think that it would be better just to bite the bullet here. There is no obvious reason why there should be any familiar (or even *un*familiar) *logical* principle that would carry us from ⌜*N*(*F*,*G*)⌝ to ⌜All *F*s are *G*s⌝. It would be enough if the second sentence had to be true whenever the first sentence was.

When we invoke ***N*** as part of the best explanation of various phenomena we have to invest it with whatever features it needs to have in order to explain those phenomena. Consider the less controversial case of conjunctive properties. An individual will have the conjunctive property of *being F and being G* just in case it has the property *being F* and it also has the property *being G*. This is just a brute fact about conjunctive properties; to postulate the existence of conjunctive properties is to hypothesize the existence of properties that behave in this way. Similarly, one of the features of the ***N***-relation is that if it relates the properties *F* and *G*, then all *F*s will be *G*s. We can say a certain amount about this relation. But its introduction is part and parcel of a philosophical account of laws, and it is supported (to whatever extent it is) by the ability of that overall account to explain the nature of laws better than any of its competitors.

The *explananda* and explanations involving laws are murkier than their counterparts in the two preceding sections. Moreover, as they stand some of the universalists' explanations leave much to be desired. But as in previous sections, I have tried to say enough to make three claims plausible. First, there are plausible (though scarcely overwhelming) arguments for universalism, and they turn on the ability of properties to *explain* various features of laws. Second, most of these explanations go hand in hand with arguments that universalism provides *better* explanations that its competitors, particularly regularity theories. Third, the arguments for, and against, current accounts of laws are *not demonstrative*, and there is no prospect of strengthening them so that they will be.

8. MORALS

8.1. Explanation and Unification

We have now seen cursory sketches of three types of explanations properties have been said to provide. What can we say about them? Even in science it seems doubtful that there is a single point to explanation, much less that there is only one format explanations can assume. In the right context we can explain something by subsuming it under general laws, by noting its causes, or by citing statistically relevant phenomena, and the last two, anyway, don't occur in philosophical explanations involving properties. But we can also explain by invoking principles or entities that unify and integrate a range of phenomena. By redescribing a host of seemingly diverse objects as bodies with inertial and gravitational mass, Newton gave a unified explanation of the motions of the planets, projectiles, colliding bodies, and the tides. And Michael Friedman (1974) and Philip Kitcher (1989) are surely right in urging that such unification is *a* key feature of explanation (though I wouldn't go on to claim that it is the only explanatory virtue).

Seeing a pattern, a common structure, yields one sort of understanding. Newton allowed us to see superficially diverse phenomena as similar in theoretically important ways. The notions, like inertial mass, gravitational mass, and force, involved in his explanations are not intrinsically clearer or more familiar than the notions to be explained, but that isn't a defect, because the explanatory gain is global.

Analogously, properties offer unified and integrated accounts of the items on our lists of mathematical, semantical, and nomological *explananda*. This way of thinking about properties may be as old as philosophical accounts of properties themselves. In a classic paper on Plato's theory of Forms, Cherniss (1936) argues that Plato saw his theory as solving difficult problems in ethics (explaining how ethical principles could be objective), epistemology (explaining the difference between knowledge and belief), and metaphysics (explaining how change is possible). We might add that it also helped him explain the semantics of general terms (cf. *Republic*, 596A; *Phaedo*, 78e; *Timaeus*, 52a; *Parmenides*, 133d). This isn't to say that all of Plato's explanations were successful—far from it. But the general pattern of *explanation by unification and integration* was at work in one of the first accounts of universals. This isn't enough to show that such explanation is legitimate, though, and I will briefly consider several challenges to it before closing.

8.2. Inference to the Best Explanation

Some philosophers have argued that explanations don't *ever* justify belief in the existence of postulated entities (at least not in entities that are in principle unobservable). Are they right? There can be no question of demonstrating that the entities postulated in an inference to the best explanation always exist (since they don't). Nor is it possible to demonstrate that such inferences will, more often than not, yield true conclusions when we start out with true premises. Inference to the best explanation is a form of ampliative inference, and Hume was surely right that such inferences cannot be justified in non-question-begging ways.

But inference to the best explanation is *not* some arcane concoction of metaphysicians. We often infer that something exists on the grounds that its existence would explain something that would otherwise be puzzling (Wilbur must have had an accomplice—there is no other way to account for his immaculate getaway). Such inferences also seem common in science. (If molecules exist, that would explain why grains of pollen dance along on the surface of water.) Moreover, we typically think that a theory must do more to save the phenomena than merely be consistent with them, and explanation seems a key addition. These issues are still being debated in discussions of scientific realism; I agree with those writers who think that explanation sometimes leads, legitimately, to inference, but since my reasons are similar to ones that are now familiar in the literature, I won't rehearse them here.

8.3. Philosophical Explanation

Even if inference to the best explanation is legitimate in science it doesn't follow that it's legitimate in philosophy. There are two obvious differences between the two. First, there are incontrovertible paradigms of successful scientific explanations. Newton explained the motions of the tides; Einstein explained gravitational phenomena. There is simply nothing comparable to such success stories in philosophy. Second, many inferences to the best explanation in science are inferences to the existence of *causes*. One of the first reasons people had for believing in the existence of molecules was that they explained Brownian motion, and they explained it because they caused it. But although properties may confer causal powers on their instances, they are not causes in the same way that the jostlings of molecules are.

Kuhn has remarked that partisans of competing scientific paradigms often disagree not only about what counts as a genuine explanation, but also about what stands in need of explanation in the first place, and it may be tempting to conclude that a similar situation obtains in philosophy. The kernel of truth here is that it typically *is* difficult to show that something is a genuine philosophical problem, and it isn't something we could ever hope to prove. Still, although philosophical explanations are not nearly as deep as our best scientific explanations, there are several reasons to think that the sorts of phenomena discussed in this paper can receive philosophical explanations.

First, many of the greatest philosophers in history have struggled to provide explanations for philosophically puzzling phenomena. They may have been misguided, but it seems unlikely that so many acute thinkers from such different historical periods were all in the grip of some simple confusion about what can, or should, be explained. Moreover, many of us still find some of these phenomena genuinely puzzling, so we needn't rely solely on authority for thinking that they are.

Second, claims that the sorts of items on our various lists cannot be given philosophical explanations are typically asserted with little argument, and the few arguments I know of are unimpressive. Not so long ago, for example, we often heard that talk about properties rested on grammatical confusions or linguistic errors, and we were assured that with the proper sort of therapy we could dissolve such pseudoproblems. But such diagnoses often turned on dubious views about meaning, for example, some sort of verificationism, which would also eviscerate much of our talk outside of philosophy.

Third, accounts involving universals are sometimes said to be vacuous, to simply introduce obscure phrases to relabel everyday phenomena like qualitative recurrence (e.g., Quine 1961, 10; Quinton 1973, 295). But many of the explanations we have seen rely on general principles about properties that have enough content to be disconfirmed. In connection with various auxiliary hypotheses, these principles can be tested, and they can certainly fail some of those tests. Nor does the fact that items on our lists call for philosophical explanation ensure that realism, much less any particular version of realism, will emerge victorious. Competing accounts that don't involve universals, for example, a resemblance theory or a theory of tropes, might turn out to afford better explanations.

Fourth, many philosophers who are not devotees of ontology nevertheless agree that there are genuine philosophical puzzles concerning mathematical truth, logical form, and natural laws. So these areas provide a less controversial testing ground for theories of properties.

Finally, it is worth remembering that it is often easier to engage in a practice than to explain it. Scientists can recognize explanations in their fields without being able to give an account of explanation; indeed, there is no generally accepted account of scientific explanation. This doesn't mean that explanations are possible in philosophy, but it does mean, I think, that we can be more certain that there are explanations than we can be about their exact nature. At all events, my aim here is not to provide an account of philosophical explanation. But I hope I have assembled enough examples to suggest that arguments for properties, though they often fall short, are best construed as attempts at inferences to the best explanation. And such examples are the kind of data on which any account of inference to the best metaphysical explanation must be based.

8.4. Good, Better, and Best

The quality of an explanation matters. The best available explanation may be too feeble to underwrite inference, and many of the debates among property-theorists concern the relative merits of rival explanations.

Sometimes straightforwardly philosophical constraints play a role in evaluating explanations in ontology. For example, empiricists like Russell sometimes endorsed a principle of acquaintance, a requirement that the primitive entities in the ontological menagerie be observable. Other philosophers have urged that if one thing is to figure in an ontological explanation of a second, it has to be *in* that second thing, or that at the very least the entities must partake of the natural, causal order. For example, this seems to lie behind Aristotle's objection that Plato separated the Forms from the natural world. The sense of *in* may be metaphorical, but the intuition here is that *x*'s standing in some (not very clearly described) relation to something outside space and time can't really explain anything about *x* and its earthly vicissitudes. Such issues can be quite complex, and some (like the principle of acquaintance) involve an entire philosophical orientation. I don't know whether anything general can be said about them, but they do play a role in our evaluations of philosophical explanation.

But less parochial, more familiar considerations are often more central. Other things being equal, we want breadth, precision, simplicity (in as many of its myriad forms as possible), freedom from ad hoc hypotheses, and an account that coheres with the rest of our views about the world. Such criteria are nebulous, and they can pull in opposite directions. But without them much ampliative inference would be impossible.

8.5. Convergence or Fragmentation

I must, alas, end with what may turn out to be bad news. It would be gratifying to find a single, unified account of properties that helped explain a wide range of phenomena. We could then build a cumulative case for the existence of properties, and we could triangulate in on their nature by seeing what they would need to be like in order to play these diverse explanatory roles. But there is a danger that the sorts of entities that are good for explaining some phenomena may not be good for explaining others. In particular, the identity and existence conditions of entities well suited to one task may be ill suited for entities with a different job to do.

For example, the identity conditions best suited to properties used to explain causation, measurement, and natural laws seem to be that properties are identical just in case they bestow the same causal (or nomological) roles on their instances. By contrast, the properties needed in semantic accounts of intentional idioms of a natural language would have to be individuated in a much more fine-grained way. Again, there may be good reasons for thinking that the properties needed to explain things like causation or laws must be instantiated in the natural world if they are to explain what they are supposed to (e.g., Armstrong 1978; Swoyer 1996). But explanations of such things as mathematical truth or the semantic values of English predicates will require a very rich realm of properties, and especially in the latter case it is unreasonable to suppose that all of them could actually be instantiated.

If such fragmentation occurs (and there is some reason to fear it will; Swoyer 1996, 1998), we could settle for the conclusion that there are several different sorts of property-like entities (as Bealer does with his concepts and qualities). But this would make it more difficult to build a cumulative case for the existence of any one sort of entity and harder to use a range of explanations to triangulate in on the natures of those with which we end up.

9. CONCLUSION

Friends and foes of properties often talk past each other. I think this frequently results from deep (and often unarticulated) disagreements about whether explanations are possible in ontology, what things (if any) can be explained, and what such explanations (if possible) would be like. These are not easy disagreements to settle, but I have tried to take one step in the direction of clarifying them.

NOTE

1. I have discussed some of these issues elsewhere (Swoyer 1983, 1996), though in less detail, without the case studies, and without drawing the morals drawn here. When I speak of *realism* I will mean realism with respect to properties unless the context makes it clear that some other sort of realism is at stake. To avoid frequent qualifications I will use "property" and "universal" interchangeably, and I will treat relations as properties; I will also use "metaphysics" and "ontology" interchangeably. Distinctions among these things are often important, but they won't matter here. I am grateful to Monte Cook, Ray Elugardo, and Jim Hawthorne for helpful comments on the first draft of this paper.

REFERENCES

Armstrong, David. 1978. *Universals and Scientific Realism*. Vol. 2, *A Theory of Universals*. Cambridge: Cambridge University Press.

_____. 1983. *What Is a Law of Nature?* Cambridge: Cambridge University Press.

_____. 1984. "Replies." In Radu Bogdan, ed., *D. M. Armstrong: Profiles*. Dordrecht, the Netherlands: D. Reidel.

_____. 1989. *A Combinatorial Theory of Possibility*. Cambridge: Cambridge University Press.

Benacerraf, Paul. 1965. "What Numbers Could Not Be." *Philosophical Review* 74:47–73.

_____. 1973. "Mathematical Truth." *Journal of Philosophy* 70:661–79.

Bealer, George. 1982. *Quality and Concept*. Oxford: Clarendon Press.

_____. 1994. "Property Theory: The Type-Fee Approach vs. the Church Approach."*Journal of Philosophical Logic* 23:139–71.

Bigelow, John, and Robert Pargetter. 1990. *Science and Necessity*. Cambridge: Cambridge University Press.

Butchvarov, Panayot. 1966. *Resemblance and Identity*. Bloomington: University of Indiana Press.

Carroll, John. 1994. *Laws of Nature*. Cambridge: Cambridge University Press.

Cherniss, H. F. 1936. "The Philosophical Economy of Plato's Theory of Ideas." *American Journal of Philology* 57:445–56.

Chierchia, Gennaro, and Raymond Turner. 1988. "Semantics and Property Theory."*Linguistics and Philosophy* 11:261–02

Davidson, Donald. 1984. *Inquiries into Truth and Interpretation*. Oxford: Clarendon Press.

Dretske, Fred. 1977. "Laws of Nature." *Philosophy of Science* 44:248–68.

Fales, Evan. 1990. *Causation and Universals*. New York: Routledge.

Friedman, Michael. 1974. "Explanation and Scientific Understanding." *Journal of Philosophy* 71:5–19.

Glymour, Clark. 1980. *Theory and Evidence*. Princeton, NJ: Princeton University Press.

Hellman, Geoffrey. 1989. *Mathematics without Numbers: Towards a Modal-Structural Interpretation*. Oxford: Clarendon Press.
Jubien, Michael. 1989. "On Properties and Property Theory." In Gennaro Chierchia, Barbara Partee, and Raymond Turner, eds., *Properties, Types, and Meaning*. Vol. I, *Foundational Issues*. Boston: Kluwer.
Kitcher, Philip. 1989. "Explanatory Unification and the Causal Structure of the World." In Philip Kitcher & Wesley Salmon, eds., *Scientific Explanation: Minnesota Studies in the Philosophy of Science*. Vol. 13. Minneapolis: University of Minnesota Press.
Lewis, David. 1970. "General Semantics," *Synthese* 22:18–67.
Linsky, Bernard. 1984. "General Terms as Designators." *Pacific Philosophical Quarterly* 65: 259–76.
Menzel, Chris. 1993. "The Proper Treatment of Predication in Fine-Grained Intensional Logic." *Philosophical Perspectives* 7:61–87.
Montague, Richard. 1974. *Formal Philosophy: Selected Papers of Richard Montague*. New Haven, CT: Yale University Press.
Mundy, Brent. 1987. "The Metaphysics of Quantity." *Philosophical Studies* 51:29–54.
Paley, William. 1802. *Natural Theology, or Evidences of the Existence and Attributes of the Deity Collected from the Appearances of Nature*. London: R. Faulder.
Pollard, Stephen, and Norman Martin. (1986). "Mathematics for Property Theorists." *Philosophical Studies* 49:177–86.
Quine, W. V. O. 1961. "On What There Is." In *From a Logical Point of View*. 2d ed. New York: Harper and Row.
Quinton, Anthony. 1973. *The Nature of Things*. London: Routledge & Kegan Paul.
Russell, Bertrand. 1912. *The Problems of Philosophy*. London: Home University Library.
Salmon, Wesley. 1989. *Four Decades of Scientific Explanation*. Minneapolis: University of Minnesota Press.
Swoyer, Chris. 1982. "The Nature of Natural Laws." *Australasian Journal of Philosophy* 60: 203–23.
_____. 1983. "Realism and Explanation." *Philosophical Inquiry* 5:14–28.
_____. 1987. "The Metaphysics of Measurement." In John Forge, ed., *Measurement, Realism and Objectivity*, 235–90. Dordrecht, the Netherlands: D. Reidel.
_____. 1991. "Structural Representation and Surrogative Reasoning." *Synthese* 87:449–508.
_____. 1993. "Logic and the Empirical Conception of Properties." *Philosophical Topics* 21: 199–231.
_____. 1996. "Theories of Properties: From Plenitude to Paucity." *Philosophical Perspectives* 10:243–64.
_____. 1997. "Complex Predicates and Conversion Principles." *Philosophical Studies* 87:1–32.
_____. 1998. "Complex Predicates and Theories of Properties and Relations." *Journal of Philosophical Logic* 27:295–325.
Tooley, Michael. 1977. "The Nature of Laws." *Canadian Journal of Philosophy* 7:667–98.
_____. 1987. *Causation*. Oxford: Oxford University Press.
van Fraassen, Bas. 1989. *Laws and Symmetry*. Oxford: Clarendon Press.
Zalta, Edward. 1983. *Abstract Objects: An Introduction to Axiomatic Metaphysics*. Dordrecht, the Netherlands: D. Reidel.
_____. 1988. *Intensional Logic and the Metaphysics of Intentionality*. Cambridge: MIT Press.

Midwest Studies in Philosophy, XXIII (1999)

Existential Relativity

ERNEST SOSA

A. THREE WAYS IN ONTOLOGY

Artifacts and natural objects are normally composed of stuff or of parts in certain ways. Those that endure are normally composed of stuff or of parts at each instant of their enduring. Moreover, the stuff or parts composing such an object right up to t must be related in certain restricted ways to the stuff or parts that compose it right after t, for any time t within its history.

Thus a snowball exists at a time t and location l only if there is a round quantity of snow at l and t sufficiently separate from other snow, and so forth; and it endures through an interval I only if, for every division of I into a sequence of subintervals I_1, I_2, . . . , there is a corresponding sequence of quantities of snow Q_1, Q_2, . . . , related in certain restricted ways. I mean thus to recall our criteria of existence and perdurance for snowballs.

So much for snowballs. The like is true of chains and constituent links, boxes and constituent sides, and a great variety of artifacts or natural entities such as hills or trees; and the same goes for persons and their constituent bodies. In each case we have criteria of existence and of perdurance, an entity of that sort existing at t (perduring through I) if and only if its criteria of existence are satisfied at t (its criteria of perdurance are satisfied relative to I).

We are supposing a snowball to be constituted by a certain piece of snow as constituent matter and the shape of (approximate) roundness as constituent form. That particular snowball exists at that time because of the roundness of that piece of snow. If at that time that piece of snow were to lose its roundness, then at that time that snowball would go out of existence.

Compare now with our ordinary concept of a snowball the concept of a "snowdiscall," which we may define as an entity constituted by a piece of snow as matter and as form any shape between being round and being disc-shaped. At any given time, therefore, any piece of snow that constitutes a snowball constitutes a snowdiscall, but a piece of snow might at a time constitute a snowdiscall without then constituting a snowball. For every round piece of snow is also in shape between disc-shaped and round (inclusive), but a disc-shaped piece of snow is of course not round.

Any snowball *SB* must hence be constituted by a piece of snow *PS* that also then constitutes a snowdiscall *SD*. Now *SB* is distinct (a different entity from) *PS*, since *PS* would survive squashing and *SB* would not. By similar reasoning, *SD* also is distinct from *PS*. And again by similar reasoning, *SB* must also be distinct from *SD*, since enough partial flattening of *PS* will destroy *SB* but not *SD*. Now, there are infinitely many shapes $S_1, S_2, \ldots$, between roundness and flatness of a piece of snow, and, for any shape S_i, having a shape between flatness and S_i would give the form of a distinctive kind of entity to be compared with snowballs and snowdiscalls. Whenever a piece of snow constitutes a snowball, therefore, it constitutes infinitely many entities all sharing its place with it.

Under a broadly Aristotelian conception, therefore, the barest flutter of the smallest leaf creates and destroys infinitely many things, and ordinary reality suffers a sort of "explosion."

This is where we are led by our first option.

We might perhaps resist this "explosion" of our ordinary world by embracing a kind of conceptual relativism. Constituted, supervenient entities do not just objectively supervene on their requisite, constitutive matters and forms, outside all conceptual schemes, with absolute independence from the categories recognized by any person or group. Perhaps snowballs do exist relative to all actual conceptual schemes ever, but not relative to all conceivable conceptual schemes. Just as we do not countenance the existence of snowdiscalls, just so another culture might be unwilling to countenance snowballs. We do not countenance snowdiscalls: conceptual scheme denies the snowdiscall form (being in shape between round and disc-shaped) the status required for it to be a proper constitutive form of a separate sort of entity—at least not with snow as underlying stuff.

That would block the explosion of reality, but the price is existential relativity. Supervenient, constituted entities do not just exist or not in themselves, free of any dependence on or relativity to conceptual scheme. What thus exists relative to one conceptual scheme may not do so relative to another. In order for such a sort of entity to exist relative to a conceptual scheme, that conceptual scheme must recognize its constituent form as an appropriate way for a distinctive sort of entity to be constituted.

Must we now conceive of the existence even of the conceptual scheme itself and of its framers and users as also relative to that conceptual scheme? And aren't we then caught in a vicious circle? The framers exist only relative to the scheme and this they do in virtue of the scheme's giving their constituent form-cum-matter the required status. But to say that the scheme gives to this form-cum-matter the required status—isn't that just to say that the *framers* of that scheme do so? Yet are not the framers themselves dependent on the scheme for their existence relative to it?

Answer: Existence *relative* to a conceptual scheme is *not* equivalent to existence *in virtue* of that conceptual scheme. Relative to scheme *C* the framers of *C* exist *in virtue* of their constitutive matter and form and how these satisfy certain criteria for existence and perdurance of such subjects (the framers). Their existence is in that way relative to *C* but not in virtue of *C*. There is hence no vicious circularity.

That is our second option.

A third option is a disappearance or elimination theory that refuses to countenance supervenient, constituted objects. But then most if not all of ordinary reality will be lost. Perhaps we shall allow ourselves to continue to use its forms of speech, "but only as a convenience or abbreviation." But in using those forms of speech, in speaking of snowballs, chains, boxes, trees, hills, or even people, we shall *not* believe ourselves to be seriously representing reality and its contents. "As a convenience" . . . to *whom* and for what *ends*? "As an abbreviation" . . . of *what*?

What follows will first develop and defend our middle, relativist, option; but we shall be led eventually to a compromise position.

Our conceptual scheme encompasses criteria of existence and of perdurance for the sorts of objects that it recognizes. Shall we say now that a sort of object *O* exists (has existed, exists now, or will exist) relative to a scheme *C* at *t* iff, at *t*, *C* recognizes sort *O* by allowing the corresponding criteria? But surely there are sorts of objects that our present conceptual scheme does not recognize, such as artifacts yet uninvented and particles yet undiscovered, to take only two obvious examples. Of course we allow that there might be and probably are many such things. Not that there could be any such entities relative to our *present* conceptual scheme, however, for by hypothesis it does not recognize them. So are there sorts of objects—constituted sorts among them, as are the artifacts at least—such that they exist but not relative to our present scheme *C*? But then we are back to our problem. What is it for there to be such objects? Is it just the in-itself satisfaction of constitutive forms by constitutive matters? That yields the explosion of reality.

Shall we say then that a constituted, supervenient sort of object *O* exists relative to our present scheme *C* if and only if *O* is recognized by *C* directly or recognized by it indirectly through being recognized by some predecessor or successor scheme? That, I fear, cannot suffice, since there might be sorts of particles that always go undiscovered by us, and sorts of artifacts in long-disappeared cultures unknown to us, whose conceptual schemes are not predecessors of ours.

Shall we then say that what exists relative to our present scheme *C* is what it recognizes directly, what it recognizes indirectly through its predecessors or successors, and what it *would* recognize if we had developed appropriately or were to do so now, and had been or were to be appropriately situated? This seems the sort of answer required, but it obviously won't be easy to say what appropriateness amounts to in our formula, in its various guises. Whether it is worth it to specify our formula further so as to assuage the foregoing concerns will depend on whether even our preliminary formulation is defensible against certain natural objections. We next formulate and answer five such objections.

B. OBJECTIONS AND REPLIES

Objection 1

Take a sort of object O recognized by our scheme C, with various instances; for example, the sort Planet, with various particular planets as instances: Mercury, Venus, etc. The instances, say we, exist, which amounts to saying that they exist relative to our scheme. But if we had not existed there would have been no scheme of ours for anything to exist relative to; nor would there have been our actual scheme C either. For one thing, we may just assume the contingent existence of our actual scheme to depend on people's actually granting a certain status to certain constitutive forms. If we had not existed, therefore, the constitutive form for the sort Planet would not have had, relative to our conceptual scheme, the status that makes it possible "that there be instances of that sort, particular planets." And from this it apparently follows that if we had not existed there would have been no planets: no Mercury, no Venus, and so on.

Reply. While existing in the actual world x we now have a conceptual scheme C_x relative to which we assert existence, when we assert it at all. Now we suppose a possible world w in which we are not to be found, in which indeed no life of any sort is to be found. Still we may, in x: (a) consider alternative world w and recognize that our absence there would have no effect on the existence or course of a single planet or star, that Mercury, Venus, and the rest would all still make their appointed rounds just as they do in x; while yet (b) this recognition, which after all takes place in x, is still relativized to C_x, so that the existence in w of whatever exists in x relative to C_x need not be affected at all by the absence from w of C_x, and indeed of every conceptual scheme and of every being who could have a conceptual scheme. For when we suppose existence in w, or allow the possibility of existence in w, *we* do so *in* x, and we do so there still relative to C_x, to our present conceptual scheme, and what it recognizes directly or indirectly, or ideally.

Objection 2

What does it matter whether we "recognize" the snowdiscall form (being in shape between round and disc-shaped, inclusive)? We are anyhow "committed" to there being such a property in any case, to there being the property or condition of being shaped in that inclusive way. If a piece of snow is in shape anywhere between disc-shaped and round then it just is a snowdiscall. So there must be lots of snowdiscalls in existence and that must be nothing new. What is the problem? Could we not even just define a "caog" as anything that is a cat or a dog, and are there not as many caogs in existence as are in the union of the set of cats and the set of dogs? Why should anyone worry about this "explosion"? Why not just admit the obvious: that, yes, there are snowdiscalls, and caogs, even if heretofore they had not been so-called?

Not only is that obvious. If anyone is misguided enough to want to avoid admitting the obvious, it does not really help to introduce some conceptually relative notion of existence according to which the entities that so exist are only those that we are committed to through the properties and kinds that we admit in our ideology and ontology. For if we admit being a dog as an ordinary, harmless enough property, and the kind dog as well, along with being a cat, and so on, then we are implicitly committed to admitting anything that is either a dog or a cat, as being "either a dog or a cat," and that is tantamount to admitting that there are caogs—not under this description, of course, but what does that matter?

Reply. That is all quite true, of course, but not in conflict with existential relativity, which is a thesis about ontological constitution, presupposing as it does that there are levels of individuals, and thus individuals on a higher level, constituted out of individuals on a lower level. How then are the constituted entities constitutable out of the constituting entities? One (partial, Aristotelian) answer: A constituted entity must derive from the satisfaction by the constituting entity (or entities) of a condition (a property or relation, a "form"). *Any* condition? That is absolutism, and leads to the "explosion." Only conditions from a restricted set? *How*, in what way, restricted? Somehow by reference to the conceptual scheme of the speaker or thinker who attributes existence? This is existential relativity (of the sort at issue here).

Returning to the examples of the objection: First, yes, of course there are snowdiscalls if all one means by this is that there are pieces of snow with a shape somewhere between disc-shaped and round. And when something is so shaped and, also, more specifically, round, then it is not only such a snowdiscall but also a round piece of snow, a "snowround," let's say. But one and numerically the same thing is then both the snowdiscall and the snowround. And this is no more puzzling than is the fact that someone can be both a mother and a daughter, or both red and round, or both an apple and a piece of fruit, and so on. When *I* introduced the term "snowdiscall" this is not what I had in mind. In my sense, a "snowdiscall" is not just any piece of snow with a shape between round and disc-shaped. Nor is a snowball just a round piece of snow, a snowround. For a round piece of snow can survive squashing, unlike the snowball that it constitutes, which is destroyed, not just changed, when it is squashed. The question is: what is special about the form of being round combined with an individual piece of snow, what is special about the ordered pair, let's say, that makes it a suitable matter-form pair for the constitution of a constituted individual, a particular snowball? Would any other shape, between roundness and flatness, also serve as such a form, along with that individual piece of snow? Could they together yield a matter-form pair that might also serve, in its own way, for the formation, the constitution of its own individual: not a snowball, presumably, but its own different kind of individual? It is to *this* question that the absolutist would answer in the affirmative, while the existential relativist might well answer in the negative.

According to existential relativity in ontology, what then is required for a matter-form pair to serve as the form and matter for the constitution of an individual, a constituted individual? Answer: that the sort of matter-form combination in question be countenanced by the relevant conceptual scheme, a conceptual scheme determined by the context of thought or utterance.

Objection 3

If it is granted that things can exist prior to the development of any conceptual scheme whatever, prior to the evolution of any thinkers who could have a conceptual scheme, is that not a concession to absolutism? Is it not being conceded that things exist "out there, in themselves," independently of conceptual schemes altogether, so that things do not exist in virtue of our conceptual choices after all. Rather things exist "in themselves." Reality itself manages somehow to cut the cookies unaided by humans. Isn't this just absolutism after all? What can be left of existential relativity after this has been granted?

Reply. Compare this. If I say, "The Empire State Building is 180 miles away," my utterance is true, but the sentence I utter is true only relative to my present position. If I had uttered that sentence elsewhere then I might well have said something false. So my sentence is true relative to my spatial position, but it is not true or false just on its own, independently of such context. And, in a sense, that the Empire State Building is 180 miles away is true relative to my present position but false relative to many other positions. However, it is not so that the Empire State Building is 180 miles from here *in virtue of* my present position. The Empire State Building would have been 180 miles from here even had I been located elsewhere. Whether I am here or not does not determine the distance of the Empire State Building relative to this place here.

Existential relativity can be viewed as a doctrine rather like the relativity involved in the evaluation of the truth of indexical sentences or thoughts. In effect, "existence claims" can be viewed as implicitly indexical, and that is what my existential relativist is suggesting. So when someone says or thinks that *O*s exist, this is to be evaluated relative to the position of the speaker or thinker in "ontological space." Relative to the thus distinguished conceptual scheme, it might be that *O*s do exist, although this is not true relative to many other conceptual schemes.

But what is it about a "conceptual scheme" that determines whether or not it is true to say that "*O*s exist"? Answer: what determines whether "there are" constituted entities of a certain sort relative to a certain conceptual scheme would be that scheme's criteria of existence (or individuation). And what are these? They are specifications of the appropriate pairings of kinds of individuals with properties or relations. Appropriate for what? For the constitution of constituted entities, *in the dispensation of that conceptual scheme*.

When one says or thinks "*O*s exist," then, according to existential relativity this is not true or false absolutely. Its truth value must be determined relative to one's conceptual scheme, to one's "conceptual position," including its criteria of existence. However, even if one's claim that "*O*s exist" must be evaluated relative to one's conceptual position, so that it can be very naturally said that "*O*s exist" relative to one's conceptual position (in that sense), it does not follow that "*O*s exist" only *in virtue* of one's conceptual position, in that if one had not existed with some such conceptual scheme, or at least if no one had existed with some such conceptual scheme, then there would have been "no *O*s in existence." This no more follows than it follows from the relativity of the truth of my statement "The Empire State Building is 180 miles from here" that the Empire State Building is that far from here as a result of *my* being here (even if I am the speaker or thinker). Despite the relativity of the truth of my statement, the Empire State Building *would have been* exactly where it is, 180 miles from here, even if I had not been here. Similarly, *O*s might have existed relative to this my (our) conceptual position, even if no one had existed to occupy this position.

Objection 4

It is not easy for me to understand what relative reference in thought would be. Relative reference in *language*, however, seems explicable in terms of conventions to refer *simpliciter* in thought. There is a rule for relative reference (for the first-person pronoun [I]): [I] refers to x relative to y iff $x = y$. But the rule only gives us truth-conditions for propositions attributing relative reference; it doesn't explain it. Correspondingly, I have trouble grasping existential relativity, even when restricted to supervenient entities. If entities in one layer of reality exist and have their properties *simpliciter*, it seems to me that either they determine *simpliciter* the existence and properties of a class of entities or they don't. What would determination relative to a conceptual scheme be? Wouldn't it be more palatable to conclude that there are snowdiscalls as well as snowballs?

Moreover, if we accept existential relativity, can we recognize disagreement between users of "rival" conceptual schemes? One population recognizes snowballs but not snowdiscalls, let us say, while another has the reverse preference. Further, suppose nothing prevents the populations from discussing this difference in what they respectively recognize. Would not each population know both what snowdiscalls would be and what snowballs would be, even if each "recognizes" only one of these. Nevertheless, shouldn't we find in the difference between them some real disagreement? If we say that to recognize *F*s is to believe there are *F*s, we can of course easily locate such disagreement. But if we say that to recognize *F*s is to use a conceptual scheme that recognizes *F*s, with no further explanation possible of recognition by schemes, wherein might reside the disagreement?

Reply. Can't one think of it as follows? There is some sort of selection function that for a community or an individual picks out the matter-form pairs that are suitable for object constitution. One's selection function determines one's position in ontological (individuation) space. "The objects that there can be"—this for our relativist view is not an absolutely and objectively denoting description; rather, it denotes relative to a position. So it is in that respect rather like "the objects that are nearby." When you and I occupy sufficiently different spatial positions, we need not disagree if you say "*X* is nearby" and I say "*X* is not nearby." Similarly we need not disagree with the alien culture if, speaking of the same place, we say, "There are only snowballs here," and they say, "There are only snowdiscalls here."

Wherein then resides our disagreement? Perhaps just in the fact that we differ in what we include in our respective ontological positions. Well, it resides at least in that. But do we not disagree also in that we believe that there are in fact snowballs and disbelieve that there are snowdiscalls, whereas they believe there are in fact snowdiscalls and disbelieve that there are snowballs? This is the move that seems questionable in the light of our analogy to judgments of what is nearby. Given that what we say is said from relevantly different positions it may just be that we are not disagreeing at all in those respective beliefs.

"There are" and, especially, "there can be" are according to this view covertly indexical. Therefore we cannot report their beliefs by saying that according to their belief there can be no snowballs. They may say, "There can be no snowballs," and they may even say, "There can be no objects composed of a chunk of snow and roundness." But we could not properly describe them as believing that there can be no snowballs or even as believing that there can be no objects so composed. We can no more do that than I (from Providence) can unambiguously describe you as believing that Boston is far away, just because you in Tokyo say sincerely, "Boston is far away."

The lack of agreement ("disagreement" may now well strike one as the wrong word here) would then reside simply in the fact that we are selecting different matter-form categories. Of course there may be reasons why it is better to select one set of categories rather than another, pragmatic reasons at least; rather as there may be reasons why it is better to be at one location rather than another. But this would not show that the actual judgments of "what is nearby" made by those poorly positioned are inferior to the judgments made by those better positioned. Nor would it show that there is any real disagreement when one says, "*X* is nearby," and the other says, "*X* is not nearby." Their only failure of "agreement" is their lack of spatial coincidence. Similarly, to have different positions in ontological space might reveal a lack of coincidence in the selected matter-form object-constituting pairs, but little else by way of real disagreement as to what there can be or what there cannot be. (There might be such disagreement anyway; but it would not derive just from the occupancy of divergent ontological positions. Rather, the disagreement might be over, say, whether there can be things that are cubical and eight-sided, or over similar property combination questions.)

That all seems compatible with its being nontrivial to determine what objects there can be relative to our position in ontological space. Nothing rules out the possibility that the selection function operate beneath the surface, such that it is far from easy to determine our implicit individuation and persistence criteria. Their being relative to the psychology of the individual or the culture of the group would seem compatible with its being a matter of difficult analysis, psychological or cultural, to tease out just what they are.

Objection 5

Surely it will prove difficult to be selective about existential relativity. Could we reasonably say that some things (atoms, perhaps) exist *simpliciter* whereas others (snowballs) exist only relative to our scheme? If we did, wouldn't we be pressed to conclude that snowballs do not *really* exist: they only "exist" courtesy of our scheme? Thus facts about atoms don't determine that there are snowballs, but they might perhaps be said to do so relative to our scheme. If so, doesn't our scheme then commit us to some falsehoods? Our scheme would then seem to attribute existence to snowballs (snowdiscalls), whereas snowballs do not exist (not *really*).

Reply. Evaluable claims as to what is or is not nearby require that the claimant be spatially located. Analogously, sensible judgments as to what objects do or do not exist, or, indeed, might or might not exist, may require a subject located in ontological space. There might still be good reasons to change our ontological position, however, just as there often is good reason to change our spatial location. And if we do move, we might in the new location be able to make true judgments that we were not in any position to make in the earlier location.

Are we precluded from supposing that there might be, or even that there definitely is, or more yet that there must be, some noumenal reality constituted in itself, with no relativity to categories or criteria of individuation and/or persistence contributed by the mind or by the culture? I can't see that we are.

Nevertheless, when we say that there are atoms, the truth of our utterance seems independent of our point of view. Whether there are atoms gives no sign of being relative to our ontological position. Would atoms be like snowballs, so that some alien culture might fail to recognize atoms, might just have some other set of categories? Surely they would just be missing something real if they miss atoms. Well, yes; but perhaps we can do justice to this fact from within existential relativity.

Consider again the analogy to judgments of distance. Boston is nearby. That's a fact I am aware of, and one I probably could not express nonperspectivally. Would someone with a different location, far from here, be unable to grasp that fact? Would they not be missing something real if they missed that fact? Here we would need to consider the coordination of thoughts, starting with simple location-relative thoughts. For example, the fact that Boston is near me now is a fact that someone else far away and in the future might still grasp even though it would be grasped, not by means of that very perspectival proposition, but by some appropriately coordinated one. Someone with a snowdiscall ontology could perhaps grasp a fact that I grasp by saying, "There are snowballs," but only by means of a coordinated proposition such as, perhaps, "There are non-disc-shaped snowdiscalls."

We can always drop down a level if our schemes coincide at the lower level: for example, if we both believe in chunks of snow and we both have a grasp of the properties of roundness and of being disc-shaped, and so on, we can compare notes at that lower level. But if a level recognizes items, be they particles or fields or whatever, and if we think of these items in terms of the matter-form model, with entailed criteria of individuation and persistence, then the same issues will recur. Nevertheless, every level might allow for agreement or disagreement determined by coordinated, perspectival propositions, such coordination among propositions to be understood in terms of some deeper ontological level, deeper in a sense suggested as follows. When I think, "Boston is near to where I am now," a fact makes that true, one involving two entities and a distance between them. Of course, if one tries to pick out the entity that is oneself, it may not be possible for *us* to do this without doing it perspectivally: either I do it, in which case I use the first-person conceptual mechanism(s), or you do it, in which case you might use some second- or third-person mechanism(s). Actually stating the fact in virtue of which my thought "Boston is nearby" is true may be a problem if one tries to do so nonperspectivally; I actually think it cannot be done, not by humans anyway. But that need not prevent us from supposing that a fact *is* stated and could be stated by any one of a large number of coordinated propositions, which would be used by different, appropriately positioned subjects; a fact, moreover, that is not mind-dependent, in the sense that its being a fact is independent of its being thought of by anyone, in any of the various perspectival ways in which it might be thought of. What is that fact, one might well ask, what could it be? Why not "the fact that Boston is nearby"? The point is that I have no way to state it except perspectivally; and of course the truth of the thought or proposition that I thereby state is not objective or mind-independent. But consider the fact thereby stated, the fact stated in that mind-dependent way, a fact that we humans may be unable to state except in some such mind-dependent way. As far as I can see, it simply does not follow that the fact itself must therefore be mind-dependent. So one single mind-independent fact can be approached from indefinitely many perspectives and can be stated in the corresponding, mutually coordinated perspectival ways. All of these statements, and the thoughts they would express, are of course mind-dependent, at least in the sense that they are not truth-evaluable except relative to the mind that uses them. But from that it does not follow that there is no mind-independent fact that is thereby stated, even if we lack access to that fact except perspectivally, and hence mind-dependently.[1]

C. SOME MIDDLE GROUND?

What then shall we say exists relative to our present scheme *C*? Assuming the success of our defense against the foregoing objections, may we answer that what so exists is what our scheme *C* recognizes directly, what it recognizes indirectly through its predecessors or successors, and what it *would* recognize if we had developed appropriately or were to do so now, and had been or were to be appropriately situated? This does seem the sort of answer required by our relativism, but we are still left wondering what "appropriateness" amounts to in our formula, in its various guises. Let us step back and reconsider.

We are pulled in several directions at once, as is typical of a paradox.

On the one hand, when a certain combination $(w + m)$ of a piece of wood w and a piece of metal m is used both as a doorstop and occasionally as a hammer, it constitutes both that doorstop and that hammer. Are there then three things there: $(w + m)$, the doorstop, and the hammer? Are these distinct entities, occupying the same location? One is drawn here to say that really there is just $(w + m)$, which might be used as a hammer, or used as a doorstop, or both.

On the other hand, why stop with $(w + m)$? Why not say that what really exists in that situation is just w and m severally, which, if properly joined, can be used for hammering, for stopping doors, and the like. But why stop even there? After all, w itself will be a combination of certain molecules, each of which in turn combines certain atoms, and so forth. Where does it all stop? What is the bottom?

How indeed can we know that there *is* a bottom? How do we know that there is a level that does not itself derive from some underlying level of reality in the way the hammer derives from $(w + m)$'s having a certain use, or in the way $(w + m)$ derives from w and m severally, when the two are relevantly joined, or the way w derives from certain molecules being arrayed a certain way? And so on.

Science, so far as I can tell, itself postulates no such bottom. Only philosophers do so. But on what basis? Is this just a metaphysical dogma?

Consider now the eliminativism that rejects the entities at any given level ontologically derivative from an underlying level. To avoid the ontological nihilism for which there is absolutely nothing ever anywhere, such eliminativism must commit itself to the existence of an ontological bottom level. But, again, this seems little better than dogma.

However, if one does therefore admit a layered reality, with ontological levels derived from underlying levels, what governs such derivation? The most general characterization of the way in which ontologically derivative particulars derive from an underlying reality would seem to be our Aristotelian conception according to which a sequence of particulars (matters) at the underlying level exemplifies a property or relation (form), giving rise thereby to a distinctive object at the higher, derived level.

But now our earlier questions recur: One would want to know what restrictions if any there might be on matter-form pairs that constitute derived entities. Why rule out entities of the sort ($w + m$) or properties of the form: having such and such a function (hammering, stopping doors, etc.)? Why not allow that these can constitute distinctive derived entities? And why not allow not only a piece of snow as matter and approximate roundness as form, but also a piece of snow as matter, and a shape anywhere between roundness and being disc-shaped as form? And if we allow these, then where does it all stop? We seem driven to the explosion.

Compare the claim that a certain irregularly shaped figure *f* drawn on a surface is "shapeless." Such a claim is interestingly relative to context. On the one hand it might be true iff figure *f* has no shape whatever, in which case it would of course be false, since *f* does have some shape or other, surely, however irregular. And yet in another context it might be evaluated as true iff *f* lacks any of the shapes in some restricted set of shapes: where the context would somehow determine the specific restriction. Thus in one context the religious background may pick out a certain irregular shape as highly significant, in which case items with that shape would not count as "shapeless," whereas in other contexts they would.

On an analogous contextual relativism of *existential* claims, the objects on the derived level relevant to the truth evaluation of an existential claim are those in some restricted set, the context somehow determining the restriction. Compare here: "There is nothing in that box." (What about the air?) Or "there is only a hammer here." (What about the doorstop?) Or even "there is only a snowball here." (What about the snowdiscall?)

So our choices, none pleasant, seem to be these:

- *Eliminativism*: Supposed entities that derive ontologically from underlying entities do not exist, not really. But this carries a commitment to an ontological bottom, one that seems little better than dogma, on pain of nihilism.
- *Absolutism*: Eliminativism is false. Moreover, there are no restrictions on the appropriate matter-form pairs that can constitute objects.[2] *Any* matter-form pair whatever, at any given ontological level, determines a corresponding derived entity at the next higher level, so long as the matter takes that form. This is the "explosion" of reality.
- *Unrestricted absolutism*: Absolutism is true. Moreover, any existential claim is to be assessed for truth or falsity relative to all objects and properties without restriction.
- *Conceptual relativism*: Absolutism is true. Moreover, existential claims are true or false only relative to the context of speech or thought, which restricts the sorts of objects relevant to the assessment. Such restrictions are governed by various pragmatic or theoretical considerations.

Note how moderate this conceptual *relativism* turns out to be. It is even absolutist and objectivist enough to accept the "explosion." Reality is objectively much richer and more bizarre than is perhaps commonly recognized. All sorts of weird entities derive from any given level of particulars and properties. Snowdiscalls are just one straightforwardly simple example. Our objective metaphysics is hence absolutist and latitudinarian, given our inability to find any well-motivated objective restriction on the matter-form pairs that constitute derived entities. Our relativism applies to the truth or falsity of existential and other ontologically committed claims. It is here that a restriction is imposed by the conceptual scheme of the claimant speaker or thinker. But the restriction is as harmless and even trivial as is that involved in a claim that some selected figure *f* is "shapeless" made in full awareness that *f* does have some specific shape, however irregular. Similarly, someone who claims that there are only snowballs at location *L* may be relying on some context-driven restriction of the totality of objects which, in full strictness, one *would* recognize at that location. Speaking loosely and popularly we may hence say that there are only snowballs there, even if strictly and philosophically one would recognize much that is not dreamt of in our ordinary talk.

Have we a robust intuition that snowballs are a different order of entity, somehow less a product of conceptual artifice, than snowdiscalls, or a robust intuition that doorstops are too dependent on the vagaries of human convenience and convention to count as distinctive kinds of entities no matter how artificial? And if doorstops do not count, how or why can cars count? Or is any such intuition displaced under reflection by corresponding intuitions about such natural kinds as animals and elements? But what exactly enables us to distinguish the distinguished classes of entities favored as objectively real, by contrast with the artificial or shadowy snowdiscalls, doorstops, hammers, snowballs, and even cars? I have here raised this question, but any claim of originality would be ludicrous. Here I have tried to frame that question in a context that rejects eliminativism on one side, and questions the "explosion" on the other. But in the end I do express a preference for the latitudinarian "explosion." This preference is motivated by the rejection of eliminativism on one side, and by my failure to find attractive and well-motivated restrictions on allowable matter-form pairs on the other. My preference can only be tentative, however, given the vast history of the issue and the subtle and intricate contemporary discussions of it. I do point to a way in which one might be able to accommodate some of the intuitions that drive the desire for restriction, through a kind of metalinguistic or metaconceptual ascent. And it is through this ascent that our relativism emerges. It remains to be seen, however, whether the accommodation thus made possible will be accommodating enough.

NOTES

1. Part A of this paper draws from part C of my "Putnam's Pragmatic Realism," *Journal of Philosophy* 90 (1993): 605–26. My thanks to Matthew McGrath for helpful comments, and also to Reginald Allen and Mitchell Green, for helpful comments at an APA Central session on my earlier paper.

2. Again, the reference should be, more strictly, to "matter(s)-form" pairs, so as to allow plural constitution.

Midwest Studies in Philosophy, XXIII (1999)

Unity without Identity: A New Look at Material Constitution

LYNNE RUDDER BAKER

It is time to rethink age-old questions about material constitution. What is the relation between, say, a lump of clay and a statue that it makes up, or between a red and white piece of metal and a stop sign, or between a person and her body? Assuming that there is a single relation between members of each of these pairs, is the relation "strict" identity, "contingent" identity or something else?[1] Although this question has generated substantial controversy recently,[2] I believe that there is philosophical gain to be had from thinking through the issues from scratch. Many of the charges and countercharges are based on the following dichotomy: For any x and y that are related as the lump of clay is to the statue that it makes up, either x is identical to y, or x and y are separate entities, independent of each other. By giving up this dichotomy, we will be able to begin to make sense, I hope, of an intermediate unity relation that holds promise for solving a raft of philosophical problems, including the problem of how persons are related to their bodies.[3] And if I am correct, then this relation—constitution without identity—is ubiquitous and interesting in its own right, apart from the light that it sheds on human persons.

My overall aim here is constructive: I want to set out and defend an explicit account of what it is for an object x to constitute an object y at time t. According to my account, if x constitutes y (at any time), then $x \neq y$. (Thus, I reject the first half of the dichotomy above.) Although I join the ranks of those who deny that the relation between the members of any of the pairs is identity in any sense, I depart from those ranks by also denying a central aspect of what has been called "the standard account."[4] Suppose that "Copper" is a name for the piece of copper that makes up a copper statue, "Statue." According to "the standard account," Copper is not (predicatively) a statue.[5] I believe that "the standard account" construes Copper and Statue as *too* separate. On my view, by contrast, the relation between Copper and Statue is so intimate that, although Copper and Statue are not identical, Copper is, nonetheless, a statue in virtue of the fact that Copper constitutes a statue. (Thus, I reject the second half of the dichotomy.) Copper borrows the property of being a statue from Statue, where "borrowing" is spelled out in detail below. The account of borrowing properties will show why, when *x* constitutes *y* at *t*, *x* and *y* share so many of their properties at *t*, without being identical. So, my account is intended as a third alternative, beyond the alternatives (either identity or separate existence) countenanced by the dichotomy.

Constitution is a relation in many ways similar to identity, but it is not the same relation as identity.[6] We need constitution to be similar to identity in order to account for the fact that if *x* constitutes *y*, then *x* and *y* are spatially coincident and share many properties; but we also need constitution to differ from identity in order to account for the fact that if *x* constitutes *y*, then *x* and *y* are of different kinds and can survive different sorts of changes. Since a large part of my task is to distinguish constitution from identity, I will be emphasizing ways in which *x* and *y* are distinct if *x* constitutes *y*. But too much emphasis on their distinctness would be misleading: for, as we see in the case of Copper and Statue, *x* and *y* are not separate, independently existing individuals. Again: I want to make sense of constitution as a third category, intermediate between identity and separate existence.[7]

My starting point is with familiar things that populate the everyday world—"moderate-sized specimens of dry goods," as J. L. Austin called them.[8] Beginning in *medias res*, I want to give a unified account of a fundamental relation—constitution—that holds everywhere one turns: Pieces of paper constitute dollar bills; DNA molecules constitute genes; hunks of metal constitute carburetors; bodies constitute persons; stones constitute monuments; pieces of marble constitute sculptures.[9] If constitution is as widespread a relation as I think it is, then there is good reason to try to develop an account of it.

AN ACCOUNT OF CONSTITUTION

Let's start with Michelangelo's *David*. *David* is a magnificent statue constituted by a certain piece of marble; call it "Piece."[10] But *David* (the piece of sculpture, the artwork) is not identical to Piece. If *David* and Piece were identical, then, by a version of Leibniz's Law, there would be no property borne by Piece but not borne by *David*, and no property borne by *David* but not borne by Piece.[11] However, Piece (that very piece of marble) could exist in a world without art. Although I do not know how to specify conditions for individuating pieces of marble, I am confident that they do not include a relation to an artworld.[12] Piece could have existed in a world without art, in which case Piece would not have had the property of being a statue. By contrast, *David* could not exist without being a statue. So, *David* has a property—being a statue wherever it exists—that Piece lacks. But if *David* were identical to Piece, then it would be impossible for "one" to have a property that "the other" lacked—even an unusual modal property like *being a statue wherever and whenever it exists*, Since *David* is essentially a statue but Piece is not, *David* has a property that Piece lacks. Therefore, "constitution" is not to be defined as identity.

The reasoning leading to the conclusion that *David* is not identical to Piece is highly controversial, and I have defended it elsewhere.[13] At this point, I am only trying to illustrate the intuitions behind the notion of constitution. The basic intuition is that, as a relation between objects, identity is necesssary: if $x = y$, then necessarily $x = y$.[14] If $x = y$, then x cannot differ from y in any respect, including respects in which x might have been, or might become, different from the way x is now. That is, if $x = y$, then x and y share their so-called "modal properties"—properties of being possibly such and such or of being necessarily such and such. I agree with Kripke when he says, "Where [*F*] is any property at all, including a property involving modal operators, and if x and y are the same object and x had a certain property F, then y has to have the same property F."[15] So, again, since Piece could exist in a world without art, but *David* could not, they differ in their (modal) properties, and hence are not identical.[16] Consequently, the corrrect account of the relation between *David* and Piece will have to be more complicated than simple identity.

On the other hand, as I think everyone would agree, *David* and Piece are not just two independent individuals. For one thing, many of *David*'s aesthetic properties depend on Piece's physical properties: *David*'s pent-up energy depends on, among other things, the way that the marble is shaped to distribute the weight. Another indication that *David* and Piece are not just two independent individuals is that they are spatially coincident. Not only are they located at exactly the same places at the same times, but also they are alike in many other ways as well: they have the same size, weight, color, smell, and so on. And their similarity is no accident: for *David* does not exist separately from Piece. Nor does *David* have Piece as a proper part. For, pretty clearly, *David* is not identical to Piece plus some other thing. *David* is neither identical to nor independent from Piece. The relation between *David* and Piece is, rather, constitution.[17]

If I am right, then instances of constitution abound: A particular school is constituted by a certain building, which in turn is constituted by an aggregate of bricks. (The same high school could have been constituted by a different building; the same building that in fact constituted the high school could have constituted an office building.) There are, of course, limits on what can constitute what, and the limits differ depending on the kind of thing in question. Not just anything could have constituted *David*: if Michelangelo had carved a 12-cm male nude out of jade and named it "David," it would not have been *David*; it would not have been the very same statue that *we* call "David." To take other examples, my car could not have been constituted by a soap bubble; nor could Kripke's lectern have been constituted by a block of ice.[18] A soap bubble is too ephemeral to constitute a car, and a block of ice, which melts fairly quickly, is unsuited to play a "lectern-role" in our temperatures. Further, some things—ships, but perhaps not statues—may be constituted by different things at different times.[19]

The basic idea behind the notion of constitution is this: when certain things with certain properties are in certain circumstances, new things with new properties come into existence. For example, when a combination of chemicals occurs in a certain environment, a new thing comes into existence: an organism. Or, when a large stone is placed in certain circumstances, it acquires new properties, and a new thing—a monument to those who died in battle—comes into being. And the constituted thing (the stone monument) has effects in virtue of having properties that the constituting thing (the stone) would not have had if it had not constituted a monument. The monument attracts speakers and small crowds on patriotic holidays; it brings tears to people's eyes; it arouses protests. Had it not constituted a monument, the large stone would have had none of these effects. When stones first came to constitute monuments, a new kind of thing with new properties—properties that are causally efficacious—came into being.

Constitution is a contingent relation between individual things. First, constitution is a relation between *individual* things.[20] Neither "stuff" (e.g., gold) nor properties (e.g., the property of having atomic number 79) are *relata* of the constitution relation.[21] As I am using the term "constitution," *David* is constituted by a *piece* of marble, not by marble as stuff.[22] Of course, *David* is made of marble, but the relation between a constituted thing and some stuff is not what I am calling constitution. What enters into the constitution relation is a marble thing (that I have named "Piece"), not mere stuff. Second, constitution is a *contingent* relation: Piece could have existed and yet failed to constitute anything at all. If x constitutes y at some time, then the existence of x at that time does not by itself entail the existence of y.[23]

Many of the relational properties that make something the thing that it is are intentional. For example, as we have seen, nothing would be *David* that failed to be a statue, and nothing could be a statue except in relation to an artworld, or an artist's intention, or something else that resists nonintentional description. Let us say that a property H is intentional if and only if H could not be exemplified in a world in which no one ever had a belief, desire, intention, hope, expectation, fear, or other propositional attitude. And let us say that a particular thing, x, is an intentional object if and only if x could not exist in a world in which no one had ever had a belief, desire, intention, hope, expectation, fear, or other propositional attitudes. ("Intentional relation" and "intentional phenomenon" may be defined similarly.) Then, artifacts and artworks, as well as persons and passports, are intentional objects.[24] Indeed, many familiar objects are intentional objects: carburetors, cathedrals, menus, birth certificates, flags, search warrants, trophies, obituaries.

But it is important to recognize that not all constituted things are intentional. Genes are constituted by DNA molecules. Something is a gene only in virtue of its relational properties. An otherwise empty world, in which a few DNA molecules coalesced, would not thereby contain genes. In order for DNA molecules to be genes, they must play a certain role in the reproduction of organisms. Although genes are constituted things, they are paradigmatically not intentional entities in the sense just specified. (Presumably, there were genes before there were any creatures with propositional attitudes.) So, appeal to constitution involves no special pleading on behalf of the intentional. Indeed, a prominent virtue of the notion of constitution is that it yields a single account of both intentional and nonintentional individuals, without reducing intentional to nonintentional individuals.

The features of constitution may be codified. For codification, I need two ideas: the idea of a primary kind, and the idea of what I'll call "circumstances." Each concrete individual is fundamentally a member of exactly one kind—call it its "primary kind." To answer the question, "What most fundamentally is x?" we cite x's primary kind by using a substance noun: for example, "a horse," or "a bowl." x's primary kind is a kind of thing, not just "stuff"; Piece's primary kind is not just marble, but a piece of marble; the Nile's primary kind is not just water, but a river (of water). Since *David*'s primary kind, for example, is a statue, call the property of being a statue *David*'s "primary-kind property." An important feature of primary kinds is this: An object could not cease to have its primary-kind property without ceasing to exist. If being a horse is a primary-kind property, then if we change the number of horses (and nothing else), we change the number of things in the world. Contrast, say, husbands, which are not a primary kind: fewer husbands may leave the number of objects in the world unchanged. So, if being an F is x's primary-kind property, then being an F is essential to x: it is impossible for anything that is not an F to be (identical to) x.[25]

It would be useful to have a theory of primary kinds. The general question that a theory of primary kinds would answer is this: under what conditions does one thing come to constitute a new entity, as opposed to simply gaining a property? For example, suppose that I buy an anvil with the intention of using it to hold open the barn door, and that I use it in that capacity for years. Is the doorstop an entity distinct from the anvil? Does the anvil now constitute a doorstop? Well, the anvil does have the property of being a doorstop, but I doubt that many would say that the doorstop is an entity distinct from the anvil. Being a doorstop is just a property that the anvil acquired. A theory of primary kinds would provide a principled way to distinguish between cases (like the anvil/doorstop) in which an object merely acquires a property and cases (like Piece/*David*) in which a new entity comes into existence. Since a theory of primary kinds would be tantamount to a theory of everything, however, it is not surprising (though still regrettable) that I do not have one. And since we are constantly bringing into existence new kinds of things—from airliners to personal computers—there is no saying in advance exactly what the primary kinds will turn out to be.

In the absence of a theory of primary kinds, let me suggest a consideration that would lead us to say whether a case is one of constitution or of mere property acquisition. If x constitutes y, then y has whole classes of causal properties that x would not have had if x had not constituted anything. The anvil acquires the property of being a doorstop by our enlisting a physical property of the anvil—its heaviness—for a special purpose: to hold open the barn door. The use of the anvil as a doorstop does not bring about instantiation of whole classes of properties that anvils per se do not have. On the other hand, *David* has many causal properties of different kinds that Piece would not have had if Piece had not constituted anything. And you and I have uncountably many causal properties that our bodies would not have had if they had not constituted anything—from having a good time at graduation, to lending money to a friend, to landing a good teaching job, to serving on a jury, and on and on. So, even without a theory of primary kinds, we have some clear cases of constitution, and we have two characteristics—the constituted thing is stable and has different kinds of causal properties than the constituting thing would have had if it had not constituted anything—that mark off constitution from mere property acquisition. In any case, in order to define "x constitutes y at t," I need the idea of a primary kind.

Second, in order to define "x constitutes y at t" in full generality, I need a variable for different answers to the question, in virtue of what is y the kind of thing that it is? For example, it is in virtue of certain legal conventions that a particular piece of paper constitutes a marriage license; it is in virtue of the arrangement of molecules that something constitutes a block of ice; it is in virtue of its evolutionary history that a particular conglomerate of cells constitutes a human heart.[26] I'll call the various answers "circumstances." It is only in certain circumstances—different circumstances for marriage licenses and human hearts—that one thing constitutes another. It is in virtue of one kind of circumstance that the piece of paper constitutes a marriage license, and it is in virtue of an entirely different kind of circumstance that the conglomerate of cells constitutes a human heart. The variable for "circumstances" (*D*) ranges over states of affairs in virtue of which something is the kind of thing that it is.

Many properties can be instantiated only in certain circumstances. For example, the property of being a national flag can be instantiated only in circumstances where there are beings with certain kinds of intentional states, certain kinds of social and political entities and certain conventions. Such circumstances are essential to national flags: nothing is a flag without them. For any primary-kind property *G*, such as the property of being a national flag, call the milieu required for something to have *G*, "*G*-favorable" circumstances. *G*-favorable circumstances are the total background conditions that must obtain for something to have *G*. For any particular place and time, the presence of *G*-favorable circumstances is necessary for the property *G* to be instantiated then and there; but the presence of *G*-favorable circumstances by itself is not sufficient for *G* to be instantiated then and there.[27]

An informal idea of material constitution is this: where *F* and *G* are distinct primary-kind properties, it is possible that an *F* exists without there being any spatially coincident *G*. However, if an *F* is in *G*-favorable circumstances, then there is a new entity, a *G*, that is spatially coincident with the *F* but not identical to it.

Now let me offer a general schema for "constitution." To allow for the possibility that *x* may constitute *y* at one time, but not at another, I have a variable for time; but I'll continue to drop the time index later where it does not matter. Let *F* be *x*'s primary-kind property, and *G* be *y*'s primary-kind property, where $F \neq G$, and *D* be *G*-favorable circumstances. Let F^* be the property of having *F* as one's primary-kind property and G^* be the property of having *G* as one's primary-kind property.[28] Then,

(C) *x* constitutes *y* at $t =_{df}$
- (a) *x* and *y* are spatially coincident at *t* and share all the same material parts at *t*; and
- (b) *x* is in *D* at *t*; and
- (c) It is necessary that $\forall z[(F^*zt$ and *z* is in *D* at $t) \rightarrow \exists u(G^*ut$ and *u* is spatially coincident with *z* at *t*)]; and
- (d) It is possible that (*x* exists at *t* and $\sim\exists w[G^*wt$ and *w* is spatially coincident with *x* at *t*]); and
- (e) If *y* has any nonspatial parts at *t*, then *x* has the same nonspatial parts at *t*.

Let me make three brief comments about (C): First, although I ultimately want to use (C) to show that human persons are material beings, (C) does not rule out there being immaterial things, or even immaterial beings that are constituted. But (e) requires that if there are immaterial constituted things, they are not constituted by wholly material things. Assuming that all the parts of human bodies are spatial parts, then (e) excludes the possibility that a human body could constitute a Cartesian person, where a Cartesian person is defined as consisting of two parts: a body and an immaterial soul.[29] Second, the modalities in (c) and (d)—"it is necessary that" and "it is possible that"—are context-dependent. For any actual situation, there will be relevant alternative situations to be considered. Although relevance will ultimately be determined by the facts of the actual situation, the laws of nature are to be held constant. Moreover, to avoid vacuous satisfaction of (c), the relevant alternatives are always to include some in which the *F* is in *G*-favorable circumstances. The examples in the next section will make clearer how to interpret the modalities. Third, (C) yields what I think are the intuitively correct properties of constitution. (C) guarantees that constitution is not identity. Constitution is an irreflexive relation: clause (d) guarantees that nothing constitutes itself. Constitution is an asymmetric relation: If *x* constitutes *y*, then *y* does not constitute *x*.[30]

To see that constitution is asymmetric, proceed by cases. Suppose that *a* (with primary-kind property *F*) constitutes *b* (with primary-kind property *G*).

> *Case 1*: Necessarily, everything with primary-kind property *G* is constituted by something with primary-kind property *F*. In Case 1, it is not possible that a *G* exists but no spatially coincident *F* exists. But if *b* also constituted *a*, then by (d) it would be possible that a *G* exists and no spatially coincident *F* exists. So, in Case 1, if *a* constitutes *b*, then *b* does not constitute *a* (since [d] is not satisfied for "*b* constitutes *a*").
>
> *Case 2*: Not necessarily everything with primary-kind property *G* is constituted by something with primary-kind property *F*. (Certain *G*-things that are instances of Case 2 are multiply realizable.) In Case 2, it is not necessary that for every *G* in *F*-favorable circumstances, there is a spatially coincident *F*. (For example, a statue may be in piece-of-marble-favorable circumstances and yet be constituted by a piece of bronze, in which case there is no piece of marble spatially coincident with the statue.) But if *b* also constituted *a*, then by (c) necessarily, for any *G* in *F*-favorable circumstances, there would be a spatially coincident *F*. So, in Case 2, if *a* constitutes *b*, then *b* does not constitute *a* (since [c] is not satisfied for "*b* constitutes *a*").

Case 1 and Case 2 exhaust the possibilities. Therefore, constitution is asymmetric.

Now let me illustrate (C) by showing how *David* and Piece satisfy it. Let *F* be the property of being a piece of marble (Piece's primary-kind property). Let *G* be the property of being a statue (*David*'s primary-kind property). Now let *D* be the circumstance of being presented as a three-dimensional figure in an artworld, given a title, and put on display (or whatever is required by the correct theory of art for something to be a statue). Then,

> (a) Piece and *David* are spatially coincident at *t*; and
>
> (b) Piece is in the circumstance of being presented as a three-dimensional figure in an artworld, given a title, and put on display at *t*; and
>
> (c) It is necessary that if anything that has being a piece of marble as its primary-kind property is presented as a three-dimensional figure in an artworld, given a title, and put on display at *t*, then there is something that

has being a statue as its primary-kind property that is spatially coincident with the piece of marble at *t*; and

(d) It is possible that Piece exists at *t* and that no spatially coincident thing that has being a statue as its primary-kind property exists at *t*; and

(e) Neither Piece nor *David* has nonspatial parts.

David would not exist but for the relational and intentional properties of the piece of marble: On (almost?) every theory of art, something is an artwork in virtue of its relations to something else—the artist, the artworld, the history of the medium.[31] The moral here is that what makes a thing the thing that it is—*David*, for example—may be its relational properties, and not always, as tradition has held, its nonrelational properties. Although a number of philosophers have discussed the relation between things like *David* and Piece, they have assumed that something is the thing that it is in virtue of its nonrelational properties.[32] I think that it is time to put aside the long-standing prejudice that what *x* really is—in itself, in its nature—is determined exclusively by *x*'s nonrelational properties. In many cases—as we have seen with *David*—there is no *x* to be considered in isolation, apart from everything else: to abstract away from all the relations would be to abstract away from the *relatum*. More strongly still, in many cases, elimination of the relations is elimination of the *relata*.

Where I depart from tradition is in taking certain relational and intentional properties to be essential properties of concrete things. Not everything that exists could exist in total isolation; hence, if there were only one thing in the world, it would not be a national flag or a gene—even if it had the characteristic pattern of three bands of red, white, and blue that in our world would constitute a national flag, or even if it had the molecular structure of a gene. Thus, I dissent from Allan Gibbard when he says, "If the statue is an entity over and above the piece of clay in that shape, then statues seem to take on a ghostly air."[33] Relational properties are in no way ghostly. (Indeed, this is the lesson of externalism in philosophy of psychology. A belief that water is wet has as an essential property that the believer is in a certain kind of environment.) And it is in virtue of its relational properties that *David* exists. Even if it is also in virtue of its relational properties that Piece exists, there remains this irreducible difference between them: Piece could exist in the absence of an artworld; *David* could not.

For a long time, philosophers have distinguished the "is" of predication (as in "Mark Twain is an author") from the "is" of identity (as in "Mark Twain is [identical to] Samuel Clemens"). If the constitution view is correct, then there is a third sense of "is," distinct from the other two. The third sense of "is" is the "is" of constitution (as in "is (constituted by) a piece of marble.")[34]

BORROWED PROPERTIES

The distinctiveness of the relation between a constituted thing and what constitutes it spills over to the properties of constituted and constituting things. Suppose that *x* has *H*, and we ask, in virtue of what does *x* have *H*? Sometimes the answer will be that *x* has *H* in virtue of constituting something that has *H* or of being constituted by something that has *H*. This important feature of constitution requires a distinction between properties that are (as I'll say) *borrowed* and properties that are not borrowed. The basic idea of borrowing properties may be stated simply like this: Say that *x* and *y* have constitution-relations if and only if either *x* constitutes *y* or *y* constitutes *x*. *H* is a borrowed property of *x* at *t* if *x*'s having *H* at *t* derives exclusively from *x*'s being constitutionally related at *t* to something that has *H* independently at *t*.

Before developing the account of borrowing properties in greater detail, I want to emphasize an important feature of borrowing that distinguishes my construal of constitution from other construals. On my account, borrowing is a two-way street: If *x* constitutes *y* at *t*, then *x* borrows some of its properties from *y* at *t*, *and y* borrows some of its properties from *x* at *t*. A constituting thing may borrow properties from the thing that it constitutes, as well as vice versa. ("Top-down" borrowing of properties is an indication of the antireductive thrust of my position.) Many philosophers are inclined to think that constituted things borrow their properties from what constitutes them, and not vice versa. Calling this the "bottom-up-borrowing-only" claim, let me give some counterexamples to it.[35] To simplify, I shall drop reference to times for a moment. Suppose that among your deceased aunt's possessions, you find a small statue. You think that it is made of a chunk of gold, and you don't know whether the statue is worth any more than the chunk of gold that constitutes it. The appraiser reports that the statue is indeed made of a chunk of gold, and that the statue is worth $10,000; the chunk of gold that constitutes the statue at *t* has a meltdown value of $1,000.[36] But the statue's property of being worth $10,000 is not borrowed from the properties of the chunk of gold that constitutes the statue. Indeed, one of the marks of a piece of fine art is that its value does not depend on the value of the materials that constitute it.

Someone may object: the chunk of gold in its present condition (in which it constitutes the statue) is worth $10,000; it is only its meltdown value (when it would no longer constitute the statue) that is $1,000. Of course, I agree: Being worth $10,000 is a property that is shared by both the statue and the chunk of gold when the chunk of gold constitutes the statue. But this is no objection to the counterexample. It just illustrates the point that I want to make: the chunk of gold in its present condition of constituting a statue is worth $10,000 *in virtue of the fact that the statue is worth $10,000, and not the other way around*. The very same chunk of gold, in the absence of the statue, is worth only $1,000. The statue does not borrow its worth from the chunk of gold that constitutes it; the chunk of gold borrows *its* worth from the statue that it constitutes.

The property of being worth $10,000 is not unusual. For a constituting thing typically borrows many of its properties from the thing that it constitutes. For example, suppose that it were illegal to destroy an American flag. In that case, we should not say that the flag borrows the property of being an *x* such that it is illegal to destroy *x* from the piece of cloth that constitutes the flag. For, clearly, the direction of fit is the other way. Its being illegal to destroy *x* is a property that the piece of cloth borrows from the flag that it constitutes. Legislators write laws to protect national symbols, not to protect pieces of cloth.

Of course, these counterexamples to the bottom-up-borrowing-only claim concern relational and intentional properties. But one of my aims is to show that such properties are crucial for understanding reality. So, on my account of constitution, borrowing goes both ways: if *x* constitutes *y* at *t*, then *x* borrows some properties from *y* at *t*, and *y* borrows other properties from *x* at *t*.

The notion of borrowing is a powerful tool for countering various objections to the idea of constitution without identity. Before showing how the notion of borrowing can deflect objections, let me set out the idea of borrowing more precisely. I'll try to make the idea clear by a couple of definitions, beginning with a definition of "*x*'s having a property at *t* independently of *x*'s constitution-relations to *y* at *t*."

We need to define three special classes of properties. (a) Call any property expressed in English with the locutions "possibly," "necessarily," or variants of such terms an "alethic property." (b) Call any property expressed in English with the locutions "is identical to" or "constitutes" ("is constituted by") or "being such that *x* would not exist if . . ." a "constitution/identity property." (c) Finally, say that a property *F* is rooted outside times at which it is had if and only if necessarily, for any *x* and for any period of time *p*, *x* has the property *F* throughout *p* only if *x* exists at some time before or after *p*.[37] A disjunctive property like being such that *x* is or was square *may be*, but need not be, rooted outside the time at which it is had. (E.g., suppose that Piece, which later came to constitute *David* at *t′*, was quarried at *t* ($t < t'$); Piece's property of having been quarried at *t* may be (indeed is) rooted outside times at which it is had.) Let *H* range over properties that neither are alethic, nor are constitution/identity, nor are such that they may be rooted outside times at which they are had. Then,

(I) *x* has *H* at *t* independently of *x*'s constitution-relations to *y* at $t =_{df}$
- (a) *x* has *H* at *t*; and
- (b) Either (1) (i) *x* constitutes *y* at *t*, and
  - (ii) *x*'s having *H* at *t* (in the given background) does not entail that *x* constitutes anything at *t*;
- or (2) (i) *y* constitutes *x* at *t*, and
  - (ii) *x*'s having *H* at *t* (in the given background) does not entail that *x* is constituted by something that could have had *H* at *t* without constituting anything at *t*.

The point of (b)(1)(ii) is that, if *x* has *H* independently of its constitution-relations to *y*, and if *x* constitutes *y*, then *x* could still have had *H* at *t* (in the given background) even if *x* had constituted nothing at *t*. The point of (b)(2)(ii) is that, if *x* has *H* independently of its constitution-relations to *y*, and if *y* constitutes *x*, then *x* could still have had *H* at *t* (in the given background) regardless of whether or not what constitutes *x* at *t* could have had *H* at *t* (in the given background) without constituting anything at *t*. To put the consequent differently: *x*'s having *H* at *t* is compatible with *x*'s being constituted by something that could not have had *H* at *t* (in the given background) without constituting something at *t*.

Clauses (b)(1)(ii) and (b)(2)(ii) are intended to capture a particular idea of dependence. The idea of dependence here concerns what is logically or metaphysically required for something to have a certain property. For example, Piece's having the shape that it has—call it "shape *S*"—is independent of Piece's constitution-relations to *David*. Clause (a) is satisfied, since Piece has shape *S*. Clause (b) is also satisfied, since Piece constitutes *David*, thus satisfying (b)(1)(i), and Piece's having shape *S* (in the given background, or any other background) does not entail that Piece constitutes anything, thus satisfying (b)(1)(ii). For Piece could still have had shape *S* even if Piece had constituted nothing; Piece's shape is not logically or metaphysically dependent on whether or not Piece ever constitutes anything. On the other hand, *David* does not have shape *S* independently of its constitution relations to Piece. Although *David* does have shape *S*, thus satisfying (a), and Piece constitutes *David*, thus satisfying (b)(2)(i), nevertheless *David*'s having shape *S* does entail that *David* is constituted by something that could have had shape *S* without constituting anything, thus violating (b)(2)(ii). (To put it another way, (b)(2)(ii) fails because *David* could not have had shape *S* unless it was constituted by something that could have had shape *S* without constituting anything.) So, *David*'s having shape *S* is not independent of *David*'s constitution relations to Piece.

The sense of "independence" here is not causal. In a causal sense, the dependence relation may go the other way: If Michelangelo hadn't wanted to carve a statue with shape *S*, Piece would not have been of shape *S*. In this causal sense of "dependence," Piece's being of shape *S* is causally dependent on *David*'s being of shape *S*. But this causal sense of "dependence" is not the one at issue. Rather, what makes it the case that *David* is of shape *S*—however it is brought about—is the fact that *David* is constituted by something of shape *S*, where what constitutes *David* is of shape *S* independently of its constitution-relations (in the relevant sense of "independence"). And the same could be said of any of *David*'s other macrophysical properties, such as weight, color, texture, height, and so on.[38] Clauses (b)(1)(ii) and (b)(2)(ii) are to be interpreted relative to a given background. The particular background played no role in the dependence of *David*'s having shape *S* on *David*'s constitution relations with Piece; for any shape of any statue depends on whatever constitutes the statue, no matter what the background. But sometimes, as we shall see, we must consider background conditions, where background conditions include relevant conventions—social, political, legal, economic.

The idea of borrowing properties shows how something can have a property by constitution. Constitution is a unity relation that allows *x* to have a property in virtue of being constitutionally related to something that has the property independently. If *x*'s having *H* at *t* depends on *x*'s constitution-relations to some *y* that has *H* at *t*, where *y* has *H* at *t* independently of *y*'s constitution-relations at *t*, then *x* borrows *H* from *y* at *t*. Let *H* range over properties that neither are alethic, nor are constitution/identity, nor are such that they may be rooted outside times at which they are had. Then,

(B) *x* borrows *H* from *y* at $t =_{df}$ There is some *y* such that:
 (a) it is not the case that *x* has *H* at *t* independently of *x*'s constitution-relations to *y* at *t*; and
 (b) *y* has *H* at *t* independently of *y*'s constitution-relations to *x* at *t*.

Note that, because of (I), satisfaction of (b) guarantees that *x* and *y* are constitutionally related at *t*. It will be convenient later to say that *x* has *H* at *t* *derivatively* if there is some *z* such that *x* borrows *H* from *z* at *t*; and *x* has *H* at *t* *nonderivatively* if *x* has *H* at *t* without borrowing it. Now let me illustrate the definitions with some examples. From now on, for simplicity, I shall drop reference to time.

I. Consider a couple of properties of Betsy Ross's first U.S. flag (call it "Flag"). Flag was constituted by a particular piece of cloth (call it "Cloth"). Flag is rectangular, but not independently of its constitution-relations. Check the definition (I): Clause (a) is satisfied since Flag is rectangular. Clause (b)(2)(i) is satisfied since Cloth constitutes Flag. But clause (b)(2)(ii) is not satisfied, for Flag's being rectangular does entail that Flag is constituted by something that could have been rectangular without constituting anything. On the other hand, Cloth does have rectangularity independently of its constitution-relations. Check the definition (I): Clause (a) is satisfied since Cloth is rectangular. Clause (b)(1)(i) is satisfied since Cloth constitutes Flag. And clause (b)(1)(ii) is satisfied since Cloth's being rectangular does not entail that Cloth constitutes something that is rectangular, for Cloth could have been rectangular without constituting anything. Notice how this example also illustrates that "depends on" is not a causal notion; for it is plausible to suppose that Cloth's being rectangular did causally depend on its constituting something rectangular. Perhaps, in the given background, Cloth would not have been cut into a rectangle if it had not been used to create a rectangular flag. But metaphysically speaking, the dependence is in the other direction. Flag's being rectangular depends (in the relevant sense) on Flag's being constituted by something that could have been rectangular even if it had not constituted anything. Now it is easy to see that Flag borrows the property of being rectangular from Cloth. Check definition (B): It is not the case that Flag is rectangular independently of its constitution relations to Cloth; and Cloth is rectangular independently of its constitution relations to Flag.

Now, to illustrate the qualification "in a given background," consider the property of being revered. Here the borrowing goes the other way: Cloth borrows the property of being revered from Flag. Check the definitions. First, Flag has the property of being revered independently of its constitution-relations: Flag has the property of being revered, so clause (a) of (I) is satisfied. Likewise, clause (b)(2)(ii) of (I) is satisfied: Flag's having the property of being revered (in the given background) does not entail that Flag is constituted by something that could have been revered without constituting anything. For Cloth could not have been revered in the given background without constituting something that was revered. This is so, because our conventions are part of the given background, and on our conventions, national symbols like flags are revered, but pieces of cloth per se are not objects of reverence. (Of course, these conventions can be abrogated by idiosyncratic revering; but in the *given* background, they were not abrogated.) If Cloth had remained in Betsy Ross's sewing basket and had never constituted a flag, it could never have been revered. So, Flag has the property of being revered independently of Flag's constitution-relations to Cloth. On the other hand, Cloth's having the property of being revered is not independent of Cloth's constitution-relations to Flag. This is so because clause (b)(1)(ii) of (I) is false. For Cloth's being revered (in the given background) does entail that Cloth constitutes something that is revered, as we have already seen. Since it is not the case that Cloth is revered independently of its constitution relations, and Flag is revered independently of its constitution relations, the clauses of (B) are satisfied, and Cloth borrows the property of being revered from Flag.

II. Consider a different kind of case that further illustrates the use of "in the given background." Buildings that constitute schools are tax-exempt, and such buildings usually borrow the property of being tax-exempt from the schools that they constitute. Typically, a building per se is not tax-exempt; it is only because it constitutes something that is tax-exempt that a building is tax-exempt. But not all situations are typical. Here is a case in which the background is not the usual one. Suppose that a certain empty building, call it "Structure," is declared tax-exempt by a corrupt tax board (the officials are "on the take" from the owner of the building). Suppose that soon thereafter, Structure is given to a community group to start a school, called "School." So, Structure comes to constitute School, and School is tax-exempt because it is a school. Now is the property of being tax-exempt borrowed by either Structure or School? No. Each has the property of being tax-exempt, in the given background, independently of the other. Since Structure was tax-exempt before it constituted anything, its being tax-exempt is independent of its constitution- relations to School. And since schools per se are tax-exempt, School's being tax-exempt is independent of its constitution-relations to Structure. (I'll leave it to the reader to check the definitions.) So, neither Structure nor School borrows the property of being tax-exempt from the other.

III. Finally, on my view, Piece is a statue, albeit derivatively.[39] *David* has the property of being a statue independently of its constitution-relations since *David*'s being a statue does not entail that *David* is constituted by something that could have been a statue without constituting anything. It is not the case that Piece has the property of being a statue independently of its constitution relations since Piece's being a statue does entail that Piece constitutes something. So, Piece borrows the property of being a statue from *David*, and Piece's being a statue depends wholly on Piece's constitution-relations to something that is a statue nonderivatively (independently of *its* constitution relations).[40] Moreover, whereas *David* is a statue essentially, Piece—which might have remained in the quarry and constituted nothing—is a statue contingently. For any primary-kind property being an *F*, if any *x* is an *F* at all, then either *x* is an *F* essentially or *x* borrows the property of being an *F* from something to which *x* has constitution-relations.

Now let me show how the idea of borrowing properties can turn aside objections to the notion of constitution without identity. First, on what one writer calls "the standard account" of the relation between copper statues and pieces of copper, *David* has the property of being a statue, but Piece does not.[41] If this is the standard account, then my construal of constitution, à la (C), is not an example of "the standard account." For, as we have just seen, I do not want to deny that Piece has the property of being a statue; rather, I want to insist that Piece is a statue and to account for that fact in terms of borrowing. The notion of borrowing opens up a distinction between two ways of being an F: nonderivatively (as *David* is a statue) or derivatively (as Piece is a statue). However, if *David* and Piece are both statues, there seems to be a problem. For consider the following argument, which aims to saddle the constitution view with an unpalatable conclusion:

(P_1) If x is an F and y is an F and $x \neq y$ and x is spatially coincident with y, then there are two spatially coincident Fs.
(P_2) *David* is a statue, and Piece is a statue, and *David* $\neq$ Piece, and *David* and Piece are spatially coincident.
$\therefore$(C_1) There are two spatially coincident statues.

(C_1) follows from a general principle, (P_1), and an instance of the constitution view, (P_2), and (C_1) is indeed an unpalatable conclusion. But the proponent of the constitution view is not committed to (C_1), for the proponent of the constitution view would reject (P_1) as begging the question against constitution. If the antecedent of (P_1) were augmented by the addition of another conjunct ("and neither x constitutes y nor y constitutes x"), then it would be acceptable. But in that case, (P_2) would not be an instance of the revised (P_1), and the argument would be invalid. The point of constitution is to open up a *via media* between identity and separateness, and as it stands, (P_1) disregards this *via media*. Given that the notion of constitution is coherent—as, I think, the definition (C) shows that it is—it is hardly effective to argue against it by ignoring it.

The reason that, where *David* is, there are not two spatially coincident statues, is that Piece *borrows* the property of being a statue from *David*. That is, Piece is a statue only in virtue of its constitution relations to something that is a statue nonderivatively. *David* and Piece are not separate statues; they are not even separable.[42] (You can't take them apart and get two statues; you can't take them apart at all.) Indeed, I want to say that Piece is the same statue as *David*. John Perry has argued that, where "F" ranges over sortals, "x is the same F as y" should be analyzed as "$x = y$ and Fx."[43] But, on my view, Piece is the same statue as *David* in virtue of constituting *David*, not in virtue of being identical to *David*. So, I suggest amending Perry's analysis to take account of constitution:

(S) x is the same F as y at $t =_{df}$ ($x = y$ or x has constitution relations to y at t) and Fxt.

(S), I believe, accords with the way that we actually count things.[44] And from (S), it follows that although Piece is the same statue as *David*, Piece might not have been the same statue as *David*. (Piece might not have been a statue at all.) In general, if x borrows being an F from y, then x and y are the same F.

Let me respond to those who take it to be intolerable to give up the principle that if x is an F and y is an F and $x \neq y$, then there are two Fs. Constitution is intended as a third alternative between identity and separate existence. How are we to count using this three-way classification? We may count either by identity ("If x and y are Fs, then there is one F only if $x = y$") or by nonseparateness ("If x and y are Fs, then there is one F only if x and y are nonseparate," where x and y are nonseparate if and only if either $x = y$ or x is constitutionally related to y). Constitution, as I have urged, is like identity in some ways and unlike identity in other ways. In counting, I believe, our practices align constitution with identity: If $x \neq y$ and *if x and y are not constitutionally related*, then x is not the same F as y. Those who adhere to the principle that I would amend ("If x is an F and y is an F and $x \neq y$, then there are two Fs") in effect insist on aligning constitution with separate existence: if $x \neq y$, then x is not the same

F as *y*. Since I do not think that we count by identity (but rather by nonseparateness), I reject (P_1).

However, another philosopher might hold on to (P_1); such a philosopher may also endorse constitution, and hence be committed to (C_1). In that case, however, she would be in a position to argue that (C_1) turns out to be acceptable. For to say that there are two spatially coincident statues in this case would only be to say this: there is one thing that is a statue nonderivatively and whatever constitutes that (nonderivative) statue borrows the property of being a statue from it. There are not two separate or independent statues. So, a proponent of the constitution view, confronted with the argument whose conclusion is (C_1), has two options: Either, with me, reject (P_1), or, more conservatively, retain (P_1) and argue that (C_1) is benign.[45]

The notion of borrowing makes sense of pretheoretical intuitions. For example, most people, including me, would agree that *David* has the property of being white. I account for this fact by saying that *David* has that property because *David* borrows the property of being white from Piece. *David*'s being white derives entirely from the fact that *David* is constituted by something that has the property of being white nonderivatively. Similarly, for (certain) other of *David*'s properties—for example, being located in Florence; being 13 ft., 5 in. high; being made of marble.

There may seem to be another problem with taking Piece to be a statue.[46] For suppose that Piece existed before *David*—in, say, 1499. *David* came into existence in 1504. Now suppose that Jones pointed to *David* in 1506 and said, "There is a statue over there that existed in 1499." If we say that Piece is a statue, and that Piece existed in 1499, then what Jones said was true. But, one may object, what Jones said was not true since Piece did not constitute a statue in 1499.

To this charge, let me reply. What Jones said is ambiguous, and on one reading what she said was true—albeit misleading. There is something over there—namely, Piece—that has the property of being a statue and that existed in 1499. Of course, since Piece acquired that property by borrowing it from *David* and since *David* did not exist in 1499, Piece did not have the property of being a statue in 1499. But this situation has a familiar structure. For "There's a statue over there that existed in 1499" is parallel to "There's a husband over there who existed in 1950," when the husband was six years old in 1950. "There's a husband over there who existed in 1950" is true on one reading and false on another. It is true if taken as $\exists x$(x is over there and x is a husband and x existed in 1950); but it is false if taken as $\exists x$(x is over there and x was a husband in 1950). Exactly the same can be said about "There's a statue over there that existed in 1499." It is true if taken as $\exists x$(x is over there and x is a statue and x existed in 1499); but it is false if taken as $\exists x$(x is over there and x was a statue in 1499). So, although Jones's sentence, "There is a statue over there that existed in 1499," is highly misleading, we need not deny that it is true (on one reading). Hence, the proposed counterexample does not impugn the claim that Piece has the borrowed property of being a statue.[47]

There are other arguments for the identity of Piece and *David*. Consider this one:[48]

> (P_3) If *David* ≠ Piece, then if *David* weighs *n* kg and Piece weighs *n* kg, then the shipping weight of the statue is 2*n* kg.
> (P_4) *David* weighs *n* kg and Piece weighs *n* kg, but the shipping weight is not 2*n* kg.
> ∴ (C_2) *David* = Piece.

Since Piece constitutes *David*, (P_3) simply ignores constitution (and hence begs the question against the view set out here). To make (P_3) true, we would have to add a clause to its antecedent: "and *David* and Piece are not constitutionally related." But with such a clause added to (P_3), the conclusion does not follow. Indeed, since Piece is the same statue as *David*, Piece's weighing *n* kg and *David*'s weighing *n* kg do not combine to entail that something weighs 2*n* kg.

The objector may persist: "If Piece weighs *n* kg, and *David* ≠ Piece, and the scales do not read 2*n*, then *David* does not genuinely have the property of weighing *n* kg. In that case, strictly speaking, *David* must be weightless. But that seems wrong." Indeed, I agree, it would be wrong; but my position does not commit me to denying that *David* has weight. *David* actually weighs *n* kg: Put *David* on the scales and see. The point is that *David* weighs *n* kg wholly in virtue of being constituted by something that weighs *n* kg. To explicate the fact that *David* weighs *n* kg is not to deny that *David* weighs *n* kg. The fact that *David* borrows its weight from the thing that constitutes it only implies that *David*'s weighing *n* kg is a matter of *David*'s being constituted by something that weighs *n* kg nonderivatively. Since *David* has its weight derivatively, from the fact that *David* weighs *n* kg and that Piece weighs *n* kg, it does not follow that anything should weigh 2*n*.

Examples could be multiplied: From the fact that Mondrian's *Broadway Boogie-Woogie* and the constituting canvas share the property of having yellow of a certain saturation at a particular location, it does not follow that at that location there is a color of twice that saturation. *Broadway Boogie-Woogie* borrows its yellow-of-that-saturation at that location from the constituting canvas. (That's why Mondrian could change the properties of the painting by changing the properties of the canvas.) The account of borrowing also shows why borrowed quantitative properties (e.g., being of a certain saturation, weighing *m* kg) cannot be added to their unborrowed sources. The reason that borrowed properties are not "additive" is that *there is nothing to add*: if *x* borrows properties from *y*, then *x* and *y* have constitution-relations. If *x* and *y* have constitution-relations and *x* is an *F*, then *x* is the same *F* as *y*. If *x* is the same *F* as *y*, then it is obvious that *x*'s quantitative properties cannot be added to *y*'s. *Piece* is the same statue as *David* (in virtue of constitution relations), and Tully is the same person as Cicero (in virtue of identity). So, neither can Tully's quantitative properties be added to Cicero's, nor can Piece's quantitative properties be added to *David*'s. It is no more legitimate to add *David*'s weight to Piece's in order to ascertain "total" weight than it would be to add the number of hairs on Cicero's head to the number of hairs on Tully's head in order to ascertain the "total" number of hairs.

Borrowing walks a fine line. On the one hand, if *x* borrows *H* from *y*, then *x* really has *H*—piggyback, so to speak. Assuming (as I shall try to show elsewhere) that persons are constituted by bodies, if I cut my hand, then *I* really bleed. It would be wrong for someone to say, "You aren't really bleeding; it's just your body that is bleeding." Since I am constituted by my body, when my body bleeds, I bleed. I borrow the property of bleeding from my body, but I really bleed. But the fact that I am bleeding is none other than the fact that I am constituted by a body that is bleeding. So, not only does *x* really have *H* by borrowing it, but also—and this is the other hand—if *x* borrows *H* from *y*, there are not two independent instances of *H*: if *x* borrows *H*, then *x*'s having *H* is entirely a matter of *x*'s having constitution-relations to something that has *H* nonderivatively.

The final worry that the notion of borrowing dissolves is that, on the view of constitution-without-identity, it seems a mystery why the statue and the piece of marble that constitutes it have in common all of what we might call "ordinary properties"—first-order properties whose instantiation is independent of what is the case at other possible worlds. It cannot be just an accident, the objection goes, that the piece of marble and the statue have the same size, weight, color, smell, value, and other ordinary properties. The notion of borrowing properties accounts for these otherwise remarkable similarities: the statue borrows its size, weight, color, and smell from the piece of marble that constitutes it; and the piece of marble borrows its astronomical value from the statue that it constitutes. So, the notion of borrowing answers the question, if *x* and *y* are nonidentical, how can they have so many properties in common?

But now a question arises from the other side: Supposing that *x* constitutes *y*, if *x* and *y* are so similar, how can they differ at all?[49] The answer is straightforward: *David* and Piece have different essential properties. If there were no artworld, there would be no *David*, but Piece could exist in a world without art.[50] As theories of art make clear, being an artwork at all—and hence being a statue—is a relational property. When Piece is in certain (statue-favorable) circumstances, a new entity (a statue, *David*) comes into existence. Piece has the property of being a statue because—and only because—Piece constitutes something that is a statue. So, despite the fact that *David* and Piece are alike in atomic structure, they differ in kind: The relational properties that *David* has essentially Piece has only accidentally. Hence, the needed asymmetry to make *David* and Piece different in kind is secured.

So, it is no mystery that *David* and Piece share so many of their properties without being identical: Constitution, defined by (C), insures nonidentity, and borrowing accounts for the fact David and Piece are alike in so many of their properties. In sum, to say that *x* borrows a property *H* from *y* highlights the difference between *x* and *y*, and hence the fact that constitution is not identity; but to say that *H* is, nevertheless, a genuine property of *x* highlights the unity of *x* and *y*, and hence the similarity of identity and constitution. (This aspect of constitution is a consequence of trying to mark off an intermediate position between identity and separateness.) Constitution is an intimate relation—almost as intimate as identity, but not quite.

CONCLUSION

The constitution view has manifold virtues. First, it achieves what contingent-identity theorists want without compromising the classical view of identity (and without using the word "identity" to mean something other than "identity"). Second, it explains the stability of constituted things: a river is constituted by different aggregates of water molecules at different times. If a river were identical to the aggregate of water molecules that made it up, then you could not step into the same river twice. By contrast, on the constitution view, you can step into the same river twice even if the water molecules that constitute the river the first time you step in it are wholly different from those that constitute it the second time. Third, and relatedly, the constitution view is nonreductive without being antimaterialistic: It is compatible with global supervenience of all properties on fundamental physical properties (and hence is not antimaterialistic), but it eschews an "intrinsicalism" that holds that the nature of a particular is determined by the properties of the fundamental physical particles that constitute it (and hence is nonreductive). Fifth, and perhaps most important, constitution highlights the genuine variety of kinds of individuals in the world. Between the big bang and now, genuinely new things of genuinely new kinds have come into existence—some of our own making (e.g., libraries, computers, space shuttles), others created without human intervention (e.g., planets, continents, organisms).

If you think that a world without organisms or art or artifacts is as ontologically rich as the actual world, then you will deny that the relation of constitution is actually exemplified. In that case, presumably, you will either assimilate cases of putative constitution to cases of mere property possession or else you will deny the existence of such things as statues and pieces of marble, schools and buildings, flags and pieces of cloth.[51] Although I hardly know what to say to those who think that a world without art or artifacts is as ontologically rich as our world, let me trim my thesis for such an audience. The idea of constitution without identity is coherent, and therefore, a world in which constitution without identity is a predominant relation is a genuinely possible world, whether such a world is ours or not.[52]

NOTES

1. For recent debate, see, for example, David Wiggins in *Sameness and Substance* (Oxford: Basil Blackwell, 1980). Also, see Mark Johnston, "Constitution Is Not Identity," *Mind* 101 (1992): 89–105. Johnston was responding to the recent work on "contingent identity" by, e.g., David Lewis, "Counterparts and Their Bodies," *Journal of Philosophy* 68 (1971): 203–11; Allan Gibbard, "Contingent Identity," *Journal of Philosophical Logic* 4 (1975): 187–221; Anil Gupta, *The Logic of Common Nouns* (New Haven, CT: Yale University Press, 1980); and Denis Robinson, "Re-Identifying Matter," *Philosophical Review* 81 (1982): 317–42.

2. For an excellent collection of articles espousing different answers to the question, see *Material Constitution: A Reader*, Michael Rea, ed. (Lanham, MD: Rowman & Littlefield, 1997).

3. Other philosophers—among them, John Locke in *Essay Concerning Human Understanding*, A. S. Pringle-Pattison, ed. (Oxford: Clarendon Press, 1924), and Sydney Shoemaker in *Identity, Cause and Mind* (Cambridge: Cambridge University Press, 1986)—have proposed that persons and bodies are related in a way similar to what I am calling "constitution." I see as kindred spirits all who construe the relation as a kind of composition without identity.

4. Michael B. Burke, "Copper Statues and Pieces of Copper: A Challenge to the Standard Account," *Analysis* 52 (1992): 12–17.

5. It is essential to the plausibility of the standard account, according to Burke, that Copper is not a statue. For if Copper were a statue, then Statue would be coextensive with *another* statue. As I shall show, my view does not have this consequence.

6. Stephen Yablo makes this point about what he calls "contingent identity," according to which things are "distinct *by nature*, but the same *in the circumstances*" (296). See his "Identity, Essence, and Indiscernibility," *Journal of Philosophy* 84 (1987): 293–314. Many who use the term "contingent identity" do distinguish that relation from genuine identity, which is construed (rightly, I think) as a necessary relation. I think that it is misleading to insist that "contingent identity" names a relation that is not identity.

7. Denial of the identity of the statue and the piece of marble does not by itself commit one to constitution. An alternative to constitution is to construe objects as four-dimensional space-time worms that have temporal parts; then, although the statue and the piece of marble are not identical, they have current temporal "stages" that are identical. I cannot discuss this alternative here. See David Lewis, "Postscripts to 'Survival and Identity,'" in *Philosophical Papers*, Vol. I (New York: Oxford University Press, 1983): 76–77. For a critique of the temporal-parts view, see Judith Jarvis Thomson, "Parthood and Identity across Time," *Journal of Philosophy* 80 (1983): 201–20.

8. I do not begin with the idea of metaphysical simples and ask under what conditions do simples constitute or compose something complex. That question is much more abstract than the one that concerns me. (For an exploration of that question, see Peter van Inwagen, *Material Beings* [Ithaca, NY: Cornell University Press, 1990].) Assuming the existence of ordinary things, my goal is to understand the relation between, say, a statue and the piece of marble that makes it up. To insist that I should first answer the abstract question about the conditions under which metaphysical simples compose something complex would be like insisting that a biologist should prove the existence of the external world before studying organisms.

9. Some philosophers (e.g., Judith Jarvis Thomson in correspondence) may agree with me about the nonidentity of an artifact with, say, a hunk of metal, though disagreeing about the nonidentity of a person and her body. Here I am only trying to work out the general idea of constitution. One can endorse this account without endorsing its range of application. I explicitly apply the constitution view to persons and bodies elsewhere.

10. I am assuming that the piece of marble that now constitutes *David* is the same piece of marble as one of a different shape that was once in a quarry. If you think that shape is essential to pieces of marble, then change the example to the one I used in "Why Constitution Is Not Identity," in which the statue *Discobolus* comes into existence at the same time as the piece of bronze that constitutes it. See my "Why Constitution Is Not Identity," *Journal of Philosophy* 94 (1997): 599–621.

Also, I am following Allan Gibbard here, who takes it that clay statues and lumps of clay "can be designated with proper names" ("Contingent Identity," 190). It is admittedly odd to name a piece of marble. The oddness stems from what we might call "the convention of naming:" If *x* constitutes *y*, and *y* constitutes nothing else, then a name of the composite object is a name of *y*. We name statues, not pieces of marble; monuments (the Vietnam Memorial), not pieces of granite; persons, not bodies. Of course, we can give a name to anything we want. And for the purpose at hand, it is useful to name the piece of marble; but I recognize that this is not what we ordinarily do.

11. According to Robert C. Sleigh, Jr., Leibniz meant his "law" to be understood like this: "if individual *x* is distinct from individual *y* then there is some intrinsic, non-relational property *F* that *x* has and *y* lacks, or vice versa" ("Identity of Indiscernibles," in *A Companion to Metaphysics*, Jaegwon Kim and Ernest Sosa, eds. [Oxford: Blackwell, 1995]: 234). I am not claiming that there is any *intrinsic, nonrelational* property *F* that *David* has but Piece lacks, or vice versa. I am claiming, rather, that *being a statue* is an essential property of *David*, but not of Piece—even though *being a statue* is a relational property, inasmuch as whether or not something is a statue depends on its relation to an artworld or to an artist. I depart from the tradition in holding that not all essential properties are intrinsic.

12. This consideration leads straight to a counterexample to the conviction that "if *y* is a paradigm *F* and *x* is intrinsically exactly like *y*, then *x* is an *F*." Using sophisticated metaphysical arguments, Mark Johnston aims to undermine this principle in "Constitution Is Not Identity"; Harold Noonan aims to rebut Johnston in "Constitution Is Identity," *Mind* 102 (1993): 133–46. I think that the principle is undermined merely by considering statues, without any fancy arguments: Suppose that something—call it "*a*"—with a microstructure exactly like *David*'s spontaneously

coalesced in outer space, light-years from any comparable mass. Now *David* is a paradigmatic statue and *a* is intrinsically exactly like *David*; but *a* is not a statue.

13. "Why Constitution Is Not Identity."

14. Cf. Ruth Barcan Marcus, "Modalities and Intensional Languages," in *Modalities: Philosophical Essays* (New York: Oxford University Press, 1993): 3–23, first published in *Synthese* 13 (1961): 303–22. So I don't take what is called "contingent identity" to be identity; and I'm unsure whether what is called "relative identity" is coherent. In any case, I am not committed to relative identity. For a defense of relative identity, see Peter Geach, "Identity," in *Logic Matters* (Oxford: Basil Blackwell, 1972): 238–49. For criticisms of relative identity, see John Perry, "The Same *F*," *Philosophical Review* 79 (1970): 181–200, and David Wiggins, *Sameness and Substance* (Oxford: Basil Blackwell, 1980).

15. Saul A. Kripke, "Identity and Necessity," in *Identity and Individuation*, Milton K. Munitz, ed. (New York: New York University, 1971): 137. Kripke continues: "And this is so even if the property *F* is itself of the form of necessarily having some other property *G*, in particular that of necessarily being identical to a certain object."

16. My commitment to the necessity of identity as a relation between objects does not imply that I have to deny either the truth or the contingency of statements of the form "the *F* is the *G*."

17. Constitution, as I am construing it, differs in important ways from Dean W. Zimmerman's construal in "Theories of Masses and Problems of Constitution," *Philosophical Review* 104 (1995): 53–110. Zimmerman takes the relata of constitution to be masses of kinds of stuff. He also permits *x* and *y* to constitute one another (74), whereas I require asymmetry. In any case, Zimmerman finds the alleged differences between coincidents ungrounded, and concludes that "coincident physical objects are not to be countenanced" (90). I believe that my account of borrowing, together with my rejection of the thesis that all essential properties are intrinsic, dissolves the difficulties that Zimmerman sees.

18. I agree with the Kripkean point that the lectern could not have been constituted by a block of ice, but not for the Kripkean reason that a thing's origins are essential properties of the thing. It is not because the lectern had a non-ice origin that it cannot be constituted by a block of ice, but because nothing constituted by a block of ice could serve the purposes of a lectern.

19. I shall discuss the temporal complications later.

20. In "The Statue and the Clay" (*Nous*, forthcoming), Judith Jarvis Thomson also sets out to define "constitution" for artifacts, but she takes constitution to be a relation between an artifact and some portion of matter. This is not my conception for two reasons: (1) The identity conditions for portions of matter don't seem to fit my intuitions about constitution. Suppose that I have a cotton dress, and suppose that it is constituted at t_1 by a certain portion of cotton, P_1. Now suppose that I cut a tiny swatch from an inside seam as a color sample that I'll use to match shoes. I take it that anything large enough to be a color sample is itself a portion; hence, after I cut my swatch, P_1 no longer exists at t_2. In that case, my dress is constituted at t_2 by a different portion of cotton, P_2. On the contrary, I have a strong intuition(!) that my dress is constituted by the same thing at t_1 and at t_2. So, I don't think that what constitutes my dress is a portion of cotton, but rather a piece of cotton (which can survive loss of a swatch). (2) I do not think that portions of matter are ontologically significant. I do not quantify over portions of matter. I see no need for an intermediate level between, e.g., pieces of cloth ("things") and bunches of molecules. (The persistence condition for a bunch of molecules is simply that the bunch persists for as long as all the molecules in the bunch persist, whatever their spatial locations; I use "bunch" because as far as I know, it's not used in the literature with some meaning that I don't intend.) Things are significant, and bunches of molecules are significant; but, on my view, portions are not. So, appeal to pieces (and other *F*s that constitute things) is not, I think, susceptible to the charge of duplication.

21. Thus, constitution must be sharply distinguished from supervenience. Failure to distinguish between supervenience and constitution has caused a great deal of confusion in the philosophy of mind. See my *Explaining Attitudes: A Practical Approach to the Mind* (Cambridge: Cambridge University Press, 1995): 132. For detailed discussions of supervenience, see Jaegwon Kim's *Supervenience and Mind* (Cambridge: Cambridge University Press, 1993).

22. For an interesting discussion of stuff and things, see Vere Chappell, "Matter," *Journal of Philosophy* 70 (1973): 679–96.

23. In many cases (though not, perhaps, in *David*'s case), the converse also holds: y constitutes x and x could have been constituted by something other than y. Although I do not endorse Kripke's doctrine of the necessity of origin as a general thesis, I would agree that in some cases a thing has its origin essentially. See Kripke's *Naming and Necessity* (Cambridge: Harvard University Press, 1980).

24. This is a different use of "intentional object" from its traditional use, in which it denotes "nonexistent" objects like Pegasus and Santa Claus.

25. As we shall see when I discuss "borrowing properties," it is possible, for some x, y, and H that x has H essentially, and y has H nonessentially. E.g., *David* has the property of being a statue essentially; Piece borrows the property of being a statue from *David*; and Piece has the property of being a statue contingently. To put it differently, being an F (e.g., being a statue) may be X's (e.g., David's) primary-kind property, and y (e.g., Piece) may have the property of being an F by borrowing that property from x. In that case, being an F is not y's primary-kind property.

26. At least, this is the view of Ruth Millikan.

27. The reason for the locution "at any particular place or time" is that perhaps the existence of an art world is required for something to be an artwork. The existence of an art world by itself may well entail that there are artworks, without entailing—for any particular place or time—that the property of being an artwork is instantiated there.

28. The reason to distinguish F^* and G^* from F and G is that some x may have the property of being an F by borrowing, in which case x is an F but being an F is not x's primary-kind property.

29. This counterexample to an earlier definition was proposed by Anil K. Gupta.

30. Constitution is also nontransitive. In order to derive "x constitutes z at t" from "x constitutes y at t" and "y constitutes z at t," the H-favorable circumstances (where H is z's primary-kind property) would have to include the G-favorable circumstances (where G is y's primary-kind property). But in general something can be in H-favorable circumstances without being in G-favorable circumstances. Even though constitution is nontransitive, there are chains of constitutionally related things all the way "down" to fundamental particles. Say that "x is constitutionally linked to y" if and only if: Either y constitutes x or $\exists z_1, \ldots, z_n$[y constitutes z_1 and z_1 constitutes z_2 and . . . and z_n constitutes x] or x constitutes y or $\exists z_1, \ldots, z_m$[x constitutes z_1 and z_1 constitutes z_2 and . . . and z_m constitutes y]. With this definition, we can formulate a weak thesis of materialism: Every concrete thing is either a fundamental particle or is constitutionally linked to an aggregate of fundamental particles.

31. Thus, I dissent from those who take statues to be determined by shape (e.g., "statuesque").

32. A recent example may be found in Michael Della Rocca, "Essentialists and Essentialism," *Journal of Philosophy* 93 (1996): 186–202. In "Why Constitution Is Not Identity," I have a direct argument against Della Rocca.

33. Gibbard, "Contingent Identity," 191.

34. A number of philosophers (e.g., Richard Boyd, Hillary Kornblith, and Derk Pereboom) hold that (token) beliefs and other attitudes are constituted by (token) brain states, without being identical to the brain states that constitute them. For reasons given in *Explaining Attitudes*, I do not endorse that claim. However, I believe that the view of constitution developed in this paper could help make clear what it might mean to say that (token) beliefs are constituted by, but not identical to, brain states.

35. E.g., with respect to nonessential properties that are such that they may not be rooted outside the times at which they are had (as defined by Chisholm), Chisholm thinks that ordinary things (like tables) borrow such properties from what constitutes them, and not vice versa. See Roderick Chisholm, *Person and Object: A Study in Metaphysics* (LaSalle, IL: Open Court Publishing, 1976): 100–101. The counterexamples that I give to the bottom-up-borrowing-only claim in the text all concern nonessential properties, and all conform to Chisholm's definition of properties that are such that they may not be rooted outside the times at which they are had. So, I think that they are counterexamples to Chisholm's view. For a detailed discussion, see my "Persons in Metaphysical Perspective" in *The Philosophy of Roderick M. Chisholm* (Library of Living Philosophers, Vol. 25) (LaSalle, IL: Open Court Publishing, 1997): 433–53.

36. And, intuitively, being worth $10,000 at t is a nonessential, present-rooted property of the *ens successivum*. It is surely not essential to the statue that it be worth $10,000 (the market could

change any day, and the statue would survive); and being worth $10,000 is a present-rooted property: "*x* is worth $10,000 at *t*" is roughly equivalent to "If you tried to sell *x* at *t*, you'd get $10,000."

37. The definition is Chisholm's. See *Person and Object*, 100. He goes on to define "*G* may be rooted outside times at which it is had" like this: "*G* is equivalent to a disjunction of two properties one of which is, and the other of which is not, rooted outside times at which it is had."

38. Although *David* borrows being of shape *S* from Piece, being of shape *S* is, I think, an essential property of *David*'s. But it is a particular essential property—a property that must be instantiated for the particular individual *David* to exist, not a property that *David* has in virtue of being the kind of individual that he is.

39. My point here is metaphysical, not linguistic. I am not postulating an ambiguity in the predicative use of "is a statue." I take it that "*a* is a statue" is true if *a* has the property of being a statue, where *a* has that property either nonderivatively (without borrowing) or derivatively (by borrowing). For any sortal, *F*, if *x* is an *F* at *t*, then $\exists y$(*y* is an *F* at *t* nonderivatively and either $x = y$ or *x* is constitutionally related to *y* at *t*).

40. None of the following properties is ever borrowed: the property of being identical to a statue, the property of constituting a statue, the property of being constituted by a statue. Necessarily, if *x* has constitution-relations to *y*, and *x* has one of these properties, then *y* does not have it.

41. Burke, "Copper Statues and Pieces of Copper, 14.

42. Philosophers who discuss constitution in terms of "spatially coincident objects" sound as if there are two independent objects that just happen to occupy the same location at the same time. Constitution, as we have seen, is a much more intimate relation than talk of "spatially coincident objects" suggests.

43. John Perry, "The Same *F*." Notice that my construal no more invokes relative identity than does Perry's.

44. Harold Noonan comments, "It is a deeply engrained conviction in many philosophical circles that if *x* is an *F* and *y* is an *F* and *x* and *y* are not identical then *x* and *y* cannot legitimately be counted as *one F*." He notes, however, that it "is perfectly possible to count by a relation weaker than, i.e., not entailing, identity." See "Constitution Is Identity," 138. In discussing fission cases of persons, David Lewis justifies counting by a weaker relation than identity in "Survival and Identity," in *The Identities of Persons*, Amelie Oksenberg Rorty, ed. (Berkeley and Los Angeles: University of California Press, 1976): 26–28.

45. This conservative option was urged on me by Hugh Benson, Monte Cook, and Ray Elugardo.

46. This was brought to my attention by Anil Gupta.

47. Husband and Piece acquired their respective properties of being a husband and being a statue in different ways. Husband is identical to something that is a husband. Piece is not identical to something that is a statue; rather, Piece constitutes something that is a statue, and borrows the (predicative) property from what it constitutes. A consequence of this is that when the property defined by a substance sortal like "statue" is borrowed, the property does not entail that its bearer is a substance of the sort: Piece could lose the (borrowed) property of being a statue and continue to exist; *David* could not lose the (unborrowed) property of being a statue and continue to exist.

48. Alvin Plantinga proposed a version of this argument.

49. Burke, "Copper Statues and Pieces of Copper," 14. Burke can imagine only two possible answers: (1) they have different histories, and (2) they have different persistence conditions. He argues that neither of these can ground a difference in sort. I discuss Burke's argument in "Why Constitution Is Not Identity."

50. I have extended discussions of this point in "Why Constitution Is Not Identity."

51. E.g., see Peter Unger, "There Are No Ordinary Things," *Synthese* 71 (1979): 117–54; and van Inwagen, *Material Beings*.

52. I am indebted to Albert Visser, Anil Gupta, Robert Hanna, Judith Jarvis Thomson, and Amie Thomasson, and to my seminar on Person and Body at the University of Massachusetts at Amherst in the fall term, 1997.

Midwest Studies in Philosophy, XXIII (1999)

Identity in the Talmud

ELI HIRSCH

I was thinking of calling this paper "How to Take the Identity of Artifacts Seriously." One of the main ideas that interests me is that in the Talmud the identity of artifacts seems to take on a kind of importance (and, in a sense, a kind of "reality") not found in any other literature with which I am familiar.

Let me say a word about how I got into this project. I was teaching a course on identity a few years ago, and I found myself feeling increasingly disconcerted by the fact that the intricate questions about identity raised by philosophers almost never have even the remotest practical significance. This seems obviously so with respect to the identity of artifacts, which, as the primary instances of the central common-sense category Austin called "moderate-sized dry goods," cannot be treated lightly in any philosophy rooted in common sense. If we ask, for instance, whether gradually replacing the planks of a wooden ship eventually gives us a different ship, we would like to take this question seriously—at least if we have any sympathy for common-sense philosophy—but part of what makes it difficult to do so is that it doesn't seem to matter what the answer to the question is. (Presumably no issue of ownership hinges on the answer, since the owner of the planks could normally claim ownership of the ship, and that won't hinge on the identity of the ship.) The practical irrelevance of such questions, I was finding, makes it harder for students to get—or to keep hold of—any intuitions about the questions. Probably one should be able to take such questions seriously even if they have no practical significance, but, I found myself mulling, wouldn't it be in a way nice if there were some general framework within which such questions did matter? What could such a framework look like?

Once having posed this question a possible answer soon dawned on me. Many years ago I studied the Talmud and found described therein an enormously elaborate structure of Halachah, or Jewish Law. Might Halachah provide a framework within which issues of identity matter? I put this question to a distinguished Talmudist of my acquaintance, and he told me that there is indeed a concept in the Talmud called *panim chadashot* that deals directly with issues of identity. The present paper summarizes some of the results of my research into this topic. I need to strongly emphasize at the outset that my knowledge of the Talmud is limited, and therefore any original interpretations suggested here are highly tentative. This is at best the beginning of a project that others more competent than I might properly complete.

In tractate *Shabbat*, folio 112b, the Gemara presents a striking position on the identity of artifacts.[1] Let me first try to explain what the position is, postponing until later an explanation of how it relates to Halachah. One example discussed in the Gemara concerns a wooden dish. We might say intuitively that a dish can be destroyed by having a sufficiently large hole made in it. Austin once asked whether a broken dish is a kind of dish. I suppose that would depend on how broken it is, and common sense of course leaves the measure of this very vague. As regards how big the hole in a (wooden) dish would have to be for the dish to be destroyed, the Mishnah in tractate *Kelim* 17.1 (i.e., chapter 17, Mishnah 1) stipulates a precisifying answer: big enough for a pomegranate to pass through. With that as the background, the Gemara in *Shabbat* considers an example in which a tiny hole forms in a dish and is effectively patched up, after which a second tiny hole forms and is again effectively patched, and this continues, with a succession of tiny holes being patched until at the end we have a patch the size of a big hole (i.e., one through which a pomegranate could have passed). Since we are imagining that the patch is effective we still have a perfectly functional dish. But is it the original dish?

To this question Rabbi Yochanan gives a negative answer, and he seems to appeal to a principle that might be summarized as follows: Suppose that, at the moment of its origin, an artifact contains certain parts the removal (without replacement) of which would destroy it by depriving it of its capacity to function in its characteristic way. Then the gradual replacement of those parts yields a functional artifact that is not the original one.[2]

Another example to which R. Yochanan applies his principle involves a leather sandal. In this example we assume as a premise that we are dealing with a kind of sandal that contains two major straps such that if both of those straps are destroyed, the sandal is destroyed. R. Yochanan's principle implies, then, that if one strap is replaced and then the second strap is replaced, the sandal we wind up with is not the original one.

In both the case of the dish and the case of the sandal what we have, says R. Yochanan, is *panim chadashot.*[3] This means literally "new faces (or appearances)," but the translation in almost every English edition of the Talmud I've seen is something like "It's a new thing." This accords with the authoritative interpretation of Rashi, who explains *panim chadashot* as meaning "This one is not the original one," which is as unambiguous a claim about identity as one can find.[4] I think it is clear that R. Yochanan was indeed making a claim about identity and I have formulated his principle accordingly.[5]

My formulation does, however, make an assumption related to a certain fundamental question that runs through the Talmudic literature in this area. The question is how exactly to understand the connection between an artifact's being "broken" (in roughly the sense of not working properly) and its going out of existence. Both notions figure in the Talmudic literature and it is certainly not to be supposed that they are equivalent. In my formulation of R. Yochanan's position what I am assuming to be obvious is that, if R. Yochanan says that replacing certain parts of a thing makes it go out of existence, then surely he would say that destroying or removing those parts without replacing them makes the thing go out of existence. (If destroying the parts without replacing them only "broke" the thing but did not make it go out of existence, then surely replacing those parts would not make the thing go out of existence.) I am assuming, therefore, that R. Yochanan's principle applies to all and only cases in which the destruction without replacement of parts makes a thing go out of existence.[6]

There are several puzzling features that I want to remark on in the Talmudic text I have just reviewed. First of all, the Gemara reports that R. Yochanan's colleagues were awed by his proposal and heaped enormous praise on him, even implying that his intelligence could be compared to that of an angel. In a culture in which intellectual demands were extraordinarily high and special praise a rarity, it needs to be explained why R. Yochanan's proposal merited such acclaim.

I think we can make some reasonable conjectures about this. We may note, to begin with, that R. Yochanan's principle affords an extremely interesting answer to what might be called "the transitivity problem." Many people are intuitively attracted to the idea that if an artifact undergoes a succession of small changes these can eventually accumulate into a large enough change to drive the object out of existence and have it be replaced by another object. On the face of it, however, this seems to violate the transitivity of identity. If the small change from x to y leaves x identical with y, and the small change from y to z leaves y identical with z, then the large(er) change from x to z must necessarily leave x identical with z. This point holds no matter how many additional small changes we add. How then can a succession of small changes add up to a loss of identity? R. Yochanan's principle answers this question by assigning a special role to an artifact's moment of origin, a distinguished moment that sets a kind of standard of identity for the thing. Although a thing may have survived the small change from x to y, the equally small change from y to z may drive it out of existence because the two changes add up to too large a change from its moment of origin.[7]

R. Yochanan's principle also provides an elegant definition of when a gradual replacement of a thing's parts eventually counts as too much to sustain the thing's identity. The fundamental idea is that if it is a requirement of a thing's identity that certain parts not be lost without replacement, then it is also a requirement of the thing's identity that those parts not be replaced. To replace them is to replace the thing. This is, I think, one natural way of explicating certain intuitions that many people have. In that sense, I think that R. Yochanan's principle can be viewed as a refinement and elaboration of commonsense ideas.

If R. Yochanan's principle is notable, I think it is his application of it that his colleagues probably found most stunning. I have thus far suppressed one feature of the sandal example. The example actually stems from a Mishnah in tractate *Kelim* 26.4, which reads in part as follows: "If one of the straps of a sandal is torn off and then repaired . . . If the second [strap] is torn off and then repaired . . ." This does not look like an example in which the straps were *replaced*. How, then, does R. Yochanan's principle apply to it?[8]

I think it is clear that R. Yochanan must be reasoning as follows: When a strap is torn off it loses its capacity to function as a strap; hence it ceases to be a strap; hence it ceases to exist; hence when the piece of leather that constituted that strap is reconstituted into a strap, what we have is a new strap. R. Yochanan is claiming that tearing a strap off a sandal makes the strap go out of existence, and that particular strap does not come back into existence.[9] Let us carefully consider what R. Yochanan's overall analysis of the sandal example comes to. We are imagining a kind of sandal that can function in some proper manner with one strap missing but not with both straps missing. Therefore at every point in the process of successively replacing the straps we have a functional sandal. And at the end of this process we have a sandal made up of the very same leather (arranged in the same way) as when we started. But it is a different sandal because it has different straps! This is surely an audacious proposal but one that, I think, continues to elaborate in a certain direction ideas that many people find immediately intuitive.

The foregoing may begin to explain the strong reaction from his colleagues elicited by R. Yochanan's proposal, but there is another difficulty that has to be addressed. The fact is that R. Yochanan does not present the doctrine of *panim chadashot* as an original contribution. Rather he says that the doctrine had already been established as the correct way to understand the Mishnah's description of the sandal example. Everyone in R. Yochanan's crowd would surely have known this. Merely repeating an established doctrine would have earned R. Yochanan no praise at all.[10]

Let me review the course of the discussion in that piece of Gemara in *Shabbat* 112b. First, a question is raised about the case of the dish. Next, R. Yochanan reminds his audience that it was already established that in the case of the sandal there is *panim chadashot*. Finally, R. Yochanan concludes that there is also *panim chadashot* in the case of the dish. I think we must surmise that what is going on here is that R. Yochanan's colleagues had not properly understood the import of the doctrine of *panim chadashot* and R. Yochanan is straightening the matter out. What could their misunderstanding have been? A clue we have is that on their faulty understanding of the doctrine's application to the case of the sandal no light was cast on the case of the dish, whereas R. Yochanan showed that when properly understood the doctrine immediately settles the case of the dish.

I will venture a suggestion as to what the misunderstanding had been. If what I say is far-fetched—as it may well be—it will in any case allow me to introduce some additional Talmudic material related to identity. R. Yochanan's principle deals with a rather complicated case in which one artifact is replaced by another as a result of compositional considerations. There is another, somewhat more obvious case in which an artifact is replaced because of *functional* considerations. If an artifact with a certain characteristic function is changed into an artifact with a different function, then we may judge that the first has gone out of existence and been replaced by the second. For example, the Mishnah in *Kelim* 28.5 implies that if a goatskin bottle is converted into a rug this is a case of *panim chadashot*, that is, the bottle goes out of existence and is replaced by the rug.[11] Now my suggestion is that R. Yochanan's colleagues had erroneously thought that *panim chadashot* in the case of the sandal was to be understood on the model of the case of the bottle-rug, as due to functional considerations. R. Yochanan explained to them that in the case of the sandal we have a new kind of instance of *panim chadashot*, one that is based on compositional rather than functional changes.

Why were they wrong? Certainly it is not implausible to imagine that the sandal in the example suffers some kind of functional change when its straps are repaired, a change, say, from being an elegant "sandal for the office" to being merely a "knockaround sandal." I take R. Yochanan's position to imply that no such change in the specific use of a sandal will permit us to say that one sandal went out of existence and was replaced by another sandal. But what is the essential difference between this kind of change and the change from a bottle to a rug? My impression is that Talmudists struggle with this question in much the way philosophers do, appealing to intuition—or what they would call *svara*—of various sorts to try to roughly demarcate a class of examples in which a functional change seems sufficiently significant to threaten an object's identity.

One interesting constraint on such examples, which I think is accepted by the majority of Talmudists, is that in order for a functional change to make a thing go out of existence, it must result from a change in the thing's intrinsic properties (e.g., its shape or structure). If an object has a certain characteristic function it does not go out of existence simply because its owners decide to assign to it some different function, without intrinsically altering it in any significant way. An example discussed in tractate *Shabbat* 58a–58b concerns a cowbell that, without suffering any intrinsic alteration, is attached to a door to serve as a doorbell. The Gemara implies that the cowbell persists through this change, and the predominant explanation given by the commentators seems to appeal to the principle that, if an object suffers no intrinsic physical change, it does not go out of existence.[12] This principle, however, will not obviously explain why the imagined functional change in the sandal, which is indeed a result of intrinsic physical changes, does not make the sandal go out of existence.

The Mishnah explains in *Kelim* 28.5 that the reason why the bottle goes out of existence when it changes into a rug is that this constitutes a change of *shem*. "*Shem*" means literally "name," and the *shem* of an artifact will presumably convey its characteristic function. R. Yochanan's colleagues, who of course knew what was said in *Kelim* 28.5, may have supposed that a change from "office sandal" to "knockaround sandal" constitutes an identity-threatening change of *shem*. And the question, again, is why that would be wrong.

I think there is no perfectly precise answer to this question, as I would expect anyone who has worked in this area of philosophy to agree. Nevertheless, the weight of *svara* seems clearly on the side of R. Yochanan's correction of his colleagues' position. There are several kinds of intuitions to which we might want to appeal, but probably the most fundamental one—or, at least, the philosophically most familiar one—has to do with our intuitive sense of what constitutes a *sort* of thing. A standard move in recent philosophy is to define a "substance sortal" as a term F that provides a natural answer to the (Aristotelian) question "What (sort of thing) is it?" An object's change from being F to being not F makes the object go out of existence only if F is a substance sortal. I think it is clear that in the Talmudic contexts under discussion the word *shem* functions very much like—and, unfortunately, with the same tribulations as—the philosophical notion of a "substance sortal." Although this notion is notoriously problematical, its application in the example of the sandal seems sufficiently clear. The proposition "It is a sandal" is a perfectly natural answer to the question "What (sort of thing) is it?" whereas "It is an office sandal" or "It is a knockaround sandal" seem inept as answers to that question. Therefore, neither "office sandal" nor "knockaround sandal" qualifies as a *shem*, and the change from being an office sandal to being a knockaround sandal is not a change that constitutes *panim chadashot*.

If the *panim chadashot* of the sandal had derived from functional changes then it would have obviously been impossible to generalize from that example to the example of the dish. The fact that a certain functional change in a sandal makes the sandal go out of existence is no evidence that a quite different functional change in a dish makes the dish go out of existence. Given, however, that the *panim chadashot* of the sandal is due to the compositional considerations described in R. Yochanan's principle, it immediately follows that, because of those very same considerations, there is *panim chadashot* in the example of the dish.

In some such manner, I conjecture, did R. Yochanan's explanations appear to his colleagues to illuminate the topic to a commendable degree.

In the next part of the paper I want to try to explain how the identity of artifacts has a very distinctive kind of significance within the context of Halachic doctrine. In the course of giving this explanation, I also want to consider a question about how a certain Halachic position of Tosafot relates to the principle of the transitivity of identity. Some of the Halachic material I am about to introduce certainly seems alien to the secular mind, but that is more reason, I think, why we have to examine it carefully if we want to understand its import.

The Halachic notion most closely related to issues of artifact identity is *tum'ah*.[13] Although this is standardly translated "impurity," I think that *"tum'ah"* in the Talmud has as much to do with impurity as "work" in theoretical physics has to do with making a living.[14] The proper way to understand the Talmudic notion is to view it as a theoretical term (a "Ramsey variable") whose content is given by its role within a highly complex theory. The theory of *tum'ah* contains four kinds of principles. First, there are principles that classify a number of different kinds of *tum'ah*. Second, there are principles that say which kinds of objects are susceptible to acquiring which kinds of *tum'ah*. Third, there are principles that describe the physical properties and relations in virtue of which objects initially acquire *tum'ah* of various kinds, and in virtue of which *tum'ah* can be transmitted from one object to another. Fourth and finally, there are principles that explain how the phenomenon of *tum'ah* relates to what is permissible and prohibited in human behavior (the most basic idea being that *tum'ah* must not be brought into the temple).

A sandal is a thing that is susceptible to certain kinds of *tum'ah*. By contrast, such parts of a sandal as the straps, bits of leather, and molecules are not independently *tum'ah*-susceptible, and, though they can acquire *tum'ah* parasitically on a sandal, they automatically lose their *tum'ah* if the sandal does. One way that a sandal can lose its *tum'ah*—and I'm inclined to think that a Talmudist would regard this as an a priori necessary fact—is by going out of existence, whereupon it loses everything, so to speak. If this happens the aforementioned parts of the sandal may persist, but they cannot retain any *tum'ah*. The point that I am attempting to highlight is the reversal of the normal order of supervenience. Normally we would expect the properties of a sandal to be supervenient on the properties of its parts, but within the context of the theory of *tum'ah* it works the other way around. Within that theory a sandal, rather than its parts, plays a primary role, and its identity therefore has a kind of theoretical significance that I doubt can be ascribed to the identity of an artifact in any secular context.

There are only a few places where the Talmud talks explicitly about *panim chadashot*, which I take to be equivalent to explicit talk about identity through time. For the most part issues of identity remain latent within Talmudic discussions whose manifest content is about *tum'ah*. For instance, I said that, according to the Gemara in tractate *Shabbat* 58a–58b, if a cowbell is reassigned the function of a doorbell it does not go out of existence. What the Gemara actually says is that the cowbell does not lose its *tum'ah*, which must imply that it does not go out of existence. I think there is little risk in my going astray by reading issues of identity into issues of *tum'ah*. I doubt that anyone could seriously examine the Talmudic material I have been reviewing without recognizing that, just below the surface, a lively dialectic about identity is transpiring. (And, of course, the most eminent Talmudic commentators do quite often talk explicitly about *panim chadashot*.)

Philosophers often distinguish between an object's identity through time and its spatial identity or unity at a moment. The latter notion corresponds closely to what is called in the Talmud *chibur*.[15] The parts of a unitary object are related to each other (and only to each other) by *chibur*. *Chibur* figures prominently in discussions of *tum'ah* because the part-whole relation is involved in various principles describing how *tum'ah* is acquired and transmitted. There are numerous explicit assertions in the Talmud about *chibur*, often based on extremely delicate and intuitively interesting criteria. I will briefly mention one illustration, drawn from a discussion in tractate *Shabbat* 48b. The Gemara describes a kind of shearing instrument that is standardly put together only when it is in the process of being used; at other times its parts are standardly kept disconnected. The Talmudic verdict is that in such a case there is *chibur* only while the object is actively used. At other times there is no *chibur*—there is no unitary object—even if the parts are, for some reason, kept connected. This difficult example is to be contrasted with two others that may seem less difficult. On one side there are typical objects such as sandals for which there is *chibur* even when they are not being actively used. On the other side are examples in which two objects are connected together for reasons unrelated to their standard functions, yielding no *chibur* at all. For instance, if two garments are temporarily sewn together in order to prevent them from being lost in the laundry, they do not make up a unitary object.[16] If I had more space—and more knowledge—I would certainly want to say more about *chibur*, but I will continue to confine myself primarily to issues of identity through time.

Earlier I gave an excerpt from the description in *Kelim* 26.4 of the example of the sandal. Let me now fill in some of the parts that I had omitted.

> If one of the straps of a sandal is torn off and then repaired, [the sandal] still retains *tum'ah* [*X*]. If the second [strap] is torn off and then repaired, [the sandal] loses *tum'ah* [*X*] but retains *tum'ah* [*Y*]."

The Mishnah mentions two specific kinds of *tum'ah*, but since their nature is not relevant to this discussion, I will simply call them *X* and *Y*.[17] So the Mishnah is saying that when the straps are successively replaced, *tum'ah X* is lost but *tum'ah Y* remains. We know why *tum'ah X* is lost. It was precisely to explain this that R. Yochanan appealed to *panim chadashot*. The explanation is that the sandal at the end is not the sandal that acquired the *tum'ah*. The obvious difficulty is to explain why *tum'ah Y* is not lost for the same reason. I want to examine an explanation given by Tosafot that appears initially to violate the principle of the transitivity of identity.[18] I pursue this matter in part for its intrinsic interest and in part to illustrate in more detail the peculiar mesh between Talmudic issues of *tum'ah* and philosophical issues of identity.

Let the *initial stage* be when the sandal has two intact straps, the *middle stage* when the first strap is replaced, and the *final stage* when the second strap is replaced. Tosafot is able to show—the details need not concern us—that, whereas *tum'ah X* is acquired by the sandal at the initial stage, *tum'ah Y* is acquired at the middle stage. Tosafot's explanation of why *tum'ah Y* is not nullified is that *panim chadashot* cannot apply with respect to *tum'ah* acquired at the middle stage.

On the face of it, this explanation is incomprehensible. We are given that (a) the sandal that exists at the initial stage is not the sandal that exists at the final stage, and (b) the sandal that exists at the initial stage is the sandal that exists at the middle stage. From (a) and (b) it follows by the transitivity of identity that (c) the sandal that exists at the middle stage is not the sandal that exists at the final stage. But it appears that Tosafot wants to assert (a) and (b) while denying (c). When I first introduced R. Yochanan's principle I said that it offers a nice solution to the transitivity problem, but it now appears that Tosafot simply ignores the demands of transitivity. On the other hand, if Tosafot does not intend to deny (c)—which is, in fact, what I will eventually maintain—then we need some other way of understanding why Tosafot holds that *tum'ah* acquired at the middle stage carries over to the final stage.[19]

A familiar controversy in recent philosophy concerns the legitimacy of "relativized" identity statements of the form "*a* is the same *F* as *b*, but *a* is a different *G* than *b*."[20] Since it is likely that certain explanations of the Mishnah under consideration appeal to the notion of relativized identity, it is worth noting that this notion seems quite irrelevant to the difficulty I have raised in Tosafot's explanation. If *a*, *b*, and *c* are, respectively, the sandal at the initial, middle, and final stage, the premise that *a* is a different sandal than *c*, in conjunction with the premise that *a* is the same sandal as *b*, certainly entail that *b* is a different sandal than *c*.[21]

I think I can explain why Tosafot's position does not violate the transitivity of identity, but I first need to introduce a few additional points. The general category of *tum'ah*-susceptible objects of which dishes and sandals are instances is called in the Talmud "*kelim*." The singular form of "*kelim*" is "*kli*" (hence, any one of the *kelim* is a *kli*).[22] The tractate *Kelim* is indeed a study of the laws of *tum'ah* as related to this category. The translation of "*kelim*" that seems to be standard in English editions of the Talmud is "utensils." This is surely a stretch, for we do not naturally apply the word "utensil" to sandals, let alone to such *kelim* as beds, shirts, and earrings. If we are looking for a word in English that gives a rough first approximation to the meaning of "*kelim*" in the Talmud, probably we can do no better than "artifacts." But certainly there is no word (or short expression) of English that can accurately convey the sense of a concept that is deeply entrenched within Talmudic theory.[23] The core idea of a *kli* is simple enough: it is the idea of an object designed by people to be used in some characteristic manner. To this core idea Talmudic theory adds various qualifying conditions.

One condition that is relevant to the present discussion is that the function of a *kli* must be in some sense independent of the functions of other things outside of it. A sandal is functionally independent in this sense, but the strap of a sandal is not, for its function depends entirely on its being part of the sandal.[24] A simplifying assumption that will be helpful in the present context and that I do not think will distort anything of relevance is that a *kli* is essentially a functionally independent artifact.

Although the relevant notion of functional independence is far from rigorous —and it may be clarified in various ways in the Talmudic literature—I think its intuitive content immediately implies that many typical parts of functionally independent objects are not themselves functionally independent. On the other hand, it seems that there are cases where some parts are functionally independent. For example, the Mishnah in *Kelim* 7.3 discusses a primitive stove or range each half of which is capable of functioning independently of the other half. Since each half is a functionally independent object, I will say that each half is an "embedded *kli*."

Although I have not found any explicit mention of embedded *kelim* in the Talmudic literature, I think this notion must be presupposed in various places where the Talmud says that, if a *kli* splits into two *kelim*, its *tum'ah* remains. An example is found in the Mishnah I have just mentioned in *Kelim* 7.3: "If a stove is split horizontally *tum'ah* is lost, if split vertically *tum'ah* remains." The obvious idea is that a vertical split leaves us with two smaller functional stoves. The question that still has to be pressed is why *tum'ah* remains given that the original stove has presumably gone out of existence. That this must be so seems to follow from considerations familiar from recent philosophical discussions of the splitting of persons. We cannot identify the original stove with each of the resultant smaller stoves, since that would blatantly violate the transitivity of identity. (If the original stove is one of the small stoves, and is also the other small stove, then it follows absurdly that each small stove is the other one.) Nor can we identify the original stove with just one of the small stoves, for that would be incoherently arbitrary. Nor is it likely to be the Talmudic position that the original stove persists (and retains *tum'ah*) in fragmented form. I think the most plausible interpretation of the Mishnah is that the halves of the original stove are embedded *kelim* that independently acquire the same *tum'ah* it does and retain that *tum'ah* after it ceases to exist.

To mention another example, the Halachah is that if a cloak is divided in half to serve as two cloaks, its *tum'ah* remains.[25] Assuming that the original cloak cannot be coherently identified with either of the resulting fragments, the Talmudic position certainly cannot be that the cloak persists in fragmented form if, say, one fragment is sent to Israel and the other stays in America. The position must be that, although the original cloak goes out of existence, it contains embedded *kelim* that independently acquire and retain the *tum'ah*, for any part of a cloak which is large enough to function as a cloak is functionally independent.[26]

Let us now reconsider the example of the sandal. Since we are dealing with a sandal that can function in the absence of one of its straps, it follows, I think, that a part of the sandal that contains everything except for one strap is functionally independent, and hence an embedded *kli*. At the initial stage we have the sandal S that contains the two straps T_1 and T_2. We also have the functionally independent object A_1 that contains T_1 but not T_2, and the functionally independent object A_2 that contains T_2 but not T_1. At the middle stage T_1 is replaced by the new strap T_1', so A_1 is replaced by the new functionally independent object A_1'. We still have S and A_2. At the final stage the second strap T_2 is replaced. Therefore, by R. Yochanan's principle, we no longer have the sandal S. We also have lost A_2. But we still have A_1'. We recall that, according to Tosafot, *tum'ah X* appeared at the initial stage, and *tum'ah Y* at the middle stage. Since, at the final stage, we no longer have any *kli* that existed at the initial stage, *tum'ah X* is gone, but since we still have the embedded *kli* A_1' that acquired *tum'ah Y* at the middle stage, that *tum'ah* is still with us. Tosafot's position, as now understood, is not threatened by the transitivity of identity.[27]

Questions remain, but they are philosophically familiar. One question concerns the fact that, between the initial and middle stages, there will be a moment when the first strap is destroyed and not yet replaced. At that moment S and A_2 coincide. This fact will not bother those philosophers—and I am one of them—who think there are many ordinary cases in which distinct objects occupy the same place at the same time.[28] Even those philosophers have generally wanted to honor the Lockean demand that coinciding objects be of different sorts. There seems no reason why the demand cannot be met in the present example. We can distinguish between a "(whole) sandal" such as S and a "partial sandal" such as A_2. A partial sandal is not a sandal, although it is capable of independently performing the function of a sandal. Even at the moment when S and A_2 coincide it remains the case that the sandal S is a sort of thing that once contained two straps and that ought to contain two straps, whereas the partial sandal A_2 is a sort of thing that never did, nor ever possibly could, contain two straps.[29]

I will conclude with a few general observations on the Talmudic material I have been discussing. This paper has been essentially a study in the history of ideas. I have offered a (traditional) reading of certain ancient and medieval Jewish texts that reveals within them—sometimes explicitly, often implicitly—a complex dialectic related to the identity of artifacts. Although the tractate *Kelim* obviously deals with many issues unrelated to identity, I think it is no distortion to say that the tractate as a whole presents an extended treatment of the identity of a wide range of artifacts. The methodology displayed in the tractate is especially noteworthy. We are given numerous examples occasionally interspersed with a *klal* or general principle that conveys in some rough way the lesson implicit in a set of examples. (One *klal* says that an object loses its *tum'ah* when there is a change of *shem*.) There is no intimation, certainly, that the examples might be rendered superfluous by the general principles applicable to them. On the contrary, it seems clear that the examples are indispensable and that it is they that bear the main explanatory burden.[30] Some of the objects dealt with by the examples in *Kelim* are boards, fire pans, tubes for roasting grain, lids for bread baskets, pitchers, jars, beds, chairs, tables, ships, lamps, lanterns, funnels used for wine or oil, covers of jars, covers of pots, trays, inkstands, spice containers, torches, candleholders, earthenware vessels for food, earthenware vessels for liquids, casks, stoppers of casks, water heaters, kettles, ovens, stoves, the brickworks surrounding ovens, the brickworks surrounding stoves, receptacles fixed to the sides of stoves, clay additions to the top of an oven, doors, locks, bolts, knockers, drains, wicker baskets, reed baskets, gloves, aprons, curtains, blinkers for an ox, bees-fumigators, swords, knives, daggers, scissors, flutes, . . . and hundreds more. Wittgensteinians, who often commend the elucidative power of examples, may especially find something of interest in this amazing tractate.

The Wittgensteinian respect for examples typically goes together with an attitude of distrust toward traditional conceptual analysis. It may initially seem wrong to attribute any such attitude to Talmudists, who are among the most analytical people on earth. But the Wittgensteinian attitude might be expressed as follows: Analysis can never be completed. We can indeed formulate criteria for determining when we have a case of *panim chadashot* or when we have a case of *chibur*, but such criteria are necessarily incomplete. There is in principle no finitary formulation that can settle once and for all every theoretical question that can reasonably be posed about the nature of artifact identity. There can be no final *klal* that brings the curtain down on this area of discourse, because around the next corner there will always be another hard case for intuition or *svara* to grapple with. Ultimately, therefore, our judgment must rest on our grasp of what is implied by the indispensable precedents or paradigm examples. Along such lines, the Wittgensteinian attitude may seem quite congenial to the Talmudist.[31]

As a philosopher who has never been able to take seriously any position that repudiates commonsense ontology, I find the Talmudist's earnest preoccupation with ordinary objects uplifting. Realism with a Talmudic face does not merely acknowledge the existence of moderate-sized dry goods but assigns to these objects a theoretical role. If we had consciously attempted to conjure up a set of theoretical properties and principles that might provide a framework for ordinary objects, we could not have done much better than the Talmudic theory of *tum'ah*. A theological hypothesis might now be that God created the phenomenon of *tum'ah* in order to make the identity of ordinary things matter. The anthropological alternative would assign the creative role to people rather than to God. (Perhaps some ancient Jew who was teaching a course on artifact identity found that in the absence of any relevant framework it was hard to get the intuitions to stick. . . .) Obviously it is not my aim to assess any such hypotheses (or more serious ones). What intrigues me philosophically is the character of a religious perspective that enhances the significance of ordinary ontology in a dramatic way. And it is certainly not just the Halachic principles of *tum'ah* that have this general effect. It appears, indeed, that the overall upshot of the way of life described in the Talmud is to achieve a distinctive kind of sanctification of the commonplace by locating every ordinary thing and event within the space of Halachic doctrine. The Rabbis of the Talmud had evidently set themselves the task of in some sense completing rather than denying the circle of the plain. From their perspective the metaphysics of the ordinary has to prevail, because their deepest theory of the world demands the existence of such things as dishes and sandals.[32]

APPENDIX:

Text from tractate *Shabbat* 112b

We learnt elsewhere: As for dishes belonging to private people, their standards are [holes as large] as pomegranates. [R.] Chizkiyah asked, What if it [a dish] acquires a hole [large enough] for an olive to fall through, and he [the owner] repairs it, then it receives another hole [large enough] for an olive to fall through, and he repairs it, [and so on] until it is made large enough for a pomegranate to fall through? R. Yochanan said to him, Rebbe, you have taught us: If one of the straps of a sandal is torn off and then repaired, [the sandal] still retains *midras tum'ah.* If the second [strap] is torn off and then repaired, [the sandal] loses *midras tum'ah* but retains *maga midras tum'ah.* Now we asked you, What is the difference between [a case in which] the first [is broken] and the second is sound and [a case in which] the second is broken and the first is repaired? And you answered us, *Panim chadashot* enters here. Here too [in the case of the dish] *panim chadashot* enters. He [R. Chizkiyah] exclaimed concerning him [R. Yochanan], He is not [merely] a man, [or] according to others, He is [genuinely] a man.

NOTES

1. The Talmud consists of many tractates, each of which deals primarily with a particular area of Halachah. Most tractates contain both "Mishnah" and "Gemara," although a few (including in particular tractate *Kelim*, to which I will be frequently referring) contain only the former. The Mishnah consists of (what appear to be) extremely sketchy notes of Halachic discussions ranging over several centuries and ending at about A.D. 200. The Gemara, which summarizes Halachic discussions from about A.D. 200–600, is a kind of running commentary on the Mishnah, somewhat less sketchy but still notoriously compressed.

2. I should emphasize that what I am calling "R. Yochanan's principle" is not explicitly stated in the Talmudic text under consideration, but as the content and meaning of that text gradually unfolds in the ensuing discussion, I think it will be clear that the principle (or some very close variant) was surely implied by R. Yochanan's remarks. The whole relevant Talmudic text is given in an appendix to this paper.

3. פנים חדשות

4. Rashi's words are: אין זו הראשון
(Rashi is Rabbi Shlomo ben Yitzhak, 1040–1105. His commentary is placed next to the Mishnah and Gemara in standard editions of the Talmud.)

5. In tractate *Eruvin* 24a the Gemara applies R. Yochanan's view to an example involving a wall in a Halachic context unrelated to the examples of the dish and sandal. I think there is no possible way of making sense of the Gemara's diverse applications of R. Yochanan's view except by supposing that *panim chadashot* means what Rashi says it does. I should mention that some Talmudic commentators apply the notion of *panim chadashot* to a discussion in tractate *Bava Kama* 65b, which may pertain to the identity of living things. I confine myself in this paper to Talmudic issues related only to the identity of artifacts.

6. The general connection between "breaking" and going out of existence is one of the themes explored in Rabbi Aharon Kotler (1892–1962), *Mishnat Rebbi Aharon* (*Zeraim, Tehorot*), chaps. 30 and 31. The assumption that I am claiming to be obvious may possibly be called into question by a remarkable statement of Tosafot Sens in tractate *Sotah* 29a. Tosafot Sens seems to say that even if we hold that a dish persists in fragmented form after it is smashed to pieces, once the fragments are reconstituted into a dish we certainly have a new dish, and the old dish has now gone out of existence. If this is so, then I suppose it might also be held that, whereas a large hole in a dish allows it to persist as a broken dish, a large patch makes one dish go out of existence and another replace it. But that does strike me as intuitively very odd. (Tosafot Sens is part of Tosafot, the latter being a collection of Talmudic commentaries from the twelfth and thirteenth centuries. Tosafot appears, together with Rashi's commentary, next to the Mishnah and Gemara in standard editions of the Talmud.)

7. I can recall seeing very few places in the philosophical literature where a thing's moment of origin is said to play a special role in its identity through time, David Wiggins explicitly makes such a claim in "On Singling Out an Object" (in P. Pettit and J. McDowell, ed., *Subject, Thought, and Context* [Oxford: Oxford University Press, 1986]), 173, and I briefly consider it in *The Concept of Identity* (New York: Oxford University Press, 1982), 216, n. 3. The idea may be connected in some intuitive way to Kripke's principle of the necessity of origins.

8. If we look into Rambam's *Mishnah Torah*, Book X, Laws of *Kelim*, chap. 7.12, we find him repeating the Mishnah's description of the sandal example and then adding the explanation, "New straps were made." How are they "new straps"? (Rambam, also known as Maimonides, is Rabbi Moshe ben Maimon, 1135–1204.)

9. Up to a point R. Yochanan's position on the strap's existence is analogous to what Aristotle says about an eye going out of existence when it ceases to function as an eye, in *De Anima*, Book 2, chap. 1, 412, B17.

10. The Gemara, in fact, depicts R. Yochanan as presenting his position to an audience including R. Chizkiyah, the person who is said to have first taught him about the doctrine of *panim chadashot*—who then praises him lavishly.

11. It is possible that I am assuming a somewhat controversial interpretation of *Kelim* 28.5. What I think is clear is that if we adopt the view attributed to Tosafot in *Mishnat Rebbi Aharon*, chaps. 30 and 31, then we must certainly interpret *Kelim* 28.5 as saying that the bottle has gone out of existence; moreover, I have no evidence that anyone would want to interpret the Mishnah differently. Note carefully that, apart from the bottle-rug example, commentators differ critically on what the correct text is with respect to the other examples in *Kelim* 28.5; see, e.g., the commentary of Rosh (Rabbi Asher ben Yeheil, c. 1250–1327), and the explanations of Chazon Ish (Rabbi A. I. Karelitz, 1878–1953) in his volume on *Kelim*, chap. 30.17. (Throughout this paper I follow the standard Talmudic practice of using a term such as "Chazon Ish" as both the name of the commentator and the name of his major work.)

12. This principle seems to be implicit in Tosafot beginning "*Af al pi*" in *Shabbat* 58a. A distinguished minority position that seems to deny the principle is advanced by Pnei Yehoshua (Rabbi Yaakov Falk, 1680–1756) in his commentary on that Tosafot.

13. טומאה

14. A number of Israelis whom I have asked about this have informed me that, in modern Hebrew, neither "*tum'ah*" nor any of its cognates is ever used in a secular context, though "*tahor*" (טהור), which is the adjectival antonym of "*tum'ah*," is used to mean "pure." I take this to be some kind of acknowledgement in modern Hebrew that the traditional notion of "*tum'ah*" has no straightforward connection to "impurity" in any ordinary sense.

15. חיבור

16.To be more accurate, what I have presented in this paragraph is the Talmudic interpretation of what is strictly the Torah rule on *chibur*; I omit various pragmatic Rabbinical revisions. For a discussion of different Talmudic notions of *chibur*, see Rabbi Chaim Soloveichik (1853–1920), *Chidushe Hagrach Al Hashas*, Part 3 (*Zeraim, Moed, Tehorot*), "*Beinyun Bet Kibul Haasu Lamalot*."

17. *X* is *midras* (מדרס), and *Y* is *maga midras* (מגע מדרס).

18. What I am taking to be the predominant position of Tosafot is attributed to Ri (Rabbi Yitzhak ben Shmuel, died c. 1185) in Tosafot beginning "*Aval*" in *Shabbat* 112b, is presented again in Tosafot beginning "*Aval*" in *Eruvin* 24a, and again in Tosafot beginning "*Ki*" in *Menachot* 24b–25a.

19. Many eminent Talmudic commentators uphold Tosafot's position. For example, Rosh presents essentially the same position in his commentary on both *Kelim* 18.6 and 26.4. In the commentary of Maharsha (Rabbi Shmuel Edels, 1555–1631) on Tosafot beginning "*Aval*" in *Shabbat* 112b, he is more explicit than Tosafot in asserting that *panim chadashot* cannot possibly nullify *tum'ah* acquired in the middle stage. An equally explicit assertion to the same effect is found in the commentary of Mishnah Lamelech (Rabbi Yehudah ben Shmuel Rosanes, 1657–1727) on Rambam's *Mishnah Torah*, Book X, Laws of *Kelim*, chap. 7.12. In the course of struggling with this problem for a number of months, I was afraid I had uncovered a massive Jewish rejection of the transitivity of identity. Eventually I found another way to see it.

20. See David Wiggins, *Sameness and Substance* (Cambridge: Harvard University Press, 1980), chap. 2. My own view on this issue is that there is nothing wrong with relativized identity, as long as one acknowledges the primacy of nonrelativized identity; see my "Identity" in J. Kim and E. Sosa, ed., *A Companion to Metaphysics* (Cambridge, MA: Basil Blackwell, 1995).

21. Relativized identity seems quite definitely to figure in the explanation of the Mishnah suggested by Ritzva (Rabbi Yitzhak ben Avrabam, 12th century), as cited in Tosafot beginning "*Aval*" in *Eruvin* 24a. Ritzva explains that *tum'ah Y* remains because, whereas there is *panim chadashot* with respect to the *shem* "sandal," there is no *panim chadashot* with respect to a certain technical *shem* that sustains *tum'ah Y*. In other words, whereas *a* is a different sandal than *c*, *a* is the same *F* as *c*, for a certain technical term *F*. Ritzva's position is clarified by Chazon Ish in his volume on *Kelim*, chap. 31.3. Let me mention that one expert Talmudist with whom I have discussed this topic expressed the opinion that Tosafot's position probably should somehow be explicated along the lines of relativized identity, but I do not see how to do this.

22. Any one of the כלים is a כלי.

23. I am not sure how "*kelim*" is used in modern Hebrew, but I suspect that this use is neither equivalent to the use of the word in the Talmud nor to the use of any English word.

24. Here I am following Chazon Ish, who states in his volume on *Kelim*, chap. 31.2, that the strap of a sandal is not a *kli* because it is functionally dependent on the sandal.

25. If a garment or large piece of cloth is cut into small pieces that do not have the function of the original, various Halachic complications arise (as discussed in *Chulin* 72b and 123a), but the simple example I describe seems to be noncontroversial; cf. *Mishnat Rebbi Aharon*, chap. 30.1.

26. I am especially interested here in examples in which an embedded *kli* has a function essentially like that of the larger *kli*, but there are important examples of other kinds to consider; see especially the discussion in *Mishnat Rebbi Aharon*, chap. 30.6, of a Gemara in *Zevachim* 95a.

27. Two technical points: (1) Because of the general principle that, if *x* is part of *y*, then *x* acquires whatever *tum'ah* is had by *y* and *y* acquires whatever *tum'ah* is had by *x* (see, e.g., *Kelim* 6.3), at the final stage the whole new sandal acquires *tum'ah Y* parasitically on A_1'; (2) Because of the principle just mentioned, at the middle stage A_1' temporarily acquires *tum'ah X* parasitically on *S*, but A_1' loses that *tum'ah* as soon as *S* ceases to exist, for even a full-fledged *kli* cannot retain parasitic *tum'ah* on its own (as shown, e.g., in *Kelim* 18.7).

28. The recent literature on the issue of coinciding objects has become overwhelming. A seminal discussion is David Wiggins, "On Being in the Same Place at the Same Time," *Philosophical Review* 77(1), January 1968, 90–95.

29. The doctrine of embedded *kelim* that I am attributing to the Talmud has something in common with the view of Roderick Chisholm, *Person and Object* (La Salle, IL: Open Court, 1976), 99, but Chisholm would say that the whole sandal contains a part that is itself a sandal. Let me add that I am leaving open some significant questions of detail concerning the identity through time of an embedded *kli*.

30. Compare with Rambam's procedure, for example, in *Mishnah Torah*, Book X, Laws of *Kelim*, chaps. 8.1 and 8.2 (my emphasis in the last sentence): "Unfinished metal *kelim* are not susceptible to *tum'ah*. And these are deemed to be unfinished metal *kelim*: any that still need to be polished, decorated, or incised, or painted, or hammered out, or that lack a handle or a rim. . . . Thus, a

sword is not susceptible to *tum'ah* until it has been furbished, nor a knife until it has been ground. *And the same applies with all like processes*." There is no indication that Rambam considers it possible to dispense with the examples in favor of a more precise characterization of the kind of process in question.

31. Needless to say, this is barely a thumbnail sketch of a possible Talmudic-Wittgensteinian attitude towards identity. Various connections between Jewish thought and Wittgenstein's philosophy are explored in Howard Wettstein, "Doctrine," *Faith and Philosophy* 14(4), October 1997, 423–43; section 3 of his paper is especially relevant to the present discussion.

32. For advice and comments on this paper, I thank John Fisher, Martin Golding, Moshe Hirsch, Amelie Rorty, David Shatz, Mark Steiner, Joel Unger, and Howard Wettstein.

Midwest Studies in Philosophy, XXIII (1999)

Distrusting Reason

HILARY KORNBLITH

The activity of reason-giving is an important part of our intellectual lives. At times, we offer reasons to justify our actions or our beliefs, both to others and to ourselves. Moreover, most of us take reason-giving to have normative force: if we are presented with good reasons in favor of a belief or a course of action, we take this to provide us with a presumption in favor of forming that belief or performing that action. This is, after all, why reason is so important: it serves, and rightly so, as a guide to both belief and action.

But there are some who are distrustful of reason, who do not take the activity of reason-giving at face value. Reason-giving may be viewed with suspicion as yet one more instrument for wielding power over the oppressed. Views of this sort have been articulated and defended by some feminists, Freudians, Marxists, and deconstructionists, and some such inchoate view may be behind a certain climate of anti-intellectualism that is currently a potent force in public debate on many issues of real import.[1]

This distrust of reason needs to be taken more seriously than it has, to my mind, not only as a political force, but as an intellectual position. In this paper, I try to show that a certain skepticism about reason-giving deserves a hearing. In coming to understand why someone might rationally be suspicious of the practice of reason-giving, those of us who place our trust in this practice may come to understand better what its presuppositions are and what it would take to ground that trust. This paper thus attempts to make a contribution to the field of social epistemology: it attempts to spell out some of the social prerequisites for the proper function of the activity of reason giving.[2]

I

Let us begin by examining a case of rationalization. Andrew has beliefs about the effectiveness of the death penalty in reducing the murder rate which are, at bottom, a product of wishful thinking. Andrew has certain views about the morality of the death penalty, views which he holds on grounds independent of his views about its deterrent effect. His views about the effectiveness of the death penalty as a deterrent are not a product of his understanding of the relevant data. Instead, it is his view about the morality of the death penalty that is driving his view about its effects. Conveniently, he has come to believe that the policy he judges to be morally correct also happens to have the best consequences. Andrew's reason for his belief about the deterrent effect of the death penalty is not a good reason. It would not withstand public, or even private, scrutiny. But Andrew is unaware that this is why he believes as he does. He sincerely believes that his reasons for belief are quite different.

Andrew is not entirely uninformed about the various empirical studies that have been done on the deterrent effect of the death penalty. Indeed, when such studies are reported in the newspapers, Andrew is extremely attentive to the details of the news story. The studies that Andrew has seen reported are mixed: some present prima facie evidence of the effectiveness of the death penalty in reducing the murder rate, whereas others present prima facie evidence of its ineffectiveness. Andrew has latched on to the stories that fit with his antecedent view. He remembers them better than the others, and when asked about the death penalty, he is often able to cite relevant statistics from them. He has less vivid memories of the other studies, those that run counter to his belief about the death penalty's effectiveness, and when he reads about these studies he is typically able to mount some perfectly plausible methodological challenge to them: some important variable was not controlled for, the number of cases involved is not statistically significant, and so on. Andrew is intelligent and articulate. He is very good at constructing reasons for his belief from the mixed evidence with which he is confronted, and he is very good at presenting these reasons to others in discussion about the issue. He believes that the reasons that he presents are the reasons for which he holds his belief. But he is wrong about this. The reasons for his belief are quite different. Thus, when Andrew offers reasons for his belief, he is offering a rationalization.[3]

Andrew's intelligence and articulateness are aids to the process of rationalization. Andrew's ability to construct and deploy arguments can be extremely convincing, both to others and to himself. Someone less sophisticated than Andrew would not be able to construct such convincing rationalizations, and opinions of such a person that were the product of wishful thinking would be more easily exposed, both to others and to the person himself. When Andrew offers rationalizations for his badly grounded opinions, his intelligence works against him.

Ordinarily, when we reflect on our reasons for one of our beliefs, we are motivated by a desire to have our beliefs conform to the truth. By scrutinizing our reasons, we hope to be able to recognize cases where our beliefs have outstripped our reasons and thus, where we should not be confident that our beliefs do indeed conform to the truth. When we consider what to believe in prospect, we reflect on our evidence, and this process of reflection is designed to guide belief fixation so as to make it likely that the beliefs we come to have also conform to the truth. Both in the case of reflection on already existing beliefs and in the case of reflection on beliefs we might come to have, our motivation for thinking about reasons is to get at the truth.

Now in the case of rationalization, our motivation for reflecting on reasons is different. Our motivation in these cases may be to make ourselves feel better, to avoid cognitive dissonance, or the like. But if our motivations in these cases are different from those in the typical case, such motivations are not transparent to us. When we rationalize, at least when we do it sincerely, we are not aware of doing so; we are not aware of being motivated by anything other than a desire to get at the truth. And it is precisely because of this that the process of scrutinizing our reasons for belief may, at times, be terribly counterproductive from an epistemological point of view. Scrutinizing our reasons, when we are engaged in sincere rationalizing, will get in the way of the goal of believing truths.

Let us return to Andrew. When Andrew reflects on his reasons for believing as he does about the effects of the death penalty, he is able to devise reasons for his belief that give the appearance of supporting it. Indeed, the reasons he is able to offer are prima facie good reasons for believing as he does. Thus, when Andrew offers these reasons to others, if they are not independently well informed on this matter, they may come, quite reasonably, to believe as Andrew does; and when others do this, their believings, unlike Andrew's, may be motivated by nothing more than a desire to believe the truth. They, unlike Andrew, are being fully responsive to the evidence, it seems. The only problem for Andrew's interlocutors is that Andrew has selectively presented the evidence; but this, of course, is not something that they are in a position to know or even have any reason to suspect. The reasons Andrew presents are, on their face, good reasons. Rational interlocutors who lack independent evidence on the questions about which Andrew speaks should come to believe as he does.

This fact about the interpersonal case of reason-giving is particularly important because it helps to explain why it is that the process of rationalization is so easy to engage in. When we scrutinize our own reasons for belief, we, like Andrew's interlocutors, take the evidence that is available to us at face value.[4] Because the biasing processes that selectively filter our evidence take place behind the scenes, as it were, unavailable to introspection, we are able to produce perfectly good reasons for belief, reasons that not only survive our private scrutiny, but would survive public scrutiny as well. The process of scrutinizing our reasons, in the case of sincere rationalization, gives the illusion of being responsive to available evidence. And the more intelligent one is and the better one is at the skills of presenting and defending arguments, the more powerful the illusion will be, if one engages in rationalizing, that one is forming beliefs in ways that are appropriately responsive to evidence.

These facts about rationalization, I believe, go some distance toward making sense of the phenomenon of distrusting reason. There are certain people who have a deep skepticism about the significance of rational argument. These people are often unmoved by rational argument, and, indeed, seem to find the activity of reason-giving less persuasive the more careful and detailed the argument given. Such people often say things like this: "I know that's a perfectly good argument for p, but I don't know whether I should believe p"; and this, on its face, seems deeply irrational. What should determine whether one should believe p, after all, if not the arguments available for and against it?[5]

But I don't think that this attitude need be irrational at all. First, the ability to form one's beliefs in a way that is responsive to evidence is not at all the same as the ability to present reasons for one's beliefs, either to others or to oneself. Reason-giving requires a wide range of skills that need not be present in the reasons-responsive person. One thing the skeptic about reason-giving may be responding to is the recognition that some people are terrifically adept at providing prima facie reasonable arguments for their beliefs, quite apart from whether those beliefs are correct. Just as a reasonable person might willfully ignore the appeals of a gifted speaker in order to avoid being misled, an intelligent person who recognizes his own weakness in distinguishing apparently good but mistaken reasoning from the genuine item might also willfully ignore detailed and subtle appeals to reason.[6]

But the second reason for thinking that skepticism about reason-giving may often be quite reasonable ties in directly with the points we have made about rationalization.[7] People who are especially intelligent and articulate and who are adept at providing reasons for their beliefs are also, in virtue of that very fact, especially well equipped at providing rationalizations for their beliefs, rationalizations that possess all of the hallmarks of good reasoning. It is not that devising a convincing rationalization for a belief is easy, even for those gifted at argument. But rationalization is often the product of very powerful motivating forces, and thus a great deal of intellectual energy may be brought to the task; the result of this is often a subtle and prima facie rational argument. This provides fuel for skepticism about rational argument, and it is precisely for this reason that the skeptic is especially wary of detailed and elaborate argument. Intricacy of argument, on this view, raises a red flag, for it raises the possibility of rationalization as the underlying source of the argument given rather than truth-responsive reason-giving. Inspection of the details of the argument would be pointless in trying to distinguish these two, for the subtle rationalizer is in a fine position to offer arguments that, on their face, are impeccable. The difference between truth-responsive reason-giving and subtle rationalization does not lie in features intrinsic to the arguments given. A reasonable person who is worried about the possibility of rationalization as a source of a particular act of reason-giving will thus not allow herself to be pulled into the intellectual task of examining the quality of reasoning offered, for this is the wrong place to look to see whether the conclusion is to be trusted. What needs to be examined is the source of the argument—its motivation—rather than its logical credentials. One needs to know whether the person offering the argument is motivated by a desire to believe truths or by something else instead.

One might object at this point that the motivation of the person offering the argument is simply irrelevant when we are trying to figure out what to believe. If the argument offered is a good one, then it doesn't matter whether it reflects the reasons for which the person offering it believes the conclusion. We shouldn't care whether the argument offered is a reflection of the arguer's reasons for belief; all we should care about is whether the argument offered is a reflection of good reasons for us to believe.

There is something right about this objection. The mere fact that an argument offered does not reflect the reasons for which the arguer believes a conclusion does not by itself undermine the value of the reasons offered. Nevertheless, as a matter of empirical fact, the phenomenon of rationalization is typically accompanied by a number of factors that do tend to undermine the value of the reasons offered by the rationalizer. As the case of Andrew illustrates, there is a tremendous selectivity in the way in which rationalizers deal with evidence: they do not present the evidence fairly, either to themselves, in memory, or to others. This point, by itself, is sufficient to show that we must be on the lookout for rationalization.

In addition, many arguments involve subtle appeals to plausibility. There can be little doubt that the rationalizer's sense of plausibility is affected in important ways by the motivation he has for rationalizing, and this does not aid in the project of coming to believe truths. Thus, if an agent suspects that he himself is rationalizing, he has reason to worry about his overall evaluations of plausibility. That an argument is born of rationalization is importantly relevant in determining what one should believe.

More than this, the extent to which inchoate judgments of plausibility come into play in evaluating arguments should be a source of concern even apart from concerns about rationalization. Our sense of plausibility is a fragile reed. There can be little doubt that it is socially conditioned. Being surrounded by people who take a particular view seriously, or, alternatively, simply dismiss a view as unworthy of serious consideration, is likely to have some effect on one's own assessments of plausibility. If those around one are well attuned to the truth, this may be a fine thing. But in less optimal circumstances, where one's epistemic community is badly misguided, one's own sense of plausibility may be distorted as a result. What passes for good reasoning in such communities may have very little connection to the truth.

In the end, the difference between the person who places his full confidence in rational argument and the person who is skeptical of it may come down, in part, to a disagreement about the frequency with which rationalization occurs and the extent to which our sense of plausibility can be distorted. If one believes that rationalization is extremely widespread and that plausibility judgments are extremely malleable, then one may be well advised to be skeptical of rational argument. Under these conditions, attending to the logical niceties of argument would be no more useful in attaining one's epistemic goals than attending to the eye color of the person offering the argument. If, on the other hand, rationalization is rare, and plausibility judgments are firmly fixed in ways that track the truth, then focusing on the logical features of reason-giving may serve as an effective guide to true belief. What divides these two views, to the extent that each is rationally held, is a disagreement about human psychology.

Let me spell out this disagreement in greater detail. The skeptic about reason-giving may view the very activity of giving reasons as far more disconnected from the truth, and indeed, in some cases, from the activity of belief fixation, than we are ordinarily accustomed to thinking. I take the traditional view to be as follows. Human beings often form their beliefs as a result of self-consciously considering reasons. When they do this, they are typically led to beliefs that are likely to be true, at least relative to the evidence available to them. Even when self-conscious consideration of reasons does not occur prior to forming a belief, we often scrutinize our reasons for belief after the fact. When we do this, we begin by determining what our reasons for holding a belief come to, and we then consider the logical credentials of our reasons. When they are good reasons, we continue to hold the belief, and when they are not good reasons, we come to give up the belief. Our reasons are, for the most part, easily available to introspection, and the activity of considering our reasons is thus deeply implicated in the fixation of belief in a way that guides it toward the truth.

But the skeptic about reason-giving may have a very different picture about the relationship among the giving of reasons, belief fixation, and the truth. On this view, belief fixation often occurs independent of self-conscious consideration of reasons. This need not make belief fixation irrational or unrelated to the truth, for we may in many cases be responsive to good reasons even without self-consciously considering them. When we do turn to self-conscious consideration of reasons, on the skeptic's view, the activity of reason-giving may often have little effect on belief fixation. Far from reasons determining which beliefs are formed, as on the traditional view, it is the beliefs we antecedently hold that largely determine the reasons we will come to find. Reason-giving, on this view, is often a matter of rationalization. From the point of view of belief fixation, reason-giving is frequently epiphenomenal.[8]

Even when reason giving is not epiphenomenal, on the skeptic's view, it may have little connection with the truth. Since our sense of plausibility is so easily affected by the standards of our community, a community whose standards have been distorted by external factors will come to taint even the judgments of those otherwise unaffected by those distorting factors prevalent elsewhere in the community. When what passes for good reason really does play a role in belief fixation, then, it does not guide the self-conscious believer toward the truth, but instead serves only to further distort that person's judgment.

The issue between the skeptic about reason-giving and the person who places his trust in it is, I believe, an important one, and I would like to examine it in more detail. But before we try to figure out who is in the right here, we need to consider an objection to the skeptic's position, an objection that challenges its internal coherence. The skeptic's position is worthy of serious consideration only if it can avoid this particular challenge.

II

The challenge I have in mind is that the skeptic's view is self-undermining, for the skeptic on the one hand proclaims that the activity of reason-giving is not connected to the truth and that we should therefore be unmoved by it, and yet, on the other hand, in order to convince us of this particular view, the skeptic offers us reasons. If the skeptic is right about the activity of reason-giving, then her argument would not, and should not, convince us. According to the challenger, skepticism about reason-giving is thus self-undermining.[9]

This challenge fails, I believe, and it fails in two different ways. First, the skeptic's argument may be seen as a simple *reductio*.[10] The skeptic about reason-giving need not be seen as endorsing the argument she gives; instead she may be seen as merely showing that the position of the person who puts his trust in reason-giving is internally inconsistent; that is, it fails to meet that person's own standards. The skeptic, on this view, demonstrates an internal tension in the view of the person who places his trust in rational argument, a tension which that person is in no position to resolve. This is sufficient to undermine the trust in rational argument.

Although this particular way of construing the skeptic's argument absolves her of the charge of undermining her own position, I think that there is a better way to represent what the skeptic is up to. I thus turn to a second response to our challenger.

As I see it, the skeptic does not mean merely to offer a *reductio* in the manner just explained. Instead, the skeptic wishes to endorse the position that reason-giving is so frequently a matter of mere rationalization, and our plausibility judgments so frequently off the mark, that reason should not be taken at face value. Indeed, this particular view of reason-giving is offered as the best available explanation of the social phenomenon of inquiring about and presenting reasons for belief. On this account of the skeptic's position, the charge of internal inconsistency, of self-defeat, is more acute. For on this account, the skeptic is presenting a rational argument *that she endorses* for the view that rational arguments should not produce conviction. How could such a position fail to be self-defeating?

The answer to this question lies in the recognition that our skeptic about reason giving is not a *total* skeptic; indeed, she is very far from it. She is not a skeptic about the possibility of rational belief. She merely denies that a certain activity, an activity that many see as paradigmatically rational, is, indeed, genuinely rational, at least in the typical case. On the skeptic's view, rational belief is not only possible, it is often actual. Beliefs that are not self-consciously arrived at are frequently responsive to reason. Moreover, although the skeptic does not accept the practice of reason-giving at face value, this does not mean that the skeptic is forced to reject every case of reason-giving as bogus. Rather, her view about the frequency of reason-giving as reason-responsive, and reason-giving as mere rationalization, is just the reverse of the person who places his trust in the practice of giving reasons.

Consider the attitude of a rational and cautious person when buying a used car. Such a person will be faced with a good deal of reason-giving on the part of the used car salesman, and it may well be that, if taken at face value, the reasons offered for various purchases are wholly convincing. From the point of view of logic alone, the used car salesman's reasoning is impeccable. But the rational and cautious person does not take the used car salesman's arguments at face value.[11] Rather, in this situation, although one does not simply ignore everything which is said, one does not simply evaluate the logical cogency of the arguments offered either. One may certainly approach argument in this way at the used car lot, while forming beliefs on the basis of argument on other occasions.

Now the skeptic about reason-giving sees the practice of reason-giving generally in much the way that we all regard the arguments of the used car salesman. The skeptic is not concerned about dishonesty or insincerity; rather, she is concerned about sincere rationalization and a distorted sense of plausibility. But just as we all regard the used car salesman's utterances and arguments with a great deal of suspicion, the skeptic sees the default situation almost everywhere as one in which rational argument should not be taken at face value. By the same token, there are situations in which we will come to believe at least some of what the used car salesman tells us because we have independent grounds for overcoming our prima facie distrust. Similarly, the skeptic will insist that the prima facie concern about rationalization and distorted judgment is one that is not only in principle but in practice surmountable, and that when these concerns are properly defeated, we should follow the arguments where they lead. Reason-giving is not automatically irrelevant epistemically, on the skeptic's view; it should simply be regarded as irrelevant until proven otherwise.

Now it is important to recognize that the skeptic does not simply apply this approach to others, assuming that she herself is immune to rationalization or distorted judgment. Rather, she approaches her own explicit reasoning with the same degree of suspicion with which she approaches that of others. After all, her reason for concern about others has to do with rationalization and misguided judgment, not lack of sincerity, and the person who offers sincere rationalizations or whose judgment is somehow misguided is not only a purveyor of misleading arguments but a consumer of them as well. Thus, on the skeptic's view, we should approach all argument, even our own, with the default understanding that it reflects rationalization or misguided judgment, a mere cover for reasons that could not pass rational scrutiny if fully exposed. If an argument is to be taken at face value, then, there must be reason for supposing that the default condition does not apply.

There is no question that it is more difficult to do this in the first-person case than it is in the third-person case. If I can take my own reasoning at face value, then when I consider the reasoning of others of whom I have reason to be suspicious, I have considerable resources on which to draw. In particular, I may reason self-consciously and explicitly about their motivations, their interests and so on, in order to try to figure out when they are most likely to offer mere rationalizations and when it is that their reasoning can be accepted on its face. But if I cannot yet trust myself, or at least cannot yet trust my own explicit reasoning, then my resources are considerably thinner. Nevertheless, I believe that we can make perfectly good sense of the project to which the skeptic is committed.

After all, even those who are not skeptics about reason-giving in general will, on occasion, have reason to treat their own reason-giving with a certain measure of skepticism. We are all familiar with factors that may frequently interfere with the operation of good reasoning, and in ways that are typically invisible to the agent who is subject to them. We not only worry that judges who have a financial stake in the outcome of a certain decision might be biased by recognition of that fact; we worry that we ourselves might also be biased when put in such a situation. Now it just won't do in such a case to introspect and ask oneself whether one is subject to any untoward influence, and then, if one passes the test, go ahead and offer a decision. This won't do simply because we know that such biases work in ways that are not typically available to introspection. No doubt the best thing to do in this kind of case is simply to opt out; one should insist that one is not in a position to make the decision. But this is not to say that the only two options here are either to opt out or to follow the casual deliverances of introspection. And if opting out is not a possibility, then one may attempt systematically to eliminate, to the best of one's ability, the various factors that might serve as a source of bias.

Any such attempt will leave open the possibility of failure. One may, in spite of sincere and responsible attempts to eliminate all possible bias, nevertheless fall victim to it. But to say that there are no guarantees of getting things right here is not to distinguish this situation, epistemically, from any other. Evidence may be gathered here that is relevant to the question of one's own bias, and one may, in some cases, gain sufficient reason to believe that one is not biased in the particular case. At least I see no reason in principle or in practice why this should not be so.[12] But if in this sort of case one may reasonably eliminate the hypothesis that one is moved by rationalization, then the skeptic may do the same. And once the skeptic can eliminate the likelihood of her own bias, in some particular case, then she may approach others in the way we all approach used car dealers. The task of evaluating reasoning for the skeptic is thus much more elaborate than it is for the person who takes reason-giving at face value, but it is not in principle impossible.[13]

In addition, it is important to point out that the skeptic about reason-giving is likely to be, as I mentioned briefly above, suspicious about pieces of reasoning in direct proportion to their logical perspicuity: the more detailed and carefully crafted the argument, the greater the suspicion that rationalization is at work.[14] Reason-giving of a more discursive sort will thus evoke little suspicion. The late Supreme Court Justice William Brennan Jr. described his own style of judicial decision making, very much in this spirit, as seeking a "range of emotional and intuitive responses" rather than "lumbering syllogisms of reason."[15] The skeptic about reason-giving will thus have substantial resources with which to address and resolve, in many cases, her concerns about rationalization. Where she cannot turn back these concerns, she will simply ignore the arguments given.

The skeptic's view is not self-undermining. More than this, I believe, it is a view that needs to be taken quite seriously. So let us do that.

III

The skeptic's view may at first sound like the mirror image of some well-known epistemic principles, principles that, though controversial, have a long history. I have in mind, for example, Thomas Reid's Principle of Credulity,[16] the idea that one should take other people's utterances to be true unless one has specific reason to believe otherwise, and Roderick Chisholm's various principles of evidence,[17] which involve accepting the "testimony of the senses" at face value, unless one has specific counterevidence. These principles are often explained by way of an analogy with the legal doctrine that one should assume a defendant innocent until proven guilty. In the case of Reid and of Chisholm, various sources of evidence are taken at face value unless there is some reason on the other side. Special reason is required to dismiss these sources of evidence; none is required if we are to follow where they seem to lead. The skeptic seems to have exactly the opposite presumption: reason-giving is to be distrusted until there is special reason to believe otherwise.

Chisholm defends his principles of evidence, however, as justified a priori, and it is important to recognize that the skeptic about reason-giving does not see her approach to reason-giving as having any such status. Rather, her presumption about reasoning is seen as an empirical hypothesis that, on her view, is well supported by available evidence. We may understand the skeptic's position only if we see it in that light.

We all recognize that sincere rationalization sometimes occurs, and that on such occasions, we would do well not to take the rationalizer's arguments, however logically impeccable, at face value. What the skeptic believes is that there is a fairly strong correlation between the logical perspicuity with which arguments tend to be offered and the amount of rationalization that underlies them. There is nothing intrinsically wrong with logic or good reasoning itself on this view; any such view would be absurd. Rather, as a matter of empirical fact, it is argued, those who tend to present their arguments with the greatest logical perspicuity are also, on those occasions, most frequently offering rationalizations, or at least so frequently offering rationalizations as to make the best epistemic policy the one of adopting the skeptic's presumption.

Consider the contemporary practice of philosophy, in which a very high premium is attached to giving detailed and logically perspicuous arguments. Surely philosophy is one of the natural homes of logical perspicuity. Is there reason to think that philosophers ought to be especially concerned about the possibility of rationalization? I think that there is. In ethics, for example, there is more than a little reason to think that a philosopher's views about right and wrong may often derive from features of that philosopher's upbringing that would do nothing at all to confer any justification on the views that result. For example, in many cases, a person's views about right and wrong are deeply influenced by that person's religious upbringing, even when that person would not appeal to any religious doctrine in support of those views. Now I do not mean to suggest that a religious origin for a view is automatically a source of distortion; but we all believe that some religious origins of moral views are an important source of distortion. When a person's view is due to some such distorting influence, and that person is able to offer detailed and logically perspicuous arguments that somehow sidestep the real source of the person's view, the worry about rationalization and its influence is particularly acute.

Nor is this peculiar to ethics. In social and political philosophy, there is also special reason to worry about the influence of distorting factors. We each have financial and personal interests that are at stake in any social and political arrangement. The idea that we might be subject to rationalization when considering which arrangements are most just is hardly a paranoid fantasy. It would, indeed, be quite remarkable if such factors rarely came to influence our views about justice, equality, and the like.

Nor do I think that this concern is rightly limited to moral philosophy broadly construed. Although the potential sources of distortion and subsequent rationalization are, I think, both most obvious and most pressing in the moral sphere, I would not wholly exempt other areas of philosophy from these concerns. Moreover, when we consider the extent to which our philosophical views are ripe for biasing influences and subsequent rationalization, it seems that, at a minimum, the responsible philosopher ought to be especially concerned about the possibility of rationalization's playing a large role in the adoption and defense of philosophical views. Here, as elsewhere, merely introspecting to see whether one's own views might have such a source is not a responsible reaction to the problem. Something much more nearly akin to the difficult project the skeptic about reason-giving is forced into may be forced on responsible philosophers as well.

Many will find this suggestion distasteful and, more to the point, epistemically counterproductive. It seems distasteful because in place of the rational discussion of substantive issues in ethics, for example, the skeptic seems to be endorsing the suggestion that when someone offers an argument for some moral view, the first thing we should think about, rather than the issue in moral philosophy that our interlocutor has attempted to raise, is the psychology of our discussant. Only by first analyzing our interlocutor's motivations may we determine whether the argument offered, and indeed, the person offering it, are to be taken seriously. It is surely distasteful to entertain such a suggestion, and it would surely be rude to behave in such a way. A person's motivations for offering an argument do sometimes need to be considered, but surely we entertain such thoughts only when the arguments offered fall very far short of logical standards. Entertaining questions about a person's motivations in offering an argument should be a last resort, not the first.

Leaving issues of etiquette aside, this strategy will also surely strike many as epistemically counterproductive, and for more than one reason. First, it will erode the quality of debate by distracting people from the issues we care most about—the moral issues, say—and focusing discussion on issues that are irrelevant to our real concerns: our interlocutors' motivations. In addition, raising these kinds of issues about people is not likely to be met with equanimity. Raising such personal issues as a subject's motivation in offering an argument, and, in effect, challenging that person's intellectual integrity, are not likely to allow for any issues at all to be discussed in ways that will allow for their resolution. But finally, and most importantly, the issue of a person's motivation in offering arguments is likely to be far more difficult to resolve than the substantive issue under investigation in, say, ethics. We have little access to the information we would need to understand fully a person's motivations, at least unless we know the individual extremely well. Moreover, there is more reason to be concerned about the possibility of rationalization in discussion of these personal issues of character than there is most any of the issues that might be under discussion in the first place. Someone who is genuinely worried about the effects of rationalization in others and in himself should recognize that even so much as entertaining the issue of a person's motivation in offering an argument dramatically increases the likelihood that rationalization will come into play. Focusing on arguments themselves does not assure that rationalization will not play a role, but it is a better strategy than our skeptic is offering, the strategy of examining people's motivations directly.

There is, I believe, a great deal of good sense in this response to the skeptic's suggestions, but before I reply on behalf of the skeptic, I wish to point out how much of the skeptic's position is already granted in this response. This response grants that the concern about rationalization and misguided judgment is a legitimate one and, indeed, does not even insist that the skeptic's assessment of the situation is terribly wide of the mark. There is a need to get around the problem with which a tendency to rationalization and bad judgment presents us, and whereas the skeptic proposes one solution to that—involving an assessment of people's motivations—our respondent has in mind a different solution: simply focusing on argument unless, in the final resort, the arguments themselves are so bad that some view about a person's motivations is rationally forced on us. Focusing on the quality of argument here is seen as a pragmatic strategy for dealing with the very problem the skeptic raises, and the skeptic's strategy, it is argued, merely exacerbates the very real problem about which she is herself concerned.

In considering this response to the skeptic, we may therefore, at least temporarily, accept the skeptic's account of the problem—that apparently rational argument is often deeply infected by rationalization—and focus on the merits of the two solutions being offered. What I wish to suggest is that neither of these two solutions is correct across the board; any reasonable response to the problem will, I believe, require a mixture of these two strategies. How much of each strategy should be used will depend, to a very large extent, on one's assessment of the ultimate source of the problem about rationalization.

Consider our respondent's suggestion that issues about a person's motivation in offering an argument are more difficult, epistemically, than the issues addressed by the argument itself; better then to focus on the issue at hand than to try to clear up questions about the person's motivation before turning to the issue he attempted to raise. This is simply not true in all cases. There are, without a doubt, cases in which a person's motivation in offering an argument is entirely transparent, and what is transparent is that the person is offering a rationalization for something believed on other grounds. Moreover, in some cases of this sort, we are in no position to address the issue that the rationalizer attempted to raise; we simply do not know enough about the issue to enter into discussion with him. In such cases, we should not take the arguments offered by the rationalizer at face value. We should adopt the skeptic's strategy and opt out of the discussion. So we do not want to adopt the respondent's strategy across the board.

But how often do situations like this occur? How often are we in a position to attribute a rationalization to someone, or at least have a strong prima facie concern about it? How often is the question about an interlocutor's motivation more easily resolved than the question the interlocutor wishes to raise? This is where, I believe, a particularly interesting difference between the skeptic and her respondent comes out.

Here is one possibility. Rationalization may well occur quite frequently, but the sources of rationalization may be many and idiosyncratic. Thus, when I offer arguments, they are distorted by my peculiar concerns and irrationalities; when others offer arguments, concerns and irrationalities peculiar to them go to work. If this is the case, then figuring out the kind of rationalization that is operative in a particular argument, or whether rationalization is operative, will require a great deal of knowledge of the particular individual involved. We will rarely have such knowledge, and thus the epistemic task of determining the extent and kind of rationalizations involved in particular arguments will typically be quite difficult. This will make the skeptic's project of examining the motivations behind individual arguments practically infeasible. At the same time, it may also make the skeptic's project unnecessary. For if the sources of distortion vary a great deal, then merely focusing on the arguments themselves may be a very good strategy. My biased recall of relevant information may be salient to others who lack my particular bias, and they will bring this into the open, not by attending to the possible sources of my bias, but simply by focusing on the issue under discussion. The public discussion of reasons here, although it brackets discussion of sources of distortion, will thereby help to overcome the problem that the distorting influences present. This, of course, is just what the respondent to the skeptic suggested.[18]

But there is another possibility, and this involves a very different picture of the sources of distortion and rationalization. Thus, suppose that instead of these sources' being varied and idiosyncratic, there are a very small number of sources of significant distortion and rationalization. Let us suppose, indeed, that there is a single major source of distortion and rationalization that is very widespread. Thus, for example, Marxists have suggested that class interests form just such a source of distortion and rationalization; some feminists have suggested that the interests of male domination play such a role.[19] If some such hypothesis is correct, then the situation is exactly the reverse of the one described above. First, we need not know much about the particular individual offering an argument to have some sense of the extent or source of rationalization likely to be playing a role; our epistemic task here, once we have come to understand the social factors at work in society at large, is easy. And second, the idea that merely focusing on argument will allow the sources of distortion to come out into the open would, on this view, be mistaken. Because the ideas that tend to be discussed, on this scenario, are all shaped by a common bias, the hope that idiosyncratic biases will cancel one another out misses the point.[20] On this view, the skeptic's strategy is not only epistemically feasible, it is the only strategy that is likely to address the problem of bias and rationalization adequately.

Note too that if the skeptic is right in thinking that public debate is largely shaped by a single source of bias, and that this bias is extremely likely to come into play and overwhelm discussion when certain members of the epistemic community are part of the debate, then a policy of isolation or exclusion will be appropriate. This is just the opposite of the policy of including as many members of the community as possible in discussion in the hope of having the various biases cancel one another out. The policy of isolation or exclusion comes with dangers of its own, of course. But which of these policies best gets at the truth is very much dependent on features of the epistemic community, and the skeptic about reason and the person confident about reason simply have differing views about the nature of that community.

Those who have placed their trust in reason and public discussion of argument are thus betting that the second of these possibilities governing the nature and distribution of bias—a small number of distorting influences affecting the entire tenor of debate—is not the case. The skeptic, on the other hand, suspects that it is precisely this problem that is responsible for our current situation. The skeptic's hypothesis, I believe, is one that we need to take seriously, and the bet that we make when we place our trust in the public discussion of reason is one of which we need to be aware. It is only by taking the skeptic's hypothesis seriously and, if possible, laying it to rest, that our trust in public reason may be fully rational. Moreover, insofar as the rational commitment to the public discussion of reasons presupposes a certain social structure—one in which the effects of bias and rationalization are canceled out—those who are committed to the public discussion of reason should also be committed to ensuring that such a social structure is more than just an ideal; we should be committed to making sure that it is realized and sustained.[21]

NOTES

1. A different, though complementary, source of distrust in reason comes from some evolutionary psychologists, who suggest that the kinds of circumstances with which our reasoning faculties are designed to deal are far narrower than the ones to which they are currently applied. For a

particularly interesting application of such a view, see Colin McGinn, *Problems in Philosophy: The Limits of Inquiry* (Oxford: Blackwell, 1993).

2. I approach the practice of reason-giving as one contingent social practice among many that, like any other, may be called into question. In this, I contrast with those who see reason-giving as different, somehow constitutive of rationality. Thus, for example, Thomas Nagel claims that the practice of reason-giving is not "merely another socially conditioned practice" ("Kolakowski: Modernity and the Devil," in his *Other Minds: Critical Essays 1969–1994* [Oxford: Oxford University Press, 1995], 212). And he goes on:

> A defender of the Kantian method must claim that it is legitimate to ask for justifying reasons for a contingent social practice in a way in which it is not legitimate to turn the tables and call reason itself into question by appealing to such a practice. The asymmetry arises because any claim to the rightness of what one is doing is automatically an appeal to its justifiability, and therefore subject to rational criticism. All roads lead to the same court of appeal, a court to which all of us are assumed to have access. Reason is universal because no attempted challenge to its results can avoid appealing to reason in the end—by claiming, for example, that what was presented as an argument is really a rationalization. This can undermine our confidence in the original method or practice only by giving us reasons to believe something else, so that finally we have to think about the arguments to make up our minds. (Ibid., 212–13. A large part of this passage is quoted, with hearty approval, by Daniel Dennett in his review of *Other Minds* in *Journal of Philosophy*, 93 [1996]: 428.)

I will not respond to this argument point by point. Instead, this paper may be viewed as presenting an alternative to Nagel's Kantian defense of reason-giving, a position that Nagel has further developed in *The Last Word* (Oxford: Oxford University Press, 1997). As will become clear presently, I believe that the point about rationalization that Nagel mentions in passing has a much deeper significance than he attaches to it and that it may be used to challenge the entire practice of reason-giving. By the same token, if this challenge can be adequately responded to, as I believe it can, then we are presented with a substantive, rather than a transcendental, defense of the practice of reason-giving. For those who are suspicious of transcendental arguments, this is an important result.

3. Andrew's resourcefulness in handling data and the convenient asymmetries in his forgetfulness are not unusual. Indeed, this example is simply adapted from the results of a study on the effects of mixed data on prior opinion: C. Lord, L. Ross, and M. R. Lepper, "Biased Assimilation and Attitude Polarization: The Effects of Prior Theories on Subsequently Considered Evidence," *Journal of Personality and Social Psychology*, 37 (1979), 2098–2110.

4. See the discussion of the availability heuristic in Richard Nisbett and Lee Ross, *Inductive Inference: Strategies and Shortcomings of Social Judgment* (Englewood Cliffs, NJ: Prentice-Hall, 1980).

5. Consider, for example, these comments of Jerry Fodor and Ernest Lepore: "It seems to us that what there is no argument for, there is no reason to believe. And what there *is* no reason to believe, one *has* no reason to believe." *Holism: A Shopper's Guide* (Oxford: Blackwell, 1992), xiii.

6. By the same token, a person who is particularly good at presenting arguments and recognizes the high regard in which such detailed reason-giving is typically held may use his ability to present detailed arguments in a coercive or oppressive manner. In such cases, it is not the logical features of the argument that are at fault, nor is it irrational that many should fail to attend to such logical features and simply dismiss arguments of this sort out of hand. This kind of concern has been raised in some of the feminist literature.

7. This concern as well has been a focus of some feminist discussions of reason-giving and the objection to what some have called "logocentrism." Although I am quite unsympathetic with most of what has been said under this label, the skeptic about reason-giving of this paper may be seen as my own reconstruction of what I take to be the most reasonable objection to so-called logocentrism. But I would not attribute the details of the position developed here to any particular feminist philosopher. For feminist philosophers who have developed such views, see, e.g., Lorraine Code, *Rhetorical Spaces: Essays on Gendered Locations* (New York: Routledge, 1995)

and Andrea Nye, *Words of Power: A Feminist Reading of the History of Logic* (New York: Routledge, 1990).

8. I defend a qualified version of this view in "Introspection and Misdirection," *Australasian Journal of Philosophy*, 67 (1989), 410–22.

9. The objection is similar to an objection frequently presented to total skepticism: that the total skeptic undermines his own position in arguing for it because the presentation of any such argument implicitly commits the skeptic to the existence some sort of knowledge whose existence he explicitly denies.

10. This follows the standard response to the claim that total skepticism is self-defeating. See, e.g., Robert Fogelin, *Pyrrhonian Reflections on Knowledge and Justification* (Oxford: Oxford University Press, 1994); Michael Frede, "The Skeptic's Two Kinds of Assent and the Question of the Possibility of Knowledge," in *Essays in Ancient Philosophy* (Minneapolis: University of Minnesota Press, 1987); and Michael Williams, "Skepticism without Theory," *Review of Metaphysics*, 41 (1988), 547–88.

11. When I speak of taking an argument at face value, I do not mean to exclude all critical evaluation; taking an argument at face value is not to be identified with gullibility. There is, however, an important difference between focusing on the subject matter of the argument given, however critically, and turning one's attention to the motivations of the person giving it. I see the first as taking the argument at face value, whereas the second is what the skeptic has in mind instead.

12. This is not to deny that individual cases may arrive in which one is not in a position to resolve the question of one's own bias. Cases must, however, be dealt with individually. There is no all-purpose argument to show either that one cannot have good evidence that one is bias-free or that one must always be able to determine whether one is influenced by bias.

13. I do not believe that this is the only way in which one might extricate oneself from the concern about rationalization. In particular, I believe that there may well be cases in which one might rationally eliminate concern about rationalization in particular others while still harboring reasonable concern about one's own propensity to rationalize. But I need not insist on this in order to extricate the skeptic about rational argument from the charge of undermining herself.

14. Even as great a champion of rational argument as W. V. Quine has expressed a sentiment that is similar in important ways to that of the skeptic. Consider Quine's account of attending the American Philosophical Association convention with Carnap:

> We moved with Carnap as henchmen through the metaphysicians' camp. We beamed with partisan pride when he countered a diatribe of Arthur Lovejoy's in his characteristically reasonable way, explaining that if Lovejoy means *A* then *p*, and if he means *B* then *q*. I had yet to learn how unsatisfying this way of Carnap's could sometimes be. ("Homage to Carnap," in *The Ways of Paradox and Other Essays*, revised and enlarged edition [Cambridge: Harvard University Press, 1976], 42.)

See also Robert Nozick's remarks about what he calls "coercive philosophy" in *Philosophical Explanations* (Cambridge: Harvard University Press, 1981), 4–8, in which he rejects the method of doing philosophy by way of "knock-down arguments" in favor of the more discursive "philosophical explanations."

15. Quoted by Alex Kozinski in "The Great Dissenter," *New York Times Book Review*, July 6, 1997, 15.

16. *Essays on the Intellectual Powers of Man* (Cambridge: MIT Press, 1969).

17. *Theory of Knowledge*, 3rd ed. (Englewood Cliffs, NJ: Prentice-Hall, 1989).

18. This is just a special case of the point that by using different measuring instruments to detect a given phenomenon, we may dramatically decrease the likelihood that our results are mere artifacts of the instruments themselves. The person who places his trust in argument sees individuals as roughly reliable detectors; their individual biases are features of the detectors that lead to experimental artifacts; and these artifacts are revealed as such by using other individuals, that is, other roughly good detectors, who are likely to exhibit a different pattern of experimental artifacts. The extent to which this method works in practice depends on the extent to which the different

detectors used are both roughly reliable and exhibit the presupposed difference in experimental artifacts.

19. Notice that these are, in effect, socialized versions of the kinds of problems suggested in the "heuristics and biases" literature of Tversky and Kahneman and Nisbett and Ross. (See Daniel Kahneman, Paul Slovic, and Amos Tversky, eds., *Judgment under Uncertainty: Heuristics and Biases* [Cambridge: Cambridge University Press, 1982]; and Nisbett and Ross, op. cit.) The social fixation of the reasoning strategies that concern the skeptic is of special concern because such a process works far faster than Darwinian methods for fixing inferential strategies. Social fixation of reasoning strategies is Lamarckian.

20. Note that Nagel's assumption in the passage quoted in note 2 that there is "equal access to the court of reason" is thus denied by many Marxists and certain feminists. Consider also Frank Sulloway's claim (*Born to Rebel: Birth Order, Family Dynamics, and Creative Lives* [New York: Pantheon Books, 1996]) that firstborns are strongly disposed to resist conceptually innovative ideas and that later-borns are strongly disposed to accept them. Add to this Sulloway's contention that firstborns tend to be disproportionately successful in their careers. Sulloway notes:

> [This] has practical implications for the selection of scientific commissions and the evaluation of their conclusions. Because commission[s] tend to be packed with eminent individuals (and hence firstborns), their votes should perhaps be "weighted" to adjust for individual biases in attitudes toward innovation. (537, n. 43)

This suggestion of Sulloway's, which I take to be emminently sensible, is just an instance of the strategy recommended by the skeptic about reason-giving.

21. I want to thank Louise Antony, David Christensen, Mark Kaplan, William Mann, Derk Pereboom, Joel Pust, Nishi Shah, Miriam Solomon, and William Talbott for especially helpful comments on drafts of this paper, often by way of vigorous disagreement. Versions of the paper were read at Middlebury College, Brigham Young University, Rutgers University, the University of Michigan, Universidad Nacional Autónoma de México, and Dalhousie University, where helpful discussions resulted in numerous changes.

Midwest Studies in Philosophy, XXIII (1999)

Reasons and the Deductive Ideal

LARRY WRIGHT

The role of deduction in reasoning seems endlessly controversial. Since the recent advent of a literature specifically devoted to reasoning and argument, deduction has variously been taken for granted,[1] made fun of,[2] denounced as irrelevant[3] or distracting,[4] and argued for as universal and basic.[5] A glance through this thoughtful commentary reveals a complex snarl of issues and motivations that no short essay can hope to untangle completely. And some of those issues are as deep as philosophy itself. Yet the matter is of some importance to the reasoning literature, since it directly or indirectly shapes so many of its analytical gambits. So I propose in the next few pages to set out two overlapping aspects of this controversy in the hope that doing so will eliminate one obstacle to clarity in this dauntingly difficult business.

ARGUMENT

The thing that is alleged to be deductive (or not) in this controversy is *an argument*, often represented in terms of premises and conclusion. Although I think the deductive associations of "premise" too strong to permit easy use in a study of the sort I propose, the general notion of argument thus captured will do perfectly well for my more pedestrian purposes. Any episode of reasons-giving may be represented in standard schematic form,

$$\frac{S}{C},$$

where S is the reason offered in support of some view or conclusion C. This very form may seem to give deduction natural hegemony because the demonstrative connections of formal and mathematical logic have produced such elaborate and elegant articulations of the relation it displays. Nothing in informal logic or other discussions of nondemonstrative reasoning can rival this body of work in size, complexity, or sheer artfulness.

We should not allow this historical accident to distract us from the broader value of schematic form, however. It may be used simply to set out what is or could easily be made explicit in *any* instance of giving reasons without further commitment. If I suggest that we should take the coast route (C) because of the snow in the mountains (S), or offer the light's ominous buzzing (S) as reason to think it's about to blow (C), or engage in any similar bit of conversational reasoning, it may usefully be displayed in simple schematic form without implying that the reason is conclusive.

I say "usefully" here not merely because it will facilitate the exercise below. The nearly effortless facility that survival requires us to develop in familiar reasoning about mundane matters allows us to miss easily the subtle complexity of the skill thus mastered. Very slight controversy can raise difficulties at the periphery of our articulation skills, so that such a simple thing as setting out what is being offered as a reason for what can have great clarificatory power. At the simplest level, both in pedagogic writing and in the philosophical literature on argument, it is sometimes easy in the din of controversy to lose track of exactly what the pertinent conclusion holds or an important qualification of the support. At a deeper analytical level, I have argued in several places[6] that explicit formulations of S and C in the standard schematic diagram provide essential elements of a rich interrogative apparatus useful in organizing and evaluating reasons in ordinary human commerce.

THE DEDUCTIVE IDEAL

In thinking about everyday reasoning our intellectual tradition makes it natural to take deduction as an ideal of one sort or another: either of clarity or of strength. But it is an ideal not commonly achieved in practice. Even deduction enthusiasts recognize that perfectly good reasons naturally schematize nondemonstrably. When I appeal to the snow as a reason to think the coast route is better or the buzzing as reason to think the light about to go, I can reasonably ignore the criticism that the reasons are not, in either case, conclusive. These are, in their familiar contexts, *good* reasons, even though I do not intend them to conflict logically with incompatible conclusions, nor even have any idea how to cast them in a form that would. Deduction might nevertheless be the ideal of clarity if properly attentive philosophers were able to *reconstruct* such arguments deductively,[7] thus making explicit everything the reasoning depends on.

A different way of thinking about deduction as an ideal arises from a standard way of *objecting* to its use in practical argument. One sensible, pragmatic view of everyday reasons holds that the question of their conclusiveness should not even arise. Since reasons offered in everyday commerce virtually never schematize deductively, we will foreclose the possibility of making any distinction between good and bad reasons if we cleave to deductive standards.[8] This is a valuable observation. But it clearly implies that the problem with deductive standards is that they are too high for routine application, so the "other" standards, whatever they are, will be inferior to deductive ones. Our reasons would be better, stronger if we *could* hold them to deductive standards. It's just too much to expect and withal we would lose the ability to discriminate better from worse among lesser arguments. Deduction on this view is an ideal of strength: the upper limit to which arguments may aspire.

In the next few pages I will try to show that each of these appreciations of deduction rests on a deep (and therefore wholly forgivable) misperception of our use of reasons. We can think of deduction as a *general* ideal only if we misunderstand the human resources that allow the institution of giving reasons to hold any interest for us.

IDEAL CLARITY

The view that deductive arrangements must represent reasoning more clearly stems from the common feeling that nondemonstrative arrangements are inherently incomplete: enthymemes. Consider an example. Driving home from work my car coughs a couple of times and dies. I manage to coast to the shoulder, where, before switching off the ignition, I notice the needle of the fuel gauge resting on "empty." In the ensuing silence my passenger restrainedly asks, "Why are we stopping?" I: "We're out of gas." Passenger: "Why do you think so?" I, again: "Because the car stopped by itself, the fuel gauge reads "empty," and, although I do not normally neglect things like this, I cannot recall filling up recently." P: "Sounds right, do you want some company on the walk?"

Here I have offered reasons in support of my diagnosis, which may be put in canonical form:

S_1 My car sputters to a stop.
S_2 The fuel gauge reads "empty."
S_3 I do not recall filling up recently.

C I am out of gas.

The reasons, in this context, are good ones, which is to say the argument is strong, even though not deductive.

Why not deductive? It fails the contradiction test. An inexhaustible list of counterexamples reveals the falsity of the conclusion to be compatible with the support. Nothing in that support, for instance, contradicts the possibility that the fuel tank is nearly full and the car was brought to a halt by an electrical failure that disabled the fuel gauge. The reasons are good ones—the argument strong—not because counterexamples are inconceivable, but because they are implausible, like this one.

The feeling that such an argument must be enthymematic articulates something like this: The whole point in my setting out reasons in schematic form is to make explicit the support I take a conclusion to have. But the plausibility of a counterexample, in cases like our illustration, obviously depends on the substantive context presumed, so the proffered support does not include everything relevant to accepting the conclusion. Other things simply being taken for granted bear crucially on the inference and should be made explicit if we are to display the support bearing on C. Perfect clarity about why we should accept a conclusion requires surfacing the considerations that allow us to ignore counterexamples not logically ruled out. Such considerations, properly framed and appended to the original support, should then rule out those counterexamples explicitly, which is to say logically. So if the reasons are actually good ones, we should always be able to *reconstruct* the argument as a valid deduction in this way. Its evaluation would then always consist in noting the plausibility of the explicit support, with no worry about its connection to the conclusion.[9]

Let us then return to the fuel exhaustion argument and try to implement the suggestion that we make it complete (and hence deductive) by surfacing contextual presuppositions. What do we take for granted that makes all the counterexamples implausible? The answer is: too much to say. An inexhaustible list of counterexamples test the understanding required to evaluate this argument in endlessly different ways. We dismiss exotic electrical failures for reasons comprehensively distinct from those that allow us to ignore conspiracies among subatomic beings. Everything we know about matter and motion, mechanisms and liquids, even the motivation and talents of creatures and gods is relevant to the judgment of fuel exhaustion.[10] A substantial change in any one of these things would change the strength of the argument, the goodness of the reasons.

How are we then to make all this explicit? An articulated list is out of the question. Some[11] have thought this might be accomplished by resort to the recursive premise, supposing this to invoke the relevant understanding without characterizing it:

S_1 My car sputters to a stop.
S_2 The fuel gauge reads "empty."
S_3 I do not recall filling up recently.
S_4 Whenever S_1, S_2, and S_3, I am out of gas.

C I am out of gas.

The problem is that no reading of S_4 does capture the understanding grounding this inference. The most natural readings actually conflict with that understanding. If "my car" in S_1 is read "a car I am driving" or "a car I own," and "whenever" covers all conceivable cases (all describable counterexamples), it is surely false, and making the argument depend on it destroys its force altogether. And if we try to tinker with S_4 to make it express whatever the conditions are in which S_1, S_2, and S_3 are sufficient for C, we go far beyond anything I or anybody else understands. Nothing we know rules out complicated electrical failures absolutely; so a reasonable formulation of everything I (or anybody) understand about this case would be *logically* compatible with not-C. Making the argument deductive by recasting it in this way inevitably overstates the case: it misrepresents the support as implausibly general, demeaning the reasoning it is supposed to articulate.

A more radical suggestion[12] is that we capture the relevant understanding noncategorically, and achieve deduction by softening C, thus:

S_1 My car sputters to a stop.
S_2 The fuel gauge reads "empty."
S_3 I do not recall filling up recently.
S_4 S_1, S_2, and S_3 constitute good reason to think I am out of gas.

C There is good reason to think I am out of gas.

But whatever the virtues of this reconstruction, it does not add clarity to the reasoning we wish to examine. That reasoning is now simply represented by S_4, and it advances nothing to say we now judge the plausibility of a sentence rather than of an inference. Any paraphrase may be useful in particular conditions, of course, but to the extent that this one makes it appear that what's essential in reasoning is a simple grammatical trick, it is actually pernicious. Forcing arguments into deductive form in either of these ways does not seem clarificatory at all, much less ideally so.

MISLEADING PICTURES

Still the alternative nags. The picture that emerges from this discussion is of reasoning resting on an understanding that is not just inarticulate, but unarticulable. Much of what we know relevant to evaluating reasons we are not even aware of in the event. This seems wholly unsatisfactory. How can we trust it?

In sober moments we all realize that understanding always outstrips articulation. Anyone who has tried to learn a complex skill from a master—even the skill of articulateness itself—confronts immediately the gulf between what someone understands and what she can put into words. So we should expect that an argument that depends on what we can *say* about our basic understanding of things will, ceteris paribus, be less secure than one that exploits that understanding unarticulated.[13] What makes this so difficult to accept on reflection? Two distinct considerations suggest themselves.

First is a useful but misleading phenomenon: the support provided in an argument can sometimes be readily supplemented to deal with incomprehension. If my interlocutor does not yet buy the fuel exhaustion diagnosis, that could simply be due to unfamiliarity with cars: something easily filled in. This may incline us to think we can thus compensate for *any* such deficiency, and, by generalization, therefore *anticipate* any deficiency simply by mentioning everything relevant in advance. But no list of reasons can remove the necessity of my interlocutor's understanding *something* to begin with; no augmentation of the list can compensate for the complete lack of competent judgment. And we need not reach for such an extreme case to see the force of this point. For when we find ourselves unprepared to appreciate an argument, only rarely can the necessary supplement be achieved by adding a few lines of support. Getting me to see a certain molecular pattern as evidence that humans and bacteria have a common thermophilic ancestor, for instance, would require a curriculum, not a proposition. Genuine increases in understanding, as any teacher knows, usually require hard work: study, exercises, training, experience. And what is gained thereby is additional competence and understanding, not something that may be exhaustively articulated. Education may enable us to appreciate the old argument, but a simple list of reasons will not have done the work.

Before we can even participate in the institution of reasons-giving we must have a fairly sophisticated grasp of our surroundings and some complicated skills grounded in that grasp. And although we can examine our take on things piecemeal, we must accept rather large chunks of it for any particular bit of articulate reflection. This is what gives the pursuit of presuppositionless reasoning an aura of surreality.

The second reason that actual limits on what we can make explicit may not seem to tell against the deductive ideal is that unachievability is characteristic of an ideal. Of course we cannot routinely achieve apodicticity in our everyday reasoning, but this is just what we should expect of an ideal: something we benefit from aspiring to even if failure is inevitable. Whether deductive form is an ideal in this sense, however, depends on what aspiring to it achieves. And that aspiration is actually deleterious if it misleads us about the credentials of our reasons, and hence leads us to recast our reasoning with indefensible categoricity. So it becomes interesting to ask whether we can represent deductive force less crudely, in a way that will allow the ideal to be a constructive aspiration.

IDEAL STRENGTH

The problem with achieving deduction by appeal to the recursive premise, or by adulterating C, is that a good argument is sullied by unwelcome augmentation. On the contrary, one might insist, the task is simply to *recognize* when deduction has been achieved without artifice. This surely happens in many useful cases, and it is here that we should find the source and nature of deduction's allure. So the task becomes to see just what achievement we recognize in such cases that has the power and clarity we attribute to the deductive ideal. And of course, tradition offers an inviting candidate: the threat of contradiction. The support in a deductive argument allows us to reject its conclusion only "on pain of contradiction"; whereas rejecting a (strong) nondemonstrative conclusion promises the pain of implausibility, incoherence, or lunacy, but not contradiction. As these things go, contradiction seems clearly the greater pain, and what could be clearer than "P and not-P"?

But in the welter of civilian life, form is an inferior guide. The practical operation of language makes genuine contradiction very hard to identify precisely when anything important hangs on it. Worse, what's required to *avoid* such a contradiction, once identified, is often even more obscure. And as we should now expect, the security of both judgments depends crucially on our substantive understanding of the matter in question.

Our shaky grasp of formal inconsistency is manifest in controversies that center on whether or not two relatively familiar theses contradict one another. The alleged clash between free will and determinism is just the most famous in which it seems endlessly controversial whether we have a contradiction or not. The same phenomenon occurs in reflections on the problem of evil and Zeno's paradoxes. Does the existence of evil logically rule out the possibility of an omnipotent, benevolent God? Is there a contradiction in our very conception of motion? We find ourselves naturally led to inconsistent-looking characterizations and do not quite know what to make of them. Have we found a mistake in our thinking? A flaw in our understanding of something familiar? Must we adjust something to avoid the inconsistency? What must we change?

This uncertainty in locating contradiction is the inevitable consequence of the profound context-sensitivity of our linguistic skill: judgments of plausibility grounded in our general understanding underpin the enterprise. Deciphering what we hear or read always requires a grasp of substantive circumstance and a disposition to ignore obviously implausible interpretations. And this is crucial not just for sorting through bad grammar and slips of the tongue, but in resolving ambiguity, determining pronoun referents, and seeing nuance. Nothing in formal linguistic training gives us the significance of "The cat is on the mat." We must understand a lot of context to see that it contradicts "The grading equipment has all been removed from the construction site." This is not to say that syntactic form and the general lexicon are not important, but they can carry only part of the characterizational burden. And the more difficult or subtle the message, the less they can do, and the more an author must ask an audience to divine from the circumstances. To make sense of

> On long winter evenings he remained indoors and did not mend harness, and he sprang out of bed at the crack of noon every day just to make certain that the chores would not be done,

we do not consult dictionaries or grammar books, but the surrounding text.

Nuance will often lie in the particular *way* an author directs attention to a context, the manner in which the crucial element is revealed. And since holding firm to both sides of a contradiction has no function in the normal communicative use of language, we commonly marshall contradictory form in this valuable task. Something of the form P and not-P can direct a reader's attention to a peculiar tension, add just the right measure of irony, or open our eyes to a neglected possibility. "He was determined to fail, even though it might be viewed as a kind of success." "In spite of her disability, she would not be a victim: she insisted on being an unhyphenated-American." In the proper setting contradictory language may have great expository value.

So inconsistent form does not even typically indicate impossibility or anything bad at all. It often just manifests the exertions required to say something subtle or difficult. It can also signal, especially in abstract rumination, that we have strayed from the confines of our linguistic competence, that our characterizational skills, honed against practical purposes, no longer provide much guidance. In any case, just what significance to attribute to contradictory language, like *any* language, is a matter of finding the most plausible reading in the context. In the normal use of language, the significance of form is subordinate to our substantive judgment.

The most revealing manifestation of this subordination in our reasoning is our reaction to philosophical puzzles like the paradox of the arrow. In attempting to articulate our understanding of it, Zeno leads us very naturally to a contradictory characterization of the arrow's motion. Our reaction, however, is not to stop worrying about arrows aimed in our direction: that would be lunacy. The stark incredibility of the conclusion that the arrow does not move is enough to rule it out as what we should learn from our characterizational misadventure. The problem obviously lies in the way Zeno's machinations test our characterizational skill, not in our understanding of missiles.[14] In a similar way, we would count it against somebody's ability to reason if Zeno's argument led him to bet on the tortoise and against Achilles. Unless buttressed by our general understanding, contradictory expressions are of little use in guiding our substantive reflection. Most reasoning gets along without them altogether.

CALCULATION

Nevertheless deduction occasionally has great value in practical reasoning. And part of its value lies in the very categorical syntax that disqualifies it from ideal status as the basic form of argument. For in the narrow range of its practical application, useful deduction is overwhelmingly algorithmic. That is, it consists in the application of a systematic inferential technique, typically some kind of arithmetic or mathematics, to a question of design or planning. And much of what makes such a technique useful is precisely the austere, well-controlled syntax of categorical generalization and transparent contradiction. This allows us to manipulatively exploit a systematic complexity in phenomena to reach conclusions otherwise inaccessible to us, at least to a certain degree of precision.

But this achievement is inevitably supervised by our grasp of the conditions allowing an algorithm-productive deployment. A bit of mathematics may provide guidance our otherwise unaided reason cannot only when representing a phenomenon in particular algorithmic terms actually allows us to derive reliably significant results. Anyone who has studied quantitative science or engineering realizes how arduously gained is the understanding required for recognizing when this is so. And its inexhaustible articulability was what Thomas Kuhn was at such pains to lay bare in giving concrete problem solutions a central place in scientific epistemology.[15] We can no more include, as part of a calculation, the understanding licensing an algorithm than we can include, as part of the out-of-gas argument, the understanding underwriting our plausibility judgment in that case.

Calculation is not an end in itself. Its value depends on what other skills and perceptions we have. A prodigal intelligence might simply make the inference without calculating, and its credentials could be as good as our calculation. And finally there is nothing special about *inference* either. If something is part of the understanding we'd use to judge an inference, that must underwrite it every bit as well as being the result of that inference. So if in educating ourselves to appreciate a difficult argument, we simply came to know the conclusion (the earth is a sphere), that would certify it as well as the argument could have.

In the business of advancing understanding and certifying belief, argument is an instrument; deductive argument is one variety. The important thing about an instrument is knowing when to exploit it, and when, despite its fascinating properties, something else works better.

SYNOPSIS

Nondemonstrative arguments play a clear and useful role in human reasoning by gaudily exploiting the whole spectrum of judgmental competencies we have developed to deal with the exigencies of life in an obtrusive world. They underwrite or advance our understanding by connecting propositions made salient by circumstance.[16] But doing so in this way guarantees a certain formal defect: a kind of intrinsic incompleteness. Nondemonstrative support does not contain everything relevant to the judgment of its strength. Its deprecation of counterexamples rests on a certain level of understanding and grasp of contextual detail, matters extrinsic to the argument itself. It turns out, however, that when we marshall demonstrative arguments in this same practical task, they suffer essentially the same defect. Judging the significance of a contradictory expression or propriety of a calculation also rests on our general understanding and grasp of contextual detail. Very little of what's required for such a judgment can ever be made explicit in argument.

When we offer deduction as an ideal, then, we simply express a preference for arguments that exploit one cluster of skills (formal or linguistic ones) over arguments that exploit others. But these are not especially good skills to rely on in civilian inference, and withal, employing them does not even avoid reliance on the understanding and judgment required for nondemonstrative reasoning. So venerating deduction with incautious generality can damage both our reasoning and our understanding of reasons. For it encourages us to cast arguments in gratuitously risky forms, and it disguises the deep dependence of reasoning on our contingent grasp of how the world works and the myriad competencies devolving thereon.

This is not to say that formal or linguistic manipulation cannot be important in bringing support to bear on practical, human matters. Perfectly rigorous calculations can be absolutely crucial in everything from design to finance. But deciding whether and how much to rely on such things always falls to our general understanding of the circumstances. And when this understanding alone is enough to decide a matter without appeal to form, it can only weaken an argument and obscure its force to recast it in a way that interposes further fallible judgments between our reasons and what they support.

NOTES

1. Perhaps most recently by Terry Parsons in "What Is an Argument?" *Journal of Philosophy* 93 (1996), 164–85.

2. See, for example, Ralph Johnson, "Logic Naturalized: Recovering a Tradition," in F. van Eemeren, R. Grootendorst, J. A. Blair, and C. Willard, eds., *Argument Illuminated: Proceedings of the Second International Society for the Study of Argumentation Conference* (1992), 47–64; and Charles L. Hamblin, *Fallacies* (London: Methuen, 1970), chap. 7.

3. For example, in Jerome E. Bickenbach, "The 'Artificial Reason' of the Law," *Informal Logic*, 12 (1990), 21–32.

4. For example in Trudy Govier, "Beyond Induction and Deduction," in F. H. van Eemeren, R. Grootendorst, J. A. Blair, and C. A. Willard eds., *Argumentation: Analysis and Practices*, forthcoming.

5. For example, in Leo Groarke, "In Defense of Deductivism: Replying to Govier," in van Eemeren et al., eds., *Argumentation: Analysis and Practices*, forthcoming; also in Jakko Hintikka, "Is Logic the Key to All Good Reasoning?" in E. Garver, ed., *Reasoning: Perspectives from the New Philosophy and History of Science*, forthcoming.

6. Most recently in "Argument and Deliberation: A Plea for Understanding," *Journal of Philosophy* 92 (1995), 565–85.

7. Here and in what follows "deductive" will normally mean "deductively valid," though occasionally the more elaborate formula will be convenient.

8. For a series of suggestions of this sort, see M. Finocchiaro, "Fallacies and the Evaluation of Reasoning," *American Philosophical Quarterly* 18 (1981), 13–22.

9. Explicit appeal to this as a virtue is made, for instance, by Groarke, op. cit.

10. Most of this we have never dwelt upon of course: it is merely reflected in the competence of judgment in cases like this. But articulating this competence is what's required to meet the demand for explicitness.

11. See, for instance, Thomas Schwartz, *The Art of Logical Reasoning* (New York: Random House, 1980), 12.

12. Made by, inter alia, Groarke, op. cit.

13. This may be what Russell had in mind in observing (almost ninety years ago) that the syllogism on "Socrates is mortal" underrepresents the reason we have to think so. See *The Problems of Philosophy* (New York: Galaxy, 1959), 80.

14. We might want to say that Zeno's ruminations show that there is *something* about missiles we do not understand. But if they do, it is not that missiles move, or when to expect them to move, or anything at all in our prudent regard of them. This makes "about missiles" a troubling way to put what we do not understand, and it seems to me to recommend locating the misunderstanding not in missiles at all, but in abstraction itself. Our great competence lies in recognizing and applying familiar concepts; we stumble easily only in trying to *talk about them* as philosophers do.

15. This is the major burden of his now legendary notion of "paradigm," introduced in *The Structure of Scientific Revolutions* (Chicago: University of Chicago Press, 1970).

16. I develop this point in some detail in "Argument and Deliberation," cited in note 6.

Midwest Studies in Philosophy, XXIII (1999)

Criteria and Truth

BERNARD HARRISON

1. WITTGENSTEIN AND "WITTGENSTEINIANISM"[1]

In the early days of Wittgenstein commentary, much attention was devoted to the term "criterion." The word occurs with some frequency in Wittgenstein's writing, often in contexts in which what the reader is to make of the general drift of the argument seems largely to depend on what he makes of its meaning. But it is seldom altogether clear whether it is being used in an "ordinary" sense, or as a term of art, and if the latter, how it should be defined.[2] Here, then, was an exegetical riddle worth tackling, and it was duly tackled, most notably, and influentially, by Rogers Albritton in "On Wittgenstein's Use of the Term 'Criterion.'"[3] Albritton's views, supported by many other writers, including P. M. S. Hacker[4] and G. P. Baker,[5] gave rise to a consensus, very widely held in the philosophical community at one time, to the effect that

1. Wittgenstein meant by the term "criterion" very much what Albritton makes him mean.
2. the concept, understood in that sense, opens the way to a new and important range of arguments against skepticism, and particularly against skepticism concerning Other Minds.

A very considerable literature, surveyed by W. Gregory Lycan[6] (to 1971) and Mark Addis[7] (subsequent discussion to 1995), accumulated around this tissue of claims. The outcome of this discussion has not, on the whole been favorable to claim (2). Few philosophers have in the event been persuaded that Wittgenstein's notion of a criterion as glossed by Albritton yields important new arguments against skepticism. Crispin Wright[8] has argued persuasively that the position ascribed to Wittgenstein by the orthodox interpretation is internally incoherent, and equally negative assessments are to be found in a range of writers as disparate in their more general philosophical commitments as Richard Rorty,[9] Charles Chihara,[10] John McDowell,[11] and Stanley Cavell.[12] This critical tradition seems to me broadly correct. I shall argue here, and have argued in more detail elsewhere,[13] that Wittgenstein does dispose of interesting new arguments against skepticism. But I do not think that they depend in the slightest upon the notion of "noninductive evidence" central to the orthodox interpretation.

By contrast, the discussions recorded by Lycan and Addis have touched very lightly on claim (1) above. Philosophers have on the whole continued to take it for granted that Wittgenstein did indeed mean by the term "criterion" something fairly close to what Albritton made of it in 1959. There is nothing surprising about this. Philosophers are not on the whole, either by temperament or by training, rummagers in obscure texts. They are not, to their credit, fascinated by cyphers or mysteries concealed in the dimensions of the Great Pyramid. They prefer rational discussions of clearly and precisely specified claims, and among the many merits of Albritton's original interpretation is that it meets these requirements. At the same time it seems clear both that philosophy cannot wholly do without interpretation, and that one principle of charity under which interpretation should proceed, especially when the work of a writer of the magnitude of Wittgenstein is in question, is that the interpreter should at least pause for reflection if he finds himself tempted by an interpretation that saddles his author with hopelessly indefensible views. By the light of that principle, the fate of the orthodox interpretation as a contribution to the discussion of skepticism must reflect some doubt back on its adequacy as an interpretation. The discussion so far, in other words, may have had less to do with Wittgenstein than with "Wittgensteinianism."

This is the issue that I hope to reopen here. I shall begin by going back all the way to Albritton's paper, with a view to identifying some interpretative questions that it, in common with later contributions to the discussion, leaves open. I shall argue that the attempt to resolve these questions suggests an alternative interpretation of Wittgenstein's use of "criterion," one whose consequences for skepticism, although interesting and important, are perhaps less important than its consequences for our understanding of the relationship between meaning and truth.

To conclude these preliminaries: a note on methodology. A natural way of approaching the question of what Wittgenstein meant by "criterion" would be to assemble all or many of the passages in which the word occurs and to attempt to distill understanding out of the immediate context of each. This procedure, indeed, has been the one most generally followed in the literature of the topic. The problem with it, it seems to me, is that it disregards the possibility that Wittgenstein's use of a given term in a specific context might be directed by considerations arising outside that immediate context of use, and for that matter outside the immediate context of any other occurrence of the term. Accordingly I shall proceed differently. I shall start by identifying some general questions, both textual and philosophical, to which an adequate interpretation ought to provide an answer. Then I shall ask whether there is to be found in Wittgenstein's work prior to the introduction of the term any body of argument that might yield answers to them. The object will be to arrive at a potential interpretation with some claim to be rooted in the prior development of Wittgenstein's thought, rather than, as has quite often happened, in the general climate and assumptions of versions of analytic philosophy, which there is reason to think Wittgenstein would have rejected. Only at that point shall we return to the familiar contexts of occurrence of "criterion" to test the power of the proposed interpretation to make sense of them.

2. SOME QUESTIONS FOR THE ORTHODOX INTERPRETATION

We need, to begin with, a summary of the orthodox interpretation. An admirably concise one, made by Crispin Wright[14] a quarter century after Albritton's paper, runs as follows:

> Orthodoxy in the interpretation of Wittgenstein attributes to criteria five cardinal features: that recognition of satisfaction of criteria for *P* can confer skeptic-proof knowledge that *P*; that *P*'s criteria determine *necessarily* good evidence for *P*, and thereby fix its content; that the criteria for *P* will typically be multiple; that satisfaction of criteria for *P* is always consistent with having, or discovering, further information whose effect is that the claim that *P* is not justified after all.

To see how this odd collection of claims originated, we need to return to Albritton's original paper of 1959, leaving aside for the moment its postscript (1966), in which he retracts some of its suggestions, most notably the proposal that to give the criterion for *X*'s being so is to state a necessary truth about *X*.

Albritton's 1959 interpretation is based very largely upon pp. 24–25 of *The Blue and Brown Books* [BB].[15] Here, Wittgenstein famously distinguishes between "criteria" and "symptoms." He does so with reference to the medical definition of "angina," meaning by that not heart pain but a sore throat. He says,

> If medical science calls angina an inflammation caused by a particular bacillus, and we ask in a particular case "why do you say this man has got angina?" then the answer "I have found the bacillus so-and-so in his blood" gives us the criterion, or what we may call the defining criterion of angina. If on the other hand the answer was, "His throat is inflamed," this might give us a symptom of angina. I call "symptom" a phenomenon of which experience has taught us that it coincided, in some way or other, with the phenomenon which is our defining criterion. Then to say "A man has angina if this bacillus is found in him" is a tautology or it is a loose way of stating the definition of "angina." But to say, "A man has angina whenever he has an inflamed throat" is to make a hypothesis.

Albritton glosses this, and other related passages, as follows:

> A criterion for a thing's being so is something that can show the thing to be so and show by its absence that the thing is not so; it is something by which one may be *justified in saying* that the thing is so and by whose absence one may be justified in saying that the thing is not so. And a criterion for a thing's being so has this relation to the thing's being so not as a matter of fact, like what Wittgenstein calls a "symptom" of its being so, but as a matter of "logical" necessity. That is, on Wittgenstein's account of such necessity, its relation to

> the thing's being so is "founded on a definition" or "founded on convention" or is a matter of "grammar."[16]

Although I think this gets Wittgenstein wrong, it comes in some respects quite close to getting him right. There are, though, some questions to be asked.

(1) Albritton says that a "criterion," as Wittgenstein uses the term, is a condition for "a given thing's being so," that "a criterion is in Wittgenstein's usage always a criterion for something or other's being the case."[17] Yet Wittgenstein in fact habitually speaks of criteria as conditions for something or other's being "*called 'X'*". Albritton in effect grants the ubiquity of this form of words in Wittgenstein's work, but has no explanation to give of its presence: "I have no exact account to give of Wittgenstein's use of such expressions as 'is called.'"[18] The suggestion is, then, that in Wittgenstein's usage "is called *X*" is no more than an obfuscatory circumlocution for "is *X*." This is certainly a possible interpretation, but again one to be adopted with caution in dealing with the work of a major philosopher. We shall return to it later.

(2) Albritton's gloss commits Wittgenstein to the existence of a class of necessary truths of the form "necessarily if *Cx* then *Fx*," where *Cx* is to be read as "*x* satisfies criterion *C*." This is surely an interpretation at best weakly supported by the textual evidence for it, which consists simply in Wittgenstein's observation that if a man's having a certain bacillus in him is the criterion (or, alternatively, a "defining criterion") of his having angina, then the statement that a man has angina if this bacillus is found in him "is a tautology or it is a loose way of stating the definition of angina." These words of Wittgenstein's do seem, at least when the resources of interpretation are confined to those available in the immediate context, depressingly vague. Albritton himself speaks of "that misery of the word 'tautology,' which Wittgenstein uses in the passage I've been discussing."[19] As readers with a full set of preexisting philosophical assumptions and commitments we naturally want to know, for instance, whether "tautology" is to be read as "analytic truth" and whether Wittgenstein's "loose way of stating the definition of angina" would, if cleaned up and made precise, amount to a statement of sufficient and necessary conditions. Lacking help from the text we naturally feel obliged to make the best we can of it, and this is what Albritton has done. But once again, that route to understanding is not a particularly safe one. The "best we can make" of a writer's words may yield too much to the natural human tendency to believe that the categorial options in terms of which a professional community tends to view things must exhaust the possible alternatives, and too little to the possibility that a more critically exacting scrutiny of a wider sample of the writer's work might reveal possibilities of thought and meaning lying outside that charmed circle.

(3) Having committed Wittgenstein to the existence of necessary truths, Albritton's gloss further commits him to a conventionalist account of the truths in question: "on Wittgenstein's account of such necessity, its relation to the thing's being so is 'founded on a definition' or 'founded on convention' or is a matter of 'grammar.'"[20] There are two problems with such an interpretation. The first is the extreme weakness of crude conventionalism as a philosophical theory. The bottom-line difficulty here is that stipulations, whether of the meanings of terms, or "conventions," or "grammar," or anything else, are implausible candidates for the status of necessarily

true statements because they are implausible candidates for the status of statements. Wittgenstein nowhere addresses this excessively obvious objection to the conventionalism about necessary truths supposedly central to his position. Is it more plausible that he was too stupid to see the need to address it, or that he was not a conventionalist and possibly not a believer in necessary truths of the required sort?

(4) The second difficulty is textual in nature; it is also a difficulty for (2). Wittgenstein makes it clear that a criterion for *X* may be satisfied without its being the case that *X* actually obtains. This is the so-called defeasibility of criteria much aired in later discussions of the topic. It is a consequence of, inter alia, Wittgenstein's further remarks about the "angina" case. "In practice," Wittgenstein says,

> if you were asked which phenomenon is the defining criterion and which is a symptom, you would in most cases be unable to answer this question except by making an arbitrary decision *ad hoc*. It may be practical to define a word by taking one phenomenon as the defining criterion, but we will easily be persuaded to define the word by means of what, according to our first use, was a symptom. Doctors will use names of diseases without ever deciding which phenomena are to be taken as criteria and which as symptoms; and this need not be a deplorable lack of clarity. For remember that in general we don't use language according to strict rules—it hasn't been taught to us by means of strict rules, either. [BB 25]

This plainly opens the possibility, among others, that the usage of the medical profession might be such that "the bacillus might be found in" someone who still fails to count as an angina sufferer because he has no sore throat. Having a sore throat on its own is not, that is, on the supposed medical usage, a "criterion" for angina, because angina is, in that usage, the disease—whose symptom is a sore throat—caused by that bacillus. But having the bacillus need not entail exhibiting any symptoms (individuals can be immune to certain bacilli), and so need not entail having the disease. That being so, Wright[21] is clearly correct to argue that "it is seriously unclear whether" the defeasibility of criteria "can be made to harmonise" with the claim that criteria offer "*necessarily* good evidence for *P*," and hence unclear whether it can be made to harmonize with the claim, also rife in the early literature of the topic, that someone who knows that face holding is a *criterion* for another person's having a toothache, knows, in a sense immune to philosophical skepticism, that the other person *has* a toothache.

It seems difficult, in short, to resist the conclusion that Albritton's initial interpretation saddles Wittgenstein with an account of the meaning of "criterion" that is actually internally incoherent. By 1966, indeed, Albritton, at least, had already granted the point. His postscript of that year concedes that

> there are no necessary or not quite contingent truths of any of the types that I suggested. There are only contingent facts of those types. But Wittgenstein never meant to deny that, and no denial of it is involved, I think now, in the observation (as he took it to be) that there are behavioural criteria of having a toothache and of other such things.[22]

(5) The result of deleting the element of necessity from Albritton's initial interpretation is, however, that the philosophical motivation of Wittgenstein's original distinction between criteria and symptoms becomes almost entirely opaque. A criterion ("for a thing's being so") is, on Albritton's account, a "phenomenon by which one may judge that it is so."[23] In other words, a truth-condition. But a symptom is also just such a phenomenon. And as Wittgenstein occasionally embarrassingly emphasises, a symptom can on occasion function as a criterion, and vice versa:

> The fluctuation in grammar between criteria and symptoms makes it look as if there were nothing at all but symptoms.[24]

But if symptoms and criteria are functionally interchangeable, and if both are truth-conditions, what conceivable philosophical motivation can there be for distinguishing between them? Why do we need to postulate two putatively distinct categories of truth-conditions? What is the ground of the distinction supposed to be?

The textually tempting answer is that "criteria" are, and "symptoms" are not, what one recurs to if one wishes to explain the *meaning* of a proposition, as distinct from merely offering reasons for taking an assertion of it to be warranted or justified. That, at any rate is the suggestion of BB 24–25. One can well imagine a conversation actually taking place along the lines of the distinction Wittgenstein sketches there. "Why do you say he has angina?" "Well, just look at that throat!" "Ah, so 'angina' means having a sore throat?" "No, angina *means* having a bacillus B infection. A sore throat is merely what happens, as a matter of empirical fact, to be what most people get if they happen to be infected with bacillus B." And no doubt people do say such things. The difficulty, however—a usual one with Wittgenstein, and one that he himself occasionally ruefully notes ("What we say will be easy, but to know why we say it will be very difficult"[25])—is to see why it should be of the slightest philosophical interest that they say such things.

That question becomes still more pointed if we contrast the position of Albritton's Wittgenstein with that of Quine. The Wittgenstein of BB 25 says that "it may be practical to define a word by taking one phenomenon as the defining criterion." If it is practical it is possible. Thus, it appears, Wittgenstein is committed to the view that one can give the meaning of a word by stating a criterion. According to Albritton's Wittgenstein, now, a criterion is a truth-condition. Albritton's Wittgenstein, it appears, is thus committed to the familiar doctrine, generally introduced with a nod to Frege, that to give the meaning of an expression is to state truth-conditions for assertions made by means of sentences in which it occurs. So is Quine. Quine in addition holds, entirely reasonably, that the enterprise of ascertaining the truth-conditions of assertions is an empirical one. But the conclusion Quine draws from those premises is, as is well known, that no distinction can be validly drawn between knowledge of meanings on the one hand and general empirical knowledge of the world on the other. There is, in other words, no distinction to be drawn between one set of truth-conditions—"criteria"—by appeal to which we establish the meaning, or the conceptual content, of "this is *X*," and another set—symptoms—that express the results of empirical investigation of *X*. All statements of truth conditions, if Quine is right, express the results of empirical investigation.

Despite the recent prestige of Quineanism, however, the literature of the topic is rich in attempts to maintain on Wittgenstein's behalf the sort of distinction between meaning-determining and non-meaning-determining truth-conditions that Quine's arguments strongly suggest to be in principle without foundation. In part this is no doubt because there seems little textual reason to doubt that in Wittgenstein's mind the ground of the distinction between symptoms and criteria is that criteria have more to do with the determination of meaning, or content, than symptoms do. The problem for the exegete is thus, it appears, to say what that more consists in. Attempts to meet this demand, however, so far as they are known to me, too often succeed merely in rephrasing the claim that criteria are in some way or other meaning-determining. One that does more is the following, from Cavell's *The Claim of Reason*:

> Criteria are not alternatives or additions to evidence. Without the control of criteria in applying concepts, we would not know what counts as evidence for any claim, nor for what claims evidence is needed.[26]

I would not wish to say that Cavell is far wrong here. Indeed, the thought that without criteria we would not know "what counts as evidence for any claim" seems to me to catch something quite central to Wittgenstein's thought on the topic. But how is that thought to be developed? Why, exactly, lacking access to "criteria," would we not know what counts as evidence for a claim? Or to put the question another way, what sort of "control" over the application of concepts do Wittgensteinian "criteria" supply, and how, exactly, do they supply it? It is time we moved on from the exegetical literature to direct discussion of these questions.

3. TRUTH, FALSEHOOD, AND MEANING

In section VIII of the Philosophical Remarks [PR],[27] we find the following remark:

> I don't describe a state of affairs by mentioning something that has nothing to do with it and stating it has nothing to do with it. That wouldn't be a negative description.

The thought here is, I take it, that a negative description, "$\sim Fx$" is, or can be, informative. To say, "x is not yellow," for instance, is at least to narrow the options for a positive characterization of x in terms of color, since if it is indeed not yellow there are only so many remaining possibilities. To say of a moving speck on the hillside, "It's not a domestic animal, certainly," is again to rule out certain options in favor of one or another of a residual collection of possibilities.

How are we to construe the notion of "possibility" at stake here? There is no simple answer to that question, because it and related notions have constituted a central bone of contention in the development of Wittgenstein's thought to this point. This is not, after all, the earliest point in Wittgenstein's work at which we find him postulating a connection between the concept of meaning and that of possibility. That there is such a connection, however it is to be explicated, is a also a central theme of the *Tractatus*. In section VIII of PR, indeed, Wittgenstein explores the issue initially by reworking the Tractarian analogy between the fully analyzed proposition and a yardstick or ruler (*Maβstab*). In the Tractarian version of the analogy [2.152–2.1521],[28] the simple signs (names) in a proposition are analogous to the graduation marks on the ruler: they reach out and touch the "objects" that they name as the marks on the ruler "*touch* the object that is to be measured." The structure of the ruler corresponds to the "logical form" of the proposition, which matches that of the "state of affairs" composed by the named objects. One consideration that, for Wittgenstein, motivates this account of the relationship between proposition and state of affairs is the need to account for the fact that [4.02] "we understand the sense of a propositional sign without its having been explained to us." Wittgenstein's favored answer to this question is introduced immediately, at 4.021: "A proposition is a picture of reality: for if I understand a proposition, I know the situation that it represents." How does treating a proposition as a kind of picture make it any easier to see how acquaintance with the propositional sign can confer knowledge of "the situation it represents"? An answer of sorts to that question has already been given, at 2.201–2.202: "A picture depicts reality by representing a possibility of existence and non-existence of states of affairs. . . . A picture represents a possible situation in logical space." We can read off from the propositional sign "the situation that it represents," in other words, because we have on the one hand access to the logical space of all *possible* states of affairs, and on the other access to mapping conventions (the "logico-syntactical employment" of the signs, which, taken together with the sign, determines a"logical form" [3.327] mirroring that of the corresponding state of affairs) that yield a unique mapping of the propositional sign on to that space.

What these passages of the *Tractatus* share, it seems to me, with the brief observation from section VIII of PR, which we began by citing, is the thought that understanding the sense, the content of a proposition is in part a matter of understanding what possibilities its truth excludes. The conclusion suggested by that thought is indeed, it seems, that to understand any proposition requires a prior grasp of a web of alternative propositional possibilities, a "logical space" within which that proposition "represents a possible situation." In the *Tractatus*, as we know, that prior grasp of the possibilities of propositional assertion is provided simply by acquaintance with the "objects" picked out by the names in fully analyzed propositions. "In logic nothing is accidental: if a thing *can* occur in a state of affairs, the possibility of the state of affairs must be written into the thing itself" [2.012]. Hence, "[i]f I know an object I know all its possible occurrences in states of affairs."

That story will only work, however, if propositions, or at any rate "elementary propositions," can be regarded as logically independent of one another. By the time he was composing PR, however, Wittgenstein had ceased to believe in elementary propositions, on the grounds that there are pairs of propositions, such as "*a* is red" and "*a* is green," that clearly stand in logical or quasi-logical relationships of exclusion to one another, but that seem too basic to admit of any plausible program of analytical reduction. He now faces two connected problems. The first is the old one, of explaining how it is possible for us to read off the content of what is asserted by a proposition *P* from the propositional sign expressing it, given that that ability must include the capacity to say what propositionally formulable possibilities the truth of

P excludes. The second is the new question of how we are to account for the existence of relations of exclusion between propositions that can by no stretch of the imagination be regarded as nonelementary.

The reworking of the Tractarian analogy between propositions and yardsticks presented in section VIII of PR offers a schematic resolution of both these problems. In the new version of the analogy propositions no longer correspond to yardsticks, but to the gradations on the yardstick:

> [P]ropositions turn out to be even more like yardsticks than I previously believed.—The fact that *one* measurement is right automatically excludes all others. I say automatically: just as all the gradation marks are on *one* rod, the propositions corresponding to the gradation marks similarly belong together, and we can't measure with one of them without simultaneously measuring with all the others.—It isn't a proposition which I put against reality as a yardstick, it's a *system* of propositions. [PR 82, p. 110]

It is easy enough to convert this analogy into a more or less realistic model of part of a natural language, if we simply interpret the propositions in question as statements of length: "*x* is 1 cm long," "*x* is 2 cm long," and so on. What holds these propositions together into "a *system* of propositions" is, of course, not the yardstick considered as a piece of engraved wood or metal, but the practice of measuring with it. By the nature of that practice, statements of length couched in terms of its modulus form a connected set such that the truth of one member of the set "automatically" entails the falsity of each of the remaining members. The answer to Wittgenstein's second question, now, is that in this context one proposition excludes another because *they are not separate propositions.*

> The situation is misrepresented if we say we may not ascribe to an object two incompatible attributes. For seen like that, it looks as if in every case we must first investigate whether two determinations are incompatible or not. The truth is, *two* determinations of the same kind (co-ordinate) are impossible. [PR 84, p. 112]

The solution to the first problem, equally, is that it is a grasp of how to measure with a yardstick, or to put it more precisely, a competent mastery of the practice of comparing distances by recording the number of iterations of the same modulus required to span each, that confers on us the ability to say what other propositional possibilities are excluded by the truth of a statement of length: they are the competing statements of length that correspond to the remaining graduations on a measuring rod of that modulus.

It is possible to see the shift in Wittgenstein's thinking that takes place between the *Tractatus* and PR as in part a shift in what Wittgenstein understands by the notion of "logical space." A central Tractarian thought is that whatever objects are picked out by the names in an elementary proposition must possess possibilities of combination into states of affairs that characterize each object internally. It follows, as he says at 2.013, that "each thing is, as it were, in a space of possible states of affairs." In PR we find:

> I should like to say: for any question there is always a corresponding *method* of finding.
> Or you might say, a question *denotes* a method of searching.
>
> You can only search in a *space*. For only in space do you stand in relation to where you are not. [PR 43, p. 77]

One could read at least the first two sentences of this as expressing a commitment to verificationism.[29] That would be to represent him as influenced, around 1929–30, by the most important philosophical tendency of the interwar years; it would also be to represent his thoughts as moving, at this point, in a direction sharply divorced from the concerns of the *Tractatus*. Suppose that, on the contrary, these remarks on "spaces" in the *Remarks* are to be understood as related to those on "logical space"in the *Tractatus*? There is textual warrant for this, after all, in the continuation of the passage from which we began.

> I don't describe a state of affairs by mentioning something that has nothing to do with it and stating it has nothing to do with it. That wouldn't be a negative description.
>
> "The sense consists in the possibility of recognition," but this is a logical possibility. I must be in the space in which what is to be expected is located.
>
> 83 The concept of an "elementary proposition" now loses all of its earlier significance.

What we have here, indeed, looks like a rejection of verificationism, at least as irrelevant to the matter in hand. Verificationism says that the meaning of a statement is the method or procedure by which its truth is to be recognized. What Wittgenstein is saying here, on the contrary, is that the meaning, the "sense" of a proposition is the *possibility* of arriving at a recognition of its truth or falsity; that this possibility has to do with the establishment of a "space" in which whatever is to constitute such a recognition is to be sought; and that the possibility of recognition established in establishing such a space is "a logical possibility." The opening of 83 now provides a further link back to the *Tractatus* in the shape of the remark "The concept of an 'elementary proposition' now loses all of its earlier significance."

Why, now, as a result of the string of remarks about propositions, yardsticks and "searching in a space" that we have been considering, should the concept of an elementary proposition lose its philosophical importance for Wittgenstein? Let us turn over the pieces of the jigsaw once more. In order to grasp what is asserted by a proposition we need to have some grasp of the propositionally formulable possibilities that its assertion excludes and that would be put into play once more by its denial. In the *Tractatus* scheme the "logical space" of propositional possibilities is constituted metaphysically, in terms of the possibilities of combination into states of affairs built internally into the nature of the "objects" picked out by the basic names that go to make up elementary propositions. On the *Tractatus* model, therefore, if there are no elementary propositions there is no access to "logical space." What Wittgenstein has realized in the *Remarks*, however, is that the semantic task performed on the level of metaphysics by "logical space" in the *Tractatus* can equally well be performed on a naturalistic level, by relating sets of propositions to practices. A yardstick, taken in connection with the practice of comparing distances by numbering the iterations of a given modulus required to span each, connects statements of length employing that modulus into a "logical space"of alternatives in terms of which it is perfectly possible to grasp what propositional possibilities are excluded by the assertion, and returned to play by the denial, of any such statement. But if the "logical space" in which a proposition is located can be constituted by the adoption of a practice or a set of conventions, then the intelligibility of a proposition, its sense, can be established by relating it to one or another such practice or convention, and so does not need to be established by relating it *via a program of philosophical analysis* to some further class of propositions taken as "basic" or "elementary." The antireductionism of Wittgenstein's later philosophy is born at this point.

But can't an obvious objection be raised? Given that Wittgenstein at this stage of his thinking has abandoned so much of the *Tractatus*, why has he chosen to retain, in any form, the notion of "logical space" at all, never mind whether it is construed metaphysically or naturalistically? For how could what he has to say in section VIII of PR have a general application to language? Some terms, doubtless, will take their meaning from the place we have assigned to them in practices, like that of measuring, established by convention. But won't many others simply pick out features of experience? And in such cases, why do we need to think of propositions as related to one another via their occupancy of "places" in any sort of "logical space"? Why can't we simply take propositions one by one, in line with the logical and semantic pluralism advanced by the early Russell (and subsequently for the most part taken as read by mainstream analytic philosophy of language) and define the meaning of each by ostensively associating it with one set of features of experience designated as assertion-conditions, and another set designated as denial-conditions?

This, it seems to me, is the question that Wittgenstein is mainly addressing in the remarks on ostensive definition that extend, roughly, from I.28 to I.39 of *Philosophical Investigations* [PI]. The basic idea of ostensive definition is, precisely, that one can give the meaning of a term *T* by ostensively indicating one or more things of which "this is *T*" is true, supplementing this, if necessary, by indicating some things of which it is false. Wittgenstein's opening point is that any such definition can be misunderstood:

> Now one can ostensively define a proper name, the name of a colour, the name of a material, a numeral, the name of a point of the compass and so on. The definition of the number two, "That is called 'two'"—pointing to two nuts—is perfectly exact.—But how can two be defined like that? The person one gives the definition to doesn't know what one wants to call "two"; he will suppose that "two" is the name given to *this* group of nuts!—He *may* suppose this; but

> perhaps he does not. He might make the opposite mistake; when I want to assign a name to this group of nuts, he might understand it as a numeral. And he might equally well take the name of a person, of which I give an ostensive definition, as that of a colour, of a race, or even of a point of the compass. That is to say: an ostensive definition can be variously understood in *every* case. [PI, I.28]

Wittgenstein then goes on to argue that the possibility of misunderstanding will be reduced or eliminated if the learner can be made to see what kind of word is being defined: a name for a color, for a race, for a point of the compass, or what:

> [W]e can prevent misunderstandings by saying: "This *colour* is called so and so," "This *length* is called so-and-so," and so on. [PI, I.29]

Why, exactly, should coming to see this help to exclude the possibilities of misunderstanding to which Wittgenstein has just drawn attention? Coming to these paragraphs from the discussions of possibility and logical space in the *Tractatus* and the *Philosophical Remarks*, it is tempting to reply that what has changed is that the learner now has some idea of what would be implied by *denying* that something, *x*, was *T*: what would be implied would be that *x* is *a group of some other number*, or *some other point of the compass*, or *some other length*, or *some other color*.

Could one, now, fill in that kind of gap in the learner's comprehension by means of another series of ostensive definitions, only negative ones this time: "That's not a *T*" ("That's not what we call '*T*'")? Evidently not. For a negative ostensive definition would, just taken in itself, be as much subject to misunderstanding as a positive one. For how is the learner, merely on the basis of the data provided by a series of ostensions, however long, to distinguish between things that fail to be *T* because they are among the alternative possibilities invoked by the denial that a thing is *T*, and those that simply have nothing to do with being *T*? It follows that negative ostensive definition—pointing to something and saying, "This is not *T*"—must remain as enigmatic a proceeding as the positive variety—unless one has already some idea of what kind of word—a color word, a name for a point of the compass, an artifact, a visual quality of surfaces—"*T*" is, and thus some idea of what alternative possibilities thus opened up would close again if one were to add, "But no, maybe it is *T* after all!"

In both the negative and the positive cases the problem is the same: that the would-be learner has no means, to the extent that the data available to him are limited to those made available by the pointing-and-saying procedure, of inferring, from the circumstances offered as true-making for "This is *T*," any conclusions regarding the circumstances that would make "This is *T*" false, and vice versa. If he is to arrive at any conclusions concerning what "This is *T*" asserts he must grasp some relationship linking what it asserts to what it denies, and correlatively for "This is not *T*." He needs what I shall call a *truth-value switch*.

In arguing against ostensive definition, Wittgenstein is sometimes taken to be arguing for the impossibility of a naturalistic account of meaning; for the irreducibility, in other words, of some form of mentalism about meaning, or better, perhaps, for a type of semantic mysticism related to that of the *Tractatus*. On this view the conclusion of the argument is that we can understand an explanation of the meaning of a word only if we already speak a language, or in other words that the question of what it is to speak a language is, at least from a naturalistic standpoint, intrinsically inscrutable, and that any attempt to offer an account of *how* we do it must therefore be misguided. This seems to me quite wrong: both wrong as an interpretation, and wrong as an estimate of the actual implications of the argument. What the argument of PI I.28–30 does *not* show is that the function of a truth-value switch cannot be performed by what Hume would have called a *natural relationship*. Indeed, throughout Wittgenstein's profoundly naturalistic later work, natural relationships are precisely what do that job. What the argument does show is that no natural relationship can *naturally possess* that function. If it could, the function of linking the assertion- and denial-conditions of a given statement would be a *natural feature* of the natural relationship that does that job, as for instance the function of linking two biochemical processes may be a *natural feature* of certain proteins. The foregoing argument shows such a supposition to be absurd. The conclusion to be drawn is that the function of linking the assertion- and denial-conditions of a statement is a logical one, not a physical or natural one. Therefore it has to be *stipulated* in some way, *as a matter of linguistic convention*, that the natural relationship in question *is to have* that function: it cannot, as the ostensive theorist would wish to persuade us, simply be *exhibited* as *possessing that function by nature*. The difficulty with the theory of ostensive definition, in other words, is not a merely practical one. It is not that what the theory proposes is, for some psychological or other reason, unworkable; it is that what it proposes is *unintelligible*. Assertion, contradiction, the contrast between assertion and denial are all, as Wittgenstein insists at PR 74, things belonging to language, or to logic, not to natural science:

> Immediate experience cannot contain any contradiction . . . [it] is beyond all speaking and contradicting.

The argument then is (1) the meaning of a proposition can be explained only by specifying an associated truth-value switch; and (2) there is no way of specifying a truth-value switch other than by stipulating a convention, or rule, or practice of some sort. That is why, at PI I.31, when Wittgenstein searches for an example of circumstances in which ostensive definition is functional—by contrast with the dysfunctional cases considered earlier—the case he considers is that of giving the explanation "this is the king" to someone who "already knows the rules of chess up to this last point: the shape of the king." Ostensive definition is not dysfunctional here because knowledge of the rules of chess has already equipped the learner with a truth-value switch. He knows, that is, what being a king is supposed to contrast with: *being another type of chess piece*. The connection of this with the observations at PR 43, about a question corresponding to a method of searching, and about that notion's in turn being unintelligible unless it can be posed relative to a "space" of some sort, now seems straightforward enough. To answer the question "Is this the king?" you need a space in which "you stand in relation to where you are not." The rules of chess, defining as they do the roles of a small array of possible types of piece, provide such a "space": a limited array of alternative options in terms of which the question becomes answerable because it becomes clear, through the linking of assertion-conditions to denial-conditions, what, exactly, is being asked. And the "space" is a *logical* space, not a natural one: a space constituted by stipulation. The rules of chess are here analogous to the yardstick of PR 82–84. Like the statements "*x* is 1 cm long," "*x* is 2 cm long," and so on, the statements "*x* is a king," "*x* is a pawn," and so on form a set of *coordinate* statements of which it can be said [PR 84], "*two* determinations of the same kind are impossible."

Significantly Wittgenstein connects abandonment of the concept of an elementary proposition to his new conception of the specification of logical spaces (the reference is presumably to *Tractatus* 2.013–2.0131):

> In my old conception of an elementary proposition there was no determination of the value of a co-ordinate; although my remark that a coloured body is in a colour-space, etc., should have put me straight on to this. [PR 83, p. 111]

And yet it could also be argued that two of the main thoughts at work in the passages we have been examining—(1) that the assertoric content of a proposition cannot be equated with the experiential content of the circumstances in which an assertion effected by uttering it is true, and (2) that the reason for this is that unless we *already* know its assertoric content we have no means of knowing what assertion, or indeed that any assertion, is effected by uttering the sign-string which *ex hypothesi* expresses it—are already clearly articulated in the *Tractatus*:

> Every proposition must *already* have a sense: it cannot be given a sense by affirmation. Indeed its sense is just what is affirmed. And the same applies to negation, etc. [4.064]

What is new in the later work, from PR onward, is the realization that these two claims entail that the relationship between what is affirmed by the assertion of a given proposition as true, what is excluded by that assertion, and what is neither affirmed nor excluded by it (what "has nothing to do with it"), is one that can only be established by stipulation.

4. THE MEANING OF "CRITERION"

Among the numerous and diverse threads of discussion that go to make up the complex tissue of Wittgenstein's transitional texts, the foregoing arguments, it seems to me, are the ones we most need to take into account as forming the background to Wittgenstein's use of the term "criterion" from the *Blue and Brown Books* onward. Against that background I can now state, baldly and briefly, what I take the term to mean in many and possibly most contexts in his later writing. A criterion, for Wittgenstein, if I read him correctly, is a conventionally stipulated truth-value switch.

5. HOW WELL DOES THE NEW INTERPRETATION FIT THE TEXT?

If the meaning of "criterion" is the one that has emerged from sections 3–4, then there is a distinction to be drawn between a criterion and either of the sorts of thing commonly understood to be intended by the expression "truth-condition." A truth-condition for "*Fx*" is simply some natural circumstance whose obtaining makes it true that *Fx*, or, in the weaker version preferred by anti-Realists, warrants the assertion of "*Fx*." A criterion, on the other hand, is some conventionally stipulated practice or condition that makes clear what is denied by asserting, and what is asserted by denying, that *Fx*: one, in other words, that links the truth- or assertion-conditions of *Fx* to its falsity- or denial-conditions. On the other hand a criterion can perfectly well *function in a given context as* a truth-condition. The criterion, in Wittgenstein's terms, of a ball's being said to be "in touch" in football is that it has been kicked, while in play, across a white line painted on the ground. The reason for calling this a criterion is that it provides a conventionally established linkage between the truth- and falsity-conditions of "*x* is in touch": if a ball in play has not crossed the line it is not in touch; if it has, it is. But of course the ball's crossing the line is also what, in most ordinary circumstances, serves the linesman, the referee, and the crowd as the main truth-condition for assertions to the effect that the ball is in touch. Now, assuming (with sufficiently obvious textual warrant, perhaps, to remove the need to labor over this bit of the argument) that Wittgenstein means by "symptom" a truth-condition in the sense just defined, we can make sense of his remarks, at BB 24–25 and PI I.354, about the distinction between symptoms and criteria.

Suppose that medicine uses the word "angina" to denote an infection by Bacillus B. In other words, as medical men use the term, someone has angina if he has a Bacillus B infection, and not if he has not. In that case, according to medical usage, being infected with Bacillus B is a *criterion* of angina in the sense of "criterion" proposed in sections 3–4. Such an infection, in other words, is the condition singled out by linguistic stipulation as the one that is to link truth-conditions to falsity-conditions for the proposition "*X* has angina." That being so, it follows that the remark that angina is a Bacillus B infection advances no claim about the nature of Reality. Rather, such a remark merely explains a bit of linguistic stipulation. It explains what conditions of use medical science attaches to the term. In the same sort of way the remark "The ball is in touch because it has crossed the touchline" is not a remark about the ball as a constituent of the natural world (cf. "The ball has vaporized because the temperature in there is now 15,000°C"), it is a remark about the rules of football. So one would expect Wittgenstein to distinguish rather carefully, as he does, between a condition for something's *being X*, and a condition for something's *being called* X, and to choose, as Albritton grants that he does almost without exception, the latter expression when he is talking about criteria.

It follows that Albritton's remark "A criterion is in Wittgenstein's usage always a criterion for something or other's being the case" is mistaken. On the contrary, a criterion is in Wittgenstein's usage always, primarily, a criterion for something or other's *being called* something, and the difference of phrasing matters: it is not just an obfuscatory circumlocution.

Furthermore one of the conclusions to be drawn from the arguments that led Wittgenstein to his later notion of a criterion is, as we have seen, that without antecedent knowledge of some conventionally stipulated relationship linking the truth-conditions to the falsity-conditions of a putative proposition "*Fx*" one could not know what was being asserted by a speaker in uttering the corresponding string of signs, or whether anything was being asserted at all. So the implications of Cavell's perceptive, though cursory, remark that

> [c]riteria are not alternatives or additions to evidence. Without the control of criteria in applying concepts, we would not know what counts as evidence for any claim, nor for what claims evidence is needed,

turn out after all to be satisfactorily explicable in detail, and the remark itself to go, as we suspected, to the heart of the matter.

"Symptoms," on the other hand, *are* evidence. If "angina" is used as we stipulated above, then to say that sufferers experience sore throats is to state a fact about angina, not merely to indicate how the term is used. Thus, if one were to ask, "Why does angina lead to people's having sore throats?" he would be asking a question about biochemistry: about the interactions between the physiology of Bacillus B and that of the human body. On the other hand, if one were to ask, "Why does Bacillus B cause angina?" no such answer would be in order: all one could do would be to reply, "How do you mean?—'Angina' is just the medical *name* for a Bacillus B infection," and if that reply failed to produce enlightenment he would be reduced to scratching his head.

Earlier, in section 2, we asked what reason there could be for postulating two distinct categories of truth-conditions, one somehow more "meaning-determining" than the other. We have now reached a point at which we can grasp the nature of the confusion concerning Wittgenstein's intentions involved in putting things this way. To Frege is due the insight that to give the meaning of an expression is to say how the truth or falsity of statements in which it figures is to be established. There are of course many ways, including verificationist ones, of spelling out what this suggestion comes to in detail. Frege's insight is often expressed, for instance, as the claim that to state the meaning of a proposition is to state its truth-conditions, in the sense of "truth-condition" noted at the start of this section. If that were Wittgenstein's position it would follow that, for him, it would be possible to give the meaning of a proposition by exhibiting its truth-conditions. But we have already seen that Wittgenstein holds the contrary and why: "Every proposition must *already* have a sense: it cannot be given a sense by affirmation. Indeed its sense is just what is affirmed. *And the same applies to negation*" (my italics). So a "criterion" for Wittgenstein is not a kind of truth-condition: rather, it is a principle or rule that establishes, necessarily by stipulation, what is denied in affirming and affirmed in denying a given proposition, and in so doing establishes the meaning, the sense, of that proposition.

At the same time a criterion, once defined, can serve as a truth-condition. Equally a truth-condition can come to function as a criterion, if it is made, by stipulation, the condition that links what is denied in asserting the proposition concerned to what is asserted in denying it. Thus the presence of a sore throat might come to be regarded as the criterion for "what is called 'angina,'" rather than merely a truth-condition for the statement that someone has angina. Such a change would of course—and here we come to another technical term of Wittgenstein's that has been found baffling—alter the "grammar" of the term: we might say, viewing it in terms of its previous "grammar," that the shift of criterion had turned it into a name for a bodily condition rather than for a disease. As Wittgenstein says in the BB passage, it is possible to get along in ordinary conversation without a pedantic regard for such shifts in grammar: "Doctors will use names of diseases without ever deciding which phenomena are to be taken as criteria and which as symptoms; and this need not be a deplorable lack of clarity." Nevertheless the shifts in "grammar" that turn on such decisions remain real, even if irrelevant in many contexts of discussion, and there is always the possibility of usage's being made more precise with respect to them if a need for resulting kinds of clarity arises.

The possibility of treating a criterion as a truth-condition creates "the fluctuation between criteria and symptoms," which, as Wittgenstein says at PI I.354, "makes it look as though there were nothing at all but symptoms." At 354 Wittgenstein illustrates the distinction between a criterion and a symptom by reference to the contrast between the falling barometer that presages rain and rain itself: "certain sensations of wet and cold." The fact that in each case our belief that it is going to rain, or that it is raining, might turn out to be mistaken, tempts us to think that in both cases we are "taught by experience," that is, that the judgment we make is in both cases based on induction. Wittgenstein's comment is that even when appearances in the second case are misleading, "the fact that the false appearance is precisely one of rain is founded on a definition."

By "definition" here Wittgenstein can't have in mind dictionary definition. Dictionaries merely record usage, and what is supposed to contrast with induction here is plainly not the recording of meanings but their constitution. And we have already traced out in Wittgenstein's earlier writings the genesis of a coherent and original structure of argument concerning the constitution of meaning. If we read him in accordance with the drift of those arguments, then to say that "rain" is *defined as* "certain sensations of wet and cold, or such-and-such visual impressions" is to say that those sensations and impressions are what link the assertion-conditions to the denial-conditions of "It's raining." That link establishes that what is affirmed by the assertion of "It's raining" is that those conditions obtain, that what is excluded is the obtaining of any weather unaccompanied by rain, and that nothing unconnected, causally or otherwise, with that difference has any bearing on the issue of whether such an assertion is true or not. So there is a difference, as Wittgenstein says, between symptom and criterion here, and the difference is the one he draws attention to in the succeeding paragraph, I. 355, to which one must go on, even though it contains no occurrence of the *word* "criterion," if one wishes to learn the conclusion aimed at by the argument of I.354:

> The point here is not that our sense-impressions can lie, but that we understand their language. (And this language, like any other, is founded on convention.)

In other words, we understand what the sound of raindrops pattering on a tin roof "is telling us" about the weather because *we* speak a language, not because Nature does. There are no books in the running brooks, and none in the falling rain either.

It follows that Albritton was right to say in 1959 that a criterion, for Wittgenstein, is "something by which one may be *justified in saying* that the thing is so *and by whose absence the thing is not so*."[30] So much squares with the suggestion we have been pursuing here: that a criterion for Wittgenstein is what we have called a truth-value switch. Where Albritton's 1959 exegesis begins to go wrong, if ours is right, is in the next step he takes, which is to go on to say,

> And a criterion for a thing's being so has this relation to the thing's being so not as a matter of fact, like what Wittgenstein calls a "symptom" of its being so, but as a matter of "logical" necessity. That is, on Wittgenstein's account of such necessity, its relation to the thing's being so is "founded on a definition" or "founded on convention," or is a matter of "grammar."[31]

The motivation for this move is, of course, the need to find some plausible reason why Wittgenstein should wish to differentiate between "criteria" and "symptoms." Since both appear to be truth-conditions in the conventional sense of that term there seems little that could differentiate them except modality, and that interpretation is fostered by Wittgenstein's choice of terminology—"founded on a definition," and so forth—vaguely redolent of Kant on analyticity or Vienna Circle positivism on the linguistic basis of necessary truth.

To take the issue of terminology first, there is no textual ground for supposing that Wittgenstein meant such terminology to mark the distinction between contingent truths or relationships and necessary ones, and every reason, as we have seen, to suppose that he meant it to mark the quite different distinction between the use of a propositional sign to express an empirically grounded judgment purporting to add to the description of reality and its use to draw attention to the nature of the conventional stipulations connecting its truth- and falsity-conditions to one another. Furthermore—moving now from terminology to substance—there is no need to appeal to modality to distinguish criteria from symptoms, since the role of criteria relative to the stipulation of truth- and falsity-conditions is already sufficient to do so. What the establishment, in terms of the actual meteorological condition, of a truth-value switch for "It's raining" does is to *give a sense to* "It's raining." What that means for the post-1929 Wittgenstein (as distinct from Frege: we shall come back to that in a moment) is specified—admittedly in Wittgenstein's habitual telegraphese, in the sentence of PR immediately following the one from which we set out:

> "The sense contains the possibility of recognition," but this is a logical possibility. I must be in the space in which what is to be expected is located. [PR 82, p. 111]

Of course, experience and inductive reasoning may teach one who hears pattering on a tin roof to expect to get wet if he goes out. Here is a "possibility of recognition" that is natural, not "logical," guaranteed by something in nature—the principles of animal learning—not by anything that one might want to call *logic*. But, as we have seen, the existence of that natural kind of possibility will not help (pace a long series of attempts to elaborate one or another type of "causal theory of meaning") in solving the problem of what is asserted in uttering a string of signs, "*xyz*." The question here is not that of what is to be expected on the basis of the occurrence of a natural phenomenon, but what is to be expected on the basis of another speaker's assertion or denial of a proposition—to which at present one can attach no meaning. In "searching" for the likely consequences of dark clouds, or the likely concomitants of pattering on a roof, one can use ordinary methods of inductive enquiry. But how do I set about "searching" for what is to be expected if my interlocutor is correct in affirming that *xyz*? He may be asserting that it is raining—heavy rain is falling, after all—but, equally, he may be asserting that the fish will be rising or that the road will be too muddy now for a jeep to get through. This is, I take it, what Wittgenstein has in mind when he says that to realize the possibilities of recognition—of recognizing that "*xyz*" has been truly asserted, or that it has not—implicit in grasping a sense, one must be "in the space in which what is to be expected is to be located." But precisely because environmental circumstances provide *in themselves* no such space—do not, that is, arrange themselves as an array of alternative possibilities relative either to the affirmation or to the denial of "*xyz*"—the space in question must be a "logical" space, and the possibilities in question "logical" possibilities, determined by antecedent stipulation to the effect that the issue of truth or falsity for "*xyz*" is to hinge on the presence or absence of certain natural circumstances: in the present instance, rain.

But if symptoms are to be differentiated, as inductively established grounds for anticipating the truth of "*xyz*" from criteria considered as the conditions, stipulatively established as such, constitutive of the possibility of anticipating either the truth or the falsity of "*xyz*," then *necessity* as the basis of the distinction simply drops out of the picture. As Wittgenstein makes clear at PI I.354, when I judge that it is raining because I can see it is, the judgment I express by remarking that it is raining is as much founded upon experience, and as fallible, as the one I make on the basis of pattering on the roof (I have never known it not to be raining, in such a downpour, but then, perhaps I am out of touch with what film crews can do to achieve lifelike atmospheric effects with modern machinery). "Grammar," "definition," "convention" come in, for Wittgenstein, not at the level of truth-determination, but earlier, at the level at which language sets up the system of truth-value switches that establish the possibility of deciding between the options of truth and falsity for given sentences; or to put it another way, that establish, for Wittgenstein, the *sense* of those sentences.

Someone might object, though, that Wittgenstein cannot get clear as easily as that of the suspicion that adopting a given criterion renders a given range of truths necessarily true. Presumably, on Wittgenstein's hypothesis at BB 25, "Angina is a Bacillus B infection" must count, if any does, as a remark "about grammar." But if so nothing, presumably, could show it to be false: indeed, Wittgenstein elsewhere speaks of related claims as "infallible." But surely the lack of any possibility of falsification is precisely the mark of a necessary truth. So why isn't "Angina is a Bacillus B infection" a necessary truth? One possible answer might be that it is a truth about "*what is called* 'angina,'" and in that capacity is clearly not necessary, precisely because the criterion for what is called "angina" might be something else: something that presently counts as a symptom of angina. But still, one might want to argue, if it *is* the criterion, then it does appear to follow that one who has a Bacillus B infection *could not fail,* in virtue of that, to have angina; so there is still an unexorcised smell of necessity about.

It cannot, plainly, be exorcised by once more invoking fallibilism. It would be a mere non sequitur, that is, to argue that "Someone who has a Bacillus B infection has angina" is not a necessary truth because no evidence that someone has a Bacillus B infection, however compelling, can exclude the possibility that in fact he has no such infection. For it still might be necessarily true that *if* someone has such an infection, *then* that person has angina. What the present objection alleges against Wittgenstein, in other words, is not that his account of criteria commits him to a denial of fallibilism, but only that it commits him to the existence of necessary truths about what *X is*, not merely to the existence of contingent ones about what *is called* "*X*."

There is, though, a deeper, as well as more authentically Wittgensteinian reason why statements "about grammar," however "infallible," are not to be construed as articulating necessary truths. A well-known statement of it occurs not far from the end of the *Philosophical Investigations:*

> I am not saying: if such-and-such facts of nature were different people would have different concepts (in the sense of a hypothesis). But: if anyone believes that certain concepts are absolutely the correct ones, and that having different ones would mean not realising something that we realise—then let him imagine certain very general facts of nature to be different from what we are used to, and the formation of concepts different from the usual ones will become intelligible to him. [PI, II.xii, p. 230]

Let us try applying this to the present case. Angina is a disease. Diseases (or some of them, including angina) are caused by interactions between human biochemistry and the biochemistry of pathogens. Suppose that, for some reason, such interactions become chemically impossible. The concepts of a human pathogen and of a pathogen-caused disease now become, in a certain sense, inaccessible to us, meaning by that that the point of making the distinctions that such concepts marked depended on the continued obtaining of "certain very general facts of nature" that have ceased to obtain. Suppose we now find Bacillus B in someone's tissues. Do we, now, continue to say that that person "has angina"? The most we can say, it appears, is that at one time he would have had angina, but now merely happens to have some Bacillus B organisms in his tissues.

Philosophy, in one way since Plato, and in another way since Kant, has enjoyed a prolonged love affair with the idea that whereas some features of the pictures we form for ourselves of Reality are contingent, other features of those pictures are noncontingent, in the sense that they would, necessarily, characterize any picture that *could* be formed of Reality; either (if we are Platonists) by any reasoning being whatsoever, or (if we are Kantians) by beings constituted as we are; and that these putatively necessary features of our world picture may therefore be taken as revelatory, either of how Reality must (metaphysically) be in itself, or of how experience must (transcendentally) be for creatures like ourselves.

If Wittgenstein's views on criteria run along the lines suggested here, then he emerges as a rooted opponent of that idea. Take, for example, the very recent reworking of it which we owe to Saul Kripke. The Kripke of *Naming and Necessity* would hold, presumably, that "Angina is a Bacillus B infection" is, precisely, a truth that holds with metaphysical necessity. According to the picture offered by Kripke (or at any rate, by the shorthand Kripke I have in mind, who may be a different character from the real one) we give a meaning to "angina" by singling out a recognizable pathological condition. Then, through scientific inquiry, we discover that angina is a Bacillus B infection. It follows that nothing not a Bacillus B infection could be, or could have been, angina. And hence it follows that the truth, that angina is that, is true "across possible worlds." In Kripke, in short, we find a recrudescence of the philosophers" dream of finding features of our way of conceptualizing the world that not only holds in the world as it is but would hold in *any possible world.*

Wittgenstein, on the present interpretation, offers a very different picture. According to him, we choose to give a meaning to the proposition "*X* has angina" by stipulating that its truth or falsity is to turn on the issue of whether *X* has a Bacillus B infection. There is nothing necessary about this: it is a pure piece of stipulation: a "convention" or a "definition," though one that determines the "grammar" of the term "angina" (turns it into a term in a classification of diseases by pathogen rather than, say, by bodily condition, that is). Under ordinary circumstances it will now follow "infallibly," or be a "tautology," that if someone exhibits the characteristic pathology engendered by a Bacillus B infection, and has such an infection, then that person has angina. But note that though, according to Wittgenstein, such a connection is "infallible" for the sort of world in which we find ourselves, that "infallibility" carries no implications for other possible worlds and thus no implications for metaphysics, of either the dogmatic or the transcendental varieties. There will always turn out to be "certain very general facts of nature" upon which the utility, and so the intelligibility, of assigning certain natural features of the world to serve as truth-value switches depends, and it will always be the case that those aspects of reality can change, come to be "different from what we are used to" in ways that overturn such putative necessities by evacuating of sense the propositions that putatively express them. Metaphysics, for Wittgenstein, is precisely the attempt to detach what we say from such demeaning practical dependencies on stipulation undertaken against a background of "general facts of nature"; to speak as though we disposed of concepts whose application to all future, and indeed to all possible, realities could be established in an eyeblink, simply by the procedure, which the early Russell thought indispensable to Realism, of pointing at something and saying, in effect, "There! *That* is what '*F*' means!"

6. WITTGENSTEIN, SKEPTICISM, AND THE PHILOSOPHY OF LANGUAGE

J. A. Fodor and Charles Chihara published in 1965 a celebrated paper attacking Albritton's rather sympathetic account of what the latter took to be Wittgenstein's argument against Other Minds skepticism. Fodor and Chihara argue that Wittgenstein's position is essentially a version of verificationalism or operationalism. From PR section VIII onward, Wittgenstein returns frequently to techniques of measurement as offering a central instance of the way in which grasping the senses of a body of related propositions is connected with learning to operate, and to grasp the point of, a practice. At PI II.xi, p. 225, Wittgenstein says "the meaning of the word 'length' is learnt by learning, among other things, what it is to determine length." Fodor and Chihara take the drift of this to be that "[reference to] relevant operations with, e.g., rulers, range-finders, etc. . . . will be essential in characterising the meaning of such predicates as 'three feet long.' It is in this manner that we are led to the view that the relevant operations for determining the applicability of a predicate are conceptually connected with the predicate."[32] Following Malcolm and others, Fodor and Chihara conclude that Wittgenstein's main argument against Other Minds skepticism is that the "meaning" (i.e., the content) of statements that someone else is in pain, or has experienced a certain sort of dream, is likewise to be explicated in terms of the public "operations" by appeal to which we determine the applicability of the corresponding predicates, with the result that the skeptic is left with nothing even putatively "private" to be skeptical about.

If we are right in what we have said so far, Fodor and Chihara entirely misconstrue the drift of remarks like the one they cite from PI p. 225. What Wittgenstein is precisely not saying, in other words, is that someone who asserts that (1) "*x* is three feet long" is asserting something "conceptually" equivalent to something along the lines of (2) "*x* fits exactly between the terminal gradations of some yardstick." Such an analysis is in any case hardly defensible, since the truth-values of (1) and (2) may in any actual situation diverge: a given yardstick may be inaccurate, a given measurer too careless or too drunk to do the job properly, and so on. What he *is* saying is something altogether different: namely, that it is only by explaining how a sentence such as "*x* is three feet long" fits into the practice of comparing distances by recording the relative numbers of iterations of a modulus required to span each that it can be made clear how the truth- and falsity-conditions of such a sentence are related to one another, or to put it another way, made clear what is denied in asserting it and what is asserted in denying it. Such a view not only fails to entail any program of reductive analysis of the sort characteristic of verificationism or operationalism, but is, as we noted earlier, hostile to philosophical reductionism in any form.

The actual strategy that Wittgenstein thinks should be adopted against philosophical skepticism is sketched, among other places, at *Philosophical Grammar* [PG] 83, p. 129:

> When one wants to show the senselessness of metaphysical turns of phrase, one often says, "I couldn't imagine the opposite of this," or "What would it be like if it were otherwise?" (When, for instance, someone has said that my images are private, that only I alone can know if I am feeling pain, etc.) Well, if I can't imagine how it might be otherwise, I can't imagine that it is *so*. For here "I can't imagine" doesn't indicate a lack of imaginative power. I can't even *try* to imagine it; it makes no sense to say "I imagine it." And that means, no

connection has been made between this sentence and the method of representation by imagination (or by drawing).

The general fit between this diagnosis of what is ultimately wrong with skepticism and the account offered here of how Wittgenstein arrived at his notion of a criterion will by now, I think, be evident. Wittgenstein's skeptic exemplifies the philosophical tendency we encountered at the end of the last section: the tendency to forget that it is clear what it is to deny some assertion, or to be mistaken in asserting it, only if there is some practice, some decision, some stipulation that we have made or adopted, that makes that clear; and to forget, also, that unless it is clear what it is for the assertion made by a propositional sign, "*xyz*," to be mistaken, it is unclear not only what assertion is made, but whether any assertion is made, by uttering "*xyz*." The skeptic, on Wittgenstein's account of the nature of skepticism, in other words, commits himself to what appear to be descriptions of possible states of affairs. But since it is crucial to skepticism that there should be no way of determining when the "descriptions" in question fail to characterize our situation, and since it must therefore remain unclear what, if one were to assert that the terms of such a description were met, one would be asserting, the alleged "descriptions" fail to describe anything at all. Wittgenstein's claim, in short, is not that skepticism can be shown to be *false*, by way of the flimsy argument often ascribed to him, to the effect that the relationship between the truth of a proposition and the circumstances that make it true is sometimes "logically" or "conceptually" certified and sometimes not. It is that the hypotheses on which the skeptic depends if he is to raise his kind of doubts are not only one and all vacuous, but necessarily vacuous, given the role assigned to them in the skeptic's plan of argument, since if they are to do the job the skeptic requires of them they must be *in principle* nonfalsifiable. Such a strategy is already sketched at *Tractatus* 6.51:

> Skepticism is *not* irrefutable, but obviously nonsensical, when it tries to raise doubts where no questions can be asked.

Its working-out, in the version developed after 1929, is exemplified in Wittgenstein's discussion, at PI I.270, of the use of a manometer to train someone to recognize an inner sensation associated with rising blood pressure. Earlier Wittgenstein has discussed the famous diarist who attempts to record in his diary, by means of the sign "S," the occurrences of an inner sensation. The sensation in question is "private," in the sense that it inhabits the Cartesian realm of the mental, and so partakes of the absolute Cartesian separation of that realm and its contents from the physical. Because of that separation, Wittgenstein has in effect argued, the diarist could have grounds for thinking he has erred in identifying S only if the *criteria* for S, the considerations that make the difference between the diarist's being right about S's having recurred and his being wrong about that, could also be inhabitants of the private realm of Cartesian inwardness. But, argues Wittgenstein, a private criterion is no criterion: I cannot, for instance, check my beliefs about a train departure time against an imaginary timetable—unless I can confirm the results of doing that by appeal to a real one. Hence the diarist can have no means of discovering that he has erred in writing "S" in his diary. And hence he cannot be correct in doing so either: the whole process is nugatory, and the "diary" a mock, or joke, diary. The conformity between the way in which Wittgenstein deploys the notion of a criterion in this, one of the central arguments of PI, and the account of the meaning of that term offered here is, I think, clear.

Now Wittgenstein turns to the manometer example as offering a case in which an inner process does dispose of an outer criterion. Using the manometer, I train myself to discriminate the sensation that accompanies the rise in blood pressure with sufficient accuracy to "be able to say that my blood pressure is rising without using any apparatus." Now, though, someone proposes a skeptical hypothesis—maybe I am mistaken in thinking that the sensation I have supposedly trained myself to "discriminate" is the same sensation at each recurrence: maybe it is a different sensation each time.

Wittgenstein's response is the following: "And now [i.e., from the point at which I can predict correctly from the occurrence of the sensation alone that my blood pressure is rising, without appealing to the manometer] it seems quite indifferent whether I have recognised the sensation *right* or not. Let us suppose I regularly identify it wrong, it does not matter in the least. *And that alone shows that the hypothesis that I make a mistake is mere show*" [PI I.270, p. 95e (my italics)].

Wittgenstein is, clearly, right that if my ability to recognize the sensation allows me to predict a rise in my blood pressure, the mere suggestion that I habitually make a mistake has no practical implications whatsoever. But why does that show that the skeptic's hypothesis is *mere show*? To say that is to say, presumably, that the hypothesis in question does not raise a genuine possibility; one that might actually be realized in the present situation. And that might seem not to have been shown. But it is at this point that we need to recall Wittgenstein's remark at PG 83—"if I can't imagine how it might be otherwise, I can't imagine that it is *so*"—and the connections between that remark and the train of argument linking the possibility of negative description to the concept of a criterion that we have been tracing out here. My power to discriminate a certain sensation as qualitatively the same at each of its recurrences appears to be established by the fact that its exercise allows me to correctly predict rises in my blood pressure that can be independently checked by means of a manometer. The skeptic wants to raise the possibility that, despite all that, I may nevertheless be mistaken: the sensation may "really" be different each time. But now one wants to ask: what sense can the skeptic attach, in this context, to "mistaken"? And if he can attach no sense to it, what sense can he attach to the adverb "really"? I know, after all, when I talk about the possibility of being mistaken about the qualitative character of a sensation, what possibility I am invoking. I would accept, other things being equal, that I was no longer able to discriminate the sensation in question from others qualitatively similar enough to be confused with it, *if I were to cease to be able to predict what a manometer would show about my blood pressure*. That is what (or at any rate, one way of putting what) a "criterion" in Wittgenstein's sense does for one: it gives one a ground for supposing that one has made a mistake. That is why, since the criterion for supposing oneself to be mistaken about an inner process can't itself be an *inner* criterion, "an 'inner process' stands in need of outward criteria" [PI I.580], and why the manometer supplies a particular inner process with just such an "outer criterion." Being in possession of such a criterion I know what it would mean to say that my assessment of the identity of my inner state fails to correspond to "reality": it would mean that I had found reason, in my failure to predict the verdict of the manometer correctly, to suppose that my powers to discriminate one sensation from another were as yet insufficiently honed. The skeptic, on the other hand, cannot say what it would be to make a mistake of the kind he envisages. He cannot say that because the qualitative differences he envisages can be assigned no "outward" criterion. And, moreover, the reason why they can be assigned no outward criterion is a reason *internal to his philosophical position.* The moment he equips the possibilities he envisages with outward criteria, that is, they become possibilities capable of being excluded by appeal to those criteria, and thus possibilities useless for the purpose of fueling *skeptical* doubt. He is thus confronted with a dilemma: either he specifies criteria for the possibilities he envisages, in which case they cease to be grist for the mill of skepticism, or else he does not, in which case they remain "mere show": a simulacrum of envisaged possibility buttressed by terms such as "mistake" or "reality" that, whatever meaning may attach to them in other contexts, remain in this one, in the absence of criteria in the sense of that term explicated above, vacuous.

That, it seems to me, is roughly how Wittgenstein intends his remarks on criteria to bear on the issue of skepticism about inner processes. A fuller development of this part of the argument will be found elsewhere.[33] But I would like to suggest, very briefly, in conclusion, that the most interesting bearings of what Wittgenstein has to say about criteria may lie elsewhere: inter alia, in what they have to teach us about the nature of the connection between meaning and truth.

The idea that there is such a connection, and that it is philosophically of the utmost importance, originates with Frege. According to Michael Dummett, Frege held that reference is not an ingredient in meaning, meaning by that that "the understanding which a speaker of a language has of a word in that language . . . can never consist merely in his associating a certain thing with its referent; there must be some particular *means* by which this association is effected, the knowledge of which constitutes his grasp of its sense."[34] And, again according to Dummett, for Frege, "the sense of an expression is . . . that part of its meaning which is relevant to the determination of the truth-value of sentences in which the expression occurs.[35]

Dummett observes[36] that this preliminary characterization of the concept of sense is largely programmatic. A long train of philosophers, beginning with Russell, have found Frege's entire doctrine of sense ultimately programmatic, and have treated it with at best caution and at worst outright rejection. What has proved most influential in Frege's account is not his doctrine of *Sinn*, but the idea that we know the meaning of an expression when we know how to determine the truth-value of sentences in which it occurs. Frege has thus come to appear as the originator of a program that might not have greatly interested him: that of providing an explication of the concept of meaning in terms of the concept of truth. The challenge posed by this program is, as we know, that of giving a reasonably precise characterization of what is known in knowing how to attach a truth-value to a sentence, and of saying how, precisely, such knowledge bears on knowledge of meanings. Around this pair of questions it has proved possible to reconstruct and reanimate a surprisingly wide range of traditional philosophical issues, as instanced by familiar disputes opposing realists to antirealists with respect to truth, supporters of Quine's version of pragmatism to reductivist versions of positivism, fallibilists to believers in the type of metaphysical necessity espoused by Kripke, and so on. The philosophy of language has become, in short, a major vehicle for the continuing discussion of issues that would in earlier ages have been classed as metaphysical.

What is not generally noticed about Wittgenstein's concept of a criterion is that it is intended to do more or less the same work as Frege's concept of *Sinn*. Thus, for instance, at PG 84, p. 130, Wittgenstein says,

> The role of a sentence in the calculus is its sense.
>
> A *method* of measurement—of length, for example—has exactly the same relation to the correctness of a statement of length as the sense of a sentence has to its truth or falsehood.

And at pp. 23–24 of the *Lectures on the Foundations of Mathematics*,[37]

> Suppose you say, "What does it mean for a man to understand a sign?—You might say, "It means he gets hold of a certain idea." . . .
>
> "Having the same idea" is only interesting if (a) we have a criterion for having the same idea, (b) this guarantees that we use the word in the same way.

A criterion then, for Wittgenstein, does much of the work that *Sinn* does for Frege. A grasp by different speakers of the criteria governing the use of a word "guarantees that [they] use the word in the same way." And it guarantees that by ensuring that they determine in the same way the "correctness"—the truth or falsity—of statements employing it. But Wittgenstein's notion of a criterion, as we have seen, is far less programmatic than Frege's notion of sense. A criterion settles the question of what is relevant to the truth or falsity of a proposition in the sort of way in which grasping a method of measurement employing a certain modulus—grasping, that is, how distances can be compared by numbering the iterations of that modulus required to span them— settles the question of what is relevant to the truth or falsity of statements of length couched in terms of that modulus. To grasp a criterion, for Wittgenstein, is to grasp how propositions fit, in terms of the kinds of thing relevant to their truth or falsity, into the context of practices, or as he is later to call them, language-games.

The connection of Wittgenstein's later philosophy to questions of sense, reference, and truth has largely been missed, mainly because of the authority of the widespread, but mistaken, belief that the later work represents a complete break with the concerns of the *Tractatus*, and that the supposed break consists in Wittgenstein's having substituted, for the interest in the relationships between meaning and truth that characterized the earlier work, a new and altogether unrelated interest in the relationships between meaning and "use." One thing about this familiar conception of Wittgenstein's intellectual development is correct, however. The later Wittgenstein is not interested in the project of explicating the concept of meaning, taken as conceptually problematic, in terms of a supposedly unproblematic concept of truth. It would be truer to say that although for the later Wittgenstein the connections between meaning and truth remain of interest, neither concept, for him, is unproblematic. Both, for him, are semimystical notions defying naturalistic understanding as they stand, and both endlessly productive of "philosophy," that is, of intrinsically interminable metaphysical dispute. His solution is to explicate both in terms of practice. In the course of such explications the "cloud of philosophy" through which gleam, dully and numinously, such entities and relations as meanings, propositions, "internal relations," truth, falsity, contradiction, condenses into "a drop of grammar." We are left confronting the prosaic landscape of our own stipulative acts, together with the background of nonnecessary "facts of nature" against which their intelligibility is buttressed, though never more than provisionally so, and the endlessly multiplying practices—counting, measurement, arranging colours in qualitative series, keeping track of direction by means of a compass, and so on, and so on—that they bring into being.

The transformation of Frege's notion of sense into that of a criterion is one of the steps toward this goal. Wittgenstein's notion carries none of the suggestions of mentalism that, as Putnam has pointed out,[38] cling obstinately to Frege's notion of sense. As Wittgenstein says [PG p. 131]:

> The sense of a proposition (or a thought) isn't anything spiritual: it's what is given as an answer to a request for an explanation of the sense. . . .
>
> The sense of a proposition is not a soul.

What Wittgenstein has in mind here, I take it, given the avenue of thought down which we have pursued him, is that the sort of explanation one gives, or might give, as an answer to a request for an explanation of the sense of "*x* is three inches long" is, or might be, an explanation of the point of the practice of comparing lengths by iterating the same modulus, with a demonstration of the modulus in question, and if necessary some practice in counting.[39] And that the sort of explanation one might give of the sense of "God, I can feel my blood pressure going up!" might take the form of recounting the details of my training in sharpening my discrimination of inner sensations by appeal to a manometer. To work through the implications of such examples, and of the view of the relationships between truth, meaning, and practice that they sustain, might lead one very close to the conclusion that, whatever may be the intrinsic interest of the essentially metaphysical disputes that have formed the main matter of the philosophy of language since Russell, they are quite inessential to the pursuit of their ostensible goal of establishing the form and content of an adequate theory of meaning.

NOTES

1. This paper is the third in a series of essays on Wittgenstein that I hope will eventually coalesce into a book. The other two are "Wittgenstein and Scepticism," in Klaus Puhl, ed., *Meaning*

Scepticism (Berlin: Walter de Gruyter, 1991), 34–69; and "Truth, Yardsticks and Language-Games,"*Philosophical Investigations* 19:2 (April 1996), 105–130.

2. Cf. Stanley Cavell, *The Claim of Reason* (Oxford: Clarendon, 1979), 7: "The thought that Wittgenstein is counting on the ordinary notion of a criterion ought to seem an unpromising line for a beginning. There seems no prospect that the ordinary notion could do all the work he can appear to count on his appeals to criteria to do, whatever that work turns out to be; . . ."

3. Rogers Albritton, "On Wittgenstein's Use of the Term 'Criterion,'" *Journal of Philosophy* 56 (1959), 845–57; reprinted in George Pitcher, ed., *Wittgenstein: The Philosophical Investigations* (New York: Doubleday, 1966), 231–50 [OWC].

4. P. M. S. Hacker, *Insight and Illusion: Wittgenstein on Philosophy and the Metaphysics of Experience* (London: Oxford University Press, 1972) [I&I].

5. G. P. Baker, "Criteria: A New Foundation for Semantics," *Ratio* 16 (1974), 156–189; "Defeasibility and Meaning," in P. M. S. Hacker and J. Raz, eds., *Law, Morality and Society* (Oxford: Oxford University Press, 1977).

6. W. G. Lycan, "Non-Inductive Evidence: Recent Work on Wittgenstein's 'Criteria,'" *American Philosophical Quarterly* 8:2 (1971), 109–25.

7. Mark Addis, "Criteria: The State of the Debate," *Journal of Philosophical Research* 20 (1995), 139–74.

8. Crispin Wright, "Second Thoughts about Criteria," *Synthese* 58 (1984), 383–405.

9. Richard Rorty, "Criteria and Necessity," *Nous* 7 (1973), 313–29.

10. Charles Chihara and J. A. Fodor, "Operationalism and Ordinary Language: A Critique of Wittgenstein," in George Pitcher, ed., *Wittgenstein: The Philosophical Investigations* (New York: Doubleday, 1966), 384–419; Charles Chihara, "Operationalism and Ordinary Language Revisited," *Philosophical Studies* 24 (1973), 137–56.

11. John McDowell, "Criteria, Defeasibility and Knowledge," *Proceedings of the British Academy* 68 (1982), 456–79.

12. Cavell, op. cit., 37–48.

13. In "Wittgenstein and Scepticism."

14. Wright, op. cit., 383.

15. Ludwig Wittgenstein, *Preliminary Studies for the "Philosophical Investigations," Generally Known as The Blue and Brown Books* (Oxford: Blackwell, 1960).

16. Albritton, op. cit., 243–44.

17. Ibid., 235n.5.

18. Ibid., 236.

19. Ibid., 236.

20. Ibid., 244.

21. Wright, op. cit., 383.

22. Albritton, op. cit., 249.

23. Ibid., 237.

24. Ludwig Wittgenstein, *Philosophical Investigations* (Oxford: Blackwell, 1958), I.354.

25. Alice Ambrose, ed., *Wittgenstein's Lectures: Cambridge 1932–35* (Oxford: Basil Blackwell, 1979), 77.

26. Cavell, op. cit., 14.

27. Ludwig Wittgenstein, *Philosophical Remarks*, ed. Rush Rhees, trans. Raymond Hargreaves and Roger White (Oxford: Blackwell, 1975), 111.

28. Ludwig Wittgenstein, *Tractatus Logico-Philosophicus*, trans. D. F. Pears and B. F. McGuinness (London: Routledge, 1961), 15.

29. As, for example, P. M. S. Hacker does in *Insight and Illusion*.

30. Albritton, op. cit., 244 (second italics mine).

31. Albritton, ibid.

32. Chihara and Fodor, op. cit., 389.

33. Bernard Harrison, "Wittgenstein and Scepticism," loc. cit.

34. Michael Dummett, *Frege: Philosophy of Language*, 2nd ed. (London: Duckworth, 1981), 93.

35. Ibid., 89.

36. Ibid.

37. Cora Diamond, ed., *Wittgenstein's Lectures on the Foundations of Mathematics, Cambridge 1939* (Hassocks, England: Harvester Press, 1976).

38. Hilary Putnam, *Mind, Language and Reality* (Cambridge: Cambridge University Press, 1975), 218.

39. Cf. L. Goddard, "Counting," *Australasian Journal of Philosophy and Psychology* 40 (1962), 222–48. Goddard's paper fits very neatly with the present account.

Midwest Studies in Philosophy, XXIII (1999)

Born Yesterday: Personal Autonomy for Agents without a Past

DAVID ZIMMERMAN

1. RUSSELL'S QUESTION, PUTNAM'S ANSWER, AND A PROBLEM ABOUT AUTONOMY

Bertrand Russell famously speculated whether it is conceptually possible for the world as it presents itself to us in perception and "memory" to have been created five minutes ago.[1] As I recall, he did sensibly reject the hypothesis, not on a priori grounds, but simply because it is a very bad empirical hypothesis. Here, I want to explore a similar question of slightly more modest dimensions: is it conceptually possible, on grounds to be established a priori, that I or even you, gentle reader, the full-fledged autonomous agents we undoubtedly are, might have been created five minutes ago, equipped with just the normal adult psychologies we actually have, replete with all of their rich and fascinating features? Or, are the very ideas of "agency," "autonomy," and "responsibility" and the like "essentially historical" and/or "essentially externalist" in a way that would block the possibility posed? Less pedantically put: is the very idea of "instant autonomy" *conceptually* incoherent?

One is inclined to respond: surely not! Let us handle this more limited question in much the same fashion Russell handled his more grand one. To be sure, neither you nor I was in fact created *that* recently. You are a "person with a past" and so am I. But the competing hypothesis is to be ruled out on entirely empirical grounds. It is a very bad hypothesis about the nature and genesis of human agency. And so, I agree, it is. But is it merely that?

Many philosophers of language and mind would be inclined to argue "no" on the grounds (inter alia) that any being capable of full-fledged conceptual thought or of reasoning of any significant complexity must *necessarily* be appropriately embodied and embedded in the spatiotemporal world. Hilary Putnam, for example, appeals to certain a priori constraints on reference-fixing to debunk the venerable skeptical idea that we might, for all we know, be brains-in-vats entertaining that very hypothesis about ourselves. He has many allies in the philosophy of language and mind, where it has become a virtual orthodoxy that propositional content must satisfy certain a priori constraints on how the references and extensions of the constituent terms have come to be fixed.[2] The constraints in question are "external" to the individual's psychology, and in most such accounts "essentially historical." (Hereafter no scare quotes around these labels.) Thus if the speaker and/or thinker is not embedded in the right sort of social, biological, or engineering context, including a history of uses of the term, then he or she will *necessarily* be unable to entertain propositional attitudes with certain kinds of content, and on more extreme versions of the view, unable to entertain any propositional attitudes at all. (The most vivid example of such putative complete failure is Davidson's "swampman." A close second are Dretskean artifacts that lack "do it yourself understanding.")[3]

This is all very well for the philosophy of language and mind, but note that this externalist orthodoxy might turn out to have important implications for the theory of autonomous agency as well. For, to count as real agents, not just mindless instruments or devices, we must (inter alia) be able to engage in genuine practical reasoning. And however that most difficult notion is ultimately to be explicated, it will surely involve some kinds of vehicles, some kinds of mental attitudes with representational content and semantic properties. In folk psychology and its cognitivist scientific heirs, wants and beliefs or states very much like them ("valences" or "expectancies," say) are the obvious candidates. (It would be nice to be able to sidestep controversies about whether elements in *connectionist* networks have representational import, and if so, what kind and whether the internalist/externalist debate has any application to them. However, this will not be completely possible. See Section 5.) But if the externalist-historicist orthodoxy about content-ascription is correct, then an individual who fails to be embodied and embedded in the right sort of physical, biological, social, engineering, and historical context *cannot* engage in real practical reasoning, on grounds that can be established a priori. But this means that if you and I are indeed genuinely autonomous and responsible agents, a conviction that I am as loath as you to give up, then it is conceptually impossible that we have been created five minutes ago. The very idea of "instant agency" is ruled out . . . on a priori grounds. Thus proponents of causal-historical semantic theories of mental content seem to be committed to a particularized version of the a priori thesis Russell so sensibly rejected on more empirical grounds. (Come to think of it, couldn't Russell himself have deployed similar reasoning to rule out his more cosmic speculation? . . . Nah! . . . Wrong theory of reference.)

2. STRUCTURALISM VERSUS HISTORICISM IN THE THEORY OF AUTONOMOUS AGENCY

My principal concern here is the nature of autonomous agency, but this brief excursus into the implications of a certain view about linguistic reference and mental content-ascription is not quite the distraction it might seem, for there is at present a vigorous debate in moral psychology between "historicists" and "structuralists" that turns on the question of what kinds of personal history and/or embeddedness in the world, if any, are necessary for genuinely autonomous agency. (Hereafter no scare quotes around these labels either.) The debate is best understood against the backdrop of Harry Frankfurt's brave attempt to establish that there can be real responsibility without avoidability, principally because the crucial conditions of personhood, autonomy, and responsibility are *internal structural* features of the person's motivational system. The central idea is by now familiar: an individual is an autonomous agent by virtue of her possession of (or capacity to form) higher-order "volitions," that is, higher-order desires that certain first-order desires actually carry into action. Autonomy and responsibility are thus grounded in structural facts about the hierarchy of desires generated by a person's capacity for critical self-reflection.[4]

What unifies the "externalists" and "historicists" against the "internalists" and "structuralists" (hereafter no scare quotes around these labels either) in this debate is the worry that no merely structural feature of a set of motivations, such as a "mesh" between its levels, could possibly be sufficient for autonomy and responsibility, because it could have been "induced" or "implanted" by some autonomy-compromising historical factor such as hypnosis, behavior control, neurological fiddling, or the like. Although Michael Slote was the first to press this worry specifically against Frankfurt, John Martin Fischer and Mark Ravizza have taken the criticism deeper, as has Alfred Mele.[5] Fischer offers an especially crisp statement of the worry:

> The problem with . . . hierarchical "mesh" theories, no matter how they are refined, is that the selected mesh can be produced via responsibility-undermining mechanisms. After all, a demonic neurophysiologist can induce conformity between the various mental elements via a sort of electronic stimulation that is not reasons-responsive. I believe that the problem with hierarchical mesh theories is precisely that they are purely structural and ahistorical. It matters what kind of process issues in an action. Specifically, the mechanism issuing in the action must be reasons-responsive . . . the mesh between various elements of different preference-systems may be induced by electronic stimulation, hypnosis, brainwashing, and so on. *Moral responsibility is a historical phenomenon*; *it is a matter of the kind of mechanism that issues in action.*[6]

Thus we see that (a specific version of) Russell's question and (precisely) Putnam's answer do indeed arise squarely within the precinct of the debate about the nature and possibility of human autonomy and responsibility. To resolve the dispute between internalist-structuralists like Frankfurt and externalist-historicists like Fischer, one attractive strategy would be to go right to the root of the matter in the psycho-semantics of reference and mental content-ascription. For, if causal-historical and externalist accounts are correct there, then the very idea of a propositional attitude-deploying creature utterly without a history and/or utterly nonembedded-or-embodied (in the "appropriate way") in the world of objects is *conceptually* incoherent. And since such attitudes are the vehicles required for practical reasoning and thus for real agency, the very idea of an instant agent would straightaway be ruled out on conceptual grounds, and the structuralist-internalist about autonomy and responsibility would be decisively and deeply refuted. We wouldn't even have to consider specific historicist arguments about responsibility per se!

This strategy does have considerable dialectical appeal. In fact, a number of contributors to the debate have noted the relevance of issues from the theory of reference and mental content-ascription to the theory of autonomous agency.[7] But without exception they have brushed aside any serious pursuit of the strategy. In the short run, this is probably the greater part of theoretical valor, since these issues are so treacherously difficult. It *would* be terribly discouraging if nothing useful could be said about the essential structural and historical conditions of autonomous agency until the truth about the representational content of the very vehicles of practical reasoning could be settled once and for all!

Happily, the ongoing debate between historicists and structuralists over the conditions of autonomy has produced useful results without going into those difficult issues about reference and mental content. Some of this work rests on intuitions about the kinds of psychological structures and personal histories which sustain or compromise autonomous agency, which is just fine. Some of it takes us deeper, into issues involving people's control and lack of control over their actions and motivations. Thus, even though there is no lack of distinctly theoretical arguments in the field, the implicit consensus has been that there is only an analogy between the internalism/externalism debates in the philosophies of language and mind, on the one hand, and of autonomy and responsibility, on the other.[8] Mele argues for the strict independence of these disputes most crisply:

> *Whatever* position one takes on the individuation of psychological states generally, internalism *and* externalism about psychological autonomy [in particular] are options. For example, an internalist about psychological states may view psychological autonomy as more than just a psychological state and as having a nonpsychological, historical component, and an externalist about psychological states might deem [doppelgangers] equally psychologically autonomous . . . , in virtue of their shared psychological capacities and abilities and their matching exercises thereof [despite their radically different personal histories, one involving the normal acquisition of values and desires through education and habituation, the other involving neurological manipulation].[9]

Call this the *Independence Thesis*. Is it true? Would it matter one way or the other if it were?

To doubt its truth and to insist that this issue does matter is not to doubt that there are other theoretical issues about the structural and historical conditions of autonomy to be explored quite independently of the structural and historical conditions of reference-fixing and semantic content. For example, there is serious work to be done about the nature of *essentially historical* phenomena and whether autonomous agency is among them.[10] And there are those theoretical issues, just alluded to, about the forms of *control* necessary and sufficient for autonomy.[11] But obviously, the more theoretical backing a view about autonomous agency can garner, the better. Therefore, if it were to turn out (contra the Independence Thesis) that externalism about mental content is *in*compatible with internalism about autonomy (or vice versa), this would be a powerful result that ought to constrain further work on the conditions of autonomous agency per se. Or so I shall argue here.

After briefly sketching in the next section what I take to be the the core of the dispute between externalists and internalists in the theory of responsibility, I explore in the rest of the paper what I take to be some of the links of mutual dependence between ideas about how reference and mental content are fixed and ideas about the conditions on autonomous agency. Although I do not have quite the courage to plump foursquare for internalism down the line, I do conclude that the Independence Thesis is false in at least one direction and that the very idea of "instant autonomous agency" is perfectly coherent (even if bizarre). Defending both ideas does, I suppose, amount to defending limited versions of internalism about both mental content and autonomous agency. (Just how limited is for the reader to judge.)

Historicists about responsibility complain that accounts like Frankfurt's give us a mere "snapshot" or "current time-slice" of the responsible agent whereas we also need "home-movies" containing "flashbacks" that provide information about how the person came to acquire the crucial components of his or her motivational system. (The first pair of quoted expressions are Fischer's and Ravizza's; the second pair are mine.) But their complaint cannot simply be that structuralists completely ignore *any* consideration of the *local* causal provenance of individual beliefs and desires, for it is hard to think of anyone who fails to acknowledge the standard excusing conditions, like ignorance, accident and coercion, or the standard exempting conditions, like extreme immaturity, severe insanity, and the various forms of "induction" and "implantation" of beliefs and desires replete in the literature.

Frankfurt certainly acknowledges them repeatedly. Moreover, even though he does reject the standard "principle of alternate possibilities," he does embrace a restricted version of it that specifies that a person is excused or exempted from responsibility for doing an action if he does it "*only because* he could not have done otherwise."[12] This is enough to entail that for him certain kinds of causal origin do matter to a person's current responsibility. Who, then, are these "pure mesh-theorists" supposed to be, and how have they completely failed to learn the lessons of personal history?

One answer, I think, is that the dispute has often been misconceived as a conflict between "current time-slice" conceptions of autonomy and those responsive to some temporal facts or other. But, as I have argued at greater length elsewhere,[13] the issue of temporal slices versus temporal stretches is strictly a red herring, for no structuralist should wish to deny that the psychological facts that ground autonomous agency involve *processes* that, of course, occupy temporal stretches. Frankfurt, for example, gives pride of place to "taking responsibility," which is clearly a psychological process involving reflection upon and adjudication among one's first-order desires and their objects.[14] The historicist's worry is better posed as a distinctly *externalist* concern that no merely internal psychological state, event, *or* process is enough to nullify the autonomy-compromising force of certain kinds of facts about an agent's *history in the world*. Thus, even though Frankfurt does acknowledge the force of such facts (via his restricted principle of alternative possibilities), he nonetheless does insist that *current internal* processes are enough to nullify them and thereby reestablish an agent's autonomy. (All the person has to do is somehow manage to identify with the inner products of these external factors.) Elsewhere, I have argued against this view, on the grounds that it makes excessive concession to objectionable Stoic ideas about freedom-as-adaptation-to-necessity.[15]

However, one can reject this aspect of Frankfurt's program without embracing the externalist-historicist idea that certain kinds of history in the world, including certain kinds of origins, are necessary if an individual is to count now as truly autonomous. The test case is the phenomenon of "instant autonomous agency." The focal question about it is whether an individual who has literally been "born (or perhaps manufactured) yesterday," equipped with the sort of complex psychology that both sides would admit would be a sufficient basis for genuine agency but for its odd origins, is nonetheless capable of autonomous agency despite those very origins. If the answer is yes, then not only is the Independence Thesis shown to be false, but limited versions of internalism about both semantic content and autonomous agency are vindicated.

3. THE INDEPENDENCE THESIS

One half of the Independence Thesis is incontrovertible. Not even the most devoted adherent of "narrow content" would wish to deny that some autonomy-subverting factors are external to a person's current psychology. Not even the most fervent adherent of "methodological solipsism considered as a research strategy in cognitive psychology" would wish to exclude facts about a person's past-in-the-world from the conditions that ground his autonomy in the present. Not even the most committed proponent of the "cluster-description" theory of reference-fixing would wish to deny that certain causal-historical stories determine (in part, anyway) whether people are autonomous now.[16]

It is the other half of the Independence Thesis that is seriously in doubt. For reasons briefly sketched in Section 1, an externalist-historicist about reference-fixing and mental content-ascription could not consistently adhere to a strict internalist-structuralism about the conditions of *all* instances of autonomous agency. Here is the argument in slightly more detail.

Semantic externalism comes in two strengths. "Industrial-strength" externalism specifies that an individual's mental states can have *any content at all* only if he has acquired them via a limited range of types of causal processes. (There are many possible variations on this necessary condition.) Thus, on this view, a creature who simply pops into existence is barred from having content-bearing states like beliefs and wants simply by virtue of lacking the right kind of history in the external world (whatever that may be). Davidson's "swampman," a creature who rises full-blown from the mire fully equipped with the semblance of a more or less complete human psychology, is the most dramatic example in the literature. Davidson famously insists that, appearances notwithstanding, such a creature does not really have any beliefs, wants, and so forth.[17]

"Regular-strength" semantic externalism, on the other hand, specifies only that *variations* in the content of propositional attitudes expressed by the use of homophonic sentences are determined (in part anyway) by the language user's spatiotemporal situation in the world. Thus, in the most celebrated thought-experiment of them all, Tim-on-Earth and Twim-on-Twin-Earth entertain different thoughts when they expostulate: "My, that glass of water was refreshing!" (The details are too familiar to need rehearsing.)

Industrial strength semantic externalism has the clearer implications for the debate over the conditions of autonomous agency, so let's start with it. The argument is pretty straightforward (as these things go):

First premise: As noted, strong semantic internalism holds that an individual can have any content-bearing propositional attitudes at all only if it is appropriately embodied and embedded in the world. (I pass over the question of what the "appropriately" amounts to, except to note that an "instant agent" like the swampman clearly fails to satisfy the condition.)

Second premise: An autonomous agent must be able to engage in practical reasoning. (That's pretty much definitive of what autonomy is all about.)

Third premise: But practical reasoning requires some kind of vehicle. In folk psychology, these are propositional attitudes like wants and beliefs.

Fourth premise: But since no individual can have content-bearing propositional attitudes unless he is appropropriately embodied and embedded, an instant agent has none, because he certainly is not so embodied and embedded.

Fifth premise: But since having such attitudes is necessary (though of course not sufficient) for functioning as an autonomous agent, the very idea of an instant autonomous agent is incoherent.

In short, the conditions of genuine autonomy demand that an autonomous agent have had "world enough and time" to establish his semantic credentials.

Of course, the most this argument establishes is an incompatibility claim: that you cannot be both a strong semantic externalist and an internalist about the autonomous agency of *certain sorts* of individuals. It certainly does not establish the truth of industrial-strength semantic internalism, and thus (assuming the argument is valid) the falsity of internalism about autonomy for those cases. That would be a tall order indeed. But perhaps we can make some headway toward establishing some nonconditional conclusions about the necessary grounding of autonomy, by considering the contrapositive of the key conditional in the argument. If a reasonably good prima facie case could be made for the coherence of instant agency, then it would provide a reasonably good prima facie case for doubting industrial-strength semantic externalism. Thus in the bargain one formidable argument for externalism about autonomy in all cases would have been tamed. (We can turn to the implications of weak semantic externalism later.)

Nor does the argument establish the incompatibility of semantic-externalism with autonomy-internalism *across the board*. (Thus the italized qualification in the first sentence of the previous paragraph.) For this combination is certainly possible in some of the test cases offered in the dispute between internalists and externalists about autonomy per se. For example, Mele invites us to consider the tale of Ann and Beth. Both are philosophy professors, but Ann is by far the more focused on the discipline itself, whereas Beth finds fulfillment, not only in writing and teaching, but also in a rich life including a wide range of other sorts of activities and relationships. The dean of the college wants more production out of Beth and does not much care how he gets it, so he sets upon her a team of neurologists who implant in her *Ann's* hierarchy of values. After the global induction, Beth is "in the relevant respect, 'a psychological twin of Ann.'"[18]

Question: Does Beth set about her single-minded daily business of teaching, writing, talking, and thinking philosophy *as autonomously* as Ann does? Mele's externalist answer is *no*, which seems quite right. But a resolute internalist about autonomy could resist this conclusion on the Frankfurtian grounds that each agent is at present fully capable of "decisive wholehearted identification" with such an intensely philosophical life. Moreover, such an autonomy-internalist could consistently embrace any externalist constraint on genuine belief-ascription that a Putnam or a Burge might care to impose, for preinduction Beth (presumably) did have the kind of embedded and embodied history in the world that semantic-externalists insist is necessary for entertaining genuine propositional attitudes. Thus in this kind of case, semantic-externalism *is* compatible with autonomy-internalism.[19] Therefore, for purposes of pursuing this inquiry into the plausibility of the Independence Thesis (in one direction), I will stick to "instant agents" who are utterly without the (allegedly) requisite external histories of concept-acquisition.

4. SEX, LIES, AND FADED PHOTOGRAPHS: AN INTUITION PUMP

There are, however, instant agents and instant agents. Some, like Davidson's swampman, spring full-blown from we know not where. Another example of agency-ex-nihilo closer to home is Mele's "Athena, who magically comes into existence with a wealth of beliefs, desires and values in place . . . [who] has and exercises a potent capacity for critical reflection . . . [and] a robust ability to shed each of her pro-attitudes."[20] Mele suggests that "other things being equal, there is no bar to Athena's autonomously possessing her pro-attitudes."[21] If this were true, then she would count as an exception to Mele's general historicist-externalism about autonomous agency.

But because Athena counts as such an exception only by virtue of conditions very specific to Mele's account of autonomy, consideration of which here would distract us from the main argument,[22] I would prefer to focus on a second kind of instant agent, one that is *manufactured or fabricated* with a number of impressive features, including the basic capacities for practical reasoning (involving, at least, procedural and instrumental rationality), a full (-ish) complement of basic values and beliefs about the world in general and beliefs about how its desires in particular are (probably) to be realized. But since I want these instant agents to be as realistic as possible, I do not stipulate that they are so adept at critical reflection that all their basic desires are (in Mele's nice phrase) "practically sheddable." Some they are simply stuck with by virtue of their "programming" (such as one science fiction author's "rule for cyborgs": "Don't harm your creator!").

On the other hand, I do not wish to rule out a realistic degree of adaptability, grounded for example in their ability to learn from the environment and thus to acquire new values as they make their way in the world. The point is that, unlike human children, they start out with psychologies more or less like those of the average adult person-in-the-street. The focal question, then, is whether the oddity of their origins, and especially of the origins of their basic wants and beliefs, bars these instant agents from immediately undertaking autonomous actions, projects, and the like that spring from the practical deliberation that their psychological capacities (prima facie, anyway) permit them to engage in.

The instant agents that already exist in artificial intelligence (AI) and in robotics are too limited in one way or another for our purposes. Either they operate in accordance with highly articulated and complex rules and heuristics, but have such narrow "interests" and not much of a *lebenswelt* (such as computers running chess-playing and medical diagnostic programs), or they are environmentally more mobile and plastic, even quite lifelike, but never manage to move beyond the behavioral repetoire of a moderately intelligent insect (such as Rodney Brooks's coke-can-collecting "mobots," celebrated for demonstrating the advantages of being "fast, cheap and out of control.")[23] It would be nice if AI and robotics could somehow manage to combine the virtues of each approach while avoiding their shortcomings, but so far this is just a dream. Therefore, in our investigation of the coherence of instant autonomous agency, we will have to resort to the philosophically time-honored method of drawing on science fiction. (Some consider this no better than "pulp philosophy," but we shall simply have to weather their scorn.)[24]

There are lots of "cyborgs" and "androids" to choose from. To fix our ideas about instant autonomous agency, let us focus on those in Ridley Scott's film *Blade Runner.*[25] In a futuristic Los Angeles, all darkly misty and claustrophobic, the title character, a professional assassin (played by Harrison Ford) is hired to track down and "retire" a group of renegade "replicants" who have rebelled against their servitude and set out upon a violent, vengeful rampage. (Perhaps they have been consumed by a wave of Kantian indignation at having been created so expressly to serve as "mere means.") These cyborgs are remarkably sophisticated, lifelike humanoids, manufactured from organic material, equipped with a large repetoire of intellectual and emotional capacities and a realistic complement of personality and character traits.

For reasons never quite explained in film or novel, some of the replicants are also equipped at creation with full and vivid "memories" of nonexistent personal pasts ("quasi memories," in the parlance of memory-continuity theories of personal identity). Perhaps Scott and Dick are slipping in a Russellian thought-experiment; more likely, they include this Proustian accessory simply to help these replicants to do their jobs more efficiently, aided by the belief that they are real human beings. Let's focus on one of the replicants for whom this utterly false conviction might well make her job easier, a young "woman" (played by Sean Young) who serves as hostess, secretary, personal assistant, and, one suspects, mistress to the powerful man who hires the blade runner. (She seems to be a kind of "intern.")

Sean Young is the one who greets Harrison Ford when he shows up to be briefed for his deadly assignment. She is elegantly beautiful and haughtily distant, but of course we can tell that she finds the blade runner curiously attractive under that gruff, crude exterior. (It's a movie, after all.) There is real sexual tension in the air as she gives him his preliminary briefing. The conversation gradually moves on to more personal matters. She tells him about her girlhood in the Midwest; she shows him her tattered box of "keepsakes" and faded photographs of her "mother" and the house she "grew up" in; she weeps a bit with nostalgia for a simpler, happier time. Harrison Ford consoles her; they are clearly heading for an affair.

The sex is real enough, but the memories, the keepsakes, the faded photographs are all lies, planted by her creators to sustain the illusion that she is a real person with a past. And sure enough, with all this talk of replicants and the tests Harrison Ford knows for distinguishing them from real human beings, Sean Young gradually comes to have doubts about herself. She persuades the blade runner to test her, with the predictable result. She is crushed by her new knowledge. Her whole "life" is a lie.

Is the idea of such intelligent, emotionally sensitive replicants even coherent? And if so, is it coherent to suppose that they would be able to function as autonomous agents, more or less as you and I do, making their way intentionally, deliberately, rationally, reasonably, sensibly, dutifully through the world? It would be most ill-advised to try to tackle such a question head on, since it lies at the epicenter of a long and contentious dispute over "artificial intelligence: the very idea."[26]

One side issue we can dispose of immediately is whether Sean Young could have functioned consistently as an autonomous agent *before* she learned that she was "born yesterday." Certainly not. Since she was so massively ignorant of the basic facts about how she acquired her basic values and motivations, and since excusable ignorance is an excusing condition, the *pre*revelation Sean Young would have been no more responsible for many of the things she did than a victim of posthypnotic suggestion is responsible for dancing around with a lampshade on his head at a professional dinner, all the time insisting that he is just trying to liven up a dull party.

It is the *post*revelation Sean Young who interests us, for she now knows full well how she came to be created and to acquire the basic features of her personality and character. (She knows a damn sight more than most of us, at that!) We should not, however, allow that she has been around too long before her access of self-knowledge because, for purposes of testing the Independence Thesis, we do not want her to have had an opportunity on her own to satisfy the externalist conditions of reference-fixing and semantic content. She is, after all, supposed to be an instant agent. So, let us simply stipulate that her debut in the world was the very moment she opened the door to greet the blade runner. Her creators carried her to the door, stood her on her legs, retreated to a discreet distance, turned on the switch, and watched the show unfold. We can imagine that after hearing the knock, she stood there for a few moments wondering who could be calling at this inconvenient hour when she would much rather be alone in her room reveling in bittersweet reminiscence about her happy but forever lost girlhood. Thereafter, the scenario unfolds as rehearsed, save that Sean Young's self-knowledge comes very quickly, and she sets about moving and acting in the world long before she herself could possibly have satisfied all those constraints imposed by semantic externalists. (Davidson would consider her no better than a "swampwoman.")

Our question, then, is whether Sean Young the replicant qualifies as an autonomous agent from the very moment she acquires her self-knowledge (and can thus no longer plead ignorance of her origins as an excuse). Before we become too intimidated by the prospect of answering one of the deepest questions in the philosophy of mind-and-language, let us remind ourselves that *our* question is not (1) whether externalism is the correct view about how referential import and semantic content get fixed. It may not even be (2) whether "narrow content" (hereafter no scare quotes) is enough for purposes of providing third-person psychological explanations of action. It *is* a question about (3) whether narrow content is enough to sustain those propositional attitudes that function as necessary vehicles for the first-person practical reasoning of autonomous agents.

To suppose that these are different issues is by no means uncontroversial. Many philosophers would insist that externalism as a view about assigning linguistic content rises or falls together with externalism as a view about ascribing mental content. Of course, if this "unifying conception" of the dialectic were true, it would be a lot harder to prise apart questions (2) and (3) from the truly daunting question (1). (Not that any of them is easy.) However, for purposes of exploring the plausibility of the Independence Thesis, I shall provisionally assume that these questions can be prised apart. Or, if not simpy assume so, at least consider some of the more formidable (alleged) obstacles to the very idea of instant psychological subjecthood, in the hope that I can render the provisional assumption more plausible and thus weaken resistance to the very idea of instant autonomous agency.

5. "HAD SHE BUT WORLD ENOUGH AND TIME": SEVERAL PSYCHO-SEMANTIC PROBLEMS WITH THE VERY IDEA OF INSTANT SUBJECTHOOD

Doubters about artificial subjecthood, instant or otherwise, have stressed several difficulties.

1. *Holistic* constraints on propositional attitude-possession render it (at worst) impossible in theory and (at best) dauntingly difficult in practice to equip a fabricated subject with *enough* beliefs about the world for it to count as having any beliefs at all.[27]
2. But even if such a subject were able to entertain enough propositional attitudes to have any propositional attitudes at all, it would still face the "frame problem" of making them *managably accessible for effective cognition.*[28]
3. And finally, the fabricated subject has (ex hypothesi) not been moving around long enough in the world of objects (including other language users) to have established the right kind of causal-historical rapport with them in order to be able to refer to them and thus to engage in meaningful discourse.[29]

In the philosophy of mind-language these are real problems, of course.[30] *Our* question is the somewhat narrower one of whether they are serious enough to prevent an instant agent from making her way around the world autonomously, *however* the general issues of linguistic reference and psychological explanation are ultimately to be settled. Our more limited question is whether Sean Young (and her creators) should worry about them (and, of course, whether an instant subject can worry about them, or anything at all).

5.1. Holistic Constraints

When Eliza Doolittle makes her famous meteorological pronouncement, do the words she utters have any referential import? (For example, does "rain" refer to rain in good Tarskian fashion?) Probably so, for word-reference is not really a problem here. But does Eliza herself express any belief at all about the incidence and location of precipitation on the flatter bits of the larger Iberian country? Probably not, for Professor Higgins has "installed" in her the capacity to utter the famous sentence in plummy King's English in order to win his wager with Colonel Pickering. Passable phonology, not referential success, is the point, and pretty much all that Eliza is capable of at the dress ball. Her principal semantic deficit, as she makes her way through the evening producing phonological strings like the famous one, is that she simply does not have enough other beliefs about relevant subjects and objects, notably Spanish geography, weather patterns in Iberia, and the like, to count as having any beliefs at all about her chosen topic of "conversation." In short, she fails to satisfy the most basic "holistic" constraints on genuine speaker-reference and belief-possession. And failing to satisfy them, she can hardly count as a "true believer" as she makes her way with *faux majesté* through the evening. And failing to count as a true believer, she can hardly count as a genuinely autonomous agent. Rather, she is the professor's puppet. Is Sean Young consigned to the same fate?

The point of my priming that intuition pump was, of course, to suggest that she is spared this fate, not for failing holistic requirements on genuine speaker-reference and belief-possession, anyway. To be sure, *before* the awful revelation that all of her "memory beliefs" are false, some accounts of belief-ascription would bar her from having any memory beliefs at all. But *after* the revelation she knows all about Sean; in any event, from the very moment her creators carry her to the door and switch her on, she is (ex hypothesi) equipped with a vast set of dispositions to utter appropriate sentences upon appropriate prompting, and even to produce her fair share of them spontaneously. *You* try to resist taking up the intentional stance toward her. Harrison Ford certainly couldn't resist (but then his intentions were less honorable than yours).

Of course, in taking my cue from an author and a film director in making this sort of stipulation about our instant agent I do run the risk of purveying "pulp philosophy," the hand-waving deployment of bizarre fictional examples without serious intellectual constraint. This is not the place to try to defend the use of odd examples and thought-experiments in philosophy,[31] but I should try to say at least a little about the continuing debate over the very possibility of creating artificial subjects with large enough belief sets to counts as intelligent cognizers, and even autonomous agents.

The issue is often taken to be about the possibility *in principle* of creating such individuals. Whether this is a particularly good way of posing the problem is itself up for grabs, because in the debates over the very possibility of building sufficiently large and effectively organized knowledge bases employing sentential elements (as opposed to distributed networks which learn more or less from the ground up), the line between the conceptual and the empirical problem, between the a priori and the a posteriori constraint on the enterprise, is never easy to draw with confidence. For example, H. Dreyfus and S. Dreyfus, among the most persistent critics of the very idea of computationalist AI, raise what look to be both kinds of worries. On the one hand, they acknowledge (grudgingly) that if certain computationalist projects were to succeed (like Douglas Lenat's CYC project, an attempt to create an enormous database of usable information—Dennett characterizes it as "the proverbial walking encyclopedia"),[32] then the computationalist framework for AI would still be in business, which makes it sound as though this approach to modeling human cognition is hostage to merely *empirical* and *practical* fortune.

On the other hand, they and other critics have more consistently pressed what look to be deep *conceptual* objections to the very possibility of classical cognitivist simulations, having to do with subtle issues involving the sententially unmodelable context-sensitivity of much human thought, the ineffability of the truly important texture of human *Dasein*.[33] One notes, however, that with the emergence of serious connectionist models of human cognition the Dreyfuses and other critics of AI have eased up a bit on the question of "what computers (still) can't do." (Evidently, Heidegger would have been quite at home with parallel distributed processing.) This suggests that the remaining conceptual objections to strong AI and thus to artificial autonomous agency may not apply to individuals designed and built as systematically related sets of connectionist networks. Committed in no particularly strong way to classical cognitivism, I have little objection to conceiving of Sean Young in this alternative fashion. (For all I know, that's how you and I should be conceived.)

There is a catch, however. Our topic is *instant* autonomous agency, our protagonist an artificial autonomous agent *without a history of her own*. But one of the principal virtues of connectionist networks as models of human cognition is supposed to be that they are so good at starting from the ground up and learning more or less on their own what they need to know, for example, how to produce acoustically recognizable phonological sequences or to recognize human faces or to distinguish torpedoes from submerged rocks. But this means that, if the conceptual difficulties with constructing sufficiently large and effectively organized conventional cognitivist systems are truly insoluble, and we must instead conceive of Sean Young as a set of such self-teaching parallel distributed processing (PDP) networks, then we have squandered an opportunity to model *instant* autonomous agency. For like all existing connectionist networks, she will start out with only the basic PDP architecture and then proceed to learn *on her own* how to make her way around in the world. But this *takes time*. Indeed, if she is eventually to learn enough about the human *lebenswelt* to function as a genuine autonomous agent who can make grown-up decisions, it will no doubt take *a lot of time*. But this would defeat the whole point of our enterprise of modeling *instant* autonomous agency.

We face here a familiar trade-off. In modeling cognition, where should the larger burden lie: on the modeler to provide the device from the very beginning with a sufficiently large knowledge base so that it can get a fair launch on its cognitive life, or on the device itself to start with only a minimal cognitive architecture and then deploy it as best it can to assemble on its own a sufficiently large knowledge base to launch its own cognitive life? Classical cognitivist theorists bear the first burden; PDP networks bear the second. Either way, there is no free launch.

My main goal in this paper is to show that the Independence Thesis is wrong (in at least one direction), so my preference would be to place the heavier burden on the cognitive modeler, in order to guarantee that the device is equipped ab initio with the resources necessary to carry on in the world as an instant autonomous agent. However, if the neo-Heideggerian Dreyfusards are correct, this may not be an option. We may be forced from the beginning to place the heavier burden on the device to do her own learning for herself, in which case there will be little that is "instant" about her resulting exercise of autonomous agency. (This is a point where one can see the link between specifically externalist theses about reference-fixing, on the one hand, and holistic constraints on belief-possession, on the other, a link that I hope justifies my expending some effort on the latter, not directly externalist, concern about modeling belief-systems.)

There may be just enough room to wiggle out of this difficulty. Commenting on the "allure of the connectionist program," Paul Smolensky remarks

> that many of the connectionist networks *program themselves*, that is, they have autonomous procedures for tuning their weights to eventually perform some specific computation. These *learning procedures* often depend on training in which the network is provided with sample input-output pairs from the function it is supposed to compute . . . the network itself "decides" what computations the hidden units will perform . . . they are never "told" what their values should be, even during training.[34]

I take away two consoling thoughts from this passage. First, "allure" is not "necessary feature" and "many" connectionist networks are not "all" of them. Therefore, Smolensky seems to leave open the possibility that there might be PDP networks, or artificial cognitive systems that include PDP networks, that start out their careers not only with labeled input nodes and learning procedures (like the "delta rule") but also with some fair amount of "a priori" substantive knowledge about their world, represented either in previously "trained up" networks or in some kind of classical cognitivist format like "frames" or "scripts." These need not involve the massively encyclopedic amount of knowledge encoded in a model like Lenat's CYC project, but they do need enough to get them up and running immediately in the exercise of recognizably autonomous agency. (However, such hybrid systems may turn out to have all the appeal of Jeff Goldblum in David Cronenberg's movie *The Fly*.) Second, Smolensky describes even those connectionist networks that lack such a priori substantive knowledge in the language of autonomous agency, which gives *some* purchase to the idea that even they might be counted as instant agents.

5.2. Frame Constraints

In John Le Carré's novel *A Murder of Quality*, spymaster George Smiley remarks of a public schoolboy who has been murdered because his cribbing for an exam made him privy to information that would compromise the person who committed the murder that got the whole plot rolling, "First the boy knew too little, and then he knew too much." This is roughly the position of our replicant if she starts out as a worldy-wise classical computational system, for having solved one problem for her (albeit by fiat), we have only created another. Our first worry was that Sean Young would not have enough beliefs to count as a true believer; now that she has so many she and her creators face a version of the "frame problem" in AI.

As before with holistic constraints on belief-possession, it is hard to say here whether frame constraints stand as a daunting conceptual problem with the very idea of instant autonomous agency or a "merely" practical problem plaguing the engineers. Dennett has remarked of it: "the 'frame problem' of Artificial Intelligence which arises for planning systems that must reason about the effects of contemplated actions . . . is either the most difficult problem AI must—and eventually can—solve, or the *reductio ad absurdum* of mental representation theory."[35] Since I do intend Sean Young to function as a "planning system that must reason about contemplated actions" ("Should I ask the blade runner to give me the replicant test?" "If it's positive should I flee from him?"), it would be wise to give the frame problem and its corollary for replicants a quick glance. Dennett usefully directs our gaze: "the minimal goal that can spawn the frame problem . . . concerns how to represent (so it can be *used*) all that *hard-won* empirical information—a problem that arises independently of the truth value, probability, warranted assertability, or subjective certainty of any of it."[36] I include the bit about the truth- and epistemic-values of the system's beliefs to prepare the way for the next section, in which we consider just how much accurate rapport with the real world an instant agent has to have had in the past in order to meet the basic constraints on successful reference in the present. But for now let's focus on a different aspect of the frame problem. Dennett notes that the information that creates it is "hard-won," but this is not a hard and fast condition on the very possibility of such action-oriented knowledge systems. For Dennett also considers the possibility that "people in AI can frankly ignore the problem of learning . . . and take the shortcut of *installing* all that an agent has to 'know' to solve a problem."[37] And though he does acknowledge that "this may be a dangerous shortcut," the existence of an "installation problem" seems inessential to the existence of the frame problem itself or to prospects for its solution. Whether the information the system will need is "hard-won" by the device itself or "installed" in one go by its creators, the problem remains the same: what can serve as a useful format for representing and efficiently deploying all that information the device will need in carrying out the general task of making its way autonomously around the world?

It would make no sense to try to say much of anything here about a problem that has puzzled, or a solution that has eluded, so many. Suffice it to note the obvious: we human beings *do* solve the frame problem somehow or other. To be sure, our solution does involve processes of *learning*, the gradual pace of which no doubt makes it more manageable for us to assemble the formats needed for the effective deployment of information about the world. (Though, of course, it does remain a vexing question in cognitive science just how many of these formats and bits of substantive knowledge are innate and how many are learned.) However, it does not follow from the fact that we do so much of this assembling *gradually* that the *instant*-installation problem for artificial knowledge systems cannot be solved with considerable help from an eventual explanation of how *we diachronically* render the frame problem tractable. To be sure, this order of explanation would thoroughly puncture the ambitions of proponents of *strong* AI to lead the way in providing illuminating models of actual human cognition, but that's no concern of mine. Absent independent arguments for the conclusion that only biological systems produced by natural selection can instantiate those psychological states needed for autonomous agency, it is an open empirical question whether a solution to the frame problem for *gradually developing* human beings will bring in its wake a solution to the installation problem for *instant* autonomous agents. A bare conceptual possibility and some empirical prospect of ultimate success are all I need for my argument here.

But Sean Young is not out of the woods yet. Even if it were to prove conceptually possible and practically feasible to install a sufficiently large number of "propositional attitudes" in her for her to satisfy the holistic constraint on having any propositional attitudes at all, and to install formats that enable her to deploy her "wants" and "beliefs" effectively as vehicles of practical reasoning (the scare quotes are meant to signal that there are questions here up for begging, quite independently of holistic and frame constraints; addressing these problems is the theme of the next section), she still might not count as a genuine instant subject, let alone an instant autonomous agent, for after all, she was born yesterday.

5.3. Causal-Historical and Teleological Constraints

But why should that be a problem for a totally fabricated, autonomous Sean Young? The suggested answers on offer are dauntingly complicated, but we can probably make do here with simplified versions of two important lines of argument that suggest that the very idea of an instant language-using, and therefore instant practical-reasoning, subject is incoherent.

The first line of argument I have already alluded to in the Introduction. Hilary Putnam (among others) insists that certain historical-externalist constraints on successful speaker-reference bar an apparent language-user from actually entertaining referentially meaningful thoughts about the objects that the words she produces seem to be about. Suppose, for example, that a brain-in-a-vat were to produce the following sentence (by means of some kind of rigged-up transducer): "If the weather is dry this afternoon and his arthritis doesn't bother him, Rodolfo and I are going to hop on the Concorde and have a delightful picnic under the elm trees in the Bois de Boulogne." Putnam and other causal-historical theorists of word- and speaker-reference would deny that the encased brain has managed to say anything at all about the topic at hand, despite the impeccable appearance of sprightly discourse, on the grounds that it completely lacks the requisite sort of causal rapport with the objects the sentence seems to be about, arthritis, Rodolfo, airplanes, Paris, picnics, elm trees, the Bois de Boulogne, and so forth. (The semantics of *self*-reference creates special problems that I shall not try to pursue here.)[38] In our dialectical context the fear is that Sean Young, our candidate for instant autonomous agency, is no better off than Putnam's brain-in-a-vat, because at the very moment she is carried to the door and switched on she has had no more rapport with the objects she proceeds to "discourse" about than the poor encased organ in Putnam's lab. And failing to have that linguistic ability would entail that she also would fail to have genuine control over the vehicles of practical reasoning.

The second line of argument maintains that any subject who is able to engage in any kind of cognition, including that which sustains genuine practical (and therefore autonomous) reasoning, must have acquired her dispositions to linguistic behavior as the result of a certain kind of selectionist history. For human beings this (presumably) involves natural selection; for language-using artifacts (if any) it involves artificial selection and the intentional design of cognitive scientists and engineers. (Though many philosophers would insist that the best that artificial selection produces is "derived intentionality.")[39]

The first line of argument is supposed to rule out as language-users organisms and artifacts that are too ill-situated in the world of objects to be able to refer to them, regardless of whether their own causal provenance involves the appropriate kind of selection. The second argument is supposed to rule out systems that, though reasonably well situated in the world of objects right now, nonetheless completely lack the right sort of selectionist history. Strictly speaking, Sean Young faces only the first putative difficulty; but we can broaden our cases to include literally instant agents who spring full-blown into existence ex nihilo and thus face the second one. Mele's "Athena" and Davidson's "swampman" are vivid examples. Both of the putative difficulties we shall consider here involve a cognizing system's history in the external world, just different aspects of it, so it is natural to consider them together.

5.3.1. *Building real rapport.* Consider one the first sentences Sean Young utters to Harrison Ford after she has been switched on, opened the door to greet him, made a bit of small talk for awhile and then offers her rebuff-excuse for not having dinner with him that evening. It's the sentence mentioned just above about her picnicking plans with "Rodolfo" (her boss). Do the *words* she utters genuinely refer? Sure. It's not as though she is spouting some Edward Lear nonsense verse to distract him from his dishonorable intentions. Does *she* successfully refer to Rodolfo, arthritis, a picnic, elm trees, Paris, and so on? That's the tricky question. I take it that Putnam would deny that she does, not on the grounds that she has never actually been *en rapport* with these items, for that is true of many of us who do refer to items in unencountered portions of the world. (Though I've never encountered a drachma or a muon, I talk about them all the time.)

The real problem seems to be that the program her creators have installed in her before getting her up and running, which is, inter alia, a set of dispositions for her to utter sentences upon appropriate prompting (from the physically proximal and culturally distal environment), has hitherto lacked the right sorts of causal input and output relations with the apparent referents of the vocables she now utters. She is not exactly like the brain-in-the-vat once she is up and running in the actual world for obvious reasons, but before she was switched on she was its cognitive equivalent. Consider this comment by Putnam about the encased organ:

> How can the fact that, in the case of the brains in the vat, the language is connected by the program with sensory inputs which do not intrinsically or extrinsically represent trees (or anything external) possibly bring it about that the whole system of representation, the language-in-use, does refer to or represent trees or anything external? The answer is that it cannot. The whole system of sense-data, motor signals to efferent endings, and verbally or conceptually mediated thought connected by "language-entry rules" to the sense-data (or

> whatever) as inputs and by "language-exit rules" to the motor signals as outputs has no more connection to *trees* than [an ant who scurries around in the sand tracing a recognizable caricature of Winston Churchill has successfully *depicted* or *represented* Churchill]. . . . Once we see that the qualitative similarity . . . between the thoughts of the brains in a vat and the thoughts of someone in the actual world by no means implies sameness of reference, it is not hard to see that there is no basis at all for regarding the brain in a vat as referring to external things.[40]

To be sure, the actual *lebenswelten* of the brain in the vat and of Sean Young *before* she is set loose in the world are pretty much the same in just the way that Putnam describes. But loath as I am to challenge a claim about the causal-historical conditions of successful speaker-reference pressed by one of the progenitors of the whole idea that "meanings ain't in the head," it does seem to me that Putnam is being a bit too restrictive here about what kinds of causal-historical paths from referents to cognitive systems are admissible for there to be genuine speaker-reference at the end of the day. Recall that Sean Young has been *designed* by a team of cognitive scientists and engineers some of whom (I presume) do satisfy any reasonable condition on successful speaker-reference that a causal-historical externalist would wish to impose. Even without dwelling on details, we may note that it is well accepted in the field that some of the paths set by these conditions are rather circuitous and, one might say, widely distributed. (After all, Putnam himself stresses the "division of linguistic labor.") Therefore, it would be unreasonable of him to deny that a brain-in-a-vat, *suitably stimulated* and *suitably programmed* by *suitably competent language-users*, would be just about as able to refer successfully to elm trees as I am to drachmas and muons. And if we are considerably better off in the external-world-representing-enterprise than Putnam's scurrying ant, then why not Sean Young as well? And if she too qualifies straightaway as a true believer, then she too has command of the vehicles of practical reasoning and is thus in a position to function as an autonomous agent, her odd history notwithstanding.[41]

It is no part of my brief for the coherence of instant autonomous agency that a creature like Sean Young can or should be held responsible for actions she "remembers" having performed in her nonexistent past or for failing to honor commitments she "remembers" having made. For example, if she feels guilty for having harshly refused to visit "her mother" in "the cancer ward" before the unfortunate woman "died," after having faithfully "promised" that she would, then she shouldn't, for the obvious reason that she never made the promise and never broke it. My interest in Sean Young is more prospective: to argue that it is perfectly coherent to suppose that from the moment she is switched on and set loose in the external world, she can function as an autonomous agent there, even though she is a subject without a (real) past.

5.3.2. *Notional worlds for instant agents.* Thus far I have pretty much conceded to causal-externalist theorists of reference everything that they demand, but perhaps this is a mistake. Perhaps we can divide the agenda of issues a bit more finely than most are prepared to accept. This would be true, for example, if some of the conditions of interest to linguists and philosophers of language for fixing word- and even speaker-reference were distinct from the conditions of interest to cognitive psychologists for fixing the mental content that enters into explanations of action. I do realize that proponents of narrow content are a bit thin on the ground these days, what with the defection even of former devotees like Fodor.[42] But the idea is worth exploring in our dialectical context, because if the agenda can be divided, then perhaps a fabricated subject like Sean Young doesn't need quite the kind of rapport with the external world in order to function as a psychological subject who acts for reasons that Putnam demands of the brain-in-a-vat, even if he should turn out to be right that it and she fail the conditions for word- and speaker-reference. Perhaps the theory of referential and intentional content is not monolithic, in a way that opens up another avenue to successful practical reasoning for an instant autonomous agent.

There is a semifamous story about British idealist philosopher F. H. Bradley, who, finding himself in a railway carriage with a persistently inquisitive fellow passenger intent upon learning his occupation, finally replies: "I'm in notions" (provenance and accuracy unknown). If the agenda of issues in the theory(ies) of content can in fact be divided in the manner just gestured at, then this would also be a nice reply for Sean Young if a persistent externalist were to challenge on causal-historical grounds her ability to engage in genuine practical reasoning.

Daniel Dennett introduces a version of the idea we might offer Sean Young in his intriguing exploration of the vicissitudes of propositional and sentential attitude psychology, "Beyond Belief."[43] A question puzzling many is how an organ that is essentially a "syntactic engine," a manipulator of formal items, can also manage to function as a "semantic engine," a cognitive system operating with items with intentionality. Dennett suggests that some of the mystery can be dispelled by a retreat to the "*organismic contribution* to the fixation of propositional attitudes," to "what we get when we subtract facts about context or embedding from the determining whole," to "psychology in the narrow sense" (134–35, emphasis in the original). After struggling with some of the vicissitudes of *this* strategy (which need not concern us here), Dennett ends up "with you might say an intermediate position—halfway between syntax and semantics, the idea of 'notional world' . . . a sort of *fictional* world devised by the theorist, a third-party observer, in order to characterize the narrow psychological states of a subject" (152–53, emphasis in the original). For, he observes, "nowhere is it written that the environment relative to which we fix such a system's semantic properties must be a real environment, or the actual environment in which the system has grown up. A fictional, an idealized or imaginary environment, might do just as well" (154). If it turned out that Putnam were right that lack of a certain rapport with the external world subverts a cognitive subject's capacity for linguistic reference, Sean Young might still seek some refuge in her own notional world as a stage on which to play out her role as a full-fledged psychological subject, even an autonomous agent.

Lest it be thought that the idea of a notional world is exclusive to a sententialist conception of the vehicles of human or artificial cognition, consider these comments in one of the founding documents of connectionism:

> One way of thinking about distributed memories is in terms of a very large set of inference rules. Each active unit represents a "microfeature" of an item, and the connection strengths stand for plausible "microinferences" between

> microfeatures. Any particular pattern of activity of the units will satisfy some of the microfeatures and violate others. A stable pattern of activity is one that violates the plausible microinferences less than any of the neighboring patterns. . . . *[T]his view of memory makes it clear that there is no sharp distinction between genuine memory and plausible reconstruction.* A genuine memory is a pattern that is stable because the inference rules were modified when it occurred before. A "confabulation" is a pattern that is stable because of the way the inference rules have been modified to store several different patterns. *So far as the subject is concerned, this may be indistinguishable from the real thing.*[44]

I do not take Hinton et al. to be writing a brief here for any kind of skepticism about memory beliefs, but rather to be capturing roughly the idea of a notional world, cast in a connectionist format.[45]

Dennett himself, however, anticipates one objection to this happy outcome, which echoes, I think, the concerns of those (like Mele, and Fischer and Ravizza) who insist on the essential externalist-historicity of autonomous agency: "The naturalists will rightly insist that the actual environment as encountered has left its mark on the organism and intricately shaped it; the organism is in its present state *because of the history it has had*, and only such a history could in fact have put it in such a state." But with only a touch of uneasiness, he provides us (and Sean Young) with the needed reply: "in a thought-experimental mood we can imagine creating a duplicate whose *apparent* history was not its actual history. . . . The notional world we describe by extapolation from the current state is thus not exactly the world we take to have created that state, but rather the apparent world of the creature, the world apparent to to the creature as manifested in the creature's total dispositonal state." And then bringing the point squarely into our dialectical context, he concludes: "The strategy is not untried. Although notional attitude psychology has been concocted here as a response to the philosophical problems encountered in propositional attitude and sentential attitude psychology, it can easily be discerned to be the tacit methodology and ideology of a major branch of Artificial Intelligence."[46] And that is precisely what we were after: notional worlds populated with objects of the mental attitudes instant subjects will need if they are to function as autonomous agents.

But how is this strategy of dividing the agenda supposed to work? With the greatest forebearance on all sides, of course. Here's the idea: Externalist philosophers of language can ecumenically acknowledge that successful *psychological* explanations can sometimes (but not always) afford to be insensitive to *linguistically* relevant referential-cum-extensional differences in the specification and/or description of the *explananda* (who does what) and of the *explanans* (what they are aiming at and what they believe about how to get it).

Here are some examples. Putnam's original Twin-Earth cases[47] were designed to show (inter alia) that part of what fixes word- and speaker-reference is outside the language-user's head, out there in the world, as it were. But it is doubtful that psychologists, jurists, and others concerned with explanation, justification, and excuse always need to be concerned with the finer-grained aspects of reference. Suppose Tim and Twim, on Earth and Twin-Earth, respectively, are doppelganger-uncles tending their two-year-old doppelganger-nephews (Tyke and Twyke) as they take baths—in tubs filled with H_2O and XYZ, respectively, of course. Being doppelgangers, both uncles have psychologies with the same narrow content, and it is not pretty. Each is clever, avaricious, and brutally unconcerned about what it takes to get what he wants, which is his nephew's considerable fortune, held in trust until Tyke (Twyke) reaches twenty-one or dies, in which case it goes to Tim (Twim). The ugly dramas unfold in predictable fashion. Each uncle stages an "accidental" bathtub drowning, claims the inheritance, and starts to live high. To make two long stories short, each uncle is caught and eventually admits what he has done. Each tells the court, "I shoved my nephew's head under the bath water until he stopped breathing. Then I called 911 in a 'panic' to report the 'accident.'" And so forth. We all hope that at trial each uncle would be convicted for his awful act, but it is most unlikely that the prosecutors on Earth and Twin-Earth would bother to call expert witnesses (Putnam and his doppelganger, perhaps) to testify about the chemical composition of the actual referent of "water" as it occurs in each uncle's confession. This information is simply not relevant to the psychological explanation of what Tim and Twim have done, nor to the assessment of the justifiability of their actions nor to each uncle's responsibility for doing what he did. For explanatory and forensic purposes, the court cares only, one might say, about narrow content. But this parochial focus shouldn't trouble an externalist, anti-individualist philosopher of *language* one whit.

One could multiply examples of this sort indefinitely (product liability cases involving bogus *arthritis* remedies in Los Angeles and Twin–Los Angeles, and the like), but I will spare the reader. I hope the point about a reasonable "division of explanatory and justificatory labor" is convincing enough on the strength of this one. However, some externalist anti-individualists about propositional-cum-mental content would still be inclined to object that introducing such a division of labor into the theory of content simply multiplies entities beyond explanatory necessity. "Why not a *univocal* notion of content?" they protest.[48] This is a perfectly sensible question, and in the end the anti-individualists may carry the day. But an equally sensible reply is that simplicity constraints often cut both ways. In the case of the murderous uncles, why burden a perfectly straightforward psychological explanation with messy and irrelevant details about the chemical composition of the murder weapon? (If the murder were a poisoning, okay, but I am assuming H_2O and XYZ are equally good asphyxiants.)[49]

5.3.3. *Semantic content without selection (natural or otherwise).* The second historicist line of argument against the very idea of instant cognitive subjecthood (and by implication, against instant autonomous agency) relies on a certain view about the teleological basis of psycho-linguistic phenomena like reference and intentionality.[50] We shall have to be satisfied here with a vastly oversimplified version of the story, which goes something like this. Reference and intentionality are theoretically grounded in the idea of *X's having a function*. That phenomenon is in turn theoretically grounded in the idea of *X's regularly* (if not necessarily invariantly) *having a certain kind of consequence C*. But that is still not enough: it must also be true that *X now exists and produces C because X was selected for precisely because it produces C.*[51] Thus certain physical event-types have reference and intentionality because they have certain functions, and they have those functions because they were selected to produce certain results. The order of explanation takes us from *content* to *function* to *history of being selected for*. No *history* of selection, no intentional or referential *content*.

That's the idea in broad outline. Here's a *slightly* more detailed version of the story. Vocable (and other appropriate physical) event-types come to have reference and meaning by virtue of a history of sufficient covariance between their tokenings and the presence of things and the obtaining of states of affairs in the world (construed broadly). This covariance need not be perfect or even very reliable, as long as it is sustained by some appropriate mechanism of selection. If the historical emergence of reference and intentionality is Darwinian, then the mechanism is natural selection: thus an event-type like the-utterance-of-"tiger" comes to have the function of referring to tigers if and only if there exists a sufficiently robust history of appropriate covariance that is sustained specifically by the fact that a sufficient number of its instances make the appropriate biological contribution to the selective advantage of the creatures who produce these tokenings . . . or something like that. To say that this is a caricature of the sort of theory that philosophers like Millikan and Dretske have been developing for some years is this year's biggest understatement. But even the caricature enables us to state the second historicist objection.

You can see how this selectionist-teleological story might tell against the cognitive subjecthood of Mele's Athena or Davidson's swampman, creatures who simply spring full-blown into existence equipped (let us say) with a complement of psychological dispositions isomorphic with those of normal adult human beings. Suppose that they are the proverbial doppelgangers, respectively, of Melina, the most popular café owner in Crete, and that garrulous guy Clem who takes tourists on boat rides through the Everglades. To be sure, Athena and the swampman are disposed to behave pretty much the same way Melina and Clem do (allowing for whatever differences in location and the like we might wish to add to the story). They can tell funny stories, order around their employees, refuse to work on Sundays, and so on. Put less question-beggingly, they are disposed to utter all the same sentence-types (merely vocable-string-types?) under all the same sorts of conditions in which Melina and Clem are disposed to utter theirs: from the very beginning of their existences, "heterophenomenologically," so to speak.[52] Athena is indistinguishable from Melina and the swampman from Clem. ("They could be twins, clones even! Have you ever seen them in the same room together?")

But there's a catch, the bio-semanticists will protest:

> Melina and Clem are members of the species *homo sapiens sapiens*, therefore products of generations of evolution, a long, arduous process involving random variations within populations of organisms, the increased rate of reproduction and thus the selective survival of some of them, under the pressures imposed by the environments they have had to contend with. In this happy instance, the species of organisms selected for includes creatures like Melina and Clem, primates who stand upright (most of the time), have large brains, are possessed of a rich range of psychological capacities, including the capacity to speak natural languages and thus to do all the other things this remarkable capacity makes possible. But Athena and the swampman? Upstarts . . . No

> breeding at all . . . mere *arrivistes* in the high society of cognition. Remember! No history of selection, no content!

I do not know if any actual proponent of teleological semantics has ever told the story in quite such stark terms. For one thing, concessions are usually made to the power of *artificial* selection in engineering design to ground reference and intentionality (sometimes with grudging labels like "derived intentionality," sometimes in a more egalitarian spirit). This qualification is, however, irrelevant to our current concern for, unlike Sean Young, neither Athena nor the swampman has been designed by anyone naturally or artificially. They are therefore cognitive parallels to Dretske's "Instant Tercel" and his "swamp-plant," neither of whose component parts manifest the functions of their morphological equivalents in their indiscernible twins, the 1981 Toyota Tercel and the Scarlet Glia. That needle-like object on Instant Tercel's dashboard-like part does not *function* as a gas gauge, however reliably its position on its dial-like background might covary with the amount of gaslike stuff in the tanklike part in its underframe. Nor does swamp-plant's change of color this spring *function* to attract pollinators, however effective it is at doing so.[53] And so the story goes with Instant Athena and Instant Swampman. They vocalize, but they don't refer or state or do anything with genuine cognitive import. And as it goes, so it ends, they cannot (*conceptually* cannot) function as autonomous agents, however perfect the illusion they create.

For all I know, the selectionist story about functions and the teleological story about reference and intentionality are correct (or at least on the right track) as *empirical* theories. But that is not their creators' sole intention: the stories are supposed to provide *conceptual* accounts of what a function is and what it is to have reference and intentionality. I am in no position to assess them *theoretically* on either basis, so my response to the very end of the story about autonomous agency will have to be about as intuition-grounded as my response to the externalist-historicist in the last section who called for a univocal account of content. The best I can do is offer a thought-experiment designed to bolster confidence in the semantic capacities of instant subjects like Athena and the swampman to function as autonomous agents.

The idea is to go public. Suppose we humans were to happen upon a community of instant beings; say we stumble upon a Twin–New York City (in a galaxy far, far away), booming and buzzing with all the apparent activity of the genuine Big Apple. (Taxi drivers volunteer their opinions about almost everything, all the waiters are *really* actors or writers, young bond traders burn out before they hit thirty, and so on.) The day we arrive, there has been a racially charged killing in Twin–Crown Heights, a neighborhood in Twin-Brooklyn within which two populations, Twin–NYC Hassidic Jews and Twin–NYC low-income blacks live together in deep mutual suspicion. A group of black youths (yelling "Get the Yid!") have pulled a Rabbinical student from a car and beaten him to death. (You can read about the details in the *Twin–New York Times*.) All of Twin–NYC is abuzz with the case. Debates rage about who is ultimately responsible for the killing, the kids themselves, some hotheaded black leaders in the district (Twin-Sharpton and the rest) who have been stirring up resentment against their Jewish neighbors, or the mayor, a former prosecutor given to inflammatory comments about the black community. (As we wander through Twin-NYC we have a strange and sad sense of déjà vu.) Enough: you get the idea.

The point, of course, is that all of Twin–New York and all of the Twin–New Yorkers sprang into existence pretty much as they are now. We learn that this happens frequently in this distant galaxy: populations of beings with the oddest habits and practices just appear. A professor at Twin-NYU explains to us that these populations are not produced by any sort of mechanism of selection at all, not natural, not artificial. They just pop into existence, last for *n* revolutions of Twin-Earth around Twin-Sun and then disappear as abruptly as they appeared. (They do leave behind records of their brief histories, for future Instant Communities to find and wonder at. That's how the professor can tell the odd tale.)

As we move around Twin-NYC we are overwhelmingly inclined to take up the *intentional* stance toward the beings we encounter. The obvious question, however, is whether we are forced by the very logic of the concepts of "function," "reference," "intentionality," "agency," "responsibility," "autonomy," and so forth to *resist* that inclination, to conclude that all the behavior we are observing, including language-like behavior, is just that, mere behavior, and to fall back on the *design* and *physical* stances in our attempt to understand what is going on in Twin-NYC.[54]

I think the answer is that one need not embrace Dennett's quasi instrumentalism about intentionality to think that it is perfectly good explanatory practice to stick to the intentional stance. It seems perfectly coherent to maintain at one and the same time that there are facts of the matter about whether a being is an intentional system and that these facts can hold true of instant agents like the Twin–New Yorkers, despite their utter lack of a selectionist history. To be sure, one would have to cash out this intuition in the hard currency of some theory of reference and intentionality or other. I myself like the market value of a story that grounds the semantic features of a speaker's utterances in his iterated Gricean-intentions supplemented by Lewis-style conventions.[55] But my proclivities in this area are neither here nor there; other semantic stories without selectionist commitments are also available. If the world of the thought-experiment is conceptually coherent, then there can be *content without selection*. (Perhaps there isn't any in fact, but this is a contingent fact about us.) And, if there can be, then Athena and the swampman can have command of the vehicles of genuine practical reasoning, and can be welcomed warmly into the community of autonomous agents. (By the way, for what it's worth, I think the ultimate bearers of responsibility in the Twin–New York atrocity are Twin-Sharpton and Twin-Giuliani.)

6. TWO CAUTIONS

In building my case against one half of the Independence Thesis, against the idea that an externalist about reference and intentionality can be an internalist about autonomous agency, I have finessed and ignored a lot of issues. Two bear special mention, one a conceptual point, the other an emotional acknowledgment. First, the conceptual coherence of the idea of instant subjecthood should not be allowed to obscure the important truth that any form of recognizably conceptual cognition has many essentially temporal aspects. Second, even if our instant subjects, Sean Young, Athena, and the swampman, can be reassured that their status as autonomous agents is secure, we should not expect them to be particularly happy or even indifferent at the revelation that they are persons without pasts. This is especially true of Sean Young, who springs full-blown into the world with all those false memories sustained so poignantly.

6.1. "Mixing Memory with Desire" (. . . and Belief and Hope and Regret and Intention and Just About Everything Else)

Paul Churchland tells the sad but intriguing story of one of Antonio Damasio's patients, Boswell, an otherwise normal adult who has one striking cognitive deficit, the complete lack of any memory (for certain sorts of facts) that extends more than forty seconds into the past.[56] For example, Boswell is a friendly, equable fellow who greets new acquaintances warmly, takes an interest in who they are, and so on. But there's a sad catch: *everyone* is a new acquaintance for Boswell, including his own doctor, members of his family, close friends, everyone. Churchland relates a meeting with Boswell in Damasio's lab, including introductions, small talk, and so on, only to be followed by a meeting with him an hour later, requiring the same introductions, the same small talk, and so on. Imprisonment in the specious present is an enduring feature of Boswell's mental life. (One might suppose that he would be deeply frustrated about constantly being reminded that you and he have already met, but evidently not. Evidently, frustration is also one of those items memory is mixed with. Another factor reducing Boswell's frustration level is also no doubt his enduring ability to recall the identities of *objects* and how, though not how he learned, to perform simple motor tasks upon them.)

Despite the enormity of his deficit, Boswell is actually a rather mild instance of the general phenomenon that I touch on here: the essential role of memory in genuinely conceptual thought. Of course, many philosophers have pursued this theme. John Campbell recently offered a crisp formulation of the general thought: "The argument of this book is that the norms governing distinctively human conceptual thought, as opposed to other types of representation, are set by the demands of self-consciousness and its interwoveness with the spatiotemporal framework, and that these norms governing conceptual thought demand a realist view of the past."[57] I would characterize the thought as "more or less Kantian," because of its emphasis on the necessity of a highly articulated set of "categories of the understanding" for genuine experience of a world of objects, but for Campbell's reference to a "realist view of the past," which may not comport all that well with Kant's own notion of time as "a purely subjective condition of our (human) intuition (which is always sensible, that is, so far as we are affected by objects), and in itself apart from the subject, is nothing."[58] How this Kantian theme plays out against Russell's famous speculation about the past with which we began, I shall not attempt to explore here.

But I will claim (admittedly, without much argument) that Campbell's thought is perfectly compatible with the coherence of instant subjecthood. Sean Young may not *have* a genuine past as a subject, but there is nothing to bar her designers from equipping her now with the *concept* of a real past (or, if you prefer, with a temporal "form of intuition"), even if they also (perversely) induce in her a set of false (prerevelation) memory beliefs about her own temporal location. Moreover, if I am right about their ability to entertain genuine propositional attitudes, then the same is true of Athena and the swampman, though they have no designers. The point is that a subject must *have and deploy temporal concepts* to engage in genuinely conceptual thought, but this does not require that the subject actually *have a past*.

6.2. "I Gotta Be Me": An Instant Agent's Identity Crisis

I end these reflections on a more emotional, less philosophical note. The *conceptual coherence* of instant subjecthood and autonomy is one thing, but an instant subject's *comfort* with the very idea is quite another. Again, Campbell puts the point well:

> Autobiographical memories are not valued principally as guides to future action. They are valued for their own sake. The fact is that identity is central to what we care about in our lives . . . one thing I care about is what I have made of my life . . . The basic point here does not have to do with achievement as such; it has to do with the way in which various incidents stack together to make a life. Fission [or instant subjecthood] would mean there could be no thinking of such things as things I have done; it would deprive me of one of the consolations of age.[59]

I am afraid that I can offer neither Sean Young, Athena nor the swampman any such consolation, but there may be others. Imagine that Sean Young goes to the keepsake-chest filled with all those faded photographs and other mementoes of her fabricated past and pulls out a tattered copy of Samuel Beckett's *The Unnameable*. She reads from it to her Instant Companions:

> perhaps it's a dream, all a dream, that would surprise me, I'll wake, in the silence, and never sleep again, it will be I, or dream, dream again, dream of a silence, a dream silence, full of murmurs, I don't know, that's all the words, never wake, all the words, there's nothing else, you must go on, that's all I know, they're going to stop, I know that well, I can feel it, they're going to abandon me, it will be the silence, for a moment, a good few moments, or it will be mine, the lasting one, that didn't last, that still lasts, it will be I, you must go on, I can't go on, you must go on, I'll go on, you must say words, as long as there are any, until they find me, until they say me, strange pain, strange sin, you must go on, perhaps it's done already, perhaps they have said me already, perhaps they have carried me to the threshold of my story, before the door that opens on my story, that would surprise me, if it opens, it will be I, it will be the silence, where I am, I don't know, I'll never know, in the silence you don't know, you must go on, I'll go on.[60]

And, somehow, they all take consolation in thinking, "and so must we all." They go on.[61]

NOTES

1. B. Russell, *The Analysis of Mind* (London: Allen and Unwin, 1921), 159–69.

2. H. Putnam, *Reason, Truth and History* (Cambridge: Cambridge University Press, 1981), chap. 1. The externalist-historicist literature on reference is by now, of course, vast, and the key contributions familiar enough to obviate the need for much bibliography. But see notes 41 and 47.

3. D. Davidson, "Knowing One's Own Mind," *Proceedings and Addresses of the American Philosophical Association*, 60 (1987), 441–58; F. Dretske, *Naturalizing the Mind* (Cambridge: MIT Press, 1995). The quoted phrase is from D. Dennett's, from "Do-It-Yourself Understanding," in his *Brainchildren: Essays on Designing Minds* (Cambridge: MIT Press, 1998), chap. 3.

4. Frankfurt's classic papers on these respective themes are "Alternate Possibilities and Moral Responsibility," *Journal of Philosophy*, 60 (1969), 829–39; and "Freedom of the Will and the Concept of a Person," *Journal of Philosophy*, 65 (1971), 5–20. He has built on this structuralist conception of responsibility in a series of essays, some of which are collected in his *The Importance of What We Care About* (Cambridge: Cambridge University Press, 1988). Other structuralists include G. Watson, "Free Agency," *Journal of Philosophy*, 75 (1977) 316–39; and C. Taylor, "Human Agency," in T. Mischel, ed., *The Self* (Oxford: Blackwell, 1977), 103–35.

5. M. Slote, "Understanding Free Will," *Journal of Philosophy*, 78 (1980), 136–51; J. M. Fischer and M. Ravizza, *Responsibility and Control* (Cambridge: Cambridge University Press, 1998), chap. 7; A. Mele, *Autonomous Agents* (Oxford: Oxford University Press, 1994), chap. 9.

6. J. M. Fischer, "Responsiveness and Moral Responsibility," in F. Schoeman, ed., *Responsibility, Character and the Emotions* (Cambridge: Cambridge University Press, 1987), 103–105, emphasis added.

7. Mele 1994, chap. 9; Fischer and Ravizza 1998, chap. 7.

8. Some contributors to the debate explicitly declare allegiance to the method of wide reflective equilibrium, which positively invites appeal to relevant background theories, even from seemingly recondite areas (Christine Swanton, *Freedom: A Coherence Theory* [Indianapolis: Hackett, 1992], chap. 2; Fischer and Ravizza 1998, 11). I do grant, however, that some of the territory I explore in this paper is pretty far off the beaten track even that grab bag of ethics known as "moral psychology."

9. Mele 1994, 147, emphasis added; bracketed interpolations also added, but consistently, I assure the reader, with Mele's text.

10. The most exhaustive and insightful is Fischer and Ravizza 1998, chap. 7.

11. Again, Fischer and Ravizza (1998) are important contributors; Mele (1994) is another.

12. Frankfurt 1969, 838.

13. Zimmerman, "Doing There: Internalism and Externalism in Theories of Autonomous Agency," forthcoming.

14. Frankfurt, "Three Concepts of Free Action," *Proceedings of the Aristotelian Society, Supplementary Volume*, 1975, 113–25; also "Identification and Wholeheartedness," in Schoeman 1987, 27–45.

15. Zimmerman, "Making Do: Nasty Stoic Tendencies in an Otherwise Compelling Theory of Autonomy," forthcoming.

16. Put it this way: even the pre-1994 Fodor could have been an avowed externalist-historicist about the conditions for autonomy (see the relevant reference in note 42), as could cluster-description theorists of reference like Russell and Searle.

17. Davidson 1987; also Mele 1994.

18. Mele 1994, 145.

19. Put it this way: a Frankfurtian structuralist could accept the externalist program in semantics and in psychology for the Ann-Beth sort of case. Accordingly, A. Mele alerted me (in personal correspondence) to the need to narrow slightly the version of the Independence Thesis up for criticism on internalist grounds.

20. Mele 1994, 173.

21. Mele 1994, 173.

22. I take up these issues in more detail in Zimmerman, "Doing There."

23. These kinds of robots are, in fact, dubbed by their creators "autonomous agents." For a good, philosophically accessible account of the research, see A. Clark, *Being There: Putting Brain, Body and World Together Again* (Cambridge: MIT Press, 1997).

24. For example, K. Wilkes, *Real People: Personal Identity without Thought-Experiments* (Oxford: Oxford University Press, 1988).

25. The film was based on Philip K. Dick's science fiction novel *Do Androids Dream of Electric Sheep?* The movie is better for my purposes, so I'll rely on it in the development of this thought-experiment.

26. Major critics include J. Haugland, *Artificial Intelligence: The Very Idea* (Cambridge: MIT Press, 1985); H. Dreyfus, *What Computers (Still) Can't Do: The Limits of Artificial Intelligence* (New York: Harper and Row, 1979); and J. Searle, "Minds, Brains and Programs," *Behavioral and Brain Sciences*, 3 (1980), 417–58.

27. Defenders of holistic constraints on belief-ascription (of one degree of strictness or another) include Davidson and Dennett.

28. This is one of Dreyfus's (1979) principal concerns. See also H. Dreyfus and S. Dreyfus, "Making a Mind versus Modelling a Brain: Artificial Intelligence Back at a Branching Point," in M. Boden, ed., *The Philosophy of Artificial Intelligence* (Oxford: Oxford University Press, 1990), 309–33. For an instructive (and considerably more optimistic) discussion, see Dennett, "Cognitive Wheels: The Frame Problem of AI," in Boden 1990, 147–70. I draw heavily on Dennett's article in section 5.3.2.

29. See the references in notes 2, 41, and 47.

30. Strictly speaking, only the last of these is a distinctly externalist concern, but for anyone who takes Russell's question seriously and hopes in the bargain to defeat (one half of) the Independence Thesis, it makes sense to tackle them all together.

31. I have already alluded to Wilkes's strong attack on the method in note 24. For a nice defense of it, see Fischer, "Stories," forthcoming, *Midwest Studies in Philosophy*. (I thank Fischer for showing me a draft of this engaging and clever paper.)

32. Dreyfus and Dreyfus, 1990, chap. 13; D. B. Lenat and R. V. Guha, *Building Large Knowledge-Based Systems: Representation and Inference in the CYC Project* (Reading, MA: Addison-Wesley, 1990). For useful discussion of the whole enterprise, see Dennett, "When Philosophers Encounter Artificial Intelligence," in Dennett 1998, 273.

33. Dreyfus 1979; Dreyfus and Dreyfus 1990; J. Haugland, *Having Thought: Essays in the Metaphysics of Mind* (Cambridge: Harvard University Press, 1998), essays 1, 8, 9, and 10.

34. Smolensky, "On the Proper Treatment of Connectionism," *Behavioral and Brain Sciences*, 11 (1988), 1–74.

35. Dennett, 1990, 158–59, emphasis added.

36. Dennett, 1990, 159, emphasis added.

37. Dennett, 1990, 159, emphasis added.

38. For a pioneering treatment of this theme, see H. N. Casteneda, "Indicators and Quasi-Indicators," *American Philosophical Quarterly*, 4 (1967): 85–100. Though I do not take up the question here, I do not offhand see why Sean Young (or even the brain-in-a-vat) could not have command of "quasi-indicators" along with their command of the other sorts of referring expressions.

39. A most vociferous advocate of this position is Searle 1980. I return to this issue in section 5.3.3.

40. Putnam, 1981, 13–14.

41. To put the point a bit differently, no one in this scenario, neither you nor I, neither the brain-in-a-vat nor Sean Young, is in the referentially unfortunate position of a devotee of unicorn lore who goes on about these mythical creatures and then triumphantly declares vindication of their reality when a paleontologist turns up the fossilized remains of a single-horned member of the genus *hippus*. The point is that the unearthed skeleton would not fall under the extension of the term "unicorn" as used for all those years in the discourse of tales and tapestries, because it lacks the right sort of causal-historical connection with those uses. I guess this means that devotees of mythology willing to bet on the paleontological odds would be better advised to opt for a cluster-description theory of reference. (This is, obviously, a clear case of the mutual nourishment of classical analytic philosophy of language and mythological speculation.) The example is, of course, in the spirit of Kripke, "Naming and Necessity," in D. Davidson and G. Harman, eds., *Semantics of Natural Language* (Dordrecht, the Netherlands: Reidel, 1972).

42. His defection came, I gather, in Fodor, *The Elm and the Expert* (Cambridge: MIT Press, 1995). Defenders of the role narrow content can play in psychological explanation are not, however, totally absent from the scene. See, for example, F. Jackson and P. Pettit, "Some Content Is Narrow," in A. Mele, ed., *Mental Causation* (Oxford: Oxford University Press, 1995), 259–82.

43. Dennett, "Beyond Belief: Reflections about Aboutness," in Dennett, *The Intentional Stance* (Cambridge, MIT Press, 1987), 172. The next few parenthetical page numbers are from this essay until it becomes obvious otherwise.

44. G. E. Hinton, J. L. McClelland, and D. E. Rumelhart, *Parallel Distributed Processing* (Cambridge: MIT Press, 1986), 80–81, emphasis added.

45. One never wishes to make too much of a good thing, but the confluence of ideas from such disparate contemporary conceptions of cognitive representation suggests that at base they have something importantly in common, which we might dub "The Woody Allen Maneuver: Ex-Characters in Search of Self-Authorship." In Allen's short story "The Kugellmass Incident," Emma Bovary emerges from Flaubert's text into the real world to charm and bewitch, but eventually to vex and plague the schlemiel of the title. This seems to be a theme close to Allen's heart, for in his film *The Purple Rose of Cairo*, the Jeff Daniels male ingenue character strides off the silver screen at first to charm and delight, but eventually to seduce and abandon the poor neglected starstruck housewife played by Mia Farrow. Allen's recurrent theme provides us with a nice way to link the comments of the cognitivist and the connectionist: both representational formats permit us to perform an *epoché*, that is, to "bracket" questions of reality from questions of intentional content (in the classical fashion of Brentano and Husserl). Thus, both representational frameworks are compatible with regarding everything Sean Young says after she is lugged to the door and switched on as amenable to the best going account of the semantics of *fictional discourse* (perhaps the one David Lewis offers in his "Truth in Fiction," *American Philosophical Quarterly* 15 (1978), especially his "Analysis 2X," 45). The idea is that the *prior and independent availability* of a semantics for fictional discourse makes the very idea that an instant agent like Sean Young might have command over semantically meaningful items conceptually more palatable for those who otherwise might have real problems even entertaining it. Of course, the spectre of *obscurum per obscurius* looms large here, but what else is new in philosophy?

46. Dennett, 1987, respectively: 157 (emphasis in original), 157 (emphasis in original), and 159.

47. Putnam, "The Meaning of 'Meaning,'" in Putnam, *Mind, Knowledge and Reality*, Philosophical Papers, Vol. 2 (Cambridge: Cambridge University Press, 1975).

48. This cross-discipline appeal to parsimony was put to me with great force by Steven Davis. Externalists also offer arguments specific to the structure and reach of psychological explanation itself. C. MacDonald, for example, argues that even where the actions of doppelgangers are type-identical (as with our two evil uncles), the deep and differing chemical structures of H_20 and XYZ will nonetheless require that the roles these kind-concepts play in the explanation of *other* actions of the doppelgangers essentially involves wide or externalist content. See MacDonald "Weak Externalism and Psychological Reduction," in D. Charles and K. Lennon, eds., *Reduction, Explanation and Realism* (Oxford: Oxford University Press: 1992), 144. This is no doubt true. I have conceded as much in the text when I acknowledged that if the doppelganger uncles had employed a different method of murder (such as poisoning) then their deeds might well not be type-identical and their respective explanations might well need to invoke the differing deep structures of the liquid media used for the poisonings. But surely that cannot support the *general* externalist claim that the content of the propositional attitudes invoked in psychological explanations is *never* narrow. MacDonald does *state* such a thesis when she suggests that "[i]t is arguable that, in order to make sense of [doppelganger's] actions on Twin Earth (as well as to make sense of [doppelganger's] on Earth, the role played by XYZ (or water) in activities *throughout the community* [including the community of chemists] must be taken into account" (145). Her reason for advancing the more ambitious thesis is that the specialists' knowledge of the wide contents of "water" on Earth and Twin-Earth "affects the attribution to [doppelganger-*non*-specialist on Earth and Twin-Earth] of dispositions to act conditionally upon the possession of such information" (145). But this is just to reiterate the already conceded weaker externalist thesis, not to argue for the stronger one, required to make the externalist case for *all* instances of psychological explanation.

49. The utter irrelevance of such fine-grained details about the composition of the crucial items in an *explanans* is an utterly routine fact about explanations even in the hardest of the sciences, physics and chemistry. For example, suppose someone's lit cigar is the only open flame that could have sparked the conflagration that completely gutted some tenant's apartment. The investigators narrow down the cause at least to that extent. But they are still puzzled because it is not clear how such a small flame could have had such a devastating effect. The obvious hypothesis is that it served to ignite some flammable material, so they set about trying to discover if there had been any in the vicinity of the cigar smoker. And sure enough, it turns out that for some time he had been cooking in his apartment on an illegal portable stove fueled with its own large tank of propane gas. The tank had sprung a small leak, the propane gas had slowly diffused through the air in the apartment until enough of it reached the lit cigar to ignite the air-propane mixture with awful consequences. That is a pretty good explanation of why the fire occurred. But suppose that the mayor is not satisfied and demands a full report on the precise physical configuration of the propane gas molecules as they diffused through the air molecules in the apartment that fated evening from the leaking tank to the lit cigar: every molecule at every spatiotemporal location it occupied on the (collectively) deadly path. ("I won't be satisfied that I really understand how that fire started until that report is on my desk!") Luckily there are no particular epistemic problems meeting the mayor's demand because the city's best investigator, Officer LaPlace, is able to come up with precisely this information, which he dutifully dumps by the truckload onto the steps of City Hall. The mayor prepares for the press conference at which he will explain to his anxious constituents how the fire occurred by sitting down as each truck arrives to read the computer printouts, which accurately describe in completely specified detail (let's say above the quantum level—the mayor isn't an obsessive-compulsive, after all) the "initial conditions" that enter into LaPlace's deductive-nomological (D-N) explanation of why the apartment went up in flames. You get the point. Even a proponent of strict D-N explanations of physical events would be prepared to admit that enough is enough. The propane molecules *could* have taken that path to the lit cigar, or that path, or that path, or. . . . To explain why the fire occurred, it simply does not matter *which* one. And so, I claim, with the actual chemical compositions of the referents of "water" in the explanations of how Tyke and Twyke became dead.

50. Developed by R. G. Millikan, *Language, Thought and Other Biological Categories* (Cambridge: MIT Press, 1984); and F. Dretske (1995).

51. The heart provides the usual example. An influential theory of the essentially etiological nature of functions is L. Wright, *Teleological Explanations: An Etiological Analysis of Goals and Functions* (Berkeley and Los Angeles: University of California Press, 1976).

52. Dennett 1987.

53. Dretske 1995, chap. 5.

54. The terms are, of course, Dennett's, from "Intentional Systems," in Dennett, *Brainstorms* (Cambridge: MIT Press, 1981), 3–22.

55. H. P. Grice,"Meaning," *Philosophical Review*, 66 (1957), 377–88; and "Utterer's Meaning and Intentions," *Philosophical Review*, 78 (1969), 147–77; also D. Lewis, *Convention* (Cambridge: Harvard University Press, 1969); and P. F. Strawson, "Intentions and Conventions in Speech Acts," *Philosophical Review*, 73 (1964), 439–60.

56. P. Churchland, *The Engine of Reason, The Seat of the Soul* (Cambridge: MIT Press, 1997), 165–66.

57. Campbell, *Past, Space, and Self* (Cambridge: MIT Press, 1994), 222.

58. I. Kant, *The Critique of Pure Reason*, 1855 (Kemp-Smith edition, MacMillan Press, 1929, A38–40).

59. Campbell 1994, 189.

60. S. Beckett, *The Unnameable* (New York: Grove Press, 1958), 178–79.

61. I thank Kathleen Akins, David Copp, Steven Davis, Francesca Derra, John Martin Fischer, Martin Hahn, Ishtiyaque Haji, Bob Solomon, Roy Slakov, Marc Smith, the late Kay Stockholder, and my students in Philosophy 321 (Topics in Moral Responsibility) at Simon Fraser University, fall term, 1993, for help and encouragement in developing some of the ideas that eventually made their way into the argument of this paper. I am especially indebted to Alfred Mele for insights into the relationship between the internalist/externalist disputes in the philosophies of

psychosemantic content and of autonomous agency. Since the ideas in this paper cross in such idiosyncratic fashion the (already porous) boundary between ethics and the philosophy of mind, the usual disavowal of the responsibility of others for how things have turned out is even more in order than it usually is. I also thank Simon Fraser University for the liberality of its research leave policy, from which I have benefited on two occasions during work on this and other papers on topics in the theory of autonomous agency.

Midwest Studies in Philosophy, XXIII (1999)

The Ethics of Belief: Off the Wrong Track[1]

JONATHAN E. ADLER

Any account of the ethics of belief should cohere with a crucial fact, which is illustrated by the ancient challenge to believe that:

The number of stars is even.[2]

We cannot meet this challenge. The crucial fact is that it is not possible that one both regard oneself as holding a belief and that one's reasons for it are inadequate.

Evidentialism, an ethics of belief advocated by David Hume, John Locke, W. K. Clifford, and many others, well coheres with the crucial fact. Stated in its most general form, evidentialism is the thesis that *the strength of one's belief ought to be proportioned to the strength of one's reasons*. Locke writes:

> For he governs his Assent right, and places it as he should, who in any Case or Matter whatsoever, believes or disbelieves, according as Reason directs him. He that does otherwise, transgresses against his own Light, and misuses those Faculties, which were given him to no other end, but to search and follow the clearer Evidence, and greater Probability.[3]

Evidentialism coheres with our crucial fact by explaining it. The explanation assumes that we grasp evidentialism's requirement of adequate reasons (or evidence) as a conceptual condition for believing properly. The explanation is then this: Since we know that we do not have adequate reasons for believing that the number of stars is even, then we cannot, in continuing awareness of that knowledge, believe that the number of stars is even. In this article I defend evidentialism and concentrate on its implication for full—rather than partial or degrees of—belief: one ought to believe that *p* only if one's evidence or reasons adequately support the truth of *p*.

Although "reason" has treacherous ambiguities for us—notably between motives or causes of believing and justification of the belief held—it belongs in the characterization of evidentialism. The rationale of evidentialism does not restrict it to empirical beliefs. The heart of evidentialism is that since believing aims at the truth of what is believed, the believer needs to grasp facts indicative of the truth of the belief. Evidence is only the most prominent kind of fact to fit this role. For beliefs whose content is not empirical, but are, say, ethical or mathematical, reasons are the appropriately broader class to draw upon for justification.

In part 1 of this paper evidentialism is defended as following from the nature of belief. This *Intrinsic* approach is contrasted in part 2 with the dominant *Extrinsic* approaches.

Early in his influential essay attacking evidentialism, Alvin Plantinga writes, "Why should we think a theist must have evidence, or reason to think there *is* evidence, if he is not to be irrational? Why not suppose, instead, that he is entirely within his epistemic rights in believing in God's existence even if he supposes he has no argument or evidence at all?"[4] In this brief passage, Plantinga implies both a blunt rejection of my crucial fact and his affirmation of rationality as the proper criterion for evaluating norms for belief.

In contrast to the Intrinsic approach that I defend, Plantinga is advancing—or assuming—an Extrinsic approach to the ethics of belief. Extrinsic approaches lead discussions of the ethics of belief onto the wrong track in that answers to the question of what one ought to believe are determined by criteria external to belief. Rationality is the most prominent criterion proposed. In part II of this article, four doctrines implied by Extrinsic approaches will be articulated and critically examined.

The right track, taken by Intrinsic approaches, is to ask what the nature of belief itself demands. On an Intrinsic approach the answer to Plantinga's second question is that his theist simply *cannot* hold such a belief if he attends to it when affirming that "he has no argument or evidence at all." The impossibility of holding such a belief, which is implied by the crucial fact cited above, is of primary importance because it is a conceptual impossibility. Only secondarily, if at all, is the belief irrational.

I. THE INTRINSIC ETHICS OF BELIEF

A. From the Subjective Principle to Evidentialism

The crucial fact can be formulated as the *subjective principle of sufficient reasons*: When one attends to any of one's beliefs, one must regard it as believed for sufficient (or adequate) reasons. The key term is "must," which should be read as governing the whole statement. Without it, there is no significance to our taking ourselves to have adequate reasons for our beliefs. Perhaps our taking ourselves to have adequate reasons is merely a gratuitous, even if widespread, expectation. With the modal "must," an argument emerges that moves from the subjective principle to the substance of evidentialism.

The main reason to believe that the subjective principle of sufficient reasons is a fact is that we do follow it, and we find ourselves compelled to do so. Consequently, I find it hard to argue with someone who would just deny the subjective principle; it is to argue with someone who, if he is sincere, is not being honest with himself. So, although I'll offer some supportive reasons to accept it, I do not expect to convince anyone who denies complying with it. For these recalcitrants, however, I can still offer a softener. If you find that the subjective principle holds for some, but not all, of your beliefs, the argument from the subjective principle to evidentialism below should still work, correspondingly limited. Further, the main role of the subjective principle is for its support of evidentialism. But independent arguments are offered for evidentialism.

We attribute acceptance of the subjective principle to others, at least for what they *assert*. If S asserts that *p* to H, H takes S to have good reasons to believe that *p*. Since S should not assert that *p* unless he has good reasons to believe it, H takes S to recognize that he has good reasons to believe *p*. But assertion is just the expression of belief. The requirement that assertions be backed by good reasons, since they claim the truth of what is asserted, is just the analogue of the requirement that beliefs be backed by good reasons, since they claim the truth of what is believed.

We would not impose the subjective principle upon ourselves by inclination. We would surely prefer to avoid the burden of sufficient reasons or evidence; this is true especially of those who hold wild or paranoid beliefs, such as that the fluoridation of water is a communist plot. But even they accept the burden, as is shown by their own (tortured) defenses of these beliefs. Similarly, as already suggested, even those who reject either evidentialism or the subjective principle typically restrict their rejection to certain contents of belief (e.g., "God is good," "Abortion is wrong"). For unproblematic contents, such as that the *cat is on the mat* or that *there are tigers*, either they do not reject, or they outright endorse, evidentialism or the subjective principle, correspondingly restricted.

Well-known experiments in social psychology reveal the workings of the subjective principle of sufficient reasons, despite their studying judgments whose underlying processes are inaccessible. For example, in one of a large number of studies, an array of identical stockings was set before subjects, and they were asked to select their favored pair.[5] Subjects preferred four to one the pair that was rightmost in the array. Typically, in these studies, subjects explained their actions or judgments with what we regard as rationalizations, such as that the stockings selected "looked better." Subjects thus displayed their appreciation that reasons should be adequate. They dismissed as preposterous the suggestion that their reason could be that the preferred stocking was rightmost, presumably because being rightmost would not be evidence that a certain stocking was preferable. Since their (confabulated) reason (that this pair looked best) claims adequacy, it explains their judgment. From their point of view, no further reasons are operative. In general, across a wide spectrum of related psychological studies, subjects are influenced to form beliefs whose causes they deny or cannot know. Yet they offer reasons for their relevant beliefs, and, though from our point of view these are rationalizations, subjects feel compelled to offer them. The felt need to rationalize is plausibly explained as reflecting the demands of the subjective principle.

As this example and these studies also show, the reasons demanded by the subjective principle are epistemic reasons, rather than mere causes or motives to believe. These are reasons indicative of the truth of the belief. We regularly employ a distinction between epistemic and nonepistemic reasons. One's wanting to be a Hollywood star may induce the belief that one is a Hollywood star. But it is not a reason that can justify believing it, since it does not indicate the truth of the belief.

The subjective principle asks us to attend to the proposition believed. The condition that we attend to our belief or become fully aware of it is for theoretical purposes, not a practical proposal that believing should be self-conscious. Much belief is acquired nonconsciously, and the normal way for a particular belief to become active is for its content to play a role in guiding action. In themselves our beliefs enter no claims of truth, and many lack adequate reasons. However, when we attend to any one belief, such a claim is made. Since the awareness is simply of one's believing, the claim of truth is taken as following from the nature of belief. Thus, the resulting demands we grasp are binding on each of our beliefs, even though we know that not each of them meets those demands.

When we do attend to a particular belief, there is no guarantee of success. Sometimes, as when we become aware of a distant memory—for example, that in a local baseball game fifteen years ago I hit a game-winning double—we do not take ourselves to have adequate reasons. It seems plausible that the memory could be the product of later suggestion or wishful thinking. What is crucial is that, as soon as we see that it is questionable, we cease to hold the belief (suspend judgment), even if we still regard it as probably correct. More obviously, we often take ourselves to have sufficient reasons when we do not, as when we rationalize.

The point of introducing the subjective principle is not to attempt any argument from our believing ourselves to have sufficient reasons to our actually having them. Obviously, one can wrongly take oneself to have adequate reasons. The purpose is to argue that we impose the demands of the subjective principle upon ourselves because these correspond to the demands of belief. That the content of the belief is true is not settled by our believing it. There is a gap between our attitude that the world is a certain way and our position to secure the correctness of this attitude. This gap can be bridged only by evidence or reasons, which link the believer to the truth-conditions of the belief.

My argument from the subjective principle (that is, when one attends to any of one's beliefs, one must regard it as believed for sufficient reasons) to full belief evidentialism (that is, one ought to believe that *p* only if one's evidence adequately supports the truth of *p*) takes the demand we impose upon ourselves for sufficient reasons as having the force of necessity. We take the source of that demand to be in the nature of belief. But the only credible reason for why we take the source of the demand to be in the nature of belief is that it is; to this extent, at least, we correctly grasp belief's nature. We impose the demand for adequate reasons on ourselves as a demand of belief. The reasoning to evidentialism from the subjective principle is explained by our finding compelling the simple, direct argument for evidentialism, sketched one paragraph back. Briefly, only evidence links believing and truth.

B. The Incoherence Test

Both the arguments from the subjective principle and the direct argument for evidentialism are confirmed as stemming from the nature of belief because overt denials of their conclusions are *incoherent* (a stark contradiction or inconsistency).

The incoherence parallels incoherences underlying *Moore's Paradox*.[6] One cannot assert statements of the form

> *p*, but I do not believe that *p*,

for example,

> It is raining, but I do not believe that it is raining.

The assertion is heard as contradictory, even though both conjuncts may be true. A rough account of the contradiction is this: Assertion expresses belief. So the assertion would be presenting the speaker as simultaneously believing both that *p* is true and that she does not believe it. But then she is believing *p* and also believing that she does not believe *p*. But if she is believing *p* and attending to it, then she must believe that she believes it.[7] The whole thought in this single consciousness would now be that I both believe that *p* and that I do not believe that *p*. But no such belief is possible, since its recognized content is a contradiction.

The unassertibility revealed in Moore's Paradox is explained by an underlying incoherence in thought,[8] rather than by conversational expectations, such as the conventional implication of "but" that a contrast is to follow. It derives from assertion as the conveyance of truth, as belief is the attitude that its content is true. (There is a familiar parallel ambiguity in "belief" and "assertion"—as referring to the attitude (action) or to its content. For brevity it is useful to exploit this ambiguity. Where danger of misunderstanding lurks, "belief" ["assertion"] will be used for the content and "believing" ["asserting"] for the attitude [action].)

The necessarily failed attempt at belief in the opening example corresponds to the Moore's Paradox–like thought or assertion:

> The number of stars is even, but I lack sufficient evidence that the number of stars is even.

In detail, the incoherence is:

> I believe that the number of stars is even. All that can secure for me the belief's claim of truth is adequate evidence (reason) of its truth. I obviously lack adequate evidence. I cannot then judge it true that the number of stars is even. So I cannot believe it. So I do not believe it. So I do not believe that the number of stars is even.

The incoherence takes the form of an explicit contradiction (between the opening and closing propositions).

The contradiction is not a further belief. The initial statement is a supposition that is implicitly rejected by the end of the reasoning. Although the reasoning unfolds as if we were entertaining a present thought or belief that the number of stars is even, what the contradiction shows is the impossibility of such a thought or belief.[9] That there is no further belief is the lesson of ordinary cases of uncovering evidence that undermines a belief. The contrary evidence thereby erases the belief. There are not separate stages: recognition (of undermining evidence), decision (to surrender the belief), and execution (by ceasing to believe).

The analysis depended only upon the recognized lack of adequate evidence, not upon the extreme lack that the opening example actually illustrates. We do not take ourselves merely to have less than adequate evidence to believe that the number of stars is even, we take ourselves to have no evidence at all. Despite the egregious nature of this particular example, however, it still serves to make the general point. The same incoherence is to arise from recognition of (just) less than adequate evidence as it does from cases where the evidence is recognized as starkly inadequate. Instances of the following are heard as Moore's Paradoxes as well:

> *p*, but I lack [sufficient] evidence [reason] that *p* is true.

The correlative explanation, in line with the subjective principle, would be that one cannot believe both that one believes that *p* and that one believes that one lacks sufficient (or any) reasons that *p* is true. For consider an (enlarged) instance of this form of Moore's Paradox in a student's assertion:

> I will receive a grade of A in logic, but I lack adequate reasons that it is true. Although I have received grades of A on all my tests and papers, I have not received a grade on the final exam.

We hear this assertion as a contradiction because its corresponding thought would be a contradiction. If the student just asserted that he will get an A in these circumstances, then if the hearer were to learn of his reasons, the hearer would no doubt have been critical: "You shouldn't have said that you will get an A, but only that it is extremely probable."

It follows that not only recognition that failures have adequate reasons, but also recognition that one's reasons are weak or impaired lead to similar incoherences. I can no longer believe that my next door neighbor's German shepherd is in my yard howling, once I discover that another neighbor also has a German shepherd, if I think that I cannot tell them apart. Extending the thought behind this example yields an instance of the following pattern of incoherent thought:

> I believe that *p* (e.g., "My next door neighbor's German shepherd is in my yard howling."). But my believing it does not render it true. All that can render the belief correct is that I have adequate evidence of its truth. I did judge that I had adequate evidence that *p* is true. However, I now realize that the judgment that my evidence is adequate was based on an insufficiently discriminating source. So I cannot judge that it is adequate for the truth of *p*. Thus, I actually lack adequate reason of the truth of *p*. Therefore I cannot believe that *p*, cognizant as I am now of that inadequacy. So I do not believe that *p*.

These incoherence tests expose not only what cannot be believed, but also what must be believed. The challenge here is to attempt *not* to believe that, for example, there are stars, and the failure is again conceptual:

> I do not believe that there are stars. But the evidence that there are stars is overwhelming. No further inquiry on its truth is needed. Since I have evidence

establishing that there are stars, I judge it true that there are stars. There are stars. So then I believe that there are stars.

Combining what we learn from each of these two incoherences in thought yields:

Necessarily, if one regards one's evidence or reasons as adequate to the truth of *p* then one believes that *p*; and if one attends to one's believing that *p*, then one regards one's evidence or reasons as adequate to the truth of *p*.

The first conditional moves from one's judgment of the strength of one's evidence to belief; the second moves in the reverse direction from awareness of one's belief to one's judgment of the strength of one's evidence. The consequent of the first conditional does not affirm merely that "one *regards* oneself as believing," but that one does believe. Once one judges that the evidence or reasons are adequate, one thereby does hold the belief, and that one does so is apparent to awareness. On this understanding, the antecedent of the second conditional is just a stylistic variant of that consequent (of the first conditional). To "attend to one's believing" is merely a certain awareness of it, not an evaluation. The combined conditional is effectively an equivalence.

So we cannot recognize ourselves as believing *p* while believing that our reasons or evidence are not adequate to its truth (and conversely). The "cannot" is conceptual, not merely psychological (an inability). The notions of higher orders of infinity or electrons shifting levels, with no intermediate position, boggle many minds. But the "cannot" or "unbelievability" that concerns us here is not rooted in (contingent) empirical or psychological barriers. We treat analogously putative cases in which one cannot hold certain beliefs, given one's upbringing and education. Familiar, if apocryphal, tales are of those who have abandoned their fundamentalist religious upbringing, but who claim to be unable to believe, for example, evolution by natural selection, despite now being persuaded by the evidence for it.[10] Even if these do describe psychological impossibilities, they remain conceptual possibilities. Conversely, what conceptually cannot be believed, cannot actually be believed.

C. Adequate Reasons

In the various formulations of evidentialism and the arguments for it, there has been a glaring vagueness in such phrases as "adequate reasons" or "evidence adequate to its truth." In firming up these vague phrases, the position I defend goes much farther out on a limb than is necessary for the central issues of the ethics of belief. The adequacy is adequacy for *knowledge*. Although this is the position I endorse, it is argued for only briefly. The excuse is the one just suggested. There are a number of weaker positions that are sufficient for defending evidentialism and for drawing a line between evidentialism and antievidentialist positions.

A short argument for this strong, determinate content for "sufficient [adequate] reasons" is again via Moore's Paradox in assertions of the form

p, but I do not know that *p*.[11]

Since Moore's Paradox is taken as implying that one should assert *p* only if one believes *p*, then, by parity of reasoning, one should assert *p* only if one knows *p*. But it is a mutual expectation (of speaker and hearer) that what is asserted is backed by adequate reasons for its truth.[12] Satisfaction of this expectation is the only place where satisfaction of the condition of knowledge can be manifest. So then the adequacy of reasons for assertion is adequacy for knowledge. In recognizing myself as believing that *p*, the sufficient reasons I take myself as having for believing it are sufficient for knowing it.

Another consideration favoring this construal of adequacy, though also going further, is that it accords with our first-personal view. That is, we take ourselves to have adequate reasons or evidence to believe that *p*, rather than merely believing it strongly or to a high degree, just when we treat it as what we know. The first-personal view leads us to the more tendentious claim that the relation of reasons or evidence and the truth of the belief in question is one of necessity. Our first-personal view is that it must be the case, given our reasons or evidence, that *p* is true. The reasons are conclusive.[13]

Consider the following ordinary exchange:

> Joey (6 years old): Dad's home.
> Mary (his 8-year-old sister): No, he's not. Why do you say that?
> Joey: The Olds just pulled into the driveway, Dad must be going through the basement.
> Mary: No. Mom just came home. Dad took the train to his office. He brought his car into the mechanic earlier, and then after work, Mom picked it up.

I assume that Joey's "must" is genuine. He is taken aback at Mary's denial. Had Joey allowed for the possibility that his reasons held, but that his dad had not returned home, he would neither have drawn his conclusion ("Dad's home"), as contrasted to "Dad is almost certainly home," nor would he have been taken aback. Since Mary turns out to be right, Joey learns that his judgment of the adequacy of his reasons is mistaken. But there would be no cause for correction if his mom's being home, rather than his dad, was only highly unexpected. So the original thought I ascribe to Joey is that it must be the case that, given his evidence, his father is home.

These ordinary first-personal judgments support our position only if we bracket our reflective or studied views of knowledge (or conclusive reasons). We are coached to understand knowledge as a high and difficult achievement. In bracketing these understandings, the assumption is that what roles the concept of knowledge plays for us and when it can play those roles are more telling of the requirements of knowledge than are our reflective judgments. The same bracketing is required for getting to the nature of belief. Our judgment about the concept of belief is subject to conflation with related concepts (belief in, inclined to believe, faith, opinion, assent), as well as to overintellectualization by salient, but problematic, content (e.g., "The universe did not exist before the Big Bang," "Abortion is immoral," "Psychic healing helps cure persons of disease"). The first-personal verification that I seek is from within our practices or activities, without admixture of theoretical musings about knowledge, conclusive reasons, or belief. With the admixture, our basic claims are defeated from the start: the standards for knowledge are too high to be commonly satisfied, and belief is too common a phenomenon to be subject to high standards.

It turns out, as a final reason favoring this construal, that if knowledge is analyzed via justification and if justification is constituted by one's reasons or evidence, then the simplest account is one in which those reasons or evidence are conclusive. The account yields a neat resolution of the "Gettier problem."[14] If justification is conclusive, then it is not possible for a belief to be justified but false. Analysis of knowledge or justification as conclusive reasons is standardly dismissed because, with inductive reasons especially, the evidence clearly does not entail the conclusion. No amount or variety of finite evidence for the proposition that "all swans are white" entails that proposition. But the fallacy is to assume that the only necessity is deductive necessity. To take a standard example: if water is H_2O, then necessarily it is H_2O. But the statement "that is water" does not deductively entail "that is H_2O."

What I find particularly attractive about the conclusive reasons account is that it sees knowledge as an ordinary and common achievement, and yet acknowledges that what is achieved meets high (epistemic) standards. As previously indicated, this is the basic claim for (full) belief that I defend: that it is ordinary and common, yet the standards to be met are very high.

It should be evident why, in adopting this position, I go much further out on a limb than is necessary. Antievidentialists of various stripes do not just deny evidentialism. They affirm that belief is proper without any reasons or evidence, or in the absence of undermining reasons or evidence, or with reasons or evidence adequate only for a probability greater than half. The denial of any of these theses does not require that evidence or reasons be adequate for knowledge, let alone that reasons be conclusive. To deny any of these positions, it would be enough to require that one properly believes that *p* only if one's evidence or reasons very strongly support the truth of *p*.

In defending evidentialism on the strongest construal, I obviously present it with the greatest challenge. If it goes through on this construal, it certainly works on the weaker, more popular construals. Those with doubts about the centrality of knowledge or its analysis as requiring conclusive reasons can still adopt my arguments against antievidentialist theses by substituting their own weaker readings of the demand for reasons or evidence.

D. Full and Partial Belief

In arguing for evidentialism I have partly acquiesced to the standard focus on full, rather than partial, belief. By acquiescing, I foreclose some natural lines of reasoning favoring evidentialism. In the case of partial (or degrees of) belief, evidentialism is virtually self-evident. If one's degree of belief that *p* is true is greater than half, one's (subjective) probability of *p* on one's evidence is greater than half and, with a qualification to come, conversely. Evidentialism, at its most general, claims:

> One ought to have a degree of belief *n* that *p* if and only if one's reasons or evidence support the truth of *p* to degree *n*.[15]

We almost imperceptibly conflate the two sides of this equivalence. We read smoothly the following declaration by Hume, just preceding his pithy expression of evidentialism ("a wise man, therefore, proportions his belief to the evidence"): "in our reasonings concerning matter of fact, there are all imaginable degrees of assurance, from the highest *certainty* to the lowest species of moral *evidence*."[16] Peter

Strawson holds that "being reasonable" *means* that one should "proportion the degree of one's convictions to the strength of the evidence."[17] Although it is not necessary that people are actually reasonable, it is necessary that, in regard to any particular conviction, the person takes himself to hold it reasonably in this way.

In putting aside partial belief in arguments for evidentialism, we put aside how the strong demands of full belief are an extension of demands hardly contestable for partial belief. We also put aside challenges both to evidentialism for full belief and to antievidentialism. The evidentialist has a familiar emergentist difficulty: How can an argument rooted in proportionality allow for a threshold (to the all-or-nothing concept of belief) beyond which further (positive) evidence or reasons cease to have an impact on the strength of belief? (Discussion below partly answers the challenge for evidentialism, but the question cannot be answered without an extensive treatment of full belief.) But the antievidentialist faces a much more serious challenge: What account of full belief will allow for the sharp discontinuity the antievidentialist posits if he accepts evidentialism for partial belief? The antievidentialist assumes that, when we get to the highest strength (full belief), we do not require correspondingly greater evidential strength, if we need evidence at all. Yet in that case the claim of truth is greater (than for any degrees of belief) and it is that claim that is the source of evidentialism's proportionality requirement.

With this contrast between full and partial or degrees of belief explicit, I can more completely state the direct argument for the strong version of (full belief) evidentialism. To fully believe that *p* is to take the world to be this way: *p*. With only a partial degree of belief that *p*, however high, one looks to the world filtered through one's attitude. Full, but not partial, belief is *transparent* to the world. When I (anyone) attend to my believing *p*, I recognize that I take *p* to be true and that this recognition makes a claim upon me. Nothing in my believing *p* itself renders it true that *p*, and so believing itself cannot satisfy the claim that *p*. Reasons or evidence indicative of the truth of *p* are required. But to satisfy the claim to truth of my belief requires not merely that I possess these reasons or evidence, but that I am in a position to appreciate their truth and their truth-conferring force on *p*. It is only then that these reasons (or evidence) count as reasons (or evidence) for me of the truth of *p*. But if they leave open possibilities that *p* is false, then I cannot yet simply look at the world transparently through my belief. So the reasons or evidence of the truth of *p* must be something like reasons or evidence that are conclusive or establish that *p* is true. One's full belief that *p* is proper only if one knows it.

II. EXTRINSIC ETHICS OF BELIEF: CRITIQUE OF FOUR DOCTRINES

Four doctrines implied by Extrinsic ethics of belief are to be set out and criticized. These doctrines are widely accepted because of the unchallenged dominance of Extrinsic approaches. The four doctrines are as follows:

1. The ethics of belief, and evidentialism, specifically, are committed to substantive views of rationality and on issues in epistemology and moral theory.
2. The ethics of belief is lax. The requirement of adequate reasons or evidence is diminished or abandoned. Characteristically, those who find evidentialism too

demanding advocate "Reidian" views in which beliefs are proper, unless they are "proven guilty."[18] William Alston advances the view that "we are permitted to believe that *p* unless we have adequate reason for supposing it false."[19] Variations on this theme allow for believing that *p* if *p* is not demonstrably false or if *p* is not shown to be false or in the absence of any specific reason to oppose *p*. The burden of proof is upon those who would deny entitlement to believe, not upon the believer. If my belief cannot be refuted in any of these ways, I am entitled to it.[20]

3. The "ought" of what it is right to believe is the "ought" of what it is right or best for a believer to do. The ethics of belief is a branch of practical or prudential ethics. (This doctrine permeates William James's influential argument as to why it could be rational to will to believe.)[21]
4. Methodology for the ethics of belief is (exclusively) either prescriptive, and hence can be indifferent to the facts of actual believing, or else descriptive, its prescriptions bounded by the facts about us as believers, particularly our finitude or limits.

In addition to these four doctrines, the next two are closely associated with Extrinsic approaches. Although these cannot be addressed here, I indicate the direction that I would take to respond to them. The first of these is *voluntarism*: belief is a matter of choice, in at least some cases. This doctrine goes along with the third and fourth. If the ethics of belief allows for "permissions" to believe and its "ought" is that of moral action, then we require the ability to exercise these permissions and to comply with the prescriptions. Contrary to the ascription of voluntarism to evidentialism,[22] the two doctrines are in conflict.

In a landmark paper, B. A. O. Williams argued for the conceptual impossibility of belief at will.[23] A variant of one of his key premises is obviously central to my arguments for evidentialism. The premise is that "[i]f in full consciousness I could will to acquire a 'belief' irrespective of its truth, it is unclear that before the event I could seriously think of it as a belief."[24] For his purposes of arguing against the conceptual possibility of belief at all, Williams had to go beyond this premise to deny voluntarism even for beliefs formed outside of full consciousness. The resulting argument has been subject to serious criticism. But I think the heart of his argument survives these criticisms, and that is the part of his argument that presumes "full consciousness." For our purposes, which are restricted to the ethics of belief, the condition of "full consciousness" or "full awareness" is proper, since, as we argued above, this imposes no restrictions on the beliefs to be considered. The condition is only a way to expose the claims inherent in belief. Consequently, it is enough for our purposes to derive the impossibility of belief at will or voluntarism under a condition of full awareness.

The other doctrine associated with Extrinsic views, which I do not examine at length here, is that evidentialism implies or requires *foundationalism*.[25] Nicholas Wolterstorff writes, "Almost always when you lift an evidentialist you find a foundationalist."[26] Foisting foundationalism and its problems onto evidentialism falls out naturally from the first doctrine, which conceives the ethics of belief as beholden to substantive views in epistemology.

The main reason evidentialism is taken as implying foundationalism is that evidentialism holds that each belief ought to be based on reasons. If reasons are themselves beliefs, and if circularity of justification is unacceptable, then we seem launched on a familiar infinite regress. Evidentialism is taken to require foundationalism in order to stop the regress. For the foundationalist posits that the justification of belief terminates with *basic* beliefs. Basic beliefs provide grounds for the nonbasic (or inferred) ones, but do not themselves require evidence or reasons (as further beliefs). They are self-justifying or groundless or justified by facts, which are not themselves reasons or beliefs. But were evidentialism to require foundationalism, evidentialism would be false. Evidentialism claims that all beliefs ought to be founded on good reasons, whereas the essence of foundationalism is that some beliefs are exempt from this demand. The alleged dependency is really a way of denying evidentialism.

The direction I would take to respond begins from the observation that evidentialism accords with our judgments. To take the foundationalist's favored case of perception, when you form a visual judgment such as that there is a red car across the street (or that it appears to you that there is), you take yourself to have good reasons to believe it. Among these reasons is something to the effect that perception is reliable. This latter reason does not have to be applied to the acceptance of the judgment through explicit reasoning. The workings of our perceptual processes are largely automatic. They do not allow for explicit reasoning (from, say, the reliability of perception to the use of the current data of perception to infer the corresponding objective judgment ["There is a red car across the street."]).

But that something like the belief that perception is reliable is a reason for you shows itself in the nature of our perceptual belief practices, in particular, that the belief formed is a full belief. In regarding the belief that perception is reliable as a good reason, you take it as justified. It is justified effortlessly through a history of largely successful uses and responsiveness to those uses. That is, it is confirmed, tacitly.[27] The proposal is not circular, even though the verification of successful uses itself requires perception, and so needs to appeal to the reliability of perception.[28] However, what matters for confirmation is simply the risk of falsification. So long as our beliefs do not control the world (such as our belief that perception is reliable), prediction is always risk.

The chain of reasons, on this view, is endless, and it goes in many directions. But it is not an infinite doing, and it does not need any particular starting point to get going. We should not confuse being justified with justifying. We expect that anywhere we stop along the chain, we have good reasons for the prior reasons we invoked, so we need retain no knowledge of the specifics. Nor is tracing the chain worthwhile in order to dig toward more secure foundations. Confirmation and our perceptual practices are self-correcting, so that past errors are likely either to be repaired or they will lead to a refining of our perceptual practices. (We have a better sense, for example, of where perception is likely to err.)[29] Endlessly grounded reasons, which is all that is implied by the combination of noncircularity and the requirement that reasons be themselves justified, does not entail an infinite regress of acts of grounding (testing, justifying). It can be norms "all the way down"[30] because it's tacit confirmation and so justification "all the way down."

I turn now to detailed examination of the four doctrines.

The first doctrine—that the ethics of belief presupposes substantive views of rationality and on issues in epistemology and moral theory—is the critical premise in Extrinsic arguments. These difficult issues come to obscure the innocent reflections that lead to evidentialism, which is arrived at by generalizing from such an unremarkable practice as asking "Why?" when someone makes a truth claim expressive of his belief. The expectation is that, in response to the why-question, reasons or evidence will be brought forth adequate to satisfy the claim.

Nevertheless, there are many routes to this first Extrinsic doctrine. The most obvious is that discussions in the ethics of belief are dominated by the familiar terms of ethics: "ought," "should," "permissible," "wrong," "justified." These terms are incorporated into talk of epistemic duties, obligations, and responsibilities. Criticism of belief is expressed in the terms of immorality ("blameworthy") or irrationality.

However, as just observed, this first doctrine is on its surface suspect. The common formulation of evidentialism, as the view that the strength of belief should be proportioned to the evidence, stands on its own. From the mere presentation of the position, we immediately grasp its rationale. The presentation does not dangle, waiting upon an elaborate defense. Evidentialism simply articulates our understanding of belief. In section I, I argued for evidentialism on conceptual grounds, explicitly assuming no substantive views of rationality, epistemology, or ethics.

The second and third doctrines (the ethics of belief is lax, and the "ought" of the ethics of belief is the practical "ought" of action, respectively) follow from taking the ethics of belief to be determined by what it is rational to believe, where the rationality assumed is that of action. Thus, the "ought" of the ethics of belief is taken as practically, ethically, or prudentially, not conceptually, based.

The second doctrine is designed to overtly relax the demands for reasons or evidence. Recall the view that

> we are permitted to believe that p unless we have adequate reason for supposing it false.[31]

According to this view, if you find yourself, for whatever reason, with the belief that the number of stars is even, you are entitled to continue to believe it. For you will surely not find adequate reason for "supposing it false."

But counterexamples are to be found in more moderate examples, such as the earlier one of the student who, let us assume, is convinced (believes) that he will receive a grade of A. Given his strong performance in the class, he has no reason to suppose that this is false. Nevertheless, once he comes to appreciate that he cannot exclude the possibility that he will not do well on the final, he ceases to hold the belief. His response is mandated: it is not just wrong or impermissible for him to hold the belief; it is not possible.

The battery of counterexamples that includes this one assumes that belief ought to be based on reasons roughly adequate for knowledge. Another form taken by a lax ethics of belief is to dispute so strong a conception. Richard Swinburne holds that:

> normally to believe that *p* is to believe that *p* is probable.[32]

But this proposal is stipulation, not analysis. If you judge it only probable (more likely true than false) that the bus leaves at 7:40, then that is your degree of belief, and you would deceive or lie if you asserted, "The bus leaves at 7:40," rather than "Probably, the bus leaves at 7:40." You cannot think "*p*, but there is a strong probability that not-*p*." If your believing that *p* implies no more than that *p* is probable, you cannot look past or through these attitudes directly to the content of the belief. Your belief is not transparent to you.

Traditionally, cases that appear to support a lax ethics of belief are those in which the support provided by the evidence or reasons for a proposition is inconclusive. If at night, we both see a single light moving rapidly toward us from the road, I come to believe a car with a broken light is coming toward us, while you come to believe that it is a motorcycle. The evidence is compatible with both views, so neither one of us is believing in opposition to our shared evidence. A gap is thought to open for the will to generate a judgment (belief). The claim of a gap where the evidence is inconclusive, but not where it is conclusive, appears plausible only when we attend just to the conclusion derived. We then ignore alternatives of weaker belief-like attitudes. But it is only the epistemic position—embracing the conclusion (belief) and the evidence for it—that is relevant. The (mistaken) thought is that when the evidence is inconclusive there is room for the will to operate, as there is not when the evidence establishes the truth of the belief. But the evidence is just as conclusive in the former case, as far as believing is concerned. The epistemic position is conclusively one of only partial support. Thus, we cannot fully, but only partially, believe.

The appeal of a lax ethics of belief depends on a stubborn conflation between the extent to which the evidence supports the truth of the belief and the strength of the belief on the evidence. One instance of this is the above equivocation on "inconclusive" as a lack of full support and as an absence of determining ground (of belief).

However, the conflation shows how readily we slide between the two, and that affinity is at one with the subjective principle of sufficient reasons. The very natural phrase "reasons [evidence] for belief" embeds the conflation. One's reasons or evidence are for the truth of the content of the belief, and it is only by virtue of the evidentialist proportionality claim, which is taken for granted, that these are thereby reasons for belief. The subjective principle is sufficiently second nature that our strength of belief, which only follows upon the judged strength of evidential support, comes to be identified with it.

The third doctrine holds that what one ought to believe is determined by the full range of practical considerations bearing on how one will act guided by that belief. As a recent article concludes, "there are occasions in which it is permissible, morally and rationally, to form beliefs not on the basis of evidence, but on the basis of pragmatic reasons."[33] The plausibility of the third doctrine resides in mistakenly moving from the fact that belief is always the belief of some agent (some doer) to the conclusion that what one ought to believe is derivative from what is right (best, optimal, rational) for one to do, all things considered.[34]

If what is meant is that the "oughts" of the ethics of belief can be overridden or outweighed by the demands of morality or prudence, then this is just the truism that "oughts" are susceptible to being overridden. You ought to speak civilly, though not if threatened by murder, if you do.[35]

The oft-repeated example supposed to favor this doctrine is of a wife who overlooks weak evidence of her husband's infidelity. She expects that, if such evidence were to undermine her belief in his faithfulness, it would destroy their marriage. She reasonably judges, we are to suppose, that the expected value of keeping her marriage together, if the evidence is misleading, well outweighs that for ending it, if the evidence is correct. The verdict is that it can be rational for the wife to continue to believe that her husband is faithful in defiance of the evidence. From these and related examples, it is concluded that if there is behavior "which one ought to prevent oneself from engaging in, and if one can . . . prevent this behavior by adopting a certain belief, then one ought to adopt that belief, apart from the epistemic warrant or lack thereof for that belief."[36] Thus the relation of evidence to what one ought to believe "needs to be justified by a practical argument."[37]

A telling concession of those who advocate the third doctrine is that, where rationality and evidentialism conflict, self-deception may be called on to serve rationality. So in the case of the justifiably suspicious wife, she might have to deceive herself in order to maintain the belief in her husband's fidelity. But advocates respond, "this only shifts the question—from whether it is wrong to believe on the basis of insufficient evidence to the question of whether self-deception is always wrong."[38] But why should self-deception be required at all unless the agent recognizes her prospective beliefs as violating their own claims? The answer is that it should not. It is because we appreciate the demands of belief that we are forced to hide from ourselves any attempt to induce belief not evidentially warranted. When we imagine self-deception lifted, the person can no longer maintain the belief, as exposing the kind of incoherence set out above.

But the unsuitability of the rationality approach to directing discoveries for the ethics of belief becomes even more glaring when we consider that one may just choose not to act rationally. So on this view, even if the wife determines that self-deception is rational, she can also decide not to comply with rationality. She will then simply believe both that there is evidence that her husband committed infidelity and that there is no evidence that he did. Our response is obvious enough. This is not merely less than perfectly rational, but incoherent, and so not merely an inferior choice. It is no choice at all.

The rationality I have been focused on is rationality of action. Some, however, would introduce as more pertinent the notion of *epistemic rationality*, as taking the best means to the end of gaining truth. This concept is much less natural and much less studied than rationality of action.[39] Still, I expect that some understandings of epistemic rationality would favor evidentialism as well. But this is not true of dominant views of epistemic rationality nor of those that give comfort to Extrinsic approaches.

The thesis to focus on, as drawing the sharpest break with evidentialism, claims that consistency, although an important advantage of a set of beliefs, is only one among others. These advantages potentially conflict, and consistency is not to be preserved at all costs. Here is a very recent expression of this broadly pragmatist perspective:

> there are criteria for rationality other than consistency, and that some of these are even more powerful than consistency. . . . These criteria are all independent

> . . . pulling in opposite directions. Now, what should one do if, for a certain belief, all of the criteria pull toward acceptance, except consistency—which pulls the other way? . . . it seems natural to suppose that the combined force of the other criteria may trump inconsistency.[40]

If this is correct, then, I assume, it should be possible to engage in the reasoning advocated openly. But it isn't. From the first-person point of view there is no coherent thought "*p*, *q*, *r* . . . are each true. However they are inconsistent. That is, at least one of them is not true. But that's OK because the collection has compensating cognitive benefits, and it would be foolish to sacrifice all the rest of these, merely for consistency. So 'yes,' each of these is true and one of them is not true." Overlooking this incoherence is a product of abstracting consistency from its central position in belief. Consistency is not just a "virtue" of a set of beliefs. Each of a set of beliefs makes a claim to truth, not to simplicity, fruitfulness, or other cognitive values. These claims can be satisfied only if the joint truth of those beliefs is possible.

The fourth doctrine assumes that the methodology of the ethics of belief is predominantly either exclusively descriptive or prescriptive. Either you infer the norms of belief from what human agents are capable of following, or else norms for belief dictate what it is right or wrong to believe, regardless of what believers actually do. The Intrinsic ethics of belief rejects this dichotomy.

Appeal to the "is-ought" distinction or to the naturalistic fallacy in order to argue for purely prescriptive approaches ignores relevant modal facts. It is erroneously assumed that the facts ("is") to which prescriptions can be indifferent are mere contingencies. But when the "cannot" is conceptual, this reasoning fails. Similarly, contrary arguments for naturalistic approaches assume that the "cannot" in the contrapositive form ("'cannot' implies not 'ought'") is that of inability. The result is an approach to the ethics of belief that is hopelessly dependent on peculiarities of human psychology ("chauvinistic"), rather than applicable to any (potential) believers.

The "cannot" of the Intrinsic ethics of belief is conceptual; it derives from the incoherence of recognizing both that one holds a belief and that one's reasons for that belief are inadequate. The incoherence is a contradiction, so there is no such thought, not merely an irrational one. The "cannot" is strongly prescriptive, generating not simply "not oughts," as entailed by the "'ought' implies 'can'" thesis, but "ought nots." Not only is it not the case that one ought to believe that *the number of stars is even*, but one ought not to believe it. And the restriction governs any believing creatures, not merely humans. For underlying the incoherence is a conflict between the nature of belief and one's epistemic position.

Because they are conceptually grounded, judgments of what one cannot believe are simultaneously normative and descriptive. The main doctrines in the ethics of belief are testable. We test them against the data of what we do (and so can) actually believe when we focus on the claims inherent in our believing a proposition and whether our epistemic position fulfills those claims. As previously noted, what we cannot believe conceptually, we cannot believe actually. So evidentialism corresponds to the facts. When we attend to any belief in clear light, it describes how we judge.[41]

An illustration of these interconnected claims is found in the *Apology*. During cross-examination, Socrates in exasperation censures his chief accuser: "You cannot be believed, Meletus, even, I think, by yourself."[42] Meletus has charged Socrates with "corrupting the young and of not believing in the gods in whom the city believes, but in other new divinities."[43] Socrates prods Meletus, in front of the jury, into admitting that one of the accusations is that of atheism: "you do not believe in the gods at all."

The unbelievability that Socrates ascribes to Meletus is on conceptual grounds. Attribution of incoherence to Meletus's beliefs follows upon the beliefs he attributes to Socrates. Meletus ascribes to Socrates beliefs that contradict—that there are gods and that there are no gods. The impossibility of holding those beliefs reflects back on Meletus, denying believability in his own attribution to Socrates. The ascription is normative: Meletus is "guilty of dealing frivolously with serious matters."[44] But the accusation is also descriptive. Once Meletus's commitments are brought to his attention, he cannot, and now does not, maintain them.

NOTES

1. This article benefited from discussion with Jeff Blustein, Sidney Morgenbesser, Michael Slote, and Michael Stocker, and from the extensive comments of Christopher Gowans, Peter Ross, Peter Unger, and especially Georges Rey. Mainly, this article is drawn from Chapter 1 of my manuscript *Belief's Ethics*.

2. See Myles F. Burnyeat, "Can the Skeptic Live His Skepticism?" in Myles Burnyeat, ed., *The Skeptical Tradition* (Berkeley and Los Angeles: University of California Press, 1983): 132.

3. John Locke, *An Essay Concerning Human Understanding*, ed. P. H. Nidditch (Oxford: Oxford University Press, 1975), bk. IV, chap. XVII, sec. 24, p. 688. Clifford's ringing motto is often quoted: "it is wrong always, everywhere, and for anyone to believe anything upon insufficient evidence." W. K. Clifford, "The Ethics of Belief," reprinted in L. P. Pojman, ed., *The Theory of Knowledge* (Belmont, CA: Wadsworth, 1993): 505. See also Brand Blanshard, *Reason and Belief* (London: Allen and Unwin, 1974), 401.

4. Alvin Plantinga, "Reason and Belief in God," in Alvin Plantinga and Nicholas Wolterstorff, eds., *Faith and Rationality* (Notre Dame, IN: University of Notre Dame Press, 1983): 30.

5. Richard E. Nisbett and Timothy DeCamp Wilson, "Telling More than We Can Know: Verbal Reports on Mental Processes," *Psychological Review*, 84 (1977): 231–59.

6. For comprehensive discussion and references see Roy Sorensen, *Blindspots* (Oxford: Oxford University Press, 1988), chap. 1.

7. For defense (of the iteration and conjunction principles) and some qualifications, see Sydney Shoemaker, "Moore's Paradox and Self-Knowledge," *Philosophical Studies*, 77 (1995): 211–28. Chapter 8 of my *Belief's Ethics* offers a more direct explanation, one without the iteration condition.

8. Shoemaker, "Moore's Paradox."

9. Contrast our analysis with those who conclude that the belief that *p* and that one does not believe that *p* violates some further principle, e.g., Jaakko Hintikka, *Knowledge and Belief* (Ithaca, NY: Cornell University Press, 1962): 64–78.

10. It is telling that rarely does one find anyone claiming compulsion by upbringing to hold a belief, while rejecting it as false.

11. Peter Unger, *Ignorance* (Oxford: Oxford University Press, 1981): 260–65. See also Robert B. Brandom, *Making It Explicit* (Cambridge: Harvard University Press, 1994): Part One, chap. 4, sec. I–II; and J. L. Austin, "Other Minds," in his *Philosophical Papers*, 2nd ed. (Oxford:

Oxford University Press, 1970): 76–116. For a forceful defense of a strong form of the connection see Timothy Williamson, "Knowing and Asserting," *Philosophical Review*, 105 (1996): 489–523.

12. A slight variation on Grice's maxim of Quality. Paul Grice, *Studies in the Way of Words* (Cambridge: Harvard University Press, 1989): 27.

13. See Fred Dretske, "Conclusive Reasons," *Australasian Journal of Philosophy*, 49 (1971): 1–22; and Robert Fogelin, *Pyrrhonian Reflections on Knowledge and Justification* (New York: Oxford University Press, 1994), chaps. 1, 4, and 5.

14. Edmund L. Gettier, "Is Justified True Belief Knowledge?" in M. D. Roth and L. Galis, eds., *Knowing* (New York: Random House, 1970): 35–38.

15. Actually, some qualifications are needed in going from right to left, since judgments of evidential support or subjective probability do not have to issue in any degree of belief. So the qualification needed is: "if any degree of belief is formed."

16. David Hume, "Of Miracles," in *An Enquiry Concerning Human Understanding*, ed. E. Steinberg (Indianapolis, IN: Hackett, 1977): 73 (emphasis added).

17. Peter F. Strawson, *Introduction to Logical Theory* (London: Methuen, 1952): 257.

18. See Nicholas Wolterstorff, "Can Belief in God Be Rational if It Has no Foundations?" in Plantinga and Wolterstorff, op. cit., 164.

19. William P. Alston, "Christian Experience and Christian Belief," in Plantinga and Wolterstorff, op. cit., 116; see also 119. Alston identifies this view with James and Reid, and it is the view that he favors. A Reidian view is endorsed in a number of Alvin Plantinga's writings; most recently it is a main theme of Plantinga's *Warrant and Proper Functioning* (Oxford: Oxford University Press, 1993). In other writings, Alston is more sympathetic to evidentialism. See the essays in parts II and III of his *Epistemic Justification* (Ithaca, NY: Cornell University Press, 1989).

20. But see Locke, op. cit., bk. IV, chap. XVII, sec. 20.

21. William James, "The Will to Believe," in A. Castelli, ed., *Essays on Pragmatism* (New York: Harner, 1951): 88–109.

22. See Alston, "Christian Experience and Christian Belief." See also his "The Deontological Conception of Epistemic Justification" in his *Epistemic Justification*: 115–52; and Plantinga, "Reason and Belief in God."

23. B. A. O. Williams, "Deciding to Believe," in his *Problems of the Self* (Cambridge: Cambridge University Press, 1973): 136–51.

24. Williams, op. cit., 148.

25. In Plantinga, "Reason and Belief in God," 39. Plantinga devotes exactly one sentence to arguing that evidentialism implies foundationalism. His argument simply assumes that evidence or reasons have to be explicitly represented and specific to each belief, rather than general or summary knowledge of the reliability of various sources of belief. He defends neither (implausible) assumption. In later works ("Coherentism and the Evidentialist Objection to Belief in God," in Robert Audi and William J. Wainwright, eds., *Rationality, Religious Belief, and Moral Commitment* [Ithaca, NY: Cornell University Press, 1986]: 109–38), Plantinga considers the possibility of evidentialism's resting on foundationalism's competitor coherentism. He even considers the evidentialist criticism to be that of a "noetic defect" (111–12). But the incoherence he looks to, and does not find, depends upon accepting a view (a further belief) incompatible with a nonevidentialist one (127–28).

26. Wolterstorff, op. cit., 142. He is here commenting favorably on Plantinga's essay, one of whose major claims is that evidentialism requires foundationalism. See also the discussion of related points by Nicholas Wolterstorff, *John Locke and the Ethics of Belief* (Cambridge: Cambridge University Press, 1996): 67–69.

27. The argument suggested, which requires extensive development, is hinted at in my "Conservatism and Tacit Confirmation," *Mind*, 99 (1990): 559–70.

28. The worry I allude to is carefully developed in William P. Alston's "Epistemic Circularity," in his *Epistemic Justification*: 319–49. However, for mitigating remarks, see, for example, sec. VIII.

29. For the broader perspective within which I locate this approach to the regress problem, see Wilfrid Sellars, "Empiricism and the Philosophy of Mind," in his *Science, Perception and Reality* (London: Routledge and Kegan Paul, 1963): 127–96.

30. Brandom, op. cit., 41; see also 178.
31. Alston, "Christian Experience and Christian Belief": 116.
32. Richard Swinburne, *Faith and Reason* (Oxford: Oxford University Press, 1981), 4.
33. Jeff Jordan, "Pragmatic Arguments and Belief," *American Philosophical Quarterly*, 33 (1996): 409.
34. In an article to which I am indebted, Richard Feldman and Earl Conee ("Evidentialism," *Philosophical Studies*, 48 [1985]: 15–34) seem moved by such a practical "ought" and our finitary predicament to offer an emasculated version of evidentialism, denuded of prescriptive force. See 17–18; however see too 19. See, further, the discussion below of the fourth doctrine.
35. See Louis P. Pojman, "Believing, Willing, and the Ethics of Belief," in Pojman, op. cit.: 573–92.
36. Jack Meiland, "What Ought We to Believe?" in Pojman, op. cit., 520.
37. Ibid., 524.
38. Ibid., 516. See too Jordan, op. cit.
39. But see Richard Foley, *The Theory of Epistemic Rationality* (Cambridge: Harvard University Press, 1987).
40. Graham Priest, "What Is So Bad about Contradictions?" *Journal of Philosophy*, 95 (1998): 420.
41. Thus, it is a fateful misstep to reason, as does Paul Helm (*Belief Policies* [Cambridge: Cambridge University Press, 1994]: 16–17): "If the idea that all bees die in the winter is incredible, this means not that such an idea cannot be believed, but that it ought not to be. It cannot mean the first, because some people do believe it. They believe it, but they ought not to."
42. Plato, *Apology* in *Five Dialogues*, trans. G. M. A. Grube (Indianapolis, IN: Hackett, 1981), 26e.
43. Ibid., 24c.
44. Ibid., 24c.

Midwest Studies in Philosophy, XXIII (1999)

Empirically and Institutionally Rich Legal and Moral Philosophy[1]

CARL F. CRANOR

The research described below began with a problem: the morality of exposing people to potentially toxic molecules. Exposure to toxic substances, created by what has become an increasingly chemical society largely in the aftermath of World War II, can harm us just as much as the grosser forms of violence, theft, and deception that have typically served as grist for philosophers' analytic mills. Indeed toxic molecules might cause more suffering than some of the things philosophers have traditionally considered to illustrate their principles or to challenge principles proposed by others. Carcinogens, for example, can kill us just as surely as, and often more agonizingly than can, a gunshot or knife wound, but we might be unaware that an invasion of our interests has occurred, unaware when it occurred, and, because such substances typically have long latency periods between an initial invasion of the body and a clinically detectable effect, unaware of the source of harm.[2] Reproductive toxins may not kill us, but might maim our children, for example, causing them to be born with stub arms or legs or worse,[3] make it impossible for men to produce children because of low sperm counts,[4] or in a kind of double whammy, give women cervical cancer and possibly give their offspring health problems as well, all because the women's mothers took the drug diethystilbestrol (DES).[5] Neurotoxins, such as lead, might lower a child's intelligence quotient or those of a whole generation. Thus, the effects caused by such substances might be as serious or more serious than the effects of the grosser forms of violence, theft, and deception in our lives. Yet philosophers for the most part have not addressed these urgent public problems. Discussions of philosophic issues in these topics appeared to be left to toxicologists, economists, risk assessors, governmental risk managers, and the like.

In what follows I sketch the nature of more than a decade's research and then address various ways in which aspects of this research might be seen as part of a new direction in philosophy, or at least one new to contemporary philosophic concerns. First, the general topic, as long as it is not characterized too abstractly, is new: philosophic issues in risk assessment and risk management and philosophic issues in science and the law for regulating toxic substances. Conceived more abstractly as issues in philosophy of law, it is similar to work that has preceded it, but extends it into some new areas. Second, the research is both empirically and institutionally rich; that is, I have learned in some detail aspects of the science needed to regulate toxic substances and aspects of the law utilized to address such issues. The empirical and institutional detail helped to reveal philosophic issues that might not have been seen, except perhaps in their most abstract formulations. This in itself is surprising given the social and legal importance of addressing philosophic approaches to toxic substances in our lives. There are philosophic issues in the science-law interface, but philosophers have not tended to address them, although others have without perhaps seeing them as philosophic problems. Finally, as we are presented with complex and multifaceted social problems with substantial philosophical content, it may be necessary to change our "organization of knowledge" to address them.[6] This is particularly true of issues concerning the environment and environmental health. By doing research that is empirically and institutionally rich, I have sought to learn "enough" of other disciplines in order to address with some care and sophistication the philosophic issues that arise at the interface of these fields and to speak with credibility to practitioners of those fields in their own terms. This approach permits philosophers to address new issues, to make a contribution to complex social problems where philosophic issues are at stake, and to have philosophy taken seriously by experts in other fields.

I

Molecules are submicroscopically small objects, unlike bullets, knives, or cars, and they can harm humans in almost vanishingly small amounts. For example, in 1978 the Occupational Safety and Health Administration (OSHA) became concerned about workplace exposures to benzene and issued a regulation lowering the permissible exposure from 10 parts per million (ppm), a level which they thought was harmful, to 1 ppm, a level that was not necessarily not harmful, but the lowest level they could reliably detect in the workplace.[7] At 10 ppm the agency was concerned that employees exposed to benzene would contract leukemia or aplastic anemia, typically both life-ending diseases. To put these amounts in perspective, the ratio of 1 ppm is equivalent to the ratio of 1 inch to 16 miles (length), 1 cent to $10,000 (money), 1 minute to 2 years (time) or 1 drop of vermouth to 80 "fifths" of gin (volume), an extraordinarily dry martini. Thus, the tiniest amounts of these substances can cause great harm to a person; they are quite potent on a unit basis.[8]

However, discovering the properties and effects of toxic substances is extremely difficult. Scientific, and some cases molecular, detective work is required. We cannot rely on our built-in "intuitive toxicology" that may serve us well when it comes to the lethal effects of speeding cars or trains or of bullets and knives.[9] However, because scientific investigation is labor-intensive, it takes time to identify and assess the toxicity of the substances involved.

We are ignorant of the scope of the problem posed by toxic substances. There are about 100,000 substances or their derivatives registered for use in commerce, but most have not been well-assessed for health effects. Moreover, for 75 percent of the 3,000 top-volume chemicals in commerce, the most basic toxicity results cannot be found in the public record; this finding is essentially unchanged from a 1984 study by the National Academy of Sciences.[10] It is difficult to get an accurate estimate of the carcinogens among them; rough estimates range from 10 percent up to 52 percent (using a relaxed criterion of carcinogenicity).[11] Finally, it is not clear how much environmental and workplace releases account for the cancer fatalities in the United States. Estimates range from 3 percent up to 30 percent of about 500,000 cancer deaths per year. One author suggests that reasonable mainstream views estimate about 10,000–50,000 deaths per year,[12] but others argue that the workplace alone might result in 50,000–70,000 deaths per year.[13]

However, even when regulatory agencies have been aware of toxic substances, they have done little by way of regulation. There are lists of carcinogens and other toxins on which there has been no or insufficient regulatory action, and often when agencies have clues about toxicity, they have not developed sufficient information about them to proceed with regulation. The U.S. Congress's Office of Technology Assessment found that of the carcinogens for which federal environmental health agencies had statutory authority, about one-half to two-thirds of the substances presumptively identified as carcinogens had not been acted upon.[14]

Inherent properties of many toxic substances make acquiring the relevant scientific information about them difficult. Carcinogens have long latency periods (the period from exposure to a substance until clinically detectable effects are manifested is from five to forty years),[15] typically operate by obscure causal mechanisms, cause diseases that are typically indistinguishable from naturally occurring diseases, and, except in rare cases, lack unique causal "signatures."[16] Moreover, different toxic substances cause different kinds of harm by different mechanisms; there are few generalizations from one substance to another; for example, compare reproductive toxins or neurotoxins with carcinogens (which sometimes cause harm by initiating the development of a tumor and sometimes by promoting the development of tumors initiated by some other nonhuman cause).

II

The above problems are exacerbated by the state of the science. Many of the scientific fields, in themselves or in application, on which we must rely for assessing the risks from toxic substances—epidemiological studies, animal studies, various short-term studies indicating toxicity, mechanisms, and so forth—are in their infancy. Some fields are not yet well-developed for identifying toxic substances and for assessing their potency (e.g., animal studies, various short-term studies indicating toxicity, and the mechanisms of action). Other fields, such as epidemiology, that have long and honorable histories must be applied anew to each example of exposure to a toxic substance to see whether there is a toxic effect compared with the occurrence of that effect in the general population.

Those who develop substances for use in commerce tend to develop information about the benefits of their products, by-products of production, or pollutants much earlier and in more detail than information about the typical health effects of those same substances. This favors permitting substances in commerce or keeping them in even though they may have as yet undiscovered adverse health effects. (Consider, for example, DDT or asbestos as older examples or something as recent as the dietary drug combination phen-fen.) In short, we might say that our information about the benefits from potentially toxic substances tends to be *asymmetrically* better than our information about potential health harms from them.[17]

Knowledge and informational asymmetries are exacerbated by political forces. Products using toxic substances, their toxic contaminants, or the toxic by-products of production have obvious constituencies, whereas potential victims are much more diffuse and less organized, and may not even constitute a constituency (because they may be unaware that a substance has caused their disease or that other persons are similarly adversely affected). Politically, it is difficult to address and deter problems posed by toxic substances.

In sum, many of the properties of toxic substances are inherently difficult to know, the tools for discovering their properties tend to be in their infancy or applied anew to each substance, and we tend to be asymmetrically better informed about their benefits than we are about their adverse health effects.

Scientific responses to ignorance and uncertainties about toxic substances can exacerbate the above problems. In assessing the risks from toxic substances as a matter of doing good science, it is presumed that substances have no properties in particular until these have been established by appropriate studies. That is, if we were to hand a scientist an unknown substance and ask her whether it was toxic or not, she would remain agnostic, as a good scientist should, until she had done appropriate tests on it. If we ask more difficult questions, such as at what exposure levels it might be toxic to humans, it would take a much longer time for her to come to a scientifically respectable conclusion. Answering questions about the mechanism of action would take even longer, if it were ever understood. Moreover, before changing the hard-earned knowledge status quo ante, scientists seek more and better information about the substance and its properties, better understanding of the mechanisms of toxicity, and good theoretical models to guide their understanding, and require that all these aspects of their research be supported with considerable certainty.[18] One concern is that the basic methodology, the presumptions, the burdens of proof and the standards of proof typically followed in science reinforce protections for potentially toxic substances.[19] Typically, the burden of proof is on a scientist who would make a claim about the world or substances in it to establish the claim by means of the appropriate methods. Moreover, these burdens of proof are typically reinforced by quite substantial standards of proof before such claims can be established.

The stringency of standards of proof is evidenced in the first instance by focusing on statistical procedures that are used to provide evidence for a departure from the current scientific knowledge status quo. In such procedures, scientists are typically quite demanding in preventing false positives (FPs), that is, their procedures are set up to prevent showing that a substance has a toxic property that in fact it does not. They typically insist that there must be less than 5 percent (or sometimes less than 1 percent) odds by chance alone (as a result of sampling error) of their evidence's showing that a substance is toxic when in fact it is not. There can also be mistakes in the other direction by chance alone, that is, procedures may fail to detect a toxic property of a substance when in fact it is toxic; this is a "false negative" (FN). However, scientists seem much less concerned about the possibility of FNs, perhaps on the view that if they fail to detect a toxic property in a particular case, it will eventually come to scientific attention. Thus, in something as fundamental as statistical support for conclusions, the foundation of most empirical research, scientists appear to devote greater attention to preventing FPs than to preventing FNs.

Scientists' epistemic conservatism concerning the knowledge status quo ante is not confined to statistical tests. Consider what a well-known toxicologist would require to establish *scientifically* that something is a human carcinogen. He argues that since an epidemiological association does not establish a causal connection, one needs not only multiple epidemiological studies, but also multiple animal studies subjected to strict experimental conditions, so there is an animal model for the toxic effect, and multiple short-term studies that might indicate the activity of the substance, the mechanism by which it works, and other detailed features of the substance.[20] The problem with this is that for few substances do we have such substantial information.[21]

Finally, consider the views of one scientist who emphasizes the importance of ruling out alternative hypotheses before drawing a conclusion. Scientists, he claims, seek to establish causal connections with "proof . . . usually accepted in science" or possibly proof "beyond a reasonable doubt" because alternative explanations will slay "a beautiful hypothesis."[22] This illustration is useful because he utilizes standard-of-proof terminology from the criminal law. We are familiar with it from other contexts and it serves as a comparison for discussing the standards of proof in science and the law. However, the "beyond a reasonable doubt" standard is one of the most demanding in the law. Accordingly, if one has "reasonable doubt" about the truth of the proposition under consideration, one should not accept it as true and presumably not act on it.

Scientific burdens of proof and the standards of proof with which they must be satisfied are reinforced by considerable skepticism and inferential caution because they play an important and legitimate role in the "institution" or "practice" of science. Scientists' responses to ignorance about toxic substances reflect important *epistemic* values and goals. They develop inferential caution to avoid mistakenly attributing properties to substances and changing the knowledge status quo. Healthy skepticism helps individual scientists by discouraging overly enthusiastic advocacy of their own ideas and by preventing them from wasting their own research efforts, and helps the profession self-regulate by discouraging it from chasing research chimeras and wasting collective efforts. More positively, scientists undergo critical training to develop virtues, skills, and techniques that lead to accurate outcomes, resist casually proposing views that overturn the hard-earned epistemic status quo, add carefully to the knowledge status quo, and improve their understanding of the mechanisms by which phenomena work.[23]

However, such skeptical attitudes, inferential caution, and epistemic virtues can have quite unintended and unexpected effects depending upon the context in which they are used. In research where we seek carefully to add to our knowledge, skepticism helps to protect against mistakenly overturning the hard-earned epistemic status quo and mistakenly adding to the stock of scientific knowledge; it helps to protect against making *certain* kinds of inferential mistakes. By contrast, in the regulatory setting or in the tort law, such skeptical attitudes reinforce the knowledge and *legal* status quo.

Legal protection from toxic substances is largely provided by two different institutions: federal and state regulatory law and private personal injury or tort law. In regulatory law, agencies use *risk assessments* to try to ascertain the risks from substances before they decide how to *manage* them. Risk assessment is the putatively factual and scientific part of the inquiry, the scientific fields and procedures used to estimate risks to human beings. The first step is to *identify* the hazard in question; for example, is it an acute toxin, a neurotoxin, a carcinogen? The second is to assess the *potency* of a substance; that is, how much of it does it take to cause a scientifically and legally worrisome effect in humans? Third, agencies need to assess the *routes and extent of exposure* to the substance, for example, via the air, water, food, and so forth, and finally to provide some overall *characterization* of the risk to humans. Risk management is concerned with managing the risks in question in accordance with the appropriate laws, taking into account the legal, political, economic, and moral considerations that bear on this issue.[24]

In the tort law the procedures are not so stylized, but the plaintiff, the person claiming injury from a toxic substance, must show that a particular defendant's substance more likely than not caused plaintiff's injuries. In this legal venue procedures similar to those used in risk assessment would be utilized to establish causal claims to the appropriate degree of certainty. However, as I discuss later, the standard of proof a plaintiff must satisfy in the tort law to establish such claims legally is not nearly as demanding as the standards of proof typically utilized in the science for research purposes.

Under a postmarket regulatory statute, that is, a statute according to which substances are permitted to remain in commerce until they are shown to pose a human health (or ecological) problem, where the burden of proof is on the government to show that a substance is harmful, skepticism and inferential caution keep a substance in commerce until a human health problem is identified with sufficient certainty to overcome the skepticism. In torts similar problems arise because the plaintiff has the burden of proof. In such circumstances if the evidentiary requirements are very high, as they are with the criminal law's "beyond a reasonable doubt" standard of proof, then it will be quite difficult to justify removing substances from commerce or reducing exposures to less harmful levels. The greater the proof barriers that must be satisfied, the harder it is to make the case for removing substances from commerce, and as in a legal trial, the more this protects one side in the regulatory or tort law debate about the proper course of action.[25] By contrast, under a premarket regulatory statute, where the burden of proof is typically on the manufacturer or registrant of a substance to show that it is safe, any skepticism and inferential caution about the extent of safety prevents a substance from commerce until the skepticism is overcome.[26]

Thus, the nature of the harms from toxic substances and the often obscure causal connections between exposures and harms forces us to discern them by means of scientific procedures and inferences (contrasted with grosser kinds of harms). However, our very reliance on these procedures exacerbates existing asymmetries concerning our knowledge about potentially toxic substances. Yet because toxic substances are by definition harmful, there is or should be a concern for discovering their effects sooner rather than later. This suggests that there may be a tension between the necessarily time-consuming, science-intensive procedures needed to discover and characterize harms and the moral and legal concerns for preventing them. As we see next, the unintended effects of scientific epistemic caution on the law are exacerbated because of the plasticity in some aspects of the science that supports regulation and tort law judgments.

III

A point less often noted is that the scientific procedures typically used in establishing risks of harm in regulatory law or the likelihood of harm in the tort law have some plasticity to them. By this I mean that two different scientists can use the same procedures and come to different conclusions depending upon how studies are designed, how the data from them are interpreted, and what science and other policy decisions guide the scientists.[27] For example, if one wanted the most accurate epidemiological studies, studies with both low chances of false positives and low chances of false negatives, that could detect relatively low relative risks for a disease,[28] such as benzene-induced leukemia, one would have to use very large samples in a prospective cohort epidemiological study. For leukemia, one would have to conduct a study of 135,000 people in the exposed group and an identical number in an unexposed group in order to detect a relative risk of three with false positive and false negative rates of .05 or less. However, such a study would likely be prohibitively expensive.[29] Thus, in order to save money, a researcher might be willing to sacrifice some of the accuracy of the study and risk higher rates of mistakes as a result of statistical chance. Smaller samples of the exposed and unexposed groups would facilitate this aim. However, once a sample smaller than the above described "ideal" is used, this forces researchers into critical trade-offs between the chances of committing a false positive mistake, the chances of committing a false negative mistake, and having a study that is too small to detect the risk of concern. In short, in such circumstances one can show mathematically that it is impossible simultaneously to have low false positives, low false negatives, and studies of sufficient power to detect the low relative risks of initial concern, for example, a relative risk of three. Like the pucker in a wall-to-wall carpet that is too large for a room, removing a pucker problem in one area merely forces it to appear somewhere else.

The major point this raises is that once a less than ideal study forces researchers into these critical trade-offs, which mistakes one risks in designing the study and interpreting it are a matter of substantial normative concern. Higher chances of false positives jeopardize scientific acceptability. Higher chances of false negatives risk failing by chance alone to detect risks of concern. If one insists on both low false positive and low false negative rates, one may not even be able to detect a relative risk remotely close to the one that motivated the study initially. Thus, decisions about the size of the study and, once that is fixed, decisions about which mistake to risk raise important normative questions. Which mistake do we risk? Which is the morally defensible risk to take? These normative issues are embedded in the very design and interpretation of such scientific studies.[30]

The other major kind of scientific study used to detect harms or risks of harm in regulatory law and to a lesser extent in torts is toxicity tests based upon animal studies. Statistical problems identical to those of epidemiology attend the use of animal studies, but there are additional ones as well. To keep costs under control relatively small groups of animals are studied. Animals (typically rats or mice) are fed several (two or three) relatively high doses of a suspected substance to see whether such doses cause statistically significant increases in tumors in the experimental as opposed to the control groups of animals. A typical study might reveal two or three data points at such dose levels, but most human exposures tend to be much lower, so researchers must extrapolate from high dose data points to much lower dose levels to project what toxic response, if any, might occur at the low dose levels typical of human exposure. This, however, would only estimate the tumor response *in animals*; thus the next step is to project from low-dose responses in animals to low-dose responses in humans by means of an animal-to-human extrapolation model. In using animal studies, then, there are two significant extrapolations: from high-dose responses in animals to low-dose responses in animals and from low-dose responses in animals to low-dose responses in humans. Which extrapolation models are appropriate? Unfortunately, there is little scientific consensus on these matters, although there appears to be considerable *normative or policy* consensus on which are appropriate. The use of extrapolation models that are radically underdetermined by existing scientific evidence adds to the controversy about whether and the extent to which there are risks to humans from substances that cause cancers in animals.[31]

The larger point is that the use of animal studies for identifying carcinogens and assessing their potencies introduces some plasticity into the ultimate judgments about whether substances pose a carcinogenic risk to humans (for regulatory purposes) and about whether they more likely than not have caused someone's cancer (for toxic tort purposes). Again there can be reasonable disagreement about these matters because they are so unsettled; someone interpreting such data must make judgments about whether to risk false positives or false negatives (or analogously overestimating or underestimating the risks from such substances) in interpreting the data and extrapolations from it, and different science and regulatory policies might guide those considering the data.

In short, there are a number of presuppositions of scientific inquiry that make seemingly "neutral" scientific research function less than fully neutral in other institutional venues such as the regulatory and tort law. For one thing, epistemic conservatism and inferential caution may contribute to delayed discovery of toxic properties. And in legal contexts, both may predispose legal debates toward one side or another in different institutional settings such as the law. Moreover, the plasticity with which scientific inferences can be drawn in risk assessment only exacerbates these problems. Automatic reversion to scientific caution in interpreting plastic evidence is likely to predispose legal disputes toward avoiding FPs and is likely to result in nonneutral effects between parties to a legal dispute (discussed below).

Scientists' typical approaches to the uncertainty and ignorance introduce other normative issues. When scientists are faced with uncertainty and ignorance they (a) acknowledge it in reporting results and (b) try to remove it with future research, but typically suspend judgment until it is removed. The *rate* at which knowledge is accumulated and uncertainty is removed is typically not critical in the scientific search for truth in research. However, for public health purposes and for purposes of justice between parties in the tort law, the rate at which substances are identified and assessed may be of considerable importance. Thus, even the approach to uncertainty and ignorance in research concerning toxic substances may raise substantial moral issues.

The previous discussion suggests the following generalizations: Difficulty in establishing information about, informational asymmetry about, and asymmetrical political constituencies favoring potentially toxic substances are all further reinforced scientifically by scientific burdens of proof, scientific standards of proof, and typical research scientific approaches to scientific ignorance and uncertainty. However, the plasticity in understanding and interpreting the evidence reveals normative issues in the utilization of science in assessing risks, and, in conjunction with certain scientific approaches to interpretation, may exacerbate some of the problems. However, the plasticity in interpreting evidence also provides opportunities for addressing some critical issues in risk assessment and the law; specifically, there are choices in how the data are utilized and inferences drawn. As I argue below, we should utilize those choices to mitigate some of the effects of asymmetries in knowledge, to address uncertainties, and to ensure that public health is protected in the different legal venues.

IV

From the above I draw several conclusions: (1) Because of ignorance, uncertainties, and the state of the science, carcinogen risk assessment differs markedly from settled areas of science, the science we tend to know from undergraduate classes and from textbooks. Simply put, it tends to be new, less well-developed and less well-settled than many of the scientific areas with which we are likely familiar. (2) However, the problems just discussed are not merely a function of newness. There are more endemic problems as a result of the introduction of new substances: the identification and assessment of the toxicity properties of substances newly introduced into commerce may always be undeveloped. For example, there is a family of dyes based on the chemical substance benzidine. If a manufacturer uses one of them and it turns out to be toxic, the firm may then turn to a different dye from the benzidine family. However, the manufacturer would argue, and a good research scientist might agree, that the second dye is at least a somewhat different substance, whose toxicity should be assessed anew. Under postmarket regulatory statutes, a whole new assessment of a structurally similar substance leaves it in commerce until the analysis is complete. There is now, however, fairly widespread agreement that this entire class of substances is carginogenic.[32] When substitute products are not from the same chemical family, such problems are exacerbated. (3) Carcinogen risk assessment is in fact substantially influenced by normative judgments; both the idea of "a risk" (the chance of an untoward or undesirable outcome) and the extent of a risk (because of the plasticity of research design and interpretation) are normatively laden. (4) In addition, the concern about preventing false positives is inconsistent in many cases with the aims of public health protections, for example, with the prevention of false negatives and prevention of disease, and with the aims of the tort law to serve justice between parties. In fact several scientific practices aimed at preventing false positives will paralyze risk assessment and regulatory activity: an insensitive demand for more and better science, for removing uncertainty, for multiple kinds of evidence, and for better understanding before regulation, including understanding of the mechanism of toxicity. Thus, in general I have argued that for environmental health protection we should find a better balance between false positives and false negatives, and we should better utilize the available scientific tools and understanding sensitively in order to achieve this. We need to recognize that our scientific and legal responses to ignorance and uncertainty may promote or frustrate the many institutional and social goals served by risk assessment and regulation. In consequence we should recognize the circumstances in which this is likely to occur and adopt policies in interpreting and utilizing scientific results in the different legal venues so that we promote and do not frustrate the legal goals of those venues.

To sum up, one problem is that scientific practices that appear neutral and that are utilized for certain purposes, when transferred to different contexts, may not be so obviously neutral: the scientific emphasis on avoiding false positives and the practice of suspending judgment until there is considerable scientific certainty or until uncertainty is removed. Another is that other scientific practices that appear to be neutral in some contexts will reinforce one side of a social debate or predispose the social debate in certain ways, for example, demanding more and better science before coming to conclusions. In addition, how research is designed and interpreted is a significant issue.

Most significant for one theme of this paper is that the above points become clear because of the empirical detail with which research into risk assessment and its use has been done. Some of the problems this poses for legal institutions and our broader social concerns becomes clearer because of the detailed description and knowledge of the regulatory law and torts. That is, although the normative or moral issues between risk assessment and the law are there whether or not we perceive them, they cannot be seen without detailed description and understanding of each of them, and they probably will not be understood without the detailed analysis. Moreover, they must be seen by someone who knows enough about both areas to detect the problems and to address them.

Having said the above, however, there is an additional issue of which we need to be aware when considering scientific accuracy and institutional decisions: there will be mistakes from the scientific procedures used to assess risks and to judge issues of causation. There will also be mistakes from the legal procedures in which the scientific evidence is used. Ideal scientific or legal procedures would result in no factual or legal mistakes: no false positives or false negatives of either kind. This is unrealistic now and into the foreseeable future, however.[33] Thus, in absence of perfect procedures for assessing and regulating toxic substances, whether in science or the law, I suggest that we should take into account the social costs of different kinds of mistakes as well as the social costs of utilizing particular procedures.[34] We clearly do this at present in many of our institutions and activities; consider, for example, the criminal law. Over time courts and legislatures have designed search and seizure procedures, presumptions, burdens of proof, standards of proof, and other protections for the general citizenry and potential defendants in light of the general aims of the law to reduce violations of the criminal law and in light of the nature of criminal punishment (as well as what wrongly punishing innocent persons will do to them). In particular, pretrial and trial procedures have been developed in order to protect strongly against innocent people being wrongly punished; there is a somewhat lesser concern to protect against guilty parties going unpunished, even though that has social costs as well. The aphorism often cited in support of this view is that it is better that ten guilty people go free (the equivalent of a legal false negative) than that one innocent person be punished (the equivalent of the legal false positive). This is a clear example of a legal/social institution that has been tailored in accordance with important social values (including those against unjust punishment of innocent persons) even though this will not always serve some of the deterrence aims of the criminal law. In short, the procedures have been designed for the context in question and for the significant social values at stake. Appellate justices and legislators have created institutional procedures to take into account the different costs of legal mistakes and the costs of the procedures themselves in designing and fine-tuning the institution. We could have greater deterrence and faster trials by removing some of the protections for defendants, but this would put in jeopardy some of our other values about justice, so we do not pursue such goals. This point can be generalized by considering the "designs" of several different institutions or activities with which we are familiar. These are summarized in Table 1, with an approximate representation of social costs of false negatives (SC_{FN}) and the social costs of false positives (SC_{FP}) or of legal FPs and legal FNs.

As an alternative example we might consider the design of breast cancer screening. Here, there is a well-founded concern for avoiding falsely identifying benign tumors as malignant (a FP), because at a minimum this will result in considerable psychological trauma and, if the mistake is not caught before an operation occurs, great costs, unnecessary operations, possible disfigurement, and additional psychological trauma. However, the greater concern is to avoid false negatives, failing to identify a malignant tumor. Positive results from screening can be followed up by additional and more sensitive tests to distinguish true from false positives,

Table 1. Designs of Some Familiar Institutions/Activities

"Institution"/Activity	False Positives	False Negatives	SC_{FP}–SC_{FN} Relation
Criminal law	Greater concern to prevent	Lesser concern to prevent	$SC_{LFP} >> SC_{LFN}$
Research science (field dependent)	Greater concern to prevent	Lesser concern to prevent	$SC_{FP} >> SC_{FN}$
Drug approval testing	Lesser concern to prevent	Greater concern to prevent	$SC_{LFN} > SC_{LFP}$
Breast cancer screening	Lesser concern to prevent	Greater concern to prevent	$SC_{FN} >> SC_{FP}$

whereas false negatives are likely to result in tumors' going undetected or going undetected for so long that once they are identified it may not be possible to prevent the tumor from causing the death of the patient. Thus, breast cancer screening is designed quite differently from the criminal law with respect to the requisite institutional false positives and false negatives.

Once we think about institutions or activities in this way, it is clear that we do not have a singular approach to institutional/activity design. This is not surprising, because, among other things, it is the values inherent in the activities and the values that we seek to secure in case mistakes are made that goes into such decisions. How such institutions should be designed is in part an institutional and social question and in part a philosophical question.

Thus, I have argued that we should adopt similar approaches toward the use of the science in the law. One common model for such purposes aims to minimize the *total social costs of mistakes*: the number and social costs of false positives, plus the number and social costs of false negatives, plus the costs of the evaluation and regulatory procedures themselves. Put technically, we can express this as

$$\min [(N_{FN} \times SC_{FN}) + (N_{FP} \times SC_{FP}) + SC_T],$$

where SC_{FN} is the social cost of a false negative, SC_{FP} is the social cost of a false positive, and SC_T is the social cost of the procedure and using it.[35] In regulating potentially toxic substances, false positives (and overregulation) will impose social and monetary costs on the manufacturers of the substances, on their shareholders, and on the consumers of their products. False negatives (and underregulation) will impose social and monetary costs on the victims or on those put at risk from the toxicity of the substances. Because of the uncertainties and normative presuppositions in risk assessment, the number and kinds of mistakes that will be made in regulating toxic substances depend upon how risk estimation tools are used for legal and public health protection purposes. Finally, there can be social costs to using institutional procedures as well. The law has an interest in relatively quick resolutions of disputes, so some legal procedures support this, whereas other procedures might favor greater time for preparation and more deliberate airing of the evidence. In regulatory procedures carcinogen risk assessment has been slow, even slower than animal studies, which are the foundation of regulation. But, if substances in commerce are harmful but unassessed, slow assessment prolongs the harm.

In short, we face normative decisions in how we design and use risk assessment procedures in different legal venues, that is, in how demanding we make data, inference, and procedural requirements for different legal purposes. A general concern is that scientific knowledge generation or knowledge accumulation activities that are subject to too many demands for science-intensive information can frustrate the public health and environmental protection goals of the regulatory law and the goals of justice between individuals in torts. How shall we err?

V

The above observations largely about risk assessment provide background for research on the use of such evidence in the law. One generic point is simple enough:

much as in different areas of the law, we need different standards of evidentiary certainty and different kinds and amounts of evidence depending upon the context of inquiry or the activity in which we are engaged. Thus, I have argued that there is a difference between the need for certain kinds of evidentiary procedures and stringent standards of certainty in science, on the one hand, and the need for evidence in the regulatory and tort law, on the other hand.

Thus, given the preceding background, it is clear that presumptions, burdens of proof, and standards of proof have important roles to play in decisions leading to action. Sometimes the burdens and standards of proof are explicit, as they are in the law, or more informal, as they tend to be in scientific inquiry; in either case insofar as they have determinative roles in decisions, what they are and how they are used will be important for decisions we make. Problems arise when we are not clear about consciously designing our institutions to recognize these issues.

In order to address some of the above problems, I have argued that we should acknowledge that risk assessment is a mixed science-policy procedure (for the reasons indicated above) and that the kind and amount of evidence needed in a particular legal or social venue is a normative issue. Both claims are relatively innocuous, but they can be liberating: freeing us from particular scientific paradigms about how scientific evidence should be used for risk assessment and regulatory and tort law activities, and freeing us to consider the possibility of other risk assessment designs and other approaches to acquiring knowledge and addressing uncertainty for the legal purposes in question. Moreover, we should be wary of an *insensitive* commitment to the epistemic values implicit in scientific inquiry (low false positive rates, demanding standards of proof, particular conceptions of rigor, and a desire not to add mistakenly to the stock of scientific knowledge) inadvertently trumping the values of the law, and the public health goals of carcinogen risk assessment and regulation. Our scientific epistemology can put these other values and goals at risk, if it is not well suited for the context. Thus, I suggest that we adopt a context-sensitive epistemology for using science and risk assessment in the law. In general we should design risk assessment, knowledge generation inquiries, and regulatory activities to serve aims of the institution in question with guidance from the norms of the institution and appropriate moral and philosophic principles.

In particular, I have argued that for regulation we should give greater attention to avoiding false negatives (appropriate to the legal context) than we have to date for two reasons: in order to protect the public health better and in order to mitigate some of the asymmetric knowledge we tend to have about toxic substances. Moreover, we should recognize that the rate of carcinogen identification and assessment is normatively important; slow knowledge accumulation per force may be harmful, especially given the large number of unassessed substances and the backlog of known animal carcinogens that may also be harmful to humans. Slow knowledge accumulation may frustrate action on a particular substance (e.g., dioxin has been under review and re-review by the U.S. Environmental Protection Agency [EPA] for decades) and it also diverts resources from acquiring information about the existing unassessed substances (in short, it has substantial opportunity costs). We should recognize the plasticity of interpretation and the mixed science-policy nature of these activities in order to address sensibly public health issues. We should consider utilizing approximations, presumptions, default assumptions, and policy choices to address uncertainties in risk assessment design, much as these devices are utilized in the law.[36] Finally, in research we should find or design scientific procedures that address the need to expedite the identification and assessment of carcinogens and other toxic substances, but with sufficiently low false negative and low false positive error rates that they can be reasonably used for legal purposes; that is, we should find replacements for animal studies, the current basis of much toxicity information, that are faster and sufficiently accurate for the purposes in question.

VI

The above generic ideas suggest a number of more specific recommendations for the use of science in the law for environmental health protection purposes. In environmental health administrative law, agencies work under laws that seek to protect our rights and interests by preventing harms from arising by specifying in advance how certain activities should be done. Typical statutes tend to be health-protective, suggesting to a greater or lesser degree a concern for preventing false negatives. Such laws tend to authorize regulation to prevent "unreasonable risks of harm to health," to prevent human health risks "with an adequate (or ample) margin of safety" or to prevent exposure to substances that cause "cancer in humans or animals."

One problem is that *potency assessments* of carcinogens, only one step in the risk assessment and regulatory process, whether done by the U.S. EPA or the California EPA, have been slow, taking, for example, from one-half to five person years per substance in the California EPA. One of the easier steps in risk assessment, this could and should be expedited, because potency assessments have not even kept pace with slow animal studies that take at least five years to complete. Thus, scientists at the University of California at Berkeley, the California EPA, and I suggested that potency assessments should be expedited in order to process information about known carcinogens faster, to provide a more consistent regulatory process, and to provide a more health-protective regulatory outcome (because unassessed carcinogens will now be more nearly fully assessed). And these procedures appear to save considerable social and governmental resources because they are less science-intensive and fewer known carcinogens go unregulated. (Thus, they appear to reduce the number of regulatory false negatives.)[37] The recommended risk assessment procedures and policy considerations aimed at mitigating social costs connected with science-intensive procedures (whose aim is to achieve a certain kind of accuracy and to minimize the number of false positives), so that the risk assessment process better served some of the health-protective aims of administrative health law. Our conclusion was that contrary to the current presumption, time-consuming, science-intensive assessments appear necessary only if there is low human exposure and the costs of regulating substances are quite high relative to the risks to human health.[38]

A second problem is that the *identification* of carcinogens and other toxic substances has also been slow. Tens of thousands of substances currently in commerce are unassessed. Some of these are of little or no import, but the most basic toxicity information is missing for 3,000 of the highest-production-volume substances, according to two different reports thirteen years apart.[39] Thus, a research group at UC

Berkeley, the California EPA, and I considered ways in which one might find quicker administrative procedures or scientific approximations to identify carcinogens (and similar things should be done for other toxic substances). We evaluated the use of quick short-term tests, such as mutagenicity tests, chemical structure-activity tests, and various in vitro tests, in order to assess them for their accuracy in comparison with animal studies for use in identifying carcinogens. The results in this area have not yet been as promising as they were for expedited potency tests, but even using less than fully accurate expedited identification procedures, the following results were suggested: if the percentage of carcinogens in the chemical universe is 10 percent or greater, and if in our considered social judgments on average the social costs of false negatives are greater than the social costs of false positives by a factor of 3.5 or greater (insofar as we can make such judgments), then there is a case for using expedited identification procedures compared with conventional science-intensive (e.g., animal) tests. Such identification procedures have relatively high false negative and false positive rates (both about .25). The false negative rates in the context of trying to protect human health are probably so high they preclude adoption of the procedures, despite their having some plausibility from a modeling exercise. (Similar high false positive rates are more tolerable, since a manufacturer or registrant of the substance upon getting a positive test result has incentives to do further testing to see whether it is a true or a false positive.) If the false negative rate for identification procedures could be reduced to more tolerable levels, such short-term tests would provide for faster screening of potentially toxic substances coming into commerce and faster surveying of unassessed substances in commerce, thus addressing one of the major shortcomings of current identification and assessment procedures.[40]

Third, susceptible subpopulations have not been well protected by environmental regulations, for example, children, the elderly, the genetically susceptible, and those whose health is already compromised. Pursuant to a National Academy of Sciences Report,[41] several pieces of legislation,[42] an agency initiative, and a Presidential Order,[43] the U.S. EPA is beginning to address this shortcoming in its regulatory science and its regulations.[44] The legal and moral case for this seems clear. Several pieces of legislation seem to support this view and several moral principles as well. Consider only one such principle that is deeply embedded in our legal system: a principle that has been part of tort law for more than 100 years suggests that if others invade our legitimately protected interests, then even if someone is more susceptible to injury than others, that person is still entitled to protection, for example, even those with eggshell skulls or particular vulnerability to disease. Thus, if the healthy are entitled to preventive measures to protect them from invasion of their interests, others who might be more susceptible to disease have equal standing to be similarly protected. For risk assessment and regulation, it is only good descriptive science to recognize the presence of factors that will make particular individuals or groups of people more at risk to disease. Moreover, pragmatically if we ignore special susceptibilities or sensitivities in risk assessment, they will surely be ignored in the management of the risks. Thus, it seems clear that susceptible subpopulations should be recognized for both risk assessment and risk management purposes.

Nonetheless, a strict research-science approach to this problem may frustrate some of the health-protective aims of protecting susceptible subpopulations. Good scientific research on the issue would identify all susceptible subpopulations potentially affected by exposure and identify the range of susceptibilities in order to set regulatory levels of exposure so that susceptible subpopulations had some appropriately low level of disease from exposures. Such an approach would involve considerable research into the particular susceptibilities, their causes and their range from most to least susceptible. This takes time and detailed information, even fundamental biological understanding of esoteric processes such as metabolic pathways and possibly genetic bases of susceptibility. And it would have to be done on a chemical-by-chemical basis for each substance under consideration. While such research is being conducted, the regulation would be held up, protections for populations would be delayed, and because resources were being spent for this purpose, they would not be available for addressing unassessed substances. In short there is the potential for considerable human and social costs, as well as great opportunity costs, from such an approach. By contrast, a context-sensitive approach to the problem would recognize such costs and recognize that the policy basis for addressing susceptible subpopulations did not have to be supported by such detailed scientific studies in order to have a good health-protective social policy. Thus, in general, agencies could shift some of the usual burdens of proof that exist in science and in postmarket regulatory processes to mitigate some of the these problems. Agencies should adopt, as some currently do, default safety factors or high-upper-confidence extrapolation models to serve as *placeholders* for variations in susceptible subpopulations until substantial, credible scientific evidence is provided to remove some of the uncertainty and change the default position.[45] Such an approach would, however, be a regulatory solution, not a scientific one. Just as in other areas of the law where certain *presumptions* are deemed appropriate for addressing a problem until there is evidence to the contrary, so similar presumptions in the form of default safety factors could be adopted in the risk assessment and regulatory contexts to address the range of susceptibilities in populations, given the legal and social policy aims in the contexts (and given the high costs of a science-intensive alternative). A more sophisticated approach might create default positions for risk assessment and regulation based upon similar classes of compounds and similar biological predispositions of certain subpopulations in order to avoid some of the gross assumptions just described. How realistic this might be is a much more open question, however. In both approaches only if there is *specific evidence* about susceptible subpopulations inconsistent with the default should it be used instead. The overall approach, contrary to the typical procedure in science, is to presume that there will be a relatively wide range of biological responses as a result of susceptible subpopulations and to change this presumption only when specific scientific evidence to the contrary is developed.[46]

VII

Finally, many of the generic concerns that led to recommendations about using science in regulatory law apply as well to the use of science in personal injury or the tort law. The tort law seeks to secure the rightful borders of our possessions and ourselves by *making us whole* should we suffer damage by "border crossings" resulting from the conduct of others. It sets public standards of conduct that must be privately enforced by the victim, who receives compensation for injuries *caused* by a defendant's acting in violation of the law. It aims to compensate wrongfully injured victims and to deter certain wrongful conduct. Injuries caused by toxic substances are one kind of legally compensable injury in torts. Establishing the cause of injury is just as much a scientific detective story in torts as it is in regulatory law.[47] Thus, similar issues arise concerning the use of scientific evidence in toxic tort cases. In particular, wholesale and insensitive adoption of scientists' burdens of proof, standards of proof, and pragmatic rules about the use of evidence in order to establish causation will distort the tort law, yet some courts and commentators urge this, suggesting that "science is science wherever you find it." Court requirements that scientific evidence satisfy the most stringent considerations take several forms. Some require multiple kinds of scientific evidence before a plaintiff can even have expert testimony admitted into court and before the plaintiff can present such testimony to a jury.[48] Some courts have instituted simple screening rules for admitting evidence into a trial, such as requiring epidemiological evidence or requiring an "epidemiological threshold"[49] for evidence of human harm, placing special restrictions on epidemiological studies before even they can be admitted into evidence.[50] Many of these considerations are typical requirements for scientific accuracy, which aims largely at preventing false positives but may increase the numbers of false negatives. Moreover, they will also distort tort law notions of accuracy,[51] which aims to achieve a much more balanced approach to preventing false positives and false negatives as the outcome of tort procedures and substantive law. In addition, such stringent scientific requirements for admitting evidence have important social and legal implications, because they, together with plaintiff's burden of proof, protect defendants at the expense of plaintiffs. Thus, failing to take into account the approximate balance of interests between plaintiffs and defendants in the tort law in designing the rules for admitting scientific evidence will over time distort the legal procedures of torts and the larger social aims they serve. Some courts have automatically excluded animal evidence, at least in the absence of epidemiological studies, for example, as was done in the Agent Orange litigation, and some commentators recommend this course of action. However, this also is too strong a requirement. It is not something a good toxicologist would do.[52]

In contrast to the above recommendations, I have suggested that courts take somewhat different approaches to the admission of scientific evidence. First, they should develop a more sensitive understanding of the science involved, including both its strengths and weaknesses and its possible effects on the law, or return to more relaxed standards for admitting scientific evidence. Second, *all* evidence on which scientists rely when making judgments about causation should be admissible in tort cases involving toxic substances: clinical studies, epidemiological studies, case studies, animal studies, structure-activity relationships, and other short-term tests. At present some courts exclude as inadmissible evidence that scientists would normally take into account. Third, the rules for admitting scientific evidence in tort law should preserve the traditional balance of interests between parties to a dispute and the traditional goals of tort law: to compensate victims for the harmful conduct of others that more likely than not harmed the victims, and to deter others from engaging in wrongful conduct that will probably harm others. Admissibility rules that explicitly or implicitly change the burdens of proof dramatically so that plaintiffs must establish a piece of scientific evidence to a very high level of certainty, approaching the criminal law's "beyond a reasonable doubt" burden of persuasion, to satisfy admissibility conditions will distort the tort law into a quite different institution. Fourth, courts should adopt evidentiary standards that give due consideration to the notion of tort law *accuracy* in decisions; that is, tort law should provide roughly equal protection to avoiding both legal false positives and legal false negatives.[53]

Finally, courts need to develop sensitivity to the subtlety, complexity, strengths, and weaknesses of different kinds of scientific evidence, and not issue overly simple rules for admitting or barring available evidence. At the same time they must learn to follow pragmatic rules about the kind and amount of evidence needed for tort law purposes, which will be somewhat different from those used by scientists. In particular, they need to develop on a case-by-case basis an idea of the minimal kinds and amounts of scientific evidence that are needed to satisfy admissibility, sufficiency, and proof requirements for the tort law.[54]

The last point can be illustrated by reference to what is now an agreed human carcinogen. Ethylene oxide, typically used as a sterilizing agent in hospitals, was for some time a suspected, but not a known, carcinogen. Human epidemiological studies had mixed results; that is, some were positive, some negative, and in general the statistical evidence based upon human data was inconclusive. Nonetheless, a scientific body, the International Agency for Research on Cancer, recently classified it as a *known* human carcinogen based upon the mixed human studies, animal studies and data about its mechanism of action.[55] Surprisingly, this was an evidentiary basis that would have been insufficient in some or many tort law jurisdictions even to persuade a court to consider a plaintiff's claim of injury meritorious enough to go to trial. Many jurisdictions would have precluded plaintiffs from trial simply because human epidemiological studies were inconclusive. Thus, if courts are going to seriously consider the science involved in deciding whether or not to admit evidence, they should at least utilize all the evidence on which scientists themselves would rely and preclude cases on the basis of overly simplified rules about the admissibility of evidence.[56]

VIII

In considering the above work and locating it on a conceptual map of developments in philosophy, we should consider both its subject matter and what might be called its "working methodology." On the issue of subject matter, the general topic, as long as it is not characterized too abstractly, is new: a cluster of philosophic issues concerning risk assessment and risk management and philosophic issues in the regulation of toxic substances with a focus on the regulatory and tort law.

Much of the work described above has had to do with the emerging field of risk assessment and with the management of risks. With others I have begun to explore philosophical issues in this increasingly important field in the contemporary world. This aspect of the research is simply an extension of long traditions in philosophy that have considered the philosophical presuppositions of different fields under the generic rubric of the philosophy of *x*, where *x* might be science, mathematics, mind, law, morality, and so forth. (That there is room in philosophy for such extensions to new areas may be evidence of an open and vibrant field.) I sought to understand risk assessment in sufficient detail, so that I could reasonably assess it and its use in the law to address the control of toxic substances. This understanding led to a diagnosis of some normative issues in (carcinogen) risk assessment and a diagnosis of some potential and actual problems in the differences between scientific approaches to evidence (as exemplified in debates about risk assessment) and evidentiary requirements of the law.

Considering this research as an aspect of philosophy of law, it is similar in many ways, but not in content, to work that preceded it. Nonetheless, even within this genus of work, it extends the scope of issues in philosophy of law to topics philosophers have not traditionally considered. Other legal philosophers have tended to write about the criminal law, the tort law, or in rarer cases, the contract and property law, in addition to such time-honored subjects as the nature of law itself. And some have written about the topics utilizing institutionally rich understandings of the relevant institutions.[57] Philosophical issues concerning the use of science in the law have not tended to be topics considered by philosophers, and philosophers have not tended to address philosophic issues in regulatory law.

Beyond these topics, this research has been partly in moral philosophy as well. A partial map on which to locate the research within some of the major issues in moral philosophy is suggested by Normal Daniels:

> "Doing ethics" involves trying to solve very different kinds of problems answering to rather different interests we may have, some quite practical, other more theoretical. [1] Sometimes we want to know what to do in this case or in developing this policy or designing this institution. [2] Sometimes our problem is in understanding the relationship between this case, policy or institution and others and making sure we adopt an approach consistent with what we are convinced we ought to do elsewhere. [3] Sometimes our problem is to provide a systematic account of some salient element in our approach to thinking about cases, such as an account of the nature of rights or virtues or consequences. [4] We can sometimes presume considerable agreement on some aspects of the problem but not others, so the practical problem may be how to leverage agreement we already have to reduce areas of disagreement. *There is no one thing we do that is always central to solving an ethical problem for there is no one paradigmatic ethical problem.*[58]

I agree with much of the above characterization; philosophers should recognize and embrace the multiplicity of activities that constitute ethics or moral philosophy. Within the above characterization, my work to date has tended to fall within [1] and [2], with some present, but even more future research aimed at [3]. That is, I have been concerned to address philosophic issues in risk assessment and risk management [1] and their use in the law [1], but also to address issues of consistency between the two institutions of science and the law [2] in order to understand philosophically the relationships between these two institutions and to articulate appropriate principles to guide the regulation and control of environmental toxins consistent with several different social goals.

This research is also partly an aspect of what we might call "institutional" morality. By that I mean research addressing appropriate moral philosophic views for assessing the joint effect of two institutions or aspects of institutions on the lives of persons.[59] In one sense, I have not for the most part addressed that issue directly, only indirectly, since I have yet to argue explicitly and fully for the moral view that should guide us on these matters (Daniels's [3] above). To date I have tended to identify and resolve incompatibilities between institutions and what their joint effect might be on persons, relying upon particular conceptions of the presuppositions of these institutions. However, hidden (for the most part) in the background of these inquiries is a concern that certain utilitarian or consequentialist approaches to the issues are not the best way to address them. I have implicitly utilized a working moral philosophic hypothesis that tends to emphasize the protection of individual persons (in something like the Kantian tradition) more than is ordinarily recommended by utilitarian kinds of justifications and arguments.

Second, on the issue of what might be called "working methodology" there are two generic points to be made. First, the research is both empirically and institutionally rich; that is, I have learned in some detail aspects of the science needed to regulate toxic substances and in considerable detail the law utilized to address such issues. Utilizing such detailed knowledge, given how philosophers of science and philosophers of law are now being trained, is not new; it is the only responsible way to proceed. One cannot engage in such research without detailed knowledge of the field involved, just as one cannot do philosophic research well in other areas of philosophy of *x* without knowing *x* well.

Second, however, the empirical and institutional detail have helped to reveal philosophic issues that might not have been seen, except perhaps in their most abstract formulations. There were philosophic issues concerning the relationship between science and the law, but perhaps they had not been seen until they were put in relief because of the detailed descriptions of each. And it is new that philosophers, as opposed to those in other disciplines, are considering them. This in itself is surprising, given the seeming importance of addressing approaches to toxic substances in our lives. Lawyers, scientists, government officials, and employees of industry have devoted considerable effort to addressing these topics, but not philosophers.

This work revealed normative judgments concealed in risk assessment and the idea that in assessing the risks from particular substances there is some plasticity in these judgments. Thus, in circumstances of less than perfect knowledge and with limited resources, we need to ensure that risk assessment is done in ways that are consistent with health protections and with our legal or moral goals, respectively. As is argued above, a major thrust of this research has been to avoid epistemic standards of one institution or area of inquiry (science) hijacking, or to change the metaphor, trumping, those of another institution (the law).

This research, however, bridging science and the law, also required detailed institutional understandings of administrative health law and the tort law. Philosophic analysis of some of the aims of the two areas was required: what are some of the aims or goals of regulatory law (and this, of course varies by statute, and by whether the particular law is a postmarket or premarket law), the relative balance of legal interests between parties, and the effect of different approaches to using scientific evidence (with all its plasticity) in regulatory law? A similar philosophical analysis is needed for the tort law, its aims and goals, the legal balance of interests between parties, and the effect of different pragmatic evidentiary rules concerning scientific evidence in torts.[60]

Finally, a much larger and somewhat vaguer point should be made about the "organization of knowledge." As different disciplines and modern university struggle with addressing pressing social problems, it has become clear that the analysis of and solutions to problems tend not to come from single fields or areas of inquiry. By their nature problems tend to be complex and multifaceted and to require the contributions of a number of different disciplines as traditionally conceived to address them. This is particularly true of issues concerning the environment and environmental health. One approach might be for teams of researchers to address such complex problems and, of course, this is done. It may be difficult, however, to create the right team of people to identify and assess a problem, especially if they are not geographically proximate. There is also a problem translating between the languages and presuppositions of different disciplines. To some extent the research described above has followed this course,[61] but for the most part it has taken a somewhat different tack. I have explicitly sought to learn "enough" of other disciplines—appropriate aspects of science and the law—in order to address with some care and sophistication the philosophic issues that arise at the interface of these fields and in order to speak to practitioners of those fields in their own terms. That is, it was necessary to acquire in modest ways appropriate understanding of other disciplines in order to address the issues. I sought in my own work to modify the organization of knowledge in order to speak to these issues. It seemed important not to be confined by traditional conceptions and boundaries of philosophy in order to address and try to resolve some of the issues that motivated the original research and in order to speak to some of the issues that emerged as it progressed. Such an approach permits philosophers to address new issues, to make a contribution to complex social problems where substantial philosophic issues are at stake, and to have philosophic contributions taken seriously by those in other fields.[62] Again, this approach is not unprecedented—both current and historical philosophers have done it—but it may be increasingly important in the future in order to come to grips with urgent and complex social problems with substantial philosophical content.

NOTES

1. Substantial sections of this paper have been taken from my Distinguished Humanist Achievement Lecture delivered to the University of California, Riverside's Center for Ideas and Society, November 20, 1997.

2. Typically, however, people who suffer from the effects of exposure to toxic substances have not been intentionally or knowingly exposed as they might be intentionally or knowingly harmed by muggers or thieves.

3. This happened to children whose mothers took the drug thalidomide during pregnancy. For a general discussion, see J. Manson, "Teratogens," chap. 7 in C. Klaassen, M. Amdur, and J. Doull, eds., *Casarett and Doull's Toxicology* (New York: Pergamon Press, 1996).

4. 1,2-DIBROMO-3-CHLOROPROPANE (DBCP) causes such harms. For a general discussion, see R. Dixon, "Toxic Responses of the Reproductive System," chap. 16 in Klaassen, Amdur, and Doull, eds., *Casarett and Doull's Toxicology*.

5. Diethystibestrol (DES) has been found to cause cervical cancer in the daughters of women who took DES during pregnancy with their daughters (*Sindell v. Abbott Laboratories*, 26 Cal. 3E 588, 607 P. 2d 924 [1980]). Some have suggested that DES might even cause third-generation effects, but this effect is not well established.

6. I borrow this term from Albert Carnesale, Chancellor, UCLA, who used it in remarks to the annual meeting of the University of California Deans of Letters and Sciences.

7. And even this level might not be low enough; see Peter F. Infante, "Benzene and Leukemia: The 0.1 ppm ACGIH Proposed Threshold Limit Value for Benzene," *Appl. Occup. Envirn. Hyg.*, 7 (1992), 253–62.

8. Subsequent analysis showed that 35 percent of leukemogenic diseases appeared to be caused by exposures below 6 ppm and that increased chromosomal breakage occurred at exposures at 1 ppm, so OSHA was hardly being too cautious in setting its exposure levels (Infante, "Benzene and Leukemia").

9. Nancy Kraus, Torbjorn Malmfors, and Paul Slovic, "Intuitive Toxicology: Expert and Lay Judgments of Chemical Risks," *Risk Analysis*, 12 no. 2 (1992), 215–32.

10. In 1984, 78 percent of chemicals in the United States with production volume greater than one million pounds per year lacked even "minimal toxicity information" (National Research Council, *Toxicity Testing* [Washington, DC: National Academy Press, 1984], 84). Little has changed in thirteen years; in 1997, 75 percent of such substances lacked minimal toxicity information (Environmental Defense Fund, *Toxic Ignorance* [New York: Author, 1997]).

11. U.S. Congress, Office of Technology Assessment, *Cancer Risk: Assessing and Reducing the Dangers in Our Society* (Boulder, CO: Westview Press, 1982), 12, 130.

12. Stephen Breyer, *Breaking the Vicious Circle: The Oliver Wendell Holmes Lectures, 1992* (Cambridge: Harvard University Press, 1993), 6.

13. Phillip J. Landrigan, "Commentary: Environmental Disease—A Preventable Epidemic," *Am. J. Public Health*, 82 (1992), 941.

14. U.S. Congress, Office of Technological Assessment, *Identifying and Regulating Carcinogens* (Washington, DC: U.S. Government Printing Office, 1987), 9–22.

15. D. Schottenfeld and J. F. Haas, "Carcinogens in the Workplace," *CA—Cancer Journal for Clinicians*, 144 (1979), 156–59.

16. Talbot Page, "A Generic View of Toxic Chemicals and Similar Risks," *Ecology Law Quarterly*, 7 no. 2 (1978), 207–44.

17. I use the term "asymmetric information or knowledge" somewhat differently than lawyers and legal scholars tend to. They refer to asymmetric knowledge differences between two or more different individuals, whereas I am concerned with the tendency for us to know asymmetrically less about some features of toxic substances (their adverse health effects) than others (their benefits).

18. Carl F. Cranor, *Regulating Toxic Substances: A Philosophy of Science and the Law* (New York: Oxford University Press, 1993), 25–28.

19. By the assignment of *burdens of proof* I mean the party or scientists who must take the argumentative initiative in persuading other scientists that the evidentiary or knowledge status quo should be changed. Typically, the burden falls on one who would argue that we are mistaken about what is currently known, on the one who would change the knowledge status quo. By *standards of proof* I mean the degree of certainty required to substantiate a claim, as established by scientific evidentiary norms and practices, that a person would have to meet who would argue to change the status quo ante.

20. Arthur Furst, "Yes, But Is It a Human Carcinogen?" *J. of the American College of Toxicology*, 9 (1990), 1–18.

21. Out of 736 substances that have been evaluated for carcinogenicity, 74 substances are known human carcinogens (these *might* satisfy Furst's criteria), 56 are "probably" human carcinogens (which would not satisfy his criteria), and 225 "possibly" human carcinogens. *IARC Monographs*, vols. 1–71 (1972–1998), summarized at the International Agency for Research on Cancer Website, http://193.51.164.11/monoeval/grlist.html (updated March 5, 1998).

22. H. J. Eysenck, "Were We Really Wrong?" *American Journal of Public Health*, 133 no. 5 (1991), 429–32.

23. Carl F. Cranor, "Discerning the Effects of Toxic Substances: Using Science without Distorting the Law," *Jurimetrics: Journal of Law, Science and Technology*, 38 (1998), 545–52.

24. National Research Council, Risk Assessment in the Federal Government (Washington, DC: National Academy Press, 1983), 3.

25. Vern R. Walker, "Preponderance, Probability and Warranted Fact-Finding," *Brooklyn L. R.*, 62 (1996), 1075, 1115.

26. Note that in the above discussion it is important what question is asked in the context. In the postmarket context, the issue is "Is the substance harmful and, if so, how harmful is it?" whereas in the premarket context, the question by contrast is "Is the substance safe, or sufficiently so that it can be permitted into commerce?" Thus, the questions are different in different contexts and the context together with the standard of proof that must be satisfied importantly affects the legal outcome.

27. This is not merely the philosophy of science problem that the evidence underdetermines conclusions, but a more serious problem resulting from the kinds of evidence in question. Cranor, *Regulating Toxic Substances*, 22–24.

28. The relative risk is the ratio of the disease rate in an exposed group divided by the disease rate in an unexposed group.

29. To put this in context, recently the *New York Times* reported that an epidemiological study of a drug thought to prevent breast cancer with a sample of 13,000 women cost $50 million. A linear extrapolation from these numbers suggests that for a study of the type described to be fully accurate it would cost at least as much as $500 million (and even this would not be adequate, if one needed that many subjects in both the experimental and control populations).

30. Carl F. Cranor, "Some Moral Issues in Risk Assessment," *Ethics*, 101 (October 1990), 123–43.

31. A National Academy of Sciences study has identified some fifty different "inferential gaps" in the chains of reasoning leading from empirically determined facts to conclusions about risks to humans. National Research Council, *Risk Assessment in the Federal Government*, 28–40. I have merely indicated some of the leading "gaps."

32. These substances are, for example, listed as known carcinogens under California's Proposition 65.

33. This concern is not just a function of ignorance in science or poorly designed institutions. Rather it would be difficult or impossible to design perfectly accurate scientific procedures and institutions that could guarantee perfect outcomes. Moreover, given the probabilistic nature of much of scientific inquiry, it is arguable that there could not be perfectly accurate scientific procedures.

34. See John Rawls, *A Theory of Justice* (Cambridge: Harvard University Press, 1971), 85–87, for a discussion of perfect and imperfect procedural justice.

35. This formulation of a unified approach to mistakes is not uncontroversial, even from my point of view, since it bears such similarity to utilitarian approaches to social problems. I tend to favor a less utilitarian and less consequentialist approach to normative and distributive issues.

36. Carl F. Cranor, "Learning from the Law for Regulatory Science," *Law & Philosophy*, 14 (1995), 115–45.

37. Sara M. Hoover, Lauren Zeise, William S. Pease, Louise E. Lee, Mark P. Henning, Laura B. Weiss, and Carl Cranor, "Improving the Regulation of Carcinogens by Expediting Cancer Potency Estimation," *Risk Analysis*, 15 no. 2 (April 1995), 267–80; and Carl F. Cranor, "The Social Benefits of Expedited Risk Assessment," *Risk Analysis*, 15 no. 4 (June 1995), 353–58.

38. The incompatibility between regulatory law and research science fields that might underlie it is expressed in the following relationships.

"Institution"/Activity	False Positives	False Negatives	SC_{FP}–SC_{FN} Relation
Research science (field dependent)	Greater concern to prevent	Lesser concern to prevent	$SC_{FP} >> SC_{FN}$
Environmental health law	Lesser concern to prevent	Greater concern to prevent	$SC_{LFN} > SC_{LFP}$

For research there is a great concern with preventing false positives *because* of the social costs to science if scientists do not have this concern, whereas for environmental health law there is priority to prevent regulatory false negatives and overregulation because of congressional mandates and the morality of protecting people from potential harms.

39. National Research Council, *Toxicity Testing*, and the Environmental Defense Fund, *Toxic Ignorance*.

40. Carl F. Cranor, "The Normative Nature of Risk Assessment: Features and Possibilities," *Risk: Health, Safety and Environment*, 8 (Spring 1997), 123–36.

41. National Research Council, *Pesticides in the Diets of Infants and Children* (Washington, DC: National Academy Press, 1993).

42. The 1992 Clean Air Act Amendment, the 1996 Food Quality Protection Act, and the Safe Drinking Water Act amendments of 1996.

43. Exec. Order No. 12,898, 3 C.F.R. 859 (1995), *reprinted in* 42 U.S.C.A. sec. 4321 (West 1994) ("Federal Actions to Address Environmental Justice in Minority Populations and Low-Income Populations").

44. Results of an EPA conference on this issue are reported in a special of *Environmental Toxicology and Pharmacology*, 4 (1998).

45. Current tenfold default safety factors may not be large enough; perhaps they should be several hundred–fold (D. Hattis and K. Barlow, "Human Interindividual Variability in Cancer Risks: Technical and Management Challenges," *Health and Ecological Risk Assessment*, 2 (1996), 194–220; F. Perera, "Molecular Epidemiology: Insights into Cancer Susceptibility, Risk Assessment, and Prevention," *J. Natl. Cancer Inst.*, 88 (1996), 496–509; S. Venitt, "Mechanisms of Carcinogenesis and Individual Susceptibility to Cancer," *Clin. Chem*, 40 (1994), 1421–25.

46. Carl F. Cranor, "Eggshell Skulls and Loss of Hair from Fright: Some Moral and Legal Principles which Protect Susceptible Subpopulations," *Environmental Toxicology and Pharmacology*, 4 (1997), 239–45.

47. There is a greater emphasis on screening evidence that purports to be scientific since the Supreme Court's decision in *Daubert v. Merrell-Dow, Inc.*, 509 U.S. 579 (1993).

48. This suggestion is analogous to the stringent scientific requirements that Professor Furst would place on judging that a substance is a human carcinogen. (See text and notes at note 20.)

49. I owe this term to Michael D. Green, *Expert Witnesses and Sufficiency of Evidence*, 86 NW. U. L. Rev. 643, 680–682 (1992).

50. Requiring that studies be statistically significant at the .05 level or below; requiring that studies exhibit a relative risk of at least two helps to provide evidence that plaintiff's injuries more likely than not resulted from exposure to defendant's substance; requiring Hill's factors or considerations, e.g., high relative risks, consistency with other studies, specificity, biological plausibility. Some courts and commentators appear to require most of Hill's factors, but Hill himself did not; he regarded none of the nine "considerations" as a necessary condition, except one requiring that the cause precede the effect. Moreover, Hill himself points out that rigid adherence to Hill's factors would have led to delay in identifying the cause of meningitis (because it had a low relative risk), and to missing that occupational exposure to nickel causes cancer (because consistency did not obtain), that soot causes scrotum cancer (because at the time it was discovered it lacked biological plausibility since it was a new biological result), and that arsenic causes skin cancer (because at the time it was discovered this result did not cohere with other scientific tests, which were still inconclusive or negative). Austin Bradford Hill, "The Environment and Disease: Association or Causation?" *Proceedings of the Royal Society of Medicine*, 58 (1965), 295, 299, reprinted in Sander Greenland, ed., *Evolution of Epidemiologic Ideas: Annotated Readings on Concepts and Methods* (Newton Lower Falls, MA: Epidemiology Resources, Inc., 1987), 15–19.

Such considerations *strengthen* the evidence and the study, but are not *necessary conditions* for a reliable or admissible study.

51. Cranor, "Discerning the Effects of Toxic Substances"; and Carl F. Cranor, John G. Fischer, and David A. Eastmond, "Judicial Boundary-Drawing and the Need for Context-Sensitive Science in Toxic Torts after *Daubert v. Merrell-Dow Pharmaceutical*," *Virginia Environmental Law Journal*, 16 (1996), 1–77.

52. Well-regarded scientific groups, such as the International Agency for Research on Cancer (IARC), always utilize animal studies, and there are substances classified as probable human carcinogens on the basis of animal and mechanistic evidence, in absence of clear epidemiological studies.

53. The distortion that might occur if scientific standards of appropriate evidence dominate tort law as an institution is indicated in the following relationships.

"Institution"/Activity	False Positives	False Negatives	SC_{FP}–SC_{FN} Relation
Research science (field dependent)	Greater concern to prevent	Lesser concern to prevent	$SC_{FP} >> SC_{FN}$
Tort law	Approximately equal concern to prevent		$SC_{LFN} = SC_{LFP}$

54. Cranor, "Discerning the Effects of Toxic Substances"; and Cranor et al., "Judicial Boundary-Drawing and the Need for Context-Sensitive Science in Toxic Torts after *Daubert v. Merrell-Dow Pharmaceutical.*"

55. IARC Monograph Series, Vol. 60 (1994). The overall evaluation of ethylene oxide was upgraded from a probable human carcinogen to a known human carcinogen with supporting evidence from other data relevant to the evaluation of carcinogenicity and its mechanisms.

56. In another interesting scientific case, investigators from the Centers for Disease Control, called in to investigate an unusual death that appeared to be murder, found that a disgruntled former lover of a woman tried to cause the slow death of her and her family by lacing lemonade in the refrigerator with a known carcinogen. The substance, dimethynitrosamine, was more potent than he anticipated, with the result that he caused acute liver disease that killed several of them within a few days. The interesting thing about this is that all the scientific evidence that the substance was a liver toxin came, not from human studies, but from animal studies, a source of evidence that would not be permitted into many tort law cases, but that formed the basis of evidence of a criminal conviction for murder. Renate D. Kimbrough, "Case Studies," in P. L. Williams and J. L. Burson, eds.), *Industrial Toxicology* (New York: Van Nostrand Reinhold, 1985), 414, 417–20.

57. H. L. A. Hart used detailed knowledge about the law to address traditional questions about the nature of law; Joel Feinberg addressed questions about responsibility in and the limits of the criminal law utilizing detailed understanding of the law; Jules Coleman has written about the tort law, its aims, and its relations to other areas of the law, which he could only do by being institutionally well-informed; and Steve Munzer has addressed philosophic issues in property law with detailed knowledge of the law as background.

58. Norman Daniels, "Wide and Narrow Reflective Equilibrium in Practice," in Norman Daniels, ed., *Justice and Justification* (New York: Cambridge University Press, 1996), 339 (Arabic numerals added).

59. A good bit (but not all) of moral philosophy has been concerned with what we might consider the morality between individuals, with a lesser focus on the effect of institutions on individuals.

60. The working methodology of much of the research described above may fit within one strand of pragmatism as described by John Dewey. Dewey, in the *Reconstruction of Philosophy* (New York: Henry Holt and Company, 1920), said that all philosophy, beginning with the Greeks to the time of his writing, was

> the significant record of the efforts of men to formulate the things of experience to which they are most deeply and passionately attached. Instead of impersonal and purely speculative endeavors to contemplate as remote beholders the nature of absolute things-in-themselves, we have a living picture of the choice of thoughtful men about what they would have life to be and to what ends they would have men shape their intelligent activities. . . . When it is acknowledged that . . . philosophy has been occupied with the precious values embedded in social traditions, that it has sprung from a conflict of inherited institutions with incompatible contemporary tendencies, it will be seen that the task of future philosophy is to

> clarify men's ideas as to the social and moral strifes of their own day. Its aim is to become so far as is humanly possible an organ for dealing with these conflicts. That which may be unreal when it is formulated in metaphysical distinctions becomes intensely significant when connected with the drama of the struggle of social beliefs and ideals. Philosophy which surrenders its somewhat barren monopoly of dealings with Ultimate and Absolute Reality will find a compensation in enlightening the moral forces which move mankind and in contributing to the aspiration of men to attain to a more ordered and intelligent happiness. (25–27)

Although I disagree with much of what Dewey says, there is a plausible pragmatism that can be discerned in his comments. The pragmatism in the research described above might be seen as follows. I have tried to address a substantial social, political, legal, and moral problem of our time—the regulation and control of toxic substances, a relatively new phenomenon in our lives. Upon investigating some of the institutions—science and the law—that are needed to address this collection of problems, I found "inherited institutions with incompatible contemporary tendencies" that reflect different "precious values," which tendencies need to be addressed if we are to use one institution, the law, to address in a timely and health-protective manner the presence of toxic substances in our lives with the necessary aid of the evidentiary tools of another institution, science. These are two important institutions in our community that have commitments to evidentiary principles and "values embedded in social traditions" that are quite appropriate for their individual purposes, but that can be and are in conflict with each other, with profound consequences for human life.

61. Several papers of the author noted throughout have been coauthored with researchers from appropriate scientific disciplines.

62. For more detail on these points, see Carl F. Cranor, "A Philosophy of Risk Assessment and the Law: A Case Study of the Role of Philosophy in Public Policy," *Philosophical Studies*, 85 (1997), 135–62.

Midwest Studies in Philosophy, XXIII (1999)

Late in the Quest: The Study of Malory's *Morte Darthur* as a New Direction in Philosophy

FELICIA ACKERMAN

Higgledy-piggledy
Sir Thomas Malory
Loved battles raging un-
Til the last breath.

Landing in jail, he was
Irreconcilable,
Writing of people who
Got bored to death.[1]

I

The new direction I have been exploring recently in philosophy is the use of Sir Thomas Malory's *Morte Darthur* as a vehicle for thinking about issues in ethics, social philosophy, philosophy of mind, and philosophy of literature.[2] This statement invites several questions. First, some philosophers will have a background question: What is Malory's *Morte Darthur*? Next are substantive questions. How is reading and reflecting on the *Morte Darthur* a new direction in philosophy? Which philosophical issues is the *Morte Darthur* a good vehicle for thinking about? Why? This introductory section discusses these questions, as well as some related general issues about the philosophical value of fiction.

The *Morte Darthur* is an English prose compilation, compression, adaptation, and supplementation of medieval French (in Malory's translation) and English

Arthurian romances. Written by Sir Thomas Malory, it was first published (and edited) by William Caxton in 1485.[3] This essay focuses on the two-volume Penguin Classics edition, which is based on the Caxton edition (and from which all my quoted Malory passages are taken),[4] as the Penguin preserves the language of the Caxton edition, but modernizes the Middle English spelling. Obviously, the distinction between changing the language and changing the spelling has borderline cases, but the net effect of focusing on the Penguin is to make the quoted Malory material readily accessible to philosophers.[5] This essay largely takes the Caxton text as a given and uses such expressions as "Malory's world" and "the Malorian notion of shame" without going into such questions as to what extent the relevant aspects of Malory's world or notions come from his sources or what editing was done by Caxton. Moreover, this essay is self-contained and hence accessible to philosophers with no background in Malory or even in Arthurian literature at all. But I urge all philosophers to read the *Morte Darthur*, not only for the philosophical value I will try to show it has, but also because, although it is one of the great classics of world literature, it has never a dull moment.

Studying works of fiction as sources of philosophical illumination is not in itself a new direction in philosophy. There is already a philosophical literature exemplifying and/or defending the practice. For example, Nussbaum argues that in moral philosophy,

> [s]chematic philosophers' [hypothetical] examples almost always lack the particularity, the emotive appeal, the absorbing plottedness, the variety and indeterminacy, of good fiction; they lack, too, good fiction's way of making the reader a participant and a friend. . . . [Such fiction characterizes] life more richly and truly.[6]

She adds that reflecting on our real lives is also insufficient, partly because, as Aristotle suggested, "we have never lived enough. Our experience is, without fiction, too confined and parochial. Literature extends it."[7] And McGinn claims that nonfiction such as biography, history, and news reports

> does not work anything like as well as fiction . . . because the techniques of *art* are missing from straight factual discourse. . . .The [fiction writer] *constructs* her story with certain aims in mind . . .; she makes her characters available to the reader so that they can be appreciated in their essence. We do not have the problem of opacity that afflicts our access to people and events in real life—the problem of what really happened, of what someone's motivation really was. The novelist can simply tell the reader what is true of her characters; she can just hand you the information you need in order to ground your moral assessments.[8]

Turning back to philosophers' schematic hypothetical test cases, Fischer says that

> the brunt of the criticism [of the use of such cases in moral philosophy] is based on the idea that schematized and abstract examples [with only a few details

> filled in]—i.e., streamlined examples—are not *realistic* . . . [where] being realistic implies a certain sort of richness of detail . . . the richness of detail present in reality.[9]

He adds that

> another way of failing to be realistic is to be far-fetched or "fantastic"; and this is quite compatible with richness of detail. Note that Nussbaum does not recommend careful perusal of the works of Robert Heinlein, for example; she prefers Henry James and Marcel Proust![10]

And what about Malory? The *Morte Darthur* includes a woman who turns herself and her retinue into "a great marble stone,"[11] a knight whose head is cut off, reattached so that he "arose lightly [quickly] up,"[12] cut off again and hewn into a hundred pieces, which are set together again—and many other equally unrealistic goings-on. So it will hardly be surprising that I reject the view that in order to provide special philosophical illumination by transcending the limitations of streamlined examples, fiction need be "realistic," at least in the sense of conforming to the laws of nature. What such fiction needs to be is psychologically realistic and compelling in the sense of having a richness of believable characterization and of event that gives the reader an emotional grasp of what it is like to be a certain sort of person in a certain sort of situation, where the "sort" of situation is defined not by physical externals, but by morally relevant conditions. The woman who turns herself and her retinue into a great marble stone is King Arthur's powerful, treacherous, and determined half-sister, Morgan le Fay. Having to deal with such a sibling is the morally relevant feature of the situation in which the enchantment occurs. Since Malory's world can bring this feature to psychological life far better than a streamlined example, the fantastic aspects of the situation are no barrier to its philosophical value. Conversely, even an example involving a long list of realistic details may fall flat if it fails to engage the reader's imagination enough to enable him to step outside his own frame of reference and assumptions. Anyone who teaches medical ethics has probably encountered nineteen-year-old athletes who take it for granted that being paralyzed or old and ill is a fate worse than death. Paralysis, old age, and illness are hardly "fantastic," but my own experience in philosophical discussion has shown me that even a long list of realistic details about such conditions often fails to make healthy young people question their assumptions about when life is worth living. Fiction that enables the reader to enter imaginatively into the life of a paralyzed person or a chronically or terminally ill old person often proves better at accomplishing this.[13]

There are other problems with the philosophical claims quoted above. Of course, fiction providing the sort of philosophical illumination under consideration here will not have "the richness of detail present in reality." No fiction has the richness of detail present in reality. Fiction is always selective. McGinn's remarks are also open to objection. Of course, philosophically illuminating fiction that "can make us *see* and *feel* good and evil in a way that no [streamlined example] can"[14] sometimes leaves open the problem of what someone's motivation really was. This sometimes occurs in Malory, but it is instead often true in the *Morte Darthur* that "appearance is to be thought of as the conscious manifestation and proper place of inward promptings, rather than a surface above hidden depths. Feelings are important, but they are displayed and perceived"[15] in behavior. Interestingly, this makes Malory's characters far more believable as people than the characters of many writers whose detailed accounts of their characters' inner lives rest on (frequently simplistic and implausible) psychological theories. It also provides a parallel between living in our world and entering imaginatively into Malory's. We know the people of Malory's world, for the most part, in a way analogous to the way we know other people in our own world, through the observable behavior, including speech, that may manifest their inner lives. But note that not everything in Malory's world is psychologically plausible; obvious sorts of counterexamples include his instances of collective discourse, where many people make complete speeches in unison, all using the same words.[16] The point is that enough about Malory's characters is rich, compelling, and believable to provide the sort of characterizations that make Malory's world useful philosophically. Instances of collective discourse by people in Malory's world, like instances of spontaneous songs by people in musical comedies, do not prevent these people from being *generally* believable as people or undermine the believability of their speech outside of such specialized circumstances.

If studying works of fiction as sources of philosophical illumination is not new, in what sense is studying Malory a new direction in philosophy? First is a trivial sense; the *Morte Darthur* is a new work for philosophers qua philosophers to be studying. As far as I know, I am the first philosopher to be writing about it.[17] Although there are literary scholars whose work on Malory has interesting philosophical implications,[18] the systematic study of the *Morte Darthur* using the methods of analytic philosophy seems to be new. But of course the important question for philosophers is, given that the philosophical study of literature is an established field, what new insights can the philosophical study of the *Morte Darthur* bring to philosophy?

One way to answer this question is by reference to what might be called a philosophers' idealized view of the proper way to engage in action. Such a view goes somewhat as follows. In deciding on a course of action, the agent amasses all the relevant available information he reasonably believes it is worth his while to obtain, thinks it over intelligently, dispassionately, carefully, and thoroughly (given whatever time constraints he has), and settles on a course of action that he reasonably believes is likely best to realize his goals, that is, a course of action he reasonably believes is such that no other course of action is more likely to do so, where his goals are not purely self-interested, but also include the aim of acting morally.

Although this idealized picture has its opponents, for example, those who see a greater role for emotion in this process,[19] it still has strong appeal, especially once modifications are made to meet the objections in question. But people in Malory's world approach this ideal even more rarely than we do. None is what we now call an intellectual. Most are not even very bright. Many, especially in the first 70 percent or so of the *Morte Darthur*, are impulsive and nonreflective.[20] With the partial exception of Dinadan, a scoffer and joker, none is an independent thinker (and even Dinadan's independence does not go much beyond mild jokes and jocular criticisms of the chivalric code). They do not value independent thinking. No one raises principled objections to the teachings of the Church. When people go against (Christian) religious authority, it is never for this reason.[21] An unpromising group for philosophers to study, it might seem, except that unintelligent, unreflective, uncritical people abound in our world as well as in Malory's, and their lives raise moral issues worthy of consideration. Such consideration is an excellent safeguard against the parochialism that comes from focusing too heavily on moral issues from the standpoint of highly intelligent, reflective, and intellectually sophisticated people.[22]

Malory's world can broaden philosophers' perspectives in other ways as well. Many of its presuppositions are very different from our own. Some will seem preposterous to many present-day philosophers. People in Malory's world take it for granted that traits of character are related to ancestry, in that honorable behavior means that one is "comen of a noble blood"[23] (although not conversely).[24] They also believe that "physical strength and success are God given . . . God speeds the right"[25] in battle, at least up to a point. This is taken seriously enough to support trial by battle as a judicial process (although King Arthur's trust in trial by battle is not complete. After his adulterous wife Guenever and her lover Launcelot are caught in Guenever's chamber, Arthur sentences Guenever to death by burning, without allowing Launcelot to fight for her in a trial by battle. Arthur's somewhat confusing rationale is that Launcelot "trusteth so much upon his hands and his might that he doubteth [fears] no man."[26])

So why should present-day philosophers look for moral insights by studying a world whose belief system rests upon such ideas? Schmitt, although an advocate of multiculturalism, has criticized the philosophical study of Malory, claiming that the presuppositions and values of Malory's world are so different from ours that they are unlikely to provide a good test of our moral intuitions and theories.[27] This claim is surprising. Would Schmitt raise similar objections to the philosophical study of Asian or African literature? Obviously, a central tenet of multiculturalism is that the study of cultures very different from our own can broaden our outlook and provide a fresh perspective on our presuppositions. (People in our world often seem almost as ready as those in Malory's to presuppose that success is deserved, although many people nowadays lack Malory's religious rationale.) Malory would never satisfy a "diversity" requirement, but even the nonblack students in my course that uses both Malory and twentieth-century American fiction generally find Malory's world far more different from their own experience than they find the fictional worlds of the two black American writers (Ernest J. Gaines and Andrea Lee) whose novels I use in the course.[28] And many characteristic values of Malory's world, however unusual they may be in mainstream twentieth-century America, are so far from being preposterous that they offer a useful corrective to currently popular ideas, or at least an alternative worth serious consideration. In Malory's world, pride is not the present-day virtue of self-confidence, but rather the "head of all deadly sins,"[29] a view that gains interest when we see that someone's confidence in his own prowess can be criticized in Malory's world not only when he "weeneth [believes] no knight so good as he, and the contrary is offtime proved,"[30] but even when his assessment of his prowess is accurate, as is illustrated by Arthur's above-quoted remark about Launcelot's trusting so much upon his hands and his might that he fears no man.[31] (This contrasts with popular present-day criticisms of the "self-esteem" movement, which focus on the evils of *overestimating* one's abilities, achievements, and/or virtues.)

The philosophical study of Malory's world offers new perspectives on many areas already important to philosophers: emotions (for example, envy, love, and pity, as well as pride), other qualities of mind (such as rationality, perceptiveness, reflectiveness, and impetuosity), and social and political concepts (such as autonomy and obedience).[32] Studying Malory's world even offers philosophers a new perspective on currently fashionable issues involving death, dying, and dignity. Knights routinely risk death to avoid shame, knights as well as ladies at times choose to die for love, and cutting one's throat is deemed preferable to the shame of being raped. When such cases are given as streamlined examples, my students often dismiss them as ridiculous. But although my students do not actually come to endorse the Malorian outlook, they often find these cases less ridiculous after reading the *Morte Darthur* and getting an emotional grasp of the characters and situations in question, especially when these are considered alongside such popular present-day reasons for wanting to die as avoidance of the "indignity" and "degradation" of incontinence or dependence.

Obviously, the richness of believable characterizations in Malory's world is of major importance here. Malory's world, like all fictional worlds, lacks the richness of detail present in reality, and in fact Malory generally does not supply much pictorial detail about what people look like, their physical surroundings, and the like.[33] Yet the *Morte Darthur* has a richness rare in fictional works, because of its length (1,000 pages in the two-volume Penguin Classics edition), large number of varied characters, frequent lifelike inconsistencies in characters' attitudes, and complexity of events and facets that ensures that virtually no casual reader and few if any scholars will be likely to keep in mind (or, in the case of casual readers, even to notice) all the various elements. This gives Malory's world, despite its fantastic aspects, a special air of verisimilitude, since the real world is of course also complex enough to be beyond our full grasp. I have read the whole book six times and many individual passages scores of times, but rereadings never fail to show me facts about Malory's world not only that I have overlooked or forgotten, but that come as surprises to me. (By contrast, with the more manageable imaginary worlds of shorter and less complex works of fiction, multiple rereadings do not keep giving me such surprises, although of course I have not memorized the works.) This point should be distinguished from the familiar claim that great literature keeps yielding new interpretations and new insights upon multiple rereadings. My point here is that even the basic facts and events of Malory's world are, like those of the real world (although to a lesser degree), too complex and extensive for our full grasp.[34]

In addition to enlarging philosophers' perspectives on already recognized concepts and issues, Malory's world also offers social and moral concepts that are likely to be unfamiliar to most twentieth-century philosophers. Two of the most important are the concept of taking the adventure, a concept frequently invoked when knights go on dangerous escapades,[35] and a highly specialized concept of stability. On the face of it, adventure may seem antithetical to stability, but on Malory's conception of stability, this is not so. Malory's conception of stability can be roughly characterized as a normatively grounded form of loyalty, so that a knight displays instability by deserting his lady for another, but not by leaving her in order to pursue a higher goal, such as seeking the Holy Grail. So a knight who takes the adventure is not sacrificing his stability unless there is a corresponding deterioration in his loyalties.

So far I have been arguing for the philosophical value of treating Malory's world as a world of real people facing real moral issues in their lives. An alternative approach, which is popular among present-day scholarly writers on Malory, is a textual approach, which treats the *Morte Darthur* "as a *text*, rather than as [a] . . . pseudo-'world'"[36] and explains characters' behavior in terms of the requirements of plot and genre, rather than by using the psychological approach I use of explaining characters' behavior in terms of these characters' personal psychologies as believable people with psychological depth, "whose motives and actions extend implicitly beyond the text, as well as explicitly within it."[37] This textual approach discourages speculation about characters' motivations or what they really mean by their words. Thus, Schroeder speaks ironically of the "critical sin of thinking of [Guenever] as an actual person,"[38] and Lynch criticizes Kennedy for an approach to the *Morte Darthur* that exhibits "a strong belief in the primacy of the demands of psychology over those of the story in the formation of 'character.'"[39]

But the textual and the psychological approaches are not necessarily in conflict; the demands of psychology need not be "over" the demands of the story at all. When a character behaves in a way that can be explained in terms of his personal psychology, this behavior also meets whatever plot requirement there is for him to behave that way.[40] (Murder mysteries offer a striking illustration of this point. Their plots require a murderer, but his motivation is generally supposed to be part of his portrayal as a believable person.) Rather than relying on a priori assumptions about whether characters in a romance are supposed to be "mimetic," it seems preferable to take an open-minded, "proof of the pudding" approach to the *Morte Darthur* and simply look and see to what extent, if at all, the book makes sense on a psychological approach that also accounts for the textual requirements in the manner I have suggested. Having first read the *Morte Darthur* just for pleasure, with no idea that "characterization *as such* is not [Malory's] aim"[41] and no beliefs that romance characters "exhibit traits depending on the demands of the context rather than being determined by any idea of a coherent individual,"[42] or that "[s]peech in Malory is not a dramatic impression, simulating what a by-stander might have heard, but rather a narration by direct means of the import of a spoken address, or, as it might be put, a continuation of the main narrative through the words of its personages,"[43] I found it natural and reasonable to see Malory's world as a world of people with psychological motivations, psychological depth, and, frequently, genuine speech by individuals. Some were people I came to know quite well (mainly in the third-person way that I know other people in the actual world), and some were people I barely knew at all, either because little information was provided or because I found them difficult to fathom, like many of my acquaintances in the actual world. And some, like Guenever, were "inconsistent in the [understandable] way 'real people' often are."[44] (This is not to make any claims about Malory's intentions along these lines.)

Premature abandonment of the psychological approach may result from setting unrealistically high standards for fictional characters to have believable personal psychologies and overlooking the all-too-human psychological inconsistencies common in real people, or from an overly narrow conception of individuality, a matter I will discuss in Section III. But an objection may arise here. Is the psychological approach (by which I mean a way of reading the text, not a hypothesis about the writer's intentions) irrefutable? Is there *any* pattern of behavior that cannot be passed off as psychologically believable by appeal to human psychological inconsistencies? Of course there is. Imagine a fictional character who continually fluctuates, in alternating 37¼-minute segments, between unexplained extreme kindness and unexplained extreme cruelty.[45] But there are also things to be gained philosophically by considering the *Morte Darthur* as a text, and I will discuss some in Section III.

I hope this overview has provided some preliminary reason to believe my claim that studying Malory will be a worthwhile new direction for philosophers. The rest of this essay will support this claim. Section II will focus on what the *Morte Darthur* has to offer philosophically concerning issues of death and dying, a matter of central current concern in philosophy and medical ethics. Section III will treat the concept of individuality in life and literature and will discuss the individuality of Malory's characters. This section will also consider some philosophical issues about the relation between a text and its readers. These are just a sampling of the many areas where Malory has much to offer philosophers. Of course, I am not claiming that the *Morte Darthur* is the *only* fictional work that can be used to make the philosophical points I am concerned with here—just that it serves this purpose particularly well.

II

At first blush, life may seem cheap in Malory's world. Knights routinely risk death to "win worship" (honor) and/or avoid shame. They even engage in dangerous jousts and tournaments for sport. Knights and ladies at times stab or starve themselves to death when their love is unrequited or their lover dies or is unfaithful. Bors chooses to save a virgin from rape rather than rescue his own brother from mortal danger; his reasoning is that "if I help not the maid she is shamed for ever, and also she shall lose her virginity the which she shall never get again."[46]

But a closer look at Malory's world suggests that matters are not so simple. The shame that knights risk death to avoid can be the shame of failing to save other people from death. Three questions offer a useful classification scheme for situations where considerations of shame and/or honor move people in Malory's world to choose or risk death. First, is the motive to gain honor or to avoid shame (or both)? Second, is the death aimed at or merely expected or risked? Third, does the honor (or shame) come from aiding (or failing to aid) people who are in mortal danger, or doesn't it?

Malory's world offers cases of both sorts for each question. When Percival's sister volunteers to bleed "a dish full of blood"[47] to heal a gentlewoman who "is but [almost] dead,"[48] she says, "and [if] I die for to heal her I shall get me great worship [honor]."[49] She does not suggest that she will be shamed if she refuses to bleed. When Guenever, on the other hand, tells Meliagaunt, who is abducting her, "I had lever [would sooner] cut mine own throat in twain rather than thou shouldest dishonor me,"[50] she is talking about a death to avoid shame, rather than to win glory. And Launcelot's final rescue of Guenever from death by burning seems to involve both elements. ("Jesu defend me from shame,"[51] he says in affirming his resolve to rescue her, but he also seems affected by the advice that he can eventually "bring again the queen to the king with great worship [honor]"[52] after King Arthur's anger has cooled.) As for the second question, Guenever would aim at death if she cut her throat, but Launcelot is merely risking death (and is not killed). As for the third question, both Percival's sister's bleeding and Launcelot's risk serve the purpose of helping people who are in mortal danger, but the suicide Guenever contemplates does not. Even risky jousting in tournaments can be undertaken to avoid shame; Dinadan "provoked Sir Tristram to do well"[53] by calling him a coward.

When I simply describe such incidents in isolation (presenting them as streamlined hypothetical cases) to people who have not read Malory, many are sympathetic to individuals who would rather risk death than suffer the shame of not helping those in mortal danger. Many, citing such cases as mountaineer Sir Edmund Hillary, trapeze artists, and race car drivers, do not dismiss out of hand people who risk their lives at least partly for glory. But a woman who would rather kill herself than suffer the shame of rape and a man who finds it shameful not to engage in a risky tournament generally do get dismissed out of hand. Such streamlined cases generally elicit predictable comments about sexism,[54] primitive conceptions of shame, and the like. The matter looks more complicated when viewed in context. One of the virtues of studying such issues in the fullness of Malory's world is that he succeeds in giving an emotionally convincing portrayal of a society with such conceptions of shame and honor, so that, rather than simply dismissing this value system as ridiculous, the reader can enter imaginatively into it to the point of being able to grasp how it would feel to accept it.

Even after several weeks of immersion in Malory's world, however, my students do not actually come to endorse a worldview that holds it is shameful to be raped, to decline to engage in a risky tournament, or to fail and be defeated.[55] But much is to be gained by a deep emotional understanding of a world where one's fighting abilities are valued to such an extent that their deficiency endangers not just one's self-concept but also one's standing among the people whose good opinion is the mainstay of one's social world. For one thing, it provides a useful perspective on our own world and on the views about death, dying, and dignity that are widespread in late twentieth-century America.

A popular figure in the present-day popular media, as well as in present-day medical ethics, is the terminally ill or severely and permanently disabled person who wants to die because he "believes that further life means only degradation."[56] The words "shame" and "honor" are not generally used in this context nowadays, but the related word "dignity" is a staple of present-day medical ethics, where it frequently follows the words "death with." "Dignity" occurs only once in the *Morte Darthur*.[57] But the phrase "death with dignity" has become so characteristic of present-day America that it belongs in a time capsule. Future generations uncovering the capsule might at first expect "death with dignity" to apply to a stately exit involving ceremonial farewells, as opposed to such ludicrous demises as that of "Chuckles the Clown" in the most famous episode of the Mary Tyler Moore show (a video of which might also be in the time capsule), who met his end dressed in a peanut suit in a parade, when an elephant mistook him for a peanut and tried to shell him. Instead, however, conventional present-day usage generally takes "death with dignity" to be what ends or prevents life without dignity, by which is meant life marked not by buffoonery but by illness and disability. Popular present-day examples of dignity depleters include incontinence, dementia, and being "dependent on machines"—provided the machines are respirators, rather than furnaces or refrigerators. For example, Dworkin sympathetically notes that people often "think it degrading to be wholly dependent. . . . At least part of what people fear about dependence is its impact . . . on their own dignity."[58] Similarly, the Philosophers' Brief for the legalization of physician-assisted suicide for the terminally ill cites many people's attitudes toward being "intubated" and "helpless" in support of its position that "it is intolerable for government to dictate that doctors may never, under any circumstances, help someone to die who believes that further life means only degradation."[59] And Dr. Timothy Quill holds that "suicide could be appropriate for patients if they did not want to linger comatose, demented, *or incontinent*."[60]

I have mentioned that, even after reading the *Morte Darthur* and gaining an emotional grasp of Malory's world, my students do not actually endorse Malorian views about honor and shame. On balance, they are still apt to think that it is barbaric to make avoidance of shame require successful participation in jousts, that such a concept of shame is apt to have unfortunate consequences (lots of injuries, not to mention corpses), and that a worldview in which being raped shames women is sexist. So it is worth considering how future generations would be justified in regarding twentieth-century conceptions of dignity embodied in the medical-ethics material I have quoted about things people consider degrading. These conceptions, like Malory's, rely heavily on the physical.[61] Honor among Malory's knights requires skill in armed combat; "dignity" on the popular present-day conception "requires the ability to walk unaided, to feed oneself, and to control one's bowels." In Malory's world a woman is shamed by penetration by a rapist's penis;[62] in our world a woman loses her dignity when she is penetrated by a feeding tube. If we think Malory's world is primitive in this respect, is our world more advanced?

Answering this question obviously requires more precise attention to the concepts of dignity and shame. *Merriam-Webster's Collegiate Dictionary* gives several definitions of "shame." Two are "a condition of humiliating disgrace or disrepute" and "something that brings censure or reproach."[63] These definitions support Lambert's suggestion that it is reasonable to suppose that Malory uses "shame" and its cognates "roughly [in the same sense] as we do now."[64] Lambert and others have stressed the idea that Malory's world is a shame-culture in the sense that external sanctions matter more than internal sanctions. Lambert adds that this ethos is not just depicted but also endorsed by Malory: "It is Malory himself, not just his characters, for whom honor and shame are more real than innocence and guilt. [The] *Morte Darthur* is *of* rather than *about* a *shame* ethos. . . . The important thing is not one's own knowledge of what one has done . . . but public recognition of one's actions."[65] In this sense, whether one's condition is shameful is a social matter. Of course, shame is also an emotion, and being in a socially shameful condition does not entail feeling the emotion of shame. It is logically possible to be in such a condition without realizing it, or to reject one's society's standards.

Like "shame," the word "dignity" has several related senses. "Dignity," however, never refers to an emotion. One may feel proud of one's dignity, but then it is the pride, not the dignity, that is the emotion. One may also feel dignified, but this seems no more an emotion than is feeling stupid. And "dignity" can refer to a personality trait, not always a desirable one. We may admire someone's dignity in the face of chaotic disaster, but one who displays "formal reserve or seriousness of manner, appearance, or language"[66] (what Chuckles the Clown lacks) is not apt to be much fun. But there is a sense of "dignity" relevant to our concerns here, "the quality or state of being worthy, honored, or esteemed."[67] This is a sense in which lack of dignity is related to degradation, as expressed in the above-quoted remarks from the Philosophers' Brief and from Dworkin about things people consider degrading. This sense of "dignity" is closely related to the Malorian notion of shame. Emanuel holds that "[s]ocial acceptance is essential to 'dignity' because dignity is a social construct. Dignity involves the gaze of others; it requires public acceptance and affirmation of one's actions."[68] But just as we have distinguished between shame as an emotion and the state of being socially shamed, we can, taking into account the second of the foregoing definitions of "dignity," distinguish between losing one's dignity in the sense of losing one's worthiness and losing one's dignity in the sense of losing one's esteem in the eyes of others. And just as the twentieth-century reader is apt to question the sources of shame in Malory's world, we can question present-day ideas about dignity and degradation. In both cases we can raise overall questions about whether these standards of shame or dignity are reasonable or desirable. Such questions are especially urgent about our present-day standards, because the desire to avoid the "degradation" or "indignity" of dependence or incontinence is a rationale frequently offered for legalizing physician-assisted suicide for the terminally ill or for the terminally ill and the severely and permanently disabled.[69]

I think we need to criticize this view of human dignity, with its suggestion that the ill and disabled have less human dignity than the healthy and able-bodied. (For simplicity of exposition, I am now using "dignity" in the sense of "the quality or state of being worthy of esteem." Of course it is true that incontinence and "dependence" reduce one's dignity in our society in the sense of reducing one's esteem in the eyes of others.) Do assisted-suicide advocates really want to endorse the view that human dignity resides in the bladder and the rectum? If being unable to control the discharge of one's urine and feces deprives one of human dignity, then what about being unable to control the discharge of one's menstrual blood? Should physician-assisted suicide also be legalized for all premenopausal women who believe that the milder "remedy" of a hysterectomy would also undermine their dignity?

Of course, the autonomy reply can be invoked here. The point is not what assisted-suicide advocates or I believe about human dignity, but what individual people believe about their own dignity. And of course, this is the position of mainstream assisted-suicide advocates, who do not endorse the "indignity" of incontinence as a reason for death except for people who themselves want to die for this reason. To be consistent, however, such a position would also have to endorse legalizing physician-assisted suicide for healthy young adults who want to die because they believe their menstruation or their irremediable stuttering or clumsiness deprives them of human dignity. Such people could doubtless use suicide assistance in the form of prescriptions for painless lethal drugs. It was not so long ago in American history that most white Americans had difficulty recognizing the human dignity of black Americans. If there are black Americans nowadays who want to die because they buy into this, should physician-assisted suicide be legalized for them? If not, why legalize physician-assisted suicide for people who believe it is their incontinence, rather than their skin color, that deprives them of human dignity?

A similar point applies to people who believe it is their "dependence," rather than their skin color, that deprives them of human dignity. In fact, the notion of "dependence" here cries out for philosophical examination. As Wendell points out, "independence" is "defined according to a society's expectations about what people 'normally' do for themselves and how they do it."[70] She adds that few people in her city would consider her a "dependent" person because she relies on other people to provide her with water out of the tap and electricity, but most people would consider her highly dependent if she needed other people to help her get out of bed or go to the toilet. This point can be extended to dependence on machines. Few people call me dependent on machines because I rely on a furnace and a refrigerator, but most people would if I relied on a respirator. I think people's "dependence" can be usefully divided into two categories: dependence on other people and dependence on animals or things. (The latter will of course often involve dependence on other people to provide or service these animals or things.) Virtually all of us are dependent on machines in present-day American society, just as knights in Malory's world are dependent upon horses. Obviously, no one has ever been entirely self-sufficient. Even Robinson Crusoe was "dependent" on food and water. Dependence upon other people raises special issues, as it may involve personal interaction with those people, who, in any case, have their own desires and agendas. But virtually all of us are subject to this sort of dependence, too. What sort of dependence on other people do people find degrading? This is partly a matter of how the others treat them, but it is also partly a matter of what their society labels as degrading. Legalizing physician-assisted suicide for those who seek to avoid the "indignity" of dependence on other people to wipe their bottoms, but not for those who seek to avoid the indignity of dependence on other people to fill or pull their teeth (another intimate, messy activity) would not only reflect but also promote such imbalances in what people are apt to find degrading. Of course, Dworkin is right that some people "think it degrading to be wholly dependent"[71] and that "[f]or [some] people, a life without the power of motion is unacceptable, not for reasons explicable in experiential terms, but because it is stunningly inadequate to the conception of self around which their own lives have so far been constructed."[72] Some people also feel this way about a life without an academic job, yet Dworkin's book does not mention legalizing suicide assistance for them.[73] And a present-day rape victim who felt shamed and degraded by rape, unlike a present-day woman who wanted to die because she felt degraded by incontinence or the "dependence" resulting from quadriplegia, would no doubt be assumed (especially by the very same "progressive" people who favor legalizing physician-assisted suicide for the severely and permanently disabled and for the terminally ill!) to be in need of counseling.[74]

At this point, one may wonder about the role of Malory's world, as opposed to streamlined hypothetical cases, in the foregoing discussion. Suppose we bypass the fullness of Malory's world and simply present the streamlined hypothetical cases *along* with explicit comparisons to our world, by asking how our present-day views about illness, disability, dependence, dignity, and degradation are an improvement over a worldview that holds that being raped shames a woman or that defeat or failure to engage in a risky tournament shames a man. When I try asking this of people unacquainted with Malory's world, however, the most common response is that the streamlined hypothetical cases are obviously ridiculous, but that of course it is degrading to need another person to wipe one's behind. One's own values seem obviously right and the alien ones absurd. I have mentioned that reading the *Morte Darthur* can give readers an emotional grasp of a world where these alien values operate. But the modern reader is unlikely to identify so closely with Malorian values that he loses sight of his original perspective as an outsider.[75] This contrast between insider and outsider perspectives can then be applied to the values of our world too, putting present-day readers of Malory in an improved position to assess whether their attachment to the values of our world is better justified than the attachment of Malory's characters to the values of their world. This illustrates how, in addition to helping us enter imaginatively into situations we do not experience in real life, fiction can improve our critical judgment about what we do experience and take for granted.

Criticizing a society's standards of dignity, degradation, or shame obviously implies criticizing the society as a whole. But the depth of such implicit social criticism will vary from case to case. Malory's world is virtually impossible to envision without its prevailing standards of shame and honor. Violating these standards would mean undermining that social world. But not all norms are as deeply embedded in a society. Refusing social endorsement of the idea that incontinence and "dependence" are degrading would not undermine our society as a whole, although it would reduce a particularly inhumane way of cutting down on medical costs. This is not to oppose physician-assisted suicide as such, just to oppose granting this right on grounds of "dignity" to the terminally ill or to the terminally ill and the severely and permanently disabled, but not to the rest of us.

Considerations of "dignity," of course, are far from the only reason people might want to die. Some people just feel miserable. Dworkin offers a useful distinction between experiential interests, that is, interests in having (or avoiding) certain sorts of experiences for their pleasant (or unpleasant) experiential qualities, and critical interests, that is, interests whose satisfaction makes one's life as a whole a better (more successful, nonwasted) life.[76] Someone who seeks death simply in order to end or avoid the experience of great unhappiness or physical pain takes himself to have an experiential interest in dying. Someone who says he would rather die than have the "indignity" of living in an irreversible coma, or someone who, overcome in battle, asks to be slain because he would rather "die with worship [honor] than live with shame,"[77] is affirming a critical interest in dying rather than living in such a state. (The battle case may also involve an experiential interest, as well as a critical one.)

Experiential interests seem to be involved in several suicides (or attempted suicides) and quasisuicides in Malory's world. Columbe stabs herself to death because Balin has slain her lover, Lanceor. (Interestingly, she blames Balin for her own death, saying, "O Balin, two bodies thou hast slain and one heart, and two hearts in one body, and two souls thou has lost.")[78] Garnish stabs himself to death after seeing the woman he loves lying with another knight (and after slaying both the woman and the knight). La Beale Isoud tries to kill herself because she (wrongly) believes her lover Tristram is dead. Elaine of Astolat (who may be more familiar to many philosophers as Tennyson's Lady of Shalott) tells Launcelot, who has rebuffed her, "then I must die for your love,"[79] and then she "made such sorrow day and night that she never slept, ate, nor drank, and ever she made her complaint unto Sir Launcelot."[80] And Launcelot himself, after the death of Guenever, "never after ate but little meat, nor drank, till he was dead."[81]

No such grounds for suicide would pass muster among today's mainstream suicide advocates. (Nor are these deaths unopposed in Malory's world. Of course, none of them needs assistance from a physician, but in fact, people in Malory's world attempt to prevent these deaths where possible.) Elaine's self-starvation, in fact, involves the sort of situation where the introduction to the Philosophers' Brief for the legalization of physician-assisted suicide for the terminally ill says suicide assistance should *not* be permitted, "a sixteen-year-old suffering from a severe case of unrequited love"[82] (although Malory does not specify Elaine's age). On the face of it, this may seem reasonable, as may the Brief's rationale that "[s]tates may be allowed to prevent assisted suicide by people who—it is plausible to think—would later be grateful if they were prevented from dying."[83] But the case of Launcelot offers a compelling illustration of why not only the terminally ill can be expected to meet this criterion. Unlike Elaine, Launcelot is no naive and inexperienced young person.[84] At the time of his death, he is a mature adult with a wide range of experiences behind him: knight, illicit lover, penitent, hermit, priest. The love of his life is dead, no other woman has ever seriously interested him, his opportunities for knightly service as a knight of the Round Table have ended, and he has already sampled religious life. How is his life likely to improve to the point where he would ever be grateful if he were prevented from dying? The vast differences between Malory's world and ours are beside the point here. The *Morte Darthur* offers a psychologically compelling portrayal of a man who is neither disabled nor terminally ill, but who has nothing left to live for. This should challenge the currently fashionable view that suicidal hopelessness can be rational only in the terminally ill, or possibly only in the terminally ill and in the severely and permanently disabled.[85] And obviously, a streamlined hypothetical case would be inadequate here. The force of the fictional case comes from the believability, compellingness, and richness of the character of Launcelot.

An objection may arise now. Why use a fictional case here? Aren't there real-life cases that can be used to make the point that conditions other than illness and disability can suffice to make suicidal hopelessness rational? In fact, don't there have to be such real-life cases if the point is supposed to be not only theoretical but also relevant to actual public-policy issues? The answer comes from adapting some remarks of De Paul (cf. note 75). In real-life cases, we may have such intense emotions (or such intense moral convictions about the issue of suicide) that this may cloud our judgments about suicides and quasisuicides of real people. A compelling fictional example may be just what we need to open our minds.

Malory's world also offers a third sort of reason for seeking death. In a state of religious joy on the quest of the Holy Grail, Galahad prays for death, saying, "Now, blessed Lord, would I not longer live, if it might please Thee, Lord."[86] Galahad's willingness—in fact, eagerness—to die is grounded in his certainty of eternal bliss in the afterlife.

This raises important questions in connection with the present-day popularity of the idea that the old and/or terminally ill should "accept death," not just in the cognitive sense of having the true belief that they do not have long to live, but also in the attitudinal sense of contemplating their impending deaths with serenity, rather than fear or resentment, and regarding "death as a friend,"[87] or at least reaching what one hospice official unaesthetically describes as "a final stage [of] acceptance . . . not a resignation but a real heartfelt feeling that what is happening is . . . not necessarily incorrect."[88]

This sort of attitude makes sense for Galahad. But why should present-day people feel this way? Some, of course, have reasons similar to Galahad's. In an interview shortly before his death, the terminally ill Joseph Cardinal Bernadin said, "I don't think I could be as tranquil [about my impending death] as I am if I didn't really believe [in an afterlife]."[89] But although serenity in the face of impending death is understandable for the Galahads and Cardinal Bernadins who are confident they are going on to a better place, why should we expect such serenity from people who believe their death will be "the unequivocal and permanent end of [their] existence"?[90] Do such expectations constitute an attempt to import religiously based attitudes—attitudes that can be reasonable on the assumption of religious belief in the afterlife—into a context where the religious beliefs that ground these attitudes are lacking? When people who do and those who do not believe in an afterlife talk about death, what they take themselves to be talking about is very different. For people who value their lives and do not believe in an afterlife, doesn't fearing death make perfect sense? We would be skeptical of people who claimed to value their marriages but faced the prospect of divorce serenely or who claimed to value their religious faith but were serene about the prospect of losing it. As Nagel points out, for those of us who do not believe in an afterlife, "it can be said that life is all we have and its loss is the greatest loss we can sustain."[91] Why, then, should we be expected to face this loss with equanimity?[92]

One possible answer, of course, is something I have already discussed: people may have (or anticipate) unhappy, "undignified," or shameful lives. Or they may just be (or expect to become) tired of living. Such people may regard death as deliverance, just as Malory in his own life sought "good deliverance"[93] from prison. Even Galahad not only displays eagerness for the afterlife, but also expresses the desire to leave "this wretched world."[94] And many nonreligious people nowadays wish to die because they regard the state of their lives as worse than nothing, or as likely to become so.

Increasingly, however, serene acceptance of death is being urged even on people who regard their lives as satisfactory or better. One of the paradoxes of the modern hospice movement is that, while claiming to enable the last months of a terminal patient's life to be comfortable, "dignified," and even "meaningful," it eschews *any* medical treatment, even if not painful or otherwise disagreeable, whose sole aim is to prolong life.[95] An obvious question arises here. As long as life can be satisfactory or better, why refuse to prolong it? Since the hospice movement is not officially religious and is intended to attract and care for nonreligious as well as religious people, recourse to the afterlife will not explain this refusal to prolong life, nor will it help answer the underlying question: Galahad's "acceptance"—in fact, courting—of death is grounded in his expectation of joy in the afterlife. What could ground serene acceptance in a nonbeliever as long as his "quality of life" is good?

One popular sort of answer is that death is natural and "renewal requires that death precede it so that the weary may be replaced by the vigorous. This is what is meant by the cycles of nature."[96] A similar claim in a social rather than a natural context is that

> [i]t should be the special role of the elderly to be the moral conservators of that which has been and the most active proponents of that which will be after they are no longer here. Their indispensable role as conservators is what generates what . . . ought to be the *primary* aspiration of the old, which is to serve the young and the future. . . . The acceptance of their aging and death will be the principal stimulus to doing this. It is this seemingly paradoxical combination of withdrawal to prepare for death and an active, helpful leave-taking oriented toward the young, which provides the possibility for meaning and significance in a contemporary context.[97]

Such grounds for serenity about one's own death require great self-abnegation on the part of the old. This can hardly be attractive to old people who are not inclined to such a sacrificial view of their old age or who consider it unfair to single them out as the group whose primary aspiration should be to serve others.[98] I have argued elsewhere against such inegalitarian expectations of altruism and sacrifice.[99] In the absence of such self-abnegation, however, the expectation that people who value their lives and do not believe in an afterlife will face their own deaths with serenity seems to be an attempt to superimpose the attitudes appropriate to a religious worldview like Galahad's on a context where the beliefs grounding such attitudes are absent.

But the philosophical value of Malory's world over streamlined examples is weaker here than in the earlier cases involving dignity or unhappiness. The present point rests less on understanding the personal psychology of Galahad (not a well-developed character in the *Morte Darthur*) than on a logical point about the relation between valuing something and serenely awaiting its soon-to-occur loss. The recourse to Galahad's beliefs about the afterlife illustrates what could ground "acceptance" of one's own death—and what is lacking when we urge serene acceptance upon the nonreligious. This contrasts with the clear inadequacy of streamlined examples in the other two sorts of cases.

III

Because rich and compelling examples are so important in forming and testing our ethical concepts, intuitions, outlooks, and theories, it is hardly surprising that Malory's world, which is rich and compelling, yet drastically different from our own, has much to offer moral philosophy. I now turn to a different but related area: the concept of individuality, where individuality is the "total character peculiar to and distinguishing an individual from others."[100] Individuality should be distinguished from individualism, in the sense of "individualism" as "a doctrine that the interests of the individual are or ought to be ethically paramount; *also*: conduct guided by such a doctrine,"[101] or "a theory maintaining the political and economic independence of the individual, and stressing individual initiative, action and interests; *also*: conduct or practice guided by such a theory."[102] The Round Table fellowship is the antithesis of individualism in this sense. The knights of the Round Table are hardly "politically independent," and they are supposed to act with the interests of the Round Table fellowship as paramount. When they fall short, this is generally due to personal failings and feuds, rather than to anything approaching individualist convictions. (The quest of the Holy Grail, however, goes against the communal ethos; it is "a solitary search for God which must be pursued in isolation.")[103]

The lack of individualism in the Round Table fellowship does not preclude individuality in its members. This is important, because characters who have enough individuality for their relationships to be rich and compelling are part of what gives Malory's world the philosophical value I have been arguing that it has. Yet Field, a Malory scholar who I will argue underestimates the level of individuality in Malory's characters, says that "if Malory's characters were more particularized, they would lose a good deal of their universality and of their symbolic suggestiveness."[104] This seems wrong, for a reason that has general implications for the philosophy of literature. Although I am not completely sure what Field means by "universality and symbolic suggestiveness," a reasonable interpretation seems to involve a universal (or at least very wide-ranging) field of application, so that readers can find analogues in their own lives to such things as the knights' quest of the Holy Grail, and can come to see the latter as symbolic of the former. But "particularizing" characters in Field's sense of giving them "distinguishing marks"[105] does not undermine universality and symbolic suggestiveness in the sense I have indicated. Moreover, even if we temporarily set aside the question of to what extent Malory's characters have marks that distinguish them from one another, the knights as a group clearly have some highly distinctive and far from universal characteristics. All are men of arms, none questions Christian religion, none is inclined toward scholarly pursuits. If these very nonuniversal traits do not deprive these knights of universality and symbolic suggestiveness, it is hard to see how individual quirks or individual styles of speech could do so.

Individual styles of speech are something Field claims that Malory's knights generally lack. He says that Malory's "lack of differentiation of individual characters"[106] is seen in that "there is little difference between [the speech of] different knights in the same mood. Defiance, affection, and defeat are expressed in very similar words by different people."[107] Field cites the partial exception of Dinadan, the scoffer and joker mentioned in Section I of the present essay, but otherwise claims that "Malory gives us a style of dialogue which stresses the similarity of all knights, not the difference between individuals."[108] To use one of Field's examples, consider these words of three knights: Uwain ("of a much more worshipfuller [honorable] man's hand might I not die"),[109] Palomides ("of a better knight's hands may I not be slain"),[110] and Gawain ("of a more nobler man might I not be slain").[111] Field calls these similarities "striking"[112] and says that this similar phrasing depicts "the generous tribute of one noble man *in extremis* to another" (in fact, to the knight who has wounded him or who he fears will do so) as "a knightly characteristic [and emphasizes] what they have in common."[113]

Similarly, Lambert holds that the fact that both Gawain and Guenever, in their farewell communications to Launcelot, use the phrase "all the love that ever was betwixt us"[114] is part of what "underlines the place of love as the common denominator of all the loyalties in the last tale [and encourages] the reader to see the likeness in various human bonds rather than look for the points of distinction."[115]

Field and Lambert thus use these examples in the service of two claims: first, obviously, that the characters in question use similar or the same language, and second, that this linguistic similarity or sameness indicates, draws the reader's attention to, and emphasizes a fundamental similarity in these characters. Field and Lambert are clearly right that having different characters use similar or the same language can highlight these characters' fundamental similarity. But I will argue that, although it is true that many of Malory's characters use much the same language, this linguistic sameness often highlights the individual *differences* among these characters, individual differences that are part of what makes Malory's world rich and compelling.

One such case of difference in sameness is the Lambert example I have already quoted, "all the love that ever was betwixt us." This example can be used to illustrate a point opposite to Lambert's own. He takes the sameness of language to illustrate the fact that "[f]or Malory there is one typical relationship, one pattern of attachment; the word *love* ties together all the loyalties in the last tale,"[116] and as I have mentioned, he says this encourages "the reader to see the likeness in various human bonds rather than look for the points of distinction."[117] But this fails to note the difference in sameness. The identical language highlights the very different values, Guenever's being romantic love[118] and Gawain's being knightly fellowship. (Guenever, of course, is bidding farewell to the man who has been her illicit lover. The dying Gawain is writing a letter of farewell and reconciliation to a man who had been his fellow knight of the Round Table, but from whom he has since become estranged. Both these farewells to Launcelot occur near the end of the *Morte Darthur*, after the following sequence of events. Launcelot and Guenever were caught together in Guenever's chamber, Arthur sentenced Guenever to death by burning, Launcelot rescued her, accidentally killing Gawain's brothers Gareth and Gaheris in the process and making an enemy of Gawain, who vowed to avenge Gareth's death and who kept Arthur from reconciling with Launcelot.)

Another case, not discussed by Field or Lambert in connection with sameness and difference, illustrates this sort of point even better. When Arthur tells the dying Gawain, "now is my joy gone . . . in Sir Launcelot and you I most had my joy . . . and now have I lost my joy of you both; wherefore all mine earthly joy is gone from me,"[119] he describes his feelings for Launcelot and Gawain, but not for his wife Guenever, in language strikingly similar to what Launcelot will say sixteen pages later (in the Penguin Classics edition) in his farewell speech to Guenever ("in you I have had mine earthly joy").[120] The similarity of language here highlights the difference between Arthur's and Launcelot's earthly joys. If Arthur and Launcelot did not use some of the same words, they would not come across so strikingly as having the same feeling about very different things. This point also applies to a related utterance of Gawain's, where his foreshadowing of Arthur's words, "now is my joy gone,"[121] arises from his learning that Launcelot has accidentally slain (Gawain's favorite brother) Gareth. So the sameness of language highlights a three-way comparison and contrast of joys, with Arthur identifying his earthly joy with his favorite nephew Gawain and best knight Launcelot (illustrating Arthur's joy in knightly fellowship and selective family love),[122] Launcelot identifying his earthly joy with Guenever (illustrating Launcelot's joy in romantic love), and Gawain identifying his joy with his favorite brother Gareth (illustrating Gawain's joy in selective family love and possibly also knightly fellowship, for, much as Gawain laments the death of Gareth, he does not actually say "now is my joy gone" until learning that *Launcelot* is the one who has slain Gareth). I indicate Gawain's *selective* family love because although, as I have mentioned, Launcelot, when rescuing Guenever, accidentally slew Gawain's brother Gaheris as well as Gareth (not to mention his earlier slayings of Gawain's brother Agravain and of Gawain's sons), Gawain indicates that Gareth's is the death that most rankles and that he is implacably determined to avenge.

But Malory's world does not arrange itself in so neat a package as what I have just said might suggest. Guenever is not Launcelot's only joy. She does not even always come first. In a state of religious ecstasy on the quest of the Holy Grail (where, of course, Guenever is absent), he says that "this joy passeth all earthly joys that ever I was in."[123] So the language Malory's characters use can illustrate not only difference in sameness, but also sameness in difference in sameness. Arthur and Launcelot may cite different things as their *earthly* joys, but the two men are similar in that neither ranks Guenever consistently first amongst his joys. But underlying this similarity is yet another individual difference, a difference in what Arthur and Launcelot are placing above Guenever: knightly fellowship and selective family love in Arthur's case, but religious ecstasy in Launcelot's. Although criticism of Launcelot's lack of stability is a major facet of the Grail quest, Brewer, in his critical discussion of the *Morte Darthur*, says Launcelot "is not unstable in the ordinary sense, because in his adulterous love for Arthur's Queen, [Guenever], he is all too stable; but unstable in his desire for moral perfection, as we all are,"[124] and McCarthy says that "[Launcelot's] love for the queen was stable, and that constitutes its greatness. He was unfailingly loyal in her service. . . . His love was sinful, if you must, but the very persistence in error is an expression of fidelity to the queen."[125] But as I indicated in Section I, Malory has a normative concept of stability. So although Launcelot's love for Guenever counts as stable in contrast to the "unstable [short-lived] love in man and woman"[126] that Malory decries in the world he actually lives in, Launcelot's love for Guenever is never acknowledged as stable, not even "all too stable," from the perspective of the Grail quest, where he is criticized for his *lack* of stability (that is, lack of stability in devoting himself to God). And in "the ordinary sense" of stability, Launcelot's remark about his joy on the Grail quest surpassing all earthly joys that ever he was in illustrates how his love for Guenever is *not* completely stable. He vacillates between his religious feelings and his illicit relationship with Guenever. His religious feelings lead him to renounce her on the Grail quest (or at least to renounce her by what Davies aptly calls the "very liberal condition"[127] of agreeing that he will "never come in that queen's fellowship as much as ye may forbear.")[128] Launcelot's religious feelings are also the subsequent partial cause of his spending less time with Guenever than she would like upon his return from the Grail quest. The Grail quest criticism of Launcelot as lacking in stability is of course directed entirely at his movement away from God, rather than at his movement away from Guenever, but Guenever (at least before her repentance) would not agree.

One illustration of Guenever's attitude toward this matter provides yet another candidate for difference in sameness. Earlier, in regard to the knights' imminent departure on the Grail quest, Arthur says, "Ah Gawain, Gawain, ye have betrayed me,"[129] and Guenever upbraids Launcelot in virtually the same language a page later in the Penguin Classics edition ("O Launcelot, Launcelot, ye have betrayed me").[130] Here, too, the sameness that leaps out at the reader is not just the sameness of content, but also the identical language, with the repetition of the name giving a note of poignant personal appeal. These are the only cases of this repeated name construction ("Ah/O _____, _____,") in the context of an accusation of betrayal in the *Morte Darthur*. It is tempting to hold that here, too, the same language strikingly highlights the different priorities, Arthur's being his fellowship of knights and Guenever's being her romantic love with Launcelot. But Guenever's full remark here is "O Launcelot, Launcelot, ye have betrayed me and put me to the death, for to leave thus my lord."[131] This makes what she says harder to interpret, although the fact that she has "departed into her chamber and held her that no man should perceive her great sorrows"[132] supports (but of course does not actually prove, especially since Arthur is sorrowing openly) the view that her great sorrow and sense of betrayal arises at least partly from the fact that her clandestine lover is departing from her. So although the identical language highlights Arthur and Guenever's similarity in taking departure on the Grail quest as a betrayal of precious, previously held values, it may also highlight a substantial individual difference in what they take these precious values to be.

And this is not the only place in the *Morte Darthur* where accusations of betrayal can indicate individual differences in character that underlie sameness in language. The final case I will use to illustrate this can also be used to raise an additional philosophical issue about the relation between a text and its readers. Consider the question, "Ah, false traitoress [or "traitress"], why hast thou betrayed me?"[133] This question, in precisely these words, occurs twice in the *Morte Darthur*, spoken by two very different knights, Segwarides and Launcelot. Both betrayals are sexual, but how different! In the first case, Segwarides finds his wife's bed "troubled and broken,"[134] where her lover Tristram has "be-bled both the over sheet and the nether, and pillows, and head sheet."[135] Segwarides correctly infers from the bloodied bedding that his wife has lain beside a wounded knight. The second occurrence of the question is from Launcelot to Elaine (not the Elaine previously mentioned in this essay, but a different woman with that name), upon his discovery that he has been tricked into having sex with her. So for Segwarides the betrayal is *his wife's* infidelity, while for Launcelot the betrayal is that he *himself* has been tricked into behavior he regards as shameful. Once again, the sameness in language highlights a fundamental individual difference, a difference that is also seen in Launcelot's and Segwarides's different responses to sexual betrayal by a "false traitoress." Segwarides threatens to kill his wife unless she tells him who was in bed with her. Upon being told, he seeks to avenge himself upon Tristram, but is easily defeated, and "all was forgiven and forgotten; for Sir Segwarides durst [dared] not have ado with Sir Tristram, because of his noble prowess, and also because he was nephew unto King Mark; therefore he let it overslip: for he that hath a privy [private] hurt is loth to have a shame outward."[136] Malory's emphasis here seems to be not on the sexual betrayal, but on Segwarides's failure in combat and subsequent fear of antagonizing those more powerful, politically or physically, than he. Whether Segwarides's reaction counts as prudence or cowardice is a matter of personal judgment. (One is reminded of Bertrand Russell's "emotive conjugations"—for example, "I am firm; you are stubborn; he is a pig-headed fool" —where the same behavior is described in successively more pejorative terms.)[137] Declining to fight when overmatched is not invariably shameful in Malory's world.[138] But whatever one's evaluation of Segwarides, his motivation contrasts sharply with Launcelot's. What keeps Launcelot from vengeance in the case of *his* "false traitoress" is not fear of having ado with the powerful, but, in large part, knightly virtue (by the standards of Malory's world). Launcelot's willingness to forgive Elaine exhibits the knightliness people in Malory's world would expect of someone pledged "to give mercy unto him that asketh mercy . . . and always to do ladies, damosels, and gentlewomen succour, upon pain of death."[139] Not that Launcelot is unerring in this succour. Shortly before forgiving Elaine, he, in an echo of Segwarides's behavior with his wife, was brandishing a sword and threatening to kill her (although Launcelot is later ashamed of doing this), and upon forgiving her, he tells her that it is Brisen, her servant who masterminded the trickery, who "shall lose her head."[140] But he never carries out this vengeance either. Overall, the fundamental individual differences between Launcelot and Segwarides —differences in the sort of sexual betrayal that leads them to call a woman a "false traitoress" and in how they deal with the situation—are strikingly highlighted by the sameness of their language.[141]

At least, these differences are strikingly highlighted for the reader with an extraordinary memory, or for the scholar or multiple rereader. The two occurrences of "Ah, false traitoress/ traitress, why hast thou betrayed me?" are so far apart (334 pages in the Penguin Classics edition) that it is worth asking just whom the sameness, or difference in sameness, is likely to impress. Clearly, the effect of an author's language on a reader is a matter not just of the language itself, but also of what the reader takes account of. This shows the importance of distinguishing two questions. First, how similar are the speech patterns of different characters in Malory's world, and how much underlying individual sameness or difference do these characters exhibit when they use the same or similar language? Second, how likely is this sameness or similarity in language to be noticed by people who are just reading Malory, as opposed to studying it?

These questions are also relevant to Field's examples of sameness in sameness, that is, similarities of speech that indicate the knights' fundamental similarities. Consider what he calls the "repeated challenge"[142] from three knights in speaking to their adversaries about what has failed and what will not fail whom. The first two occurrences—"Then anon Sir Blamor . . . bad Sir Tristram alight, 'For though an horse hath failed me, I trust to God the earth will not fail me'"[143] and Lamorak's "though a mare's son hath failed me, now a queen's son shall not fail thee"[144]—occur just twenty pages apart in the Penguin Classics edition. But this is over 600 pages before the third instance, Gawain's "if this mare's son hath failed me wit [know] thou well a king's son and a queen's son shall not fail thee."[145] Following his presentation of these examples and then of another trio of examples —the speeches of knights *in extremis* that were the first quoted Malory examples in this section—Field says that the similarities in the knights' speeches provide "a cumulative effect as we read on."[146] But since these three utterances are the only cases of the "though/if *x* hath failed me, *y* will/shall not fail *z*" construction in the *Morte Darthur*, there are no intervening instances to bridge the 600-page gap and keep this manner of phrasing in the mind of the reader who reads the work in order. This again illustrates the importance of distinguishing what is in a text from its likely effect on the reader and of recognizing that this effect may well be very different for the ordinary reader and the scholar.

Of course, the effect on the reader of repeated phrasings need not be limited to what arises from the sharp awareness of isolated occurrences. Language and details one does not explicitly keep in mind may combine to have an overall force. Thus, Lambert says that Malory "links the [next-to-last tale of the *Morte Darthur*] and the [final tale, which deals with the destruction of the Round Table fellowship] with a large number of situational and verbal echoes which *en masse* create for the reader a haunting remembrance of the [former] in the [latter]."[147] Lambert adds that these echoes "differ widely in audibility"[148] and that at times "the reader will have only the faintest sense of *déjà vu* (or *déjà entendu*)."[149] But the material he refers to, taken together, is only 160 pages in the Penguin Classics edition. The Field examples about what has failed and what will not fail whom involve, as I have mentioned, a 600-page gap. It is worth asking what sort of memory the casual and sequential reader, as opposed to the painstaking scholar, would need for such similarities to affect him at all, even unconsciously, or in terms of providing the faintest sense of *déjà vu* or *déjà entendu*.

It is also worth looking more carefully at what sorts of assumptions might underlie the view that sameness or similarity of different characters' language betokens a basic lack of individuality in these characters. Academic intellectuals, especially in the humanities, are apt to set great store by their distinctive ways of expressing themselves in language and to prize such distinctiveness as a fundamental expression of their individuality. But in a world like Malory's, where action is valued more than words and where the characters are, to put it mildly, not intellectuals, I think that lack of individuality in use of language is no more an indication of a basic lack of individuality in the characters than is lack of individuality in clothing among people who set little store by dress. In fact, as I have argued, the identical language of different characters in the *Morte Darthur* often highlights their substantial individual differences. Inferring a lack of individuality in Malory's characters from the sameness of their language suggests an overly intellectual conception of human personality, although it would be unfair to attribute the full-blown form of this view to Field or Lambert, who also mention ways in which sameness in language is associated with a contrast in the characters, despite the emphasis on the opposite phenomenon.[150]

IV

The preceding two sections have aimed to illustrate in detail how the *Morte Darthur* can provide philosophical enlightenment in diverse areas. Along with the issues mentioned in Section I, these are only a sampling of the ways in which studying the *Morte Darthur* can be a new direction in philosophy, even though philosophers will be, albeit in a different sense from Launcelot, "late in the quest."[151]

NOTES

1. This meets the requirements for double dactyls. For details of these requirements, see Anthony Hecht and John Hollander (eds.), *Jiggery-Pokery: A Compendium of Double Dactyls* (New York: Atheneum, 1967), 26–31.

2. The first essay in this series, "Flourish Your Heart in This World: Emotion, Reason, and Action in Malory's *Le Morte D'Arthur*," appeared in volume 22 of this journal (1998), 182–226. A third essay on philosophical themes in Malory is forthcoming in volume 24 of this journal. See also my short story, "Flourish Your Heart in This World," in Martha C. Nussbaum and Cass R. Sunstein (eds.), *Clones and Clones: Facts and Fantasies about Human Cloning* (New York: Norton, 1998), 310–31, which uses and discusses Malory themes.

3. A different edition of Malory, the Vinaver edition, is based mainly on the Winchester manuscript, a Malory manuscript (believed to be in the handwriting of scribes rather than of Malory himself) discovered at Winchester College in 1934 and subsequently edited by Eugène Vinaver—a sequence of events that, unsurprisingly, transformed Malory scholarship. Although the Winchester manuscript and Caxton's edition contain basically similar material, they also have significant differences, and debate continues over which is more authentic in the sense of being closer to what Malory actually wrote. (For discussion of this issue, see Walter Kendrick, "Which Malory Should I Teach?" in Maureen Fries and Jeanie Watson [eds.], *Teaching the Arthurian Tradition* [New York: Modern Language Association of America, 1992, 100–105]; Ingrid Tieken-Boon van Ostade, *The Two Versions of Malory's Morte Darthur* [Cambridge: D. S. Brewer, 1995], and Eugène Vinaver [ed.], *The Works of Sir Thomas Malory*, third edition, revised by P. J. C. Field [Oxford: Oxford University Press, 1990], especially Vinaver's preface to his first edition and chapters 2–4 of his introduction.) Reflecting his (highly controversial) view that Malory wrote eight separate romances rather than one unified work, Vinaver called his edition not *Le Morte D'Arthur* (Caxton's title) but *The Works of Sir Thomas Malory*. The general term "the *Morte Darthur*," which I use in this essay, covers both versions. Vinaver's edition uses unmodernized Middle English spelling. There is also a text based on the Winchester manuscript but using modernized spelling (Sir Thomas Malory, *Le Morte Darthur: The Winchester Manuscript*, edited with an introduction and explanatory notes by Helen Cooper [Oxford: Oxford University Press, 1998]), but it is abridged, with various wonderful episodes omitted.

4. For the sake of Malory scholars (whom I hope this essay will also interest, despite the practical necessity of my including background information already familiar to them), I include references to Vinaver's three-volume *The Works of Sir Thomas Malory* for all quoted Malory passages. But I very rarely discuss differences between the Caxton and Vinaver editions here. I am using a three-way reference system, giving first the volume and page numbers in the Penguin Classics volumes (e.g., v. 2, 314), then the book and chapter numbers for the Caxton edition (e.g., C XVIII, 25), then the page and line numbers of the corresponding passages in the third edition of Vinaver's three-volume *The Works of Sir Thomas Malory* (e.g., V 874:3–4), whose continuous pagination makes specifying the volume number unnecessary. The spelling of all proper names is from the Penguin Classics volumes.

5. To appreciate the problems that the Middle English spelling poses for philosophers, try to guess what "heete sone keelyth" means. None of the philosophers I asked got it right, even when I supplied the context, "for where they bethe sone accorded and hasty, heete sone keelyth. And ryght

so faryth the love nowadayes, sone hote sone colde" (*The Works of Sir Thomas Malory* 1119:33–1120:2). The answer is "for where they be soon accorded and hasty, heat soon cooleth. And right so fareth the love nowadays, soon hot, soon cold."

6. Martha C. Nussbaum, *Love's Knowledge: Essays on Philosophy and Literature* (New York: Oxford University Press, 1990), 46–47.

7. Ibid., 47.

8. Colin McGinn, *Ethics, Evil, and Fiction* (Oxford: Oxford University Press, 1997), 176–77 (italics in original).

9. John Martin Fischer, "Stories," *Midwest Studies in Philosophy*, 20 (1996), 5–6 (italics in original).

10. Ibid., 6. Fischer quotes a far-fetched streamlined example disparaged by Anscombe, "what you ought to do if you had to move forward, and stepping with your right foot meant killing twenty-five [fine] young men, while stepping with your left foot would kill fifty drooling old ones" (G. E. M. Anscombe, "Does Oxford Moral Philosophy Corrupt the Youth?" *The Listener*, February 14, 1957, 267), quoted (with the word "fine" omitted) in Fischer, "Stories," 4. Note the casual bigotry here; it is taken for granted that one (fine?) young man is worth two drooling old ones. (What justifies the inequity: the age, the "fineness," or the drooling?)

Note also that McGinn is quite willing to use "fantastic" fiction as a vehicle for philosophical discussion. His book includes philosophical discussions of *The Picture of Dorian Gray* and *Frankenstein*.

11. Sir Thomas Malory, *Le Morte D'Arthur* (London, 1969), v.1, 140; C IV, 14; V 151:19–20. (The Vinaver edition has them turned into great marble stones [plural].)

12. Ibid., v. 1, 274; C VII, 22; V 334:25.

13. Examples of such fiction include the novels *Tender Mercies*, by Rosellen Brown (New York: Knopf, 1994), and *The Diary of a Good Neighbor*, by Jane Somers, a.k.a. Doris Lessing (New York: Knopf, 1983), as well as Mary Gordon's novella "Immaculate Man" (in Gordon, *The Rest of Life*, New York: Penguin Books, 1993, 3–76).

14. McGinn, *Ethics, Evil, and Fiction*, 176 (italics in original).

15. Andrew Lynch, *Malory's Book of Arms* (Cambridge: D. S. Brewer, 1997), 135. For details and complications, see the discussion in ibid., chap. 6.

16. For example, see v. 2, 492; C XX, 17; V 1203:29. For discussion of this construction, see my "Flourish Your Heart in This World: Emotion, Reason, and Action in Malory's *Le Morte D'Arthur*," n. 208; as well as Jeremy Smith, "Language and Style in Malory," in Elizabeth Archibald and A. S. G. Edwards (eds.), *A Companion to Malory* (Cambridge: D. S. Brewer, 1996), 102–3; Terence McCarthy, *An Introduction to Malory* (Cambridge: Boydell & Brewer, 1991) 130–31; and Mark Lambert, *Malory: Style and Vision in Le Morte Darthur* (New Haven: Yale University Press, 1975), 16–19.

17. A check of the *Philosophers' Index* (going back for 31 years) yields only one listing under "Malory": Beverly Kennedy's "The Re-Emergence of Tragedy in Late Medieval England," in A. Tymieniecka (ed.), *Existential Coordinates of Human Condition* (Boston: D. Reidel, 1984), 363–78. Beverly Kennedy is a professor of English at Marianapolis College in Quebec, and the article deals with the concept of tragedy. (I thank Timothy Chambers and David Matheson for the computer searches, and I invite readers to blame them if the searches are in error.)

18. For example, see ibid. as well as Kennedy, *Knighthood in the Morte Darthur*, 2nd ed. (Cambridge: D. S. Brewer, 1992) and "Notions of Adventure in Malory's *Morte Darthur*," *Arthurian Interpretations*, 3 no. 2 (1989): 39–59; Felicity Riddy, *Sir Thomas Malory* (Leiden: E. J. Brill, 1987); C. S. Lewis, "The English Prose *Morte*," in J. A. W. Bennett (ed.), *Essays on Malory* (Oxford: Oxford University Press, 1963); D. S. Brewer, Introduction to *The Morte Darthur, Parts Seven and Eight* (Evanston, IL: Northwestern University Press, 1968); Lynch, *Malory's Book of Arms*; and Lambert, *Malory*.

19. See Nussbaum, *Love's Knowledge*, 40–43.

20. For detailed discussion of these matters, see my "Flourish Your Heart in This World: Emotion, Reason, and Action in Malory's *Le Morte D'Arthur*."

21. For example, Gawain defends his refusal to do penance on the quest of the Holy Grail not by claiming ideological disagreement with the Church but on the grounds that such penance

would be redundant, "for we knights adventurous oft sufferen [often suffer] great woe and pain" (Malory, *Le Morte D'Arthur*, v.2, 266; C XIII, 16; V 892:19–20). (Peter Schroeder has suggested in correspondence that even this nonideological justification should not be taken at face value, but should rather be seen as just Gawain's way of brushing off the hermit who is trying to get him to do penance. I think this interpretation is reasonable, especially in light of the wording of Gawain's later refusal to stay for a hermit's counsel: "and I had leisure I would speak with you, but my fellow here, Sir Ector, is gone, and abideth me yonder beneath the hill" [ibid., v.2, 308–09; C XVI, 5; V 949:10–12].) Palomides the Saracen delays being christened not because of disbelief ("in my heart I am christened," ibid., v.2, 92; C X, 47; V 666:26–7), but because he wants to wait until he is worthy. Even the persistence of Arthur's evil son, Mordred, in his plan to marry his father's wife, Guenever, in defiance of the Bishop of Canterbury, comes across as sheer wickedness and contrariness ("'Do thou thy worst,' said Sir Mordred, 'wit thou well I shall defy thee,'" ibid., v.2, 506; C XXI, 1; V 1228:8–9), rather than as any sort of principled disagreement.

22. For example, in reply to the objection that utilitarianism is unworkable as a practical guide to conduct because of the difficulty of determining what will promote happiness, John Stuart Mill says, "There is no difficulty in proving any ethical standard whatever to work ill, if we suppose universal idiocy to be conjoined with it" ("Utilitarianism," in John Plamenatz (ed.), *The English Utilitarians* [Oxford: Basil Blackwell, 1949, 186]), although he does grant that "the multitude" can rely on "rules" (ibid.) instead of having to determine for themselves the utility of particular actions.

23. This is a statement by Persant in Malory, *Le Morte D'Arthur*, v.1, 254; C VII, 12; V 315:19–20.

24. See the discussion in my "Flourish Your Heart in This World: Emotion, Reason, and Action in Malory's *Le Morte D'Arthur*," as well as Kennedy, *Knighthood in the Morte Darthur*; and Lynch, *Malory's Book of Arms*, 62–68.

25. McCarthy, *An Introduction to Malory*, 83. For further discussion of these issues, see Kennedy, *Knighthood in the Morte Darthur*, 39–47, 155–61, 281–82; as well as Brewer, Introduction to *The Morte Darthur*.

26. Malory, *Le Morte D'Arthur*, v.2, 470; C XX, 7; V 1175:21–22. See the discussion in Kennedy, *Knighthood in the Morte Darthur*, 314–21.

27. Richard Schmitt expressed this view in remarking on a draft of the philosophy honors thesis of Cornelius Simons, Brown University, 1997–98.

28. The novels are Ernest J. Gaines's *A Lesson Before Dying* (New York: Knopf, 1993), which is set in a black community in rural Louisiana around fifty years ago, and Andrea Lee's *Sarah Phillips* (Boston: Northeastern University Press, 1993), which is set among upper-middle-class blacks in the 1960s and 1970s.

29. Malory, *Le Morte D'Arthur*, v.2, 261; C XIII, 14; V 886:23–24.

30. Ibid., v. 1, 216; C VI, 12; V 275:18–19.

31. This is not to claim that thinking well of oneself or one's abilities always comes in for criticism in Malory's world. See the discussion in my "Flourish Your Heart in This World: Emotion, Reason, and Action in Malory's Le *Morte Darthur*," 201.

32. I discuss Malory's treatment of the first two areas in "Flourish Your Heart in This World: Emotion, Reason, and Action in Malory's *Le Morte D'Arthur*."

33. For a discussion of this, see P. J. C. Field, *Romance and Chronicle* (Bloomington, IN: Indiana University Press, 1971), chap. 5.

34. I thank Sara Ann Ketchum for the objection that gave rise to this distinction.

35. For discussions of Malory's concept of taking the adventure, see Jill Mann, "Taking the Adventure: Malory and the *Suite du Merlin*," in T. Takamiya and D. S. Brewer (eds.), *Aspects of Malory* (Cambridge: D. S. Brewer, 1981), 90; and Kennedy, *Knighthood in the Morte Darthur* and "Notions of Adventure in Malory's *Morte Darthur*."

36. Lynch, *Malory's Book of Arms*, 33. Italics in original. For additional complexities, see Lynch's discussion of "name," ibid., chap. 1.

37. Ibid., 2.

38. Peter R. Schroeder, "Hidden Depths: Dialogue and Characterization in Chaucer and Malory," *PMLA*, 98 (1983), 376.

39. Lynch, *Malory's Book of Arms*, 3.

40. See the discussion in ibid., 112–13 and 126–29. This sort of consideration can also be used to criticize Ann Dobyns's claim that "[t]o assume that [Guenever] is a complex character whose words illustrate psychological depth is to disregard her many shifts in role and concurrently in voice" (*The Voices of Romance* [Newark: University of Delaware Press, 1989], 29). A complex explanatory psychology can underlie the speech of a character that also serves textual requirements of role and voice. Similarly, consider Dobyns's further claim that "[i]f, instead, one tries to account for [a particular speech of Guenever's] as words spoken by a romance character, the question changes. No longer does one wonder what the queen means but rather how the words work rhetorically within the larger framework of *Le Morte Darthur*" (ibid.). This further claim invites the reply that the first question does not preclude the second.

41. Brewer, Introduction to *The Morte Darthur*, 24 (italics in original).

42. Dobyns, *The Voices of Romance*, 9.

43. Lynch, *Malory's Book of Arms*, 135.

44. Schroeder holds that "[t]he demands of the story and the techniques by which Malory tells it enable him to make [Guenever] plausible, individual, and inconsistent in the way 'real people' often are." ("Hidden Depths," 375.)

45. Perhaps a less drastic form of this idea is behind Lynch's (in my view, exaggerated) claim that "in order to prolong the narrative . . . [t]he [section of the *Morte Darthur* comprising Books VIII–XII in the Caxton edition] releases multiple possibilities, several Tristrams, several [Palomideses], not often simultaneously, in the manner of the psychological novel, but sequentially, or alternately, in its sequence of episodes" (*Malory's Book of Arms*, 90–1). But later Lynch acknowledges that eventually, as the narrative progresses, "[Palomides's] story becomes gradually easier to discuss in terms of [Palomides's] character . . . and centres a growing effect of interiority and autonomy" (ibid., 127).

46. Malory, *Le Morte D'Arthur*, v.2, 315; C XVI, 9; V 961:16–17. See the discussion in the explanatory notes of Helen Cooper's abridged edition of *Le Morte Darthur*, 553.

47. Ibid, v.2, 348; C XVII, 11; V 1002:20.

48. Ibid., v.2, 349; C XVII, 11; V 1002:26.

49. Ibid, v.2, 349; C XVII, 11; V 1002:30–31.

50. Ibid, v.2, 429; C XIX, 2; V 1122:14–15.

51. Ibid, v.2, 466; C XX, 6; V 1172:1.

52. Ibid, v.2, 467; C XX, 6; V 1173:8–9.

53. Chapter heading of ibid., C X 72 (v.2, 150). This heading is not found in the Vinaver edition, but the material it describes is.

54. The charge of sexism also seems to come almost automatically to many present-day students who do read Malory. This charge is in a sense true—in fact, Malory's world even holds that having sex with a virgin shames her *father* (see ibid., v.1, 254; C VII, 12; V 315:9–16)—but it is oversimplified and unimaginative. It is hardly surprising that the view of women in the writings of a fifteenth-century English gentleman who was reactionary in his own time will fail to pass muster with progressive people nowadays. But detailing the ways Malory falls short in this area has a paint-by-numbers quality that distracts the reader from the deeper imaginative, moral, and psychological richness of Malory's world. And Malory's view of women is often more complex than might be supposed. See the discussion in my "Flourish Your Heart in This World: Emotion, Reason, and Action in Malory's *Le Morte D'Arthur*."

55. For a poignant example of a shameful defeat, see Palomides's defeat by Tristram in a tournament in Ireland: Malory, *Le Morte D'Arthur*, v.1, 319–21; C VIII, 10; V 387–89.

56. This formulation is from Ronald Dworkin, Thomas Nagel, Robert Nozick, John Rawls, Thomas Scanlon, and Judith Jarvis Thomson, "Assisted Suicide: The Philosophers' Brief," *New York Review of Books*, March 27, 1997, 44.

57. The second tale in the Vinaver edition ends with "HERE ENDETH THE TALE OF THE NOBLE KING ARTHUR THAT WAS EMPEROR HIMSELF THROUGH DIGNITY OF HIS HANDS" (V 247:3–5, capitalization in original, but I have modernized the spelling); this (minus the first two words) is also given as the title of the second tale in Vinaver. The word "dignity" does not occur in the Caxton edition. The glossary in the Vinaver edition defines "dygnyté of his hondys" ("dignity of his hands") as "his fighting abilities" (*The Works of Sir Thomas Malory*, 1713.)

58. Ronald Dworkin, *Life's Dominion* (New York: Knopf, 1994), 210.

59. Dworkin et al., "The Philosophers' Brief," 44.

60. Jane Gross, "Quiet Doctor Finds a Mission in Assisted Suicide Case," *New York Times*, January 2, 1997, B1 (italics added). The phrase "death with dignity" and its cognates are also sometimes used at least partly to denote control over one's own death. For example, U. S. Supreme Court Justice Stephen Breyer has claimed that the " 'right to die with dignity' has at its core three components [one of which is] personal control over the manner of death": Ezekiel J. Emanuel, "The Future of Euthanasia and Physician-Assisted Suicide: Beyond Rights Talk to Informed Public Policy," *Minnesota Law Review*, 82 (1998), 988. Lack of dignity in this sense should be distinguished from the sense of lack of dignity that I am concerned with here, a sense in which lack of dignity can be a *reason* for exercising one's control over one's death by choosing to die. (I thank Sara Ann Ketchum for this formulation.)

61. J. David Velleman, "Against the Right to Die," *Journal of Medicine and Philosophy*, 17 (1992), 666. Dementia and unconsciousness, as well as purely physical disabilities, figure prominently in present-day philosophical discussions of death and dignity. See Dworkin, *Life's Dominion*, chap. 7–8. The present essay's discussion of our notion of dignity focuses on the concept of dignity in connection with purely physical disabilities, as these are the sorts of cases where my comparison with Malory's world is most relevant.

62. This view of Guenever's above-quoted remark when Meliagaunt abducts her involves some interpretation on my part, as Guenever's actual words do not specify just what the dishonor she would cut her throat to avoid actually is. But note also Bors's above-quoted reflection that if he does not protect a virgin from rape, "she is shamed for ever" (Malory, *Le Morte D'Arthur*, v.2, 315; C XVI, 9; V 961:16), a clear case of the view that rape shames the victim in Malory's world—a view that the potential victim shares, for Bors acts in response to her plea, "suffer me not to be shamed of this knight" (ibid., v.2, 315; C XVI, 9; V 961:11–12).

63. *Merriam-Webster's Collegiate Dictionary*, 10th ed. (Springfield, MA: Merriam-Webster, 1993), 1076.

64. Lambert, *Malory*, 184.

65. Ibid., 179 (italics in original). See also the discussions in Brewer, Introduction to *The Morte Darthur*; McCarthy, *An Introduction to Malory*, 72–100; and Stephen U. Miko, "Malory and the Chivalric Order," *Medium Aevum*, 24 (1966), 211–30. This is not to endorse all that these authors say along these lines. For example, in my view, McCarthy drastically exaggerates when he claims that

> Malory's characters worry about public opinion because it is only in public opinion that they exist. . . . No one in the *Morte Darthur* is thoughtful, tolerant, understanding, tender, or kind. . . . [Launcelot], of course, accuses himself of unkindness toward Arthur and [Guenever] . . . but even this is not a private failing. He is upbraiding himself for his lack of the proper, natural behavior to his lord and lady. (*An Introduction to Malory*, 89)

This overlooks such instances of private kindness as Tristram's seeking out the distraught Palomides and saying "such kind words that Sir Palomides went with him to his lodging" (Malory, *Le Morte D'Arthur*, v.1, 443; C IX, 31; V 529:22–23).

Like other aspects of Malory's world, the shame-culture is not monolithic. As Field points out in a different context, "few generalizations about Malory are not subject to exceptions" (*Romance and Chronicle*, 119). The Grail quest obviously involves concern with the morality of the inner life; Launcelot confesses not only to wrongful behavior, such as "[doing] battle were it right or wrong" (Malory, *Le Morte D'Arthur*, v.2, 272; C XIII, 20; V 897:19), but also to wrongful motives ("never did I battle all only for God's sake, but for to win worship and to cause me to be the better beloved," ibid., V 897:19–21). This is not to claim that the shame-culture is entirely absent from the Grail-world; see the discussion in Lambert, *Malory*, 184–87.

66. This is the fourth definition of "dignity" in *Merriam-Webster's Collegiate Dictionary*, 324.

67. This is the first definition of "dignity," ibid.

68. Emanuel, "The Future of Euthanasia and Physician-Assisted Suicide," 993.

69. See the references given in notes 56, 58, and 60.

70. Susan Wendell, *The Rejected Body: Feminist Philosophical Reflections on Disability* (New York: Routledge, 1996), 145.

71. Dworkin, *Life's Dominion*, 210.

72. Ibid., 210–11.

73. Although Dworkin is one of the signatories to the Philosophers' Brief and the author of its introduction, the Brief takes a weaker position than Dworkin takes in *Life's Dominion*. It is only for the terminally ill that the Brief advocates legalizing physician-assisted suicide. It explicitly leaves open the question of physician-assisted suicide for the severely and permanently disabled. *Life's Dominion* discusses cases of both sorts and does not differentiate between them in its claim that "a true appreciation of dignity argues decisively . . . for individual freedom . . . for a régime of law and attitude that encourages each of us to make mortal decisions for himself" (ibid., 239). As this remark suggests, Dworkin sometimes also uses the word "dignity," as does Justice Breyer (see note 60), to apply to personal control over one's own death. Note also Dworkin's claim that "[t]he most important feature of [Western political] culture is a belief in individual human dignity: that people have the moral right—and the moral responsibility—to confront the most fundamental questions about the meaning and value of their own lives for themselves, answering to their own consciences and convictions" (ibid., 166). The book does not suggest this applies to people whose affliction is the inability to get an academic job, as well as to people whose affliction is severe disability or terminal illness.

74. I thank Sara Ann Ketchum for the parenthetical observation.

75. As De Paul points out, "when we encounter situations requiring moral discernment in real life, we are often so emotionally involved that it is difficult to determine whether our moral faculty is operating freely or is clouded by intense feeling. Literature supplies cases remote enough to minimize the effects of personal bias and excessive emotion, while still sufficiently realistic to engage our emotions to the degree necessary for the proper functioning of our moral judgment." Michael De Paul, "Argument and Perception: The Role of Literature in Moral Inquiry," *Journal of Philosophy*, 85 (1988), 563. See also Nussbaum, *Love's Knowledge*, 48.

76. Dworkin, *Life's Dominion*, 201ff.

77. Malory, *Le Morte D'Arthur*, v. 1, 343; C VIII, 23; V 409:28–29.

78. Ibid., v.1, 68, C II, 6, V 69:22–3.

79. Ibid., v. 2, 411; C XVIII, 19; V 1089:24.

80. Ibid., v. 2, 413; C XVIII, 19; V 1092:9–12.

81. Ibid., v.2, 528; C XXI, 12; V 1257:1–2. Helen Cooper points out that "suicide, other than to avoid rape, was regarded as incurring damnation" (Explanatory notes to *Le Morte Darthur*, 554). But this consideration does not seem to deter these characters. La Beale Isoud says, "Sweet Lord Jesu, have mercy upon me, for I may not live after the death of Sir Tristram de Liones, for he was my first love and he shall be the last" (Malory, *Le Morte D'Arthur*, v.1, 417; C IX, 19; V 499:17–19), as she is about to try to run upon a sword and kill herself. And Elaine even says of her quasisuicide, "sithen [since] it is the sufferance of God that I shall die for the love of so noble a knight, I beseech the High Father of Heaven to have mercy upon my soul" (ibid., v.2, 413; C XVIII, 19; V 1093:11–13).

82. Dworkin, Introduction to "The Philosophers' Brief," 41.

83. Ibid. For discussion of a philosophical problem with this criterion, see my "Death, Dying, and Dignity," in Klaus Brinkmann (ed.), *The Paideia Project: Proceedings of the XXth World Congress of Philosophy* (Bowling Green, OH: Philosophy Documentation Center, forthcoming 1999).

84. Malory never tells us Launcelot's age either, but he provides the following information. At the start of the quest of the Holy Grail, Launcelot's son Galahad is fifteen. On the quest, Launcelot spends twenty-four days and nights "as still as a dead man" (Malory, *Le Morte D'Arthur*, v.2, 357; C XVII, 16; V 1017:2–3), as punishment for the twenty-four years he has been a sinner, and near the end of the *Morte Darthur*, after the dissolution of the Round Table, he spends six years as a hermit and one as a priest.

85. There are some other cases (confinement in a death camp, for example) in which conventional wisdom might grant that suicidal hopelessness can be rational, but I am concerned with less extreme cases here.

86. Malory, *Le Morte D'Arthur*, v.2, 370; C XVII, 22; V 1034:25–28.

87. See Joseph Cardinal Bernadin, "Death as a Friend," *New York Times Magazine*, December 1, 1996: 112–15.

88. These are the words of hospice medical director Dr. Fred Schwartz in the Home Box Office documentary *Letting Go: A Hospice Journey*.

89. Bernadin, "Death as a Friend," 114.

90. The phrase comes from Thomas Nagel, "Death," in Nagel, *Mortal Questions* (New York: Cambridge University Press, 1996), 1. Note also that disbelief in an afterlife is not even necessary for a rational fear of death. Even believers in an afterlife may rationally fear death, for example, because they do not want to leave their familiar lives and loved ones, because they fear a bad fate in the afterlife, or because their belief in the afterlife is shaky, rather than being as strong and unswerving as that of Galahad and Cardinal Bernadin. Aversion to death seems to be quite common among believers in heaven. Although 90 percent of Americans profess belief in heaven (*The Gallup Poll* [Wilmington, DE: American Institute of Public Opinion, 1995], 8), even Sherwin B. Nuland, a doctor who is very unsympathetic to last-ditch high-tech medical treatment for the terminally ill, grants that "[a]lmost everyone seems to want to take a chance with the slim statistics that oncologists give to patients with advanced disease. . . . Though everyone may yearn for a tranquil death, the basic instinct to stay alive is a far more powerful force" (*How We Die* [New York: Knopf, 1994], 233–34).

91. Nagel, "Death," 1.

92. See my "Goldilocks and Mrs. Ilych: A Critical Look at the 'Philosophy of Hospice,'" *Cambridge Quarterly of Healthcare Ethics*, 6 (1997): 314–24, as well as my short story, "Buddies," *Commentary*, December 1994: 54. Shannon French has pointed out in discussion that even a disbeliever in the afterlife who wants to stay alive may have practical reasons for acting serenely in the face of his own impending death; such a way of acting may be pleasanter than bewailing his fate. This point can be expanded to apply even to the feeling of serenity, insofar as one has control over his feelings. (He may choose to take Prozac, for example.) But I want to distinguish between whether serenity is *epistemically* justified, in the sense of being grounded in a justified belief that one is not facing a terrible loss, and whether serenity is *practically* justified, in the sense of having desirable consequences. (This parallels a distinction made by Alfred Mele [*Irrationality*, New York: Oxford University Press, 1987, 110ff].) This essay deals only with whether such serenity would be epistemically justified, a reasonable restriction, as many people have a critical interest (in the sense defined above) in not having attitudes that are epistemically unjustified.

93. Malory, *Le Morte D'Arthur*, v.2, 531; C XXI, 13; V 1260:23. Malory wrote the *Morte Darthur* while in prison, a fact he refers to in the book.

94. Ibid., V 1034:26. (I have modernized the spelling.) The reference to "this wretched world" is not in the Caxton edition, although, right before dying, Galahad asks Bors to "bid" [Launcelot] remember of this unstable world" (ibid., v.2 370; C XVII, 22; V 1035:11–12).

95. See B. Manard and C. Perrone, *Hospice Care: An Introduction and Review of the Evidence* (Arlington, VA: National Hospice Organization, 1994). The National Hospice Organization states that "hospice will neither seek to hasten [death] nor to postpone it" (ibid., 4) for its patients. I have argued elsewhere that this amounts to an arbitrary "Goldilocks Principle" for the terminally ill, that is, "death by assisted suicide is too soon, death after high-tech life-prolonging treatment is too late, [but] 'natural' death is just right" ("Goldilocks and Mrs. Ilych," 317). After all, hospices do not eschew intervention through technology in other areas, such as regulating the temperature of a room. For further critical treatment of the hospice approach to death and dying, see my short story, "Flourish Your Heart in This World."

96. Nuland, *How We Die*, 58.

97. Daniel Callahan, *Setting Limits* (New York: Simon and Schuster, 1987) 43 (italics in original).

98. Although Callahan specifies responsibilities for other age groups as well, these are less self-sacrificial. For example, he says, "The mature adult has the responsibility to procreate and rear the next generation and to manage the present society" (ibid.). These responsibilities, unlike what Callahan thinks should be the primary aspiration of the elderly, do not consist entirely in serving

others; the "mature adult" is part of and shares in the benefits of the society he is supposed to be managing.

99. See "No Exit," my review of Nuland's book, *The American Scholar*, 64 no. 1 (1995): 131–34, as well as my "What Is the Proper Role for Charity in Healthcare?" *Cambridge Quarterly of Healthcare Ethics*, 5 no. 3 (1996): 428.

100. *Merriam-Webster's Collegiate Dictionary*, 593.

101. Ibid. (italics in original).

102. Ibid. (italics in original). The dictionary also lists "individuality" as an additional meaning of "individualism," but I am concerned here with specifying senses of "individualism" that distinguish it from individuality.

103. Riddy, *Sir Thomas Malory*, 127. See the discussion in ibid., chap. 5.

104. Field, *Romance and Chronicle*, 140.

105. Ibid.

106. Ibid., 131.

107. Ibid.

108. Ibid., 135.

109. Malory, *Le Morte D'Arthur*, v.2, 305; C XVI, 3; V 945:8–9.

110. Ibid., v.2, 184; C X, 87; V 781:31–32. (This is the version of the remark in the Caxton edition; the Vinaver edition, which Field uses, has "myght [might] I never" instead of "may I not.")

111. Ibid., v.2, 509; C XXI, 2; V 1231:22–23.

112. Field, *Romance and Chronicle*, 132.

113. Ibid. (italics in original).

114. Malory, *Le Morte D'Arthur*, v.2, 509; C XXI, 2; V 1231:24–25; and v.2, 523; C XXI, 9; V 1252:18–19.

115. Lambert, *Malory*, 212.

116. Ibid.

117. Ibid.

118. For convenience of exposition, I use the term "romantic love" broadly enough to apply in Malory's world, despite the view of some scholars that "Romantic love is part and parcel of Romanticism, a distinctly modern movement" (Robert Solomon, "The Virtue of Love," *Midwest Studies in Philosophy* 13 [1988], 22).

119. Malory, *Le Morte D'Arthur* v.2, 508; C XXI, 2; V 1230:14–17.

120. Ibid., v.2, 524; C XXI, 9; V 1253:20.

121. Ibid., v.2, 475; C XX, 10; V 1185:8.

122. Further evidence that by the final tale of the *Morte Darthur*, Arthur cares little for Guenever comes from his notorious remark, "much more I am sorrier for my good knights' loss than for the loss of my fair queen; for queens I might have enow [enough], but such a fellowship of good knights shall never be together in no company" (ibid., v.2, 473; C XX, 9; V 1184:1–5). McCarthy claims that

> Arthur is not expressing his indifference to [Guenever], but his inconsolable grief at the loss of his fellowship. That loss is so terrible that even his exceptional and dearly loved queen takes second place in his thoughts. If the loss of [Guenever] had brought little pain to Arthur, it could be no point of reference here (*An Introduction to Malory*, 76).

This seems wrong. It ignores the obviously slighting words "queens I might have enow," words both inappropriate and inexplicable if Arthur dearly loves his queen and is just trying to convey that the Round Table fellowship ranks even higher in his affections.

123. Malory, *Le Morte D'Arthur*, v.2, 352; C XVII, 13; V 1011:18.

124. Brewer, Introduction to *The Morte Darthur*, 10.

125. McCarthy, *An Introduction to Malory*, 66.

126. Malory, *Le Morte D'Arthur*, v.2, 426; C XVIII, 25; V 1119:15–16.

127. R. T. Davies, "The Worshipful Way in Malory," in John D. Lawlor (ed.), *Patterns of Love and Courtesy: Essays in Memory of C. S. Lewis* (London: Edward Arnold, 1966), 167. See also R. T. Davies, "Malory's Vertuouse Love," *Studies in Philology* 53 (1956): 466.

128. Malory, *Le Morte D'Arthur*, v.2, 272; C XIII, 20; V 897:25–26.

129. Ibid., v.2, 250; C XIII, 8; V 870:12.

130. Ibid., v.2, 251; C XIII, 8; V 872:10.

131. Ibid., v.2, 251; C XIII, 8; V 872:10–12.

132. Ibid., v.2, 251; C XIII, 8; V 872:6–7.

133. Ibid., v.1, 327; C VIII, 14; V 394:35–395:1; and v.2, 193; C XI, 3; V 796:4. The spelling "traitress" occurs in the first of these passages and "traitoress" in the second in the Penguin Classics edition. Both are modernized spellings of "traitresse," the spelling that occurs in both passages in the original Caxton edition.

134. Ibid., v.1, 327; C VIII, 14; V 394:32.

135. Ibid., v.1, 327; C VIII, 14; V 394:25–26.

136. Ibid., v.1, 328; C VIII, 14; V 396:11–16.

137. Russell used this example in a BBC Radio "Brains' Trust" discussion in 1948. See the entry under "Emotive Conjugation" in Robert Audi (ed.), *The Cambridge Dictionary of Philosophy* (New York: Cambridge University Press, 1995), 223.

138. For example, Tristram is not considered cowardly in an episode where he yields to Galahaut the Haut Prince when outnumbered. (As I mentioned in note 65, generalizations about Malory have exceptions.) And Dinadan, the perennial scoffer, says that "it is ever worship to [honorable for] a knight to refuse that thing that he may not attain" (Malory, *Le Morte D'Arthur*, v.2, 18; C X, 8; V 581:24–26), although this view is not widely shared in Malory's world.

139. This is part of the Oath of the Round Table, ibid., v.1, 115–16, C III, 15; V 120:18–23.

140. Ibid., v.2, 193; C XI, 3; V 796:15.

141. This point is worth stressing in light of Brewer's claim that what he calls the *Morte Darthur*'s "almost complete absence of 'characterisation' (i.e., of specifically identifying idiosyncratic traits of personality [such as Gawain's fondness for fruit])" ("Malory: The Traditional Writer and the Archaic Mind," *Arthurian Literature* 1 [1981]: 107) indicates a lack of individuality in the characters. A natural objection is that individuality consists not only in idiosyncrasies, but also (and more deeply) in the sort of differences in values and propensities that Launcelot and Segwarides exhibit in the passages under consideration. (But see also Brewer's discussion of Malory's characters, Introduction to *The Morte Darthur*, 18–20 and 23–24.)

142. Field, *Romance and Chronicle*, 131.

143. Malory, *Le Morte D'Arthur*, v. 1, 342; C VIII, 22; V 409:8–11.

144. Ibid., v.1, 362; C VIII, 33; V 429:15–17.

145. Ibid., v.2, 502; C XX, 22; V 1219:35–36. (The first volume of the Penguin Classics edition has 468 pages.)

146. Field, *Romance and Chronicle*, 132.

147. Lambert, *Malory*, 145 (italics in original).

148. Ibid. (italics in original).

149. Ibid.

150. See Field, *Romance and Chronicle*, chap. 6–7, and Lambert, *Malory*.

151. Malory, *Le Morte D'Arthur*, v.2, 374; C XVIII, 1; V 1046: 5–6. The phrase is embedded in Launcelot's statement "I was but late in the quest [of the Holy Grail]," where "late" has the sense of "lately," that is, "recently."

I am indebted to many people for discussions of the material in this essay, especially Shannon French, D. Thomas Hanks, Jr., Donna Harvey, Jean Jost, Sara Ann Ketchum, Alfred Mele, Carole Roos, Peter Schroeder, James Van Cleve, and the students in my 1999 graduate seminar on Malory, especially Simon Feldman, who saved me from a serious blooper about trial by battle. Part of Section III was read at the 33rd International Congress on Medieval Studies, Kalamazoo, Michigan, May 1998.

Contributors

Felicia Ackerman, Department of Philosophy, Brown University
Jonathan E. Adler, Department of Philosophy, Brooklyn College
Lynne Rudder Baker, Department of Philosophy, University of Massachusetts
Carl F. Cranor, Department of Philosophy, University of California, Riverside
Kit Fine, Department of Philosophy, New York University
Richard Foley, Department of Philosophy, Rutgers University
Richard Fumerton, Department of Philosophy, University of Iowa
Bernard Harrison, East Sussex, England
John Heil, Department of Philosophy, Davidson College
Eli Hirsch, Department of Philosophy, Brandeis University
Hilary Kornblith, Department of Philosophy, University of Vermont
C. B. Martin, Department of Philosophy, Davidson College
Ernest Sosa, Department of Philosophy, Brown University
Chris Swoyer, Department of Philosophy, University of Oklahoma
Peter Unger, Department of Philosophy, New York University
Larry Wright, Department of Philosophy, University of California, Riverside
David Zimmerman, Department of Philosophy, Simon Fraser University

Peter A. French holds the Cole Chair in Ethics at the University of South Florida. He has taught at the University of Minnesota, Morris, served as Distinguished Research Professor in the Center for the Study of Human Values at the University of Delaware, and most recently served as Lennox Distinguished Professor of Philosophy at Trinity University in San Antonio, Texas. His books include *The Scope of Morality* (1980), *Collective and Corporate Responsibility* (1980), and *Responsibility Matters* (1992). He has published numerous articles in the philosophical journals. **Howard K. Wettstein** is chair and professor of philosophy at the University of California, Riverside. He has taught at the University of Notre Dame and the University of Minnesota, Morris, and has served as visiting associate professor of philosophy at the University of Iowa and Stanford University. He is the author of *Has Semantics Rested on a Mistake? and Other Essays* (1992).